Fodor's 2001

Ireland

P9-APN-522

Fodor's Travel Publications • New York, Toronto, London, Sydney, Auckland
www.fodors.com

CONTENTS

MAPS

Circled letters in text correspond to letters on the photographs. For more information on the sights pictured, turn to
the indicated page number ⓐ on each photograph.

DESTINATION
IRELAND

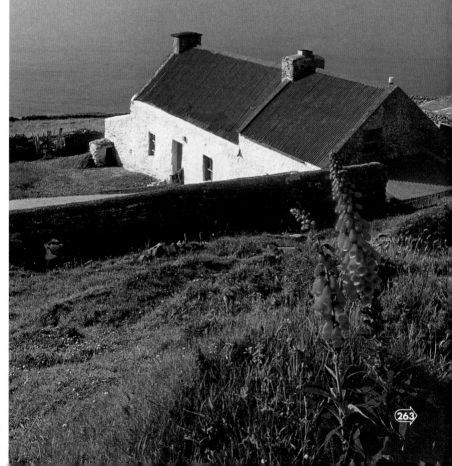

All the talk in Ireland these days is of change: an affluence previously unknown in the nation's history has led to a boom in the creation of luxury hotels, innovative restaurants, first-class golf courses, and stylish nightclubs. But beneath all the excitement and hurly-burly of newness, something essential and magical endures. This quintessence of Irishness is hard to define, but it has something to do with the myriad shades of green coloring a landscape that can shift suddenly from fertile plain to rugged coastal mountains. It's visible in the pace at which the locals live their lives, even in the middle of unprecedented prosperity, always taking time to laugh, sip a pint, and extend a warm welcome to a stranger.

263

DUBLIN

Ⓐ 48

Dublin is 1,000 years and more of history neatly packaged for your convenience. The port city on a deep bay has long attracted the attention of European invaders, and the fingerprints of her conquerors are everywhere. The gray, majestic Ⓓ**St. Patrick's Cathedral** stands on the site of the earliest Celtic settlement, where the man himself is said to have baptized locals in the 5th century. Nearby is the more austere Christ Church, built by the Viking king Sigtyggr Silkbeard in

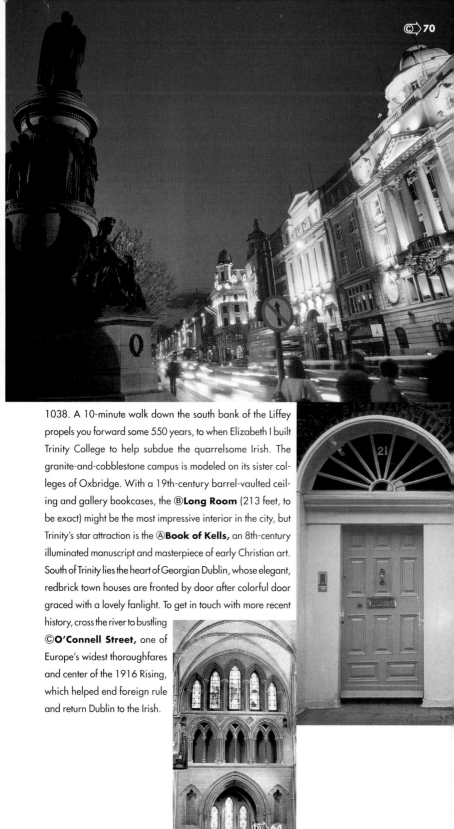

1038. A 10-minute walk down the south bank of the Liffey propels you forward some 550 years, to when Elizabeth I built Trinity College to help subdue the quarrelsome Irish. The granite-and-cobblestone campus is modeled on its sister colleges of Oxbridge. With a 19th-century barrel-vaulted ceiling and gallery bookcases, the ®**Long Room** (213 feet, to be exact) might be the most impressive interior in the city, but Trinity's star attraction is the ®**Book of Kells,** an 8th-century illuminated manuscript and masterpiece of early Christian art. South of Trinity lies the heart of Georgian Dublin, whose elegant, redbrick town houses are fronted by door after colorful door graced with a lovely fanlight. To get in touch with more recent history, cross the river to bustling ©**O'Connell Street,** one of Europe's widest thoroughfares and center of the 1916 Rising, which helped end foreign rule and return Dublin to the Irish.

DUBLIN

E ⊳77

"Me darlin' Dublin's dead and gone," laments the popular ballad, and indeed the pace of change in the old city has been breakneck over the last decade. A robust economy and a deluge of European Union money have transformed the once sleepy city into a cosmopolitan capital. The cast-iron Ⓗ**Ha'penny Bridge** (the name comes from the toll once charged to cross) leads to Ⓙ**Temple Bar,** a few cobblestoned blocks rezoned to stir up a red-hot cocktail of wild nightlife and highbrow culture. The area is at the heart of a city-wide dining renaissance that has brought diverse ethnic cuisines and a more daring approach to

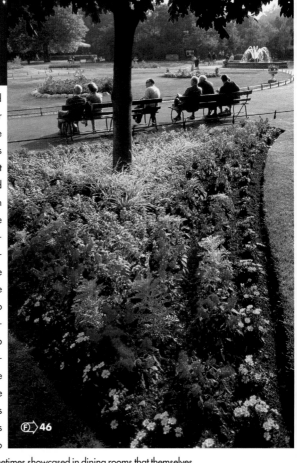

F ⊳46

local dishes all over town, sometimes showcased in dining rooms that themselves represent the best of modern Dublin design, such as Ⓔ**Patrick Guilbaud** in Center City. If Temple Bar is emblematic of all that is quirky and offbeat in this newly vital Dublin, Ⓘ**Grafton Street** reveals the mainstream side of prosperity—this is where new money is spent, in department stores and chain boutiques. Flower sellers and high-spirited buskers drawn by the promise of excess spending keep the streetscape lively. Alongside the getting and spending, traditional pleasures endure. A long, slow, conversation-rich evening

G ⊳46

in any of the city's nearly 1,000 public houses is as delicious as ever; from the brass-and-marble Stag's Head to the café-like Globe, Guinness is always the poison of choice and good-humored banter is the background music. A night at W. B. Yeats's historic Abbey Theatre or an afternoon investigating the Dublin Writer's Museum offers a little time with the city's literary notables, including Joyce, Shaw, and Beckett. High tea in the light-flooded Lord Mayor's Lounge at the ⒼShelbourne Méridien Hotel is almost a ritual for Dubliners. Right outside the front door of the Shelbourne is flower-filled ⒻSt. Stephen's Green. A stroll around this Victorian park is the perfect end to a day in a city that is "all changed, changed utterly" since poet W. B. Yeats wrote those words in 1921.

Ⓘ 110

DUBLIN ENVIRONS

ⓑ 155

Like the city's great garden, the counties around Dublin—Louth, Meath, Kildare, and Wicklow—draw visitors by the thousands with a concentration of ancient sights, natural wonders, stately homes, and historic towns. The classic, English-style seaside resort town of ⒺBray is a favorite of day-trippers. The 85-mile ⒸWicklow Way, the nation's premier long-distance footpath—has led generations of more adventurous travelers out of the city and 1,600 feet up into the harsh splendor of the Wicklow Mountains. Nestled in a fecund valley in the middle of those mountains is the serene, early Christian St.

Ⓐ 147

Ⓒ 133

Ⓔ 146

Kevin's Monastery at Ⓓ**Glendalough.** Along with the Cistercian abbey at Mellifont in Louth and the solemn neolithic burial mounds at Newgrange in Meath, Glendalough testifies to the region's role as the cradle and nursery of religion in Ireland. In Louth's historic Ⓕ**Drogheda** town, the head of the martyred saint Oliver Plunkett sits preserved for all time in a glass case. Flat, grassy County Kildare is home to three first-class horse-racing tracks: the Curragh, Naas, and Ⓑ**Punchestown.** Dublin's 18th-century Protestant Ascendancy had ideas about building its own temples amid the natural splendor that encircles the capital. Its great houses and adjoining formal gardens rose up in Palladian style to honor Mammon: Russborough, Castletown, and Ⓐ**Powerscourt House** are nonpareil monuments to this brash, decorous age.

Ⓕ 141

11

Overlooked and underrated, the Midlands beckon to travelers who like to stray from the beaten path. Although the area lacks a coastline, its waterways are a pleasure; many Irish people refer to the region as the Lakelands. Wild, unpolluted ©**Lough Derg** is the jewel of Ireland's 800 ancient, dark blue lakes and pools and draws all those who love fishing and other water sports. The moisture in the area's rich soil supports the for-

THE MIDLANDS

Ⓐ 167

mation of chocolate-brown peat bogs; take the Ⓑ**Bord na Mona Bog Rail Tour** in County Offaly to gain some insight into the complex ecosystem underlying the mysterious landscape. The bog lands' isolation protected one of early Christian Ireland's foremost monastic settlements, Clonmacnoise. As around Dublin, Protestant landowners in the Midlands built great houses to display their wealth: Strokestown and Belvedere houses are splendid examples, but Ⓐ**Emo Court and Gardens** in County Laois, designed by James Gandon, is the

Ⓑ 180

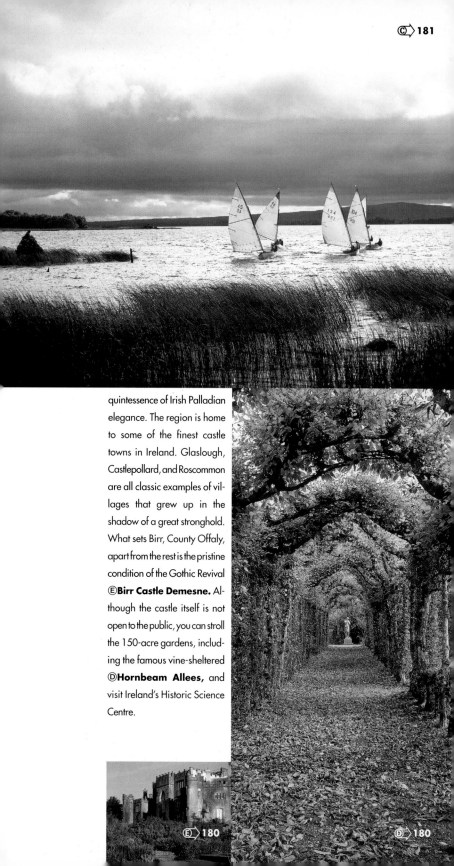

quintessence of Irish Palladian elegance. The region is home to some of the finest castle towns in Ireland. Glaslough, Castlepollard, and Roscommon are all classic examples of villages that grew up in the shadow of a great stronghold. What sets Birr, County Offaly, apart from the rest is the pristine condition of the Gothic Revival Ⓔ**Birr Castle Demesne.** Although the castle itself is not open to the public, you can stroll the 150-acre gardens, including the famous vine-sheltered Ⓓ**Hornbeam Allees,** and visit Ireland's Historic Science Centre.

Ⓔ 180

Ⓓ 180

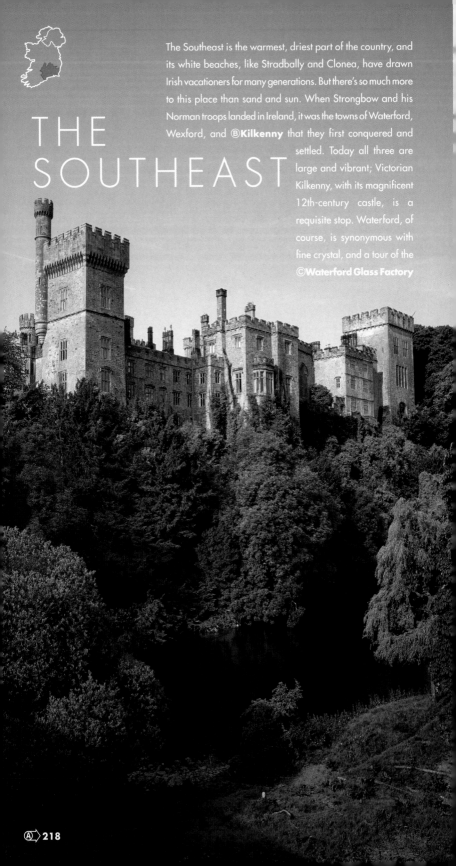

THE
SOUTHEAST

The Southeast is the warmest, driest part of the country, and its white beaches, like Stradbally and Clonea, have drawn Irish vacationers for many generations. But there's so much more to this place than sand and sun. When Strongbow and his Norman troops landed in Ireland, it was the towns of Waterford, Wexford, and ®**Kilkenny** that they first conquered and settled. Today all three are large and vibrant; Victorian Kilkenny, with its magnificent 12th-century castle, is a requisite stop. Waterford, of course, is synonymous with fine crystal, and a tour of the ©**Waterford Glass Factory** is an hour well spent. Modern, bustling Wexford is a repository of historic Irish churches, including 12th-century Selskar Abbey. Outside Ⓓ**Wexford** and the other cities lies some of the most fertile countryside in Ireland—a quiet place dotted with thatched cottages where the sheep often outnumber the people. Numerous fish-rich rivers also wind through this area before spilling into the Irish Sea. On the banks of the Blackwater lies enchanting

Ⓒ▷212

Lismore. As you cross the bridge to enter the town you'll be struck by a dramatic view of mighty Ⓐ**Lismore Castle,** one of many turreted, gray, stone battlements the Normans erected in the Southeast, rebuilt from ruins in the 19th century.

Going south from Lismore the land starts to rise at last, and you enter the Knockmealdown Mountains, from which, on a good day, you can see all the way to the mist-shrouded, 200-foot Rock of Cashel.

Ⓓ▷202

THE SOUTHWEST

"My Own Lovely Lee," "The Lakes of Killarney," "The Rose of Tralee"—when great tenors sing about Ireland it is usually the glories of the Southwest they are praising. The awesome coast and mountains of west Cork and the three peninsulas of Kerry (the Dingle, Iveragh, and Beara) make for postcard-perfect scenery. On the Iveragh Peninsula, a short drive outside touristy Killarney, you can view the sunset from the 12th-century ruined church on the shore of ⒟**Lough Leane.** From there a foray into the MacGillycuddy's Reeks, Ireland's highest mountains, brings you to the glacially formed ⒜**Gap of Dunloe,** just off the scenic Ring of Kerry loop drive where five lakes are strung beside sky-scraping road. Cars are banned from the Gap, but in summer it's busy with horse and foot traffic. Dingle is the most spectacular of the peninsulas, and cozy, pub-filled, music-crazy ⒝**Dingle Town** is a pleasant alternative to hectic Killarney. Native Irish speakers occupy much of the ancient peninsula, and historic sites range from Dunbeg, the Iron Age promontory fort, to 7th-century ⒞**Gallarus Oratory,** still watertight after a millennium.

⒝ 273

⒞ 277

⒟ 268

SOUTHWEST

E 237

Disney himself couldn't have designed a better place for exploring some of the key sights of modern Irish history than "the Rebel County," as County Cork is proud to call itself. Patrick Street in E **Cork City,** now an upscale shopping district, saw some of the worst fighting during the 1919–21 War of Independence. And it was from nearby G **Cobh,** so picturesque

F 244

and tranquil today, that many of the infamous "coffin ships" carried a million immigrants to the New World. Cobh was also the last port of call for the doomed *Titanic.* Kinsale, now an affluent tourist town known for its good restaurants, was, in 1601, the site of a decisive battle that pitted the Irish and Spanish against the English and spelled the beginning of the end of Gaelic Ireland. To guard against future foreign intervention, the victorious British built imposing J **Charles Fort,** one of Europe's best preserved star forts, on top of a cliff looking out to sea. Elizabeth I settled

G 245

Ⓗ 246

Ⓘ 258

Cork with her followers, presenting to Sir Walter Raleigh 40,000 acres, including the elegant harbor town of Ⓗ**Youghal,** famed for its beautiful clock tower, in the Blackwater Valley 30 miles east of Cork City. Here as in the rest of Ireland, this new Anglo-Irish Ascendancy proceeded to build for itself some of the finest houses in Europe: few are more spectacular than Ⓘ**Bantry House,** whose fine Italianate gardens overlook the sea. In the rolling, fertile hills between Kinsale and Bantry, Michael Collins, the greatest Irish rebel of them all, was assassinated, only a few miles from Clonakilty, the town of his birth. Cork men and women developed a secret weapon to defy their British rulers, the fabled "gift of the gab." Legend has it that the source of the Irish gift for conversation and wit is the

Ⓕ**Blarney Stone,** set into the walls of Blarney Castle. Lie down, throw your head back with abandon, kiss the stone, and never again will you be stuck for a word, be it praise or scorn.

Ⓙ 251

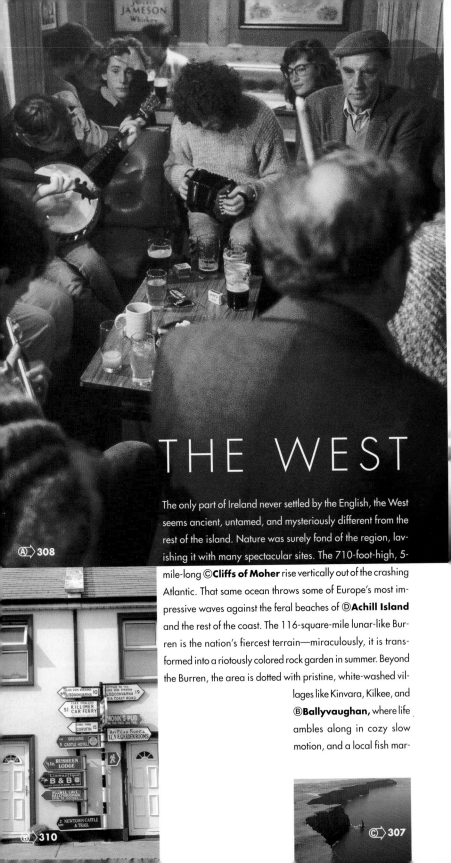

THE WEST

The only part of Ireland never settled by the English, the West seems ancient, untamed, and mysteriously different from the rest of the island. Nature was surely fond of the region, lavishing it with many spectacular sites. The 710-foot-high, 5-mile-long ©**Cliffs of Moher** rise vertically out of the crashing Atlantic. That same ocean throws some of Europe's most impressive waves against the feral beaches of ⑩**Achill Island** and the rest of the coast. The 116-square-mile lunar-like Burren is the nation's fiercest terrain—miraculously, it is transformed into a riotously colored rock garden in summer. Beyond the Burren, the area is dotted with pristine, white-washed villages like Kinvara, Kilkee, and ⑧**Ballyvaughan,** where life ambles along in cozy slow motion, and a local fish mar-

Ⓐ〉308

Ⓑ〉310

Ⓒ〉307

Ⓓ337

Ⓔ321

ket is the height of excitement. But put your ears up against a door or two and you might be in for a surprise: the West, especially the Gaeltacht—as the Irish-speaking regions of Connemara are known— is the heartland of traditional Irish music and dance. In the tiny coastal village of Doolin, ⒶGus O'Connor's pub is known as the high temple of the jig and reel with its free-for-all sessions. In lively Galway City, folks gambol to a different beat, now that foreign residents have introduced an exotic flavor to the ancient city at a slew of new clubs like the salsa-inspired ⒺCuba.

THE NORTHWEST

Ⓐ▷ 379

Like the West, the rugged Northwest of Ireland was pretty much left to its own devices by the land-hungry English settlers. What could they possibly want with Counties Donegal and Sligo—a region of rock and stone typified by Ⓐ**Malin Head,** Ireland's northernmost, most desolate point? The barren moorland surroundings and the great distance from civilization enticed St. Columba and his followers to build a monastery here, at the heart of the region in Ⓑ**Glencolumbkille,** in the 6th century. Driving from village to village through the Derryveagh Mountains, you encounter the savage coastal beauty of the

Ⓒ▷ 367

Ⓑ▷ 368

Gweedore Headland and Horn Head. In these relatively unspoiled villages you can still see locals go about their everyday lives, from the pubs of tiny Fal Carrach to the harbor of the fishing town of ©**Killybegs.** Irish is still the first language in many parts of isolated northern Donegal. When fin-de-siècle poets attempted to revive native Irish culture they often sought inspiration in the Northwest. William Butler Yeats was

among the most eloquent to celebrate the lakes, farms, woodland, and dramatic mountains around the now-prosperous market center of ©**Sligo Town.** "The Lake Isle of Innisfree" is his lament, written from exile, for the island at the center of serene ©**Lough Gill,** as popular today among fishermen as it once was with writers. In "Under Ben Bulben" the poet talked of where he wanted to be buried and the words he wanted on his gravestone, which you can see today in small ©**Drumcliff** churchyard, under the shadow of the mountain he loved so well.

NORTHERN IRELAND

Ⓐ 397

In Northern Ireland one of the so-called peace dividends has been the opening up of this undiscovered province to adventurous travelers. The former splendor of Belfast, a boomtown in Victorian times, is on view at the restored Grand Opera House and the exuberant, Renaissance Revival Ⓑ **City Hall.** Symbols and scars of the recent troubles are still apparent in the cityscape and well-rendered murals carry on a still-lively propaganda war; staunchly Republican Ⓐ **Falls Road** is home to the finest examples of this urban art. However disturbing, the tribulations of men can seem somehow temporary when you ponder the beauty of the North's varied landscape. Along the coast of County Antrim, the hazy sea pounds at the base of high, green hills dotted with lush, gently curved glens carved out by glaciers at the end of the Ice Age. Hidden in the glens, small towns like Ballycastle carry on an older, less hurried way of life typified by the ⒹOul' Lammas Fair, a modern version of the ancient harvest festival of Lughnasa. Another wonder, the 37,000 hexagonal basalt pillars known as the ⒺGiant's Causeway, is the North's premier tourist attraction. Walled Derry and massive Lough Neagh dominate the middle and western sections of the province, and south of Belfast and scenic Strangford Lough, songwriter Percy French's rolling ©Mountains of Mourne "sweep down to the sea"—the most peaceful place in this new province of peace.

25

GREAT ITINERARIES

Public transportation in rural Ireland is too unreliable and expensive to make it worth-while. Trains go only to major towns, and bus service is infrequent to many of the more interesting sights and villages off the beaten path. You really need a car to get the most out of your visit.

Highlights of Ireland: The East and the South

5 days

The classical splendor of the great buildings in and around Dublin, the lush Southwest, rugged County Wicklow, and the historic Meath plains are all just a few hours' drive apart. Listen for the variety of accents along the way—proof (if you needed it) that

there is no such thing as a "typical" Irish person.

DUBLIN

1 day. Head straight to Dublin's center. Spend the morning exploring 400-year-old Trinity College. After lunch and a "swift one" in a pub, stroll around the rest of the compact city center, taking in the elegant Georgian architecture around St. Stephen's Green, the austere Ⓐ Dublin Castle, and the national treasures in the museums around Merrion Square and pedestrian Grafton Street. Stop for tea and scones at the Shelbourne Méridien Hotel and wind up the day with a show at the Abbey Theatre.
☞ *Exploring Dublin in Chapter 1*

BOYNE VALLEY AND COUNTY WICKLOW

2 days. Rent a car or join an organized tour and head out to the Boyne Valley, a short trip north of the capital. Spend the morning walking among the Iron Age ruins of

the rolling Hill of Tara. After a picnic lunch on top of the hill, drive through ancient Kells and then to Ⓑ New-grange, one of Europe's most spectacular prehistoric tombs. One thousand years older than Stonehenge, the great white-quartz structure merits two or three hours. Spend the rest of your day driving through the low hills and valleys of verdant County Meath and on to the Georgian village of Slane. Domi-nating the town are elegant Slane Castle and 500-ft Slane Hill. The following day, drive through the County Wicklow mountains. You might want to get out of your car in one of the small, quiet towns along the Wicklow Way, Ireland's premier hiking trail, and go for a short hike. Drive on to stately Powerscourt House, whose grounds are perhaps the finest in the country. On the way to Glendalough and the medieval monastery of the hermit St. Kevin, stop

for a bite in Roundwood, Ireland's highest village.
☞ *North of Dublin in the Boyne Valley, and County Wicklow's Coast and Mountains in Chapter 2*

WEST CORK AND KERRY

2 days. Head south to Cork City, perfect for half a day of walking. Drive directly south to Kinsale, an old fishing town turned resort with many good restaurants. A slow three- or four-hour drive along the coast and up through the small towns of west County Cork takes you through the kind of lush landscape that inspired Ireland's nickname, the Emerald Isle. Spend the night in the market town of Skibbereen. Next morning, cross into County Kerry and head

straight for popular, bustling Killarney, right at the center of a scattering of azure lakes and heather-clad mountains. It's a good base for exploring your pick of three great Atlantic-pounded peninsulas: the Beara Peninsula, the Ring of Kerry, and the Dingle Peninsula. All offer stunning ocean views, hilly landscapes, and welcoming towns with good

B&Bs. The five-hour drive back to Dublin takes you through Limerick City and the lakes of the Midlands.
☞ *Cork City, Kinsale to Glengarriff via Bantry Bay, the Ring of Kerry, Killarney and Environs, the Dingle Peninsula, and North Kerry and Shannonside in Chapter 5*

Great Irish Houses and Castles
5 to 7 days

If you have an interest in architecture, interior design, and history (including the sinister and macabre kind), then a tour of Ireland's great houses and castles is for you. You might even decide to splurge and stay at one of the grand country-house hotels along the way. It's best to go between June and September, when the maximum number of houses are open. In other months expect to make an appointment a day or so in advance to view a house.

DUBLIN AND ENVIRONS

2 days. Right in the center of Dublin are historic Dublin Castle and the elegant, 18th-century Royal Hospital Kilmainham. Walk along the inner-city stretch of the River Liffey for excellent views of two of architect James Gandon's Georgian masterpieces, the Custom House and the Four Courts. South of the river, Georgian domestic town architecture is at its best on Merrion Square and Fitzwilliam Street. On day two go west of Dublin to Castletown House, one of Ireland's most magnificent Georgian structures, in Celbridge, County Kildare; it serves as the headquarters of the Irish Georgian Society. From here head south into County Wicklow to visit Russborough House near Blessington.
☞ *Exploring Dublin in Chapter 1 and County Kildare and West Wicklow in Chapter 2*

THE ROAD TO CORK

1 day. Leave early from Dublin, heading southwest on the road to Cork. Stop on the way at Emo Court and Gardens, another James Gandon design and one of the finest large country houses near Dublin open to the public. You'll pass the Rock of Cashel on your way to Cahir Castle. Continue to Cork City. If you have time, stop at the coastal bulwark ©Charles Fort, about half an hour south of the city. Spend the night in Cork.
☞ *The Eastern Midlands in Chapter 3; The Nire Valley, The Blackwater Valley, and County Tipperary in Chapter 4; and Cork City and Kinsale to Glengarriff via Bantry Bay in Chapter 5*

AROUND KILLARNEY

2 days. From Cork City, a short detour off the main road to Killarney leads to ruined 15th-century Blarney Castle, where you can kiss the famed Blarney Stone. Nearby Blarney House was built in 1784 in Scottish baronial style. In Killarney National Park, Muckross House, a mid-Victorian manor, is worth seeing for its grounds full of flowers and outstanding rock garden. After a night in Killarney, head north to the Shannon estuary, on whose shore looms Glin Castle, ancestral home of the great Anglo-Norman Fitzgeralds. Continue to Rathkeale and Castle Matrix. Stop for tea or dinner at Adare Manor. Stay overnight in or near Limerick City or Ennis.
☞ *Cork City, Killarney and Environs, and North Kerry and Shannonside in Chapter 5*

Highlights of Ireland: The West and the North

6 to 7 days

"To hell or to Connaught" was the choice given the native population by Cromwell, and indeed the harsh, barren landscape of parts of the west and north might appear cursed to the eye of an uprooted farmer. But there is an appeal in the very wildness of counties

Ⓓ❯307

Ⓔ❯330

Clare, Galway, Mayo, Sligo, and Donegal—their stunning, steep coastlines hammered for aeons by the Atlantic. Here, in isolated communities, you'll hear locals speaking Irish as they go about their everyday lives. To the east, in the lusher pastures of long-suffering Northern Ireland, the arrival of peace has opened a treasure trove of gems for travelers.

GALWAY AND CLARE

2 days. A three-hour drive west from Dublin leads straight to the 710-ft Ⓓ Cliffs of Moher, perhaps the single most impressive sight in Ireland. Using the waterside village of Ballyvaughan as your base, spend a day exploring the lunar landscape of the harsh, limestone Burren. In spring it becomes a mighty rock garden of exotic colors. The next morning head north out of Ballyvaughan toward Galway City. On the way you'll pass 2-million-year-old Ailwee Cave and picture-perfect Kinvara. Galway City, spectacularly overlooking

Galway Bay, is rapidly growing, vibrant, and packed with culture and history. If time allows, drive west to Ros an Mhil (Rossaveal) and take a boat to the fabled Aran Islands. Spend the night in Galway City.
☞ *The Burren and Beyond— West Clare to South Galway,*

(F) 413

Belfast

and Galway City and the
Aran Islands in Chapter 6

CONNEMARA, MAYO, SLIGO, AND DONEGAL

2 days. Northwest of Galway City is tiny ⒺClifden, with some of the country's best Atlantic views. From here, head east through one of the most beautiful stretches of road in Connemara—through Kylemore Valley, home of Kylemore Abbey, a huge Gothic Revival castle. After seeing the castle and its grounds, head north through tiny Leenane (the setting of the hit Broadway play *The Beauty Queen of Leenane*) and on to the most attractive town in County Mayo, Westport. It's the perfect spot to spend the night: the 18th-century planned town is on

an inlet of Clew Bay, and some of the west coast's finest beaches are nearby. Your drive north leads right through the heart of Yeats Country in Sligo. Just north of cozy Sligo Town is the stark outline of a great hill, Ben Bulben, in whose shadow poet W.B. Yeats wanted to be buried. South of town, follow the signposted Yeats Trail around woody, gorgeously scenic Lough Gill. Continuing north, you pass Yeats's simple grave in unassuming Drumcliff, a 3000 BC tomb in Creevykeel, and small Donegal Town. Head north through Letterkenny on the tight, meandering roads, into the windswept mountains and along the jagged coastline of northern Donegal. A trip on a fishing boat to one of the many islands off the coast is a must, as is a slow drive along the coast from the Gweedore Headland, covered with heather and gorse, to the former plantation village of Dun Fionnachaid (Dunfanaghy), heart of Donegal's Gaelic-speaking Gaeltacht region and a friendly place to spend the night.
☞ *Through Connemara and County Mayo in Chapter 6,*

Yeats Country—Sligo Town and Environs, Around Donegal Bay, and Northern Donegal in Chapter 7

NORTHERN IRELAND

2 days. Begin exploring the province in historic, divided Derry City (called Londonderry by Unionists), Northern Ireland's second city. A few hours is sufficient to take in the views from the old city walls and the fascinating murals of the Catholic Bogside district. Continue on to two of the region's main attractions, the 13th-century Norman fortress of ⒻDunluce Castle and the ⒼGiant's Causeway, shaped from volcanic rock some 60 million years ago. Heading south, sticking to coastal roads for the best scenery, you'll soon pass through the Glens of Antrim, whose green hills roll down into the sea. Tucked away in the Glens are a number of small, unpretentious towns with great hotels. Early in the morning, head straight to Northern Ireland's capital, Belfast. The old port city, gray and usually wet, is a fascinating place recovering from years of war. A morning of driving through its streets will have to suffice before you head west through the rustic, pretty countryside to Lough Neagh, the largest lake in the British Isles. It's time to head back to Dublin, but if you're ahead of schedule, take the longer route that passes though the glorious Mountains of Mourne and around icy-blue Carlingford Lough. ☞ *Around Counties Antrim and Derry, and Belfast in Chapter 8*

(G) 412

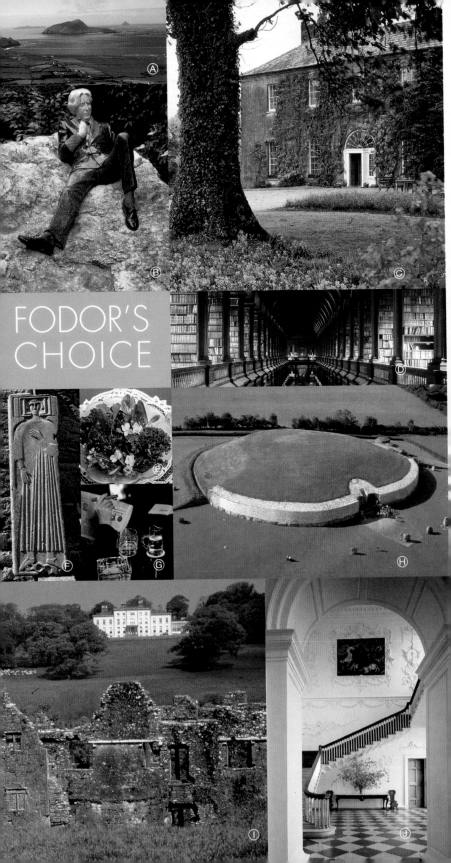

FODOR'S
CHOICE

Even with so many special places in Ireland, Fodor's writers and editors have their favorites. Here are a few that stand out.

QUINTESSENTIAL IRELAND

Ballyhack village from Passage East, Waterford. The view of the village and its imposing castle at the top of the harbor is inspiring. ☞ p. 209

Ⓐ **Blasket Islands from Slea Head, near Dingle.** The view of these rugged—and now uninhabited—islands from the top of these towering cliffs is stunning. ☞ p. 276

Dusk over Killarney's Lower Lake from Aghadoe. Queen Victoria was reputedly overwhelmed by the vista. ☞ p. 267

Ⓑ **Georgian squares on a Sunday, Dublin.** Sit beside Oscar Wilde in tranquil Merrion Square. ☞ p. 53

Glendalough Valley, County Wicklow. This valley with two lakes is home to some of the country's most significant monastic ruins. ☞ p. 149

HISTORIC BUILDINGS AND MONUMENTS

Ⓙ **Castletown House, Celbridge.** Begun in 1722, this Palladian-style house is one of the country's architectural glories. ☞ p. 153

Clonmacnoise, County Offaly. One of Ireland's most important monastic settlements, it was famous throughout Europe as a center for learning. ☞ p. 179

Crown Liquor Saloon and the Grand Opera House, Belfast. These two edifices represent the height of the city's Victorian splendor. ☞ p. 394

Glenveagh Castle, County Donegal. This 19th-century house is grand and luxurious, with delightful gardens. ☞ p. 377

Ⓗ **Newgrange, County Meath.** A spectacular prehistoric tomb, it dates from the 4th millennium BC. ☞ p. 139

Ⓕ **Rock of Cashel, Cashel.** These ruins—cathedral, chapel, and round tower—

are perched dramatically atop a hill. ☞ p. 220

Ⓓ **Trinity College, Dublin.** Ireland's oldest university is full of genteel charm. ☞ p. 47

FLAVORS

Cromleach Lodge, Castlebaldwin. The food is excellent, and every table has panoramic views of Lough Arrow. $$$$ ☞ p. 355

Patrick Guilbaud, Dublin. Guilbaud's chef and staff are French, and the cooking is *magnifique!* $$$$ ☞ p. 77

Peacock Alley, Dublin. Chefowner Conrad Gallagher cooks with great brio and style. $$$$ ☞ p. 76

Rathsallagh House, Dunlavin, County Wicklow. The culinary talents of owner Kay O'Flynn have become legendary. $$$$ ☞ p. 156

The Vintage, Kinsale. Owners Raoul and Seiko de Gendre, a Swiss-Japanese couple, bring sophistication to classical cuisine. $$$$ ☞ p. 251

Deane's, Belfast. Michael Deane trained in Thailand, as you can tell from his innovative cuisine. $$$ ☞ p. 400

Ⓘ **Longueville House, Mallow.** William O'Callaghan trained with leading European chefs before returning to Ireland to cook in his family's 18th-century country-house hotel. $$$ ☞ p. 250

Shanks, Clandeboye, Bangor, County Down. The Millars run one of Northern Ireland's best restaurants. $$$ ☞ p. 400

Ⓒ **Ballymaloe House, Shanagarry, County Cork.** Myrtle Allen continues to refine contemporary Irish cooking at her elegant inn. $$$ ☞ p. 248

Casino House, Timoleague. In this stylish farmhouse, the Reljas have brought new standards of casual elegance to Irish country cooking. $$$ ☞ p. 255

The Wineport, Athlone. The cuisine is wonderfully imaginative in this informal restaurant on the shore of Lough Ree. $$$ ☞ p. 178

Erriseask House, Ballyconneely, County Galway. In this rambling, two-story modern house, Stefan Matz creates sublime contemporary Irish fare. $$ ☞ p. 331

COMFORTS

Kildare Hotel and Country Club, Straffan, County Kildare. The lush Arnold Palmer–designed golf course is among many attractions here. $$$$ ☞ p. 155

Merrion, Dublin. Four Georgian town houses make up this luxurious hotel. $$$$ ☞ p. 87

Mount Juliet, Thomastown, County Kilkenny. This Georgian mansion on 1,500 acres has a championship golf course and extensive riding trails. $$$$ ☞ p. 200

Ⓖ **Park Hotel, Kenmare.** Formerly a bishop's palace, it's now one of Ireland's premier country-house hotels. $$$$ ☞ p. 260

St. Ernan's House, Donegal Town. On its own wooded island in Donegal Bay, this 19th-century country house is unbeatable. $$$$ ☞ p. 365

Ballynahinch Castle, Recess. This river's-edge hotel has long been a favorite retreat of statesmen and stars. $$$ ☞ p. 330

Ash-Rowan Guest House, Belfast. Every room at this Victorian B&B has its own individual style. $$–$$$ ☞ p. 404

Delphi Lodge, Leenane. This comfortable sporting lodge is surrounded by spectacular mountains-and-lakes scenery. $$ ☞ p. 334

Ⓔ **Old Rectory Country House, Wicklow Town.** The comforts at this Greek Revival inn prove that you can be treated like royalty without spending a king's ransom. $$ ☞ p. 151

Ballymakeigh House, Youghal. In lush dairy country, this is the sort of creeper-clad Irish farmhouse you dream of finding. $ ☞ p. 247

1 DUBLIN

Ask any Dubliner what's happening and you may hear echoes of one of W. B. Yeats's most-quoted lines: "All changed, changed utterly." You can practically hear the roar as Western Europe's most intimate capital transforms itself into its fastest-growing urban tourist destination—a boomtown of new construction and restoration. Nowhere are the changes more apparent than in Temple Bar—the cobblestoned arts and culture quarter. But the city's pleasures are uncontainable: historic Georgian buildings, 1,000-odd pubs, buzzing cafés and restaurants, museums of quiet glory, lovely green parks, and, best of all, the easy friendliness of the people.

I **N HIS INIMITABLE, IRRESISTIBLE WAY,** James Joyce immortalized
Dublin in his *Ulysses, Dubliners,* and *A Portrait of the Artist as a
Young Man,* filling his works with the people he knew, with their
own words, and with not a few of his own. As it turns out, he became
one of Dublin's most famous exiles. Disappointed with the city's
provincial outlook and small-town manners, he departed in 1902, at
the age of 20 (his famed peers Sean O'Casey and Samuel Beckett soon
followed). If, however, Joyce was to return to his genteel hometown
today and take an extended, quasi-Homeric odyssey through the city
(as he does so famously in *Ulysses*), would he even recognize Dublin
as his "Dear Dirty Dumpling, foostherfather of fingalls and dot-
thergills"?

Updated by
Anto Howard

What would he make of Temple Bar—the city's erstwhile down-at-heels
neighborhood now crammed with chic restaurants and stylish hotels
in its reborn state as Dublin's "Left Bank"? Or the Liffey quays, whose
makeover have them standing in for Hollywood backlots? (Not so long
ago, he would have found Daniel Day-Lewis acting in Jim Sheridan's
film *The Boxer* near the Ha'penny Bridge.) Or of the new Irishness,
where every aspect of Celtic culture is hot-hot: Frank McCourt's *Angela's Ashes* has dominated American best-seller lists (the movie version was shot in the city and elsewhere around the country), as has its
sequel, *'Tis; Riverdance,* the old Irish mass-jig, has gone global; and
even patriot Michael Collins has become a movie icon. Plus, the returned Joyce would be stirred by the songs of Sinéad O'Connor, fired
up by the films of Neil Jordan, and moved by the poems of Nobel lau-
reate Seamus Heaney. In short, Irish is way in. As for Ireland's capital, elegant shops and hotels, galleries, art-house cinemas, coffeehouses,
and a stunning variety of restaurants are springing up on almost every
street in Dublin, transforming the genteel capital that once suffocated
Joyce into a city every bit as cosmopolitan as the Paris to which he fled.

Forget the Vikings and the English. Fast-forward to the new Dublin,
where the army of invaders landing at the intersection of O'Connell
Street and Temple Lane are London lads on a wild bachelor night, Europeans in search of a chic weekend getaway, and representatives from
America of the "FBI"—or foreign-born Irish. Thanks to "the Celtic
Tiger"—the nickname given to the roaring Irish economy—this most
intimate capital city in Western Europe has become a boomtown (with
unemployment at an all-time low of 6%, Ireland's per-capita economy
is now ranked 19th in the world, higher than that of Great Britain).

No doubt about it: the new millennium belongs to Dublin. Yet, a
goodly number of its citizens protest that the rapid globalization of the
heretofore tranquil capital is forever changing its spirit and character.
Some observers view the openings of Planet Hollywood on elegant St.
Stephen's Green and the 400-seat Sports Bar in Temple Lane as signs
of the corporatization of Ireland's fair city. These skeptics await the
outcome of "Dublin: The Sequel"—can the "new Dublin" get beyond
the rage stage and sustain its rate of phenomenal growth or will it, like
London, have to suffer recession and crisis to rediscover its soul?

Happily, enough of the old Dublin remains to enchant. After all, it's
the fundamentals—the Georgian elegance of Merrion Square, the Norman drama of Christ Church Cathedral, a foamy pint at an atmospheric
pub—that still gratify. Fittingly, some of the more recent developments
hark back to the earliest. Two multimedia shows in the downtown area
remind us that Norsemen (various neighborhood names, such as
Howth, Leixlip, and Dalkey, echo their historic presence) were re-

sponsible for the city's original boom. In ancient days, more than 1,500 years ago, Dublin had been little more than a crossroads—albeit a critical one—of four of the main thoroughfares that traversed the country. Then, it had two names: Baile Atha Cliath, meaning City of the Hurdles, which was bestowed by Celtic traders in the 2nd century AD and which you can still see on buses and billboards throughout the city, and Dubhlinn, or "dark pool" (the murkiness of the water was caused by peat), which is believed to have been where Dublin Castle now stands.

In 837, Norsemen from Scandinavia carried out the first invasion on Dublin, only to be followed by other waves of warriors staking their claim to the city—from the 12th-century Anglo-Normans to Oliver Cromwell in 1651. Not until the 18th century did Dublin reach a period of glory, when a golden age of enlightened patronage by wealthy nobles turned the city into one of Europe's most prepossessing capitals. Streets and squares, such as Merrion and Fitzwilliam squares, were constructed with neoclassic dignity and Palladian grace. If, today, Dublin is still redolent in parts of the elegance of the 18th century, it is due to the imminently refined Georgian style of art and architecture, which flowered in the city between 1714 and 1820 during the English reigns of the three Georges. To satisfy the taste for luxury of the often-titled, unusually wealthy members of society, lemon-color chintz borders, gilded Derbyshire pier tables, and Adamesque wood paneling were installed in the salons of town houses. The arts also flourished: Handel, the German-born English composer, wrote much of his great oratorio *Messiah* here, where it was first performed in 1742. But the aura of "the glorious eighteenth" was short-lived; in 1800, the Act of Union brought Ireland and Britain together in a common United Kingdom, and political power moved from Dublin to London. Dublin quickly lost its cultural and social sparkle, as many members of the nobility moved to the new power center, turning Ireland practically overnight into "the Cinderella of all nations," in historian Maurice Craig's words.

The 19th century proved to be a time of political turmoil and agitation, although Daniel O'Connell, the first Catholic lord mayor of Dublin (his statue dominates O'Connell Street), won early success with the introduction of Catholic emancipation in 1829. During the late 1840s, Dublin escaped the worst effects of the famine, caused by potato blight, that ravaged much of southern and western Ireland. As an emerging Victorian middle class introduced an element of genteel snobbery to the city, Dublin began a rapid outward expansion to the new suburban enclaves of Ballsbridge, Rathgar, and Rathmines on the southside and Clontarf and Drumcondra on the northside.

The city entered a period of cultural ferment (☞ Literary Dublin *in* Pleasures and Pastimes, *below*) in the first decade of the 20th century—an era that had its political apotheosis in the Easter Uprising of 1916. A war aimed at winning independence from Britain began in County Tipperary in 1919 and lasted for three years. During the Civil War, which followed the setting up of the Irish Free State in December 1921, the Four Courts and the Custom House both came under fire and were severely damaged. The capital had to be rebuilt during the 1920s. After the Civil War was over, Dublin entered a new era of political and cultural conservatism, which continued until the late 1970s. Amazingly, the major turning point in Dublin's fortunes occurred in 1972, when Ireland, emerging from 40 years of isolationism, joined the European Economic Community. In the 1980s, while the economy remained in the grasp of recession, Dublin and Ireland once again turned to the cultural sphere to announce themselves to the rest of the world. Irish musicians stormed the American and British barricades of rock-and-roll. Bob Geldof and the Boomtown Rats ("I Don't Like Mondays") and Chris de Burgh were among the most prominent of the musicians who found audiences well beyond their native shores, but it was U2, which climbed to the topmost heights of rock-and-roll stardom, that forged a permanent place in international popular culture for Irish musicians. Sinéad O'Connor and the Cranberries have since followed, and more are on the fast track.

If the 1980s saw the ascent of Irish rock stars, the 1990s were truly the boom years—a decade of broadly improved economic fortunes, major capital investment, declining unemployment, and reversing patterns of immigration—all set in motion to a great extent by Ireland's participation in the EEC (now the European Union, or EU). When Ireland overwhelmingly approved the new EU treaty in 1992, it was one of the poorest European nations; it qualified for EU grants of all kinds. Since then, money has, quite simply, *poured* into Ireland—nowhere more so than in Dublin. The International Financial Services Centre, gleaming behind the two-centuries-old Custom House, is one of the most overt signs of the success the city has had in attracting leading multinational corporations, particularly those in telecommunications, software, and service industries. In the spring of 1998, the Irish overwhelmingly voted in favor of membership in the Single European Currency; since in January 1999, all prices have been quoted in pounds and euros, even though the European supercurrency as of press time was not yet in circulation. In January 2002, Ireland's main currency is to become the euro and the pound is to be faded out altogether.

Today, roughly half of the Irish Republic's population of 3.6 million people live in Dublin and its suburbs. It's a city of young people—astonishingly so. Students from all over Ireland attend Trinity College and the city's dozen other universities. On weekends, their counterparts from Paris, London, and Rome fly in, swelling the city's youthful contingent, crowding its pubs and clubs to overflowing. After graduating, more and more young people are sticking around rather than emigrating to New York or London, filling the raft of new jobs set up by multinational corporations and contributing to the hubbub that's evident everywhere.

All this development has not been without growing pains; with soaring house prices, increased crime, and major traffic problems, Dubliners are at last suffering the woes so familiar to city dwellers around the world. But you won't find many locals complaining, and progress steamrolls on. A new state-of-the-art Opera House and National Convention Center are both planned along the quays. "Me darlin' Dublin's dead and gone," so goes the old traditional ballad, but the rebirth, at times difficult and a little messy, has been a spectacular success.

Pleasures and Pastimes

Literary Dublin

Dublin packs more literary punch per square foot than practically any other spot on the planet—largely because of the ferment that took hold at the end of the 19th century, when two main cultural movements emerged. In 1893, Douglas Hyde, a Protestant and later the first president of Ireland, founded the Gaelic League (Conradh na Gaelige), whose goal was to preserve the Irish language and Gaelic traditions. At the same time, W. B. Yeats played a pivotal role in the Irish literary renaissance. With the foundation of the **Abbey Theatre** (☞ The Arts, *below*) in 1904 and the growing prominence of such playwrights as Sean O'Casey and J. M. Synge, Irish literature thrived. The **Dublin Writ-**

ers Museum (☞ Exploring Dublin, *below*) gives a terrific introduction to this story and to the more than two dozen major writers Ireland subsequently produced (at least the dead ones—living legends have to wait to be included). To go further back in literary history, head for **Trinity College** (☞ Exploring Dublin, *below*), where you can see a few pages of the legendary 9th-century *Book of Kells* and stroll through the hallowed campus where Samuel Beckett studied and where a theater now bears his name. If you're an Oscar Wilde fan, you can pay homage at 1 Merrion Square. The "ReJoyce! A Walk through *Ulysses* and James Joyce's Dublin" Close-Up box (☞ *below*) guides you through some key sites connected with Joyce and *Ulysses*. And if you want to stock up on anecdotes about the relationship between the pint and the pen, check out the *Dublin Literary Pub Crawl* or take a guided tour of literary pubs (☞ Guided Tours *in* Dublin A to Z, *below*).

Musical Dublin

Music fills Dublin's streets (especially Grafton Street) and its pubs, where *talk* of music is as popular as the tunes themselves. Dubliners are obsessed with music of every kind and will happily discuss anything from Elvis's earliest recordings (remember Jimmy's father in *The Commitments*?) to U2's latest incarnation. The city has been the stomping ground of so many big-league rock and pop musicians that Dublin Tourism has created a "Rock 'n Stroll" Trail (☞ Guided Tours *in* Dublin A to Z, *below*), which covers 16 sites, most of them in the city center and Temple Bar. It includes spots like **Bewley's Oriental Café** (☞ Exploring Dublin, *below*), where Bob Geldof and the other members of the Boomtown Rats hung out, and the Bad Ass Café, where Sinéad O'Connor once worked. You're forgiven if you think some connections between the trail sites and the musicians seem hokey, but you're not if you don't seek out Dublin's lively, present-day music scene. A number of small pubs and larger halls host live music, but the best places are midsize venues such as the **Olympia Theatre** (☞ Exploring Dublin, *below*) and the **Temple Bar Music Centre** (☞ The Arts, *below*), where you can hear well-established local acts *and* leading international artists (including world-renowned Irish musicians), playing everything from traditional and folk rock to jazz-funk and "Dubcore," a term coined to describe the city's many noisy alternative bands. **Ceol** (☞ Exploring Dublin, *below*), a new museum dedicated to traditional Irish music, is the perfect place to explore the uniquely Celtic rhythms of native music and dance.

A Thousand Pubs

Even if you only order an Evian, a visit to an Irish pub (or two or three) is a must. The Irish public house is a national institution—down to the spectacle, at some pubs, of patrons standing at closing time to the playing of Ireland's national anthem. Samuel Beckett would often repair to one, believing a glass of Guinness stout was the best way to ward off depression. Indeed, Dublin is for the stout of heart—the city has one pub for every 450 of its 500,000 adults. There are actor's pubs, sports pubs, even pubs for "less famous literary types" (Grogan's on South William Street). And any occasion—be it "ordinations, liquidations, cremations," as one storefront puts it—is the right occasion. Today, Irish pubs are being exported at an unprecedented rate all around the world, but in Dublin, it's a different story altogether. Here, surprisingly, modern, European-style café-bars are fast replacing the capital's traditional drinking spots. The extraordinary prices being offered for the old pubs by new entrepreneurs have proven hard to resist for the longtime owners. The city center is now dotted with high-concept designer pubs with bright, arty facades and a pervasive scent of affluence. To be sure, in the City of 1,000 Pubs, you're still certain of finding a good, old-fashioned watering hole. And if you do find yourself in a new spot, surrounded by the trappings of European chic, you'll soon discover that Dubliners still enjoy good *craic*—quintessentially Irish friendly chat and lively, irony-laced conversation. Wherever you go, remember that when you order a Guinness, the barman first pours it three-quarters of the way, lets it settle, then tops it off and brings it over to the bar. You should then wait again until the top-up has settled, at which point the brew turns a deep black. The mark of a perfect pint? As you drink the glass down, the brew will leave thin rings to mark each mouthful.

EXPLORING DUBLIN

In Dublin's fair city—"where the girls are so pretty" went the centuries-old ditty. Today, parts of the city—particularly the vast, uniform housing projects of the northern suburbs—may not be fair or pretty. But even if you're not conscious of it while you're in the city center, Dublin is in a beautiful setting: it loops around the edge of Dublin Bay and on a plain at the edge of the gorgeous, green Dublin and Wicklow mountains, rising softly just to the south. From the famous Four Courts building in the heart of town, the sight of the city, the bay, and the mountains will take your breath away. From the city's noted vantage points, such as the South Wall, which stretches far out into Dublin Bay, or from choice spots in the suburbs of south and north County Dublin, you can nearly get a full measure of the city. From north to south, Dublin stretches 16 km (10 mi). From its center, immediately adjacent to the port area and the River Liffey, the city spreads westward for an additional 10 km (6 mi); in total, it covers 28,000 acres. But its heart is far more compact than these numbers indicate. As in Paris, London, and Florence, and as in so many other cities throughout the world, a river runs right through Dublin. The River Liffey divides the capital into the "northside" and the "southside," as everyone calls the two principal center-city areas, and almost all the major sights in the area are well within less than an hour's walk of one another.

Coverage is organized into eight walks of the city center and the areas immediately surrounding it, and two excursions into County Dublin—the first to the southern suburbs, the latter to the northern. The first two walks—The Center City: Around Trinity College and The Georgian Heart of Dublin—cover many of the southside's major sites: Trinity College, St. Stephen's Green, Merrion Square, and Grafton Street. It makes sense to do these walks first, as they will quickly orient you to a good portion of the southside. The third walk—Temple Bar: Dublin's "Left Bank"—takes you through this revived neighborhood, which is the hottest, hippest zone in the capital. The fourth walk—Dublin West: From Dublin Castle to the Four Courts—picks up across the street from Temple Bar and gets you to the Guinness Brewery, the city's most popular attraction. The fifth walk—The Liberties—takes you on a brief stroll through working-class Dublin, a historic but often overlooked part of the city. A word about these five walks: although we've split the southside into five, you'll soon realize that the distance between the areas in all these walks is not very great. The sixth walk—North of the Liffey—moves to the northside of the city center and covers all the major cultural sites there, including the James Joyce Cultural Centre, Gate Theatre, Dublin Writers Museum, and Hugh Lane Municipal Gallery of Modern Art. It also includes the rapidly developing Smithfield district, which locals are already hailing as the future "Temple Bar of the northside." The seventh walk—Along the Grand Canal—covers noteworthy sites along the canal, beginning in the northeast part of the city, and ending in the southwest. Phoenix Park and Environs, at the western fringe of the northside city center, is the main focus of the eighth Dublin walk.

If you're visiting Dublin for more than two or three days, you'll probably want to explore farther afield. There's plenty to see and do a short distance from the center city—in the suburbs of both north and south County Dublin—but since you need either a car or public transportation to reach these destinations, we cover them in our Side Trips section (☞ *below*).

Because of its compact size and traffic congestion (brought on in the last few years by an astronomical increase in the number of new vehicles), *pedestrian* traffic—especially on the city center's busiest streets during commute hours—is astonishing. Watch where you stop to consult your map or you're liable to be swept away by the ceaseless flow of the bustling crowds.

Numbers in the text correspond to numbers in the margin and on the Dublin City Center, Dublin West, County Dublin–Southside, and County Dublin–Northside maps.

Great Itineraries

In a week, you should be able to cover almost all of our Dublin Exploring suggestions, including the Side Trips. But in three or even two days, you can see many city-center sites and probably come away with a greater familiarity of the city than you could establish in a similar length of time in any of Europe's other capitals.

IF YOU HAVE 1 DAY

Touring the largest city in Ireland in the space of a single day sounds like an impossible goal, but it can actually—almost—be done in the span of one sunrise to sunset. Think Dublin 101. South of the Liffey are graceful squares and fashionable terraces from Dublin's elegant Georgian heyday; interspersed with some of the city's leading sights, this area is perfect for an introductory city tour. You might begin at O'Connell Bridge—as Dublin has no central focal point, most natives regard it as the city's Piccadilly Circus or Times Square—then head south down Westmoreland Street on your way to view one of Dublin's most spectacular buildings, James Gandon's 18th-century Parliament House, now the Bank of Ireland building. To fuel up for the walk ahead, however, first stop at 12 Westmoreland Street and go into Bewley's Oriental Café, an institution that has been supplying Dubliners with coffee and buns since 1842. After you drink in the grand colonnade of the Bank of Ireland building, head west to the genteel, elegant campus of Trinity College—the oldest seat of Irish learning. Your first stop should be the Library, to see the staggering Long Room and Ireland's greatest art treasure, the *Book of Kells,* one of the world's most famous— and most beautiful—illuminated manuscripts.

Leave the campus and take a stroll along Grafton Street, Dublin's ritziest shopping street and—"Who will buy my beautiful roses?"—open-air flower market. Appropriately enough, one of the city's favorite relaxation spots, the lovely little park of St. Stephen's Green, is nearby. Head over to the northeast corner of the park to find ground zero for the city's cultural institutions. Here, surrounding the four points of Leinster House (built by the Duke of Kildare, Ireland's first patron of Palladianism), are the National Museum, replete with artifacts and exhibits dating back to prehistoric times; the National Gallery of Ireland (don't miss the Irish collection and the Caravaggio *Taking of Christ*); the National Library; and the Natural History Museum. Depending on your interests, pick one to explore, and then make a quick detour westward to Merrion Square—among Dublin's most famous Georgian landmarks.

For a lovely lunch, head back to Stephen's Green and the Victorian Shelbourne Méridien Hotel—the lobby salons glow with Waterford chandeliers and blazing fireplaces. From Stephen's Green head west to pay your respects to St. Paddy—St. Patrick's Cathedral. If, instead, the Dublin of artists and poets is more your speed, hop a double-decker bus and head north of the Liffey to the Dublin Writers Museum. End the day with a performance at the nearby Gate Theatre, another Georgian eye-knocker, or spend the evening exploring the cobbled streets, many cafés, and shops of Dublin's bohemian quarter, the compact Temple Bar area. Because you couldn't fit in a stop at the Guinness Brewery, top the evening off with a pint at the Norseman pub. By the time the barman says "Finish your pints" to announce closing time at 11 PM, you'll agree that although this day was a lightning tour of the city's main sights, it will have left an indelible impression of what Dublin is all about.

IF YOU HAVE 3 DAYS
The above tour is the grand curtain-raiser for this itinerary. Dedicate your second day to the north and west of the city center. In the morning, cross the Liffey via O'Connell Bridge and walk up O'Connell Street, the city's widest thoroughfare, stopping to visit the General Post Office—the besieged headquarters of the 1916 rebels—on your way to the Dublin Writers Museum and the Hugh Lane Municipal Gallery of Modern Art. Be sure to join the thousands of Dubliners strolling down Henry, Moore, and Mary streets, the northside's pedestrian shopping area. In the afternoon, head back to the Liffey for a quayside walk by Dublin's most imposing structure, the Custom House; then head west to the Guinness Brewery. Hop a bus or catch a cab back into the city and a blow-out dinner at the glamorous Tea Room in the Temple Bar's Clarence hotel. Spend the evening on a literary pub crawl to see where the likes of Beckett and Behan held court, perhaps joining a special guided tour. On the third day tour the northern outskirts of Dublin from Glasnevin Cemetery and the National Botanic Gardens across to the sublime Marino Casino in Marino and the quaint fishing village of Howth. Back in the city, have tea at Bewley's and catch a musical performance at the Olympia Theatre or a play at the Abbey Theatre.

IF YOU HAVE 5 DAYS
Start your fourth day at Dublin's dawn—a living history of Dublin can be seen at medieval Dublinia, across the street from ancient Christ Church Cathedral, whose underground crypt is Dublin's oldest structure. Head north, jumping across the Liffey to the Four Courts, James Gandon's Georgian masterpiece and the home of the Irish judiciary. Continue northward to visit the Royal Kilmainham Hospital—the home of the Irish Museum of Modern Art—and Kilmainham Gaol, where the leaders of the Easter Rising were executed following their capture. Return via Dublin Castle, residence of British power in Ireland for nearly 800 years, and new home of the Chester Beatty Library, containing Chinese and Turkish exhibits. On your fifth and final day explore the southern outskirts of the city, accessible by DART train, including the suburban areas of Dalkey and Sandycove (where you can visit the James Joyce Martello Tower), and the busy ferry port of Dun Laoghaire. Before returning to the city center, take a stroll along the 5-km (3-mi) beach of Sandymount Strand—that is, if Irish skies are smiling!

The Center City: Around Trinity College

The River Liffey provides a useful aid to orientation, flowing as it does through the direct middle of Dublin. If you ask a native Dubliner for directions—from under an umbrella, as it will probably be raining in the approved Irish manner—he or she will most likely reply in terms of "up" or "down," up meaning away from the river, and down toward it. Until recently, Dublin's center of gravity was O'Connell Bridge, a diplomatic landmark in that it avoided locating the center to the north or south of the river, as strong local loyalties still prevailed among "northsiders" (who live to the north of the river) and "southsiders," and neither would ever accept that the city's center lay on the other's side of the river. But by the early 1990s, diplomacy had gone by the wayside. Now, Dublin's heart beats loudest southward across the Liffey, due, in part, to a large-scale refurbishment and pedestrianization of Grafton Street, which made this already upscale shopping address *the* street to shop, stop, and be seen. At the foot of Grafton Street is the city's most famous and recognizable landmark, Trinity College; at the top of it is Dublin's most popular strolling retreat, St. Stephen's Green, a 27-acre landscaped park replete with flowers, lakes, bridges, and—most of all—Dubliners enjoying a time-out.

A Good Walk

Numbers in the text correspond to numbers in the margin and on the Dublin City Center map.

Start at **Trinity College** ①, exploring the quadrangle as you head to the Old Library to see the *Book of Kells*. If you want to see modern art, visit the collection housed in the Douglas Hyde Gallery, just inside the Nassau Street entrance to the college. If you're interested in the Georgian era, try to view the Provost's House and its salon, the grandest in Ireland. Trinity can easily eat up at least an hour or more, so when you come back out the front gate, you can either stop in at the **Bank of Ireland** ②, a neoclassic masterpiece that was once the seat of the Irish Parliament, or make an immediate left and head up **Grafton Street** ③, the pedestrian spine of the southside. The **Dublin Tourism** ④ office is just off Grafton Street, on the corner of Suffolk Street. If Grafton Street's shops whet your appetite for more browsing and shopping, turn right down Wicklow Street, then left up South William Street to **Powerscourt Townhouse Centre** ⑤, where a faux-Georgian atrium (very dubiously set within one of Dublin's greatest 18th-century mansions) houses high-priced shops and pleasant cafés. The **Dublin Civic Museum** ⑥ is next door to Powerscourt, across the alley on its south flank. If you're doing well on time and want to explore the shopping streets farther east, jog via the alley one block east to Drury Street, from which you can access the Victorian **George's Street Arcade** ⑦. Whether or not you make this excursion, you should head back to Grafton Street, where **Bewley's Oriental Café** ⑧, a Dublin institution, is another good place for a break. Grafton Street ends at the northwest corner of **St. Stephen's Green** ⑨, Dublin's most popular public gardens; they absolutely require a stroll-through. **Newman House** ⑩ is on the south side of the green. Amble back across the green, exiting onto the northeast corner, at which sits the grand **Shelbourne Méridien Hotel** ⑪, a wonderful place for afternoon tea or a quick pint at one of its two pubs. The **Huguenot Cemetery** ⑫ is just down the street from the hotel, on the same side. If you want to see more art, make a detour to the **RHA Gallagher Gallery** ⑬.

TIMING

Dublin's city center is so compact you could race through this walk in an hour, but in order to gain full advantage of what is on offer, we recommend that you set aside at least half a day—if you can—to explore the treasures of Trinity College and amble up and around Grafton Street to Stephen's Green.

Sights to See

🕾 *following the text of a review is your signal that the property has a Web site, where you will find details and, usually, images; for a link, visit www.fodors.com/urls.*

❷ Bank of Ireland. Across the street from the west facade of **Trinity College** (☞ *below*) stands one of Dublin's most striking buildings, now the Bank of Ireland but formerly the original home of the Irish Parliament. The building was begun in 1729 by Sir Edward Lovett Pearce, who designed the central section; three other architects would ultimately be involved in its construction. A pedimented portico fronted by six massive Corinthian columns dominates its grand facade, which follows the curve of Westmoreland Street as it meets College Green, once a Viking meeting place and burial ground. Two years after the Parliament was abolished itself in 1801 under the Act of Union, which brought Ireland under the direct rule of Britain, the building was bought for £40,000 by the Bank of Ireland. Inside, stucco rosettes adorn the coffered ceiling in the pastel-hue, colonnaded, clerestoried **main banking hall,** at one time the Court of Requests, where citizens' petitions were heard. Just down the hall is the original **House of Lords,** with tapestries depicting the Battle of the Boyne and the Siege of Derry, an oak-paneled nave, and a 1,233-piece Waterford glass chandelier; ask a guard to show you in. Visitors are welcome during normal banking hours; a brief guided tour is given every Tuesday at 10:30, 11:30, and 1:45 by the Dublin historian and author Éamonn Mac Thomáis. Accessed via Foster Place South, the small alley on the bank's east flank, the **Bank of Ireland Arts Center** frequently exhibits contemporary Irish art and has a permanent exhibition devoted to "The Story of Banking." ⊠ *2 College Green,* ☎ *01/677–6801, 01/671–1488 arts center.* ⊘ *Mon.– Wed. and Fri. 10–4, Thurs. 10–5; Arts Center Tues.–Fri. 10–4, Sat. 2– 5, Sun. 10–1.*

❽ Bewley's Oriental Café. The granddaddies of the capital's cafés, Bewley's has been serving coffee and buns to Dubliners since it was founded by Quakers in 1842 and now has four locations. Bewley's trademark stained-glass windows were designed by Harry Clarke (1889–1931), Ireland's most distinguished early 20th-century artist in this medium. They all make fine places in which to observe Dubliners of all ages and occupations; the aroma of coffee is irresistible, and the cafés' dark interiors—with marble-top tables, bentwood chairs, and mahogany trim—evoke a more leisurely Dublin. The food is overpriced and not particularly good, but people-watching here over a cup of coffee or tea is a quintessential Dublin experience. If you're interested in a more modern cup of coffee, check out the Metro Café, nearby at 43 South William Street—it's one of Dublin's best haunts for the caffeine-addicted and its staff is devoid of the devil-may-care, pseudo-existential inefficiency that seems to plague so many other Dublin cafés. ⊠ *78 Grafton St.,* ☎ *01/677–6761 (for all locations except Great George's St.);* ⊘ *Sun.–Thurs. 7:30 AM–1 AM, Fri.–Sat. 7:30 AM–4 AM.* ⊠ *13 Great George's St.,* ☎ *01/679–2078;* ⊘ *Mon.–Thurs. 7:45 AM–6 PM, Fri.– Sat. 7:45 AM–6 PM and 10:30 PM–4 AM.* ⊠ *12 Westmoreland St.;* ⊘ *Mon.–Sat. 7:30 AM–9 PM, Sun. 9:30 AM–9 PM.* ⊠ *40 Mary St.;* ⊘ *Mon.–Wed. and Fri.–Sat. 7 AM–6 PM, Thurs. 7 AM–9 PM.*

❻ Dublin Civic Museum. Built between 1765 and 1771 as an exhibition hall for the Society of Artists, this building later was used as the City Assembly House, precursor of City Hall. The museum's esoteric collection includes Stone Age flints, Viking coins, old maps and prints of the city, and the sculpted head of British admiral Horatio Nelson, which used to top Nelson's Pillar, beside the General Post Office (☞

North of the Liffey, *below*) on O'Connell Street; the column was top-pled by an explosion in 1966 on the 50th anniversary of the Easter Uprising. The museum holds exhibitions relating to the city. ⊠ *58 S. William St.,* ☎ *01/679–4260.* ⊡ *Free.* ☉ *Tues.–Sat. 10–6, Sun. 11–2.*

❹ Dublin Tourism. Churches are not just for prayers, as this deconsecrated medieval church proves. Resurrected as a visitor center, St. Andrew's, fallen into ruin after years of neglect, now houses Dublin Tourism, a private concern that offers the most complete information on Dublin's sights, restaurants, and hotels; you can even rent a car here. The office provides reservations facilities for all Dublin hotels, as well as guided tours, a plethora of brochures, and a gift shop (beware the exorbitant prices). Upstairs is a pleasant café serving sandwiches and drinks. ⊠ *St. Andrew's Church, Suffolk St.,* ☎ *01/605–7700 or 1850/230330 (within Ireland).* ☉ *July–Sept., Mon.–Sat. 8:30–6, Sun. 11–5:30; Oct.–June, daily 9–6.*

❼ George's Street Arcade. This Victorian covered market fills the block between Drury Street to the west and South Great George's Street to the east. It's changed little, despite a restoration. You'll find two dozen or so stalls selling books, prints, clothing (mostly secondhand), exotic foodstuffs, and trinkets. ⊠ *S. Great George's St.* ☉ *Mon.–Sat. 9–6.*

....

NEED A   One of Dublin's most ornate traditional taverns, the **Long Hall Pub** (⊠
BREAK?   51 S. Great George's St., ☎ 01/475–1590) has Victorian lamps, a
           mahogany bar, mirrors, chandeliers, and plasterwork ceilings, all more
           than 100 years old. The pub serves sandwiches and an excellent pint of
           Guinness.

....

★ **❸ Grafton Street.** It's no more than 200 yards long and about 20 ft wide, but brick-lined Grafton Street, open only to pedestrians, can make a claim to be the most humming street in the city, if not in all of Ireland. It is one of Dublin's vital spines: the most direct route between the front door of Trinity College and Stephen's Green, and the city's premier shopping street, home to Dublin's two most distinguished department stores, **Brown Thomas** and **Marks & Spencer** (☞ Shopping, *below*). Both on Grafton Street itself and in the smaller alleyways that radiate off it, there are also dozens of independent stores, a dozen or so colorful flower sellers, and some of Dublin's most popular watering holes (☞ Pubs *in* Nightlife and the Arts, *below*). In summertime, buskers from all over the country and the world line both sides of the street, pouring out the sounds of drum, whistle, pipe, and string.

⑫ Huguenot Cemetery. One of the last such burial grounds in Dublin, this cemetery was used in the late 17th century by French Protestants who had fled persecution in their native land. The cemetery gates are rarely open, but you can view the grounds from the street. It stands on the northeast corner across from the square. ⊠ *27 St. Stephen's Green N.*

❿ Newman House. One of the greatest glories of Georgian Dublin, Newman House is actually two imposing town houses joined together. The earliest, No. 85 St. Stephen's Green (1738), was designed by Richard Castle, favored architect of Dublin's rich and famous, and features a winged Palladian window on the Wicklow granite facade. Originally known as Clanwilliam House, it features two landmarks of Irish Georgian style: the Apollo Room, decorated with stuccowork depicting the sun god and his muses; and the magnificent Saloon, "the supreme example of Dublin Baroque," according to scholars Jacqueline O'Brien and Desmond Guinness, crowned with an exuberant ceiling aswirl with cupids and gods, created by the Brothers Lafranchini, the finest *stuccadores* (plasterworkers) of 18th-century Dublin. Next door at No. 86

44

Dublin City Center

KEY

i Tourist Information

(1765), the staircase is one of the city's most beautiful rococo examples, with floral swags and musical instruments picked out in cake-frosting white on pastel-color walls. Catholic University (described by James Joyce in *A Portrait of the Artist as a Young Man*) was established in this building in 1850, with Cardinal John Henry Newman as its first rector. At the back of Newman House lie **Iveagh Gardens,** a delightful hideaway with statues and sunken gardens that remains one of Dublin's best-kept secrets (you can enter via Earlsfort Terrace and Harcourt Street). The Commons Restaurant (☞ *Dining, below*) is in the basement. ⊠ *85–86 St. Stephen's Green,* ☎ *01/475-7255.* ⊠ *£2.* ☉ *June–Aug., weekdays 9–5, but visitation limited to supervised tours, daily June–Aug. at noon, 2, 3, and 4 PM.*

⑤ Powerscourt Townhouse Centre. Lucky man, this Viscount Powerscourt. In the mid-18th century, not only did he build Ireland's most spectacular country house, in Enniskerry, County Wicklow (which bears the family name; ☞ Chapter 2), but he also decided to rival that structure's grandeur with one of Dublin's largest stone mansions. Staffed with 22 servants and built of granite from the viscount's own quarry in the Wicklow Hills, Powerscourt House was a major statement in the Palladian style designed by Robert Mack in 1774—a massive, Baroque-style edifice that towers over the little street it sits on (note the top story, framed by massive volutes, that was once intended as an observatory). The interior decoration runs from rococo salons by James McCullagh to Adamesque plasterwork by Michael Stapleton to—surprise—an imaginative shopping atrium, installed in and around the covered courtyard. The stores here include high-quality Irish crafts shops and numerous food stalls (☞ *Shopping, below*). The mall exit leads to the Carmelite **Church of St. Teresa's** and **Johnson's Court.** Beside the church, a pedestrian lane leads onto Grafton Street. ⊠ *59 S. William St.* ☉ *Mon.–Sat.*

⑬ RHA Gallagher Gallery. The Royal Hibernian Academy, an old Dublin institution, is housed in a well-lit building, one of the largest exhibition spaces in the city. The gallery holds adventurous exhibitions of the best in contemporary art, both from Ireland and abroad. ⊠ *15 Ely Pl. off St. Stephen's Green,* ☎ *01/661-2558.* ⊠ *Free.* ☉ *Mon.–Wed. and Fri.–Sat. 11–5, Thurs. 11–9, Sun. 2–5.*

★ **⑪ Shelbourne Méridien Hotel.** The ebullient, redbrick, white wood-trimmed facade of the Shelbourne has commanded "the best address in Dublin" from the north side of St. Stephen's Green since 1865. In 1921 the Irish Free State's constitution was drafted here in a first-floor suite. The most financially painless way to soak up the hotel's old-fashioned luxury and genteel excitement is to step past the entrance—note the statues of Nubian princesses and attendant slaves—for afternoon tea (£13.50 per person, including sandwiches and cakes) in the green-wallpapered **Lord Mayor's Lounge** or for a drink in one of its two bars, the **Shelbourne Bar** and the **Horseshoe Bar** (☞ *Pubs, below*), both of which are thronged with businesspeople and politicos after the workday ends. Elizabeth Bowen, famed novelist, wrote her novel *The Hotel* about this very place. ⊠ *27 St. Stephen's Green,* ☎ *01/676-6471.* ☏

★ **⑨ St. Stephen's Green.** Dubliners call it simply Stephen's Green, and green it is (year-round)—a verdant, 27-acre city-center square that was an open common used for the public punishment of criminals until 1664. After a long period of decline, it became a private park in 1814—the first time in its history that it was closed to the general public. Its fortunes changed again in 1880, when Sir Arthur Guinness, later Lord Ardiluan (a member of the Guinness brewery family), paid for it to be laid out anew. Flower gardens, formal lawns, a Victorian bandstand,

and an ornamental lake that is home to many waterfowl are all within the park's borders, connected by paths guaranteeing that strolling here or just passing through will offer up unexpected delights (be sure to look out for palm trees). Among the park's many statues are a memorial to Yeats and another to Joyce by Henry Moore, and the *Three Fates,* a dramatic group of bronze female figures watching over man's destiny. In the 18th century the walk on the north side of the green was referred to as the Beaux Walk because most of Dublin's gentlemen's clubs were in town houses here. Today it is dominated by the **Shelbourne Méridien Hotel** (☞ *above*). On the south side is another alluring attraction, Georgian-gorgeous Newman House (☞ *above*). 🖾 *Free.* ☉ *Daily sunrise–sunset.*

★ ❶ **Trinity College.** Founded in 1592 by Queen Elizabeth I to "civilize" (Her Majesty's word) Dublin, Trinity is Ireland's oldest and most famous college. The memorably atmospheric campus is a must; here you can enjoy tracking the shadows of some of the more noted alumni, such as Jonathan Swift (1667–1745), Oscar Wilde (1854–1900), Bram Stoker (1847–1912), and Samuel Beckett (1906–89). Trinity College, Dublin (familiarly known as TCD) was founded on the site of the confiscated Priory of All Hallows. For centuries Trinity was the preserve of the Protestant church. A free education was offered to Catholics—provided that they accepted the Protestant faith. As a legacy of this condition, until 1966 Catholics who wished to study at Trinity had to obtain a dispensation from their bishop or face excommunication. Today more than 70% of Trinity's students are Catholics, an indication of how far away those days seem to today's generation.

Trinity's grounds cover 40 acres. Most of its buildings were constructed in the 18th and early 19th centuries. The extensive **West Front,** with a classical pedimented portico in the Corinthian style, faces College Green and is directly across from the **Bank of Ireland** (☞ *above*); it was built between 1755 and 1759, possibly the work of Theodore Jacobsen, architect of London's Foundling Hospital. The design is repeated on the interior, so the view is the same both from outside the gates and from the quadrangle inside. On the lawn in front of the inner facade are **statues** of orator Edmund Burke (1729–97) and dramatist Oliver Goldsmith (1728–74), two other alumni. Like the West Front, **Parliament Square** (commonly known as Front Square), the cobblestoned quadrangle that lies just beyond this first patch of lawn, also dates from the 18th century. On the right side of the square is Sir William Chambers's **theater,** or **Examination Hall,** dating from the mid-1780s, which contains the college's most splendid Adamesque interior (designed by Michael Stapleton). The hall houses an impressive organ retrieved from an 18th-century Spanish ship and a gilded oak chandelier from the old House of Commons; concerts are sometimes held here. The **chapel,** which stands on the left of the quadrangle, has stucco ceilings and fine woodwork. Both the theater and the chapel were designed by Scotsman William Chambers in the late 18th century. The looming **Campanile,** or bell tower, is the symbolic heart of the college; erected in 1853, it dominates the center of the square. To the left of the campanile is the **Graduates Memorial Building,** or GMB. Built in 1892, the slightly Gothic building is now home to both the Philosophical and Historical Societies, Trinity's ancient and fiercely competitive debating groups. At the back of the square stands old redbrick **Rubrics,** looking rather ordinary and out of place among the gray granite and cobblestones. Rubrics, now used as rooms for students and faculty, dates from 1690, making it the oldest building still standing.

Ireland's largest collection of books and manuscripts is housed in **Trin-**
★ **ity College Library.** Its principal treasure is the *Book of Kells,* generally considered the most striking manuscript ever produced in the
Anglo-Saxon world and one of the greatest masterpieces of early Christian art. Once thought to be lost—the Vikings looted the book in 1007
for its jeweled cover but ultimately left the manuscript behind—the book
is a splendidly illuminated version of the Gospels. In the 12th century,
Guardius Cambensis declared that the book was made by an angel's
hand in answer to a prayer of St. Bridget; in the 20th century, scholars decided instead that the book originated on the island of Iona in
Scotland, where followers of St. Colomba lived until the island came
under siege in the early to mid-9th century. They fled to Kells, County
Meath (☞ Chapter 2), bringing the book with them. The 680-page work
was rebound in four volumes in 1953, two of which are usually displayed at a time, so you typically see no more than four original pages.
(Some wags have taken to calling it the "Page of Kells.") However, such
is the incredible workmanship of the *Book of Kells* that one folio contains the equivalent of many other manuscripts. On some pages, it has
been determined that within a quarter inch, no fewer than 158 inter-
lacements of a ribbon pattern of white lines on a black background
can be discerned—little wonder some historians feel this book contains
all the designs to be found in Celtic art. Note, too, the extraordinary
colors, some of which were derived from shellfish, beetles' wings, and
crushed pearls. The most famous page shows the "XPI" monogram
(symbol of Christ), but if this page is not on display, you can still see
a replica of it, and many of the other lavishly illustrated pages, in the
adjacent exhibition—dedicated to the history, artistry, and conservation of the book—through which you must pass to see the originals.

Because of the fame and beauty of the *Book of Kells,* it is all too easy
to overlook the other treasures in the library. They include the *Book
of Armagh,* a 9th-century copy of the New Testament that also contains St. Patrick's Confession, and the legendary *Book of Durrow,* a
7th-century Gospel book from County Offaly. You may have to wait
in line to enter the library; it's less busy early in the day.

The **Old Library,** aptly known as the Long Room, is one of Dublin's
most staggering sights, at 213 ft long and 42 ft wide. It contains in its
21 alcoves approximately 200,000 of the 3 million volumes in Trinity's collection. Originally the room had a flat plaster ceiling, but in
1859–60 the need for more shelving resulted in a decision to raise the
level of the roof and add the barrel-vaulted ceiling and the gallery bookcases. Since the 1801 Copyright Act, the college has received a copy
of every book published in Britain and Ireland, and a great number of
these publications must be stored in other parts of the campus and beyond. Of note are the carved Royal Arms of Queen Elizabeth I, above
the library entrance—the only surviving relic of the original college buildings—and, lining the Long Room, a grand series of marble busts, of
which the most famous is Roubiliac's portrait of Jonathan Swift. The
Trinity College Library Shop sells books, clothing, jewelry, and postcards. ☎ *01/608–2308.* 🖃 *£4.50.* ☉ *June–Sept., Mon.–Sat. 9:30–5,
Sun. 9:30–4:30; Oct.–May, Mon.–Sat. 9:30–5, Sun. noon–4:30.*

Trinity College's stark, modern Arts and Social Sciences Building, with
an entrance on Nassau Street, houses the **Douglas Hyde Gallery of Modern Art,** which concentrates on contemporary art exhibitions and has
its own bookstore. Also in the building, down some steps from the gallery,
there's a snack bar with coffee, tea, sandwiches, and students willing
to talk about life in the old college. ☎ *01/608–1116.* 🖃 *Free.* ☉
Mon.–Wed. and Fri. 11–6, Thurs. 11–7, Sat. 11–4:45.

The **New Berkeley Library,** the main student library at Trinity, was built in 1967 and named after the philosopher and alumnus George Berkeley. The small open space in front of the library contains a spherical brass sculpture designed by Arnaldo Pomodoro. The library is not open to the general public. ⊠ *College Green,* ☎ *01/677–2941.* ⊙ *Grounds daily 8 AM–10 PM.*

In the Thomas Davis Theatre in the arts building, the **"Dublin Experience"** is a 45-minute audiovisual presentation devoted to the history of the city over the last 1,000 years. ☎ *01/608–1688.* ⊠ *£3; in conjunction with Old Library (☞ above), £6.* ⊙ *May–Oct., daily 10–5; shows every hr on the hr.*

The Georgian Heart of Dublin

If there's one travel poster that signifies "Dublin" more than any other, it's the one that pictures 50 or so Georgian doorways—door after colorful door, all graced with lovely fanlights upheld by columns. A building boom began in Dublin in the early 18th century, as the Protestant ascendancy constructed town houses for themselves and civic structures for their city in the style that came to be known as Georgian, for the four successive British Georges who ruled from 1714 through 1830. The Georgian architectural rage owed much to architects like James Gandon and Richard Castle. They and others were influenced by Andrea Palladio (1508–80), whose *Four Books of Architecture* were published in the 1720s in London and helped to precipitate the revival of his style that swept through England and its colonies. Never again would Dublin be so "smart," so filled with decorum and style, nor its visitors' book so full of aristocratic names. (For an introduction to Dublin's Georgian heyday, *see* the Close-Up box "The Age of Elegance: Dublin's Georgian Style," *below.*) Note that while Dublin's southside is a veritable shop window of the Georgian style, there are many other period sights to be found northside—for instance, the august interiors of the Dublin Writers Museum and Belvedere College, or James Gandon's great civic structures, the Custom House and the Four Courts, found quayside. These, and other Georgian goodies, are described in the Exploring sections of Dublin West and the North of the Liffey, *below.*

A Good Walk

Numbers in the text correspond to numbers in the margin and on the Dublin City Center map.

When Dublin was transformed into a Georgian metropolis, people came from all over to admire the new pillared and corniced city. Today, walking through Fitzwilliam Square or Merrion Street Upper, you can still admire vistas of calm Georgian splendor. Begin your Palladian promenade at the northeast corner of Stephen's Green—here, in front of the men's clubs, was the Beaux Walk, a favorite 18th-century gathering place for fashionable Dublin. Chances are you won't bump into a duke on his way to a Handel concert or an earl on his way to a rout, ball, and supper, but then, you won't have to dodge pigs, which used to dot the cityscape back then. Walk down Merrion Street to **Merrion Square** ⑭—one of Dublin's most attractive squares. The east side of Merrion Square and its continuation, Fitzwilliam Street, form what is known as "the Georgian mile," which, unlike some Irish miles, in fact measures less than a kilometer. On a fine day the Dublin Mountains are visible in the distance and the prospect has almost (thanks to the ugly, modern office block of the Electricity Supply Board) been preserved to give an impression of the spacious feel of 18th-century Dublin. Walk down the south side of the square to **Number Twenty-Nine** ⑮. Cut back through the square to visit the refurbished **Govern-**

ment Buildings ⑯, the **Natural History Museum** ⑰, **Leinster House** ⑱, and/or the **National Gallery of Ireland** ⑲. The last leg of this walk is up Kildare Street to the **National Library** ⑳, passing the back of Leinster House to the **National Museum** ㉑. Stop in at the **Genealogical Office** ㉒ if you're doing research about your ancestors. Walk back to Stephen's Green and down Dawson Street, which runs parallel to Grafton Street. The **Mansion House** ㉓, **Royal Irish Academy** ㉔, and **St. Ann's Church** ㉕ are on the left as you walk down toward Trinity College's side entrance.

TIMING

Dublin is so compact you could race through this walk in two hours, if you don't linger anywhere or set foot in one of the museums. But there are treasures galore at the National Gallery and the National Museum; the green tranquillity of Merrion Square; and many of Dublin's finest sites along the way (not to mention dozens of the city's most historic pubs)—so if you can, this is a good walk to do over the course of a half day.

Sights to See

㉒ **Genealogical Office.** Are you a Fitzgibbon from Limerick, a Cullen from Waterford, or a McSweeney from Cork? This reference library is a good place to begin your ancestor-tracing efforts. If you're a total novice at genealogical research, you can meet with an advisor (£25 for an hour consultation) who can help get you started. It also houses the **Heraldic Museum** (☉ weekdays 10–8:30, Sat. 10–12:30), where displays of flags, coins, stamps, silver, and family crests highlight the uses and development of heraldry in Ireland. Note that a map detailing the geographical origin of the hundred or so most common Irish surnames can be found at the back of this book (☞ Chapter 10). ✉ *2 Kildare St.,* ☎ *01/603–0200.* ☉ *Genealogical Office weekdays 10–4:30, Sat. 10–12:30.* 🎫 *Free. Guided tours by appointment.*

⑯ **Government Buildings.** The swan song of British architecture in the capital, this enormous complex was the last neoclassic edifice to be erected by the British government. A landmark of "Edwardian Baroque," it was designed by Sir Aston Webb—who did many of the similarly grand buildings in London's Piccadilly Circus—as the College of Science in the early 1900s. Following a major restoration in the early 1990s, these buildings became the offices of the Department of the *taoiseach* (the prime minister, pronounced *tea*-shuck) and the *tánaiste* (the deputy prime minister, pronounced tawn-*ish*-ta). Fine examples of contemporary Irish furniture and carpets now decorate the offices. A stained-glass window, known as "My Four Green Fields," was originally made by Evie Hone for the 1939 World Trade Fair in New York. It depicts the four ancient provinces of Ireland: Munster, Ulster, Leinster, and Connacht. The government offices are accessible only via 45-minute guided tours given on Saturday (tickets are available on the day of the tour from the National Gallery), though they are dramatically illuminated every night. ✉ *Upper Merrion St.,* ☎ *01/662–4888.* 🎫 *Free.* ☉ *Sat. 10:30–3:30.*

⑱ **Leinster House.** Built in 1745, Leinster House was commissioned by the Duke of Leinster and almost singlehandedly helped to ignite the Georgian style that dominated Dublin for 100 years. It was not only the largest private residence in the city but the first structure in Ireland by Richard Castle, a follower of Palladio, who was to design some of the country's most important Palladian country houses (☞ Powerscourt House and Russborough *in* Chapter 2). Inside, the grand salons were ornamented with coffered ceilings, Rembrandts, and Van Dycks, fitting settings for the parties often given by the duke's wife, Lady Emily

THE AGE OF ELEGANCE: DUBLIN'S GEORGIAN STYLE

EXTRAORDINARY DUBLIN!" sigh art lovers and connoisseurs of the 18th century. It was during the "gorgeous eighteenth" that this duckling of a city was transformed into a preening swan, largely by the Georgian style of art and architecture that flowered between 1714 and 1820 during the reigns of the three English Georges. Today, Dublin remains in good part a sublimely Georgian city, thanks to enduring grace notes: the commodious and uniformly laid out streets, the genteel town squares, the redbrick mansions accented with demilune fan windows. The great 18th-century showpieces are **Merrion, Fitzwilliam, Mountjoy,** and **Parnell squares**. Merrion Square East, the longest Georgian street in town, reveals scenes of decorum, elegance, polish, and charm, all woven into a "tapestry of rosy brick and white enamel," to quote the 18th-century connoisseur Horace Walpole. Setting off the facades are fan-lighted doors (often lacquered in black, green, yellow, or red) and the celebrated "patent reveal" window trims, thin plaster linings painted white to catch the light. These demilune fanlights—as iconic of the city as clock towers are of Zurich—are often in neoclassic Adamesque style.

Many exteriors appear severely plain, but don't be fooled: these town houses can be compared to bonbons whose sheaths of hard chocolate conceal deliciously creamy centers. Just behind their stately front doors are entry rooms and stairways aswirl with tinted rococo plasterwork, often the work of *stuccadores,* or plaster-workers imported from Italy (including the talented Lafranchini brothers). Some of the very finest of these houses are open to the public, such as the **Newman House** (☞ *below*); others are open by appointment, like **Belvedere College** (⊠ 6 Great Denmark St.).

The Palladian style—as the Georgian style was then called—began to reign supreme in domestic architecture in 1745 when the Croesus-rich Earl of Kildare returned from an Italian Grand Tour and built a gigantic Palladian palace called **Leinster House** in the seedy section of town. "Where I go, fashion will follow," he declared, and indeed it did. By then, the Anglo-Irish elite had given the city London airs by building the **Parliament House** (now the Bank of Ireland), **Royal Exchange** (now City Hall), the **Custom House,** and the **Four Courts** (☞ *above* and *below*) in the new style. But this phase of high fashion came to an end with the Act of Union: according to historian Maurice Craig, "On the last stroke of midnight, December 31, 1800, the gaily caparisoned horses turned into mice, the coaches into pumpkins, the silks and brocades into rags, and Ireland was once again the Cinderella among the nations." It was nearly 150 years before the spotlight shone once again on 18th-century Dublin, thanks to the conservation efforts of the **Irish Georgian Society** (⊠ 74 Merrion Sq., ☎ 01/676–7053).

ANCESTOR-HUNTING

THE LATE PRESIDENT KENNEDY and, more recently, former President Reagan are only two among many thousands of Americans who have been drawn to Ireland in an attempt to track down their ancestors. So popular has this become that Ireland today has numerous facilities for those in search of their past. However, before you begin some genealogical Sherlock Holmesing, you'll need some detailed information, not just the fact that your last name is Murphy, Kelly, or O'Donnell. The memories of elderly relatives about the place which they or their forebears emigrated, for example, is often a useful starting point. The county name is an aid, but the name of their village or town is even better. It can lead quickly to parish registers, often going back 200 years or more, which the local clergy will usually be very glad to let you see (keep in mind that, recently, many of these parish registers have been moved to regional town halls and government agencies). Best of all, however, is to organize some professional help. The Genealogical Office in Dublin is the best source of information on family names and family crests. Similarly, the Office of the Registrar General in Dublin's Custom House has details of many births, deaths, and marriages after 1864, and some marriages dating back to 1845 (a substantial part of their records were destroyed, however, in the Troubles of 1921). The Public Record Office at the Four Courts and the Registry of the Deeds in Henrietta Street, both in Dublin, are two other potentially useful sources of information. Of course, if your great-grandfather's name was Blarney Killakalarney, you should have an easy time sleuthing your family roots. Chances are, however, your name is one of the more prominent surnames in Ireland (☞ Irish Family Names, *in* Chapter 10), so you'll have a longer time tracking down your ancestors among all the Ahernes.

Lennox, a celebrated beauty. The building has two facades: the one facing Merrion Square is designed in the style of a country house; the other, on Kildare Street, is that of a town house. This latter facade—if you ignore the ground-floor level—was a major inspiration for Irishman James Hoban's designs for the White House in Washington, D.C. Built in hard Ardbracan limestone, the house's exterior makes a cold impression, and, in fact, the duke's heirs pronounced the house "melancholy" and fled. Today, the house is the seat of Dáil Éireann (the House of Representatives, pronounced dawl e-rin) and Seanad Éireann (the Senate, pronounced shanad e-rin), which together constitute the Irish Parliament. When the Dáil is not in session, tours can be arranged weekdays; when the Dáil is in session, tours are available only on Monday and Friday. The Dáil visitors' gallery is included in the tour, although it can be accessed on days when the Dáil is in session and tours are not available. To arrange a visit, contact the public relations office at the phone number provided. ⊠ *Kildare St.,* ☎ *01/618–3000.*

㉓ Mansion House. Home to the mayor of Dublin, the Mansion House dates from 1710, when it was built for Joshua Dawson, who later sold the property to the government on condition that "one loaf of double refined sugar of six pounds weight" be delivered to him every Christmas. In 1919 the Declaration of Irish Independence was adopted here. Dawson Street (named for the house's original tenant) is the site of the annual and popular **August Antiques Fair.** ⊠ *Dawson St.*

★ ⓮ **Merrion Square.** Created between 1762 and 1764, this tranquil square a few blocks to the east of St. Stephen's Green is lined on three sides by some of Dublin's best-preserved Georgian town houses, many of which have brightly painted front doors above which sit intricate fanlights. Leinster House—Dublin's Versailles—along with the Natural History Museum and the National Gallery line the west side of the square, but it is on the other sides that the Georgian terrace streetscape comes into its own, with the finest houses located on the north border. Even when its flower gardens are not in bloom, the vibrant, mostly evergreen grounds, dotted with sculpture and threaded with meandering paths, are worth a walk-through. The square has been the home of several distinguished Dubliners, including Oscar Wilde's parents, Sir William and "Speranza" Wilde (No. 1); Irish national leader Daniel O'Connell (No. 58); and authors W. B. Yeats (Nos. 52 and 82) and Sheridan LeFanu (No. 70). Walk past the houses and read the plaques on the house facades, which identify the former inhabitants. Until 50 years ago, the square was a fashionable residential area, but today most of the houses are offices. At the south end of Merrion Square, on Upper Mount Street, stands **St. Stephen's Church.** Known locally as the "pepper canister" church because of its cupola, the structure was inspired in part by Wren's churches in London. ⊠ *Merrion Sq.* ☉ *Daily sunrise–sunset.*

★ ⓳ **National Gallery of Ireland.** Caravaggio's *The Taking of Christ* (1602), Reynolds's *First Earl of Bellamont* (1773), Vermeer's *Lady Writing a Letter with Her Maid* (ca. 1670) . . . you get the picture. The National Gallery of Ireland—the first in a series of major civic buildings on the west side of Merrion Square—is one of Europe's finest smaller art museums, with more than 3,000 works. Unlike Europe's largest art museums, which are almost guaranteed to induce Stendhal's syndrome, the National Gallery can be thoroughly covered in a morning or afternoon without inducing exhaustion. An 1854 Act of Parliament provided for the establishment of the museum, which was helped along by William Dargan (1799–1867), who was responsible for building much of Ireland's railway network in the 19th century (he is honored by a statue on the front lawn). The 1864 building was designed by Francis Fowke, who was also responsible for London's Victoria & Albert Museum. More art than ever before is on display following the completion in 1996 of a four-year renovation and expansion.

A highlight of the museum is the major collection of paintings by Irish artists from the 17th through 20th centuries, including works by Roderic O'Conor (1860–1940), Sir William Orpen (1878–1931), William Leech (1881–1968), and Jack B. Yeats (1871–1957), the brother of W. B. Yeats and by far the best-known Irish painter of the 20th century. Yeats painted portraits and landscapes in an abstract expressionist style not dissimilar from that of the later Bay Area Figurative painters of the 1950s and 1960s. His *The Liffey Swim* (1923) is particularly worth seeing for its Dublin subject matter (the annual swim is still held, usually on the first weekend in September).

The collection also claims exceptional paintings from the 17th-century French, Dutch, Italian, and Spanish schools. Among the highlights that you should strive to see are those mentioned above (the spectacular Caravaggio made headlines around the world when it was found hanging undiscovered in a Jesuit house not far from the museum) and Rembrandt's *Rest on the Flight into Egypt* (1647), Poussin's *The Holy Family*

(1649) and *Lamentation over the Dead Christ* (ca. 1655–60), and, somewhat later than these, Goya's *Portrait of Doña Antonia Zárate* (ca. 1810). Don't forget to check out the amazing portrait the *First Earl of Bellamont,* by Reynolds; the earl was among the first to introduce the Georgian fashion to Ireland and this portrait stunningly flaunts the extraordinary style of the man himself. The French Impressionists are represented with paintings by Monet, Sisley, and Pissarro. The northern wing of the gallery houses the British collection and the Irish National Portrait collection, and the amply stocked **gift shop** is a good place to pick up books on Irish artists. An addition on nearby Clare Street was to be completed by early 2001. Free guided tours are available on Saturday at 3 PM and on Sunday at 2:15, 3, and 4. ⊠ *Merrion Sq. W,* ☎ *01/661–5133.* ☒ *Free.* ☉ *Mon.–Wed. and Fri.–Sat. 10–5:30, Thurs. 10–8:30, Sun. 2–5.* ✥

NEED A
BREAK?
Fitzer's (⊠ Merrion Sq. W, ☎ 01/661–4496), the National Gallery's self-service restaurant, is a find—one of the city's best spots for an inexpensive, top-rate lunch. The 16–20 daily menu items are prepared with an up-to-date take on new European cuisine. It's open Thursday until 8 and Sunday 2–5 in addition to Monday–Saturday lunch.

⓴ **National Library.** Ireland is one of the few countries in the world where one can happily admit to being a writer. And few countries as geographically diminutive as Ireland have garnered as many recipients of the Nobel Prize for Literature. Along with works by W. B. Yeats (1923), George Bernard Shaw (1925), Samuel Beckett (1969), and Seamus Heaney (1995), the National Library contains first editions of every major Irish writer, including books by Jonathan Swift, Oliver Goldsmith, and James Joyce (who used the library as the scene of the great literary debate in *Ulysses*). In addition, of course, almost every book ever published in Ireland is kept here, as well as an unequaled selection of old maps and an extensive collection of Irish newspapers and magazines—more than 5 million items in all. The main **Reading Room** opened in 1890 to house the collections of the Royal Dublin Society. Beneath its dramatic domed ceiling, countless authors have researched and written their books over the years. ⊠ *Kildare St.,* ☎ *01/661–8811.* ☒ *Free.* ☉ *Mon. 10–9, Tues.–Wed. 2–9, Thurs.–Fri. 10–5, Sat. 10–1.*

★ ㉑ **National Museum.** On the other side of Leinster House from the National Library, Ireland's National Museum houses a fabled collection of Irish artifacts, dating from 7000 BC to the present. The museum is organized around a grand rotunda and elaborately decorated, with mosaic floors, marble columns, balustrades, and fancy ironwork. It has the largest collection of Celtic antiquities in the world, including an array of gold jewelry, carved stones, bronze tools, and weapons. The Treasury collection, including some of the museum's most renowned pieces, is open on a permanent basis. Among the priceless relics on display are the 8th-century **Ardagh Chalice,** a two-handle silver cup with gold filigree ornamentation; the bronze-coated, iron **St. Patrick's Bell,** the oldest surviving example (5th–8th centuries) of Irish metalwork; the 8th-century **Tara Brooch,** an intricately decorated piece made of white bronze, amber, and glass; and the 12th-century bejeweled oak **Cross of Cong,** covered with silver and bronze panels. The Road to Independence Room is devoted to the 1916 Easter Uprising and the War of Independence (1919–21); displays here include uniforms, weapons, banners, and a piece of the flag that flew over the General Post Office during Easter Week, 1916. Upstairs is a permanent exhibit on the Vikings, featuring a full-size Viking skeleton, swords, leather works recovered in Dublin and surrounding areas, and a replica of a small Viking boat. In contrast to the ebullient late-Victorian architecture of the main museum building, the design of the **National Museum Annexe** is purely functional; it houses temporary shows of Irish antiquities. The 18th-century **Collins Barracks** (☞ Phoenix Park and Environs, *below*), the most recent addition to the museum, houses the collection of glass, silver, furniture, and other decorative arts. ⊠ *Kildare St.; Annexe: 7–9 Merrion Row;* ☎ *01/677-7444.* ☒ *Free.* ☉ *Tues.–Sat. 10–5, Sun. 2–5.*

⑰ Natural History Museum. Dr. Stanley Livingstone inaugurated this museum when it opened in 1857. Today, it is little changed from Victorian times and remains a fascinating repository of mounted mammals, birds, and other flora and fauna. The most famous exhibits are the skeletons of Ireland's extinct, prehistoric giant "Irish elk" and the 65-ft whale skeleton suspended from the roof. The museum is next door to the ☞ **Government Buildings.** ⊠ *Merrion Sq. W,* ☎ *01/677-7444.* ☒ *Free.* ☉ *Tues.–Sat. 10–5, Sun. 2–5.*

⑮ Number Twenty-Nine. Everything in this carefully refurbished 1794 home, known simply as Number Twenty-Nine, is in keeping with the elegant lifestyle of the Dublin middle class between 1790 and 1820, the height of the Georgian period, when the house was owned by a wine merchant's widow. From the basement to the attic, in the kitchen, nursery, servant's quarters, and the formal living areas, the National Museum of Ireland has re-created the period's style with authentic furniture, paintings, carpets, curtains, paint, wallpapers, and even bellpulls. ⊠ *29 Lower Fitzwilliam St.,* ☎ *01/702-6165.* ☒ *£2.50.* ☉ *Tues.–Sat. 10–5, Sun. 2–5.*

㉔ Royal Irish Academy. Adjacent to the **Mansion House** (☞ *above*), the country's leading learned society houses important manuscripts in its 18th-century library, including a large collection of ancient Irish manuscripts such as the 11th–12th century *Book of the Dun Cow* and the library of the 18th-century poet Thomas Moore. ⊠ *19 Dawson St.,* ☎ *01/676-2570.* ☒ *Free.* ☉ *Weekdays 9:30–5.*

㉕ St. Ann's Church (Church of Ireland). St. Ann's plain, neo-Romanesque, granite exterior, erected in 1868, belies the church's rich Georgian interior, designed in 1720 by Isaac Wills. Among the highlights of the interior are polished-wood balconies, ornate plasterwork, and shelving in the chancel dating from 1723 and still in use for the distribution of bread to the poor of the parish. ⊠ *Dawson St.,* ☒ *Free.* ☉ *Weekdays 10–3 and Sun. for services.*

Temple Bar: Dublin's "Left Bank"

More than anywhere else in Dublin, it is Temple Bar that represents the dramatic changes (good and bad) and ascending fortunes of Dublin in the 1990s. Named after one of the streets of its central spine, the area was targeted for redevelopment in 1991–92 after a long period of neglect, having survived widely rumored plans to turn it into a massive bus depot and/or a giant parking lot. Temple Bar took off—*fast*—into Dublin's version of New York's SoHo, Paris's Bastille, London's Notting Hill: a thriving mix of high and alternative culture distinct from that in every other part of the city. Dotting the area's narrow cobblestone streets and pedestrian alleyways are new apartment buildings (inside they tend to be small and uninspired, with sky-high rent), vintage-clothing stores, postage-stamp-size boutiques selling £200 sunglasses and other expensive gewgaws, art galleries galore, a hotel resuscitated by U2, hip restaurants, pubs, clubs, European-style cafés, and a smattering of cultural venues.

Temple Bar's regeneration was no doubt abetted by that one surefire real estate asset: location, location, location. The area is bordered by Dame Street to the south, the Liffey to the north, Fishamble Street to the west, and Westmoreland Street to the east. In fact, Temple Bar is so perfectly situated between everywhere else in Dublin that it's difficult to believe this neighborhood was once largely forsaken. It's now sometimes called the "playing ground of young Dublin," and for good reason: on weekend evenings and daily in the summer it teems with young people—not only from Dublin but from all over Europe—who fly into the city for the weekend, drawn by its pubs, clubs, and lively craic. It has become a favorite of young Englishmen on "stag" weekends, 48-hour bachelor parties heavy on drinking and debauching. Some who have witnessed Temple Bar's rapid gentrification and commercialization complain that it's losing its artistic soul—*Harper's Bazaar* said it was in danger of becoming "a sort of pseudoplace," like London's Covent Garden Piazza or Paris's Les Halles. Over the next few years the planned Smithfield development (☞ North of the Liffey, *below*) may replace Temple Bar at the cutting edge of Dublin culture, but for the moment there's no denying that this is one of the best places to get a handle on the city.

A Good Walk

Numbers in the text correspond to numbers in the margin and on the Dublin City Center map.

Start at O'Connell Bridge and walk down Aston Quay, taking in the terrific view west down the River Liffey. Alleys and narrow roads to your left lead into Temple Bar, but hold off turning in until you get to **Ha'penny Bridge** ㉖, a Liffey landmark. Turn right and walk through Merchant's Arch, the symbolic entry into Temple Bar (see if you can spot the surveillance cameras up on the walls), which leads you onto the area's long spine, named Temple Bar here but also called Fleet Street (to the east) and Essex Street (both east and west, to the west). You're right at Temple Bar Square, one of the two largest plazas in Temple Bar. Just up on the right are two of the area's leading art galleries, the Temple Bar Gallery (at Lower Fownes Street) and, another block up, the Original Print Gallery and Black Church Print Studios (☞ Art Galleries *in* Nightlife and the Arts, *below*). Turn left onto Eustace Street. If you have children, you may want to go to the **Ark** ㉗, a children's cultural center. Across the street from the Ark, stop in at the Temple Bar Information Centre (☞ Visitor Information *in* Dublin A to Z, *below*) and pick up a handy *Temple Bar Guide*. Farther down Eustace Street is the **Irish Film Centre** ㉘, Temple Bar's leading cultural venue and a great place to catch classic or new indie films. In summer, the IFC organizes Saturday-night outdoor screenings on **Meeting House Square** ㉙, behind the Ark, accessed via Curved Street. The street is dominated on one side by the **Arthouse** ㉚ and on the other by the Temple Bar Music Centre (☞ Nightlife and the Arts, *below*). Dublin's leading photography gallery, the **Gallery of Photography** ㉛, is also here. Walk a few steps west to the narrow, cobbled Sycamore Street, and then turn right and walk to Dame Street, where you'll find the **Olympia Theatre** ㉜. Farther down Dame Street, the ultramodern **Central Bank** ㉝ rises above the city. Head for the corner of Parliament Street, where you can stop for a break or begin the next walk.

TIMING

You can easily breeze through Temple Bar in an hour or so, but if you've got the time, plan to spend a morning or afternoon here, drifting in and out of its dozens of stores and galleries, relaxing at a café over a cup of coffee or at a pub over a pint, maybe even seeing a film if you're looking for a change from sightseeing.

Sights to See

The Ark. If you're traveling with children and looking for something fun to do, be sure to stop by the Ark, Ireland's children's cultural center, housed in a former Presbyterian church. Its theater opens onto Meeting House Square for outdoor performances in summer. A gallery and workshop space host ongoing activities. ⊠ *Eustace St.,* ☎ *01/670–7788.* ⊡ *Free.* ۞ *Weekdays 9:30–4, Sat. 10–4.*

Arthouse. This is one of the first purpose-built multimedia centers for the arts in the world. Its modern design—all glass, metal, and painted concrete—is the work of esteemed architect Shay Cleary Doyle, who intended the building to reflect the object glorified within: the computer. Inside is a training center, a performance venue, a creative studio, and an exhibition space that plays host to a variety of art exhibitions. Pride of place, however, goes to the Art Information Bureau and the Artifact artist's database, featuring the work of more than 1,000 modern Irish artists working in Ireland and abroad. This useful catalog is open to anyone wishing to buy or admire the work of the listed artists, and it is set up in such a way that you can search for work according to specific criteria; just press a few buttons and a list of artists and images of their work fitting your description will appear. An Internet café, Cyberia, is on the top floor. ⊠ *Curved St.,* ☎ *01/605–6800.* ⊡ *Free.* ۞ *Weekdays 9:30–6.*

Central Bank. Designed by Sam Stephenson in 1978, the controversial, ultramodern, glass and concrete building suspends huge concrete slabs around a central axis. Skateboarders and in-line skaters have taken up residence on the little plaza in front of the building. ⊠ *Dame St.,* ☎ *01/671–6666.* ⊡ *Free.* ۞ *Weekdays 10–6.*

Gallery of Photography. Dublin's premier photography gallery has a permanent collection of early 20th-century Irish photography and also puts on monthly exhibits of contemporary Irish and international photographers. The bookstore is the best place in the city to browse for photography books and pick up arty postcards. ⊠ *Meeting House Sq. S,* ☎ *01/671–4654.* ⊡ *Free.* ۞ *Mon.–Sat. 11–6.*

Ha'penny Bridge. This heavily trafficked footbridge crosses the Liffey at a prime spot: Temple Bar (☞ *above*) is on the south side, and the bridge provides the fastest route to the thriving Mary and Henry Street shopping areas to the north (☞ *Shopping, below*). Until early in the 20th century, a half-penny toll was charged to cross it. Yeats was one among many Dubliners who found this too high a price to pay—more a matter of principle than of finance—and so made the detour via O'Connell Bridge. Congestion on the bridge has been relieved with the opening of the Millennium Footbridge a few hundred yards up the river.

Irish Film Centre (IFC). The opening of the IFC in a former Quaker meetinghouse in 1992 helped to launch the revitalization of Temple Bar. It has two comfortable art-house cinemas showing revivals and new independent films, the Irish Film Archive, a bookstore for cineastes, and a "happening" bar, all of which make this one of the neighborhood's most vital cultural institutions. ⊠ *6 Eustace St.,* ☎ *01/679–5744.* ⊡ *Free.* ۞ *Weekdays 9:30–late, weekends 11–late.*

NEED A BREAK? The creamiest, frothiest coffees in all of Temple Bar can be had at the **Joy of Coffee/Image Gallery Café** (⊠ 25 E. Essex St., Temple Bar, ☎ 01/679–3393); the wall of windows floods light onto the small gallery with original photographs adorning the walls.

㉙ **Meeting House Square.** Behind the Ark (☞ *above*) and accessed via Curved Street, Meeting House Square has become something of a gathering place for Dublin's youth and artists. Throughout the summer, seats are erected and a wide variety of events—including classic movies (every Saturday night), theater, games, and family programs—are held here. It's also a favorite site for the continuously changing street sculpture that pops up all over Temple Bar. All year round it's a great spot to sit and relax and engage in a bit of people-watching. It hosts an organic food market every Saturday morning. The square gets its name from a nearby Quaker meetinghouse.

★ ㉜ **Olympia Theatre.** One of the best places anywhere in Europe to see live musical acts, the Olympia is Dublin's second oldest and one of its busiest theaters. Built in 1879, this classic Victorian music hall has a gorgeous red wrought-iron facade. Conveniently, two pubs are situated through doors directly off the back of the theater's orchestra section. The Olympia's long-standing Friday and Saturday series, "Midnight at the Olympia," has brought a wide array of musical performers to Dublin, and the theater has also seen many notable actors strut its stage, including Alec Guinness, Peggy Ashcroft, Noël Coward, and even Laurel and Hardy. In November 1996, when Van Morrison played Dublin, he chose to perform here rather than in a larger venue. If you have a chance to catch a favorite performer (or to discover someone new), go!—you won't regret it. ⊠ *72 Dame St.,* ☎ *01/677–7744.*

NEED A
BREAK?

The trendy **Irish Film Centre Café** (⊠ 6 Eustace St., ☎ 01/679–5744) is a surprisingly pleasant place for a lunchtime break. Sandwiches are large and healthy, with plenty of nonmeat choices, and the people-watching is nonpareil.

Dublin West: From Dublin Castle to the Four Courts

This section of Dublin takes you from the 10th-century crypt at Christ Church Cathedral—the city's oldest surviving structure—to the modern plant of the Guinness Brewery. It also crosses the Liffey for a visit to Smithfield, the old market area being billed as the next hot location in the city. Dublin is so compact, however, that to separate out the following sites from those covered in the two other city-center southside walks is potentially to mislead by suggesting that this area is at some remove from the heart of the city center. In fact, this tour's starting point, City Hall, is just across the street from Thomas Read's, and Christ Church Cathedral is a very short walk farther west. However, the westernmost sites covered here—notably the Royal Hospital and Kilmainham Gaol—*are* at some distance, more so than may be comfortable if you're not an enthusiastic walker, so you may want to drive or catch a cab or a bus out to them.

A Good Walk

Numbers in the text correspond to numbers in the margin and on the Dublin West map.

Begin with a brief visit to **City Hall** ㉞, and then walk up Cork Hill to the Castle Street entrance to **Dublin Castle** ㉟, whose highlights—the grand salons that show off Viceregal Dublin at its most splendid—are only visitable via a guided tour. The castle is also the new home of the **Chester Beatty Library** ㊱, a world-renowned collection of Oriental art. Leave via the same gate, turn left, and walk up Castle Street to ancient **Christ Church Cathedral** ㊲, picturesquely situated on one of the few hills in the city. At the southeast corner of the cathedral, connected via an utterly beguiling Victorian-era bridge, **Dublinia** ㊳ gives you a chance to experience life in medieval Dublin. And just down Nicholas Street is—begorrah!—**St. Patrick's Cathedral** ㊵. If you're eager to venture back to the 17th century or love old books, visit the quaint **Marsh's Library** ㊶, next door to St. Patrick's. You can then stroll through the old artisan redbrick dwellings in the Liberties, home to the heaviest concentration of the city's antiques stores, to Thomas Street and—just follow your nose—the **Guinness Brewery** ㊷, where you can keep your spirits up in more ways than one. At this point, if you want to see more architecture and modern art, proceed farther west to the Irish Museum of Modern Art in the elegant 18th-century **Royal Hospital Kilmainham** ㊸, and the **Kilmainham Gaol** ㊹. If you don't elect to head this way, turn back down Thomas Street, crossing the Liffey at Bridge Street, which on its north side becomes Church Street. On your left is the **Four Courts** ㊹. A little farther up on the left is **St. Michan's Church** ㊺ and the beginning of the Smithfield area, which includes the brand-new **Ceol** ㊻, a museum dedicated to traditional Irish music. A quick jog over to Bow Street (via Mary's Lane) brings you to the **Old Jameson Distillery** ㊼—here you'll learn all there is to learn about Irish whiskey.

TIMING

Allow yourself a few hours, especially if you want to include the Guinness Brewery and the Irish Museum of Modern Art at the Royal Hospital. Keep in mind that if you want to cover the easternmost sites—Dublin Castle, City Hall, Christ Church Cathedral, and environs—you can easily append them onto a tour of Temple Bar.

Sights to See

★ ✋ ㊻ **Ceol.** At the heart of the new Smithfield Village development is Chief O'Neill's complex, consisting of a hotel (☞ Lodging, *below*) and Ceol, a new interactive museum of Irish music. The museum tells the ancient story of Celtic music in a thoroughly modern fashion. The History of Irish Music area consists of five rooms dedicated to different periods from the age of myth and legend to the present. Computerized exhibits allow you to pick and choose as much detail as you want. The Stories Room contains a priceless oral history of musicians and storytellers from early in the last century. The Song Room illustrates the centuries-old Irish love of lyrics, from the haunting, unaccompanied sean nós style to the scatological Dublin ballad. The four major instruments of Irish music—fiddle, flute, button accordion, and *uilleann* (elbow) pipes (small, bellow-blown bagpipes played sitting down)—are displayed on the ground floor. Throughout the museum, touch screens allow access to recordings of the masters of the genre plus hundreds of film clips of them performing. A children's area has an ingenious game of musical twister that allows kids to play along with a tune, using parts of their body to play the notes. ✉ *Smithfield Village,* ☎ *01/817–3820.* ☞ *£3.75.* ☉ *Mon.–Sat. 9:30–6.* ✇

㊱ **Chester Beatty Library.** Formerly in the suburb of Ballsbridge, the library is now housed in the clock tower building of **Dublin Castle** (☞ *below*). Sir Alfred Chester Beatty (1875–1968), a Canadian mining millionaire, assembled one of the most significant collections of Islamic and Far Eastern art in the Western world, which he then donated to Ireland. Among the library's exhibits are clay tablets from Babylon dating from 2700 BC, Japanese color wood-block prints, Chinese jade books, and Turkish and Persian paintings. It also has 250 manuscripts of the Koran from throughout the Moslem world. Guided tours of the library are available on Tuesday and Saturday at 2:30 PM. ✉ *Castle St.,* ☎ *01/269–2386.* ☞ *Free.* ☉ *Tues.–Fri. 10–5, Sat. 2–5.*

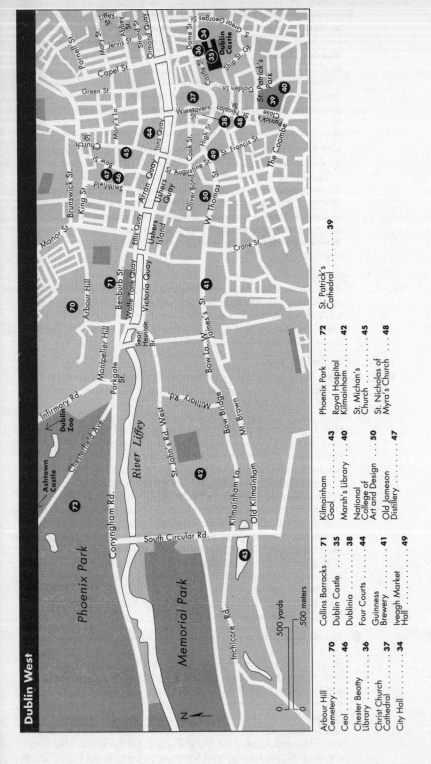

Dublin West

★ ㊲ **Christ Church Cathedral.** You'd never know from the outside that the first Christianized Danish king built a wooden church at this site in 1038; thanks to the extensive 19th-century renovation of its stonework and trim, the cathedral looks more Victorian than Anglo-Norman. Construction on the present Christ Church—the flagship of the Church of Ireland and one of two Protestant cathedrals in Dublin (the other is St. Patrick's just to the south; ☞ *below*)—was begun in 1172 by Strongbow, a Norman baron and conqueror of Dublin for the English crown, and went on for 50 years. By 1875 the cathedral had deteriorated badly, so a major renovation gave it much of the look it has today, including the addition of one of Dublin's most charming structures: a Bridge of Sighs–like affair that connects the cathedral to the old Synod Hall, which now holds the Viking extravaganza, Dublinia (☞ *below*). Remains from the 12th-century building include the north wall of the nave, the west bay of the choir, and the fine stonework of the transepts, with their pointed arches and supporting columns. Strongbow himself is buried in the cathedral beneath an impressive effigy. The vast, sturdy **crypt**, with its 12th- and 13th-century vaults, is Dublin's oldest surviving structure and the building's most notable feature. ⌂ *Christ Church Pl. and Winetavern St.,* ☎ *01/677–8099.* ⌾ *£2.* ⊙ *Daily 9:30–5.* ⌖

㉞ **City Hall.** Facing the Liffey from Cork Hill at the top of Parliament Street, this grand Georgian municipal building (1769–79), once the Royal Exchange, was designed by Thomas Cooley and marks the southwestern corner of Temple Bar. Today it's the seat of the Dublin Corporation, the elected body that governs the city. Twelve columns encircle the domed central rotunda, which has a fine mosaic floor and 12 frescoes depicting Dublin legends and ancient Irish historical scenes. Just off the rotunda is a gently curving staircase, a typical feature of most large Dublin town houses. ⌂ *Cork Hill,* ☎ *01/679–6111 ext. 2807.* ⌾ *Free.* ⊙ *Weekdays 9–1 and 2:15–5.*

㉟ **Dublin Castle.** Neil Jordan's film *Michael Collins* captured Dublin Castle's near-indomitable status well: seat and symbol of the British rule of Ireland for 7½ centuries, the castle figured largely in Ireland's turbulent history early in the 20th century. After extensive renovations, it's now used mostly for Irish and EU governmental purposes. The sprawling **Great Courtyard** is the reputed site of the Black Pool (Dubh Linn, pronounced *dove*-lin) from which Dublin got its name, though today it is lined with stretch limos and security guards. In the Lower Castle Yard, the **Record Tower,** the earliest of several towers on the site, is the largest remaining relic of the original Norman buildings, built by King John between 1208 and 1220. The clock tower building now houses the **Chester Beatty Library** (☞ *above*). Guided tours are available around the principal **State Apartments** (on the southern side of the Upper Castle Yard), formerly the residence of the English viceroys. Now used by the president of Ireland to host visiting heads of state and EU ministers, they are lavishly furnished with rich Donegal carpets and illuminated by Waterford glass chandeliers. The largest and most impressive of these chambers, **St. Patrick's Hall,** with its gilt pillars and painted ceiling, is used for the inauguration of Irish presidents. The **Round Drawing Room,** in Bermingham Tower, dates from 1411 and was rebuilt in 1777; a number of Irish leaders were imprisoned in the tower, from the 16th century to the early 20th century. The blue oval **Wedgwood Room** contains Chippendale chairs and a marble fireplace. The **Castle Vaults** now holds an elegant little patisserie and bistro.

On the grounds of the castle is the **Church of the Holy Trinity** (formerly called Chapel Royal), designed in 1814 by Francis Johnston, who also designed the original General Post Office building on O'Connell

Street. Carved oak panels and stained glass depicting viceroys' coats of arms grace the interior. Look up to view the elaborate array of fan vaults that decorates the ceiling. On the outside more than 100 carved heads adorn the walls. St. Peter and Jonathan Swift preside over the north door, St. Patrick and Brian Boru over the east. One-hour guided tours of the castle are available every half hour, but the rooms are closed when in official use, so phone first. The easiest way in to the castle today is via the **Cork Hill Gate,** just west of City Hall. ✉ *Castle St.,* ☎ *01/ 677–7129.* ▣ *State Apartments £3, including tour.* ⊙ *Weekdays 10– 5, weekends 2–5.*

🕭 ㊳ **Dublinia.** In the old Synod Hall (formerly a meeting place for bishops of the Church of Ireland), attached via a covered stonework Victorian bridge to **Christ Church Cathedral** (☞ *above*), Dublin's Medieval Trust has set up an entertaining and informative reconstruction of everyday life in medieval Dublin. The main exhibits use high-tech audiovisual and computer displays; there are also a scale model of what Dublin was like around 1500, a medieval maze, a life-size reconstruction based on the 13th-century dockside at Wood Quay, and a fine view from the tower. For a more modern take on the city, study the noted James Malton series of prints of 18th-century Dublin hanging on the walls of the coffee shop. ✉ *St. Michael's Hill,* ☎ *01/679–4611.* ▣ *Exhibit £3.95.* ⊙ *Apr.–Sept., daily 10–5; Oct.–Mar., Mon.–Sat. 11– 4, Sun. 10–4:30.*

㊹ **Four Courts.** Today the seat of the High Court of Justice of Ireland, the Four Courts are James Gandon's second Dublin masterpiece, built between 1786 and 1802, close on the heels of his **Custom House** (☞ *below*), downstream on the same side of the River Liffey. The Four Courts replaced a 13th-century Dominican abbey that stood here earlier. In 1922, during the Irish Civil War, the Four Courts was almost totally destroyed by shelling, and the adjoining Public Records Office was gutted, with many of its priceless legal documents destroyed, including innumerable family records; efforts to restore the building to its original state spanned 10 years. Today the stately Corinthian portico and the circular central hall are well worth viewing. Its distinctive copper-covered dome atop a colonnaded rotunda makes this one of Dublin's most instantly recognizable buildings; the view from the rotunda is terrific. Although there is no tour of the building, you are welcome to sit in while the courts are in session. ✉ *Inns Quay,* ☎ *01/872–5555.* ⊙ *Daily 10–1 and 2:15–4.*

★ ㊶ **Guinness Brewery.** Founded by Arthur Guinness in 1759, Ireland's all-dominating brewer—in fact, at one stage the largest stout-producing brewery in the world—is on a 60-acre spread west of Christ Church Cathedral. It happens to be the most popular tourist destination in town—not surprisingly, since the Irish national drink is Guinness stout, a dark brew made with roasted malt. If you're used to lighter, lager-type beers you may find this rich dark concoction, with its thick creamy "head" or "collar," somewhat unusual at first taste. But once the taste is acquired, it soon becomes an addiction. The brewery itself is closed to the public, but the 19th-century **Hop Store,** on Crane Street, part museum and part gift shop, puts on an 18-minute audiovisual presentation. The show ends with the curtain rising on the kind of old-fashioned pub—with mahogany decor, mirrors, and snugs—that is fast becoming hard to find in modern Dublin. You then receive two complimentary glasses (or one pint) of the famous black stout (a smile and a polite request might get you a couple more). The Guinness Zone, an interactive exhibit on the second floor, highlights the history of the beer's remarkably successful advertising campaigns, from the famous

"Guinness is Good for You" poster ads to the ultrasleek television commercials of the present day. A gift shop sells the best of Guinness memorabilia: posters, bar towels, beer mats, and garments. ⊠ *James' Gate,* ☎ *01/453–3645.* 🖭 *£4.* ⊘ *Daily 9:30–5.* 🐌

43 Kilmainham Gaol. Even farther west than the Royal Hospital, this is a grim, forbidding structure where leaders of the 1916 Easter Uprising, including Pádrig Pearse and James Connolly, were held before being executed in the prison yard. In the 19th century, other inmates here were the revolutionary Robert Emmet and Charles Stewart Parnell, a leading politician (☞ Avondale House, *in* Chapter 2). You can visit the cells, a chilling sight, while the guided tour and a 30-minute audiovisual presentation relate a graphic account of Ireland's political history over the past 200 years from a Nationalist viewpoint. You can only visit the prison as part of a guided tour, which leaves every hour on the hour. There is also a small tearoom on the premises. ⊠ *Inchicore Rd.,* ☎ *01/453–5984.* 🖭 *£3.* ⊘ *Apr.–Sept., daily 9:30–5; Oct.–Mar., weekdays 9:30–4, Sun. 10–5.*

40 Marsh's Library. A short walk west from St. Stephen's Green and accessed through a tiny but charming cottage garden lies a gem of old Dublin: the city's—and Ireland's—first public library, founded and endowed in 1701 by Narcissus Marsh, the Archbishop of Dublin, then open to "All Graduates and Gentlemen." The two-story, brick, Georgian building has been practically unchanged inside since it was built. It houses a priceless collection of 250 manuscripts and 25,000 16th- to 18th-century books. Many of these rare volumes are locked inside cages, as are the readers who wish to peruse them. The cages were to discourage students who, often impecunious, may have been tempted to make the books their own. The library has been restored with great attention to its original architectural details, especially in the book stacks. ⊠ *St. Patrick's Close off Patrick St.,* ☎ *01/454–3511.* 🖭 *£1.* ⊘ *Mon. and Wed.–Fri. 10–12:45 and 2–5, Sat. 10:30–12:45.*

47 Old Jameson Distillery. Founded in 1791, this distillery produced one of Ireland's most famous whiskeys for nearly 200 years until 1966, when local distilleries merged to form Irish Distillers and moved to a purpose-built, ultramodern distillery in Middleton, County Cork. Part of the complex was converted into the group's head office, and the distillery itself was turned into a museum. You can watch a short audiovisual history of the industry, which actually had its origins 1,500 years ago in Middle Eastern perfume making, and tour the old distillery, where you can learn about the distilling of whiskey from grain to bottle. You can also view a reconstruction of a former warehouse, where the colorful nicknames of former barrel makers are recorded. There's a 20-minute audiovisual show, a 40-minute tour, and a complimentary tasting (remember: Irish whiskey is best drunk without a mixer—try it straight or with water); four attendees are invited to taste different brands of Irish whiskey and compare them against bourbon and Scotch. If you have a large group and everyone wants to do this, phone in advance to arrange it. ⊠ *Bow St.,* ☎ *01/807–2355.* 🖭 *Tour £3.95.* ⊘ *Daily 9:30–5:30; tours every ½ hr.*

★ **42 Royal Hospital Kilmainham.** A short ride by taxi or bus from the city center, this replica of Les Invalides in Paris is regarded as the most important 17th-century building in Ireland. Commissioned as a hospice for disabled and veteran soldiers by James Butler, the Duke of Ormonde and Viceroy to King Charles II, it was completed in 1684, making it the first classical building in the city and a precursor of Dublin's golden age. It survived into the 1920s as a hospital, but after the founding of the Irish Free State in 1922, the building fell into disrepair. Over the last 15 years or so, restoration has returned the entire edifice to what it once was.

The structure consists of four galleries around a courtyard and includes a grand dining hall, 100 ft long by 50 ft wide. The architectural highlight is the hospital's Baroque **chapel,** distinguished by its extraordinary plasterwork ceiling and fine wood carvings. "There is nothing in Ireland from the 17th century that can come near this masterpiece," raves cultural historian John FitzMaurice Mills. Today the Royal Hospital houses the **Irish Museum of Modern Art.** The museum displays works by non-Irish, 20th-century greats like Picasso and Miró but concentrates on the work of Irish artists. Richard Deacon, Richard Gorman, Dorothy Cross, Sean Scully, Matt Mullican, Louis Le Brocquy, and James Colman are among the contemporary Irish artists represented. The Café Musée has soups, sandwiches, and other light fare. ⊠ *Kilmainham La.,* ☎ *01/612–9900.* ⌖ *Royal Hospital free, but individual shows may have separate charges; Museum of Modern Art permanent collection free, small charge for special exhibitions.* ⊙ *Royal Hospital Tues.–Sat. 10–5:30, Sun. noon–5:30, tour every ½ hr; Museum of Modern Art Tues.–Sat. 10–5:30, Sun. noon–5:30; tours Wed. and Fri. 2:30, Sat. 11:30.* 🐾

㊺ St. Michan's Church. Built in 1685 on the site of an older, 11th-century Danish church (Michan is a Danish saint), this Anglican church is architecturally undistinguished except for its 120-ft-high bell tower. But its 18th-century organ was supposedly played by Handel for his first-ever performance of the *Messiah,* and its Stool of Repentance is the only one still in existence in the city; parishioners who were judged to be "open and notoriously naughty livers" used it to do public penance. St. Michan's main claim to notoriety, however, is down in the vaults, where the totally dry atmosphere has preserved a number of corpses in a remarkable state of mummification. They lie in open caskets, and if you're strong-hearted, you can shake hands with a former religious crusader or nun! Most of the preserved bodies are thought to have been Dublin tradespeople. ⊠ *Lower Church St.,* ☎ *01/872–4154.* ⌖ *£2.* ⊙ *Weekdays 10–12:45 and 2–4:45, Sat. 10–12:45, Sun. service at 10 AM.*

㊴ St. Patrick's Cathedral. The largest cathedral in Dublin and also the national cathedral of the Church of Ireland, St. Patrick's is the second of the capital's two Protestant cathedrals (the other is Christ Church; ☞ *above*). (The reason that Dublin has two cathedrals is that St. Patrick's originally stood outside the walls of Dublin, while its close neighbor was within the walls and belonged to the see of Dublin.) Legend has it that St. Patrick baptized many converts at a well on the site of the cathedral in the 5th century. The original building, dedicated in 1192 and early English Gothic in style, was an unsuccessful attempt to assert supremacy over Christ Church Cathedral. At 305 ft, it is the longest church in the country, a fact that Oliver Cromwell's troops—no friends to the Irish—found useful, as they made the church's nave into their stable in the 17th century. Their visit left the building in a ruinous state, and its current good repair is largely due to the benevolence of Sir Benjamin Guinness, of the brewing family, who started to finance major restoration work in 1860. Be sure to view the gloriously heraldic **Choir of St. Patrick's,** hung with colorful medieval banners, as well as find the tomb of the most famous of St. Patrick's many illustrious deans, Jonathan Swift, immortal author of *Gulliver's Travels,* who held office from 1713 to 1745. **Swift's tomb** is in the south aisle, not far from that of his beloved "Stella," Mrs. Esther Johnson. Swift's epitaph is inscribed over the robing-room door. Yeats—who translated it thus: "Swift has sailed into his rest; Savage indignation there cannot lacerate his breast"—declared it the greatest epitaph of all time. Other memorials include the 17th-century **Boyle Monument,** with its numerous painted figures of family members, and the **monument to Turlough O'Carolan,** the last of the Irish bards and one of the country's finest harp players. To the immediate north of the cathedral is a small park, with statues of many of Dublin's literary figures and St. Patrick's Well. Matins (9:45 AM) and evensong (5:35 PM) are still sung on most days, a real treat for the music lover. ✉ *Patrick St.,* ☎ *01/475–4817.* 🎟 *£2.* ⊘ *May and Sept.–Oct., weekdays 9–6, Sat. 9– 5, Sun. 10–11 and 12:45–3; June–Aug., weekdays 9–6, Sat. 9–4, Sun. 9:30–3 and 4:15–5:15; Nov.–Apr., weekdays 9–6, Sat. 9–4, Sun. 10– 11 and 12:45–3.*

The Liberties

A stroll through the Liberties is a walk through working-class Dublin, past and present, good and bad. The name derives from Dublin of the Middle Ages, when the area south and west of Christ Church Cathedral was outside the city walls and free from the jurisdiction of the city rulers. A certain amount of freedom, or "liberty," was enjoyed by those who settled here, and it often attracted people on the fringes of society, especially the poor.

A Good Walk

Numbers in the text correspond to numbers in the margin and on the Dublin West map.

Start on Patrick Street, in the shadow of St. Patrick's Cathedral (☞ *above*). Look down the street toward the Liffey and a glorious view of Christ Church (☞ *above*). Take a right on Dean Street, where you'll find John Fallons pub (☞ Pubs *in* Nightlife and the Arts, *below*). Take a right off Dean Street onto Francis Street and walk uphill. A number of quality antiques shops (☞ Shopping, *below*) line both sides of the thoroughfare. Halfway up Francis Street, on the right, behind hefty wrought-iron gates, is one of Dublin's most-overlooked treasures, **St. Nicholas of Myra's Church** ㊽. Continue up Francis Street and take the next right onto Thomas Davis Street (named after a famous patriot and revolutionary—the Liberties has long had a close association with Irish Nationalism). The street is full of classic, two-story redbrick houses. The area, once the heart of "Darlin' Dublin" and the holy source of its distinctive accent, is rapidly becoming yuppified. Back on Francis Street, in an old factory building with its chimney stack intact, is the exciting **Iveagh Market Hall** ㊾. At the top of Francis Street turn left onto Thomas Street. Across the road, on your right side, stands the wonderfully detailed exterior of St. Augustine and St. John, with its grandiose spire dominating the area around. You'll notice churches all over the Liberties; the bishops thought it wise to build holy palaces in the poorest areas of the city as tall, shining beacons of comfort and hope. Farther up Thomas Street in another converted factory is the **National College of Art and Design** ㊿.

TIMING

Unless you intend on doing some serious antiques shopping, this is a relatively quick stroll—perhaps two hours—as the Liberties is a compact area of small, winding streets.

Sights to See

㊾ **Iveagh Market Hall.** One of numerous buildings bestowed upon the city of Dublin by Lord Iveagh of the Guinness family, the cavernous, Victorian, redbrick-and-granite Iveagh Market Hall holds a regular, eclectic market from Tuesday to Saturday. ⊠ *Francis St.,* ⊙ *Tues.–Sat. 9–5.*

50 National College of Art and Design. The delicate welding of glass and iron onto the redbrick Victorian facade of this onetime factory makes this school worth a visit. Walk around the cobblestone central courtyard, where there's always the added bonus of viewing some of the students work in mediums such as glass, clay, metal, and stone. ⊠ *Thomas St.,* ☎ *01/671–1377.*

48 St. Nicholas of Myra's Church. This church was completed in 1834 in grand neoclassic style. Inside, the highly ornate chapel includes ceiling panels of each of the 12 apostles and a pietà raised 20 ft above the marble altar, which is guarded on each side by angels sculpted by John Hogan while he was in Florence. The tiny nuptial chapel to the right has a small Harry Clarke stained-glass window. ⊠ *St. Nicholas St.* ✉ *Free.* ⊙ *Hrs vary.*

North of the Liffey

If you stand on O'Connell Bridge or the pedestrian-only Ha'penny span, you'll get excellent views up and down the Liffey, the *abha na life,* which James Joyce transcribed phonetically as Anna Livia in *Finnegan's Wake.* Here, framed with embankments just like those along Paris's Seine, the river is near the end of its 128-km (80-mi) journey from the Wicklow Mountains into the Irish Sea. And near here, you begin a pilgrimage into James Joyce Country and the fascinating sights of Dublin's northside.

Today the northside—a mix of densely thronged shopping streets and run-down sections (though the property boom is rapidly refurbishing these areas) of once-genteel homes—absolutely warrants a walk for three reasons: its major cultural institutions (which include the Gate Theatre, the James Joyce Cultural Centre, the Dublin Writers Museum, and the Hugh Lane Municipal Gallery of Modern Art), the number of sites of significance with ties to Irish Republicanism, and its busy streets. During the 18th century, most of the upper echelons of Dublin society lived in the Georgian houses around Mountjoy Square and shopped along Capel Street, which was lined with stores stocking fine furniture and silver. The construction of Merrion Square on the southside (completed in 1764) and nearby Fitzwilliam Square (completed in 1825), and the decision by Ireland's grandest duke to build Leinster House on the southside, permanently changed the northside's fortunes. The city's fashionable social center crossed the Liffey, and although some of the northside's illustrious inhabitants clung to their houses, this area gradually became more run-down. The northside's fortunes may be changing, though. Once-derelict swaths of houses, especially on and near the Liffey, are being rehabilitated, and a large new shopping center opened on Mary Street in late 1996. Now a huge shopping mall and entertainment complex are planned for O'Connell Street, right where the defunct Cartlon Cinema stands. Still, the redevelopment that has swept through Temple Bar is only in its early stages here, but precisely because it's a place on the cusp of transition, it's an interesting part of town to visit.

A Good Walk

Numbers in the text correspond to numbers in the margin and on the Dublin City Center map.

Begin at O'Connell Bridge—if you look closely at it you will notice that it is wider than it is long—and head north up **O'Connell Street** ⑤①. Stop to admire the monument to Daniel O'Connell, "The Liberator," erected as a tribute to the great orator's achievement in securing Catholic Emancipation in 1829 (note the obvious scars from the fighting of 1916 on the figures). Then continue north to the **General Post Office** ⑤②, a major site in the Easter Uprising of 1916. O'Connell leads to the southeastern corner of Parnell Square. Heading counterclockwise around the square, you'll pass in turn the **Gate Theatre** ⑤③ and **Abbey Presbyterian Church** ⑤④ before coming to the **Dublin Writers Museum** ⑤⑤ and the **Hugh Lane Municipal Gallery of Modern Art** ⑤⑥, both on the north side of the square and both housed in glorious neoclassic mansions; these are the two sites where you should plan to spend most of your time on the northside. Either before you go in or after you come out, you might want to visit the solemn yet serene **Garden of Remembrance** ⑤⑦.

From here, you have two choices: to continue exploring the cultural sights that lie to the northeast of Parnell Square and east of O'Connell Street or to head to Moore, Henry, and Mary streets for a flavor of middle-class Dublin that you won't get on the spiffier southside. If you decide to continue your cultural explorations, jump two blocks northeast of Parnell Square to the **James Joyce Cultural Centre** ⑤⑧, then head farther northeast to the once-glamorous **Mountjoy Square** ⑤⑨. From here, turn south, stopping in at the **St. Francis Xavier Church** ⑥⓪ on Gardiner Street. Head back west to Marlborough Street (parallel to and between Gardiner and O'Connell streets) to visit the **Pro-Cathedral** ⑥①. Continue down to the quays and jog a block east to the **Custom House** ⑥②. If you decide to shop with the locals, leave Parnell Square via the southwestern corner, stopping first to check out the chapel at the **Rotunda Hospital** ⑥③. Moore Street is your first left off Parnell Street and leads directly to Henry Street.

TIMING

The northside has fewer major attractions than the southside and, overall, is less picturesque. As a result, you're unlikely to want to stroll as leisurely here. If you zipped right through this walk, you could be done in less than two hours. But the two major cultural institutions covered here—the Dublin Writers Museum and the Hugh Lane Municipal Gallery of Modern Art—easily deserve several hours each, so it's worth doing this walk only if you have the time to devote to them. Also, a number of additional sights connected with James Joyce and *Ulysses*—covered in "ReJoyce! A Walk through *Ulysses* and James Joyce's Dublin"—are in the vicinity, so if you're a devoted Joycean, you should consult the Close-Up box (☞ *below*) before setting out on this walk.

Sights to See

⑤④ **Abbey Presbyterian Church.** A soaring spire marks the exterior of this church, popularly known as Findlater's Church, after Alex Findlater, a noted Dublin grocer who endowed it. Completed in 1864, the church stands on the northeast corner of Parnell Square; the inside has a stark Presbyterian atmosphere, despite stained-glass windows and ornate pews. For a bird's-eye view, take the small staircase that leads to the balcony. ⊠ *Parnell Sq.* ▣ *Free.* ☉ *Hrs vary.*

⑥② **Custom House.** Seen at its best reflected in the waters of the Liffey during the short interval when the high tide is on the turn, the Custom House is the city's most spectacular Georgian building. Extending 375 ft on the north side of the river, this is the work of James Gandon, an English architect who arrived in Ireland in 1781, when construction commenced (it continued for 10 years). Crafted from gleaming Portland stone, the central portico is linked by arcades to the pavilions at either end. Too bad the dome is on the puny side and out of proportion. A statue of Commerce tops the graceful copper dome; statues on the main facade are based on allegorical themes. Note the exquisitely carved lions and unicorns supporting the arms of Ireland at the far ends of the facade. Republicans set the building on fire in 1921, but it was completely restored and now houses government offices. The building opened to the public in mid-1997 after having been closed for many years, and with it came a new exhibition tracing the building's history and significance. ⊠ *Custom House Quay,* ☎ *01/679–3377.* ▣ *£1.50.* ◷ *Weekdays 9:30–5, weekends 2–5.*

★ **⑤⑤ Dublin Writers Museum.** "If you would know Ireland—body and soul— you must read its poems and stories," wrote Yeats in 1891. Further investigation into the Irish way with words can be found here at this unique museum, set within a magnificently restored 18th-century town house on the north side of Parnell Square. Once the home of John Jameson (of the Irish whiskey family), the mansion is centered on an enormous drawing room, gorgeously decorated with paintings, Adamesque plasterwork, and a deep Edwardian lincrusta frieze. Rare manuscripts, diaries, posters, letters, limited and first editions, photographs, and other mementoes commemorate the life and works of the nation's greatest writers (and there are *many* of them, so leave plenty of time), including Joyce, Shaw, J. M. Synge, Lady Gregory, Yeats, Beckett, and many others. On display are an 1804 edition of Swift's *Gulliver's Travels,* an 1899 first edition of Bram Stoker's *Dracula,* and an 1899 edition of Wilde's *Ballad of Reading Gaol.* There's even a special "Teller of Tales" exhibit showcasing Behan, O'Flaherty, and O'Faolan. Readings are periodically held. The bookshop and café make this an ideal place to spend a rainy afternoon. If you lose track of time and stay until the closing hour, you might want to dine at Chapter One, a highly regarded restaurant in the basement (☞ Dining, *below*), which would have had Joyce ecstasizing about its currant-sprinkled scones. ⊠ *18 Parnell Sq. N,* ☎ *01/872–2077.* ▣ *£3.* ◷ *June–Aug., Mon.–Sat. 10–6, Sun. 11– 5; Sept.–May, Mon.–Sat. 10–5, Sun. 11–5.*

⑤⑦ Garden of Remembrance. Opened in 1966, 50 years after the Easter Uprising of 1916, the garden, within Parnell Square, commemorates all those who died fighting for Irish freedom. A large plaza is at the garden's entrance; steps lead down to the fountain area, graced with a sculpture by contemporary Irish artist Oisín Kelly based on the mythological Children of Lír, who were turned into swans. The garden serves as an oasis of tranquillity in the middle of the busy city. ⊠ *Parnell Sq.* ◷ *Daily 9–5.*

⑤③ Gate Theatre. The Gate has been one of Dublin's most important theaters since its founding in 1929 by Mícheál MacLiammóir and Hilton Edwards, who also founded Galway City's An Taibhdhearc as the national Irish-language theater (☞ Chapter 6). Many innovative productions by Irish playwrights have been staged here, and Dublin audiences have encountered foreign playwrights and actors here as well, including Orson Welles (his first paid performance) and James Mason, who also performed here early in his career. The show actually begins as soon as you walk into the auditorium—a Georgian masterwork designed by Richard Johnston in 1784 as an assembly room for the Rotunda Hospital complex. Today the theater plays it safe with a major repertory of European and American drama and new plays by established Irish writers. ⊠ *Cavendish Row,* ☎ *01/874–4045.*

⑤② General Post Office. Known as the GPO, it is one of the great civic buildings of Dublin's Georgian era, but its fame derives from the role it played during the Easter Uprising. It has an impressive facade in the neoclassic style and was designed by Francis Johnston and built by the British between 1814 and 1818 as a center of communications. This gave it great strategic importance and was one of the reasons why it was chosen by the insurgent forces in 1916 as a headquarters. Here, on Easter Monday, 1916, the Republican forces, about 2,000 in number, and under the guidance of Pádrig Pearse and James Connolly, stormed the building and issued the Proclamation of the Irish Republic. After a week of shelling, the GPO lay in ruins; 13 rebels were ultimately executed (including Connolly, who was dying of gangrene from a leg shattered in the fighting and had to be propped up in a chair before the firing squad). Most of the original building was destroyed, though the facade survived (you can still see the scars of bullets on the its pillars). Rebuilt and subsequently reopened in 1929, it is still a working post office, with an attractive two-story main concourse. A bronze sculpture depicting the dying Cuchulainn, a leader of the Red Branch Knights in Celtic mythology, sits in the front window. The 1916 Proclamation and the names of its signatories are inscribed on the green marble plinth. ⊠ *O'Connell St.,* ☏ *01/872–8888.* ⊙ *Mon.–Sat. 8–8, Sun. 10:30–6.*

★ 56 **Hugh Lane Municipal Gallery of Modern Art.** Built originally as a town house for the Earl of Charlemont in 1762, this residence was so grand its Parnell Square street was nicknamed "Palace Row" in its honor. Designed by Sir William Chambers (who also built the Marino Casino for Charlemont) in the best Palladian manner, its delicate and rigidly correct facade, extended by two demilune arcades, was fashioned from the "new" white Ardmulcan stone (now seasoned to gray). Charlemont was one of the cultural locomotives of 18th-century Dublin—his walls were hung with Titians and Hogarths, and he frequently dined with Oliver Goldsmith and Sir Joshua Reynolds—so he would undoubtedly be delighted that his home is now the Hugh Lane Gallery, named after a nephew of Lady Gregory (Yeats's aristocratic patron; ☞ Coole Park *in* Chapter 6). Lane collected both Impressionist paintings and 19th-century Irish and Anglo-Irish works. A complicated agreement with the National Gallery in London (reached after heated diplomatic dispute) stipulates that a portion of the 39 French paintings amassed by Lane shuttle back and forth between London and here. You can see Pissarro's *Printemps,* Manet's *Eva Gonzales,* Morisot's *Jour d'Été,* and, the jewel of the collection, Renoir's *Les Parapluies.*

Between the collection of Irish paintings in the **National Gallery of Ireland** (☞ *above*) and the superlative works on view here, you can quickly become familiar with Irish 20th-century art. Irish artists represented here include Roderic O'Conor, well known for his views of the West of Ireland; William Leech, including his *Girl with a Tinsel Scarf* (ca. 1912) and *The Cigarette*; and the most famous of the group, Jack B. Yeats (W. B.'s brother). The museum has a dozen of his paintings, including *Ball Alley* (ca. 1927) and *There Is No Night* (1949). There is also strikingly displayed stained-glass work by early 20th-century Irish master artisans Harry Clarke and Evie Hone. ⊠ *Parnell Sq. N,* ☏ *01/874–1903.* 🎟 *Free.* ⊙ *Sept.–Mar., Tues.–Thurs. 9:30–6, Fri.–Sat. 9:30–5, Sun. 11–5; Apr.–Aug., Tues.–Wed. 9:30–6, Thurs. 9:30–8, Fri.–Sat. 9:30–5, Sun. 11–5.* ✒

58 **James Joyce Cultural Centre.** Not everyone in Ireland has read James Joyce, but everyone has heard of him—especially since a copy of his censored and suppressed *Ulysses* was one of the top status symbols of the early 20th century. Today, of course, Joyce is acknowledged to be one of the greatest modern authors, and his *Dubliners, Finnegan's Wake,* and *A Portrait of the Artist as a Young Man* can even be read as poetic "travel guides" to Dublin. Now open to the general public, this restored, 18th-century Georgian town house, once the dancing academy of Professor Denis J. Maginni, is a center for Joycean studies and

events related to the author. It has an extensive library and archives, exhibition rooms, a bookstore, and a café. Along with housing the **Joyce Museum** (☞ *below*) in Sandycove, the center is the main organizer of "Bloomstime," which marks the week leading up to June 16's Bloomsday celebrations. For a tour of Joyce's Dublin, *see* the Close-Up box "ReJoyce!" A Walk through *Ulysses* and James Joyce's Dublin," *below.* ⊠ *35 N. Great George's St.,* ☎ *01/878–8547.* ⊡ *£2.75.* ☉ *Mon.–Sat. 9:30–5, Sun. 12:30–5.*

❺❾ **Mountjoy Square.** Built over the two decades before 1818, this square was once surrounded by elegant, terraced houses, but today only the northern side remains intact. The once-derelict southern side has been restored and converted into apartments. Irishman Brian Boru, who led his soldiers to victory against the Vikings in the Battle of Clontarf in 1014, was said to have pitched camp before the confrontation on the site of Mountjoy Square. Playwright Sean O'Casey once lived here at No. 35 and used the square as a setting for *The Shadow of a Gunman.*

❺❶ **O'Connell Street.** Dublin's most famous thoroughfare, 150 ft wide, was previously known as Sackville Street, but its name was changed in 1924, two years after the founding of the Irish Free State. After the devastation of the 1916 Easter Uprising, the street had to be almost entirely reconstructed, a task that took until the end of the 1920s. The main attraction of the street, **Nelson's Pillar,** a Doric column towering over the city center and a marvelous vantage point, was blown up in 1966, the 50th anniversary of the Easter Uprising. The large **monument** at the south end of the street is dedicated to Daniel O'Connell (1775–1847), "The Liberator," and was erected in 1854 as a tribute to the orator's achievement in securing Catholic Emancipation in 1829. Seated winged figures represent the four "Victories,"—courage, eloquence, fidelity, and patriotism—all exemplified by O'Connell. Ireland's four ancient provinces—Munster, Leinster, Ulster, and Connacht—are identified by their respective coats of arms. Look closely and you'll notice that O'Connell is wearing a glove on one hand, as he did for much of his adult life, a self-imposed penance for shooting a man in a duel. Alongside O'Connell is another noted statue, a modern rendition of Joyce's **Anna Livia,** seen as a lady set within a waterfall and now nicknamed by the natives the "floozy in the Jacuzzi." **O'Connell Bridge,** the main bridge spanning the Liffey (wider than it is long), marks the street's southern end.

NEED A BREAK?   You have a number of good alternatives for a break on the northside. One of Dublin's oldest hotels, the **Gresham** (⊠ Upper O'Connell St., ☎ 01/874–6881), is a pleasant old-fashioned spot for a morning coffee or afternoon tea. **Conway's** (⊠ Parnell St. near Upper O'Connell St., ☎ 01/873–2687), founded in 1745, is reputed to be Dublin's second-oldest pub. For a real Irish pub lunch, stop in at **John M. Keating** (⊠ 14 Mary St. and 23 Jervis St., ☎ 01/873–1567), at the corner of Mary and Jervis streets; head upstairs, where you can sit at a low table and chat with locals.

❻❶ **Pro-Cathedral.** Dublin's principal Catholic cathedral (also known as St. Mary's) was built between 1816 and 1825. Although the severely classical church design is on a suitably epic scale, the building was never granted full cathedral status, nor has the identity of its architect ever been discovered; the only clue is in the church ledger, which lists a "Mr. P." as the builder. The church's facade, with a six-Doric-pillared portico, is based on the Temple of Theseus in Athens; the interior is modeled after the Grecian-Doric style of St-Philippe du Roule in Paris. A Palestrina choir, in which the great Irish tenor John McCormack began

71

Close-Up

CLOSE-UP: REJOYCE! A WALK THROUGH JAMES JOYCE'S DUBLIN AND *ULYSSES*

JAMES JOYCE'S genius for fashioning high art out of his day-to-day life brought him literary immortality and makes him, even today and possibly for all time, the world's most famous Dubliner. He set all of his major works—*Dubliners, A Portrait of the Artist as a Young Man, Ulysses,* and *Finnegan's Wake*—in the city where he was born and spent the first 22 years of his life, and although he spent the next 36 in self-imposed exile, he never wrote about anywhere else. Joyce knew and remembered Dublin in such detail that he claimed that if the city were destroyed, it could be rebuilt in its entirety from his written works.

Joyceans flock to Dublin annually on June 16 to commemorate **Bloomsday,** the day in 1904 on which Leopold Bloom wanders through the city in *Ulysses.* Why *this* day? It had been an important one for Joyce—when he and his wife-to-be, Nora Barnacle, had their first date. Today Bloomsday has evolved into "Bloomstime," with events taking place in the days leading up to the 16th, then all day and well into the night. Even if you don't make it to Dublin on Bloomsday, you can still roam its streets, sniffing out Bloom's—and Joyce's—haunts.

Begin in the heart of the northside, on **Prince's Street,** next to the **GPO** (☞ Exploring Dublin, *above*), where the office of the old and popular *Freeman's Journal* newspaper (published 1763–1924) was located before it was destroyed during the 1916 Easter Uprising. Bloom was a newspaper advertisement canvasser for the *Journal.* Leopold and Molly Bloom's fictional home stood at **7 Eccles Street,** north of Parnell Square. On Great Denmark Street, **Belvedere College** (☎ 01/874–3974)

is housed in a splendid 18th-century mansion. Between 1893 and 1898, Joyce studied here under the Jesuits. A few steps away, the **James Joyce Cultural Centre** (☞ Exploring Dublin, *above*) is the hub of Bloomsday celebrations. Also on the northside is the site of **Bella Cohen's Brothel** (✉ 82 Railway St.), in an area that in Joyce's day contained many such houses of ill-repute. Across town on the western edge of the northside, the **New Ormond Hotel** (✉ Upper Ormond Quay, ☎ 01/872–1811) was an afternoon rendezvous spot for Bloom.

Across the Liffey, walk up Grafton Street to **Davy Byrne's Pub** (☞ Pub Food *in* Dining, *above*) and then proceed to the **National Library** (☞ Exploring Dublin, *above*)—where Bloom has a near meeting with Blazes Boylan, his wife's lover, and looks for a copy of an advertisement—via **Molesworth Street.** No establishment mentioned by Joyce has changed less since his time than **Sweny's Pharmacy** (✉ Lincoln Pl.), at the back of Trinity College, which still has its black-and-white exterior and an interior crammed with potions and vials.

A NUMBER OF KEY JOYCE SITES lie outside the city center. On February 2, 1882, Joyce was born in the genteel southern suburb of Rathgar, at **41 Brighton Square,** where he spent the first two years of his life. (Bus 15A and Bus 15B make the 5-km/3-mi journey.) Other sites are covered elsewhere in our guide: **Sandymount Strand** and the **James Joyce Martello Tower** (☞ County Dublin—Southside, *below*) and **One Martello Terrace** (☞ Bray *in* Chapter 2).

his career, sings in Latin here every Sunday at 11. ✉ *Marlborough St.,* ☎ *01/874–5441.* 🆓 *Free.* ◷ *Daily 8–6.*

㊻ **Rotunda Hospital.** Founded in 1745 as the first maternity hospital in Ireland or Britain, the Rotunda was designed on a grand scale by architect Richard Castle (1690–1751), with a three-story tower and a copper cupola. It's now most worth a visit for its **chapel,** with elaborate plasterwork executed by Bartholomew Cramillion between 1757 and 1758, appropriately honoring motherhood. The **Gate Theatre** (☞ *above*), in a lavish Georgian assembly room, is also part of the complex. ✉ *Parnell St.,* ☎ *01/873–0700.*

㊿ **St. Francis Xavier Church.** One of the city's finest churches in the classical style, the Jesuit St. Francis Xavier's was begun in 1829, the year of Catholic Emancipation, and was completed three years later. The building is designed in the shape of a Latin cross, with a distinctive Ionic portico and an unusual coffered ceiling. The striking, faux-marble high altarpiece, decorated with lapis lazuli, came from Italy. The church appears in James Joyce's story "Grace." ✉ *Upper Gardiner St.,* ☎ *01/836–3411.* 🆓 *Free.* ◷ *Daily 7 AM–8:30 PM.*

Along the Grand Canal

At its completion in 1795, the 547-km (342-mi) Grand Canal was celebrated as the longest in Britain and Ireland. It connected Dublin to the River Shannon, and horse-drawn barges carried cargo (mainly turf) and passengers to the capital from all over the country. By the mid-19th century the train had arrived and the great waterway slowly fell into decline, until the last commercial traffic ceased in 1960. But the 6-km (4-mi) loop around the capital is ideal for a leisurely stroll.

A Good Walk
Numbers in the text correspond to numbers in the margin and on the Dublin City Center map.

Begin by walking down the Pearse Street side of Trinity College until you arrive at the Ringsend Road Bridge. Raised on stilts above the canal is the **Waterways Visitors Centre** ㊽. Head west along the bank until you reach the **Mount Street Bridge** ㊾. On the southside is Percy Place, a street with elegant, three-story, terraced houses. On the northside, a small lane leads up to the infamous **Scruffy Murphy's** ㊿ pub. Taking a little detour at the next right, you'll pass a road that leads up to St. Stephen's (☞ *above*). Another right takes you into Powerscourt, a classic, inner-city estate of two-up, two-down terraced houses. Return to the canal and continue your walk along Herbert Place. You can get really close to the dark green water here as it spills white and frothy over one of the many wood-and-iron locks (all still in working order) that service the canal. James Joyce lost his virginity to a prostitute on the next stretch of the Canal, around Lower Baggot Street Bridge, but these banks belong to the lonesome ghost of another writer, Patrick Kavanagh. A life-size **statue of Patrick Kavanagh** ㊿ sits here, contemplative, arms folded, legs crossed on a wooden bench. Less than a mile past Kavanagh's statue the canal narrows as it approaches Richmond Bridge. Just beyond the bridge is the **Irish Jewish Museum** ㊿. To finish your walk in style, take a right onto Richmond Street, past a few antiques stores, until you arrive at **Bambrick's** ㊿, a public house in the best tradition of Dublin.

TIMING
You could walk this section of the canal in half an hour if you hurried, but what's the point? A leisurely pace best suits a waterside walk,

so give yourself a couple of hours to visit the Jewish Museum and explore the old streets off the canal.

Sight to See

69 Bambrick's. This is a pub in the best Irish tradition: a long, dark-wood bar, half-empty, frequented mostly by men over 50, with a staff whose sharp, grinning humor borders on being rude.

68 Irish Jewish Museum. Though Ireland has never had a large Jewish population (it hovers around 1,800 today), in the late 19th century and early 20th century it did become home to roughly 5,000 European Jews fleeing the pogroms of Eastern Europe. Opened in 1985 by Israeli president Chaim Herzog (himself Dublin-educated), the museum has a restored synagogue and a display of photographs, letters, and personal memorabilia culled from Dublin's most prominent Jewish families, though the exhibits trace the Jewish presence in Ireland back to 1067. In homage to Leopold Bloom, the Jewish protagonist of Joyce's *Ulysses*, every Jewish reference in the novel has been identified. The museum is a 20-minute walk or so from St. Stephen's Green. ⊠ *3–4 Walworth Rd.,* ☎ *01/453–1797.* ⊡ *Free.* ☉ *Oct.–Apr., Sun. 10:30–2:30; May–Sept., Tues., Thurs., and Sun. 11–3:30. Also by appointment.*

65 Mount Street Bridge. This bridge has a wooden lock on either side and is the perfect spot to watch these original gateways to the canal in operation. On the southwest corner of the bridge a small stone monument commemorates the battle of Mount Street Bridge in 1916 and the Irish Volunteers who died on this spot.

66 Scruffy Murphy's. Many a backroom deal by the country's political power brokers has been made in the back room of this classy wood-and-brass pub. It's the perfect spot for a pint and a snack.

67 Statue of Patrick Kavanagh. Patrick Kavanagh, Ireland's great lyric poet, spent the later years of his life sitting on a bench here writing about the canal, which flowed from his birthplace in the Midlands to the city where he would die. In one such poem he tells those who outlive him, "O commemorate me with no hero-courageous tomb, just a canal-bank seat for the passerby." Acknowledging Kavanagh's devotion to this spot, his friends commissioned a life-size bronze of the poet here. ⊠ *Canal bank along Wilton Terr.*

64 Waterways Visitors Centre. In the airy, wood-and-glass building you can learn about the history of Irish rivers and canals through photos, videos, and models. ⊠ *Grand Canal Quay,* ☎ *01/677–7501.* ⊡ *£2.* ☉ *June–Sept., daily 9:30–6:30; Oct.–May, Wed.–Sun. 12:30–5.*

Phoenix Park and Environs

Far and away Dublin's largest park, Phoenix Park (the name is an anglicization of the Irish *Fionn Uisce,* meaning clear water) is a vast, green arrowhead-shape oasis north of the Liffey, a 20-or-so-minute walk from the city center. Today—Heaven send what weather it may—Dubliners flock here to "take it aisy." It remains the city's main lung, escape valve, sports center (cricket, soccer, Gaelic games, and polo), and home to the noble creatures of the Dublin Zoo. A handful of other cultural sites near the park are also worth visiting, but to combine a visit to any of them with any of our other walks would be a bit difficult. Ceol and the Old Jameson Distillery, at the end of the Dublin West walk (☞ *above*), are the sites closest (the Guinness Brewery [☞ *above*], across the river, is also fairly close). So if you do make it to any of those, be sure to evaluate whether you have enough time to append a visit to one or another of these sites. Otherwise, plan to make a special trip out here, either walking or going by car or cab.

A Good Walk

Numbers in the text correspond to numbers in the margin and on the Dublin West map.

Beginning at the Custom House, walk down the quays on the north side of the Liffey until you come to Blackhall Place. Walk up to Arbour Hill and turn left: the **Arbour Hill Cemetery** ⑦ will be on your left. Directly across Arbour Hill are the **Collins Barracks** ⑦, now a branch of the National Museum (the main entrance is on Benburb Street on the south side). On its east side Benburb becomes Parkgate Street, and it's just a short stroll farther down to the main entrance of **Phoenix Park** ⑦.

TIMING

Phoenix Park is *big*; exploring it on foot could easily take the better part of a day. If you're looking for a little exercise, head here: jogging, horseback riding, and bicycling (☞ Outdoor Activities and Sports, *below*) are the ideal ways to explore the park more quickly than you can simply by strolling.

Sights to See

⑦ **Arbour Hill Cemetery.** A total of 14 Irishmen were executed by the British following the 1916 Easter Uprising. They were all buried here, including Pádrig Pearse, who led the rebellion; his younger brother Willie, who played a minor role in the uprising; and James Connolly, a socialist and labor leader wounded in the battle. Too weak from his wounds to stand, Connolly was tied to a chair and then shot. The burial ground is a simple but formal area, with the names of the dead leaders carved in stone beside an inscription of the proclamation they issued during the uprising. ⊠ *Arbour Hill.* 🖾 *Free.* ☉ *Mon.–Sat. 9–4:30, Sun. 9:30–noon.*

⑦ **Collins Barracks.** Until fairly recently, this was the oldest purpose-built military barracks in the world still in use. Now it's home to the National Museum's collection of glass, silver, furniture, and other decorative arts, exhibitions on Irish military history, and an exhibition of 200 years of Irish costumes and jewelry. ⊠ *Benburb St.,* ☎ *01/677–7444.* 🖾 *Free.* ☉ *Tues.–Sat. 10–5, Sun. 2–5.*

★ ☺ ⑦ **Phoenix Park.** Europe's largest public park, extending about 5 km (3 mi) along the Liffey's north bank, encompasses 1,752 acres of verdant green lawns, woods, lakes, and playing fields. It's a jogger's paradise, but Sunday is the best time for everyone to visit: games of cricket, soccer, polo, baseball, hurling—a combination of lacrosse, baseball, and field hockey—and Irish football are likely to be in progress. Old-fashioned gas lamps line both sides of **Chesterfield Avenue,** the main road that bisects the park for 4 km (2½ mi), which was named for Lord Chesterfield, a lord lieutenant of Ireland, who laid out the road in the 1740s. To the right as you enter the park, the **People's Garden** is a colorful flower garden designed in 1864.

Among the park's major monuments are the **Phoenix Column,** erected by Lord Chesterfield in 1747, and the **198-ft obelisk,** built in 1817 to commemorate the Duke of Wellington, the Irish general who defeated Napoleon for the British. (Wellington was born in Dublin but, true to the anti-Irish prejudice so prevalent in 19th-century England, balked at the suggestion that he was Irish: "If a man is born in a stable, it doesn't mean he is a horse," he is reputed to have said.) A tall **white cross** marks the spot where Pope John Paul II addressed more than a million people during his 1979 visit to Ireland. Wild deer can be seen grazing in the many open spaces of the park, especially near here.

You're guaranteed to see wildlife at the **Dublin Zoo,** the third-oldest public zoo in the world, founded in 1830, and just a short walk beyond the People's Garden (☞ *above*). The place looks a little dilapidated, but the government has allocated money for a five-year renovation that is now under way. Many animals from tropical climes are housed in barless enclosures, while Arctic species swim in the lakes close to the reptile house. The zoo is one of the few places in the world where lions will breed in captivity. Some 700 lions have been bred here since the 1850s, one of whom became familiar to movie fans the world over when MGM used him for its trademark. (As they will tell you at the zoo, he is in fact yawning in that familiar shot: an American lion had to be hired to roar and the "voice" was dubbed.) The children's corner has goats, guinea pigs, and lambs. In summer, the Lakeside Café serves ice cream and drinks. ⊠ *Phoenix Park,* ☎ *01/677–1425.* ⊡ *£6.* ⊙ *Apr.–Oct., Mon.–Sat. 9:30–6, Sun. 10:30–6; Nov.–Mar., weekdays 9:30–4, Sat. 9:30–5, Sun. 10:30–5.*

Both the president of Ireland and the U.S. ambassador have official residences in the park (the president's is known as Aras an Uachtarain), but neither building is open to the public. The Garda Siochana (police) has its headquarters in the park; a small **Garda Museum** contains many relics of Irish police history, including old uniforms. ⊠ *Phoenix Park,* ☎ *01/ 677–1156 ext. 2250.* ⊡ *Free.* ⊙ *Weekdays 9–5; call to confirm.*

Also within the park is a **visitor center,** in the 17th-century fortified Ashtown Castle; it has information about the park's history, flora, and fauna. ⊠ *Phoenix Park,* ☎ *01/677–0095.* ⊡ *£1.50.* ⊙ *Mar.–May, daily 10–1 and 2–5; June–Sept., daily 9:30–6:30; Oct., daily 2–5; Nov.–Feb., weekends 9:30–4:30.*

NEED A
BREAK?

Just before the entrance to Phoenix Park, **Ryan's Pub** (⊠ 28 Parkgate St., ☎ 01/677–6097) is one of Dublin's last remaining genuine, late-Victorian-era pubs.

DINING

Revised by
Orna Mulcahy

Once upon a time, and it wasn't too long ago, dining out in Dublin was a limited pleasure. Even 10 years ago, the city had lots of pubs but few interesting restaurants. All that has changed in recent years. With the Irish economy booming, everyone wants to eat out, and, not surprisingly, the Dublin dining scene has exploded with dazzling new places. Growing international interest and a more diverse local palate have also widened the range of restaurants and triggered new developments in Irish cuisine. So if you arrive thinking you're going to be eating potatoes, potatoes, and more potatoes, be prepared to have your preconceptions overturned—and to be very happily sated.

Many Dublin restaurateurs have trained in top restaurants in France, Switzerland, and Germany; others have worked in New York and Chicago; some have been much farther afield—to Thailand, Hong Kong, New Zealand, and Australia. The result is a dizzying choice of restaurants to suit every mood and situation. You can eat superb French or Italian food, often with an Irish twist; you can have all the fusion you want, with menus that experiment with Asian, Mediterranean, and Californian cuisine; and you'll find plenty of elegant dining rooms, stylish bistros, relaxing hideaways, and late-night eateries to boot.

Irish food is enjoying a renaissance, thanks to talented, imaginative chefs determined to put a fresh spin on traditional ingredients. Organic is the buzzword in Irish cuisine, and you'll find some restaurants specializing in organic and free-range food. Fresh produce is being imaginatively treated, too, giving stalwart Irish ingredients such as potatoes, onions, carrots, and cabbage new life. Seafood, lamb, beef, and pork and bacon still provide the backbone for many signature dishes, but there is also great interest in venison, quail, and other game—both wild and farmed. There are dozens of excellent cheeses—such as St. Tola goat cheese from County Clare or Carrigburne Brie from Wexford—most produced by small artisan cheese makers. If one of these farmhouse varieties appears on a menu, make a point of trying it.

While few restaurants in Dublin have dress requirements, men may feel more comfortable in a jacket and tie at fancier places.

We have included some of the city's best addresses for a hearty pub lunch, a popular dining option among Dubliners.

Prices

For price ranges, *see* Dining *in* Smart Travel Tips A to Z. Value Added Tax (VAT) will automatically be added to your bill—a 12.5% tax on food and a government excise tax on drinks. Before paying, check to see whether service has been included. If it has been included, you can pay it with a credit card; but if it has not, it's more considerate to the staff to leave the tip in cash (10% to 15%) if paying the main bill by credit card.

A word of warning—you will pay for your dining pleasure here: high overheads and staffing costs have pushed up prices, especially in more upscale places. The good news is that, while Dublin doesn't have Starbucks, there are scores of local cafés serving excellent coffee, often with a good sandwich. Small bakeries are beginning to spring up, borrowing trends from all around the world, offering inexpensive pizzas, focaccia, pitas, tacos, and wraps (taking over for the sandwich as the favorite snack).

It's worthwhile to see if the restaurant of your choice offers an early-bird and/or pre- or post-theater menu, with significantly lower set prices at specific times, often from 6 to 7:30 PM.

City Center (Southside)

CONTEMPORARY

$$$$ ★ X **Peacock Alley.** Conrad Gallagher ran away from school at 12 to be a cook in his native County Donegal. By 18 he was sous-chef at the Plaza in New York, and at 19 *chef de cuisine* at the Waldorf-Astoria's Peacock Alley, whose name he has borrowed. His elegant, modern restaurant has a large, airy 120-seat room with a spectacular view over St. Stephen's Green at one end and a view of the white-tiled open kitchen at the other. Gallagher has a penchant for high food, building up food on the plate and dabbing multicolored oils and garnishes with painterly precision. Strikingly inventive dishes include smoked salmon with basmati rice, pear, preserved ginger, soy sauce, and quesadilla; deep-fried crab cakes with katifi (shredded phyllo pastry); and daube of pot-roasted beef. The excellent service and strong wine list add to the experience, as does the towering presence of Gallagher himself. ⊠ *Fitzwilliam Hotel, St. Stephens Green,* ☎ *01/478–7015. Reservations essential. AE, DC, MC, V. Closed Sun.*

$$$ X **Cooke's Café.** Johnny Cooke's Mediterranean bistro is a cool spot for visiting movie stars. Sit out in summer under an awning and watch the people go by, enjoying elegantly presented dishes on huge white

Wedgwood plates. Favorites here include pasta with a rich bubbling Gorgonzola sauce, lobster simply grilled with garlic-herb butter, salad scattered with pieces of tender roast duck, and crab salad with spinach, coriander, mango salsa, and lime dressing. Try not to be in a hurry, because the service, through charming, is slow. Upstairs is the grill bar Rhino Room, also owned by Cooke. ⊠ *14 S. William St.,* ☎ *01/679–0536. Reservations essential. AE, DC, MC, V.*

$$$ ✕ **La Stampa.** One of the most dramatic dining rooms in Dublin, La
★ Stampa has huge gilt mirrors and elaborate candelabra that are gloriously over the top and give a sense of occasion to the simplest meal. The menu changes frequently to reflect an eclectic, international style. For a main course, you may get rack of organic lamb with braised beans, tomatoes, and rosemary jus, roast scallops with artichoke mash and a tomato vinaigrette, or giant prawns served with garlic or mango mayonnaise. Service is brisk but friendly, and there's always a fun atmosphere. ⊠ *35 Dawson St.,* ☎ *01/677–8611. AE, DC, MC, V. No lunch weekends.*

CONTINENTAL

$$$$ ✕ **Locks.** Claire Douglas's town-house restaurant, overlooking the Grand Canal, offers a genuinely warm welcome. The dining room is comfortable and old-fashioned, with seating on banquettes, starched table linen, and hearty portions served on antique, ironstone plates. Classic starters include Locks's special potato skins—dished up with a fabulous cream, cheese, and bacon sauce—and excellent smoked salmon. For the main course, there's a choice of traditional fish dishes, Irish lamb, and fillet of beef. Although slightly off the beaten path (a 20-minute walk or a short taxi ride southwest of St. Stephen's Green), it's worth the trip. ⊠ *1 Windsor Terr., Portobello,* ☎ *01/454–3391. Reservations essential. AE, DC, MC, V. Closed Sun. No lunch Sat.*

FRENCH

$$$$ ✕ **Patrick Guilbaud.** This fine restaurant combines superb French
★ cooking with impeccable service. The best food here is simple but flawless: juicy prawns wrapped in a light swaddling of phyllo; roast squab stuffed with cabbage and served with a spicy Madeira jus; and the house specialty dish, Challans duck with honey, lemon, and soy. Follow that if you can with the *assiette au chocolate* (a plate of five different hot and cold chocolate desserts). The walls of the marvelously lofty dining room are hung with paintings from the owners' private collection. ⊠ *Hotel Merrion, Upper Merrion St.,* ☎ *01/676–4192. Reservations essential. AE, DC, MC, V. Closed Sun.–Mon. and late Dec.–mid-Jan.*

$$$$ ✕ **Thornton's.** Owner Kevin Thornton is one of the very best chefs in
★ Ireland, and if you are passionate about food, then this place is a must. The upstairs dining room is simply decorated, creating few distractions from the exquisite cuisine. Thornton's cooking style is light, and his dishes are small masterpieces of structural engineering. In season, he marinates legs of partridge, then debones and reforms the bird, with the breasts presented as a crown. Desserts range from fig ice cream to chocolate mousse. The enormous selection of cheeses is shipped in weekly from the Rungis market in Paris. ⊠ *1 Portobello Rd.,* ☎ *01/454–9067. Reservations essential. AE, DC, MC, V. Closed Sun.–Mon. No lunch.*

INDIAN

$$ ✕ **Khyber Tandoori.** Just a short walk from St. Stephen's Green is this gem of a tandoori restaurant. Although it specializes in Pakistani cuisine, it serves a broad range of Indian dishes. Try the shami kebabs—dainty, spiced patties of minced lamb and lentils—or *kabuli chicken*

78

Dublin Dining

KEY

DART Railway Station

tikka shashlik, marinated, diced chicken with onions and red and green peppers, which comes bright red and sizzling on an iron platter. Settle in and admire the richly embroidered wall hangings and the great gusts of steam coming from the tandoori oven in the glassed-in area. ⊠ *44 S. William St.,* ☏ *01/670–4855. AE, DC, MC, V.*

IRISH

$$$$ ✕ **The Commons Restaurant.** This large, elegant dining room is in the basement of historic Newman House (☞ The Center City: Around Trinity College, *in* Exploring Dublin, *above*). The patio doors open onto a paved courtyard for summer aperitifs and alfresco lunches. Typical dishes include Irish lamb baked in thyme and black pepper pastry, and loin of rabbit with prawns from Dublin Bay. If you have time, take a stroll in the Iveagh Gardens, an enclosed park that is one of Dublin's best-kept secrets. ⊠ *85–86 St. Stephen's Green,* ☏ *01/478–0530. Reservations essential. AE, DC, MC, V. Closed Sat.–Sun.*

$$$ ✕ **Brownes Brasserie.** In a Georgian town house on St. Stephen's Green, now converted to a luxury hotel, is this lovely spot for an intimate lunch or dinner. Huge mirrors reflect the light from crystal chandeliers, glowing on jewel-color walls and upholstery. The food is rich and heartwarming, with classics like Irish smoked salmon, served on warm blini with cream, and confit of duck with lentils. Treat yourself to the lemon tart for dessert. ⊠ *Brownes Townhouse, 22 St. Stephen's Green,* ☏ *01/638–3939. Reservations essential. AE, DC, MC, V. No lunch Sat.*

$$–$$$ ✕ **Dobbins.** Don't be deceived by the sawdust on the floor and the simple decor. It's popular with businesspeople who like the combination of cozy booth seating, friendly service, and classic bistro food. Owner John O'Byrne presides over an impressive cellar with hundreds of wines from around the world. Goat cheese salad and scallops or crab claws drenched in butter are popular starters, while boned brace of quail, with black pudding and foie gras stuffing, is a typical entrée. Lunch can stretch into dinner, which can last well into the night. There is valet parking and the staff are expert at summoning taxis. ⊠ *15 Stephens La., off Mount St.,* ☏ *01/676–4679. Reservations essential. AE, DC, MC, V. Sun.–Mon.*

$$–$$$ ✕ **The Lord Edward.** Creaking floorboards and an old fireplace give the impression of being in someone's drawing room at this establishment, one of the oldest in the city. Start with traditional fish dishes such as prawn cocktail or smoked salmon, followed by simply cooked Dover sole, salmon, or lobster. Vegetables and potatoes are almost incidental to the fish, but the French fries are excellent, and there's fresh brown bread throughout the meal. The restaurant is named after Irish revolutionary Lord Edward Fitzgerald, whose remains are buried in St. Werburgh's Church across the road. ⊠ *23 Christ Church Pl.,* ☏ *01/454–2420. Reservations essential. AE, DC, MC, V. Closed Sun.*

$ ✕ **Burdock's.** Right next door to the Lord Edward is Dublin's famous take-out fish-and-chips shop. Join the inevitable queue and eat in the gardens of St. Patrick's Cathedral, a five-minute walk away. ⊠ *21 Werburgh St.,* ☏ *01/454–0306. No credit cards.*

$ ✕ **Kilkenny Kitchen.** On the upper floor of the Kilkenny Shop (☞ Shopping, *below*), this big self-service restaurant is an ideal place to take a break from shopping and sightseeing. Homemade soup, casseroles, cold meats, and salads are arranged on a long buffet, along with lots of tasty breads and cakes. Try to get a table by the window overlooking the playing fields of Trinity College. Lunchtime is busy, but it's very pleasant for morning coffee or afternoon tea. ⊠ *6 Nassau St.,* ☏ *01/677–7066. AE, DC, MC, V.*

ITALIAN

$$ ✗ Milano. The big open kitchen at this bright, cheerful place turns out a wide array of tasty, flashy pizzas, with combinations like tomato and mozzarella, ham and eggs, Cajun with prawns and Tabasco, spinach and egg, or ham and anchovies. There are also simple salads, like tomato and mozzarella with dough balls, and a couple of baked pasta dishes. This is a good place to dine late, with last orders at midnight. Two branches have recently opened up, one in Temple Bar and another on Bachelors Walk along the Quays. ⊠ *38 Dawson St.,* ☎ *01/670–7744; 18 Essex St. E, Temple Bar,* ☎ *01/670–3384; 38/39 Lower Ormond Quay,* ☎ *01/872–0003. AE, MC, V.*

$–$$ ✗ Il Primo. Old wooden tables and chairs give it a casual feel, and the friendly, if cramped, atmosphere attracts a devoted clientele. The Irish-Italian cuisine is imaginative and reassuring at the same time. Among the main courses, a delicious creamy risotto with chunky chicken breasts, a scattering of chicken livers, and wild mushrooms is a standout. Wine is a specialty. ⊠ *Montague St., off Harcourt St.,* ☎ *01/478–3373. AE, DC, MC, V. Closed Sun.*

$–$$ ✗ Pasta Fresca. This stylish little Italian restaurant and deli off Grafton Street squeezes a surprising number of people into a fairly small space. Antipasto *misto* (assorted sliced Italian meats) makes a good appetizer—or go for carpaccio *della casa* (wafer-thin slices of beef fillet, with fresh Parmesan, olive oil, lemon juice, and black pepper). The main courses consist of Pasta Fresca's own very good versions of well-known dishes such as spaghetti *alla Bolognese,* cannelloni, and lasagna *al forno.* The pasta is freshly made each day. You'll find lines at lunchtime. ⊠ *3–4 Chatham St.,* ☎ *01/679–2402. AE, DC, MC, V. Closed Sun.*

$–$$ ✗ The Steps of Rome. Just a few steps from Grafton Street, it's perfect for a late-night bite or quick lunch. Slices of homemade pizza can be eaten on the spot or wrapped for takeout. The handful of tables is usually full, but it's worth waiting for classic Italian pasta dishes like pasta parmigiano or pesto, and good fresh salads with focaccia. Follow with zabaglione or tiramisu and good strong espresso. ⊠ *1 Chatham Ct.,* ☎ *01/670–5630. No credit cards.*

JAPANESE

$ ✗ Yamamori. Ramen noodle bars offer a staple diet for budget travelers to Japan, but this is the first in Ireland. The meals-in-a-bowl are a splendid slurping experience, and although you will be supplied with a small Chinese-style soup spoon, the best approach is with chopsticks. You can also get an authentic spin on sushi and sashimi dishes, as well as delicious chicken teriyaki. ⊠ *71 S. Great George's St.,* ☎ *01/475–5001. AE, DC, MC, V.*

PAN-ASIAN

$$$ ✗ Diep le Shaker. Slightly off the beaten track, on a narrow lane off Pembroke Street, this big, flamboyant restaurant serving Chinese and Thai food opened in 1999 and was an instant success. Comfortable high-back chairs, pristine table linen, and elegant stemware make this a lovely place to dine—and that's before you experience the superb food. Try the steamed scallops and ginger, or Dover sole served off the bone and encased in a light batter. Don't be surprised to see people ordering champagne to go with their meal. There's a permanent party feel that attracts Ireland's new wealthy set in droves. ⊠ *55 Pembroke La.,* ☎ *01/661–1829. AE, DC, MC, V. Closed Sun.*

$$ ✗ Mao. Everything is Asian fusion at this bustling café, from the little Andy Warhol pastiche of Chairman Mao on the washroom door to the Ho Fun noodles, stir-fried with shaved beef sirloin, pak choy, garlic, and black beans. It pays homage to Thai, Vietnamese, and other Southeast Asian cuisines. Red snapper is served with a tempura batter, chili mussels come in a large bowl with lemongrass, and vegetarian rice-paper rolls arrive stuffed with shiitake mushrooms and bean-thread noodles. Reservations aren't accepted, so go early to be sure of a seat. ⊠ *2 Chatham Row,* ☎ *01/670–4899. MC, V.*

RUSSIAN AND SCANDINAVIAN

$$$ ✕ **Old Dublin.** Unlikely as it might seem, this brasserie-style restaurant near St. Patrick's Cathedral specializes in Russian and Scandinavian food. A series of cozy but elegant low-ceilinged rooms are decorated with pristine white linens and candlelit tables and warmed by glowing fires in the evening. Familiar dishes such as blini, borscht, chicken Kiev, and beef Stroganoff feature alongside good Irish staples such as roast lamb and fresh baked salmon. The lunch menu tends to be more conventional, while the evening menu has surprises like planked sirloin Hussar, a steak baked between two oak planks, served on an oak platter with salad and sweet pickle. After your meal explore the antiques shops on Francis Street. ⊠ *90–91 St. Francis St.,* ☎ *01/454–2028. AE, DC, MC, V. Closed Sun. No lunch Sat.*

VEGETARIAN

$ ✕ **Nude.** This place is such a good idea that owner Norman Hewson—brother of U2's Bono—will probably open a chain. A sleek fast-food café, though not fully vegetarian, it serves organic and free-range foods. There are homemade soups, like roasted Italian vegetable or mushroom, and you can get vegetable wraps as well as smoothies and freshly squeezed juices. ⊠ *21 Suffolk St.,* ☎ *01/672–5577. MC, V.*

Temple Bar

AMERICAN/CASUAL

$$ ✕ **Elephant & Castle.** One of Temple Bar's most popular and established eateries, Elephant & Castle serves up traditional American food—charcoal-grilled burgers, salads, omelets, sandwiches, and pasta. The brunch on Sunday is always packed. The crowds and absence of soft surfaces mean the noise level can be high. When the service is good, the turnover tends to be quick, although you may be inclined to linger, as its formula—an atmosphere that's both bustling *and* relaxed, generous portions of unfussy and well-prepared food—makes it a casual Dublin standout. New Yorkers take note: yes, this is a cousin of the restaurant of the same name in Greenwich Village. ⊠ *18 Temple Bar,* ☎ *01/679–3121. Reservations not accepted. AE, DC, MC, V.*

$–$$ ✕ **Belgo.** Part of a Belgium chain of restaurants, it's the perfect place to go if you want a large serving of comfort food and are prepared to be adventurous with what you drink. The menu has dozens of different beers, and the French fries, served alongside omelets, burgers, *saucissons* (large, flavored Belgian sausages), and steaks, are the best you'll eat in Temple Bar. Go early in the evening (between 5:30 and 7:30) and your bill will match the time you arrived: if you sit down at 6:30 PM you pay £6.30. ⊠ *17–20 Sycamore St.,* ☎ *01/672–7554. AE, DC, MC, V.*

$ ✕ **Bad Ass Café.** Sinéad O'Connor used to wait tables at this lively spot in a converted warehouse between the Central Bank and Ha'penny Bridge (a "Rock 'n Stroll" tour plaque notes O'Connor's past here). Old-fashioned cash shuttles whiz around the ceiling of the barnlike space, which has bare floors and is painted in primary colors inside and out. A wall of glass makes for great people-watching. Although the food—mostly pizzas and burgers—is unexceptional, the Bad Ass can be a lot of fun and is popular with appetites of all ages. ⊠ *9–11 Crown Alley,* ☎ *01/671–2596. AE, MC, V.*

CONTEMPORARY

$$$–$$$$ ✕ **The Tea Room.** This restaurant is a good place to go if you have something to celebrate, or if you're hoping to spot some celebrities: it is part of the Clarence hotel (☞ *below*), where stars of stage and screen stay when they're in town. The bright, lofty dining room has spectacular flower arrangements and elegant, modern table settings. The food is adventurous and consistently good, although the menu is not extensive. Try a smoked duck salad or a spectacular baked cheese soufflé, and hope that risotto is on the menu because it always arrives perfectly cooked and superbly flavored. Mouthwatering entrées may include roast scallops, served with new potatoes and seasonal leaves, or grilled corn-fed chicken with goat cheese, pancetta, roast beetroot, and red onion. ⊠ *Clarence hotel, 6–8 Wellington Quay,* ☎ *01/670–7766. Reservations essential. AE, MC, V.*

$$$ ✕ **Eden.** The young owners of several of Dublin's café-style bars, in-
★ cluding the Front Lounge and the Globe (☞ Pubs, *below*), have followed those successes with a popular brasserie-style restaurant with an open kitchen and high wall of glass looking out onto one of Temple Bar's main squares. Patio-style doors lead to an outdoor eating area—a major plus in a city with relatively few alfresco dining spots. Chef Eleanor Walsh creates such dishes as duck leg confit with lentils and braised hock of ham served with mustard crust and *champ* (creamy, buttery mashed potatoes with scallions). Desserts include rhubarb crème brûlée and homemade ice creams and sorbets. ⊠ *Meeting House Sq.,* ☎ *01/670–5372. Reservations essential. AE, MC, V.*

$$–$$$ ✕ **Mermaid Cafe.** One of the chef-owners dabbles in fine art, and a couple of the large canvases on the walls are carried over into painterly bistro cooking. Lunch, ordered from a blackboard of specials, is an exceptional value—piquant crab cakes, hearty seafood casseroles, venison sausage, or vegetables roasted in a clay dish. Good attention to detail and a thoughtful wine list make this modest restaurant with tall windows looking onto busy Dame Street one of the best eateries in Temple Bar. ⊠ *69 Dame St.,* ☎ *01/670–8236. MC, V.*

FRENCH

$$$–$$$$ ✕ **Les Frères Jacques.** This restaurant brings a little bit of Paris to Tem-
★ ple Bar: old prints of Paris and Deauville hang on the green-papered walls, and the French waiters, dressed in white Irish linen and black bow ties, exude a Gallic charm without being excessively formal. Expect traditional French cooking that nods to the seasons. Seafood is a major attraction, and lobster, from the tank, is a specialty, typically roasted and flambéed with Irish whiskey. Also recommended is the *magret de canard* (roast breast of duck served with a ginger and grapefruit sauce). A piano player performs Friday and Saturday evenings and the occasional weeknights. ⊠ *74 Dame St.,* ☎ *01/679–4555. Reservations essential. AE, DC, MC, V. Closed Sun. No lunch Sat.*

ITALIAN

$–$$ ✕ **Osteria Romano.** Members of the Italian community congregate in the evenings at this cheerful eatery, dishing up authentic Roman cuisine. Specialties include *melanzane parmigiani,* a delicious dish of baked eggplant and cheese, while the pasta list has excellent cream-based dishes, like spaghetti alfredo and carbonara. Beware of finishing the meal with too many flaming *sambucas* (anise-flavored, semisweet Italian liqueur). The best table is by the window overlooking the street. ⊠ *5 Crow St.,* ☎ *01/670–8662. AE, DC, MC, V.*

MEDITERRANEAN

$$–$$$ ✕ **Bruno's.** Experienced French-born restaurateur Bruno Berta has a hit on his hands with his French-Mediterranean bistro on one of the busiest corners in Temple Bar. Low-slung windows let you watch passersby. Simple but stylish dishes range from starters of fresh crab claws with chilies, lemongrass, and tomato concassé to main dishes of grilled chicken with raisins, dried prunes, Moroccan semolina, and walnut dressing. Friendly service and a relaxed atmosphere make this one of the best bets in the area. ✉ *30 Essex St. E,* ☎ *01/670–6767. AE, DC, MC, V. Closed Sun.*

South City Center: Ballsbridge, Donnybrook, and Stillorgan

CONTEMPORARY

$$–$$$ ✕ **O'Connells.** This recently opened restaurant puts an emphasis on fresh Irish produce and baked goods. The dining room is a vast, modern space with sleek timber paneling and floor-to-ceiling windows. Go for the spit-roasted chicken, or anything baked in the huge clay oven that came all the way from Australia. Other tasty dishes are warm salad of kidneys with greens and oyster mushrooms, or monkfish with a lively pepper, tomato, and coriander salsa. The wine list gives interesting notes on each of the reasonably priced French and New World wines. A huge array of fresh breads is on display in the open kitchen, which turns into a buffet for breakfast and lunch. ✉ *Merrion Rd., Ballsbridge,* ☎ *01/647–3400. AE, DC, MC, V.*

CONTINENTAL

$$$$ ✕ **Le Coq Hardi.** For many years John Howard has been running one
★   of Dublin's best restaurants. Meeting the challenge posed by newer restaurants and younger chefs, he continues to refine and reinvent his own cooking. One of Howard's signature dishes—a little old-fashioned, perhaps, but still popular—is Coq Hardi, chicken stuffed with potatoes and mushrooms, wrapped in bacon before going into the oven, and finished off with a dash of Irish whiskey. The cheese boards are among the best in the country, and desserts tend to be rich and sumptuously classical French. Service is friendly and relaxed in the plush, comfortable, and quietly elegant dining room. The wine cellar holds many of the world's great wines. ✉ *35 Pembroke Rd., Ballsbridge,* ☎ *01/668–9070. Reservations essential. AE, DC, MC, V. Closed Sun.*

$$$ ✕ **Beaufield Mews.** A 10-minute taxi ride from the city center, this 18th-century coach house with stables still has its original cobbled courtyard and is even said to be haunted by a friendly monk. Inside it's all black beams, old furniture, and bric-a-brac. The more desirable tables overlook the courtyard or the garden or are, less predictably, "under the nun" (the nun in question is a 17th-century portrait). While the main attraction is the atmosphere, the food is based on fresh ingredients, and you'll find old favorites like roast duckling à l'orange as well as wild-salmon steaks simply grilled. ✉ *Woodlands Ave., Stillorgan,* ☎ *01/288–0375. Reservations essential. AE, DC, V. Closed Mon.*

IRISH

$$$ ✕ **Ernie's Restaurant.** High-quality ingredients, attention to detail, and consistency are the hallmarks of this long-established restaurant only a few minutes by taxi from the city center. Built around a large tree and fountain, the place has a welcoming atmosphere; it's also well known for the late Ernie Evans's large collection of paintings of the West of Ireland. Blue Irish linen and sparkling crystal decorate tables. The seasonal menu always has a variety of catches of the day—grilled sole with spring onion and thyme butter and poached wild salmon on

a bed of creamed potato—as well as four or five meat and poultry entrées such as roasted rack of Wicklow lamb with a caramelized onion
tart. ⊠ *Mulberry Gardens, Donnybrook,* ☎ *01/269–3300. AE, DC,
MC, V. Closed Sun.–Mon. and 1 wk at Christmas. No lunch Sat.*

City Center (Northside)

CONTEMPORARY

$$$$ ✕ **The Halo.** This restaurant in the chic Morrison hotel (☞ Lodging,
below) has been an instant hit with the fashion crowd and lawyers from
the nearby Four Courts. The dramatic dining room with a soaring ceiling and minimalist decor, devised by fashion designer John Rocha, looks
moody and mysterious by night, a little forbidding by day. The emphasis here is on complex dishes that look as good as they taste:
salmon with a divine hollondaise sauce, served in a Chinese spoon resting on a black platter; fish and vegetable tempura; and chicken stuffed
with fresh greens, served with shiitake mushrooms and black bean sauce,
are among the specialties. Desserts are miniature works of art on enormous China platters. ⊠ *Morrison hotel, Ormond Quay,* ☎ *01/887–
2421. AE, DC, MC, V.*

$$–$$$ ✕ **Chapter One.** In the vaulted, stone-walled basement of the Dublin
Writers Museum, just down the street from the Hugh Lane Municipal
Gallery of Modern Art (☞ North of the Liffey *in* Exploring, *above*), this
is one of the most notable restaurants in northside Dublin. Try the pressed
duck and black pudding terrine with pear chutney as well as the roast
scallops with smoked bacon and potato-herb salad in a chili dressing. The
rich bread-and-butter pudding and the apple and pecan crumble are two
stellar desserts. ⊠ *18–19 Parnell Sq.,* ☎ *01/873–2266. Reservations
essential. AE, DC, MC, V. Closed Sun.–Mon. No lunch Sat.*

$$ ✕ **Harbour Master.** The main attraction of this big, airy restaurant and
bar in the Irish Financial Services Centre north of the Liffey is its set-
ting overlooking a canal basin. At lunch the place is packed with
stockbrokers and lawyers; dinner is more subdued. There's a cav-
ernous bar where you can dine bistro style, but head for the newly built
section, which serves hearty food such as seafood risotto, braised lamb
shank with lentils and mash, and rib-eye steak with chips. ⊠ *Custom
House Docks,* ☎ *01/670–1688. AE, DC, MC, V.*

Pub Food

Most pubs serve food at lunchtime, some throughout the day. Food
ranges from hearty soups and stews to chicken curries, smoked-salmon
salads, and sandwiches, and much of it is surprisingly good. Expect to
pay £4–£6 for a main course. Some of the larger, more popular pubs
may take credit cards.

✕ **Davy Byrne's.** James Joyce immortalized Davy Byrne's in his sprawl-
ing novel *Ulysses*. Nowadays it's more akin to a cocktail bar than a
Dublin pub, but it's good for fresh and smoked salmon, salads, and a
hot daily special. ⊠ *21 Duke St.,* ☎ *01/671–1298.*

✕ **Old Stand.** Conveniently close to Grafton Street, the Old Stand serves
grilled food, including steaks. ⊠ *37 Exchequer St.,* ☎ *01/677–7220.*

✕ **O'Neill's.** This fine pub, a stone's throw from Trinity College, has the
best carvery (open from noon to 2:30) of any pub in the city, serving up
a hearty lunch for about £5–£6. ⊠ *2 Suffolk St.,* ☎ *01/679–3614.*

✕ **Stag's Head.** With one of Dublin's best pub lunches, the Stag's
Head is a favorite of both Trinity students and businesspeople. ⊠ *1
Dame Ct.,* ☎ *01/679–3701.*

✕ **Zanzibar.** This spectacular and immense bar on the northside of the Liffey looks as though it might be more at home in downtown Marrakesh. While away an afternoon on one of its many wicker chairs and enjoy freshly made sandwiches, salads, and cocktails. ✉ *34–35 Lower Ormond Quay,* ☎ *01/878–7212.*

LODGING

"An absolute avalanche of new hotels" is how the *Irish Times* characterized Dublin's hotel boom. It's unlikely that there have ever been more hotels under construction at one time in the capital than there are now, while at the same time, at least one-quarter of the existing hotels are being renovated. New lodgings have sprung up in all areas of the city, including the much-talked-about one in Smithfield, and some in Ballsbridge, an inner "suburb" that's a 20-minute walk from the city center. Demand for rooms means that rates are still high at the best hotels by the standards of any major European or American city (and factoring in the exchange rate means a hotel room can take a substantial bite out of any traveler's budget). Service charges range from 15% in expensive hotels to zero in moderate and inexpensive ones. Be sure to inquire when you make reservations.

Many hotels have a weekend, or "B&B," rate that's often 30%–40% cheaper than the ordinary rate; some hotels also have a midweek special that provides discounts of up to 35%. These rates are available throughout the year but are harder to get in high season. Ask about them when booking a room (they are available only on a prebooked basis), especially if you plan a brief or weekend stay. If you've rented a car and you're not staying at a hotel with secure parking facilities, it's worth considering a location out of the city center, such as Dalkey or Killiney, where the surroundings are more pleasant and you won't have to worry about parking on city streets, which can be difficult.

Dublin has a decent selection of less-expensive accommodations—including many moderately priced hotels with basic but agreeable rooms. As a general rule of thumb, lodgings on the northside of the river tend to be more affordable than those on the south. Many B&Bs, long the mainstay of the economy end of the market, have upgraded their facilities and now provide rooms with private bathrooms or showers, as well as multichannel color televisions and direct-dial telephones, for around £25 a night per person. B&Bs tend to be in suburban areas—generally a 10-minute bus ride from the center of the city. This is not in itself a great drawback, and savings can be significant. For lodging prices and information, *see* Lodging *in* Smart Travel Tips A to Z.

City Center (Southside)

$$$$ 🏨 **Conrad Dublin International.** In a seven-story redbrick and smoked-glass building just off St. Stephen's Green, the Conrad, owned by the Hilton Group, is firmly aimed at international business travelers. Gleaming, light marble graces the large, formal lobby. Rooms are rather cramped and have uninspiring views of the adjacent office buildings, but they are nicely outfitted with natural wood furnishings, painted in sand colors and pastel greens, and graced with Spanish marble in the bathrooms. A note to light sleepers: the air-conditioning/heating system can be noisy. The hotel has two restaurants: the informal Plurabelle and the plusher Alexandra Room. The main bar, Alfie Byrne's, named in honor of Dublin's lord mayor for most of the 1930s (a renowned teetotaller), attempts to re-create a traditional Irish pub atmosphere. ✉ *Earlsfort Terr., Dublin 2,* ☎ *01/676–5555, 800/*

HILTONS in the U.S., FAX *01/676–5424. 182 rooms with bath, 9 suites. 2 restaurants, bar, in-room data ports, in-room safes, in-room VCRs, minibars, no-smoking floor, no-smoking rooms, room service, exercise room, concierge, business services, meeting rooms, free parking. AE, DC, MC, V.* 🕾

$$$$ 🏨 **Fitzwilliam Hotel.** A relative newcomer to the luxury circuit, the Fitzwilliam has been dubbed a "designer" hotel for its impeccable decor: everything from light fixtures to luggage racks to staff uniforms is the work of international design leaders. The modern glass building has a large roof garden and overlooks the park. The spacious rooms are furnished in a contemporary, comfortable style. Conrad Gallagher, one of Ireland's young up-and-coming chefs, presides over the rooftop restaurant. ⊠ *St. Stephen's Green, Dublin 2,* ☎ *01/478–7000,* FAX *01/ 478–7878. 135 rooms with bath, 2 suites. Restaurant, bar, brasserie, in-room data ports, no-smoking rooms, room service, exercise room, laundry service, business services, meeting rooms. AE, DC, MC, V.* 🕾

$$$$ 🏨 **Merrion.** The home of Arthur Wellesley, the Duke of Wellington and ★ hero of the Battle of Waterloo, is one of four exactingly restored Georgian town houses that make up part of this luxurious hotel. The stately rooms are richly appointed in classic Georgian style down to the last detail—from the crisp linen sheets to the Carrara marble bathrooms. Some are vaulted with delicate Adamesque plasterwork ceilings, and others are graced with magnificent, original marble fireplaces. The Garden Wing, at the back of the hotel behind the elegant gardens laid out by Irish landscape designer Jim Reynolds, has smaller rooms than the main house, but they are just as ornate. You know this place has to be one of Dublin's best—after all, leading Dublin restaurateur Patrick Guilbaud (☞ *Dining, above*) moved his eponymous restaurant here. ⊠ *Upper Merrion St., Dublin 2,* ☎ *01/603–0600,* FAX *01/603–0700. 127 rooms with bath, 18 suites. 2 restaurants, 2 bars, in-room data ports, in-room safes, in-room VCRs, minibars, no-smoking floor, no-smoking rooms, room service, indoor pool, barbershop, beauty salon, massage, steam room, dry cleaning, laundry service, concierge, business services, meeting rooms, free parking. AE, DC, MC, V.* 🕾

$$$$ 🏨 **Shelbourne Méridien Hotel.** Paris has the Ritz, New York has the ★ Plaza, and Dublin has the Shelbourne. The grand old history (Ireland's constitution was signed in Room 112 in 1921) of this grand old place was written by no less than celebrated novelist and wit Elizabeth Bowen. One step past the ornate, redbrick and white-gingerbread facade and you know you're in Dublin: Waterford chandeliers, gleaming Old Masters on the wall, and Irish Chippendale chairs invite you to linger in the lobby—as many fabled names have done so since this city showplace opened in 1824 (☞ The Center City: Around Trinity College, *above*). Each guest room is unique; all have fine, carefully selected furniture and luxurious drapes, with splendid antiques in the older rooms. Those in front overlook St. Stephen's Green, but rooms in the back, without a view, are quieter. The impressive suites have separate sitting rooms and dressing areas. The restaurant, 27 The Green, is one of the most elegant rooms in Dublin; Lord Mayor's Lounge, off the lobby, is a perfect rendezvous spot and offers a lovely afternoon tea— a real Dublin tradition. ⊠ *27 St. Stephen's Green, Dublin 2,* ☎ *01/ 676–6471, 800/543–4300 in the U.S.,* FAX *01/661–6006. 194 rooms with bath, 9 suites. 2 restaurants, 2 bars, indoor pool, hot tub, sauna, health club, free parking. AE, DC, MC, V.* 🕾

$$$$ 🏨 **Westbury.** This comfortable, modern hotel is in the heart of southside Dublin, right off the city's buzzing shopping mecca, Grafton Street. Join elegantly dressed Dubliners for afternoon tea in the spacious mezzanine-level main lobby, furnished with antiques. Alas, the utilitarian rooms—painted in pastels—don't share the lobby's ele-

gance. More inviting are the suites, which combine European decor with tasteful Japanese screens and prints. The flowery Russell Room serves formal lunches and dinners; the downstairs Sandbank, a seafood restaurant and bar, has decor resembling a Joycean-period establishment. ⊠ *Grafton St., Dublin 2,* ☎ *01/679–1122,* FAX *01/679–7078. 203 rooms with bath, 8 suites. 2 restaurants, bar, minibars, no-smoking rooms, room service, dry cleaning, laundry service, free parking. AE, DC, MC, V.*

$$$ ⊞ **Davenport, Mont Clare, and Alexander.** The Davenport's gorgeous, bright-yellow neoclassic facade was built in the 1860s to front a church, but a 1993 conversion remade the building into this hotel, just behind Trinity College. The reasonably spacious rooms and larger suites are fitted in tasteful, deep colors and functional furnishings. The hotel restaurant, Lanyon's, serves breakfast, lunch, and dinner amid traditional Georgian decor. In the comfortable President's Bar, see how many heads of state you can identify in the photos covering the walls. ⊠ *Merrion Sq., Dublin 2,* ☎ *01/661–6800, 800/327–0200 in the U.S.,* FAX *01/ 661–5663. 118 rooms with bath, 2 suites. Restaurant, bar, air-conditioning, in-room VCRs, minibars, no-smoking rooms, room service, dry cleaning, laundry service, concierge, business services, meeting rooms, free parking. AE, DC, MC, V.*

$$ ⊞ **Central Hotel.** Established in 1887, this grand, old-style redbrick hotel is in the heart of the center city, steps from Grafton Street, Temple Bar, and Dublin Castle. Rooms are small but have high ceilings and practical but tasteful furniture. Adjacent to the hotel is Molly Malone's Tavern, a lively hotel-bar with plenty of regulars who come for the atmosphere and the live, traditional Irish music on Friday and Saturday nights. The restaurant and Library Bar—one of the best spots in the city for a quiet pint—are on the first floor. ⊠ *1–5 Exchequer St., Dublin 2,* ☎ *01/679–7302,* FAX *01/679–7303. 67 rooms with bath, 3 suites. Restaurant, 2 bars, room service, dry cleaning, laundry service, concierge, business services, meeting rooms. AE, DC, MC, V.* ✆

$$ ⊞ **Drury Court Hotel.** A two-minute walk from Grafton Street and just around the corner from some of the city's best restaurants, this small hotel opened in March 1996. Rooms are done in subtle greens, golds, and burgundies. The parquet-floored rathskeller dining room serves breakfast and dinner; lunch is served in the casual Digges Lane Bar, frequented by many young Dubliners. ⊠ *28–30 Lower Stephens St., Dublin 2,* ☎ *01/475–1988,* FAX *01/478–5730. 30 rooms with bath, 2 suites. Restaurant, bar, room service, dry cleaning, laundry service, meeting room. AE, DC, MC, V.* ✆

$$ ⊞ **Stephen's Hall All-Suite.** Dublin's only all-suite hotel is in a tastefully modernized Georgian town house just off Stephen's Green. The suites, considerably larger than the average hotel room, include one or two bedrooms, a separate sitting room, a fully equipped kitchen, and bath. They are comfortably equipped with quality modern furniture. Top-floor suites have spectacular city views, and ground-floor suites have private entrances. Morel's Restaurant serves breakfast, lunch, and dinner. ⊠ *14–17 Lower Leeson St., Dublin 2,* ☎ *01/661–0585,* FAX *01/ 661–0606. 37 suites. Restaurant, 2 bars, room service, no-smoking rooms, meeting rooms, free parking. AE, DC, MC, V.*

$ ⊞ **Avalon House.** Many young, independent travelers rate this cleverly restored, Victorian redbrick building the most appealing of Dublin's hostels. A 2-minute walk from Grafton Street and 5–10 minutes from some of the city's best music venues, the hostel has a mix of dormitories, rooms without bath, and rooms with bath. The dorm rooms and en-suite quads all have loft areas that offer more privacy than you'd typically find in a multibed room. The Avalon Café serves food until 10 PM but is open as a common room after hours. ⊠ *55 Aungier St.,*

Dublin 2, ☎ *01/475–0001,* ℻ *01/475–0303. 35 4-bed rooms with bath, 5 4-bed rooms without bath, 4 twin rooms with bath, 4 single rooms without bath, 22 twin rooms without bath, 5 12-bed dorms, 1 10-bed dorm, 1 26-bed dorm. Bar, café. AE, MC, V.* 🐾

$ 🖭 **Jurys Christchurch Inn.** Expect few frills at this functional budget hotel, part of a Jurys minichain that offers a low, fixed room rate for up to three adults or two adults and two children. (The **Jurys Custom House Inn** [⊠ Custom House Quay, Dublin 1, ☎ 01/607–5000, ℻ 01/829–0400], at the International Financial Services Centre, operates according to the same plan.) The biggest plus is the pleasant location, facing Christ Church Cathedral and within walking distance of most city-center attractions. The rather spartan rooms are decorated in pastel colors and utilitarian furniture. ⊠ *Christ Church Pl., Dublin 8,* ☎ *01/454–0000,* ℻ *01/454–0012. 182 rooms with bath. Restaurant, bar, no-smoking rooms, parking (fee). AE, DC, MC, V.* 🐾

$ 🖭 **Kilronan House.** A five-minute walk from St. Stephen's Green, ★ Deirdre and Noel Comer's guest house is a favorite—thanks in large measure to the friendly welcome. The large, late-19th-century terraced house, with a white facade, was carefully converted, and the furnishings are updated each year. Richly patterned wallpaper and carpets grace guest rooms, while orthopedic beds (rather rare in Dublin hotels, let alone guest houses) help to guarantee a restful night's sleep. If you have a dog back home whom you're pining after, you'll appreciate Homer, the Labrador. ⊠ *70 Adelaide Rd., Dublin 2,* ☎ *01/475–5266,* ℻ *01/478–2841. 12 rooms with bath. Free parking. MC, V.*

$ 🖭 **Number 31.** Two Georgian mews strikingly renovated in the early '60s as the private home of Sam Stephenson, Ireland's leading modern architect, are now connected via a small garden to the grand town house they once served. Together they form a marvelous guest house a short walk from St. Stephen's Green. Owners Deirdre and Noel Comer, who also own Kilronan House (☞ *above*), serve made-to-order breakfasts at refectory tables in the balcony dining room. The white-tiled sunken living room, with its black leather sectional sofa and modern artwork that includes a David Hockney print, will make you think you're in California, not Dublin. ⊠ *31 Leeson Close, Dublin 2,* ☎ *01/676–5011,* ℻ *01/676–2929. 18 rooms with bath. No-smoking rooms, dry cleaning, laundry service, free parking. AE, MC, V.*

Temple Bar

$$$$ 🖭 **The Clarence.** You might well bump into celebrity friends of co-owners Bono and the Edge of U2 at this contemporary hotel, understated to the point of austerity. Stone floors, unadorned oak wainscoting, and a leather-lined elevator set the slightly chaotic tone downstairs, where the Octagon Bar and the Tea Room Restaurant are popular Temple Bar watering holes. Guest rooms are done in a mishmash of earth tones accented with deep purple, gold, cardinal red, and royal blue. With the exception of those in the penthouse suite, rooms are small; but *very* comfortable beds, sparkling bathrooms, and views of the Liffey, from the front rooms, compensate. The laissez-faire service seems to take its cue from the minimalist decor, so if you like to be pampered, stay elsewhere. ⊠ *6–8 Wellington Quay, Dublin 2,* ☎ *01/670–9000,* ℻ *01/670–7800. 46 rooms with bath, 4 suites. Restaurant, bar, no-smoking rooms, minibars, dry cleaning, laundry service, meeting rooms, free parking. AE, DC, MC, V.*

$$ 🖭 **Arlington Hotel.** A converted auction house on the quays is the setting for this privately owned boutique hotel. Pass between the gold lions guarding the door and enter a medieval great hall with suits of armor, sumptuous swags, and creaky floors. The theme continues in the bar;

boisterous and echo-filled, it's more mead hall than cozy pub. Rich up-holstery, romantic lighting, and hearty Irish fare (full breakfast is included in the rates) make the restaurant more intimate. Upstairs the corridors and rooms have a Georgian feel, with soothing pastel yellow or lavender walls; spreads and drapes are awash in golds, rusts, and blues and have patterns and details evocative of tapestries. The hotel also has limited off-street parking, though your way might be blocked by a Guinness truck. ⊠ *23–25 Bachelor's Walk, O'Connell Bridge, Dublin 1,* ☎ *01/804–9100,* 🖾 *01/804–9112. 115 rooms with bath. Restaurant, bar, in-room data ports, no-smoking rooms, dance club, baby-sitting, laundry service, meeting rooms, free parking. AE, DC, MC, V.*

$$ 🏨 **Parliament.** Although the Parliament is in one of Dublin's finest Edwardian buildings, its interior is very much functional, if tidy, and attracts a mostly business clientele. They are drawn by the location, on Dame Street near the Central Bank and a few blocks down from Trinity College. Rooms are a good size, with a simple, slightly monotonous beige and off-white scheme. The Senate Restaurant and Forum Bar keep up the democratic theme. ⊠ *Lord Edward St., Dublin 2,* ☎ *01/670–8777,* 🖾 *01/670–8787. 63 rooms with bath. Restaurant, bar, no-smoking rooms. AE, DC, MC, V.*

$$ 🏨 **Temple Bar.** In a former bank building just around the corner from Trinity College, this hotel has an Art Deco lobby with a large and old-fashioned cast-iron fireplace, natural-wood furniture, and lots of plants. Off the lobby are a small cocktail bar and the bright, open, glass-roofed Terrace Restaurant, which serves sandwiches, pastas, omelets, and fish all day. Mahogany furnishings and autumn green and rust colors adorn guest rooms, nearly all of which have double beds, making them more than a little cramped. The Boomerang nightclub on the premises is open to both guests and the public. ⊠ *Fleet St., Dublin 2,* ☎ *01/677–3333,* 🖾 *01/677–3088. 129 rooms with bath, 1 suite. Restaurant, 2 bars, nightclub, parking (fee). AE, DC, MC, V.*

South City Center—Ballsbridge

$$$$ 🏨 **Berkeley Court.** The most quietly elegant of Dublin's large modern hotels, Berkeley Court has a glass-and-concrete exterior designed in a modern, blocklike style set in verdant grounds. Inside, the vast white-tiled and plushly carpeted lobby has roomy sofas and antique planters. The large rooms are decorated in golds, yellows, and greens, with antiques or reproductions of period furniture; bathrooms are tiled in marble. The five luxury suites have a Jacuzzi. The Berkeley Room restaurant has table d'hôte and à la carte menus; the more informal Conservatory Grill, with large windows, serves grilled food and snacks. ⊠ *Lansdowne Rd., Dublin 4,* ☎ *01/660–1711, 800/550–0000 in the U.S.,* 🖾 *01/661–7238. 157 rooms with bath, 29 suites. 2 restaurants, bar, room service, no-smoking rooms, barbershop, beauty salon, exercise room, shops, dry cleaning, laundry service, business services, meeting rooms, free parking. AE, DC, MC, V.*

$$$$ 🏨 **Herbert Park Hotel.** The Herbert Park sits adjacent to a park of the same name and beside the River Dodder. The large lobby has floor-to-ceiling windows and a slanted glass roof. The spacious bar, terrace lounge, and restaurant are Japanese-inspired. Relaxing shades of blue and cream predominate in the nicely sized rooms, which are brightened by green, red, or white bedspreads; all have individually controlled air-conditioning, a large desk, and two telephone lines. Some look onto the park. Two of the suites have large balconies with views of the park or the leafy suburbs. The restaurant has a large terrace where you can dine in warm weather. ⊠ *Ballsbridge, Dublin 4,* ☎ *01/667–2200,* 🖾

01/667–2595. 150 rooms with bath, 3 suites. Restaurant, bar, exercise room, business services, free parking. AE, DC, MC, V. 🕸

$$$$ 🏨 **Jurys and The Towers.** These adjacent seven-story hotels, a short cab ride from the center of town, are popular with businesspeople and vacationers. They have more atmosphere than most comparable modern hotels, though the Towers has an edge over Jurys, its older (it dates from 1962), larger, less-expensive companion. Jurys has large, plainly decorated rooms with light walls and brown drapes; furnishings are functional but uninspired. The Towers' rooms are a third larger than those of Jurys, decorated in blue and gold with built-in, natural wood furniture; the large beds and armchairs are comfortable. All the suites in both hotels have their own sitting rooms and kitchenettes. The Dubliners Bar, modeled on an old country kitchen, is popular with upwardly mobile locals and guests. ✉ *Ballsbridge, Dublin 4,* ☎ *01/660–5000,* FAX *01/660–5540. Jurys: 288 rooms with bath, 3 suites; the Towers: 100 rooms with bath, 4 suites with kitchenettes. Restaurant, coffee shop, 2 bars, indoor-outdoor pool, hot tub, shop, cabaret (May–Oct.), dry cleaning, laundry service, business services, meeting rooms, free parking. AE, DC, MC, V.* 🕸

$$$ 🏨 **Doyle Burlington.** Dublin's largest hotel, popular with American tour groups and Irish and European business travelers, is about five minutes by car from the city center. Its impersonal, 1972 glass-and-concrete facade contrasts with the friendly and attentive staff. Public rooms, especially the large bar, have mahogany counters and hanging plants that enhance the conservatory-style setting. The generous-size rooms, in the usual modern plush in neutral tones, have large picture windows. At night, Annabel's nightclub and the seasonal Irish cabaret are both lively spots. Although the Burlington has no sports and health facilities, the Doyle hotel group (☞ Doyle Tara, *below*) has an arrangement that allows you to use the RiverView Sports Club in nearby Clonskeagh for £5 a visit. ✉ *Upper Leeson St., Dublin 4,* ☎ *01/660–5222,* FAX *01/660–8496. 523 rooms with bath. 2 restaurants, 3 bars, room service, shops, cabaret (May–Oct.), nightclub, dry cleaning, laundry service, business service, meeting rooms, free parking. AE, DC, MC, V.*

$$$ 🏨 **Hibernian.** Only a 15-minute walk from the city center, this early
★ 20th-century Edwardian nurses' home designed by Albert E. Murray—one of the architects of the Rotunda Hospital—is now a small luxury hotel. One of the city's most elegant and intimate hostelries, it has retained the distinctive red-and-amber brick facade and has smallish rooms, nicely done in pastels, with deep-pile carpets and comfortable furniture. The public rooms, in cheerful chintz and stripes, include a period-style library and a sun lounge—both comfortable spaces to relax before or after a dinner in the hotel's intimate restaurant, the Patrick Kavanagh Room. Amid all this Victorian elegance, the owners haven't forgotten the warming touches. ✉ *Eastmoreland Pl. off Upper Baggot St., Dublin 4,* ☎ *01/668–7666 or 800/414243,* FAX *01/660–2655. 40 rooms with bath. Restaurant, bar, parking (fee). AE, DC, MC, V.*

$$ 🏨 **Lansdowne.** This small Ballsbridge hotel has cozy rooms in Geor-
★ gian style with deep floral-pattern decor. Photos of sports personalities hang on the walls of the Green Blazer bar in the basement, a popular haunt for local businesspeople and fans of the international rugby matches held at nearby Lansdowne Road; you can get a bite to eat here all day. Next to the bar is Parker's Restaurant, which specializes in seafood and grilled steaks. ✉ *27 Pembroke Rd., Dublin 4,* ☎ *01/668–2522,* FAX *01/668–5585. 37 rooms with bath, 2 suites. Restaurant, bar, free parking. AE, DC, MC, V.*

Dublin Lodging

KEY

DART Railway
Station

Eccles St.

Berkeley Rd.

Blessington St.

Wellington St.

Phibsborough Rd.

Royal Canal Bank

Western Way

Upper Dominick St.

Constitution Hill

Upper Grangegorman

Lower Grangegorman

N. Brunswick St.

King St.

Smithfield

Bow St.

Church St.

Mary's La.

Coleraine St.

Beresford St.

Green St.

Capel St.

Parnell St.

Upper Dorset St.

Lower Dorset St.

Lower Gardiner St.

Temple St.

Great Denmark St.

N. Great George's St.

Parnell Square

Parnell St.

O'Connell St.

Marlborough St.

Summerhill

Mountjoy
Square

Belvidere Pl.

Hill St.

Earl St. N.

Henry St.

Mary St.

Liffey St.

Prince's St. N.

Abbey St.

Jervis St.

Strand St. Great

Upper Abbey St.

Middle Abbey St.

Lotts

Sackville Pl.

Eden Quay

Bachelor's Walk

Burgh Q.

Pool

Mary's Abbey

Ormond Quay

Arran Quay

Usher's Quay

Whitworth Br.

Inns Quay

Merchant's Quay

Ormond Quay

River Liffey

Aston Quay

Wellington Quay

Temple Bar

Fleet St.

Westmoreland St.

College St.

Doiler St.

Anglesea St.

Fownes St.

College
Green

Suffolk St.

Nassau St.

Oliver Bond

Cook St.

Wood Quay

Essex Quay

St. Augustine St.

High St.

W. Thomas St.

St. Francis St.

Winetavern St.

St. Nicholas St.

Fishamble St.

Lord Edward St.

Castle St.

Dame St.

City
Hall

Castle

Ship St. Great

Werburgh St.

S. Great George's St.

Exchequer St.

Drury St.

William St.

Clarendon St.

Wicklow St.

Duke St.

Anne St.

Molesworth St.

Kildare St.

Dawson St.

Golden La.

Patrick St.

St. Patrick's
Park

St. Patrick's Close

Aungier St.

York St.

Mercer St.

Cuffe St.

St. Stephen's Green N.

ST. STEPHEN'S
GREEN

St. Stephen's
Green W.

St. Stephen's
Green S.

The Coombe

New Row

Bride St.

New Bride St.

Lower
Kevin St.

Camden St.

Camden Row

Mill St.

N

Lower Clanbrassil St.

Heytesbury St.

Pleasants St.

Grantham St.

Charlotte St.

Upper Hatch St.

Lower Ha...

Harcourt St.

Earlsfort Ter.

Victoria St.

Camden St.

S. Richmond St.

S. Circular Rd.

Harrington St.

Harcourt Rd.

Adelaide Rd.

Charlemont St.

0   330 yards

0   300 meters

North Circular Rd.

Charleville Ave.

Strand Rd.

Tolka River

Royal Canal

River Tolka Promenade

Ballybough Rd.

Great Charles St.

Mountjoy Square

West Rd.

Church Rd.

E. Wall St.

Killarney St.

Amiens St.

Seville Pl.

Church Rd.

East Rd.

Sean McDermott St.

Railway St.

Gardiner St.

Foley St.

Connolly Station

Lower Sheriff St.

Talbot St.

Inner Dock

Busaras Bus Station

Upper Sheriff St.

Lower Abbey St.

Custom House

George's Dock

Commons St.

New Wapping St.

Mayor St.

Castleforbes Rd.

Custom House Quay

Butt Br.

George's Quay

North Wall Quay

Quay

Poolbeg

Tara St. Station

City Quay

Gloucester St.

Sir John Rogerson's Quay

Townsend St.

Pearse St.

Lombard St. E.

Magennis Pl.

Cardiff's La.

Hanover Quay

Trinity College

Westland Row

Pearse Station

Pearse St.

Macken St.

Ringsend Rd.

Lincoln Place

Clare St.

18

Fenian St.

Hogan Pl.

South Lotts Rd.

Frederick La. S.

Leinster St.

18   18

Merrion Sq. N.

Lower Grand Canal St.

Kildare St.

Upper Merrion St.

Merrion St.

Merrion Square

Merrion Sq. S.

Upper Mount St.

Upper Grand Canal St.

19

Merrion Row

20

Fitzwilliam Ln.

Lower Mount St.

St. Stephen's Green E.

Pembroke St.

Fitzwilliam St.

Lower Baggot St.

Lad La.

Herbert Pl.

Herbert St.

Grand Canal

Shelbourne Rd.

21

Lower Fitzwilliam St.

Haddington Rd.

Northumberland Rd.

35

22

Upper Hatch St.

24

Wilton Terrace

Upper Baggot St.

31

32 33 34

Lower Leeson St.

Waterloo Rd.

26

Lansdowne Rd.

30

Pembroke Rd.

29

27

25

28

$ ⊞ **Ariel Guest House.** This redbrick, 1850 Victorian guest house is one
★ of Dublin's finest, just a few steps from a DART stop and a 15-minute
walk from St. Stephen's Green. Recently restored rooms in the main
house are lovingly decorated with Victorian and Georgian antiques,
Victoriana, and period wallpaper and drapes. The 13 rooms at the back
of the house are more spartan, but all are immaculate. A Waterford-
crystal chandelier hangs over the comfortable leather and mahogany
furniture in the gracious, fireplace-warmed drawing room. Owner
Michael O'Brien is an extraordinarily helpful and gracious host. ⊠ *52
Lansdowne Rd., Dublin 4,* ☎ *01/668–5512,* ℻ *01/668–5845. 40
rooms with bath. Breakfast room, free parking. MC, V.*

$ ⊞ **Mount Herbert Hotel.** This sprawling accommodation is made up
of a number of large Victorian-era houses. It overlooks some of Ballsbridge's fine rear gardens and is right near the main rugby stadium;
the nearby DART will have you in the city center in seven minutes.
The simple rooms are painted in light shades and contain little besides
beds, but all have bathrooms and 10-channel TVs. You can relax in
the lounge; the large restaurant, overlooking the English-style back garden (floodlit at night) and children's play area, serves three meals a
day, with unpretentious dinners of steaks and stews. ⊠ *7 Herbert Rd.,
Dublin 4,* ☎ *01/668–4321,* ℻ *01/660–7077. 200 rooms with bath.
Restaurant, bar, sauna, shop, business services, meeting rooms, free parking. AE, DC, MC, V.* ✍

City Center (Northside)

$$$$ ⊞ **The Morrison.** Halfway between the Ha'penny and Capel Street
bridges, it's no more than 10 minutes from Trinity College. The highly
modern interior—designed by John Rocha, Ireland's most acclaimed
fashion designer—can be a bit cold. He had the last word on everything down to the toiletries and staff uniforms. Rooms are standard
in decor but high-tech, with top-of-the-line entertainment units, satellite TV, and ISDN lines. The Halo restaurant (☞ Dining, *above*) has
an Asian theme. ⊠ *Ormond Quay, Dublin 1,* ☎ *01/879–2999 or
800/447–7462,* ℻ *01/878–3185. 88 rooms with bath, 7 suites. 2
restaurants, 2 bars, in-room data ports, in-room VCRs, minibars, no-
smoking rooms, room service, dry cleaning, laundry service, concierge,
business services, meeting rooms, free parking. AE, DC, MC, V.* ✍

$$ ⊞ **Chief O'Neill's.** Named after a 19th-century Corkman who became
chief of police in Chicago, Dublin's newest hotel dominates Smithfield
Village. It is part of the complex that also houses Ceol (☞ Exploring,
above), the traditional music museum. Like the museum, the hotel has
a modern design, with a huge lobby-bar area overlooking a cobbled
courtyard. Smallish, high-tech rooms all have ISDN lines and thoroughly
up-to-date decor with chrome fixtures and minimalist furnishings.
Top-floor suites have delightful roof-top gardens with views of the city
on both sides of the Liffey. The café-bar has live traditional music and
contemporary Irish food, and Asian cuisine is available in Kelly & Ping,
a bright, airy restaurant off Duck Lane, an integral shopping arcade.
⊠ *Smithfield Village, Dublin 7,* ☎ *01/817–3838,* ℻ *01/817–3839. 70
rooms with bath, 3 suites. Restaurant, bar, in-room data ports, mini-
bars, no-smoking rooms, room service, in-room VCRs, exercise room,
shops, dry cleaning, laundry service, free parking. AE, DC, MC, V.* ✍

$$ ⊞ **Royal Dublin Hotel.** O'Connell Street is not what it once was, but
this renovated, quality hotel has just about a perfect location at the
top of the old thoroughfare. All of the northside's major attractions
are nearby, and you can walk south to Trinity College in 10 minutes.
The public spaces are all well lit glass and brass, rooms are spacious,
and the hotel has a reputation for extrafriendly service. The Georgian

Room and Raffles bar try to put on posh English airs, but the casual warmth of the Irish manages to heat up the slightly stuffy atmosphere. ⊠ *O'Connell St., Dublin 1,* ☎ *01/873–3666,* ℻ *01/873–3120. 117 rooms with bath, 3 suites. Restaurant, bar, in-room data ports, in-room VCRs, minibars, no-smoking rooms, room service, dry cleaning, laundry service. AE, MC, V.* ✏

$ 🔃 **Dublin International Youth Hostel.** In a converted convent, Dublin's major hostel has a total of 420 beds divided between private rooms and dorm rooms with 8, 12, 15, or 22 beds. Bathroom facilities are communal, even for private rooms. This is a spartan, low-cost alternative to hotels; if you're not a member of the International Youth Hostel organization, you can stay for a small extra charge. The hostel is north of Parnell Square, near the Mater Hospital. ⊠ *51 Mountjoy St., Dublin 1,* ☎ *01/830–1766,* ℻ *01/380–1600. 2 twin rooms, 3 3-bed rooms, 2 4-bed rooms, 9 6-bed rooms, and 8-, 12-, 15-, and 22-bed dorms. Restaurant. MC, V.*

South County Dublin Suburbs

$$$ 🔃 **Doyle Tara.** On the main coast road 10–15 minutes from the Dun Laoghaire ferry terminal and 6½ km (4 mi) from the city center, this unpretentious, informal seven-story hotel is also near the Booterstown Marsh Bird Sanctuary (☞ County Dublin—Southside *in* Side Trips, *below*). The best rooms are in the original section and face Dublin Bay; rooms in the addition have slightly more modern decor. The restaurant serves grilled fish, steaks, and omelets. The hotel staff is very personable. ⊠ *Merrion Rd., Dublin 4,* ☎ *01/269–4666,* ℻ *01/269–1027. 114 rooms with bath. Restaurant, bar, no-smoking rooms, dry cleaning, laundry service, free parking. AE, DC, MC, V.*

$$$ 🔃 **Royal Marine.** This 1870 seaside hotel has been completely modernized. The comfortable, capacious rooms have also been refurbished with contemporary decor, though the eight suites with four-poster beds and sitting rooms preserve the lofty ceilings of the original building. Ask for a room at the front of the hotel, facing Dun Laoghaire harbor. ⊠ *Marine Rd., Dun Laoghaire, Co. Dublin,* ☎ *01/280–1911,* ℻ *01/280–1089. 95 rooms with bath, 8 suites. Restaurant, 2 bars, room service, no-smoking rooms, business services, free parking. AE, DC, MC, V.*

$$ 🔃 **Fitzpatrick Castle Dublin.** With its sweeping views over Dun Laoghaire
★ and Dublin Bay, the Fitzpatrick is worth the 15-km (9-mi) drive from the city center. The original part of the hotel is an 18th-century stone castle, with a substantial modern addition housing rooms; many are furnished with antiques and four-poster beds and have large bathrooms. The hotel is convenient to golfing, horseback riding, and fishing; the fitness facilities include an 82-ft heated pool. The views from Killiney Hill, behind the hotel, are spectacular; the seaside village of Dalkey and Killiney Beach are both in walking distance. ⊠ *Killiney, Co. Dublin,* ☎ *01/284–0700,* ℻ *01/285–0207. 113 rooms with bath. Restaurant, bar, indoor pool, sauna, steam room, health club, meeting rooms, free parking. AE, DC, MC, V.*

$ 🔃 **Bewleys at Newlands Cross.** On the southwest outskirts of the city, this 1998 four-story hotel is a good option if you're planning to head out of the city (especially to points in the Southwest and West) early and don't want to deal with morning traffic. The hotel is emulating the formula recently made popular by Jurys Inns, in which rooms—here each has a double bed, a single bed, and a sofa bed—are a flat rate for up to three adults or two adults and two children. ⊠ *Newlands Cross, Naas Rd., Dublin 22,* ☎ *01/464–0140,* ℻ *01/464–0900. 200 rooms with bath. Café, free parking. AE, MC, V.* ✏

Dublin Airport

$$$ ⊞ **Forte Posthouse.** The only hotel at Dublin Airport, this low-rise, red-brick structure with a plain exterior has rooms that are basic but spacious. The Bistro Restaurant serves fish and meat entrées, as well as a selection of vegetarian dishes; Sampans serves Chinese cuisine at dinner only. There's live music in the bar on weekends. You have access to a nearby health club. ⊠ *Dublin Airport,* ☎ *01/844–4211,* 𝐅𝐀𝐗 *01/844–6002. 249 rooms with bath. 2 restaurants, bar, room service, free parking. AE, DC, MC, V.*

$$ ⊞ **Doyle Skylon.** This modern, five-story hotel with a concrete-and-glass facade is on the main road into Dublin city center from the airport. The generous-size rooms are plainly decorated in cool pastels; double beds and a pair of easy chairs are almost the only furniture. A glass-fronted lobby with a large bar and the Rendezvous Room restaurant dominate the public areas. The cooking is adequate but uninspired, with dishes such as grilled steak, poached cod, and omelets. ⊠ *Upper Drumcondra Rd., Dublin 9,* ☎ *01/837–9121,* 𝐅𝐀𝐗 *01/837–2778. 88 rooms with bath. Restaurant, bar, free parking. AE, DC, MC, V.*

NIGHTLIFE AND THE ARTS

Long before Stephen Daedalus's excursions into nighttown (read Joyce's *A Portrait of the Artist as a Young Man*), Dublin was proud of its lively after-hours scene, particularly its thriving pubs. Lately, however, with the advent of Irish rock superstars (think U2, the Cranberries, Sinéad O'Connor, Bob Geldof) and the resurgence of Celtic music (think *Riverdance,* the soundtrack to *Titanic*), the rest of the world seems to have discovered that Dublin is one of the most happening places in the world. Most nights the city's pubs and clubs overflow with young cell phone–toting Dubliners and Europeans who descend on the capital for weekend getaways. The city's 900-plus pubs are its main source of entertainment; many public houses in the city center have live music—from rock to jazz to traditional Irish.

A number of newspapers have informative listings: the *Irish Times* has a daily guide to what's happening in Dublin and in the rest of the country, as well as complete film and theater schedules. The *Evening Herald* lists theaters, cinemas, and pubs with live entertainment. *In Dublin* and the *Big Issue* are weekly guides to all film, theater, and musical events around the city. The *Event Guide,* a weekly free paper that lists music, cinema, theater, art shows, and dance clubs, can be found in pubs and cafés around the city. In peak season, consult the free Bord Fáilte leaflet "Events of the Week."

The Arts

Theater and popular music are the dominant performing arts in Dublin, but by no means the only ones; they are supplemented by a handful of cinemas, an opera company, classical music, art galleries, and the city's vibrant pub life.

Art Galleries

Green on Red Galleries. This rather unprepossessing gallery, near the back of Trinity College, is one of Dublin's best, with constantly changing exhibitions featuring the work of some of the country's—and Britain's—most promising up-and-coming artists. ⊠ *26–28 Lombard St. E,* ☎ *01/671–3414.* ⊙ *Weekdays 11–6, Sat. 11–5.*

Kerlin Gallery. Perhaps Dublin's most important commercial gallery, this large space behind Grafton Street exhibits the work of many of

Ireland's most important contemporary artists, including such internationally recognized figures as New York–based Sean Scully, Kathy Prendergast, Paul Seawright, and Stephen McKenna. ⊠ *Anne's La., S. Anne St.,* ☎ *01/670–9093.* ⊘ *Weekdays 10–5:45, Sat. 11–4:30.*

Original Print Gallery. An ultramodern building by the same prominent Dublin architect who designed Temple Bar Gallery (☞ *below*), this place specializes in handmade, limited editions of prints by Irish artists. Also in the building, the **Black Church Print Studio** (☎ 01/677–3629) exhibits prints. ⊠ *4 Temple Bar,* ☎ *01/677–3657.* ⊘ *Tues.–Fri. 10:30–5:30, Sat. 11–5, Sun. 2–6.*

National Photographic Archive. A real treasure trove of Irish photographs from the last century, the Archive also hosts exhibits of work from contemporary Irish photographers, North and South. ⊠ *Temple Bar,* ☎ *01/603–0200.* ⊘ *Mon.–Fri. 10–5, Sat. 10–2.*

Rubicon Gallery. This second-floor gallery overlooking St. Stephen's Green holds a number of yearly exhibitions featuring work in all media from sculpture to photography. ⊠ *10 St. Stephen's Green,* ☎ *01/670–8055.* ⊘ *Mon.–Sat. 11–5:30.*

Solomon Gallery. Not exactly a risk taker, the Solomon has slowly developed a name as one of Dublin's leading fine-art galleries. ⊠ *Powerscourt Townhouse Centre, S. William St.,* ☎ *01/679–4237.* ⊘ *Mon.–Sat. 10–5:30.*

Temple Bar Gallery. A flagship of the Temple Bar redevelopment project, this gallery exhibits the work of emerging Irish photographers, painters, sculptors, and other artists in monthly rotating shows. ⊠ *5–9 Temple Bar,* ☎ *01/671–0073.* ⊘ *Mon.–Sat. 11–6, Sun. 2–6.*

Classical Music and Opera

The **Bank of Ireland Arts Center** (⊠ Foster Pl. S, ☎ 01/671–1488) is the perfect sport for a regular lunchtime recital.

National Concert Hall (⊠ Earlsfort Terr., ☎ 01/475–1666), just off St. Stephen's Green, is Dublin's main theater for classical music of all kinds, from symphonies to chamber groups. It's also home to the National Symphony Orchestra of Ireland.

Opera Ireland (⊠ John Player House, 276–288 S. Circular Rd., ☎ 01/453–5519) performs at the Gaiety Theatre (☞ *below*); call to find out what's on and when.

Opera Theatre Company (⊠ 18 St. Andrew St., ☎ 01/679–4962) is Ireland's only touring opera company, performing at venues in Dublin and throughout the country.

Royal Hospital Kilmainham (⊠ Military Rd., ☎ 01/671–8666) presents frequent classical concerts in its magnificent historic interior.

St. Stephen's Church (⊠ Merrion Sq., ☎ 01/288–0663) has a regular program of choral and orchestral events in its glorious setting.

Film

Dublin has two dozen cinema screens in the city center and a number of large, multiscreen cinema complexes in the suburbs, showing current releases made in Ireland and abroad.

Irish Film Centre (⊠ 6 Eustace St., ☎ 01/677–8788; ☞ Temple Bar *in* Exploring, *above*) shows classic and new independent films.

Savoy Cinema (⊠ O'Connell St., ☎ 01/874–6000), just across from the General Post Office, is a four-screen theater with the largest screen in the country.

Screen Cinema (⊠ 2 Townsend St., ☎ 01/671–4988), between Trinity College and O'Connell Street Bridge, is a popular three-screen arthouse cinema.

Virgin Multiplex (⊠ Parnell Center, Parnell St., ☎ 01/872–8400), a 12-screen theater just off O'Connell Street, is the city center's only multiplex movie house and shows the latest commercial features.

Jazz
The **Globe** (⊠ 11 S. Great George's St., ☎ 01/671–1220) has live jazz on Sundays from 5 to 7 PM. The emphasis is on funk fusion and acid jazz, interspersed with classic '50s–'60s sounds. The quality of the music varies, and the audience is often less than attentive.

JJ Smyth's (⊠ 12 Aungier St., ☎ 01/475–2565) is an old-time jazz venue where Louis Stewart, the granddaddy of Irish jazz, has a regular slot.

Pendulum Club (⊠ The Norseman, at Eustace St. and E. Essex St., Temple Bar) is the place to go for good jazz, with some of Ireland's top acts featured as well as guest appearances by internationally recognized musicians.

Rock and Contemporary Music
The long established **International Bar** (⊠ Wicklow St., ☎ 01/677–9250) has a tiny, get-close-to-the band venue upstairs. It hosts theater in the afternoons.

Mean Fiddler (⊠ Wexford St., ☎ 01/475–8555) is the small Dublin cousin of the famous London venue. There's plenty of room here for rising Irish and international acts who draw young, lively crowds. After the gig, there's usually a late-night club; your ticket gets you in free.

Olympia Theatre (⊠ 72 Dame St., ☎ 01/677–7744; ☞ Temple Bar *in* Exploring, *above*) puts on its "Midnight from the Olympia" shows every Friday and Saturday from midnight to 2 AM, with everything from rock to country.

The **Point** (⊠ Eastlink Br., ☎ 01/836–3633), a 6,000-capacity arena about 1 km (½ mi) east of the Custom House on the Liffey, is Dublin's premier venue for internationally renowned acts. Call or send a self-addressed envelope to receive a list of upcoming shows; tickets can be difficult to obtain, so book early.

Temple Bar Music Centre (⊠ Curved St., ☎ 01/670–0533)—a music venue, rehearsal space, television studio, and pub rolled into one—buzzes with activity every day of the week. Live acts range from rock bands to ethnic music to singer-songwriters.

Whelan's (⊠ 25 Wexford St., ☎ 01/478–0766), just off the southeastern corner of St. Stephen's Green, is one of the city's best—and most popular—music venues, featuring well-known acts performing everything from rock to folk to traditional.

Theater
Abbey Theatre (⊠ Lower Abbey St., ☎ 01/878–7222), the home of Ireland's national theater company, stages mainstream, mostly Irish traditional, plays. Its sister theater at the same address, the **Peacock**, offers more experimental drama. W. B. Yeats and his patron, Lady Gregory, opened the theater in 1904, which became a major center for the Irish literary renaissance—the place that first staged works by J. M. Synge and Sean O'Casey, among many others. The original theater burned down in 1951, but it reopened with a modern design in 1966.

Andrew's Lane Theatre (⊠ 9–11 Andrew's La., ☎ 01/679–5720) presents experimental productions.

Gaiety Theatre (⊠ S. King St., ☎ 01/677–1717) is the home of Opera Ireland (☞ *above*) when it's not showing musical comedy, drama, and revues.

Gate Theatre (⊠ Cavendish Row, Parnell Sq., ☎ 01/874–4045; ☞ North of the Liffey *in* Exploring, *above*), an intimate 371-seat theater in a jewel-like Georgian assembly hall, produces the classics and contemporary plays by leading Irish writers.

Olympia Theatre (⊠ 72 Dame St., ☎ 01/677–7744; ☞ Temple Bar *in* Exploring, *above*) is Dublin's oldest and premier multipurpose theatrical venue. In addition to its high-profile musical performances, it has seasons of comedy, vaudeville, and ballet.

Project Arts Centre (⊠ 39 E. Essex St., ☎ 01/671–2321) is an established fringe theater.

Samuel Beckett Centre (⊠ Trinity College, ☎ 01/608–2266) is home to Trinity's Drama Department as well as visiting groups from around Europe. Dance is often featured.

Tivoli (⊠ 135–138 Francis St., ☎ 01/454–4472) brings culture to the heart of old working-class Dublin, the Liberties. Lighter, comedy-based shows and the occasional Shakespeare play are favored.

Nightlife

Dublin has undergone a major nightlife revolution in the last few years and now, for better or worse, bears more than a passing resemblance to Europe's nightclub mecca, London. The old-fashioned discos, once the only alternative for late-night entertainment, have been replaced by a plethora of internationally known dance clubs where style and swagger rule. The streets of the city center, once hushed after the pubs had closed, are the scene of what appears to be a never-ending party; indeed, you're as likely to find crowds at 2 AM on a Wednesday as you are at the same time on a Saturday. Although the majority of clubs cater to an under-30 crowd of trendy students and young professionals eager to sway to the rhythmic throb of electronic dance music, there are plenty of alternatives, including a number of nightclubs where the dominant sounds range from soul to salsa. And if you're looking for something less strenuous, Dublin doesn't disappoint: there are brasseries, bistros, cafés, and all manner of late-night eateries where you can sit, sip, and chat until 2 AM or later.

A relatively new introduction to Dublin's nightclub scene is the professional promoter who organizes theme "parties" and rents space from nightclub owners, paying them a share of the door receipts as rent.

Another trend has been the "reinventing" of some of the old classic pubs—arguably some of the finest watering holes in the world—as popular spots. Despite the changes, the traditional pub has steadfastly clung to its role as the primary center of Dublin's social life. The city has nearly 1,000 pubs ("licensed tabernacles," writer Flann O'Brien calls them). And while the vision of elderly men enjoying a chin wag over a creamy pint of stout has become something of a rarity, there are still plenty of places where you can enjoy a quiet drink and a chat. Last drinks are called at 11:30 PM in spring and summer, and 11 PM in fall and winter; some city-center pubs even have extended opening hours from Thursday through Saturday and don't serve last drinks until 1:45 AM.

A word of warning: Although most pubs and clubs are extremely safe, the lads can get lively—public drunkenness is very much a part of Dublin's nightlife. While this is for the most part seen as the Irish form of unwinding after a long week (or day!), it can sometimes lead to regrettable incidents such as fighting. In an effort to keep potential trouble at bay, bouncers and security men maintain a visible presence in all clubs and many pubs around the city. At the end of the night, the city center is full of young people trying to get home, which makes for extremely long lines at taxi stands and light-night bus stops, especially on weekends. The combination of drunkenness and impatience can sometimes lead to trouble, so act cautiously. If you need late-night transportation, try to arrange it with your hotel before you go out.

Pubs

For the famous "Dublin Literary Pub Crawl," *see* Guided Tours *in* Dublin A to Z, *below.*

SOUTH CITY CENTER

Byrnes (⊠ Galloping Green, Stillorgan, ☎ 01/288–7683) has the airy atmosphere of an old-fashioned country pub, even though it's only 8 km (5 mi) from the city center. It's one of the few pubs that haven't been renovated.

Dubliner Pub (⊠ Jurys Hotel, Ballsbridge, ☎ 01/660–5000) has been remade as an old-fashioned Irish pub; it's a busy meeting place at lunch and after work.

John Fallons (⊠ 129 Dean St.), a classy public house in the Liberties, has one of the finest snugs in the city and great photos of old Dublin.

Kiely's (⊠ Donnybrook Rd., ☎ 01/283–0208), at first glance, appears to be just another modernized pub, but go up the side lane, and you'll find a second pub, Ciss Madden's, in the same building. Even though it was built in 1992, it's an absolutely authentic and convincing reconstruction of an ancient Irish tavern, right down to the glass globe lights and old advertising signs.

Kitty O'Shea's (⊠ Upper Grand Canal St., ☎ 01/660–9965) has Pre-Raphaelite–style stained glass, complementing its lively, sports-oriented atmosphere. Its sister pubs are in Brussels and Paris; this is the original.

O'Brien's (⊠ Sussex Terr., ☎ 01/668–2594), beside the Doyle Burlington hotel, is a little antique gem of a pub, scarcely changed in 50 years, with traditional snugs.

CITY CENTER

Brazen Head (⊠ Bridge St., ☎ 01/677–9549), Dublin's oldest pub (the site has been licensed since 1198), has stone walls and open fires that have changed little over the years. It's renowned for traditional-music performances and for lively sing-along sessions on Sunday evenings. A little difficult to find, the Brazen Head is located on the south side of the Liffey quays; turn down Lower Bridge Street, and then make a right into the old lane.

Café-en-Seine (⊠ 40 Dawson St., ☎ 01/677–4369) is a Parisian-style "locale," with a wrought-iron balcony, art deco furniture, a vaulted ceiling, and a clientele to match: most are young, cell phone–carrying professionals. Café au lait and alcoholic drinks are served all day until closing.

Cassidy's (⊠ 42 Lower Camden St., ☎ 01/475–1429) is a quiet neighborhood pub with a pint of stout so good that President Bill Clinton dropped in for one during a visit to Dublin.

Chief O'Neill's (✉ Smithfield Village, ☎ 01/817–3838), Dublin's newest hotel, has a large bar-café with an open, airy atmosphere and often hosts traditional Irish sessions.

The **Cobblestone** (✉ N. King St., ☎ 01/872–1799) is a glorious house of ale in the best Dublin tradition. Popular with Smithfield market workers, its chatty atmosphere and live music are attracting a wider crowd.

Davy Byrne's (✉ 21 Duke St., ☎ 01/671–1298) is a pilgrimage stop for Joyceans (☞ Close-Up: "ReJoyce! A Walk through *Ulysses* and James Joyce's Dublin," *above*). In *Ulysses,* Leopold Bloom stops in here for a glass of burgundy and a Gorgonzola cheese sandwich. He then leaves the pub and walks to Dawson Street, where he helps a blind man cross the road. Unfortunately, the much-altered pub is unrecognizable from Joyce's day, but it still serves some fine pub grub.

Dockers (✉ 5 Sir John Rogerson's Quay, ☎ 01/677–1692) is a trendy quayside spot east of city center, just around the corner from Windmill Lane Studios, where U2 and other noted bands record; at night the area is a little dicey, so come during the day.

Doheny & Nesbitt (✉ 5 Lower Baggot St., ☎ 01/676–2945), a traditional spot with snugs, dark wooden decor, and smoke-darkened ceilings, has hardly changed over the decades.

Doyle's (✉ 9 College St., ☎ 01/671–0616), a small, cozy pub, is a favorite with journalists from the *Irish Times,* just across the street.

The **Globe** (✉ 11 S. Great George's St., ☎ 01/671–1220), one of the hippest café-bars in town, draws arty, trendy Dubliners who sip espresso drinks by day and pack the place at night. There's live jazz on Sunday.

Grogans (✉ 15 S. William St., ☎ 01/677–9320), also known as the Castle Lounge, is a small place packed with creative folk.

GUBU (✉ Capel St., ☎ 01/874–0710) is the newest venture north of the river by the hugely successful owners of the Globe (☞ *above*). The pool table downstairs is a bonus.

Hogan's (✉ 35 Great St. Georges St., ☎ 01/6677–5904), a huge floor space on two levels, is jammed on most nights, but the old place maintains its style through it all and the beer is top class.

Horseshoe Bar (✉ Shelbourne Méridien Hotel, 27 St. Stephen's Green, ☎ 01/676–6471) is a popular meeting place for Dublin's businesspeople and politicians, though it has comparatively little space for drinkers around the semicircular bar.

Kehoe's (✉ 9 S. Anne St., ☎ 01/677–8312) is popular with Trinity students and academics. The tiny back room is cozy.

McDaid's (✉ 3 Harry St., ☎ 01/679–4395) attracted boisterous Brendan Behan and other leading writers in the 1950s; its wild literary reputation still lingers, although the bar has been discreetly modernized and the atmosphere is altogether quieter.

Mother Redcap's Tavern (✉ Back La., ☎ 01/453–8306) is an authentic re-creation of a 17th-century Dublin tavern, with stone walls from an old flour mill, beams, and old prints of the city.

Neary's (✉ 1 Chatham St., ☎ 01/677–7371), which has an exotic Victorian-style interior, was once the haunt of music-hall artists, as well as of a certain literary set including Brendan Behan. Join the actors from the adjacent Gaiety Theatre for a good pub lunch.

Dublin Pubs

Brazen Head 6	The George 13	Mother Redcap's Tavern 11
Byrnes 28	The Globe 15	Neary's 21
Café-en-Seine 22	Grogans 17	O'Brien's 33
Cassidy's 23	GUBU 3	O'Donoghue's 25
Chief O'Neill's 1	Hogan's 16	Oliver St. John Gogarty 8
The Cobblestone 2	Horseshoe Bar 24	
Davy Byrne's 18	John Fallons 34	Out on the Liffey 4
Dockers 10	Johnnie Fox's 30	Palace Bar 7
Doheny & Nesbitt 26	Kehoe's 20	Ryan's Pub 5
	Kiely's 31	Stag's Head 14
Doyle's 9	Kitty O'Shea's 32	Toner's 27
Dubliner Pub 29	McDaid's 19	
The Front Lounge 12		

O'Donoghue's (✉ 15 Merrion Row, ☎ 01/676–2807), a cheerful, smoky hangout, has impromptu musical performances that often spill out onto the street.

Ryan's Pub (✉ 28 Parkgate St., ☎ 01/677–6097) is one of Dublin's last genuine, late-Victorian-era pubs and has changed little since its last (1896) remodeling.

Stag's Head (✉ 1 Dame Ct., ☎ 01/679–3701) dates from 1770 and was rebuilt in 1895; theater people from the nearby Olympia, journalists, and Trinity students turn up around the unusual counter, fashioned from Connemara red marble.

Toner's (✉ 139 Lower Baggot St., ☎ 01/676–3090), though billed as a Victorian bar, actually goes back 200 years, with an original flagstone floor to prove its antiquity, as well as wooden drawers running up to the ceiling, a relic of the days when bars doubled as grocery shops. Oliver St. John Gogarty accompanied W. B. Yeats here, in what was purportedly the latter's only visit to a pub.

COUNTY DUBLIN—SOUTHSIDE

Johnnie Fox's (✉ Glencullen, Co. Dublin, ☎ 01/295–5647), 12 km (8 mi) from the city center, sits 1,000 ft up in the Dublin Mountains, making it the highest licensed premises in Ireland. It's approached by a winding and steeply climbing road that turns off the main Dublin–Enniskerry road at Stepaside. Steadfastly refusing to bow to the whims of modernization, it has maintained all of its traditional character—oak tables, rough-stone floor flags strewn with sawdust, and ancient bric-a-brac, including copper kettles, crockery, old prints, and guns—appearing very much as it did in the early 19th century, when Daniel O'Connell used it as a safe house for his seditious meetings. Lunch and dinner are served; the specialty is seafood, which is alone worth the journey. In the evenings there is traditional Irish music.

TEMPLE BAR

The **Front Lounge** (✉ 33 Parliament St., Temple Bar, ☎ 01/679–3988), a modern, well-appointed pub, caters to a mixed crowd of young professionals, both gay and straight.

Oliver St. John Gogarty (✉ 57 Fleet St., Temple Bar, ☎ 01/671–1822) is a lively bar that attracts all ages and nationalities and overflows in summer. On most nights there is traditional Irish music upstairs.

Palace Bar (✉ 21 Fleet St., Temple Bar, ☎ 01/677–9290), scarcely changed over the past 60 years, is tiled and rather barren looking but popular with journalists and writers (the *Irish Times* is nearby). The walls are hung with cartoons drawn by the illustrators who used to spend time here.

Gay and Lesbian Pubs

The **George** (✉ 89 S. Great George's St., ☎ 01/478–2983), Dublin's two-floor main gay pub, draws an almost entirely male crowd; its nightclub stays open until 2:30 AM nightly except Tuesday.

Out on the Liffey (✉ 27 Ormond Quay, ☎ 01/872–2480) is Dublin's second gay pub; it draws a mixed crowd of men and women.

Irish Cabaret

BALLSBRIDGE/SOUTH CITY CENTER

Doyle Burlington Hotel (✉ Upper Leeson St., ☎ 01/660–5222) is a high-class lounge featuring a well-performed Irish cabaret, with dancing, music, and song.

Jurys Hotel (⊠ Ballsbridge, ☎ 01/660–5000) stages a cabaret show similar to that at the Doyle Burlington hotel (☞ *above*).

CITY CENTER

Castle Inn (⊠ Christ Church Pl., ☎ 01/475–1122) is really just a huge pub that has traditional Irish music and dancing with dinner in a medieval-style banquet hall.

COUNTY DUBLIN—NORTHSIDE

Abbey Tavern (⊠ Howth, ☎ 01/839–0307) has a rip-roaring cabaret with rousing, traditional Irish songs.

Clontarf Castle (⊠ Castle Ave., Clontarf, ☎ 01/833–2321) offers a spectacular setting for a traditional night of song and comedy.

Irish Music and Dancing

SOUTH DUBLIN

Comhaltas Ceoltóiri Éireann (⊠ 35 Belgrave Sq., Monkstown, ☎ 01/280–0295) has boisterous summer evenings of genuine Irish music and dancing.

Harcourt Hotel (⊠ Harcourt St., ☎ 01/478–3677) is where some of the best traditional musicians gather for wild jam sessions.

Nightclubs

The dominant sound in Dublin's nightclubs is electronic dance music, and the crowd that flocks to them every night of the week is of the trendy, under-25 generation. However, there are a couple of clubs where you're more likely to hear tango than techno, such as the weekend nightclub at the Gaiety Theatre, Thursday nights at the Pod, and Sunday nights at Lillie's Bordello. **Velure** (☎ 01/670–3750) is one of Dublin's most successful nightclub promoters, organizing live music, DJs, and theme parties; call to find out what's going on.

CITY CENTER

The **Da Club** (⊠ 3–5 Clarendon Market, ☎ 01/670–5116), in the refurbished Dublin Arts Club, is one of the most popular spots in town. Despite its small capacity, it has a wide variety of nightly entertainment—from comedy acts to live bands to dance clubs—often running concurrently on its two floors. The venue attracts a young bohemian crowd. It has full bar facilities.

Leeson Street—just off St. Stephen's Green and known as "the strip"—is a main nightclub area from pub closing time to 4 AM, although it has lost its gloss in recent years. Dress at these places is informal, but jeans and sneakers are not welcome. Most of these clubs are licensed only to sell wine, and the prices can be exorbitant (up to £20 for a mediocre bottle); the upside is that most don't charge to get in.

Lillie's Bordello (⊠ Grafton St., ☎ 01/679–9204) is a popular spot for a trendy, professional crowd, as well as for rock and film stars. On Sunday nights, the strict dress code is relaxed for a night of live music and DJs.

The **Pod** (⊠ Harcourt St., ☎ 01/478–0166), also known as the "Place of Dance," is Dublin's most-renowned dance club, especially among the younger set. Entry is judged as much on clothing as on age; it helps to look either stylish or rich, except on Thursday nights, when the club hosts a no-frills, no-nonsense night of dance-floor jazz and funk.

The **Red Box** (⊠ Old Harcourt St. Station, Harcourt St., ☎ 01/478–0166), adjacent to the Pod (☞ *above*) and the Chocolate Bar, can pack in more than 1,000 people and surround them with state-of-the-art sound and light. It regularly hosts Irish and international rock acts as well as celebrity DJs from Europe and the United States. As do most other Dublin rock venues, the Red Box has full bar facilities.

Rí Ra (✉ Dame Ct., ☎ 01/677–4835) is part of the hugely popular Globe bar (☞ *above*). The name means "uproar" in Irish, and on most nights the place does go a little wild. It's one of the best spots in Dublin for no-frills, fun dancing. Upstairs is more low key.

TEMPLE BAR

The **Kitchen** (✉ E. Essex St., ☎ 01/677–6359) is in the basement of the Clarence hotel (☞ Lodging, *above*); its popularity, mainly with an under-30s crowd, owes much to its owners, Bono and the Edge of U2.

OUTDOOR ACTIVITIES AND SPORTS

Health clubs are relatively new to the city, but they are starting to flourish (especially at hotels). Yet there are plenty of other ways to get out and move about. You can explore a beach; cheer on a hometown team; or walk, run, horseback-ride, or bike through Phoenix Park.

Beaches

To the north of Dublin city is **North Bull Island,** created over the years by the action of the tides and offering an almost 3-km-long (2-mi-long) stretch of fine sand. Bus 130 from Lower Abbey Street stops by the walkway to the beach (☞ County Dublin—Northside *in* Side Trips, *below*). **Malahide,** a charming village on the northside DART line, has a clean and easily accessible beach, though the current can be strong. The main beach for swimming on the south side of Dublin is at **Killiney** (✉ 13 km/8 mi south of the city center), a shingly beach stretching for 3 km (2 mi). The DART train station is right by the beach; the stop is called Killiney. Near Dublin city center, **Sandymount Strand** is a long expanse of fine sand where the tide goes out nearly 3 km (2 mi), but it's not suitable for swimming or bathing because the tide races in so fast. The strand can be reached easily by the DART train.

Participant Sports

If it's essential that you get in a daily workout, you should be able to do so while you're in Dublin, although it will probably take some careful planning. For all its recent changes, the city has only recently embraced health clubs and fitness centers. Check the service information provided for each hotel (☞ Lodging, *above*) for particular fitness amenities; if none are listed, call to inquire, as many of the hotels are adding these amenities.

Bicycling

Bicycling is not recommended in the city center, as traffic is heavy and most roads don't have shoulders, much less bike lanes. Phoenix Park and some suburbs (especially Ballsbridge, Clontarf, and Sandymount), however, are pleasant for biking once you're off the main roads. To the immediate south of Dublin, the Dublin and Wicklow mountains provide plenty of challenging terrain (☞ Chapter 2). Care should always be taken in securing your bicycle when it's left unattended.

Bicycles can be rented for about £35 a week, with an equivalent amount charged for deposit. Nearly 20 companies in the Dublin region rent bicycles; Tourist Information Offices (TIOs) have a full list. Some of the best include the following: **Joe Daly** (✉ Lower Main St., Dundrum, ☎ 01/298–1485); **McDonald's** (✉ 38 Wexford St., ☎ 01/475–2586); **Mike's Bike Shop** (✉ Dun Laoghaire Shopping Center, ☎

01/280–0417); and **Tracks Cycles** (⊠ 8 Botanic Rd., Glasnevin, ☎ 01/ 873–2455).

Bowling

Bowling is a popular sport in Dublin; two kinds are played locally. The sedate, outdoor variety is played at **Herbert Park** (⊠ Ballsbridge, ☎ 01/660–1875) and at **Kenilworth Bowling Club** (⊠ Grosvenor Sq., ☎ 01/497–2305). The city has six indoor 10-pin bowling centers: **Bray Bowl** (⊠ Quinsboro Rd., ☎ 01/286–4455); **Leisureplex Coolock** (⊠ Malahide Rd., ☎ 01/848–5722; ⊠ Village Green Center, Tallaght, ☎ 01/459–9411); **Metro Bowl** (⊠ 149 N. Strand Rd., ☎ 01/855–0400); **Stillorgan Bowl** (⊠ Stillorgan, ☎ 01/288–1656); and **Superdome** (⊠ Palmerstown, ☎ 01/626–0700).

Golf

The Dublin region is an idyllic place for golfers, with 30 18-hole courses and 15 9-hole courses, and several more on the way. For detailed information about Dublin's championship courses, including **Portmarnock, St. Margaret's,** and **Royal Dublin,** see Chapter 9. Other major 18-hole courses include the following: **Deer Park** (⊠ Howth, ☎ 01/832–6039); **Edmonstown** (⊠ Rathfarnham, ☎ 01/493–2461); **Elm Park** (⊠ Donnybrook, ☎ 01/269–3438); **Foxrock** (⊠ Torquay Rd., ☎ 01/289–3992); **Hermitage** (⊠ Lucan, ☎ 01/626–4781); **Newlands** (⊠ Clondalkin, ☎ 01/459–2903); **Sutton** (⊠ Sutton, ☎ 01/832–3013); and **Woodbrook** (⊠ Bray, ☎ 01/282–4799).

Health Clubs

The health craze has reached laconic Dublin, and health clubs are springing up all over the city. The **Iveagh Fitness Club** (⊠ Christ Church St., Dublin 8, ☎ 01/454–6555) is right next to Christ Church Cathedral and has a pool, sauna, and full weight room. Just off Grafton Street, the **Jackie Skelly Fitness Centre** (⊠ 41–42 Clarendon St., Dublin 2 ☎ 01/677–0040) is perfect if you're staying in a city-center hotel without a gym.

Horseback Riding

Dublin's environs are excellent for horseback riding. Stables on the city outskirts give immediate access to suitable riding areas. In the city itself, Phoenix Park provides superb, quiet riding conditions away from the busy main road that bisects the park. About 20 riding stables in the greater Dublin area have horses for hire by the hour or the day, for novices and experienced riders; a few also operate as equestrian centers and have lessons. Major stables in the area include the following: **Brittas Lodge Riding Stables** (⊠ Brittas, ☎ 01/458–2726) and **Deerpark Riding Center** (⊠ Castleknock Rd., Castleknock, ☎ 01/820–7141). Outside Dublin, Counties Dublin, Kildare, Louth, Meath, and Wicklow all have unspoiled country territory ideal for horseback riding (☞ Chapter 2).

Jogging

Traffic in Dublin is heavy from early morning until late into the night and it's getting worse, so if you're used to jogging the streets back home be aware that here you'll have to dodge vehicles and stop for lights. (Remember *always* to look to your right *and* your left before crossing a street.) If you're staying in Temple Bar or on the western end of the city and you can run 9 km (5½ mi), head to Phoenix Park, easily the nicest place in the city for a jog. If you're on the southside, Merrion Square, St. Stephen's Green, and Trinity College are all good places for short jogs, though be prepared to dodge pedestrians; if you're looking for a longer route, ask your hotel to direct you to the Grand

Canal, which has a pleasant path you can run along as far east as the Grand Canal Street Bridge.

Swimming

Dublin has 12 public pools; recommended are **Townsend Street** (⌧ Townsend St., ☎ 01/677–0503) and **Williams Park** (⌧ Rathmines, ☎ 01/496–1275). Private pools open to the public for a small fee are located at **Dundrum Family Recreation Center** (⌧ Meadowbrook, Dundrum, ☎ 01/298–4654), **Fitzpatrick Castle Hotel** (⌧ Killiney, ☎ 01/285–0328), **St. Vincent's** (⌧ Navan Rd., ☎ 01/838–4906), and **Terenure College** (⌧ Templeogue Rd., ☎ 01/490–7071). For a hardier dip, there's year-round sea swimming at the **Forty Foot Bathing Pool** in Sandycove (☞ Side Trips, *below*).

Tennis

Tennis is one of Dublin's most popular participant sports, and some public parks have excellent tennis facilities open to the public. Among the best are **Bushy Park** (⌧ Terenure, ☎ 01/490–0320); **Herbert Park** (⌧ Ballsbridge, ☎ 01/668–4364); and **St. Anne's Park** (⌧ Dollymount Strand, ☎ 01/833–8898). Several private tennis clubs are open to the public, including **Kilternan Tennis Centre** (⌧ Kilternan Golf and Country Club Hotel, Kilternan, ☎ 01/295–3729); **Landsdowne Lawn Tennis Club,** (⌧ Londonbridge Rd., Dublin 4, ☎ 01/668–0219); and **West Wood Lawn Tennis Club** (⌧ Leopardstown Racecourse, Foxrock, Dublin 18, ☎ 01/289–2911). For more information, contact **Tennis Ireland** (⌧ 22 Argyle Sq., Donnybrook, Dublin 4, ☎ 01/668–1841).

Spectator Sports

Gaelic Games

The traditional games of Ireland, Gaelic football and hurling, attract a huge following, with roaring crowds cheering on their county teams. Games are held at **Croke Park,** the national stadium for Gaelic games, just north of the city center. For details of matches, contact the **Gaelic Athletic Association** (⌧ Croke Park, ☎ 01/836–3222). A museum dedicated to the history of Gaelic games, with plenty of footage from famous games, has recently opened at Croke Park (⌧ £3, ☉ May–Sept., daily 9:30–5; Oct.–Apr., Tues.–Sat. 10–5, Sun. 12–5).

Greyhound Racing

As elsewhere in the world, Greyhound racing is a sport in decline in Ireland. But the track can still be one of the best places to see Dubliners at their most passionate, among friends, and full of wicked humor. **Harolds Cross** (⌧ Harolds Cross, Dublin 6, ☎ 01/497–1081) is dilapidated but serves its purpose. **Shelbourne Park** (⌧ Shelbourne Park, Dublin 4, ☎ 01/668–3502) is a more stylish place where you can book a table in the restaurant overlooking the track.

Horse Racing

Horse racing—from flat to hurdle to steeplechase—is one of the great sporting loves of the Irish. The sport is closely followed and betting is popular, but the social side of attending racing is also important to Dubliners. The main course in Dublin is **Leopardstown** (☎ 01/289–3607), an ultramodern course on the southside and home of the Hennessey Gold Cup in February, Ireland's most prestigious steeplechase. In the greater Dublin region, other courses include **Fairyhouse** (⌧ Co. Meath, ☎ 01/825–6167), which every Easter Monday hosts the Grand National, the most popular steeplechase of the season; the **Curragh** (☎ 045/441205; ☞ Chapter 2), southwest of Dublin, home of the five Classics, the most important flat races of the season, which are run from May to September; and **Punchestown** (☎ 045/897704) outside Naas,

County Kildare, home of the ever-popular Punchestown National Hunt Festival in April (☞ Festivals and Seasonal Events *in* Smart Travel Tips A to Z).

Rugby

International rugby matches are staged during the winter and spring at the vast **Lansdowne Road Stadium.** Local matches are played every weekend, also in winter and spring. For details, contact the **Irish Rugby Football Union** (⊠ 62 Lansdowne Rd., ☎ 01/668–4601).

Soccer

Although soccer—called football in Europe—is very popular in Ireland (largely due to the euphoria resulting from the national team's successes throughout the late 1980s and early '90s), facilities for watching it are not so ideal; they tend to be small and out of date. **Lansdowne Road,** the vast rugby stadium, is the main center for international matches. For details, contact the **Football Association of Ireland** (⊠ 80 Merrion Sq. S, ☎ 01/676–6864).

SHOPPING

In days gone by, travelers would arrive in Ireland, land of leprechauns, shillelaghs, and shamrocks, and quickly realize that the only known specimens of leprechauns or shillelaghs were those in souvenir-shop windows, while shamrocks mainly bloomed around the borders of Irish linen handkerchiefs and tablecloths. All of this is still true, of course, but today you'll find so much more. The variety and sophistication of stores in Dublin now are quite remarkable, as a walk through Dublin's central shopping area, from O'Connell to Grafton Street, proves. Department stores stocking internationally known fashion-designer goods and housewares stand beside small boutiques that make shopping in the city a personalized and pleasurable experience. Prices can be higher in the smaller shops, but the department stores are less likely to stock specifically Irish crafts. Shopping in central Dublin can mean pushing through crowds, especially in the afternoons and on weekends. Most large shops and department stores are open Monday–Saturday 9–6. Although nearly all department stores are closed on Sunday, some smaller specialty shops stay open. Those with later closing hours are noted below. You're particularly likely to find sales in January, February, July, and August. Don't get confused by the two prices quoted on all goods. As of January 1, 1999, all items had to be listed in euros as well as Irish pounds.

Shopping Streets

Dublin's dozen or so main shopping streets each have a different character, and it's only by visiting them all that you can really appreciate just how wide a range of items are for sale here. The main commercial streets north of the river have chain stores and lackluster department stores that tend to be less expensive and less design-conscious than their counterparts in the city center on the other side of the Liffey.

City Center (Northside)

Henry Street. Running westward from O'Connell Street, this is the spot where middle-class Dublin shops. Arnotts department store is the anchor; a host of smaller, specialty stores sell CDs, footwear, and fashion. Henry Street's continuation, Mary Street, has a branch of Marks & Spencer and the Jervis Shopping Centre (☞ *below*).

O'Connell Street. One of Dublin's largest department stores, Clery's, faces the GPO across the city's main thoroughfare—more downscale than southside city streets but still worth a walk. On the same side of

Dublin Shopping

the street as the post office is Eason's, a large book, magazine, and stationery store.

City Center (Southside)

Dawson Street. Just east of Grafton Street between Nassau Street to
the north and St. Stephen's Green to the south, this is the city's primary bookstore avenue, with Waterstone's and Hodges Figgis facing
each other on different sides of the street (☞ Books, *below*).

Grafton Street. Dublin's bustling pedestrian-only main shopping street
has two upscale department stores, Marks & Spencer and Brown
Thomas. The rest of the street is taken up by smaller shops, many of
them branches of international chains such as the Body Shop and
Bally, and many British chains. This is also the spot to buy fresh flowers, available at reasonable prices from a number of outdoor stands.
Smaller streets off Grafton Street, especially Duke Street, South Anne
Street, and Chatham Street, have worthwhile crafts, clothing, and designer housewares shops.

Francis Street. The Liberties, the oldest part of the city, is the hub of
Dublin's antiques trade. This street and surrounding areas, such as the
Coombe, have plenty of shops where you can browse. If you're looking for something in particular, dealers will gladly recommend the appropriate store to you.

Nassau Street. Dublin's main tourist-oriented thoroughfare has some
of the best-known stores selling Irish goods, but you won't find many
locals shopping here. Still, if you're looking for classic Irish gifts to take
home, you should be sure at least to browse along here.

Temple Bar. Dublin's hippest neighborhood is dotted with small, precious boutiques—mostly intimate, quirky shops that traffic in a small
selection of *très* trendy goods, from vintage wear to some of the most
avant-garde Irish clothing you'll find anywhere in the city.

Specialty Shopping Centers

City Center (Northside)

Ilac Center (✉ Henry St.) was Dublin's first large, modern shopping
center, with two department stores, hundreds of specialty shops, and
several restaurants. The stores are not as exclusive as at some of the
other centers, but there's plenty of free parking.

Jervis Shopping Centre (✉ Jervis and Mary Sts.), opened in late 1996,
is Dublin's newest city-center shopping mall; it brought with it the major
British chain stores.

City Center (Southside)

Powerscourt Townhouse Centre (✉ 59 S. William St.), the former
town home of Lord Powerscourt and built in 1771, has an interior courtyard that has been refurbished and roofed over; a pianist often plays
on the dais at ground-floor level. Coffee shops and restaurants share
space with a mix of antiques and crafts stores, including the **HQ
Gallery,** the main showcase of the Irish Craft Council and one of the
finest places in Dublin to buy contemporary crafts. You can also buy
original Irish fashions here by young designers like Gráinne Walsh.

Royal Hibernian Way (✉ off Dawson St. between S. Anne and Duke
Sts.) is on the former site of the two-centuries-old Royal Hibernian Hotel,
a coaching inn that was demolished in 1983. The stylish shops are small
in scale and include a branch of Leonidas, the Belgian chocolate firm.

St. Stephen's Green Centre (✉ northwest corner of St. Stephen's Green),
Dublin's largest and most ambitious shopping center, resembles a giant

greenhouse, with ironwork in the Victorian style. On three floors over-looked by a vast clock, the 100 mostly small shops sell a variety of crafts, fashions, and household goods.

Tower Design Centre (⊠ Pearse St., ☎ 01/677–5655), east of the heart of the city center (near the Waterways Visitor Centre), has more than 35 separate crafts shops in a converted 1862 sugar-refinery tower. On the ground floor, you can stop at workshops devoted to heraldry and Irish pewter; the other six floors feature hand-painted silks, ceramics, hand-knit items, jewelry, and fine-art cards and prints.

County Dublin Suburbs

Blackrock (⊠ Blackrock, Co. Dublin), to the south, is technically out-side of Dublin's city center, but it deserves special mention as one of the most customer-friendly shopping centers around. It's built on two levels, looking onto an inner courtyard, with the giant Superquinn Food-store, cafés, and restaurants. Blackrock can be reached conveniently on the DART train line; it has its own stop.

Blanchardstown (⊠ Blanchardstown, Dublin 15) is the biggest shop-ping center in the country. It's a good spot for bargains and a chance to see Dublin families about their everyday lives. The No. 39 bus from Lower Abbey Street goes to Blanchardstown.

Department Stores

Arnotts (⊠ Henry St., ☎ 01/872–1111) has a wide variety of cloth-ing, household, and sporting goods filling three complete floors; the smaller Grafton Street branch (⊠ Grafton St., ☎ 01/872–1111) stocks only new fashion and footwear.

A-Wear (⊠ Grafton St., ☎ 01/671–7200; ⊠ Henry St., ☎ 01/872–4644) is a line of shops specializing in fashion for men and women. Many of the items are seasonal and closely follow the ever-changing styles. A steady stream of clothing is supplied by leading Irish design-ers, including John Rocha.

Brown Thomas (⊠ Grafton St., ☎ 01/679–5666), Dublin's most ex-clusive department store, stocks the leading designer names in cloth-ing and cosmetics and a wide variety of stylish accessories. It also carries clothing by Irish designers.

Clery's (⊠ O'Connell St., ☎ 01/878–6000) was once the city's most fashionable department store and is still worth a visit, despite its rapidly aging decor. It has four floors of all types of merchandise—from fashion to home appliances—and caters to a distinctly modest, traditional sense of style.

Dunnes Stores (⊠ St. Stephen's Green Centre, ☎ 01/478–0188; Henry St., ☎ 01/872–6833; Ilac Shopping Center, Mary St., ☎ 01/873–0211) is Ireland's largest chain of department stores. All stores stock fashion, household, and grocery items and have a reputation for value and variety.

Eason's (⊠ O'Connell St., ☎ 01/873–3811; Ilac Shopping Center, Mary St., ☎ 01/872–1322) is known primarily for its wide variety of books, magazines, and stationery; its larger O'Connell Street branch now sells tapes, CDs, records, videos, and other audiovisual goodies.

Marks & Spencer (⊠ Grafton St., ☎ 01/679–7855; ⊠ Henry St., ☎ 01/872–8833), perennial competitor to Brown Thomas (☞ *above*), stocks everything from fashion (including lingerie) to tasty, unusual gro-ceries. The Grafton Street branch even has its own bureau de change, which doesn't charge commission.

Outdoor Markets

Dublin has a number of open-air markets. **Moore Street,** behind the
Ilac center, is open Monday–Saturday 9–6. Stalls lining both sides of
the street sell fruits and vegetables; it's also a good spot to come to
buy shoes and boots. The traditional Dublin repartee here is renowned
in the city. Other open markets are only open on weekends. A variety
of bric-a-brac is sold at the **Liberty Market** on the north end of Meath
Street, open on Friday and Saturday 10–6, Sunday noon–5:30. The indoor **Mother Redcap's Market,** opposite Christ Church, is open Friday–Sunday 10–5; come here for antiques and bric-a-brac. Outside the
city center, weekend markets take place in Blackrock and Dun Laoghaire
(☞ Side Trips, *below*).

Specialty Shops

Antiques

Dublin is one of Europe's best cities in which to buy antiques, largely
due to a long and proud tradition of restoration and high-quality
craftmanship. The Liberties, Dublin's oldest district, is fittingly the hub
of the antiques trade and is chock-a-block with shops and traders. Bachelor's Walk, along the quays, also has some decent shops. Although
the economic boom has created quite a seller's market, bargains are
still possible.

Antiques and Collectibles Fairs (☎ 01/670–8295) take place at Newman House (✉ 85–86 St. Stephen's Green) every second Sunday
throughout the year.

Conlon Antiques (✉ 21 Clanbrassil St., ☎ 01/453–7323) has a wide
selection of antiques, from sideboards to fanlights.

Ha'penny Bridge Galleries (✉ 15 Bachelor's Walk, ☎ 01/872–3950)
has four floors of curios, with a particularly large selection of bronzes,
silver, and china.

O'Sullivan Antiques (✉ 43–44 Francis St., ☎ 01/454–1143 or 01/453–
9659) specializes in 18th- and 19th-century furniture and has a high-
profile clientele, including Mia Farrow and Liam Neeson.

Books

You won't have any difficulty weighing down your suitcase with books:
Ireland, after all, produced four Nobel literature laureates in just under
75 years. If you're at all interested in modern and contemporary literature, be sure to leave yourself time to browse through the bookstores, as you're likely to find books available here you can't find back
home. Best of all, thanks to an enlightened national social policy,
there's no tax on books, so if you only buy books, you don't have to
worry about getting VAT slips.

Books Upstairs (✉ 36 College Green, ☎ 01/679–6687) carries an excellent range of special-interest books, including gay and feminist literature, psychology, and self-help books.

Cathach Books (✉ 10 Duke St., ☎ 01/671–8676) sells first editions
of Irish literature and many other books of Irish interest, plus old maps
of Dublin and Ireland.

Dublin Bookshop (✉ 24 Grafton St., ☎ 01/677–5568) is an esteemed,
family-owned bookstore.

Fred Hanna's (✉ 29 Nassau St., ☎ 01/677–1255) sells old and new
books, with a good choice of works on travel and Ireland.

Greene's (✉ Clare St., ☎ 01/676–2544) carries an extensive range of secondhand volumes.

Hodges Figgis (✉ 56–58 Dawson St., ☎ 01/677–4754), Dublin's leading independent, stocks 1½ million books on three floors; there's also a pleasant café on the first floor.

Hughes & Hughes (✉ St. Stephen's Green Centre, ☎ 01/478-3060), has strong travel and Irish interest sections. There is also a store at Dublin Airport.

Waterstone's (✉ 7 Dawson St., ☎ 01/679–1415), a large branch of the British chain, has two floors featuring a fine selection of Irish and international books.

Winding Stair (✉ 40 Ormond Quay, Dublin 1, ☎ 01/873–3292) is a charming new- and used-book store overlooking the Liffey. The little upstairs café is the perfect spot for an afternoon of reading.

China, Crystal, Ceramics, and Jewelry
Ireland is synonymous with Waterford crystal, which is available in a wide range of products, including relatively inexpensive items. But other lines are now gaining recognition, such as Cavan, Galway, and Tipperary crystal. **Brown Thomas** (☞ *above*) is the best department store for crystal; the best specialty outlets are listed below.

Blarney Woollen Mills (✉ 21–23 Nassau St., ☎ 01/671–0068) is one of the best places for Belleek china, Waterford and Galway crystal, and Irish linen.

Crafts Centre of Ireland (✉ Stephen's Green Centre, ☎ 01/475–4526) has an impressive inventory of Ireland's most famous contemporary designers, including Michael Kennedy and Diane McCormick (ceramics), Glen Lucas (woodturning), and Jerpoint Glass (glassworks).

Crannóg (✉ Crown Alley, ☎ 01/671–0805), in Temple Bar, specializes in ceramics and contemporary Irish jewelry, especially silver pendants and rings.

Designyard (✉ E. Essex St., ☎ 01/677–8453) carries beautifully designed Irish and international tableware, lighting, small furniture, and jewelry.

House of Ireland (✉ 37–38 Nassau St., ☎ 01/671–6133) has an extensive selection of crystal, jewelry, tweeds, sweaters, and other upscale goods.

Kilkenny Shop (✉ 5–6 Nassau St., ☎ 01/677–7066) specializes in contemporary Irish-made ceramics, pottery, and silver jewelry and also holds regular exhibits of exciting new work by Irish craftspeople.

McDowell (✉ 3 Upper O'Connell St., ☎ 01/874–4961), a jewelry shop popular with Dubliners, has been in business for more than 100 years.

Tierneys (✉ St. Stephen's Green Centre, ☎ 01/478–2873) carries a good selection of crystal and china. Claddagh rings, pendants, and brooches are popular buys.

Weir & Sons (✉ 96 Grafton St., ☎ 01/677–9678), Dublin's most prestigious jewelers, sells a wide range of goods in addition to jewelry and watches, including china, glass, lamps, silver, and leather.

Museum Stores
National Gallery of Ireland Shop (✉ Merrion Sq. W, ☎ 01/678–5450) has a terrific selection of books on Irish art, plus posters, postcards, note cards, and a wide array of lovely bibelots.

National Museum Shop (✉ Kildare St., ☎ 01/677–7444 ext. 327) carries jewelry based on ancient Celtic artifacts in the museum collection, contemporary Irish pottery, a large selection of books, and other gift items.

Trinity College Library Shop (✉ Old Library, Trinity College, ☎ 01/ 608–2308) sells Irish-theme books, *Book of Kells* souvenirs of all kinds, plus clothing, jewelry, and other lovely Irish-made items.

Music
An increasing amount of Irish-recorded material—including traditional folk music, country-and-western, rock, and even a smattering of classical music—is available.

Celtic Note (✉ 12 Nassau St., ☎ 01/670–4157), **Claddagh Records** (✉ 2 Cecilia St., Temple Bar, ☎ 01/679–3664), and **Gael Linn** (✉ 26 Merrion Sq., ☎ 01/676–7283) specialize in traditional Irish-music and Irish-language recordings.

HMV (✉ 65 Grafton St., ☎ 01/679–5334; ✉ 18 Henry St., ☎ 01/872–2095) is one of the larger record shops in town.

McCullogh Piggott (✉ 25 Suffolk St., ☎ 01/677–3138) is the best place in town for instruments, sheet music, scores, and books about music.

Tower Records (✉ 6–8 Wicklow St., ☎ 01/671–3250) is the best-stocked international chain.

Virgin Megastore (✉ 14–18 Aston Quay, ☎ 01/677–7361) is Dublin's biggest music store and holds in-store performances by Irish bands.

Sweaters and Tweeds
If you think Irish woolens are limited to Aran sweaters and tweed jackets, you'll be pleasantly surprised by the range of hats, gloves, scarves, blankets, and other goods you can find. If you're traveling outside of Dublin, you may want to wait to make purchases elsewhere, but if Dublin is it, you still have plenty of good shops to choose from. The tweed on sale in Dublin comes from two main sources, Donegal and Connemara; labels inside the garments guarantee their authenticity. Following are the largest retailers of traditional Irish woolen goods in the city.

An Táin (✉ 13 Temple Bar Sq. N, ☎ 01/679–0523) carries hyperstylish handmade Irish sweaters, jackets, and accessories.

Blarney Woollen Mills (✉ 21–23 Nassau St., ☎ 01/671–0068) has a good selection of tweed, linen, and woolen sweaters in all price ranges.

Cleo Ltd. (✉ 18 Kildare St., ☎ 01/676–1421) sells hand-knit sweaters and accessories made only from natural fibers; it also carries its own designs.

Dublin Woollen Mills (✉ Metal Bridge Corner, ☎ 01/677–5014) at Ha'penny Bridge has a good selection of hand-knit and other woolen sweaters at competitive prices.

Kevin and Howlin (✉ 31 Nassau St., ☎ 01/677–0257) specializes in handwoven tweed men's jackets, suits, and hats and also sells tweed fabric.

Monaghan's (✉ Grafton Arcade, 15–17 Grafton St., ☎ 01/677–0823) specializes in cashmere.

Vintage
Flip (✉ 4 Upper Fownes St., ☎ 01/671–4299), one of the original stores in Temple Bar, sells vintage and retro clothing from the '50s, '60s, and '70s.

SIDE TRIPS

Dubliners are undeniably lucky. Few populaces enjoy such glorious—and easily accessible—options for day trips. Just outside the city, some of the region's most unique sights—the Joyce Tower, the Marino Casino, Malahide Castle, to name a few—beckon. Once you cross over the Grand Canal, which defines the southern border of the city center, you enter exclusive Ballsbridge and other southern areas of the city and its suburbs. If you do set out for points south and you don't have time to see everything, plan to begin in Ballsbridge. If you have a car, then head to Rathfarnham, directly south of the city. Alternatively, head east and follow the coast road south to Dun Laoghaire (and points even farther south, covered in Chapter 2). Beyond Ballsbridge, these areas are too spread out to cover on foot, and either a car or public transportation (the bus or DART) is the only way to get around. Traveling to and from each of the suburbs will take up most of a day, so you need to pick and choose the excursions you prefer.

County Dublin—Southside

Rathfarnham

Bus 47A from Hawkins St. in the city center goes to both parks in Rathfarnham. Or drive, leaving the city center via Nicholas St. just west of Christ Church Cathedral and following it south through Terenure.

❶ Two parks lie in the suburb of Rathfarnham, due south of the city at the edge of the Dublin Mountains. The 18th-century house in **St. Enda's National Historic Park** has been turned into the **Pearse Museum**, commemorating Pádrig Pearse, leader of Dublin's 1916 Easter Uprising. In the early 20th century, the house was a Irish-language boys' school, which Pearse and his brother Willie founded. The museum preserves Pearse family memorabilia, documents, and photographs. A lake and nature trails are also on the park's 50-acre grounds, and guides are available for tours of the park or simply for information. ⊠ *Grange Rd.,* ☎ *01/493–4208.* ⌨ *Free.* ⊘ *Park daily 8:30–dusk. Museum May–Aug., daily 10–1 and 2–5:30; Sept.–Apr., daily 10–1 and 2–4.*

❷ To get to **Marlay Park,** leave St. Enda's Park via Grange Road and walk up the hill for about 1 km (½ mi), turning left at the T junction and continuing another ½ km (¼ mi). The park marks the start of the **Wicklow Way,** a popular walking route that crosses the Wicklow Mountains for 137 km (85 mi), through some of the most rugged landscapes in Ireland (☞ Chapter 2). In addition to its woodlands and nature walks, the 214-acre park has a cobbled courtyard, home to brightly plumaged peacocks. Surrounding the courtyard are crafts workshops, where you are welcome to observe bookbinding, jewelry making, and furniture making in process. Every Saturday from 3 to 5, kids can take a free ride on the model steam railway. ⊠ *Grange Rd.,* ☎ *01/493–4059.* ⌨ *Free.* ⊘ *Nov.–Jan., daily 10–5; Feb.–Mar., daily 10–6; Apr. and Oct., daily 10–7; May and Sept., daily 10–8; June–Aug., daily 10–9.*

Ballsbridge

Take the DART train to Sidney Parade, or Bus 7 or Bus 8 from Burgh Quay (on the south bank of the Liffey, just east of O'Connell Bridge).

Many of Dublin's best hotels and restaurants are in the northern reaches of Ballsbridge, a leafy suburb that is directly across the Grand Canal from the city center. Its major cultural sites, however, are considerably farther south—a bit too far to reach on foot unless you're really an ambitious walker.

County Dublin — Southside

Dublin Bay

Dun Laoghaire Harbour

Scotsman's Bay

James Joyce Martello Tower

Georges St.

Scrsmans Bay

DUN LAOGHAIRE

Monkstown Rd.

Main Temple Rd.

BLACKROCK

Bootersown Ave.

Rock Rd.

SANDY-MOUNT

Merrion Rd.

MERRION

Aylesbury Rd.

Nutley Ln.

Stillorgan Rd.

Mount Merrion Ave.

N11

MOUNT MERRION

Drumartin Rd.

Kilmacud Rd.

DONNY-BROOK

Sandford Rd.

Milltown Rd.

Dundrum Rd.

Ranelagh Rd.

Adelaide Rd.

RATHMINES

RATHGAR

Rathmines Rd.

Rd.

CHURCHTOWN

Churchtown Rd.

Main Sandyford Rd.

DUNDRUM

S. Circular Rd.

Grand Canal

Crumlin Rd.

Clonard Rd.

Harold's Cross Rd.

TERENURE

Terenure Rd.

Nutgrove Ave.

RATH-FARNHAM

Rathfarnham Rd.

Ballyboden Rd.

N17

DRIMNAGH

Crumlin Rd.

Kildare Rd.

Drimnagh Rd.

Cromwell Rd.

CRUMLIN

Kimmage Rd.

Templeville Rd.

Templeogue Rd.

N81

TEMPLEOGUE

KEY

DART Railway Stations

N

0   1 km
0   1 mile

Blackrock **5**
Booterstown
Marsh Bird
Sanctuary **4**
Dalkey **8**
Dun Laoghaire and
Sandycove **7**
Marlay Park **2**

Monkstown **6**
Sandymount
Strand **3**
St. Enda's
National
Historic Park **1**

❸ **Sandymount Strand,** stretching for 5 km (3 mi) from Ringsend to Booterstown, can be accessed a few blocks west of the Sydney Parade DART station. It was cherished by James Joyce and his beloved from Galway, Nora Barnacle, and it figures as one of the settings in *Ulysses.* (The beach is "at the lacefringe of the tide," as Joyce put it.) When the tide recedes, the beach extends for 1½ km (1 mi) from the foreshore, but the tide sweeps in again very quickly. A sliver of a park lies between the main Strand Road and the beach.

OFF THE
BEATEN PATH

SOUTH WALL – East of the city is the South Wall, a long breakwater that stretches 1½ km (1 mi) out into Dublin Bay from the Ringsend power station. The wall is punctuated at its end by **Poolbeg Lighthouse.** On a nice day, it's a wonderful place for a walk and affords stunning views of North Bull Island to the north, Dublin to the west, and the entirety of the bay. It's too far to walk to the wall from the city center, and public transportation runs sporadically, so your best bet is to come out here if you have a car.

Booterstown

Take the DART local train from either Tara St. or Pearce St. Or take R118 from the corner of Lower Merrion St. and Merrion Sq.

❹ Booterstown lies along Dublin Bay south of Sandymount. The **Booterstown Marsh Bird Sanctuary** is the largest wildlife preserve in the Dublin area. Curlews, herons, kingfishers, and other fairly rare migratory species come to nest here; information boards along the road describe the birds for visitors. Also on this main road you'll pass **Glena,** the house where Athlone-born John McCormack, one of the best and most popular tenors in the first quarter of the 20th century, died on September 16, 1945. ⊠ *Between the DART line and Rock Rd.,* ☎ *01/454–1786.*

Blackrock

❺ *3 km (2 mi) south of Booterstown. Take the DART line from the city center to Blackrock.*

Fine sea views, swimming, and a major shopping center (☞ Shopping, *above*) draw Dubliners down to Blackrock, a bedroom community where James Joyce's parents lived with their large brood for most of 1892. Above the Blackrock DART station, **Idrone Terrace,** lined with restored, old-fashioned lamps, provides a lovely view across the bay to Howth Peninsula.

Monkstown

❻ *3 km (2 mi) south of Blackrock on R119. Take the DART train from the city center to the Monkstown and Seapoint stations.*

One of Dublin's most exclusive suburbs, Monkstown has two architectural curiosities. John Semple, the architect of Monkstown's **Anglican parish church,** was inspired by two entirely different styles, the Gothic and the Moorish, which he joined into an unlikely hybrid of towers and turrets. Built in 1833 in the town's main square, the church is only open during Sunday services. The well-preserved ruins of **Monkstown Castle** lie about 1 km (½ mi) south of the suburb; it's a 15th-century edifice with a keep, a gatehouse, and a long wall section, all surrounded by greenery.

☾ The **Lambert Puppet Theatre** (⊠ Clifton La., ☎ 01/280–0974) stages regular puppet shows and has a puppetry museum.

Dun Laoghaire and Sandycove

❼ *2½ km (1½ mi) beyond Monkstown along R119, the Monkstown Crescent.*

After the British monarch King George IV disembarked for a brief visit in 1821, Dun Laoghaire (pronounced dun *lear*-ee) was renamed Kingstown, but it reverted to its original Irish name 99 years later. Its Irish name refers to Laoghaire, the High King of Tara who in the 5th century permitted St. Patrick to begin converting Ireland to Christianity. The town was once a Protestant stronghold of the old ruling elite; in some of the neo-Georgian squares and terraces behind George's Street, the main thoroughfare, a little of the community's former elegance can still be felt.

Dun Laoghaire has long been known for its great harbor, enclosed by two piers, each 2½ km (1½ mi) long. The harbor was constructed between 1817 and 1859, using granite quarried from nearby Dalkey Hill; the west pier has a rougher surface and is less favored for walking than the east pier, which has a bandstand where musicians play in summer. The workaday business here includes passenger-ship and freight-services sailings to Holyhead in north Wales, 3½ hours away (☞ Arriving and Departing by Ferry *in* Dublin A to Z, *below*). Dun Laoghaire is also a yachting center, with the members-only Royal Irish, National, and Royal St. George yacht clubs, all founded in the 19th century, lining the harbor area.

West of the harbor and across from the Royal Marine Hotel and the People's Park, the **National Maritime Museum** is in the former Mariners' church. Its nave makes a strangely ideal setting for exhibits like the French longboat captured during an aborted French invasion at Bantry, County Cork, in 1796. A particularly memorable exhibit is the old optic from the Baily Lighthouse on Howth Head, across Dublin Bay; the herringbone patterns of glass reflected light across the bay until several decades ago. ⊠ *Haigh Terr.,* ☎ *01/280–0969.* ⊡ *£1.50.* ⊙ *May–Sept., Tues.–Sun. 1–5.*

From the harbor area Marine Parade leads alongside Scotsmans Bay for 1¼ km (¾ mi), as far as the **Forty Foot Bathing Pool,** a traditional bathing area that attracts mostly nude older men. Women were once banned from here, but now hardy swimmers of both genders are free to brave its cold waters.

A few steps away from the Forty Foot Bathing Pool stands Sandycove's other claim to fame, the **James Joyce Martello Tower.** Originally built in 1804 when Napoleon's invasion seemed imminent, it was demilitarized in the 1860s along with most of the rest of the 34 Martello towers that ring Ireland's coast. (Martello towers were originally Italian and were constructed to protect the Italian coastline against the possibility of a Napoleonic naval invasion. In Ireland, they were built by the British to protect Irish shores from the same threat and were remarkable for their squat and solid construction, rotating cannon at the top, and—most importantly—their proximity to one another, so that each one is within visible range of the one next to it.) In 1904, this tower was rented to Oliver St. John Gogarty, a medical student who was known for his poetry and ready wit, for £8 a year. He wanted to create a nurturing environment for writers and would-be literati. Joyce spent a week here in September 1904 and described it in the first chapter of *Ulysses,* using his friend as a model for the character Buck Mulligan. The tower now houses the **Joyce Museum,** founded in 1962 thanks to Sylvia Beach, the Paris-based first publisher of *Ulysses.* The exhibition hall contains first editions of most of Joyce's works. Joycean memorabilia include his waistcoat, embroidered by his grandmother, and a tie that he gave to Samuel Beckett (who was Joyce's onetime secretary). The gunpowder magazine stores the Joyce Tower Library, including a death mask of Joyce taken on January 13, 1941. ⊠ *Sandycove,* ☎ *01/280–*

9265. ▣ £2. ⊘ *Apr.–Oct., Mon.–Sat. 10–1 and 2–5, Sun. 2–6; Nov.–Mar. by appointment.*

$$$–$$$$ ✕ **Morel's Bistro.** Alan O'Reilly has a stylish, first-floor restaurant over the Eagle House pub on the north side of Dun Laoghaire. The summery Mediterranean colors, striking paintings—large and specially commissioned—and curvaceous (albeit uncomfortable) metal chairs at classically white-clothed tables all create a dashing impression. The seared fillet of salmon with crispy pancetta and savoy cabbage is a terrific entrée. ✉ *18 Glasthule Rd.,* ☏ *01/230–0210. AE, DC, MC, V. No lunch Mon.–Wed. and Sat.*

$$$ ✕ **Brasserie Na Mara.** The first railway in Ireland, opened in 1834, was built from Westland Row (now Pearse Station) in Dublin to Dun Laoghaire. Much of the original station's entrance and ticketing area has been converted into this restaurant, now a brasserie (*na mara* means "of the sea" in Gaelic; the name was kept but the emphasis on seafood jettisoned). Tall Georgian windows overlook the busy Dun Laoghaire ferryport. The menu highlights international dishes with a modern twist, such as confit of Barbary duck with pesto potatoes. ✉ *Dun Laoghaire Harbour,* ☏ *01/280–6767. Reservations essential on weekends. AE, DC, MC, V. Closed Sun. and 1 wk at Christmas.*

$ ✕ **Caviston's.** Stephen Caviston and his family have been dispensing fine fare for years from their fish counter and delicatessen in Sandycove. The fish restaurant next door is a lively and intimate place. Typical entrées include panfried scallops served in the shell with a Thermidor sauce and steamed Dover sole with mustard sauce. You can also get a halved lobster with a simple butter sauce for an exceptionally good price. ✉ *58–59 Glasthule Rd.,* ☏ *01/280–9120. MC, V. Closed Sun.–Mon. and late Dec.–early Jan. No dinner.*

Dalkey

❽ *From the James Joyce Tower in Sandycove, it's an easy walk or quick drive 1 km (½ mi) south to Dalkey. Or take the DART line from the city center to Dalkey.*

Along Castle Street, the town's main thoroughfare, are the substantial stone remains, resembling small, turreted castles, of two 15th- and 16th-century fortified houses. In summer, small boats make the 15-minute crossing from Coliemore Harbour to **Dalkey Island,** covered in long grass, uninhabited except for a herd of goats, and graced with its own Martello tower. From Vico Road, beyond Coliemore Harbour, are astounding bay views as far as Bray in County Wicklow (☞ Chapter 2). On Dalkey Hill is **Torca Cottage,** home of the Nobel Prize–winning writer George Bernard Shaw from 1866 to 1874. You can return to Dalkey Village by Sorrento Road.

County Dublin—Northside

Dublin's northern suburbs remain predominantly working class and largely residential, but there are a few places worth the trip. As with most other suburban areas, walking may not be the best way to get around. A car is recommended but not essential. Buses and trains service most of these areas, the only drawback being that to get from one suburb to another by public transportation means returning back through the city center. Even if you're traveling by car, visiting all these sights will take a full day, so plan your trip carefully before setting off.

Glasnevin

Drive from the north city center by Lower Dorset St., as far as the bridge over the Royal Canal. Turn left, go up Whitworth Rd., by the side of the canal, for 1 km (½ mi); at its end, turn right onto Prospect Rd. and then left onto the Finglas road, N2. You may also take Bus 40 or Bus 40A from Parnell St., next to Parnell Sq., in the north city center.

⑨ **Glasnevin Cemetery,** on the right-hand side of the Finglas road, is the best-known burial ground in Dublin. Here you'll find the graves of many distinguished Irish leaders, including Eamon De Valera, a founding father of modern Ireland and a former Irish taoiseach and president, and Michael Collins, the celebrated hero of the Irish War of Independence. Other notables interred here include late-19th-century poet Gerard Manley Hopkins and Sir Roger Casement, an Irish rebel hanged for treason by the British in 1916. The large column to the right of the main entrance is the tomb of "The Liberator" Daniel O'Connell, perhaps Ireland's greatest historical figure, renowned for his nonviolent struggle for Catholic rights and emancipation, which he achieved in 1829. The cemetery is freely accessible all day.

⑩ On the northeastern flank of Glasnevin Cemetery, the **National Botanic Gardens** date from 1795 and have more than 20,000 different varieties of plants, a rose garden, and a vegetable garden. The main attraction is the **Curvilinear Range,** 400-ft-long greenhouses designed and built by a Dublin ironmaster, Richard Turner, between 1843 and 1869. The Palm House, with its striking double dome, was built in 1884 and houses orchids, palms, and tropical ferns. ⊠ *Glasnevin Rd.,* ☎ *01/837–4388.* 🎟 *Free.* ☉ *Apr.–Sept., Mon.–Sat. 10–6, Sun. 11–6; Oct.–Mar., Mon.–Sat. 10–4:30, Sun. 11–4:30.*

Marino Casino

⑪ *Take the Malahide road from Dublin's north city center for 4 km (2½ mi). Or take Bus 20A or Bus 24 to the Casino from Cathal Brugha St. in the north city center.*

One of Dublin's most exquisite, yet also most underrated, architectural landmarks, the Marino Casino (the name has nothing to do with gambling—it means "little house by the sea") is a small-scale, Palladian-style Greek temple, built between 1762 and 1771 from a plan by Sir William Chambers. Often compared to the Petit Trianon at Versailles, it was commissioned as a summerhouse overlooking Dublin harbor by that great Irish grandee, Lord Charlemont (☞ Hugh Lane Municipal Gallery of Modern Art *in* North of the Liffey, *above*). While his estate's grand mansion was tragically demolished in 1921, this sublime casino was saved and has now been lovingly restored (thankfully, Sir William's original plans survived). Inside, highlights are the china-closet boudoir, the huge golden sun set in the ceiling of the main drawing room, and the signs of the zodiac in the ceiling of the bijou-size library. When you realize that the structure has, in fact, 16 rooms—there are bedrooms upstairs—Sir William's sleight-of-hand is readily apparent: from its exterior, the structure seems to contain only one room. The tricks don't stop there: the freestanding columns on the facade are hollow so they can drain rainwater, while the elegant marble urns on the roof are chimneys. Last but not least, note the four stone lions on the outside terrace—they were carved by Joseph Wilson, who created the famous British royal coronation coach back in London. All in all, this remains, to quote Desmond Guinness, "one of the most exquisite buildings in Europe." It makes a good stop on the way to Malahide, Howth, or North Bull Island. ⊠ *Malahide Rd., Marino,* ☎ *01/833–1618.* 🎟 *£2.* ☉ *June–Sept., daily 9:30–6.*

County Dublin — Northside

KEY
DART Railway Stations

0 — 1 km
0 — 1 mile

N

Glasnevin Cemetery **9**
Howth. **13**
Malahide Castle . . **14**
Marino Casino **11**

National Botanic Gardens **10**
Newbridge House . **15**
North Bull Island . **12**

North Bull Island

⑫ *From Dublin's north city center, take the Clontarf road for 4 km (2½ mi) to the causeway.*

A 5-km-long (3-mi-long) island created in the last century by the action of the tides, North Bull Island is one of Dublin's wilder places, a nature conservancy with vast beach and dunes. The island is linked to the mainland via a wooden causeway that leads to **Bull Wall,** a 1½-km (1-mi) walkway that stretches as far as the **North Bull Lighthouse.** The island is also accessible via a second, northerly causeway, which gives access to **Dollymount Strand.** (The two routes of entry do not meet at any point on the island.) It's reached from the mainland via James Larkin Road. A small **visitor center** is largely devoted to the island's bird life. ✉ *Off the northerly causeway,* ☎ *01/833–8341.* ☞ *Free.* ⊙ *Mar.–Oct., Mon.–Wed. 10:15–1 and 1:30–4, Thurs. 10:15–1 and 1:30–3:45, Fri. 10:15–1 and 1:30–2:30, weekends 10–1 and 1:30–5:30; Nov.–Feb., same hrs except 4:30 closing time weekends.*

On the mainland directly across from North Bull Island is **St. Anne's Park,** a public green with extensive rose gardens (including many prize hybrids) and woodland walks; it is freely accessible all day. ✉ *James Larkin Rd. and Mt. Prospect Ave.*

Howth

★ ⑬ *From Dublin, take the DART train, which takes about 30 mins; Bus 31B from Lower Abbey St. in the city center; or, by car, take the Howth road from the north city center for 16 km (10 mi).*

A fishing village at the foot of a long peninsula, Howth (derived from the Norse *hoved,* meaning head; it rhymes with "both") was an island inhabited as long ago as 3250 BC. Between 1813 and 1833, Howth was the Irish terminus for the sea crossing to Holyhead in north Wales, but it was then superseded by the newly built harbor at Kingstown (now Dun Laoghaire; ☞ *above*). Today, a marina graces its harbor, which supports a large fishing fleet. Both arms of the harbor pier form extensive walks. Separated from Howth Harbour by a channel nearly 1½ km (1 mi) wide, **Ireland's Eye** has an old stone church on the site of a 6th-century monastery and an early 19th-century Martello tower. In calm weather, local boatmen make the crossing to the island.

At the King Sitric restaurant on the East Pier (☞ Dining, *below*), a 2½-km (1½-mi) cliff walk begins, leading to the white **Baily Lighthouse,** built in 1814. In some places, the cliff path narrows and drops sheerly to the sea, but the views out over the Irish Sea are terrific. Some of the best views in the whole Dublin area await from the parking lot above the lighthouse, looking out over the entire bay as far south as Dun Laoghaire, Bray, and the north Wicklow coast. You can also see much of Dublin.

Until 1959, a tram service ran from the railway station in Howth, over Howth Summit, and back down to the station. One of the open-topped ⊙ Hill of Howth trams that plied this route is now the star at the **National Transport Museum,** a short, 800-yard walk from Howth's DART station. Volunteers have spent several years restoring the tram, which stands alongside other unusual vehicles, including old horse-drawn bakery vans. ☎ *01/848–0831 or 01/847–5623.* ☞ *£1.50.* ⊙ *Easter–Sept., daily 10–5:30; Oct.–Easter, weekends 2–5:30.*

Next door to the Transport Museum and accessible from the Deer Park Hotel, the **Howth Castle Gardens** were laid out in the early 18th century. The many rare varieties of its fine rhododendron garden are in full flower April–June; there are also high beech hedges. The rambling castle, originally built in 1654 and considerably altered in the intervening centuries, is not open to the public, but you can access the ruins of a tall, square, 16th-century castle and a Neolithic dolmen. ⊠ *Deer Park Hotel,* ☎ *01/832–2624.* ☜ *Free.* ⊙ *Daily 8–dusk.*

DINING

$$$ ✕ **Abbey Tavern.** The original stone walls, flagged floors, blazing turf fires, and old gaslights of the ancient building that houses this old-world tavern all contribute to the historic atmosphere. The upstairs restaurant serves traditional Irish and Continental cuisine and specializes in fish dishes. Sole Abbey (filleted and stuffed with prawns, mushrooms, and herbs) is a house specialty, and fresh Dublin Bay prawns can be cooked to order. Traditional Irish music is performed in a different part of the building. The restaurant is a five-minute walk from the DART station; call for directions. ⊠ *Abbey St.,* ☎ *01/839–0307. Reservations essential. AE, DC, MC, V. No dinner Sun.*

$$$ ✕ **King Sitric.** This well-known seafood restaurant is one of Howth's main attractions. It's in a Georgian house on the harbor front, with the yacht marina and port on one side, and with sea views from the upstairs seafood bar, where informal lunches are served in summer. A house specialty is black sole meunière, grilled and finished with a nut-brown butter sauce, but lobster, caught just yards away in Balscadden Bay, is the big treat; it's best at its simplest, in butter sauce. Crab is equally fresh, dressed with mayonnaise or Mornay sauce. ⊠ *East Pier,* ☎ *01/832–5235. AE, DC, MC, V. Closed Sun.*

Malahide

To get here by car, drive from the north city center on R107 for 14½ km (9 mi). Or catch the hourly train from Connolly Station, which takes about 20 mins. Or board Bus 42 to Malahide, which leaves from Beresford Pl. behind the Custom House (service runs every 15 mins; the ride takes about 40 mins).

★ ☾ ⑭ Malahide is chiefly known for **Malahide Castle,** a picture-book castle occupied by the Anglo-Irish and aristocratic Talbot family from 1185 until 1976, when it was sold to the Dublin County Council. The great expanse of parkland around the castle includes a botanical garden with more than 5,000 species and varieties of plants, all clearly labeled. The castle itself is a combination of styles and periods; the earliest section, the three-story tower house, dates from the 12th century. The medieval great hall is the only one in Ireland that is preserved in its original form, while the National Portrait Gallery features many fine paintings of the Talbot family and 18th- and 19th-century Irish notables. Other rooms are well furnished with authentic 18th-century pieces. Also in the castle is the **Fry Model Railway Museum,** with rare, handmade models of the Irish railway. The castle's self-service restaurant serves good homemade food all day. ⊠ *6 mi north of Howth on the Coast Road,* ☎ *01/846–2184.* ☜ *£3.* ⊙ *Apr.–Sept., weekdays 10–6, Sat. 11–6, Sun. 2–6; Oct.–Mar., weekends 2–5.*

☾ ⑮ **Newbridge House,** in nearby Donabate, was built between 1740 and 1760 for Charles Cobbe, Archbishop of Dublin. Newbridge was owned by the Cobee family until 1985, when it, along with most of its furnishings, was purchased by the state. One of the finest Georgian interiors in Ireland, the **Red Drawing Room** is hung with dozens of paintings and decorated with many fine antiques. The **kitchens** of the house still have their original utensils. Crafts workshops and some examples of old-style transportation, such as coaches, are in the courtyard. Beyond the walled garden are 366 acres of parkland and a restored 18th-century animal farm. **Tara's Palace,** a dollhouse that was made to raise funds for children's charities, is also here; it has 25 rooms, all fully furnished in miniature. The exterior of the dollhouse is based on the facades of three great Irish houses—Carton, Castletown, and Leinster. The **coffee shop** is renowned for the quality and selection of its homemade goods. You can travel from Malahide to Donabate by train, which takes about 10 minutes. From the Donabate train station, the walk to the Newbridge House grounds takes 15 minutes. ⊠ *Donabate, 8 km (5 mi) north of Malahide, signposted from N1,* ☎ *01/843–6534.* ▣ *House £2.75, farm £1.* ☺ *Apr.–Sept., Tues.–Fri. 10– 5, Sat. 11–6, Sun. 2–6; Oct.–Mar., weekends 2–5.*

DINING

$$$ ✕ **Bon Appetit.** Owner-chef Patsy McGuirk brought a loyal following from his previous city-center restaurant of the same name when he moved, in 1989, to this substantial Georgian terraced building. The striking floral decor creates a cozy, traditional atmosphere, an impression heightened by the staff of black-jacketed waiters. The traditional Continental menu includes such entrées as warm salad of Dublin Bay king prawns with pine nuts, prawn oil, and shavings of Parmesan, and a generous selection of desserts. Especially recommended are sole McGuirk (filleted, stuffed with prawns and turbot, and baked with white wine and cream) and duckling Grand Marnier (double-roasted duck served on a potato-and-herb stuffing). ⊠ *9 James's Terr.,* ☎ *01/845–0314. Jacket and tie. AE, DC, MC, V. Closed Sun. No lunch Sat.*

DUBLIN A TO Z

Arriving and Departing

By Bus
Busaras (☎ 01/830–2222) is Dublin's main bus station, just behind the Custom House on the northside.

By Car
Renting a car in Dublin is very expensive, with high rates and a 12½% local tax. Gasoline is also expensive by U.S. standards, at around 70p a liter. Peak-period car-rental rates begin at around £200 a week for the smallest stick models, like a Ford Fiesta. Dublin has many car-rental companies, and it pays to shop around and to avoid "cowboy" outfits (☞ Car Rentals, *below*).

By Ferry
Irish Ferries (⊠ Merrion Row, ☎ 01/661–0511) and **Stena Sealink** (⊠ Ferryport, Dun Laoghaire, ☎ 01/204–7777) have regular car and passenger service between Dublin and Wales (Holyhead). Irish Ferries sails directly into Dublin port. Stena Sealink docks in Dublin port (3½-hour service to Holyhead) and in Dun Laoghaire (**High Speed Service,** known as "HSS," which takes 99 minutes). Prices and departure times vary according to season, so call either company to confirm. In summer reservations are strongly recommended. Dozens of taxis wait to take you into town from both ports, or you can take DART or a bus to the city center.

By Plane
Dublin Airport (☎ 01/844–4900), 10 km (6 mi) north of the city center, serves international and domestic airlines.

AIRPORT SHUTTLE

Dublin Bus (☎ 01/873–4222) operates a shuttle service between Dublin Airport and the city center with departures outside the arrivals gateway; pay the driver inside the coach. The single fare is £3. Service runs from 6:40 AM to 11 PM, at intervals of about 20 minutes (after 8 PM buses run every hour), to as far as **Busaras** (☎ 01/830–2222), Dublin's main bus station, behind the Custom House on the northside. Journey time from the airport to the city center is normally 30 minutes, but it may be longer in heavy traffic.

A taxi is a quicker alternative than the bus to get from the airport to Dublin center. A line of taxis waits by the arrivals gateway; the fare for the 30-minute journey to any of the main city-center hotels is about £14 plus tip (tips don't have to be large but they are increasingly expected). It's advisable to ask about the fare before leaving the airport.

FROM THE U.K.
Five airlines now serve destinations in Ireland: Aer Lingus, Ryanair, City Jet, British Airways, and British Midland Airways. There are daily services to Dublin from all major London airports; Aer Lingus operates 12 flights from Heathrow Airport, with British Midland operating an additional 10 flights; Ryanair operates several flights from Luton and Stanstead airports, and Cityjet flies from London City Airport. In addition, flights to Dublin leave from Birmingham, Bristol, East Midlands, Liverpool, Luton, Manchester, Leeds/Bradford, Newcastle, Edinburgh, and Glasgow. Prices vary a great deal between companies and at different seasons. Ryanair is known for being the cheapest, but this means cutting back on comfort and services. For reservations and information in Dublin, contact **Aer Lingus** (☎ 01/844–4747), **British Airways** (☎ 800/626747), **British Midland** (☎ 01/283–8833), **City Jet** (☎ 01/844–5566), or **Ryanair** (☎ 01/844–4411).

FROM ELSEWHERE IN EUROPE
Major European carriers, such as Air France, Lufthansa, Sabena, SAS, and Alitalia, run direct services to Dublin from most European capital cities and major regional airports, especially those in Germany.

FROM THE U.S.
The three airlines with regularly scheduled flights from the United States to Dublin are **Aer Lingus** (☎ 01/844–4747), which flies direct from New York, Boston, Los Angeles, and Chicago to Dublin; **Continental** (☎ 0800/321324), which flies from New York (Newark Airport) to Dublin daily; and **Delta** (☎ 01/844–4166 or 01/676–8080), which flies from Atlanta to Dublin via New York.

FLYING WITHIN IRELAND
Aer Lingus (☎ 01/844–4747) and **Ryanair** (☎ 01/844–4411) operate flights from Dublin to Cork, Kerry, Shannon, Galway, Knock in County Mayo, Donegal, and Sligo.

By Train
The main train stations in Dublin are **Connolly Station** (✉ Amiens St.) and **Heuston Station** (✉ end of Victoria Quay). The former provides train services to the north and northwest, the latter to the south and west. Contact the **Irish Rail Travel Centre** (✉ 35 Lower Abbey St., ☎ 01/836–6222) for information.

Getting Around

Traveling around Dublin by public transportation is comparatively easy, although a car is useful for getting to the outlying suburbs. If you're just planning to visit city-center Dublin, definitely plan to do it without a car.

By Bus
Dublin has an extensive network of buses—most of them are green double-deckers. Timetables (£1.50) are available from **Dublin Bus** (✉ 59

Upper O'Connell St., ☎ 01/873–4222), staffed weekdays 9–5:30, Saturday 9–1. Fares begin at 55p and are paid to the driver, who will accept inexact fares, but you'll have to go to the central office in Dublin to pick up your change as marked on your ticket. Change transactions and the city's heavy traffic can slow service down considerably. Some bus services run on cross-city routes, including the smaller "Imp" buses, but most buses start in the city center. Buses to the north of the city begin in the Lower Abbey Street/Parnell Street area, while those to the west begin in Middle Abbey Street and in the Aston Quay area. Routes to the southern suburbs begin at Eden Quay and in the College Street area. A number of services are links to DART stations, and another regular bus route connects the two main provincial railway stations, Connolly and Heuston. If the destination board indicates AN LÁR, that means that the bus is going to the city center. Late-night buses run weekends, on the hour from midnight to 3 PM; the fare is £3.

Museumlink is a new shuttle service linking up the Natural History Museum, National Museum, and Collins Barracks (☞ The Georgian Heart of Dublin *and* Phoenix Park and Environs, *above*). You can catch it outside any of the three museums.

By Car
The number of cars in Ireland has grown exponentially in the last few years, and nowhere has their impact been felt more than in Dublin, where the city's complicated one-way streets are congested during the morning and evening rush hours and often during much of the rest of the day. If you can, avoid driving a car except to get you into and out of the city, and be sure to ask your hotel or guest house for clear directions to get you out of the city.

By Taxi
Official licensed taxis, metered and designated by roof signs, do not cruise. Taxi stands are located beside the central bus station, at train stations, O'Connell Bridge, St. Stephen's Green, College Green, and near major hotels; the Dublin telephone directory has a complete list. The initial charge is £1.80 with an additional charge of about £1.60 a kilometer thereafter. The fare is displayed on a meter (make sure it's on). Alternatively, you may phone a taxi company and ask for a cab to meet you at your hotel, but this may cost up to £2 extra. Hackney cabs, which also operate in the city, have neither roof signs nor meters and will sometimes respond to hotels' requests for a cab. Negotiate the fare before your journey begins. Although the taxi fleet in Dublin is large, the cabs are nonstandard and some cars are neither spacious nor in pristine condition. Local taxi companies include **Cab Charge** (☎ 01/677–2222), **Metro** (☎ 01/668–3333), and **VIP Taxis** (☎ 01/478–3333).

By Train
An electric railway system, the **DART** (Dublin Area Rapid Transit; ☎ 01/836–6222) connects Dublin with Howth to the north and Bray to the south on a fast, efficient line. There are 25 stations on the route, which is the best means of getting to seaside destinations such as Howth, Blackrock, Dun Laoghaire, Dalkey, Killiney, and Bray. The service starts at 6:30 AM and runs until 11:30 PM; at peak periods, 8–9:30 AM and 5–7 PM, trains arrive every five minutes. At other times of the day, the intervals between trains are 15 to 25 minutes. Tickets can be bought at stations, but it's also possible to buy weekly rail tickets, as well as weekly or monthly "rail-and-bus" tickets, from the **Irish Rail Travel Centre** (✉ 35 Lower Abbey St., ☎ 01/836–6222). Individual fares begin at 65p and range up to £1.30. There are heavy penalties for traveling the DART without a ticket. Train services run from **Heuston Station** (✉ End of Victoria Quay) to Kildare Town west of

Dublin via Celbridge, Sallins, and Newbridge, and from **Connolly Station** (⊠ Amiens St.) to more distant locations like Malahide, Maynooth, Skerries, and Drogheda to the north of Dublin and Wicklow and Arklow to the south.

Contacts and Resources

B&B Reservation Agencies

For a small fee, **Bord Fáilte** will book accommodations anywhere in Ireland through its central reservations system; have your credit card ready. B&Bs can be booked at local visitor information offices when they are open; however, even these reservations will go through the central reservations system. For more information, *see* Lodging *in* Smart Travel Tips A to Z.

Car Rentals

A dozen car-rental companies have desks at Dublin Airport; all the main national and international firms also have branches in the city center. Some reliable agencies include the following: **Avis** (⊠ 1 Hanover St. E, ☎ 01/677–5204; Dublin Airport, ☎ 01/844–5204); **Budget** (⊠ 151 Lower Drumcondra Rd., ☎ 01/837–9802; Dublin Airport, ☎ 01/844–5919); **Dan Dooley** (⊠ 42–43 Westland Row, ☎ 01/677–2723; Dublin Airport, ☎ 01/844–5156); **Hertz** (⊠ Leeson St. Bridge, ☎ 01/660–2255; Dublin Airport, ☎ 01/844–5466); **Murray's Rent-a-Car** (⊠ Baggot St. Bridge, ☎ 01/668–1777; Dublin Airport, ☎ 01/844–4179).

Embassies

Embassies are open weekdays 9–1 and 2–5. **Australia** (⊠ Fitzwilton House, Wilton Terr., ☎ 01/676–1517). **Canada** (⊠ 65 St. Stephen's Green, ☎ 01/478–1988). **United Kingdom** (⊠ 29 Merrion Rd., ☎ 01/205–3700). **United States** (⊠ 42 Elgin Rd., ☎ 01/668–8777).

Emergencies

Gardai (police), ambulance, or fire (☎ 999).

DOCTORS AND DENTISTS

Dublin's **Eastern Help Board** (☎ 01/679–0700) can provide the names of doctors. The **Dublin Dental Hospital** (⊠ 20 Lincoln Pl., ☎ 01/662–0766) has emergency facilities and lists of dentists offering emergency care.

HOSPITALS

Beaumont (⊠ Beaumont Rd., ☎ 01/837–7755). **Mater** (⊠ Eccles St., ☎ 01/830–1122). **St. James's** (⊠ 1 James St., ☎ 01/453–7941). **St. Vincent's** (⊠ Elm Park, ☎ 01/269–4533).

PHARMACIES

Hamilton Long (⊠ 5 Upper O'Connell St., ☎ 01/874–8456) is open Monday–Wednesday and Saturday 8:30–6, Thursday 8:30–8, and Friday 8:30–7.

Temple Bar Pharmacy (⊠ 20 E. Essex St., Temple Bar, ☎ 01/670–9751) is open Monday–Wednesday and Friday–Saturday 9–7, Thursday 9–8.

Guided Tours

BEYOND THE CITY

Bus Éireann (☎ 01/836–6111) organizes day tours out of Busaras, the main bus station, to country destinations such as Glendalough.

ORIENTATION

Dublin Bus (☎ 01/873–4222) has three- and four-hour tours of the city center that include Trinity College, the Royal Hospital Kilmainham, and Phoenix Park. The one-hour City Tour, with hourly departures, allows you to hop on and off at any of the main sites. Tickets are avail-

---

able from the driver or Dublin Bus. From mid-April through September Dublin Bus runs a continuous guided open-top bus tour (£5) that allows you to hop on and off the bus as often as you wish and visit some 15 sights along its route. The company also conducts a north-city coastal tour, going to Howth, and a south-city tour, traveling as far as Enniskerry.

Gray Line Tours (☎ 01/670–8822) runs city-center tours that cover the same sights as the Dublin Bus itineraries (☞ *above*).

TRAIN AND CARRIAGE TOURS

Guided tours of Dublin using the DART system are organized by **Views Unlimited** (✉ 8 Prince of Wales Terr., Bray, ☎ 01/286–0164 or 01/285–6121).

Horse-drawn carriage tours are available around Dublin and in Phoenix Park. For tours of the park, contact the **Department of the Arts, Culture and the Gaeltacht** (☎ 01/661–3111). Carriages can be hired at the Grafton Street corner of St. Stephen's Green, without prior reservation.

WALKING TOURS

Historical and Literary Tours: Historical Walking Tours of Dublin (☎ 01/878–0227), run by Trinity College history graduate students, are excellent two-hour tour introductions to Dublin. The Bord Fáilte–approved tour assembles at the front gate of Trinity College mid-May–mid-October, daily at 11, noon, and 3, with an extra tour on Sunday at 2, and mid-October–mid-May on weekends at noon. The cost is £5. A **Georgian/Literary Walking Tour** (☎ 01/496–0641) leaves from Bewley's Oriental Café (☞ The Center City: Around Trinity College, *above*) June–September daily at 11; each tour lasts approximately two hours and costs £5. **Trinity Tours** (☎ 01/608–2320) organizes walks of the Trinity College campus on weekends from March 17 (St. Patrick's Day) through mid-May and from mid-May to September daily; the half-hour tour costs £3.50 and includes admission to the *Book of Kells* (☞ Trinity College *in* City Center: Around Trinity College, *above*); tours start at the college's main gate. The **Zozimus Experience** (☎ 01/661–8646) is an enjoyable walking tour of Dublin's medieval past, with a particular focus on the seedy, including great escapes, murders, and mythical happenings. Led by a guide in costume, tours are by arrangement only and run from the main gate of Dublin Castle from 6:45 PM; the cost is £5 per person. Prepare yourself for a surprise!

Musical Tours: Dublin Tourism (☞ Visitor Information, *below*) has a booklet to its self-guided **"Rock 'n Stroll" Trail,** which covers 16 sites with associations to performers such as Bob Geldof, Christy Moore, Sinéad O'Connor, and U2. Most of the sites are in the city center and Temple Bar. The **Musical Pub Crawl** (✉ Discover Dublin, 20 Lower Stephens St., ☎ 01/478–0191) begins at **Oliver St. John Gogarty's** (✉ Fleet St., Temple Bar) and moves on to three other pubs. Led by two professional musicians who perform songs and tell the story of Irish music, the tour is given May–October, Monday–Thursday and weekends at 7:30 PM; the cost is £6.

Pubs: Colm Quilligan (☎ 01/454–0228) arranges highly enjoyable evening walks of the literary pubs of Dublin, where "brain cells are replaced as quickly as they are drowned." The *Dublin Literary Pub Crawl* is a 122-page guide to those Dublin pubs with the greatest literary associations; it's widely available in Dublin bookstores.

Internet

In the city center are a number of Internet cafés that allow you access to the Internet and e-mail. All charge between £5 and £8 an hour. **Betacafe** (✉ Arthouse, Curved St., Temple Bar, ☎ 01/671–5717) is a Internet café serving coffee and sandwiches. **Cyberia** (✉ The Granary, Temple La. S, Temple Bar, ☎ 01/679–7607) is very popular with students, who tend to spend hours playing computer games. **Planet Cyber Café** (✉ 23 S. Great George's St., ☎ 01/679–0583), in the basement of a video store, is the city's best, with top-of-the-range computers and a good coffee bar.

Lost and Found

Dublin Bus: Contact its headquarters (✉ 59 Upper O'Connell St., ☎ 01/873–4222). **Railways and DART:** Contact **Iarnród Éireann/Irish Rail** (✉ Travel Centre, 35 Lower Abbey St., ☎ 01/836–6222).

Opening and Closing Times

Dublin is gradually becoming a 24-hour city, even though the bus and DART train services close down for the night at 11:30. (A few lines run until dawn on the weekends, and late buses go until 3 AM.) Many taxis run all night, but the demand, especially on weekends, can make for long lines at taxi stands. Many clubs on the Leeson Street strip and elsewhere stay open until 4 AM or later.

Banks are open weekdays 10–4 and remain open on Thursday until 5. All stay open at lunchtime. Most branches have ATMs that accept bank cards and MasterCard and Visa credit cards (☞ Money *in* Smart Travel Tips A to Z). **Museums** are normally open Tuesday–Saturday and Sunday afternoon. **Post offices** are open weekdays 9–1 and 2–5:30, Saturday 9–12:30. Main post offices are open Saturday afternoons, too (look for green signs that say "An Post"). The General Post Office (GPO) on O'Connell Street, which has foreign exchange and general delivery facilities, is open Monday–Saturday 8–8, Sunday 10:30–6:30. To send a postcard to the United States costs 38p, to the United Kingdom 28p.

Pubs open Monday–Saturday at 10:30 AM and 12:30 PM on Sunday. They must stop serving at 11 PM in winter and 11:30 PM in summer, but most pubs take another hour to empty out. A number of bars in the center of the city have permission to serve until 1 AM on weekend nights. **Stores** are open Monday–Saturday 9–5:30 or 9–6, and Thursday until 8. Smaller city-center specialty stores open on Sunday as well, usually 10–6. Most department stores are closed on Sunday.

Safety

What crime there is in Dublin is often drug-related. Sidestreets off O'-Connell Street can be dangerous, especially at night. When you park your car, *do not* leave any valuables inside, even under a raincoat on the backseat or in the trunk; be especially careful parking around the Guinness Brewery and the Old Jameson Distillery (☞ Dublin West: From Dublin Castle to the Four Courts, *above*), neither of which is in a great neighborhood.

Travel Agencies

American Express (✉ 116 Grafton St., ☎ 01/677–2874). **Thomas Cook** (✉ 118 Grafton St., ☎ 01/677–1721).

Visitor Information

The main **Dublin Tourism** (✉ Suffolk St., just off Grafton St., ☎ 01/605–7700 or 1850/230330 within Ireland, FAX 01/605–7787) is open July–September, Monday–Saturday 8:30–6, Sunday 11–5:30, and October–June, daily 9–6; at Dublin Airport, daily 8 AM–10 PM; and at the Ferryport, Dun Laoghaire, daily 10–9. **Bord Fáilte,** the Irish Tourist Board, has its own visitor information offices in the entrance hall of its head-quarters (⌧ Baggot St. Bridge, ☎ 1850/230330 [within Ireland] or 01/602-4000, FAX 01/602–4100), open weekdays 9:15–5:15. A suburban tourist office in Tallaght is open March–December, daily 9:30–5. The **Temple Bar Information Centre** (⌧ 18 Eustace St., ☎ 01/671–5717, FAX 01/677–2525) produces the easy-to-use, annually updated *Temple Bar Guide,* which provides complete listings of the area's hundreds of stores, pubs, restaurants, clubs, galleries, and other cultural venues.

2 DUBLIN ENVIRONS

*The Boyne Valley and
Counties Wicklow and Kildare*

Both glory and grandeur are tucked into the folds of the Pale—the counties north, south, and west of Dublin. Here, the scenic-hungry traveler will find some of the richest treasure houses in the land: Castletown, Russborough, and Powerscourt Houses. But there are more than just 18th-century Palladian porticoes here. Celtic crosses, historic churches, the ancient passage graves at Newgrange, and the "monastic city" of Glendalough await—all time-burnished sites that still guard the roots of Irishness.

Updated by
Anto Howard

O NE OF THE LOVELIEST REGIONS in this land of loveliness, the Pale—the counties immediately north, south, and west of Dublin—constitutes an area that seems expressly designed for the sightseer. The entire region is an open-air museum filled with legendary Celtic sites, grand gardens (little wonder the air is flower-scented), and elegant Palladian country estates. France may have its châteaux of the Loire Valley, England the treasure houses of Kent and Sussex, Germany its castles of the Rhine, but today, more and more travelers are discovering that the grand estates of the Pale rank nearly as high in the galaxy of stately style.

Dublin environs comprise three basic geographical regions: County Wicklow's coast and mountains, the Boyne Valley, and County Kildare. Lying tantalizingly close to the south of Dublin is the mountainous county of Wicklow, which contains some of the most *et-in-arcadia-ego* scenery in the Emerald Isle. Here, the gently rounded Wicklow Mountains—to some tastes Ireland's finest—contain the evocative monastic settlement at Glendalough, many later abbeys and churches, and such noted 18th-century estates as Powerscourt and Russborough. Nearby is an impressive eastern coastline that stretches from Counties Wicklow to Louth, punctuated by delightful harbor towns and fishing villages. The coast is virtually unspoiled for its entire length.

North of Dublin lies the Boyne Valley, with its abundant ruins of Celtic Ireland stretching from Counties Meath to Louth. Some of the country's most evocative Neolithic ruins—including the famous passage graves at Newgrange—are nestled into this landscape, where layer upon layer of history penetrates down into earlier, unknowable ages. It was west of Drogheda—a fascinating town settled by the Vikings in the early 10th century—that the *Tuatha De Danann,* onetime residents of Ireland, went underground when defeated by the invading Milesians and became, it is said, "the good people" or fairies of Irish legend. In pagan times this area was the home of Ireland's high kings and the center of religious life. In those days, all roads led to Tara, the fabled Hill of Kings. Today, time seems to stand still there—and you should do so, too, for it is almost sacrilegious to introduce a note of urgency. At any of the religious sites of the Boyne Valley—Tara, Mellifont Abbey, Monasterboice—be sure to feast your ears on the quietude of centuries gone by.

Southwest of Dublin are the flat pastoral plains of County Kildare, which stretch between the western Midlands and the foothills of the Dublin and Wicklow mountains—both names actually refer to one mountain, but each marks its county's claim to the land. Kildare has the reputation of being the flattest part of Ireland, a playing field for the breeding, training, and racing of some of the world's premier Thoroughbreds.

Of all the artistic delights that beckon both north and south of Dublin, few are as enchanting as the imposing country estates of County Wicklow. Here, during the "glorious eighteenth," great Anglo-Irish estates were built by Irish "princes of Elegance and Prodigality." Only an hour or two from Dublin, these estates were profoundly influenced by the country villas of the great Italian architect Andrea Palladio, who erected the estates of the Venetian aristocracy only a short distance from the city on the lagoon. As in other parts of Ireland, the ancestral homes of the dwindling members of the Anglo-Irish ascendancy dot the landscape in the Pale. Today, lords and baronets down on their luck have turned into hoteliers who welcome guests to castle holidays with adaptable grace.

Pleasures and Pastimes

Dining

Dining out in the area is still essentially a casual affair, but the innovations and experimentation of Dublin's top restaurateurs are influencing the cooking at the finer establishments outside the capital. As in the Southwest (☞ Chapter 5), chefs hereabouts have a deep respect for fresh, locally grown and raised produce. You'll find everything from Continental-style meals to hearty ploughman's lunches. For price ranges, *see* Dining *in* Smart Travel Tips A to Z.

Lodging

Counties Wicklow and Kildare offer excellent accommodations, even if the choice may not be vast. If you have only a night or two outside Dublin, try to stay at least one night in one of the area's country-house or manor-house hotels, where some of Ireland's finest hosts welcome you into sometimes glorious, sometimes rustic, but almost invariably comfortable homes. Old-style hotels in Counties Meath and Louth are showing signs of improvement and are becoming ever more popular. Bed-and-breakfasts, as elsewhere in Ireland, are always a delightful option. For price ranges, *see* Lodging *in* Smart Travel Tips A to Z.

Prehistoric and Monastic Sites

The Boyne Valley, which straddles the county of Louth and runs through the flat heartland of Meath, is home to 10% of all prehistoric monuments in Ireland. Foremost among these is Neolithic Newgrange, passage graves built between 2800 and 2400 BC. The Hill of Tara, one of the focal points for the ancient high kings of Ireland, was where disputes between clans were settled, new laws were passed, and, eventually, Christianity was proclaimed from the summit by St. Patrick. The advent of Christianity led to the construction of County Wicklow's Glendalough monastery, founded by one of St. Patrick's followers, St. Kevin. Later in the 12th century, the first Cistercian house in Ireland, the monastery of Mellifont, was founded. North of Mellifont are the ruins of Monasterboice, another monastic site where one of the finest high crosses in Ireland stands in the shadow of a 9th-century round tower.

Walking, Hiking, and Biking

Whether you're a novice or veteran hiker, Wicklow's gentle, rolling hills are a terrific place to begin an Irish walking vacation. Devoted hikers come from all over the world to traverse the 137-km (85-mi) Wicklow Way, the first long-distance trail to open in Ireland and one of the best. Beginning in Marlay Park (☞ Side Trips *in* Chapter 1), just a few miles south of Dublin, much of the route lies above 1,600 ft and follows rough sheep tracks, forest firebreaks, and old bog roads; rain gear, windproof clothing, and sturdy footwear are essential. Consider participating in one of the walking festivals held at Easter, in May, and in autumn. Biking is also an excellent way to see the area.

Exploring Dublin Environs

All of the towns and sites in the Dublin environs region can be visited on a day trip from the city. This chapter is organized into three different sections, each of which makes a reasonable day trip. Keep in mind that it's easy to lose an hour or so making detours, chatting with locals, and otherwise enjoying the unexpected. The itineraries below cover the area's highlights; if you have fewer than three days, use parts of each day's suggested itinerary to plan your excursion. A car is essential to visit most sights—and don't plan on visiting both the north and south of Dublin in the same day. You can also reach some points of interest by public transport: bus tours from Dublin cover County

Wicklow as far as Glendalough in the southwest and the Boyne Valley to the north; suburban bus services reach into the foothills of the Dublin Mountains; and Bus Éireann services take in the outlying towns. Some popular sites have direct connections to Dublin, including Enniskerry and Powerscourt House, Gardens, and Waterfall, which can be reached by taking the No. 44 bus from the Dublin quays area.

Numbers in the text correspond to numbers in the margin and on the Dublin Environs map.

Great Itineraries

IF YOU HAVE 3 DAYS

Begin your first day by traveling southward along N11 to **Powerscourt House, Gardens, and Waterfall** ⑲, the opulent Palladian mansion and garden estate, set under the great Sugar Loaf. Keep your spirits up, literally, by taking the road to **Roundwood** ⑳, the highest village in Ireland. Move on to the early Christian monastic settlement of **Glendalough** ㉑, set amid the tranquil Wicklow Mountains' forests. Follow R752 south to Rathnew and proceed to **Avoca** ㉕, where you can browse for wool fabric and apparel at Ireland's oldest mill. End your day in 🏨 **Wicklow Town** ㉓, north of Avoca on R754; or, if you want to remain Dublin based, return to the capital via N11.

Begin your second day with a visit to one of Ireland's grandest mansions, **Castletown House** ㉗ near Celbridge, easily reached via N4, with a left turn at Leixlip, followed by a 8-km (5-mi) drive down R403. Continue south and turn left at Clane until you reach **Naas** ㉙, where you turn left along R410 and go the short distance to Sir Alfred Beit's sumptuous **Russborough House** ㉚—a feast of Old Master paintings, Regency armoires, and Georgian stuccowork. Or, continue west toward **Kildare Town** ㉝, an elegant, prosperous town surrounded by the broad, flat plains of the **Curragh** ㉜. The **National Stud and Japanese Gardens,** just outside Kildare Town, are the real highlight of the area. If you spent your first night in Wicklow, return to Glendalough and proceed onward toward Kildare via the wonderfully scenic Wicklow Gap, a maze of winding roads that take you through the villages of Granabeg, Hollywood (no relation to its American namesake), and Kilcullen. Spend your second night either in nearby 🏨 **Straffan** ㉘ or back in 🏨 **Dublin.**

On your third day, head north of Dublin to Counties Meath and Louth via N3, which will take you to the **Hill of Tara** ②, one of Ireland's most important Celtic sites and home of the Irish kings just after the birth of Christ. Travel back another 2,000 years in time with a visit to **Newgrange** ⑤, home to the most important Neolithic passage tombs in Europe. On your way north to **Monasterboice** ⑩, where one of the finest high crosses in all of Ireland awaits, be sure to visit the small Georgian village of **Slane** ⑥. Make a stop along N51 at **King William's Glen** ⑦, site of the Battle of the Boyne in 1690 between the Catholic forces of King James II and the Protestant army of King William of Orange—a battle that shaped the course of Irish history. Return to Dublin via N2.

IF YOU HAVE 5 DAYS

Five days should give you ample opportunity to "take it aisy"—or, at least, to take it as easy as you can, considering the array of beautiful sights found in this part of the country. Make a stop in the coastal town of **Bray** ⑱, a Victorian seaside resort founded in the 1850s, before heading south toward **Powerscourt House, Gardens, and Waterfall** ⑲, **Roundwood** ⑳, and on to **Glendalough** ㉑. (If you haven't already explored the towns along Dublin Bay north of Bray but south of Dublin, consult the Side Trips section in Chapter 1 to decide whether or not to visit the County Dublin sights we cover in that section on your way

Dublin Environs

farther south.) For a taste of more recent history, follow N11 a few miles south to Rathnew and drive inland on R752 until you reach **Avondale Forest Park and House** ㉔, the home of the 19th-century Irish leader Charles Stewart Parnell. Stay overnight in 🖪 **Wicklow Town** ㉓, which dates back to Viking days, or near the 🖪 **Poulaphouca Reservoir** ㉛, home of the wonderful Rathsallagh House. If you have time, you may want to visit the seaside resort of **Arklow** ㉖ or the **Mount Usher Gardens** ㉒ northwest of Wicklow Town, off N11 beyond Rathnew. Spend your second day visiting the broad flatland of County Kildare, venturing as far south as **Ballytore** ㉟ and **Castledermot** ㊱ before spending the night in 🖪 **Straffan** ㉘. On your third day, set off for the Celtic and prehistoric sights of County Meath. Be sure to visit the 12th-century remains of **Mellifont Abbey** ⑨ near **Slane** ⑥, and the town of **Kells** ④, where Ireland's greatest treasure was unearthed from a bog. Overnight in historic 🖪 **Drogheda** ⑧. The following morning, travel north to 🖪 **Dundalk** ⑭, the border town of **Omeath** ⑰, and **Inniskeen** ⑬, home of poet Patrick Kavanagh. After lunch, take the **Cooley Peninsula Drive** ⑮ and visit the medieval fishing town of **Carlingford** ⑯, which should take up most of the afternoon. If possible, spend the night in Drogheda, returning to Dublin the next day via the ancient town of **Louth** ⑫ and the market town of **Ardee** ⑪.

When to Tour the Dublin Environs

The wild mountains of Wicklow and the flat pasturelands of Kildare are at their best in spring and summer. However, there is often higher rainfall in March and April. If you're planning to tour the towns and historic sites, winter is a good time to avoid the crush; bring warm clothing and boots, and be prepared for light snow on the hills.

NORTH OF DUBLIN IN THE BOYNE VALLEY

The great prehistoric, pagan, and Celtic monuments of the wide arc of fertile land known as the Boyne Valley excite a grand sense of wonder. As you'll discover, you don't have to be an archaeologist to be awed by Newgrange, Knowth, and Dowth—all set beside the River Boyne— or the sites of the Hill of Tara, Mellifont Abbey, and the high cross of Monasterboice. You might, as we suggest here, begin at Trim, the locale closest to Dublin, and work your way north. Keep in mind that Omeath and the scenic Cooley Peninsula at the end of this section are on the border of Northern Ireland. If you make it this far north, consult Chapter 8, particularly our coverage of the Mountains of Mourne, which are just across Carlingford Lough.

Trim

❶ *51 km (32 mi) northwest of Dublin via N3 to R154.*

Resting on the River Boyne, Trim has some of the finest medieval ruins in Ireland. In 1359, on the instructions of King Edward III, the town was walled and its fortifications strengthened; in the 15th century several parliaments subsequently were held here. Oliver Cromwell massacred most of its inhabitants when he captured the town in 1649. **Trim Castle,** the largest Anglo-Norman fortress in Ireland, dominates present-day Trim from its 2½-acre site, which slopes down to the river's placid waters. Built by Hugh de Lacy in 1173, the castle was soon destroyed and then rebuilt from 1190 to 1200. The ruins include an enormous keep with 70-ft-high turrets flanked by rectangular towers. The outer castle wall is almost 500 yards long, and five D-shape towers survive. The castle remains are freely accessible at all times. Facing the river is the **Royal Mint,** another ruin that illustrates Trim's political importance in the Middle Ages.

The **Yellow Steeple** overlooks Trim from a ridge opposite the castle. The structure was built in 1368 and is a remnant of the 13th-century Augustinian abbey of St. Mary's, which itself was the sight of a great medieval pilgrimage to a statue of the Blessed Virgin. Much of the tower was destroyed in 1649 to prevent its falling into Cromwell's hands, and today only the striking, 125-ft-high east wall remains. The Church of Ireland **St. Patrick's Cathedral** (⊠ Loman St.) dates from the early 19th century, but the square tower belongs to an earlier structure built in 1449. The Trim **visitor center's** "The Power and the Glory" audiovisual display tells the story of the arrival of the Normans and of medieval Trim. ⊠ *Mill St.,* ☎ *046/37227.* ⊡ *£2.50.* ⊙ *May–Sept., Wed.– Sun. 9:30–5; Oct.–Apr. by appointment.*

If your ancestors are from County Meath, take advantage of the family-history tracing service at the **Meath Heritage and Genealogy Center.** ⊠ *Mill St.,* ☎ *046/36633.* ⊡ *Free.* ⊙ *Mon.–Thurs. 9–5, Fri. 9–2.*

Several places east and south of Trim are also of interest. At **Newtown,** 1¼ km (¾ mi) east of Trim on the banks of the River Boyne, lie the ruins of what was the largest cathedral in Ireland, built beginning in 1210 by Simon de Rochfort, the first Anglo-Norman bishop of Meath. At **Laracor,** 3 km (2 mi) south of Trim on R158, a wall left of the rectory is where Jonathan Swift (1667–1745), the satirical writer, poet, and author of *Gulliver's Travels,* was rector from 1699 until 1714, when he was made dean of St. Patrick's Cathedral in Dublin. Nearby are the walls of the cottage where Esther Johnson, the "Stella" who inspired much of Swift's writings, once lived. One of the most pleasant villages of south County Meath, **Summerhill,** 8 km (5 mi) southeast of Laracor along R158, has a large square and a village green with a 15th-century cross. South of Summerhill is **Cnoc an Linsigh,** an attractive area of forest walks with picnic sites, ideal for a half day's meandering. Many of the lanes that crisscross this part of County Meath provide delightful driving between high hedgerows and afford occasional views of the lush, pastoral countryside.

Hill of Tara

❷ *14½ km (9 mi) east of Trim, 33 km (21 mi) northwest of Dublin on N3.*

At the meeting point of the five ancient roads of Ireland and known in popular folklore as the seat of the High Kings of Ireland, the Hill of Tara is one of the country's most important historic sites. The 19th-century ballad by Thomas Moore, "The Harp That Once Through Tara's Halls," was a factor in the over-romanticized view of Tara nearly up to recent times. Systematic excavation by 20th-century archaeologists has led to the less-exciting conclusion that the remains are those of an Iron Age fort that had multiple ring forts, some of which were ruined in the 19th century by religious zealots from England who believed they would find the Ark of the Covenant here. The "Mound of the Hostages," a Neolithic passage grave, most likely gave the place its sacred character. During the hill's reign as a royal seat, which lasted to the 11th century, a great *feis* (national assembly) was held here every three years, when laws were passed and tribal disputes were settled. Tara's decline was predicted one eventful Easter Eve in the 5th century on a night when, according to the Druid religion, no fires could be lit. Suddenly on a hillside some miles away, flames were spotted. "If that fire is not quenched now," said a Druid leader, "it will burn forever and will consume Tara." The fire seen by the court at Tara was lit by St. Patrick at Slane to celebrate the Christian rites of the Paschal. Tara's influence waned with the arrival of Christianity; the last king to live here was Malachy II, who died in 1022.

But like so many of the most prominent sites of the pagan, pre-Christian era, Christianity remade Tara in its own image. Today a modern statue of St. Patrick stands here, as does a pillar stone that may have been the coronation stone (it was reputed to call out in approval when a king was crowned). In the graveyard of the adjacent Anglican church, you'll find a pillar with the worn image of a pagan god and a Bronze Age stone standing on end. However, the main attraction is the Hill of Tara's height: it rises more than 300 ft above sea level, and from its top on a clear day, you can see across the flat central plain of Ireland, with the mountains of east Galway rising nearly 160 km (100 mi) away. In the mid-19th century, the nationalist leader Daniel O'Connell staged a mass rally that is said to have drawn more than a million people—nearly a third of Ireland's population today. In an old Church of Ireland church on the hillside, the **interpretative center** tells the story of Tara and its legends. This can be truly informative, for without expert assistance, it is difficult to identify many of the earthworks at Tara. ⊠ *Hill of Tara,* ☎ *046/25903.* ⊞ *£1.50.* ⊘ *May–mid-June and mid-Sept.– Oct., daily 10–5; mid-June–mid-Sept., daily 9:30–6:30.*

Navan

❸ *10 km (6 mi) northwest of the Hill of Tara on N3, 48 km (30 mi) north of Dublin on N3.*

A busy market and mining town with evidence of prehistoric settlements, Navan lies at the crucial juncture of the Rivers Blackwater and Boyne. It took off in the 12th century, when Hugh de Lacy, Lord of Trim, had the place walled and fortified, making it a defensive stronghold of the English Pale in eastern Ireland. It is now the administrative center of Meath. The Catholic **St. Mary's Church,** built in 1839, features a late-18th-century wood carving of the Crucifixion, the work of a local artist, Edward Smyth, who at the time was the greatest sculptor Ireland had produced since the Middle Ages. On Friday, the **Fair Green,** beside the church, is the site of a bustling outdoor market. ⊠ *Trimgate St.* ⊞ *Free.* ⊘ *Daily 8–8.*

The best views of town and the surrounding area are from the top of the **Motte of Navan,** a grassy mound that tradition—most likely apocryphal—holds to be the tomb of Odhbha, the deserted wife of a Celtic king who died of a broken heart. D'Angulo, the Norman baron, adapted it into a motte and baily.

Lodging

✑ *following the text of a review is your signal that the property has a Web site, where you will find details and, usually, images; for a link, visit www.fodors.com/urls.*

$$ 🏨 **Ardboyne Hotel.** Conveniently situated on its own grounds beside the main Dublin road (N3), this modern hotel is a good base for golfing, angling, and horse racing, as well as visiting local heritage sites, such as Newgrange (☞ *below*). The whole place has a casual, airy feel and rooms are a good size. ⊠ *Dublin Rd., Co. Meath,* ☎ *046/23119,* 🖷 *046/22355. 29 rooms with bath. Restaurant, bar. AE, MC, V.* ✑

Kells

4 *16 km (10 mi) northwest of Navan on N3.*

In the 9th century, a group of monks from Iona in Scotland took refuge at Kells (Ceanannus Mór) after being expelled by the Danes. St. Columba had founded a monastery here 300 years earlier, and while some historians think the indigenous monks wrote and illustrated the *Book of Kells*—the Latin version of the four Gospels and one of Ireland's greatest medieval treasures—most scholars now believe that the Scottish monks brought it with them. Reputed to have been fished out of a watery bog at Kells, the legendary manuscript was removed for safekeeping during the Cromwellian wars to Trinity College, Dublin, where it remains. A large exhibit is now devoted to it in the college's Old Library, where a few of the original pages at a time are on view (☞ Exploring Dublin *in* Chapter 1). A facsimile copy of the *Book of Kells* is on display in the Church of Ireland **St. Columba's,** in Kells. Four elaborately carved high crosses stand in the church graveyard, while the stump of a fifth is in the marketplace; during the 1798 uprising against British rule, it was used as a gallows.

St. Colmcille's House, a small, two-story, 7th-century church measuring about 24 ft square and nearly 40 ft high, with a steeply pitched stone roof, is similar in appearance to St. Kevin's Church at Glendalough (☞ County Wicklow's Coast and Mountains, *below*) and Cormac's Chapel at Cashel (☞ Chapter 4). Adjacent to St. Colmcille's House, the nearly 100-ft-high **round tower,** which dates prior to 1076, is in almost perfect condition. Its top story has five windows, each facing an ancient entrance to the medieval town.

Dining and Lodging

$ ✕⌑ **Lennoxbrook.** This fine, 200-year-old-plus farmhouse is run by Pauline Mullan, whose children are the fifth generation of the family to occupy the home. A casual, friendly mood prevails throughout the house. Upstairs, the four rooms are decorated with finely patterned wallpaper and period furniture. Lamb and produce are often on the dinner menu (£12 extra). The house, 5 km (3 mi) north of Kells on N3, is convenient to Newgrange. The prehistoric forts, passage graves, and other remains dating from 2000 BC on the Loughcrew Hills are a 15-minute drive away. ✉ *Co. Meath,* ☎ *046/45902. 4 rooms with bath. Dining room. MC, V.*

Newgrange

★ **5** *11⅓ km (7 mi) east of Navan on N51, 24 km (15 mi) east of Kells.*

Newgrange is one of the most spectacular prehistoric tombs in Europe. Built in the 4th millennium BC, which makes it roughly 1,000 years older than Stonehenge, Newgrange was constructed with some 250,000 tons of stones, the nearest source of which was the Wicklow Mountains south of Dublin. How the people who built this tumulus transported the stones here remains a mystery. The mound above the tomb measures more than 330 ft across and is 36 ft high at the front. White quartz stones—somehow hauled the 80 km (50 mi) from the mountains of Wicklow to the south—were used for the retaining wall, while egg-shape gray stones were studded at intervals. The passage grave may have been the world's earliest observatory. It was so carefully constructed that, for five days on and around the winter solstice, the rays of the rising sun still hit a roof box above the lintel at the entrance to the grave.

The rays then shine for about 20 minutes down the main interior passageway to illuminate the burial chamber. The site was first restored in 1962 after years of neglect and quarrying. A visit to the passage grave during the winter solstice is considered by many to be the most memorable experience of all, in part due to the luck needed to witness the illumination. There is a nine-year waiting list for one of the 24 places available on each of the five mornings (December 19–23)—and even if you have a place, there is no guarantee that the sun won't be obscured by clouds! However, visitors to the interior of this Bronze Age tomb can also see the effect artificially re-created. The geometric designs on some stones at the center of the burial chamber continue to baffle experts.

The prehistoric sites of nearby Dowth and Knowth have been under excavation since 1962, and although Dowth is still closed to the public, the partially excavated site at **Knowth** is open between May 1 and October 31. It is far larger and more diversified than the more famous Newgrange tomb, with a huge central mound and 17 smaller ones. About one-third of the site has been excavated, and you can watch archaeologists at work on the rest of the site. The earliest tombs and carved stones date from the Stone Age (3000 BC), although the site was in use until the early 14th century. In the early Christian era (4th–8th centuries AD) it was the seat of the High Kings of Ireland. Access to Newgrange and Knowth is solely via **Brú na Bóinne** ("palace of the Boyne"), the Boyne Valley visitor center. ⊠ *Donore, off N2, signposted from Slane,* ☎ *041/982–4488.* 🎟 *Newgrange and interpretive center £3; Knowth and interpretive center £2; Newgrange, Knowth, and interpretive center £5.* 🕙 *Newgrange May, daily 9:30–6:30; June–mid-Sept., daily 9:30–7; mid-Sept.–Feb., daily 10–4:30; Mar.–Apr., daily 10–5. Knowth June–mid-Sept., daily 9–7; May and mid-Sept.–end of Sept., daily 9–6:30; Mar., Apr., and Oct., daily 9:30–5:30; Nov.–Feb., daily 9:30–5.* 🐾

Slane

❻ *2½ km (1½ mi) north of Newgrange, 46 km (29 mi) northwest of Dublin on N2.*

The small, Georgian village of Slane was built in the 18th century around a crossroads on the north side of the River Boyne. The **Conyngham Arms Hotel** (☎ 041/988–4444), at the crossroads in Slane, is an agreeable, family-run establishment that serves a buffet from noon to 3 and a bar menu throughout the day. The 16th-century building known as the **Hermitage** was constructed on the site where St. Erc, a local man who was converted to Christianity by St. Patrick, led a hermit's existence. All that remains of his original monastery is the faint trace of the circular ditch that surrounded it. **Slane Castle,** beautifully situated overlooking a natural amphitheater, was badly damaged in a 1991 fire and is now closed to the public. Back in 1981, the castle's owner, Anglo-Irish Lord Henry Mountcharles, staged the first of what have been some of Ireland's largest rock concerts; U2, still only one album old, had second billing to Thin Lizzy that year. Most of rock's greatest names have performed here since, including Bob Dylan, Bruce Springsteen, David Bowie, and the Rolling Stones—REM's 1995 show holds the record for attendance, with 70,000. The venue was closed indefinitely following the 1995 show, due in part to protests by locals, who complained that the masses of fans descending upon this quiet town were like marauding armies bent on destruction.

North of Slane town is the 500-ft-high **Slane Hill,** where St. Patrick proclaimed the arrival of Christianity in 433 by lighting the Paschal Fire.

From the top, you have sweeping views of the Boyne Valley. On a clear day, the panorama stretches from Trim to Drogheda, a vista extending 40 km (25 mi).

King William's Glen

❼ *7½ km (4½ mi) east of Slane on N51.*

On the northern bank of the River Boyne, King William's Glen is where a portion of King William's Protestant army hid before the Battle of the Boyne in 1690. They won by surprising the Catholic troops of James II, who were on the southern side, but many of the Protestant-Catholic conflicts in present-day Northern Ireland can be traced to the immediate aftermath of this battle. The site is marked with an orange and green sign, while part is also incorporated in the nearby, early 19th-century **Townley Hall Estate,** which has forest walks and a nature trail.

Drogheda

❽ *6½ km (4 mi) east of King William's Glen on N51, 45 km (28 mi) north of Dublin on N1.*

One of the most enjoyable historic towns on the east coast of Ireland, Drogheda (pronounced draw-*hee*-da) was colonized in 911 by the Danish Vikings. Two centuries later, the town was taken over by Hugh de Lacy, the Anglo-Norman lord of Trim (☞ *above*) who was responsible for fortifying many locales up and down the River Boyne. At first, two separate towns existed on the northern and southern banks of the river. In 1412, already heavily walled and fortified, Drogheda was unified, making it the largest English town in Ireland. Today, large 18th-century warehouses line the northern bank of the Boyne. Towering over the river is the long **railway viaduct.** Built around 1850 as part of the railway line from Dublin to Belfast, it is still used and is a splendid example of Victorian engineering. Because of its height above the river, the viaduct remains Drogheda's most prominent landmark.

The center of the town, around West Street, is the historic heart of Drogheda. The bank building on the corner of West and Shop streets, called the **Tholsel,** is an 18th-century, square granite edifice with a cupola. **St. Laurence's Gate,** one of the two surviving entrances from Drogheda's original 11 gates in its town walls, has two four-story drum towers and is one of the most perfect examples in Ireland of a medieval town gate. **Butler's Gate,** near the Millmount Museum (☞ *below*), predates St. Laurence's Gate by 50 years or more.

The Gothic Revival, Roman Catholic **St. Peter's Church** (✉ West St.) houses the preserved head of St. Oliver Plunkett. Primate of all Ireland, he was martyred in 1681 at Tyburn in London, where his head was pulled from the execution flames. A severe, 18th-century church within an enclosed courtyard, the Anglican **St. Peter's** (✉ Fair St.) is rarely open except for Sunday services. It's worth a peek for its setting and the fine views over the town from the churchyard.

Off the Dublin road (N1) south of Drogheda, the **Millmount Museum** shares space in a renovated British Army barracks with crafts workshops, including a pottery and picture gallery and studio. Relics of eight centuries of Drogheda's commercial and industrial past are on display, including painted banners of the old trade guilds; a circular willow and leather coracle (the traditional fishing boat on the River Boyne); and many instruments and utensils from domestic and factory use. Surprisingly, the museum does not have many mementos of the most infamous episode in Drogheda's history, when the English leader Oliver Cromwell sacked the town in 1649, killing 3,000 people. During the attack, Sir Arthur Aston, the town garrison leader and a staunch royalist, was beaten to death with his own wooden leg. ⊠ *Millmount,* ☎ *041/983–3097.* ⛆ *£2.50.* ☉ *Mon.–Sat. 10–6, Sun. 2:30–5:30.*

Dining and Lodging

$$ ✕ **Buttergate.** Traditional Irish dishes are served at lunch and dinner, while tasty "light bites" are available throughout the day. If plans to extend the small conservatory go forward, the splendid view over the town and the River Boyne will make this one a must-visit while you're in Drogheda. It's next to the Millmount Museum. ⊠ *Millmount,* ☎ *041/983–4759. MC, V.*

$$ ✕🖭 **Boyne Valley Hotel and Country Club.** Once owned by a Drogheda brewing family, this 19th-century mansion sits on 16 acres and is approached via a 1-km (½-mi) drive. The newer wing of the hotel has double rooms, all with contemporary furnishings. A large conservatory houses a bar and overlooks the grounds, while a large hall is decorated with antiques and comfy chairs. The Cellar Restaurant specializes in fresh fish. ⊠ *Dublin Rd., Co. Louth,* ☎ *041/983–7737,* 𝖥𝖠𝖷 *041/983– 9188. 71 rooms with bath. Restaurant, bar, indoor pool, hot tub, sauna, steam room, 18-hole golf course, 2 tennis courts, health club. AE, DC, MC, V.* ✎

En Route   From Drogheda's center, follow R167 north along the northern bank of the River Boyne for 11 km (7 mi) to **Baltray,** which still closely resembles an 18th-century Irish fishing village. From here, continue north another 8 km (5 mi) to the fishing village of **Clogherhead.** Take a walk above the local harbor to the heights of Clogher Head for outstanding views north to the Mountains of Mourne (☞ Chapter 8) and south to Skerries.

Mellifont Abbey

❾ *11 km (7 mi) north of Newgrange on N2, 8 km (5 mi) west of Drogheda on R168.*

On the eastern bank of the River Mattock, which creates a natural border between Counties Meath and Louth here, lie the remains of Mellifont Abbey, the first Cistercian monastery in Ireland. Founded in 1142 by St. Malachy, Archbishop of Armagh, it was inspired by the formal structure around a central courtyard of St. Bernard of Clairvaux's monastery, which St. Malachy had visited. Among the substantial ruins are the two-story chapter house, built in 12th-century English-Norman style and once a daily meeting place for the monks; it now houses a collection of medieval glazed tiles. Four walls of the 13th-century octagonal lavabo, or washing place, still stand, as do some arches from the Romanesque cloister. At its peak Mellifont presided over almost 40 other Cistercian monasteries throughout Ireland, but all were suppressed by Henry VIII in 1539 after his break with the Catholic Church. Adjacent to the car park is a small **architectural museum** depicting the history of the abbey and the craftsmanship that went into its construction. ⊠ *Near Collon,* ☎ *041/982–6459.* ⛆ *£1.50.* ☉ *May–mid-June and mid-Sept.–Oct., daily 10–5; mid-June–mid-Sept., daily 9:30–6:30.*

Dining

$$$ ✕ **Forge Gallery Restaurant.** In a converted forge in Collon, north of Slane on N2, this well-established restaurant is decorated in warm rose and plum tones and antique furnishings, while an old fireplace throws comforting warmth and light. The cuisine mixes French Provençale with

a strong hint of traditional Irish cooking. Two popular specialties are salmon and crab in phyllo pastry and prawns and scallops in a cream and garlic sauce. Be sure to try one of the seasonal homemade soups. Paintings in the reception area, done by local artists, are for sale. ⊠ *Collon,* ☎ *041/982–6272. Reservations essential on weekends. AE, DC, MC, V. Closed Sun.–Mon. and last two wks. of Jan.*

Monasterboice

⑩ *8 km (5 mi) northeast of Mellifont Abbey on N1, 17 km (11 mi) northeast of Slane.*

Ireland has more carved-stone high crosses than any other European country, and an outstanding collection is in the small, secluded village of Monasterboice. Dated to AD 923, the **Muireadach Cross** stands nearly 20 ft high and is considered to be the best-preserved example of a high cross anywhere in Ireland. Its elaborate panels depict biblical scenes, including Cain slaying Abel, David and Goliath, and a centerpiece of the Last Judgment. (Figurative scenes are not a characteristic of earlier high crosses, such as those found in Ahenny, County Clare, which are elaborately ornamented but without figures.) From the adjacent, 110-ft-high **round tower,** the extent of the former monastic settlement at Monasterboice is apparent. The key to the tower door is held at the nearby gate lodge.

Ardee

⑪ *14½ km (9 mi) north of Monasterboice on N2.*

The market town of Ardee, formerly at the northern edge of the Pale, has a broad main street and two 13th-century castles. **Ardee Castle** (the one with square corners) was converted into a courthouse in the 19th century. **Hatch's Castle** (with rounded corners) is a private residence and not open to the public. **St. Mary's Church of Ireland** on Main Street incorporates part of a 13th-century Carmelite church burned by Edward Bruce in early 1316.

Dining

$$ ✕ **Gables House and Restaurant.** Off N2, not far from the Dundalk junction, this family-run spot has traditional decor, with antique mahogany furniture, deep-burgundy velvet curtains, and oil paintings by local artists. Polished tables, silver cutlery, linen napkins, lace coasters, and gleaming leaded-crystal glasses add elegance. Expect generous portions and a French-influenced cooking style. The catch of the day is often monkfish, halibut, or sole. The Gables Medley, made up of cheesecake, profiteroles, and homemade ice cream, is a satisfying way to get a sugar rush. ⊠ *Dundalk Rd.,* ☎ *041/985–3789. MC, V.*

Louth

⑫ *11½ km (7 mi) north of Ardee on R171.*

St. Patrick, Ireland's patron saint, was reputed to have built his first church in the hilltop village of Louth in the 5th century and to have made St. Mochta (d. 534) the first bishop of Louth. Standing at the center of the village is the excellently preserved **St. Mochta's House,** an oratory dating from the 11th century, which has a steeply pitched stone roof that can be reached by a stairway. The house is freely accessible, but visitors should watch out for cattle in the surrounding field.

Inniskeen

 6½ km (4 mi) north of Louth.

On the road to Dundalk and just over the Louth county boundary in Monaghan, Inniskeen is a small farming town that acts as a social hearth for the area's far-flung community. Patrick Kavanagh (1906–69), the area's most famous poet, is commemorated at the **Inniskeen Folk Museum,** housed in a converted church next to a round tower. Born and raised here, Kavanagh immortalized the town in his early poem "Inniskeen Road"—where as a child he spied on young lovers and their "wink and elbow language of delight"—before becoming one of Ireland's leading poets. He was brought back to the village for burial. ☎ *042/937-8109. ⌑ Donations accepted. ☺ May–Sept., Sun. 3–6, or by appointment.*

Dundalk

 14½ km (9 mi) east of Inniskeen, 80 km (50 mi) north of Dublin on N1.

Dundalk, the main town of County Louth (Ireland's smallest county), dates from the early Christian period, around the 7th century. The area near the town is closely connected with Cuchulainn (pronounced coo-cullen)—"a greater hero than Hercules or Achilles," as Frank McCourt, in *Angela's Ashes,* recalls his father claiming. Today, Dundalk is a thriving, if uninspiring, frontier town—only 9½ km (6 mi) from the Northern Ireland border—with some fine historic buildings. On Mill Street, the **bell tower** of a Franciscan monastery with Gothic windows dates from the 13th century. The **Market House,** the **Town Hall,** and the **Courthouse** are examples of the town's 19th-century heritage; the Courthouse is the most impressive of the three, built in the 1820s in a severe Greek Revival style, with Doric columns supporting the portico. It stands north of St. Patrick's Cathedral.

The Catholic **St. Patrick's Cathedral** was built between 1835 and 1847, when the Gothic Revival was at its height. It is modeled on the 15th-century King's College Chapel (at Cambridge, England), with its buttresses and mosaics lining the chancel and the side chapel walls. The fine exterior was built in Newry granite, and the high altar and pulpit are of carved Caen stone. ⌑ *Town center. ☺ Daily 8–6.*

The Church of Ireland's **St. Nicholas** incorporates a 15th-century tower. The church was rebuilt in 1707 and has a large, early 19th-century transept. In the graveyard lies the tomb of Agnes Galt, sister of Robert Burns, the 18th-century Scottish poet. ⌑ *Market Sq. ☺ During services only.*

The **Dundalk County Museum** is dedicated to preserving the history of the dying local industries, such as beer brewing, cigarette manufacturing, shoe and boot making, and railway engineering. Other exhibits deal with the history of Louth from 7500 BC to the present. ⌑ *Joycelyn St.,* ☎ *042/932-7056. ⌑ £3. ☺ May–Sept., Mon.–Sat. 10:30–5:30, Sun. 2–6; Oct.–Apr., Tues.–Sat. 10:30–5:30, Sun. 2–6.*

OFF THE
BEATEN PATH
ARDGILLAN DEMESNE – Across the Louth border in County Dublin, 18 km (13 mi) south of Dundalk, Ardgillan Demesne is one of the prettiest parks along the coast. Its 194 acres consist of rolling pastures, mixed woodland, and gardens overlooking the Bay of Drogheda, with splendid views of the coastline. The castle was built in 1738 for the Taylor family, one of the principal landowners of the northeast, and consists of two stories over a basement that extends out under the south lawns. The

ground-floor rooms are decorated in Georgian and Victorian styles; the first-floor rooms are home to a permanent display of 17th-century maps and host an annual program of exhibitions. ⊠ *Balbriggan,* ☎ *01/849–2212.* 🖭 *£2.75.* ☉ *Apr.–June and Sept., Tues.–Sun. 11–6; Oct.–Mar., Tues.–Sun. 11–4:30.*

Dining and Lodging

$$ ✕🏨 **Ballymascanlon House Hotel.** On 130 acres on the scenic Cooley Peninsula just north of Dundalk, this converted Victorian mansion has long had a fine reputation for comfort and good cuisine. Rooms are large and furnished with reproduction period pieces. The restaurant serves Irish and French cuisine and specializes in fresh seafood entrées, such as lobster in season; vegetarian plates are also available. ⊠ *Dundalk, Co. Louth,* ☎ *042/937–1124,* 𝔽𝔸𝕏 *042/937–1598. 74 rooms with bath. Restaurant, 2 bars, indoor pool, hot tub, sauna, steam room, 18-hole golf course, 2 tennis courts, health club. AE, DC, MC, V.* 🐾

Cooley Peninsula Drive

⓯ *Beginning in Dundalk, 80 km (50 mi) north of Dublin, 35 km (22 mi) north of Drogheda.*

If you have a car and three or four free hours, the scenic drive around the Cooley Peninsula has some of the finest views of the east coast of Ireland. This is a 64-km (40-mi) round-trip beginning and ending in Dundalk. Beyond the Carlingford Lough on the north side of the peninsula, the Mountains of Mourne rise in the distance. From **Gyles Quay,** a small coastal village with a clean, safe beach, you'll have excellent views southward along the County Louth coast to Clogher Head. A road winds east around the Cooley Peninsula to **Greenore,** a town built in Victorian times as a ferryboat terminal. Today it has become a port for container traffic.

Carlingford

⓰ *6½ km (4 mi) south of Omeath on R173, 21 km (13 mi) from Dundalk.*

The small, medieval fishing town of Carlingford still has some striking thatched cottages, but what makes it particularly attractive is its natural setting. The mountains of the Cooley Peninsula back right up to the town, the Carlingford Lough lies at its feet, and the Mountains of Mourne rise only 5 km (3 mi) away across the lough.

A massive, 13th-century fortress that rises up over the entrance to Carlingford Lough, **King John's Castle** has an unusual feature: its west gateway is only wide enough to admit one horseman. At present, of the historic buildings in the town, only the castle is freely accessible to the public. Other remnants from the area's medieval days include a tower from the town wall and one of its gates, which later became the town hall; the 15th-century **Mint Tower House,** with mullioned windows; and **Taaffe's Castle,** a 16th-century fortified town house.

Omeath

⓱ *6½ km (4 mi) northwest of Carlingford on R173.*

The northernmost town on Cooley Peninsula, Omeath was until recently the last main Gaeltacht (Irish-speaking) village in this part of Ireland (most extant Gaeltacht villages are in the Southwest and the West). On the eastern side of the village, you'll find open-air **stations of the cross** at the monastery of the Rosminian Fathers. Jaunting cars (traps pulled by ponies) take visitors to the site from the quayside, which has stalls selling all kinds of shellfish from the nearby lough, including oysters and mussels. A ferry service runs from the quay to Warrenpoint, across the lough in Northern Ireland.

A narrow road climbs the mountains behind Omeath. As you climb higher, the views become ever more spectacular, stretching over the Mountains of Mourne in the north and as far south as Skerries, 32 km (20 mi) north of Dublin. This narrow road leads back to Dundalk.

COUNTY WICKLOW'S COAST AND MOUNTAINS

Make your way to the fourth or fifth story of almost any building in Dublin that faces south and you'll see off in the distance—though amazingly not *that* far off in the distance—the green, smooth hills of the Dublin and Wicklow mountains. On a clear day the mountains are even visible from some streets in and around the city center. If your idea of solace is green hills, and your visit to Ireland is otherwise limited to Dublin, County Wicklow—or Cill Mhantain, as it is known in Irish—should be on your itinerary.

Not that the secret isn't out: rugged and mountainous with dark, wooded forests, central Wicklow is known as the "garden of Ireland" and is a popular picnic area with Dubliners. Set with some of Ireland's grandest 18th-century mansions, it also cradles one of the country's earliest Christian retreats: Glendalough. Nestled in a valley of dense woods and placid lakes, Glendalough and environs can seem (at least during the off-season) practically untouched since their heyday 1,000 years ago. The same granite mountains that have protected Glendalough all these years run into the sea along the east coast, which is home to several popular sandy beaches. Journey from Dublin down to Arklow, sticking to the east side of the Wicklow Mountains. A quick note about getting here: it takes stamina to extract yourself from the unmarked maze of the Dublin exurbs (your best bet is to take N11, which becomes M11, and then again N11), but once you've accomplished that feat, this gorgeous, mysterious terrain awaits.

Bray

⑱ *22 km (14 mi) south of Dublin on N11, 8 km (5 mi) east of Enniskerry on R755.*

One of Ireland's oldest seaside resorts, Bray is a trim village known for its dilapidated summer cottages and sand-and-shingle beach, which stretches 2 km (1 mi). When the trains first arrived from Dublin in 1854, Bray became the number one spot for urban vacationers and subsequently took on the appearance of an English oceanfront town. Some Dubliners still flock to the faded glory of Bray's boardwalk to push baby carriages and soak up the sun. It's the terminus of the DART train from Dublin, so it's easy to get here without a car. Opposite the Royal Hotel, the **heritage center** in the town hall houses artifacts from Bray's history, including old photographs and household items. ⊠ *Lower Main St.,* ☎ *01/286–6796.* ☑ *Free.* ☉ *May–Sept., weekdays 9–5, Sat. 10–4; Oct.–Apr., weekdays 9:30–1 and 2–4:30, Sat. 10–4.*

One Martello Terrace (☎ 01/286–8407), at the harbor, is Bray's most famous address. James Joyce (1882–1941) lived here between 1887 and 1891 and used the house as the setting for the Christmas dinner in *A Portrait of the Artist as a Young Man* (☞ Close-Up: ReJoyce! A Walk through James Joyce's Dublin and *Ulysses in* Chapter 1). Today the house is privately owned by an Irish Teachta Dála (member of Parliament, informally known as a "TD"). The phone number we list rings into her constituency office, and someone there should be able to help scholars and devotees arrange a visit; call on Thursday 10 AM–1 PM. Although the residence has been renovated, the dining room portrayed in Joyce's novel still maintains the spirit of his time.

National Sealife is an aquarium and museum dedicated to the creatures of the sea, with an emphasis on those that occupy the waters around Ireland. Besides massive sea tanks containing all manner of swimming things, there's a major conservation project with captive breeding of sea horses. FinZone is an undersea adventure trail perfect for kids, with puzzles to solve. Touch-screen computers and video games give the whole thing a high-tech feel. In winter check opening times before visiting. ⊠ *Strand Rd.,* ☎ *01/286–6939.* ☜ *£5.50.* ☉ *Daily 10–6.*

At **Killruddery House** you'll find rare, 17th-century gardens, precisely arranged, with fine beech hedges, Victorian statuary, and a parterre of lavender and roses. The estate, which still belongs to the Earl of Meath, also has a Crystal Palace conservatory. ⊠ *Killruddery, off the Bray–Greystones Rd., 3 km (2 mi) south of Bray,* ☎ *01/286–2777.* ☜ *House and gardens £4, gardens only £2.* ☉ *Gardens Apr.–Sept., daily 1–5; house May–June and Sept., daily 1–5; by appointment at other times.*

Dining

$$$ ✕ **Tree of Idleness.** This Greek-Cypriot restaurant, a 10-minute walk
★ from Bray's DART train station, is a pleasant dining spot on the ground floor of a Victorian house along the seafront. It specializes in classic dishes and tasty, hearty portions. The roast suckling pig with caramelized apples is highly recommended. The extensive wine list includes Greek and Cypriot house wines. ⊠ *Seafront,* ☎ *01/286–3498. AE, MC, V. Closed Mon., last wk in Aug., 1st wk in Sept. No lunch.*

$ ✕ **Poppies Country Cooking.** Following the success of their remark-
★ able restaurant in Enniskerry (☞ Powerscourt House, Gardens, and Waterfall, *below*), the owners of Poppies decided to open a second restaurant with the same name in Greystones, an old-fashioned seaside resort only a couple of miles south of Bray along the coast. The ceilings are high, the space is airy and bright, and the food is absolutely delicious. If you can, dine here in summer, when you can avail yourself of the sun-drenched garden terrace. ⊠ *1 Trafalgar Sq., Greystones,* ☎ *01/287–4228. No credit cards.*

Outdoor Activities and Sports

The mountains bordering Bray to the south are laced with uncrowded hiking and mountain-bike trails. One of the best is a well-marked path that leads from the beach to the 10-ft-tall cross that crowns the spiny peak of Bray Head, a rocky outcrop that rises 791 ft from the sea. The semidifficult, one-hour climb affords stunning views of Wicklow Town and Dublin Bay.

Powerscourt House, Gardens, and Waterfall

★ ☺ ⑲ *25 km (16 mi) south of Dublin on R117, 22 km (14 mi) north of Glendalough on R755.*

Within the shadow of the famous Sugar Loaf mountain and one of the prettiest villages in Ireland, **Enniskerry** is built around a sloping central triangular square and surrounded by the wooded Wicklow Mountains. The main reason to visit the area around Enniskerry is the **Powerscourt Estate.** The grounds were originally granted to Sir Richard Wingfield, the first viscount of Powerscourt, by King James I of England in 1609. Richard Castle, the architect of Russborough House (☞ *below*), designed Powerscourt House in a grand Palladian style, and it was constructed between 1731 and 1743. Alas, the house was gutted in a fire in 1974 immediately following a long period of restoration by the Slazenger family. It's undergoing an extensive re-restoration; the original ballroom on the first floor— once "the grandest room in any Irish house," according to historian Desmond Guinness— is the only room that gives a sense of the house's former life.

Powerscourt Gardens, considered among the finest in Europe, were first laid out from 1745 to 1767 following the completion of the house and then were radically redesigned in the Victorian style from 1843 to 1875. The redesign was the work of the eccentric, boozy Daniel Robertson, who liked to be tootled around the gardens-in-progress in a wheelbarrow while nipping at his bottle of sherry. He was inspired by the Villa Butera in Sicily, and the gardens thus comprise sweeping terraces, antique sculptures, and a circular pond and fountain flanked by winged horses. There is a celebrated view of the Italianate patterned ramps, lawns, and pond across the beautiful, heavily wooded Dargle Valley, which stairsteps to the horizon and the noble profile of Sugar Loaf mountain. The grounds include many specimen trees (plants grown for exhibition), an avenue of monkey puzzles, a parterre of brightly colored summer flowers, and a Japanese garden. The kitchen gardens, with their modest rows of flowers, are a striking antidote to the classical formality of the main sections. A self-serve restaurant, crafts center, garden center, and a children's play area are also on the grounds. (Enniskerry can also be reached directly from Dublin by taking the No. 44 bus from the Dublin quays area.) ⊠ *Enniskerry,* ☎ *01/204–6000.* ▦ *Mar.–Oct. £5, Nov.–Feb. £3.50.* ⊙ *Mar.–Oct., daily 9:30–5:30; Nov.–Feb., daily 9:30–dusk.* ✎

One of the most inspiring sights to the writers and artists of the Romantic generation, the 400-ft **Powerscourt Waterfall,** 5 km (3 mi) south of the gardens (☞ *above*), is the highest in the British Isles. ⊠ *Enniskerry.* ▦ *£2.* ⊙ *Mar.–Oct., daily 9:30–7; Nov.–Feb., daily 10:30–dusk. Closed 2 wks before Christmas.*

Dining

$ ✕ **Poppies Country Cooking.** Like something out of a fairy tale, this
★ charming café is the perfect spot for breakfast, lunch, or late-afternoon tea. It's a cozy place, with a low, pine-paneled ceiling; floral wallpaper and matching cloth lamp shades; and pine farmhouse furniture. Potato cakes, shepherd's pie, lasagna, vegetarian quiche, a variety of house salads (you can order a sampler plate), and the day's soup are the usual fare. The homemade desserts—caramel squares, lemon meringue pie, pavlova—are terrific. You'll be tempted to sit here for hours writing postcards and daydreaming. ⊠ *The Square, Enniskerry,* ☎ *01/282–8869. No credit cards.*

Roundwood

⓴ *18 km (13 mi) south of Enniskerry on R755.*

At 800 ft above sea level and set amid spectacular scenery, Roundwood is the highest village in Ireland. The Sunday-afternoon market held in the village hall, where cakes, jams, and other homemade goods are sold, livens up what is otherwise a sleepy place. From the broad main street, by the Roundwood Inn (☞ Dining, *below*), a minor road leads west for 8 km (5 mi) to two lakes, **Lough Dan** and **Lough Tay,** lying deep between forested mountains like Norwegian fjords.

Dining

$$$ ✕ **Roundwood Inn.** This 17th-century inn, furnished in a traditional
★ style, with wooden floors, dark furniture, and diamond-shape windows, is best known for good, reasonably priced bar food ($) eaten at sturdy

tables beside an open fire. The restaurant offers a combination of Continental and Irish cuisines, reflecting the traditions of the German proprietor, Jurgen Schwalm, and his Irish wife, Aine. The separate bar and lounge also serve an excellent menu that includes a succulent seafood platter of salmon, oysters, lobster, and shrimp. ⊠ *Main St., Roundwood village center,* ☎ *01/281–8107. Reservations essential for restaurant. AE, MC, V. Restaurant closed Sun. dinner and Mon. except public holidays.*

Glendalough

★ ㉑   *54 km (34 mi) south of Dublin on R117 and R755, 9½ km (6 mi) southwest of Roundwood.*

One of Ireland's premier monastic sites, Glendalough is nestled in a lush, quiet valley deep in the rugged Wicklow Mountains. Set around two lakes, evergreen and deciduous trees, and acres of windswept heather, Glendalough flourished as a monastic center from the 6th century until 1398, when English soldiers plundered the site, leaving the ruins that you see today. (The monastery survived earlier 9th- and 10th-century Viking attacks.) Glendalough's founder was St. Kevin (Coemghein, or "fair begotten" in Irish), a descendant of the royal house of Leinster, who renounced the world and came here to live as a hermit before opening the monastery in 550. Note that in high season, hordes of visitors to Glendalough can make it difficult to appreciate the quiet solitude that brought Kevin to this valley. The **visitor center** is a good place to orient yourself and pick up a useful pamphlet. Many of the ruins are clumped together beyond the visitor center, but some of the oldest surround the Upper Lake, where signed paths direct you through spectacular scenery absent of crowds. Most ruins are open all day and are freely accessible.

Probably the oldest building on the site, presumed to date from St. Kevin's time, is the **Teampaill na Skellig** (Church of the Oratory), on the south shore of the **Upper Lake.** A little to the east is **St. Kevin's Bed,** a tiny cave in the rock face, about 30 ft above the level of the lake, where St. Kevin lived his hermit's existence. It is not easily accessible; you approach the cave by boat, but climbing the cliff to the cave can be dangerous and is not recommended. At the southeast corner of the Upper Lake is **Reefert Church,** also dating from the 11th century, whose ruins consist of a nave and a chancel. The saint also lived in the adjoining, ruined beehive hut with five crosses, which marked the original boundary of the monastery. There's a superb view of the valley from here.

The ruins by the edge of the **Lower Lake** are the most important of those at Glendalough. The **gateway,** beside the Glendalough Hotel (☞ Lodging, *below*), is the only surviving entrance to an ancient monastic site anywhere in Ireland. An extensive graveyard lies within, with hundreds of elaborately decorated crosses, as well as a perfectly preserved, six-story **round tower.** Built in the 11th or 12th century, it stands 100 ft high, with an entrance 25 ft above ground level.

The largest building at Glendalough is the substantially intact, 7th- to 9th-century **cathedral,** where you'll find the nave (small for a large church, only 30 ft wide by 50 ft long), chancel, and ornamental oolite limestone window, which may have been imported from England. South of the cathedral is the 11-ft-high Celtic **St. Kevin's Cross.** Made of granite, it is the best-preserved such cross on the site. **St. Kevin's Church** is an early, barrel-vaulted oratory with a high-pitched stone roof.

A note about getting here directly from Dublin: you can take the **St. Kevin's** bus service (☞ Getting Around *in* Dublin Environs A to Z, *below*). If you're driving from Dublin, consider taking the scenic route along R155 (☞ Dublin Environs A to Z, *below*), which includes awesome, austere mountaintop passes. Don't drive this route if you're in a hurry, and don't look for a lot of signage—just concentrate on the glorious views. ☎ *0404/45325.* ⌷ *£2.* ⊙ *Mar.–May and Sept.–Oct., daily 9:30–6; June–Aug., daily 9–6:30; Nov.–Feb., daily 9:30–5; last admission 15 mins before closing.* ✎

Dining and Lodging

$$ ✕⊞ **Glendalough Hotel.** Purists object to how close this old-fashioned, early 19th-century hotel lies to the ruins at Glendalough, but to others it's a convenience. Some of the bedrooms, decorated in quiet, pastel colors, overlook the monastery and the wooded mountain scenery; the burble of running water from the Glendassan River audibly enhances the experience. The restaurant also has views of the grounds. The menu is simple but portions are hearty, and the pub is the only one for miles around. ⊠ *Co. Wicklow,* ☎ *0404/45135,* FAX *0404/45142. 44 rooms with bath. Restaurant, bar, fishing. AE, DC, MC, V. Closed Jan. and 2nd wk in Dec..* ✎

Mount Usher Gardens

㉒ *14½ km (9 mi) southeast of Roundwood on R764, 13 km (8 mi) east of Glendalough.*

Settled into more than 20 acres on the banks of the River Vartry, Mount Usher Gardens were first laid out in 1868 by Edward Walpole, who owned a Dublin textile firm. Succeeding generations of the Walpole family further planted and maintained the grounds, which today have more than 5,000 species. Eucalypti, azaleas, camellias, and rhododendrons make the most of the riverside locale. Water is visible from nearly every place in the gardens, while bridges span the river. A cluster of crafts shops, including a pottery workshop, and a bookstore and self-service restaurant stand at the entrance. The twin villages of Ashford and Rathnew are to the south and east, and Newtownmountkennedy is to the north. ⊠ *Ashford,* ☎ *0404/40205.* ⌷ *£3.50.* ⊙ *Mid-Mar.–Oct., daily 10:30–6.*

Dining and Lodging

$$$$ ✕⊞ **Tinakilly House.** William and Bee Power have lovingly restored this Victorian-Italianate mansion, built in the 1870s by Captain Robert Halpin (1836–94), who laid the first transatlantic cable lines as captain of *The Great Eastern,* then the biggest ship in the world. The lobby has mementos of Captain Halpin and his nautical exploits, including paintings and ship models; impeccable Victorian antiques fill the house. Some bedrooms have four-poster beds, Jacuzzis, sitting areas, and views of the Wicklow landscape, the Irish Sea, or the lovely gardens on the 7-acre grounds. The dining room spotlights French-influenced Irish cuisine, with fresh vegetables from the garden; brown and fruit breads are baked daily. ⊠ *Rathnew, Co. Wicklow,* ☎ *0404/69274,* FAX *0404/67806. 52 rooms with bath. Restaurant, bar, tennis court. AE, DC, MC, V.* ✎

$$ ✕⊞ **Hunter's Hotel.** One of Ireland's oldest coaching inns, first opened in the early 1700s, sits in a lovely rural setting on the banks of the River Vartry, only 1 km (½ mi) east of Rathnew Village. Period prints, beams, and antiques lend an old-world feel enjoyed by both locals and guests. All bedrooms have delicate flower-print wallpaper and are superbly furnished with Victorian-style pieces. There is a fine restaurant, and in the summer, afternoon tea with homemade scones and jams is served in the magnificent garden that stretches down to the river. ✉ *Rathnew, Co. Wicklow,* ☎ *0404/40106,* FAX *0404/40338. 16 rooms with bath. Restaurant, bar. AE, DC, MC, V.* 🍴

Wicklow Town

㉓ *26 km (16 mi) east of Glendalough on R763, 51 km (32 mi) south of Dublin on N11.*

At the entrance to the attractive, tree-lined Main Street of Wicklow Town—its name, from the Danish *wyking alo,* means "Viking meadow"—lie the extensive ruins of a 13th-century Franciscan friary. The **friary** was closed down during the 16th-century dissolution of the monasteries in the area, but its ruins give a sense of Wicklow's stormy past, which began with the unwelcome reception given to St. Patrick on his arrival in AD 432. Inquire at the nearby priest's house (✉ Main St., ☎ 0404/67196) to view the ruins.

The old town jail, just above Market Square, has been converted into a museum and **heritage center,** where visitors can trace their genealogical roots in the area. Using computer displays and life-size models, the gruesome history of the jail is told, from the local rebellion in 1798 right up to the late 19th century. ✉ *Market Square,* ☎ *0404/61599.* 🎟 *£3.75.* ◷ *Daily 10–6.*

The **harbor** is Wicklow Town's most appealing area. Take Harbour Road down to the pier; a bridge across the River Vartry leads to a second, smaller pier, at the northern end of the harbor. From this end, follow the shingle beach, which stretches for 5 km (3 mi); behind the beach is the broad lough, a lagoon noted for its wildfowl. Immediately south of the harbor, perched on a promontory that has good views of the Wicklow coastline, is the ruin of the **Black Castle.** This structure was built in 1169 by Maurice Fitzgerald, an Anglo-Norman lord who arrived with the English invasion of Ireland. The ruins (freely accessible) extend over a large area; with some difficulty, you can climb down to the water's edge.

Between one bank of the River Vartry and the road to Dublin stands the Protestant **St. Lavinius Church,** which incorporates a variety of earlier elements and unusual details: a Romanesque door, 12th-century stonework, fine pews, and an atmospheric graveyard. The church is topped off by a copper, onion-shape cupola, added as an afterthought in 1771. 🎟 *Free.* ◷ *Daily 10–6.*

Dining and Lodging

$ ✗ **Pizza del Forno.** With its red-and-white-check tablecloths, low lighting, and pizza oven blazing away, this is a great vantage point for people-watching on Main Street. Inexpensive pizzas, pasta, steaks, and vegetarian dishes appeal to a wide array of appetites. ✉ *Main St.,* ☎ *0404/67075. AE, MC, V. Closed Christmas–mid-Feb.*

$$ ✗🏠 **Old Rectory Country House.** Once a 19th-century rectory, this small,
★ charming Greek Revival country house stands on a hillside just off the main road from Dublin on the approach to Wicklow Town. Owners Paul and Linda Saunders have a splendid touch. Black-and-white marble fireplaces, bright colors, original oil paintings, and antique and contemporary furniture decorate the house; the light, spacious guest rooms are done in white and pastel shades with antique Victorian and country-house furniture. Linda's "Green Cuisine" makes use of fresh ingredients; don't miss her salads and desserts, often made or garnished with edible flowers and herbs. ✉ *Wicklow Town, Co. Wicklow,* ☎ *0404/67048,* FAX *0404/69181. 8 rooms with bath. Restaurant. AE, MC, V. Closed Jan.–Feb.* 🍴

Avondale Forest Park and House

㉔ *17 km (11 mi) southwest of Wicklow Town on R752.*

Outside the quaint village of Rathdrum, on the west bank of the Avondale River, the 523-acre **Avondale Forest Park** was, in 1904, the first
forest in Ireland to be taken over by the state. There's a 5½-km (3½-
mi) walk along the river, as well as pine and exotic-tree trails. **Avondale House**, on the grounds of the park, resonates with Irish history.
The house was the birthplace and lifelong home of Charles Stewart Parnell (1846–91), "The Uncrowned King of Ireland," the country's leading politician of the 19th century and a wildly popular campaigner for
democracy and land reform. His career clattered to a halt after he fell
in love with a married woman, Kitty O'Shea. When her husband in-
stituted divorce proceedings in 1890, the revelation of Parnell's affair
during court hearings ruined his political career, and he died a year later
under the strain of the controversy. (In Joyce's *A Portrait of the Artist
as a Young Man,* the controversy is dramatized as a keenly contested
argument during the Daedalus family dinner.) The house, built in
1779, was acquired by John Parnell, great-grandfather of Charles
Stewart, in 1795. It has been flawlessly restored, with the reception
and dining rooms on the ground floor filled with Parnell memorabilia,
including some of his love letters to Kitty O'Shea and political cartoons
portraying his efforts to secure home rule for Ireland. ☎ *0404/46111.*
⌨ *£3, parking £2.* ☉ *May–Sept., daily 10–6; Oct.–Apr., daily 11–5.*

Avoca

㉕ *6½ km (4 mi) south of Avondale Forest Park on R754.*

The small hamlet of Avoca is set amid heavily forested hills at the confluence of the Rivers Avonbeg and Avonmore. Beneath a riverside tree
here, the Irish Romantic poet Thomas Moore (1779–1852) composed
his 1807 poem "The Meeting of the Waters." There are some pleasant forest walks nearby, with scenic views of the valley. The oldest hand-
weaving mill in Ireland, **Avoca Handweavers,** offers a short tour of
the mill, which is still in operation. The store sells a wide selection of
its own superb fabrics and woven and knit apparel, some of which is
difficult to find elsewhere. ☎ *0402/35105.* ⌨ *Free.* ☉ *Shop daily 9:30–
5:30, mill weekdays 8–4:30.*

Arklow

㉖ *11 km (7 mi) southeast of Avoca on R754.*

Arklow's long, bustling main street winds its way down a gently sloping hill. Bread lovers and those with a sweet tooth should stop in at
Stone Oven Bakery (✉ 65 Lower Main St., ☎ 0402/39418) at the bottom of the hill. The German-born baker, Egon Friedrich, turns out sour-
dough breads and delicious sweet treats, including hazelnut-chocolate
triangles; the shop can prepare simple cheese and bread sandwiches to
go or to eat in the tiny, slightly haphazard café. Down on the waterfront at the **Arklow Pottery Factory** (well signed throughout the town),
you can take guided tours and shop for crafts. ☎ *0402/32401.* ☉ *Weekdays 9–5, weekends 10–5.*

The **Maritime Museum,** in the public library building near the railway
station, traces Arklow's distinguished seafaring tradition; exhibits include old photographs, some original boats, and the logs of long-dead
captains. To get here, take a left at St. Peter's Church as you're heading out of town in the direction of Gorey and Wexford. ✉ *St. Mary's*

Rd., ☎ 0402/32868. ✉ £2.50. ⊙ May–Sept., Mon.–Sat. 10–1 and 2–5; Oct.–Apr., weekdays 10–1 and 2–5.

Ⓢ Immediately north of Arklow is **Brittas Bay,** an area of white sand, quiet coves, and rolling dunes. It is popular in summer with vacationing Dubliners and is perfect for adventurous kids.

COUNTY KILDARE AND WEST WICKLOW

Horse racing is a passion in Ireland—you'll notice every little town has its betting shop—and County Kildare is the country's horse capital. Nestled between the basins of the River Liffey to the north and the River Barrow to the east, its gently sloping hills and grass-filled plains are perfect for breeding and racing Thoroughbreds. For first-time visitors, the National Stud just outside Kildare Town offers a fascinating glimpse into the world of horse breeding. The Japanese Gardens, adjacent to the National Stud, are among Europe's finest, while Castletown House, in Celbridge to the north, is one of Ireland's foremost Georgian treasures. We make Dublin your starting point, but you may want to pick up this leg from Glendalough (☞ *above*). The spectacular drive across the Wicklow Gap, from Glendalough to Hollywood, makes for a glorious entrance into Kildare. One last note: consult Chapter 4 if you make it as far south as Castledermot (the southernmost point in this section), since Carlow and environs are only 10 km (6 mi) farther south.

OFF THE
BEATEN PATH

MAYNOOTH – Before heading to Castletown House, make a quick detour slightly farther west to Maynooth, a tiny Georgian town 24 km (15 mi) west of Dublin. Here you'll find **St. Patrick's College,** once exclusively a center for the training of Catholic priests and now also one of Ireland's most important lay universities. It was established in 1795 on the site of an earlier college founded by the Earl of Kildare in the 16th century, which was suppressed by Henry VIII. The visitor center chronicles the college's history and the history of the Catholic Church in Ireland. The university gardens are worth a stroll; choose between the Path of Saints and the Path of Sinners. ☎ 01/628–5222. ⊙ May–Sept., Mon.–Sat. 11–5, Sun. 2–6; guided tours every hr.

At the entrance to St. Patrick's College lie the ruins of **Maynooth Castle,** the ancient seat of the Fitzgerald family. The Fitzgeralds' fortunes changed for the worse when they led the failed rebellion of 1536, and the castle was finally dismantled in Cromwellian times. The castle keep, the oldest part, dates from the 13th century, and the keep and the great hall are still in reasonable condition. The key can be obtained from Mrs. Saults at 9 Parson Street. ✉ Free.

Castletown House

㉗ *24 km (15 mi) southwest of Dublin via N7 to R403, 6½ km (4 mi) south of Maynooth.*

In the early 18th century, a revival of the architectural style of Andrea Palladio (1508–80) swept through England, where architects built dozens of houses reinterpreting a style already 150 years old. The rage swept through Ireland among the Anglo-Irish aristocracy (*see also* Russborough House, *below,* for another fine example nearby, and for references to others). Arguably the largest and finest example of an Irish Palladian-style house is Castletown, begun in 1722 for William Conolly (1662–1729), the Speaker of the Irish House of Commons and then the country's wealthiest man (he made his fortune in forfeited estates after the Battle of the Boyne). Conolly first hired the Italian architect Alessandro Galilei, who designed the facade of the main block; in 1724, the young Irish architect Sir Edward Lovett Pearce completed the house by adding the colonnades and side pavilions. Conolly's death brought construction to a halt; it wasn't until his great-nephew, Thomas Conolly, and his wife, Lady Louisa (née Lennox), took up residence in 1758 that work on the house picked up again. Throughout the 1760s and '70s, Lady Louisa oversaw the alteration and redecoration of the house. Today Castletown is the largest house built as a private residence. The poet Robert Lowell lived here for a time in the 1960s. The house was rescued in 1967 by Desmond Guinness (of the brewing family), then the president of the Irish Georgian Society, and it is now the property of the Irish state. It's also the headquarters of the Irish Georgian Society and contains many examples of its original furniture.

Inside, there are many splendid features, including hall plasterwork by the Lafranchini brothers, Swiss-Italian craftsmen who were active in Dublin in the mid-18th century. The ground-floor **Print Room** is the only 18th-century example in Ireland of this elegant fad. Like oversize postage stamps in a giant album, black-and-white prints were glued to the walls by fashionable young women who unwittingly anticipated the universal impulse among teenagers to cover their bedroom walls with posters. Upstairs at the rear of the house, the **Long Gallery**, almost 80 ft by 23 ft, is the most notable of the public rooms. In the 1770s it was redecorated in Pompeian style and with three Venetian Murano glass chandeliers. ⊠ *Celbridge,* ☎ *01/628–8252.* ⊠ *£2.50.* ☼ *Apr.–Sept., weekdays 10–6, Sat. 11–6, Sun. 2–6; Oct., Mon.–Sat. 10–5, Sun. 2–5; Nov.–Mar., Sun. 2–5.*

Dining and Lodging

$$$$ ✕🏠 **Moyglare Manor.** Set on 16 pastoral acres dotted with sheep and cows, reached via a short tree-lined drive, this majestic Georgian manor house is 29 km (18 mi) west of Dublin. Owner Nora Devlin has exuberantly decorated the house with her renowned antiques collection; fresh flowers further enliven the decor. Velvet chairs, oil paintings, and thickly draped windows are in the drawing room, while the grand bedrooms have four-poster canopy beds, roomy wardrobes, marble fireplaces, and comfortable, chintz-covered armchairs. Lamp-shaded wall sconces add a romantic touch to the formal dining room, where a traditional French menu is served. Rich desserts match the spirit of the house. ⊠ *Maynooth, Co. Kildare,* ☎ *01/628–6351,* 📠 *01/628–5405. 17 rooms with bath. Restaurant, 2 bars. AE, DC, MC, V.*

Straffan

㉘ *5 km (3 mi) southwest of Castletown House on R403, 25½ km (16 mi) southwest of Dublin.*

Attractively situated on the banks of the River Liffey, Straffan is home to the Kildare Hotel and Country Club (☞ Dining and Lodging, *below*), where Arnold Palmer designed the K Club, one of Ireland's most renowned 18-hole golf courses (☞ Chapter 9). The only one of its kind in Ireland, the **Straffan Butterfly Farm** has a tropical house with exotic plants, butterflies, and moths. Mounted and framed butterflies are available for sale. ☎ *01/627–1109.* ⊠ *£2.50.* ☼ *May–Aug., daily noon–5:30.*

The **Steam Museum** covers the history of Irish steam engines, handsome machines used in Ireland industrially as well as agriculturally, in such operations as churning butter and threshing corn. There's also a collection of model locomotives. Engineers are present on "live steam days"; phone in advance to confirm. ✉ *Lodge Park,* ☎ *01/627–3155.* 🎫 *Live steam days £4, other times £3.* ☉ *Easter–May and Sept., Tues.–Sun. 2–6; June–Aug., Mon.–Sat. 2–6, Sun. 2:30–5:30.*

Dining and Lodging

$$$$ ✕🏠 **Kildare Hotel and Country Club.** Manicured gardens and the
★ renowned Arnold Palmer–designed K Club golf course (☞ Chapter 9) surround this mansard-roofed former residence built in the 1830s for Hugh Barton, an Irishman who had to flee his extensive vineyards in France after the French Revolution and then decided to create a French country mansion here in Ireland. The spacious, very comfortable guest rooms are each uniquely decorated with antiques and have large windows that overlook either the Liffey or the golf course. (The rooms in the old house are highly recommended). The hotel also has a leasing agreement with several privately owned cottages on the property, which guests can rent when they're available—although most look as though they belong on a Florida golf course, not in Ireland. Chef Michel Flamme serves an unashamedly French menu—albeit with the hint of an Irish flavor—at the Byerly Turk Restaurant (named after a famous racehorse). ✉ *Co. Kildare,* ☎ *01/601–7200,* FAX *01/601–7299. 45 rooms with bath, 20–30 apartments. 2 restaurants, 3 bars, beauty salon, indoor pool, 18-hole golf course, 4 tennis courts, horseback riding, squash, fishing. AE, DC, MC, V.* 🐎

$$$ ✕🏠 **Barberstown Castle.** With a 13th-century castle keep at one end, an Elizabethan central section, and a large Georgian country house at the other, Barberstown effortlessly blends 750 years of Irish history. Turf fires blaze in beautifully ornate fireplaces in the three sumptuously decorated lounges. Bedrooms are furnished with reproduction pieces; some have four-poster beds. The restaurant—half Georgian, half medieval (the latter part is in the ground floor of the castle keep)—serves creatively prepared fare. ✉ *Co. Kildare,* ☎ *01/628–8157,* FAX *01/627–7027. 22 rooms with bath. Restaurant, bar. AE, DC, MC, V.*

En Route County Kildare has two major canal systems that connect Dublin with the Rivers Shannon and Barrow and the interior Lakelands. Sixteen kilometers (10 miles) southwest of Straffan, **Robertstown** sits on the **Grand Canal** (the other major canal is the **Royal,** which heads to the northeast from Dublin), where you can take scenic walks and, during the summer, barge trips. Built in the early 19th century to accommodate passengers on the canal, the **Grand Canal Hotel** (☎ 045/870005) offers candlelit dinners and musical entertainment.

Naas

㉙ *13 km (8 mi) south of Straffan on R407, 30 km (19 mi) southwest of Dublin on N7.*

The seat of County Kildare and a thriving market town in the heartland of Irish Thoroughbred country, Naas (pronounced Nace) is full of pubs with high stools where short men (trainee jockeys) discuss the merits of their various stables. Nass has its own small racecourse, but **Punchestown Racecourse** (✉ 3 km/2 mi from Naas) has a wonderful setting amid rolling plains, with the Wicklow Mountains forming a spectacular backdrop. Although horse races are held regularly here, the most popular event is the Punchestown National Hunt Festival in April.

Russborough House

㉚ *16 km (10 mi) southeast of Naas on R410.*

One of the highlights of the western part of County Wicklow, Russborough House is among the finest of the Palladian-style villas built throughout Ireland by the Anglo-Irish ascendancy in the first half of the 18th century. (Castletown House [☞ *above*], Emo Court [☞ Chapter 3], and Castle Coole [☞ Chapter 8] are the other bright stars in this constellation.) In 1741, a year after Joseph Leeson inherited a vast fortune from his father, a successful Dublin brewer, he commissioned Richard Castle (architect of Leinster House [☞ Exploring Dublin *in* Chapter 1] and Powerscourt [☞ *above*]) to build this palatial house, and he worked on it until his death (after which Francis Bindon took over). They pulled out all the stops to create a confident, majestic house with a silver-gray Wicklow granite facade that extends for more than 700 ft and encompasses a seven-bay central block, off which radiate two semicircular loggias connecting the flanking wings.

Baroque exuberance reigns in the house's main rooms, especially in the lavishly ornamented plasterwork ceilings executed by the Lafranchini brothers (they also worked at Castletown House). After a long succession of owners, Russborough was bought in 1952 by Sir Alfred Beit, the nephew of the German cofounder (with Cecil Rhodes) of the De Beers diamond operation, and it now belongs to Lady Beit, his widow. In 1988, after two major robberies, the finest works in the Beits' art collection were donated to the National Gallery of Ireland (☞ Exploring Dublin *in* Chapter 1). However, works by Gainsborough, Guardi, Reynolds, Rubens, and Murillo remain, as well as bronzes, silver, and porcelain. The views from Russborough's windows take in the foothills of the Wicklow Mountains and a small lake in front of the house; the extensive woodlands on the estate are open to visitors. ⊠ *Blessington, off N81,* ☎ *045/865239.* ✆ *£3, upstairs bedrooms £1.* ☉ *June–Aug., daily 10:30–5:30; Apr.–May and Oct., Sun. 10:30–5:30; Sept., Mon.–Sat. 10:30–2:30, Sun. 10:30–5:30.*

Poulaphouca Reservoir

③ *33 km (21 mi) west of Glendalough on R758 via R756, 3 km (2 mi) southeast of Russborough House.*

Known locally as the **Blessington Lakes,** Poulaphouca (pronounced pool-a-*fook*-a) Reservoir is a large, meandering artificial lake that provides Dublin's water supply minutes from Russborough House. You can drive around the entire perimeter of the reservoir on minor roads; on its southern end lies Hollywood Glen, a particularly beautiful natural spot.

The small market town of **Blessington,** with its wide main street lined on both sides by tall trees and Georgian buildings, lies on the western shore of the lakes and is one of the most charming villages in the area. Founded in the late 17th century, it was a stop on the Dublin–Waterford mail-coach service in the mid-19th century; until 1932, a steam train ran from here to Dublin, along the side of the main road.

Beyond the southern tip of the Poulaphouca Reservoir, 13 km (8 mi) south of Blessington on N81, you will spot a small sign for the **Piper's Stones.** A short walk from the road, this Bronze Age stone circle was probably used in a ritual connected with worship of the sun.

Dining and Lodging

$$$$ ✕🏠 **Rathsallagh House.** Set amid 530 acres of parkland, these low-
★   slung, ivy-covered Queen Anne stables, converted to a farmhouse in 1798, await at the end of a long drive that winds through a golf course. Kay and Joe O'Flynn oversee a stellar staff and an impeccably run operation. Two drawing rooms are adorned with enveloping couches and chairs, fresh flower arrangements, large windows, fireplaces, and lots of lamps providing ample light to read or relax by day or night. In the elegant wood-paneled dining room, sconces with silk-covered lamp

shades, an open fireplace, and candles softly illuminate the beautifully set tables. Kay's outstanding haute Irish dinner menu changes daily; specialties include paupiette of herb-filled salmon with onion and chive beurre blanc. The route to the house, 49 km (31 mi) southwest of Dublin, is well signposted and is not far from where N756 meets N81, but call ahead for precise directions. ⊠ *Dunlavin, Co. Wicklow,* ☎ *045/ 403112,* FAX *045/403343. 17 rooms with bath. Restaurant, bar, indoor pool, massage, sauna, 18-hole golf course, tennis court, croquet, meeting rooms. AE, DC, MC, V.* ✇

Outdoor Activities and Sports

There are splendid views of the Blessington Lakes from the top of **Church Mountain,** which you reach via a vigorous walk through **Woodenboley Wood,** at the southern tip of Hollywood Glen. Follow the main forest track for about 20 minutes and then take the narrow path that heads up the side of the forest to the mountaintop.

The Curragh

32 *8 km (5 mi) southwest of Naas on M7, 25½ km (16 mi) west of Poulaphouca Reservoir.*

The broad plain of the Curragh, bisected by the main N7 road, is the biggest area of common land in Ireland, encompassing about 31 square km (12 square mi) and devoted mainly to grazing. It's also Ireland's major racing center, home to **Curragh Racecourse** (☎ 045/441205), where the Irish Derby and other international horse races are run.

The **Curragh Main Barracks,** a large camp where the Irish Army trains, has a small museum. One of its prize relics is the armored car once used by Michael Collins, the former head of the Irish Army who, in December 1921, signed the Anglo-Irish Treaty designating a six-county North to remain in British hands, in exchange for complete independence for Ireland's remaining 26 counties. The car can be seen with permission from the commanding officer. ☎ *045/445000; ask for the command adjutant.*

Kildare Town

33 *5 km (3 mi) from the Curragh on M7, 51 km (32 mi) southwest of Dublin via N7 and M7.*

Horse breeding is the basis of Kildare's thriving economy. Right off Kildare's main market square, the **Silken Thomas** (☎ 045/522232) re-creates an old-world atmosphere with open fires, dark wood decor, and leaded lights; it's a good place to stop for lunch before exploring the sights here.

St. Brigid's Cathedral (Church of Ireland) is where the eponymous saint founded a religious settlement in the 5th century. The present cathedral, with its stocky tower, is a restored 13th-century structure. It was partially rebuilt about 1686, but restoration work wasn't completed for another 200 years. The stained-glass west window of the cathedral depicts three of Ireland's greatest saints: Brigid, Patrick, and Columba. ⊠ *Off Market Sq.* 🎟 *50p.* ⊙ *Daily 10–6.*

The 108-ft-high **round tower,** in the graveyard of St. Brigid's Cathedral, is the second highest in Ireland and dates from the 12th century. Extraordinary views across much of the Midlands await those energetic enough to climb the stairs to the top. ☎ *045/521229.* 🎟 *£2.* ⊙ *May–Sept., daily 10–1 and 2–5.*

If you're a longtime horse aficionado, or just curious, the **National Stud Farm,** a main center of Ireland's racing industry, is well worth a visit. Founded in 1900 by Colonel William Hall-Walker (later Lord Wavertree), a brewing heir, and transferred to the Irish state in 1843, the Stud is home to breeding stallions who are groomed, exercised, tested, and bred within the neat white buildings, which are set around immaculately kept green lawns. Spring and early summer, when mares will have new foals, are the best times to visit. Walker believed in astrology; thus, every new foal had its "chart done," and those with unfavorable results were sold right away. He even built the stallion boxes with lantern roofs that allow the moon and stars to work their magic on the occupants. Also on the grounds, the **National Stud Horse Museum** recounts the history of horses in Ireland. Its most outstanding exhibit is the skeleton of Arkle, the Irish racehorse that won major victories in Ireland and England during the late 1960s. The museum also contains medieval evidence of horses, such as bones from 13th-century Dublin, and some early examples of equestrian equipment. ⊠ *South of Kildare Town about ½ km (⅓ mi),* ☎ *045/521617.* ☞ *£5, including entry to the Japanese Gardens.* ☉ *Mid-Feb.–mid-Nov., daily 9:30–6.*

★ Adjacent to the National Stud, the **Japanese Gardens** were created between 1906 and 1910 by the Stud's founder, Colonel Hall-Walker, and laid out by a Japanese gardener, Tassa Eida, and his son Minoru. The gardens are recognized as among the finest in Europe, although they're something of an East-West hybrid rather than authentically Japanese. The Scots pine trees, for instance, are an appropriate stand-in for traditional Japanese pines, which signify long life and happiness. The gardens symbolically chart the human progression from birth to death, although the focus is on the male journey, not that of the female. A series of landmarks are situated on a meandering path: the Tunnel of Ignorance (No. 3) represents a child's lack of understanding; the Engagement and Marriage bridges (Nos. 8 and 9) span a small stream; and from the Hill of Ambition (No. 13), you can look back over your past joys and sorrows. It ends with the Gateway to Eternity (No. 20), beyond which lies a Buddhist meditation sand garden. It's a worthwhile destination any time of the year, though it's particularly glorious in spring and fall. ⊠ *South of Kildare Town about 2½ km (1½ mi), clearly signposted to left of market square,* ☎ *045/521617.* ☞ *£5, including entry to the National Stud.* ☉ *Mid-Feb.–mid-Nov., daily 9:30–6.* ✎

Athy

❸❹ *24 km (15 mi) south of Kildare Town on R417, 33½ km (21 mi) south of Naas.*

The River Barrow widens considerably at Athy, an industrial town; though it has seen better days, a recent designation as a heritage town has spiffed things up. Overlooking the river, by the bridge, 16th-century **White's Castle,** now a private house, was built by the earl of Kildare to defend this strategic crossing. The modern pentagonal **Catholic church** (1963–65) has a striking interior with statues, a crucifix by local artist Brid ni Rinn on the high altar, and stations of the cross by George Campbell. ☞ *Free.* ☉ *Daily 8–6.*

Ballytore

❸❺ *8 km (5 mi) east of Athy, 26 km (16 mi) south of Naas on N9.*

In the 18th and 19th centuries, Ballytore was a Quaker settlement. An old schoolhouse is now a small **Quaker Museum.** Among the pupils at the school was Edmund Burke (1729–97), the orator and political philosopher who was close to Samuel Johnson and Sir Joshua Reynolds. ☎ 045/431109. ⌑ Free. ⊙ Tues.–Fri. 11–6, Sat. 11–1.

An old mill was converted into the **Crookstown Heritage Centre,** a museum of the flour-milling and baking industries with a functioning water mill. Built in 1840, the center helped reduce the effects of the Great Famine in this area. You can get a quick bite in its coffee shop. ☎ 0507/23222. ⌑ £2.50. ⊙ Apr.–Sept., daily 10–7; Oct.–Mar., Sun. 2–5:30.

Dining

$ ✕ **Moone High Cross Inn.** Down the road from the Moone High Cross (☞ below), about 7½ km (5 mi) south of Ballymote, this old pub is packed with a cornucopia of local artifacts, newspaper clippings, and old photographs—all fascinating browsing while you nosh on the eclectic bar food that includes steak, salmon, and bacon and cabbage. Save room for the homemade apple pie. On sunny days, you can sit outside and admire the old signs in158 the beer garden. ⊠ Bolton Hill, Moone, ☎ 0507/24112. MC, V. Closed Jan.

En Route From Ballytore take the main N9 road south for 3 km (2 mi) to Timolin, where the **Irish Pewter Mill** pays splendid tribute to an old Irish craft with its showrooms, factory, and museum. Jugs, plates, and other pewter items are for sale. ☎ 0507/24164. ⊙ May–Sept., weekdays 9:30–5, weekends 11–4.

South Kildare is home to several well-preserved high crosses, set amid monastic ruins. On N9, 1½ km (1 mi) beyond Timolin, take the signposted right turn at the Moone Post Office and continue for 3 km (2 mi) to the **Moone High Cross,** an ancient Celtic cross that stands 17½ ft high, with 51 sculptured panels showing scriptural scenes.

Castledermot

㊱ 13 km (8 mi) south of Ballytore on N9.

On the left side of the village of Castledermot, you'll find an almost perfectly preserved 10th-century **round tower** together with two 10th-century **high crosses,** equally well preserved, on the grounds of the local church. From the church gate, you can walk back to the main road along the footpath that is totally enclosed by trees. On the right side of the road in the village, the substantial ruins of a Franciscan friary, mostly dating from the 14th century, are freely accessible.

Dining and Lodging

$$$ ✕🖭 **Kilkea Castle.** Built in 1180 as a defensive Anglo-Norman castle, Kilkea was the longtime home of the FitzGerald family; it was modified in the 17th century and later restored. Eleven rooms are in the castle itself, while the rest are set around an adjacent courtyard; those in the castle are more luxuriously furnished. The restaurant is in what was the great hall of the castle; dishes are based on fresh, seasonal produce, some of it from the old, walled gardens below. The hotel has an extensive sports complex, including an 18-hole golf course and clubhouse. ⊠ Castledermot, near Athy, Co. Kildare, ☎ 0503/45156, FAX 0503/45187. 36 rooms with bath. Restaurant, 2 bars, indoor pool, hot tub, sauna, steam room, 18-hole golf course, 2 tennis courts, archery, health club, fishing. AE, DC, MC, V.

DUBLIN ENVIRONS A TO Z

Getting Around

By Bus

Bus services link Dublin with main and smaller towns in the environs. All bus services for the region depart from Busaras, the central bus station, at Store Street. For bus inquiries, contact **Bus Éireann** (☎ 01/836–6111). **St. Kevin's** (☎ 01/281–8119), a private bus service, runs daily from Dublin (outside the Royal College of Surgeons on St. Stephen's Green) to Glendalough, stopping off at Bray, Roundwood, and Laragh en route. Buses leave Dublin daily at 11 AM and 6 PM (7 PM on Sunday); buses leave Glendalough weekdays at 7:15 AM and 4:15 PM (9:40 AM and 4:15 PM on Saturday, 9:40 AM and 5:30 PM on Sunday). One-way fare is £6; round-trip, £10.

By Car

The easiest and best way to tour Dublin's environs is by car, because many sights are not served by public transportation, and what service there is, especially to outlying areas, is infrequent. If you need to rent a car, *see* Car Rentals *in* Dublin A to Z *in* Chapter 1.

To visit destinations in the **Boyne Valley,** follow N3, along the east side of Phoenix Park, out of the city and make Trim and Tara your first stops. Alternatively, leave Dublin via N1/M1 to Belfast. Try to avoid the road during weekday rush hours (8 AM–10 AM and 5 PM–7 PM); stay on it as far as Drogheda and start touring from there.

To reach destinations in **County Kildare,** follow the quays along the south side of the Liffey (they are one-way westbound) to St. John's Road West (N7); in a matter of minutes, you're heading for open countryside. Avoid traveling this route during the evening peak rush hours, especially on Friday, when Dubliners are themselves making their weekend getaways.

To reach destinations in **County Wicklow,** N11/M11 is the fastest and most clearly marked route. The two more scenic routes to Glendalough are R115 to R759 to R755, or R177 to R755.

By Train

Iarnród Éireann (✉ Irish Rail, ☎ 01/836–6222) trains run the length of the east coast, from Dundalk to the north in County Louth to Arklow along the coast in County Wicklow. Trains make many stops along the way; there are stations in Drogheda, Dublin (the main stations are **Connolly Station** [✉ Amiens St.], and **Pearse Station** [✉ Westland Row]), Bray, Greystones, Wicklow, and Rathdrum. From Heuston Station (✉ Victoria Quay and St. John's Road W.), the Arrow, a commuter train service, runs westward to Celbridge, Naas, Newbridge, and Kildare Town. Contact Iarnród Éireann for schedule and fare information.

Contacts and Resources

B&B Reservation Agencies

For a small fee, **Bord Fáilte** will book accommodations anywhere in Ireland through its central reservations system. B&Bs can be booked at local visitor information offices when they are open; however, even these reservations will go through the central reservations system. For more information, *see* Lodging *in* Smart Travel Tips A to Z.

Car Rentals

See Car Rentals *in* Dublin A to Z *in* Chapter 1.

Emergencies
Police, fire, and **ambulance** (☎ 999).

Guided Tours
Bus Éireann (☎ 01/836–6111) runs guided bus tours to many of the historic and scenic locations throughout the Dublin environs daily during the summer. Visits include trips to Glendalough in Wicklow; Boyne Valley and Newgrange in County Louth; and the Hill of Tara, Trim, and Navan in County Meath. All tours depart from Busaras Station, Dublin; information is available by phone Monday–Saturday 8:30–7, Sunday 10–7.

Gray Line (☎ 01/661–9666), a privately owned touring company, also runs many guided bus tours throughout the Dublin environs between May and September. **Wild Wicklow Tours** (☎ 01/280–1899) has a small, 26-seater coach that can take you to the more off-the-beaten-track sites in the mountains and along the coast.

HORSEBACK RIDING
Wicklow Trail Rides (✉ Grainne Sugars, Calliaghstown Riding Center, Ratcoole, Co. Dublin, ☎ 01/458–9236, FAX 01/458–8171) takes experienced adult horseback riders on weeklong rides through the Wicklow Mountains (May–September), with overnight stays in country homes and guest houses. Instructional holidays for children and adults at the riding center are also available.

WALKING AND HIKING
The **Wicklow Way** is Ireland's most popular walking route, a 137-km (85-mi) trek through the Dublin and Wicklow mountains. The walk begins in Marlay Park, just south of Dublin city center (☞ Chapter 1), where there are a selection of different trails. For information call 01/493–4059. County Wicklow also sponsors three annual walking festivals. The two-day **Rathdrum Easter Walking Festival** (☎ 0404/46262) includes hill walks of varying lengths over Easter weekend. The first weekend of May, the **Wicklow Mountains May Walking Festival** (☎ 0404/66058) is centered on Blessington. The **Wicklow Mountains Autumn Walking Festival** (☎ 0404/66058) is based in the Glenmalure area.

Visitor Information
For information on travel in the Dublin environs and for help in making lodging reservations, contact one of the following Tourist Information Offices (TIOs): **Dublin Tourism** and **Bord Fáilte** (☞ Visitor Information *in* Dublin A to Z *in* Chapter 1); **Dundalk** (☎ 042/933–5484, FAX 042/933–8070); **Mullingar** (☎ 044/48761, FAX 044/40413); or **Trim** (☎ 046/37227, FAX 046/31595).

Mullingar is the head office of tourism for Counties Wicklow, Louth, Meath, and Kildare; it can give you contact information for temporary TIOs in these areas. During the summer, temporary TIOs are open throughout the environs, in towns such as Arklow and Wicklow Town in County Wicklow; Drogheda and Dundalk in County Louth; and Kildare Town in County Kildare.

3 THE MIDLANDS

*Counties Offaly, Roscommon,
Longford, Cavan, Monaghan,
Westmeath, the North Tipperary,
Laois, and the south of Leitrim*

Unspectacular and unsung, the flat plains of
the Midlands form the geographical heart of
Ireland. There's water at every turn in this
landscape of wide lakes and fast rivers,
including the mighty Shannon, Ireland's
central artery and the longest river in the
British Isles. Among the highlights are
Clonmacnoise, Ireland's most important
monastic ruins; historic towns with age-
old industries such as lace making and
crystal; the gardens of Birr Castle; and
some of Ireland's finest Anglo-Irish houses—
Strokestown House, Castle Leslie, and
Emo Court.

Updated by
Alannah
Hopkin

IRISH SCHOOLCHILDREN WERE ONCE TAUGHT to think of their country as a saucer, with mountains around the edge and a dip in the middle. The dip is the Midlands—or the Lakelands, as it is sometimes also referred to—and this often-overlooked region comprises seven counties: Cavan, Laois (pronounced leash), Westmeath, Longford, Offaly, Roscommon, and Monaghan, in addition to North Tipperary and Leitrim.

A fair share of Ireland's 800 bodies of water speckle this lush countryside. Many of the lakes formed by glacial action some 10,000 years ago are quite small, especially in Cavan and Monaghan. Anglers who come to the area have learned to expect to have a lake to themselves, and many return year after year to practice the sport. Because of all the water, much of the landscape lies under blanket bog, a unique ecosystem that's worth exploring. The River Shannon, one of the longest rivers in Europe and the longest in the British Isles, bisects the Midlands from north to south, piercing a series of loughs (lakes): Lough Allen, Lough Ree, and Lough Derg. The Royal Canal and the Grand Canal cross the Midlands from east to west, ending in the Shannon north and south of Lough Ree. Stretches of both canals have been developed for recreational purposes.

The main roads from Dublin to the south and the west cross the area—and these roads ultimately came to eclipse the Shannon and the canals as important transportation arteries—but there is also a network of minor roads linking the more scenic areas. You'll find more conventionally attractive hill and lake scenery in the forest parks of Killykeen and Lough Key. The towns themselves—including Nenagh, Roscommon, Athlone, Boyle, Mullingar, Tullamore, Longford, and Cavan—are not among Ireland's most distinctive, but they are likely to appeal to people hungry for a time when the pace of life was slower and every neighbor's face was familiar. A Midland town's main hotel is usually the social center, a good place from which to experience life as the locals do. You might witness a wedding reception (generally a boisterous occasion for all age groups), a First Communion supper, a meeting of the local Lions Club, or even a gathering of the neighborhood Weight Watchers group. By now you've probably realized: night owls and thrill seekers should probably head elsewhere.

The Midlands are, last but not least, dotted with some of Ireland's most impressive heritage properties from disparate eras: Strokestown Park House, Birr Castle Gardens, Emo Court and Gardens, Castle Leslie, and the magnificent monastic ruins of Clonmacnoise on the banks of the Shannon.

Pleasures and Pastimes

Dining
Most of the restaurants are simple eateries, ranging in price from inexpensive ($) to moderate ($$), and are often attached to a family hotel. Mullingar, in the center of the Midlands, is the beef capital of Ireland, and the many lakes and rivers of the region provide an abundance of fresh salmon and trout. And since no place in Ireland is more than an hour and a half from the sea, you can also expect to find fresh ocean fish. The approach to cooking may often be conventional, but the ingredients will always be first-rate. For price ranges, *see* Dining *in* Smart Travel Tips A to Z.

Lodging

Although there are some beautifully opulent country-house hotels in the region, accommodations for the most part are often modest affairs. The choice is usually between a small-town hotel offering a reasonable standard of basic comfort or a scenically located, country-house bed-and-breakfast, perhaps overlooking a small lake or river. Either way, informality is the order of the day. For price ranges, *see* Lodging *in* Smart Travel Tips A to Z.

Outdoor Activities and Sports

BICYCLING

One of the best ways to immerse yourself in the Midlands is to tour the region on a bicycle. Although the area may not have the spectacular scenery of the more hilly coastal regions, its level terrain means a less-strenuous ride. The twisting roads are generally in good condition, and there are pleasant picnic spots in the many state-owned forests just off the main roads. Bord Fáilte recommends two long tours: one of the Athlone-Mullingar-Roscommon area and another of the Cavan-Monaghan-Mullingar region. Whenever possible, try to avoid the major trunk roads that bisect the region.

BOATING

With 485 km (300 mi) of navigable rivers and numerous island-studded lakes in the region, a boat is the best way to see the Midlands at a leisurely pace and from an unusual and memorable angle. Several companies rent out charter boats of varying sizes for vacations on the water. Most of these vessels hold from six to eight people, and all are operated by the parties who rent them, meaning everyone can be captain for a day.

FISHING

Anglers worldwide are attracted to the region's River Shannon and its system of lakes. Beam, rudd, tench, roach, perch, and hybrids are the main varieties, while pike roam select waters. Monaghan, Cavan, Boyle, and the small lakes to the east and west of Lough Derg are the best coarse fishing areas, while brown-trout lakes and rivers can be found around Birr, Banagher, Mullingar, and Roscommon. For pike, you'll find the most fruitful areas around Cavan, Clones, Cootehill, Castleblaney, Kingscourt, Carrick-on-Shannon, Boyle, Belturbet, and Butlersbridge. The Midlands region hosts several angling festivals, with prize money and fringe events such as sing-alongs, dart games, and card competitions. Castleblaney has a tournament in March; Carrickmacross and Ballinsasloe, in May; Athlone, in July and October; and Cootehill, in September.

GOLF

Although the parkland courses of the Midlands may lack the spectacular challenge of Ireland's more famous scenic and coastal greens, they have a quiet charm all their own. On weekdays, at least, you are unlikely to have any trouble booking a tee time. Six 18-hole courses have opened in the Midlands in recent years, considerably reducing the pressure on facilities. Many of the older courses are inexpensive, costing as little as £8; greens fees at newer courses are generally moderate at around £15–£25.

HIKING AND WALKING

Forest park trails (at Killykeen, Lough Key, and Dun a Ri) and narrow country roads invite visitors to tour parts of the Midlands on foot. One impressive walking trail to the east of Birr, called the Slieve Bloom Way, runs through the Slieve Bloom Mountains on a 50-km (30-mi) circular route; its attractions include deep glens, rock formations, waterfalls, and views from mountain peaks.

Exploring the Midlands

Our coverage of the Midlands is organized into three sections: the Eastern Midlands; the Northern Midlands; and North Tipperary and the West Midlands. The first two areas can easily be covered in an extended visit to the Midlands, as they chart a course almost due north from the initial starting point in Portarlington, County Laois. Because our third section includes sights west of those in the first two, keep it in mind if you're flying into Shannon and beginning your explorations of Ireland in the western half of the country. In fact, because the Midlands border virtually every major county of Ireland, there are three places in this chapter where you should be alert to nearby locales we cover in other chapters: the easternmost sites in the Midlands (Emo Court and Coolbanagher) are within a few miles of the westernmost sites in Dublin Environs (☞ Chapter 2); the westernmost sites in the Midlands (Boyle and Lough Key Forest Park) are just across the border from County Sligo (☞ Chapter 7); and the northernmost sites and towns of the Midlands are just across the border from Northern Ireland (☞ Chapter 8).

Numbers in the text correspond to numbers in the margin and on the Midlands map.

Great Itineraries

The Midlands is a relatively small region, but part of its attraction lies in the temptation to follow a loose itinerary and spend time off the beaten path. Ten days would allow for a leisurely exploration of the region by bicycle. Car drivers could cover the same route in five days with plenty of time to improvise. Three days would be enough to sample the central area of the region, which is probably more sensible than driving long distances on small roads in an effort to see everything.

IF YOU HAVE 3 DAYS

Heading east from Shannon Airport, turn off the N7 Limerick–Dublin road for ⊞ **Birr** ㉑, a quiet Georgian town built around its magnificent castle and gardens. Then take the nearby **Bord na Mona Bog Rail Tour** ⑲ near Shannonbridge, a good introduction to the flora and fauna of Ireland's many bogs. While you're in the area, stop at **Clonmacnoise** ⑱, Ireland's most important monastic settlement, which overlooks the River Shannon, and return to Birr for the night. The next day head for **Strokestown** ⑮ and its namesake house, where a museum documents the causes and effects of the 1845–49 Great Famine. Spend the night back in **Longford** ⑦, and visit the nearby **Carrigglas Manor**, a romantic, 1837 Tudor-Gothic house that has Jane Austen associations. If the weather is good, take some fresh air in **Lough Key Forest Park** near **Boyle** ⑭, from where you will be well positioned to explore the West or Northwest (☞ Chapters 6 and 7, respectively).

IF YOU HAVE 5 DAYS

Heading from Dublin or from points east in Wicklow and Kildare, start at ① **Portarlington,** making sure to visit the nearby **Emo Court and Gardens.** This is the only large-scale country house designed by James Gandon, the architect responsible for much of Georgian Dublin. Move north to the Gothic Revival Charleville Castle outside **Tullamore** ②, then to **Kilbeggan** ③, where you can learn about whiskey making at the Kilbeggan Distillery; if you have time, stop in at the beautiful lakelands setting of the **Belvedere House Gardens** to the north. Stay in or around ⊞ **Mullingar** ④ for the night. In the morning of day two, briefly ex-

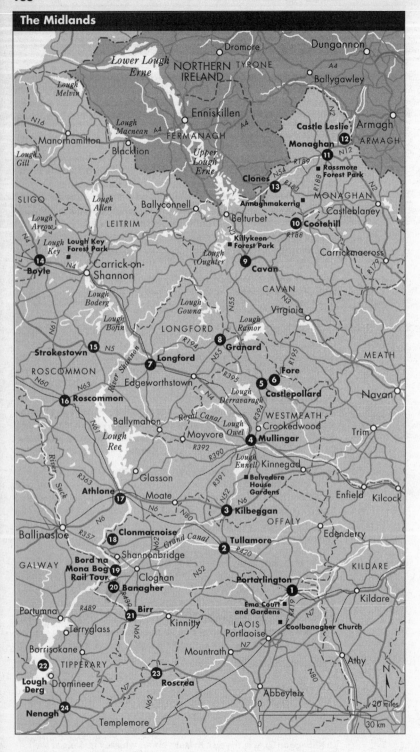

Dromore
Dungannon
Lower Lough Erne
NORTHERN IRELAND
TYRONE
A4
Ballygawley
Lough Melvin
Enniskillen
N16
Lough Macnean
A4
FERMANAGH
Castle Leslie 12
Armagh
Manorhamilton
Blacklion
Upper Lough Erne
Monaghan 11
ARMAGH
N12
Lough Gill
Rossmore Forest Park
R188
N2
SLIGO
Ballyconnell
Clones 13
R183
N5A
MONAGHAN
LEITRIM
Belturbet
Annaghmakerrig
Castleblaney
Lough Arrow
Lough Allen
Cootehill 10
R188
Carrickmacross
N4
Lough Key
Killykeen Forest Park
R179
Lough Key Forest Park
Lough Oughter
9 Cavan
14 Boyle
N4
Carrick-on-Shannon
Lough Boderg
CAVAN
N3
Lough Gowna
Virginia
N61
Lough Bofin
LONGFORD
N55
Lough Ramor
R194
Strokestown 15
N5
River Shannon
8 Granard
R195
MEATH
7 Longford
N55
ROSCOMMON
Edgeworthstown
R395
N60
N63
N4
Lough Derravaragh
5 6 Fore
16 Roscommon
Castlepollard
Navan
N61
Ballymahon
Royal Canal
WESTMEATH
Lough Ree
Moyvore
Lough Owel
Crookedwood
Trim
R392
R390
4 Mullingar
Lough Ennell
Kinnegad
River Suck
R363
Glasson
R391
N52
Belvedere House Gardens
Enfield
Kilcock
Athlone
Moate
N6
3 Kilbeggan
17
N6
N80
OFFALY
Edenderry
Ballinasloe
R357
18 Clonmacnoise
Grand Canal
2 Tullamore
R420
GALWAY
Shannonbridge
N62
KILDARE
Bord na Mona Bog Rail Tour 19
Cloghan
N52
Portarlington
1
Portumna
20 Banagher
R489
R489
Ema Court and Gardens
Kildare
Terryglass
21 Birr
N62
Kinnitty
LAOIS
Coolbanagher Church
N7
Borrisokane
TIPPERARY
Portlaoise
Athy
22
Dromineer
23 Roscrea
Mountrath
N7
N80
Lough Derg
N62
Abbeyleix
20 miles
24 Nenagh
Templemore
30 km

plore Mullingar, and then head north on scenic R394 to **Castlepollard** ⑤ and the massive Tullynally Castle and Gardens. Crystal aficionados will want to stop in **Cavan** ⑨, while nature buffs can easily spend the afternoon exploring the nearby water-laced **Killykeen Forest Park**. Spend the night in ⛨ **Cootehill** ⑩, an old-fashioned, friendly County Cavan town popular with the many anglers who frequent this area. Begin your third day visiting ⛨ **Castle Leslie** ⑫, beautifully situated on the shores of Glaslough (the "Green Lake"). If you're ready for some downtime, you can extend your visit and stay the night. Alternatively, you can either jump across the border to explore the southernmost sights in Northern Ireland (☞ Chapter 8) or head southwest, making a brief stop at **Rossmore Forest Park** on your way to the border town of **Clones** ⑬, a lace-making center. On your fourth day, return to Cavan and pick up the road to ⛨ **Longford** ⑦, where the nearby **Carrigglas Manor,** a romantic Tudor-Gothic house, has associations with Jane Austen. To the west lies **Strokestown** ⑮ and its namesake house; its museum devoted to the Great Famine is not to be missed, and the house and restored gardens are also worth a look. ⛨ **Athlone** ⑰ is a convenient place to spend the night—from here you're well positioned for an early morning visit to **Clonmacnoise** ⑱, the most important early Christian monastic site in Ireland. Stop at the **Bord na Mona Bog Rail Tour** ⑲ near Shannonbridge on your way to **Banagher** ⑳, where you can either take a two-hour Shannon cruise (a great trip in good weather) or drive around **Lough Derg** ㉒. Depending on your time, you can choose to end up in either ⛨ **Birr** ㉑, ⛨ **Roscrea** ㉓, or ⛨ **Nenagh** ㉔; from any of these towns you're not far from Shannon Airport and points to the west and southwest.

When to Tour the Midlands

The Midlands are a good year-round choice because, unlike those in the more popular destinations in the West and Southwest, their restaurants, accommodations, and major attractions remain open all year. The area is usually quiet, except at the boating resorts on the Shannon and its loughs, which are heavily booked by Irish vacationers in July and August.

THE EASTERN MIDLANDS

The eastern fringe of the Midlands is about an hour's drive from Dublin, and a visit to the area could easily be grafted onto a trip to the Dublin Environs (☞ Chapter 2). We begin at Portarlington, the closest village to Dublin in the chapter, and move northwest to Castlepollard and environs, stopping just short of Longford, the jumping-off point for the Northern Midlands.

☙ *following the text of a review is your signal that the property has a Web site, where you will find details and, usually, images; for a link, visit www.fodors.com/urls.*

Portarlington

❶ *72 km (43 mi) southwest of Dublin.*

If you enjoy large-scale, domestic architecture, drive to Portarlington, which until recently had a sizable bilingual (English-French) population of Huguenot origin. A quintessential landmark of Irish Palladian
★ elegance lies just 7 km (4½ mi) south of Portarlington: **Emo Court and Gardens,** one of the finest large-scale country houses near Dublin open to the public. (If you elect to skip over much of the Midlands, at least try to tack on a visit to Emo, especially if you're in County Kildare or Wicklow [☞ Chapter 2].) To come upon the house from the main drive,

an avenue lined with magisterial Wellingtonia trees, is to experience one of Ireland's great treasure-house views. Begun in 1790 by James Gandon, architect of the Custom House and the Four Courts in Dublin, Emo (the name derives from the Italian version of the original Irish name Imoe) is thought to be Gandon's only domestic work on as grand a scale as his Dublin civic buildings. Construction continued on and off for 70 years, as family money troubles followed the untimely death of the Emo's first patron and owner, the first Earl of Portarlington.

In 1996, Emo's English-born owner, Mr. Cholmeley Dering Cholmeley-Harrison, donated the house to the Irish nation. The ground-floor rooms have been beautifully restored and decorated. Among the highlights are the **entrance hall,** with trompe l'oeil in the apses on each side, and the **library,** which has a carved Italian marble mantle with putti frolicking among grapevines. But the showstopper, and one of the finest rooms in Ireland, is the domed **rotunda**—in fact the work of one of Gandon's successors, the Irish architect William Caldbeck—inspired by the Roman Pantheon. The rotunda's blue-and-white coffered dome is supported by marble pilasters with gilded Corinthian capitals. Emo's 55 acres of grounds include a 20-acre lake, lawns planted with yew trees, a small garden (the Clocker) with Japanese maples, and a larger one (the Grapery) with rare trees and shrubs. ⊠ *Emo,* ☎ *0502/26573.* ⛱ *Gardens free, house £2.* ⊙ *Gardens daily 10:30–5:30; house mid-June–mid-Sept., Tues.–Sun. 10–6, last tour 5:15.* ⚜

Coolbanagher Church, the familiar name for the exquisite Church of St. John the Evangelist, was, like Emo Court and Gardens, designed by James Gandon. On view inside are Gandon's original 1795 plans; there's also an elaborately sculpted 15th-century font from an earlier church that once stood nearby, and adjacent is Gandon's mausoleum for Lord Portarlington, his patron at Emo. The church is open daily in the summer; during other months, ask around in the tiny village for a key, or call the rectory (☎ 0502/24143), which is a 10-minute drive away. ⊠ *8½ km (5½ mi) south of Portarlington on R419.* ⊙ *May–Oct., daily 9–6.*

Dining and Lodging

$ ✕🖫 **Preston House.** This ivy-clad Georgian schoolhouse on the main Cork–Dublin road is a popular lunch and coffee stop by day, renowned for home baking, while in the evening the restaurant (closed Sunday and Monday) takes on a more formal aspect. Owner Allison Dowling prepares local beef and lamb in traditional Irish style—roast or grilled— and offers lighter dishes such as baked cheese soufflé and warm chicken salad. The guest rooms are spacious, furnished with solid Victorian antiques, and all have working fireplaces. They also have views of the long back gardens and fields beyond. ⊠ *Main St., Abbeyleix, Co. Laois,* ☎ FAX *0502/31432. 4 rooms with bath. Restaurant. MC, V.*

$ 🖫 **Roundwood House.** Just off N7 at the foot of the Slieve Bloom Moun-
★   tains, this is a warm, relaxed, classically beautiful 1730s house. Behind the symmetrical Palladian facade lies a simple interior, with family antiques and Persian rugs on well-worn wooden floors in the study, drawing room, and other common rooms. You can stay in one of the large rooms in the main house or in a smaller, cozy room in the original house, which dates from 1650 and is just beyond an herb garden at the back. There are 18 acres of woodland to explore and more strenuous hill walks in the Slieve Blooms. Hosts Frank and Rosemarie Kennan are likely to share a table with you at dinner (for residents only), which consists of a multicourse set menu with Continental cuisine. ⊠ *Mountrath, Co. Laois,* ☎ *0502/32120,* FAX *0502/32711. 10 rooms with bath. Dining room. AE, DC, MC, V.* ⚜

Tullamore

❷ *27 km (17 mi) northwest of Portarlington.*

Tullamore, the county seat of Offaly, is a big country town on the Grand Canal. The main reason to pass through is the **Charleville Forest Castle,** a castellated, Georgian–Gothic Revival manor house set on about 30 acres of woodland walks and gardens. This magnificent building dates from 1812 and is a fine example of the work of architect Francis Johnston, who was responsible for many of Dublin's stately Georgian buildings. Look for the William Morris–designed dining room with its original wallpaper. Guided tours of the interior are available. ✉ *1½ km (1 mi) outside Tullamore on N52 to Birr,* ☎ *0506/21279.* 🎫 *£2.50.* ☉ *May, weekends 2–5; June–Sept., Wed.–Sun. 2–5; Oct.–Apr., groups of 4 or more by appointment.*

Outdoor Activities and Sports

BOATING

A river cruiser for a floating holiday can be rented from **Celtic Canal Cruisers Ltd.** (✉ 24th Lock, ☎ 0506/21861).

GOLF

Esker Hills Golf & Country Club (☎ 0506/55999) is a challenging 18-hole, par-71 championship course with natural lakes and woodlands.

Tullamore Golf Club (✉ Brookfield, ☎ 0506/21439) is an 18-hole, par-71 parkland course.

Kilbeggan

❸ *11 km (7 mi) north of Tullamore.*

Kilbeggan is known mainly for the **Kilbeggan Distillery,** which was established in 1757 to produce a traditional Irish malt whiskey. It closed down in 1954 and was reopened in 1987 by Cooley Distillery, which now makes its whiskey in County Louth but brings it here to be matured in casks. The distillery has been restored as a museum of industrial archaeology illustrating the process of Irish pot-whiskey distillation and the social history of the workers' lives. ☎ *0506/32134.* 🎫 *£3.25.* ☉ *Apr.–Oct., daily 9–6; Nov.–Mar., daily 10–4.*

En Route **Belvedere House Gardens** is remarkable for its beautiful setting on the northeast shore of Lough Ennel. Terraced gardens descend in three stages to the waters of the lake and provide a panoramic view of its islands. The estate also contains a walled garden with many varieties of trees, shrubs, and flowers landscaped in the 18th-century style. ✉ *19 km (12 mi) north of Kilbeggan on N52,* ☎ *044/40861.* 🎫 *£1.* ☉ *Apr.–Oct., daily noon–6.*

Mullingar

❹ *24 km (15 mi) northeast of Kilbeggan.*

County Westmeath's major town, Mullingar is a busy commercial and cattle-trading center on the Royal Canal, midway between two large, attractive lakes, Lough Owel and Lough Ennel. This is an area of rich farmland, and the town is known as Ireland's beef capital; farmers all over Ireland describe a good young cow as "beef to the ankle, like a Mullingar heifer." The buildings in Mullingar date mostly from the 19th century.

The large, Renaissance-style Catholic **Cathedral of Christ the King** was completed in 1939. Finely carved stonework decorates the front of the cathedral, and the spacious interior has mosaics of St. Patrick and St.

Anne by the Russian artist Boris Anrep. ⊠ *Mary St.,* ☎ *044/48391.*
🕑 *Daily 9–5:30.*

Mullingar's **Military Museum in Columb Barracks** has a surprisingly wide
array of artifacts that includes weapons from the two world wars; long,
canoelike boats of oak from the 1st century AD found in the surrounding lakes; and uniforms and other articles of the old IRA, including
a pistol said to have been the property of Michael Collins, chief of staff
during the War of Independence and the Civil War. ⊠ *Columb Barracks,* ☎ *044/48391.* 🎟 *Free.* 🕑 *By appointment only.*

Dining and Lodging

$$$ ✕🏠 **Crookedwood House.** This large rectory, more than 200 years old,
★   overlooks Lough Derravaragh and is 13 km (8 mi) north of Mullingar
        on R394 Castlepollard road. Nine spacious bedrooms are in a wing
        of the main house, with another nine available nearby in a fine period
        house. The dining room is particularly notable, as Noel is recognized
        as a leading Irish chef. Irresistible delights include a trio of salmon, sole,
        and scallops with lobster sauce. ⊠ *Mullingar, Co. Westmeath,* ☎ *044/
        72165,* 🗚 *044/72166. 18 rooms with bath. Restaurant. AE, DC, MC,
        V. Closed 2 wks in Nov.* ✍

$ ✕🏠 **Temple.** Along N6, almost equidistant from Mullingar, Tullam-
        ore, and Athlone, Temple is a superb Victorian farmhouse in a park-
        land setting. The Fagan family warmly welcomes visitors into large rooms
        furnished with modest antiques. Children can enjoy watching a work-
        ing sheep farm, while adults can indulge in a relaxation program that
        includes yoga, aromatherapy, and massage. The house is ideally situ-
        ated for outdoor activities, such as cycling, golfing, horseback riding,
        and dinghy sailing. Most guests choose to sample Bernadette Fagan's
        renowned cooking at dinner (book by 10 AM). ⊠ *Horseleap, Moate,
        Co. Westmeath,* ☎ *0506/35118,* 🗚 *0506/35008. 8 rooms with bath.
        Sauna, steam room, bicycles. MC, V. Closed Nov.–Feb..* ✍

$$ 🏠 **Bloomfield House Hotel.** A rambling two-story former convent with
        a castellated roof on the shores of Lough Ennell has been converted
        into this comfortable hotel with excellent fitness center. The decor is
        cheerful, with modern furniture upholstered in various warm shades
        of plaid. Rooms are spacious and all have peaceful country views. The
        Brinsley Restaurant has tall Georgian-style windows overlooking the
        lake and features renowned local beef as well as seafood dishes. The
        hotel is 3 km (2 mi) south of Mullingar on N52. ⊠ *Tullamore Rd.,
        Mullingar, Co. Westmeath,* ☎ *044/40894,* 🗚 *044/43767. 57 rooms
        with bath, 8 suites. Restaurant, bar, indoor pool, hot tub, sauna, steam
        room, exercise room. AE, DC, MC, V.* ✍

Outdoor Activities and Sports

GOLF

Delvin Castle Golf Club (⊠ Delvin, ☎ 044/64315) is a 9-hole course.
The **Heath Golf Club** (⊠ Portlaoise, ☎ 0502/46533) is a challenging,
18-hole parkland course. **Mullingar Golf Club** (⊠ Belvedere, ☎ 044/
48629) is an 18-hole parkland course.

HORSEBACK RIDING

Mullingar Equestrian Centre (⊠ Athlone Rd., ☎ 044/48331) has riding on the shores of Lough Derravaragh and lessons at all levels. The
center also organizes residential riding holidays.

Castlepollard

⑤ *21 km (13 mi) north of Mullingar.*

Castlepollard is a pretty village of multihued, 18th- and 19th-century
houses laid out around a large, triangular green. The biggest (literally!)

nearby attraction is **Tullynally Castle and Gardens,** the largest castle in Ireland still lived in as a family home. The total circumference of the building's masonry adds up to nearly ½ km (¼ mi)—an astonishing agglomeration of towers, turrets, and battlements that date from the first early fortified building, circa 1655, up through the mid-19th century, when additions in the Gothic Revival style went up one after another. Two wings designed by Sir Richard Morrison in 1840 that joined the main block to the stable court had dramatically different purposes: one was given over entirely to luxurious quarters for the Dowager Countess; the other housed 40 *indoor* servants. It was one of the first houses in the British Isles to have central heating.

Tullynally—the name, literally translated, means "Hill of the Swans"—has been the home of 10 generations of the literary Pakenham family and the seat of the earls of Longford. Among the living Pakenhams are the current earl of Longford, Frank Pakenham, the prison reformer and anti-pornography campaigner; wife Elizabeth and daughter Antonia Fraser, both historical biographers; and Antonia's brother Thomas, a historian. In addition to a fine collection of portraits and furniture, the house contains an immense kitchen furnished with many fascinating 19th-century domestic gadgets, including a marmalade cutter and an oversize contraption designed to take the buttermilk out of the freshly churned butter. The grounds also include a landscaped park and formal gardens. ⊠ *1½ km (1 mi) west of Castlepollard on the road to Granard (R395),* ☎ *044/61159.* ⌑ *Castle and gardens £4, gardens only £2.50.* ☉ *Gardens May–Sept., daily 2–6; castle rooms mid-June–July and mid-Sept.–end Sept., guided tours daily 2:30–6.*

Fore

❻ *5 km (3 mi) east of Castlepollard.*

The simple village of Fore is dominated by the remains of **Fore Abbey. St. Fechin's Church,** dating from the 10th century, has a massive, cross-inscribed lintel stone. Nearby are the remains of a 13th-century Benedictine **abbey,** whose imposing square towers and loophole windows resemble a castle rather than an abbey.

THE NORTHERN MIDLANDS

This section starts in Longford and works its way north, leaving the ancient kingdom of Leinster for Ulster's two most southerly counties, Cavan and Monaghan. (Ulster's four other counties, which now constitute Northern Ireland, are covered in Chapter 8.) The land north of Cavan is characterized by small, round hills called drumlins and is known as "drumlin country."

Longford

❼ *37 km (24 mi) west of Castlepollard, 124 km (77 mi) northwest of Dublin.*

Longford, the county seat of County Longford, is a typical little market-town community. Jane Austen fans should consider making a visit to **Carrigglas Manor.** The romantic, Tudor-Gothic house, built in 1837 by Thomas Lefroy, offers a glimpse into gracious country living in 18th-century surroundings. His descendants, who still reside here, note that as a young man in England Lefroy was romantically involved with the novelist. Why they never married is a mystery, but it is believed that Austen based the character of Mr. Darcy in *Pride and Prejudice* on Mr. Lefroy. The house still has high-quality plasterwork and many of its original, mid-19th-century furnishings. A magnificent stable yard, part of an earlier house on the site, was designed in 1790 by James Gandon, architect of Dublin's Custom House and Four Courts. Visitors to the stable yard and gardens also have access to a small **costume museum,** which displays mostly 18th-century apparel found in the house. ⊠ *5 km (3 mi) northeast of Longford on R194 to Granard,* ☎ *043/ 45165.* 🖼 *Stable yard, gallery, and shop free; gardens and museum £3.* ⊘ *Stable yard, gardens, and museum daily 11–6; house, by appointment only, early June–early Sept., Thurs.–Mon. 2–6.*

Granard

8 *18 km (11 mi) northeast of Longford.*

The market town and fishing center of Granard stands on high ground near the Longford–Cavan border. The **Motte of Granard** at the southwest end of town was once the site of a fortified Norman castle. In 1932, a statue of St. Patrick was erected here to mark the 15th centenary of his arrival in Ireland.

Outdoor Activities and Sports
County Longford Golf Club (⊠ Glack, ☎ 043/46310) is an 18-hole parkland course.

Cavan

9 *30 km (19 mi) north of Granard, 114 km (71 mi) northwest of Dublin.*

A small, quiet, undistinguished town serving the local farming community, Cavan has two central streets—Main and Farnham—that are parallel to one another. With its pubs and shops, Main Street is like many others in similar Irish towns, while Farnham Street is decorated with Georgian houses, churches, and a courthouse. **Cavan Crystal** is an up-and-coming rival to Waterford in the cut-lead-crystal line; the company offers guided factory tours and access to its factory shop. This is a good opportunity to watch skilled craftspeople at work if you can't make it to Waterford. There is a major building attached to the factory, housing a visitor center, glass museum, restaurant, and coffee shop. ⊠ *Dublin Rd.,* ☎ *049/433–1800.* 🖼 *Free.* ⊘ *Guided tour weekdays at 9:30, 10:30, and 11:30.*

OFF THE
BEATEN PATH

KILLYKEEN FOREST PARK – This park lies among the beautiful, mazelike network of lakes called Lough Oughter. Within the park's 600 acres are a number of signposted walks and nature trails, stables offering horseback riding, and boats and bicycles for rent. Twenty-eight fully outfitted two- and three-bedroom cottages are available for weeklong, weekend, or midweek stays; everything is provided except towels. Rates vary according to season; call for details. ⊠ *11 km (7 mi) north of Cavan,* ☎ *049/433–2541.* 🖼 *Free, parking £1.50.* ⊘ *Feb.–Dec., daily 9–5.*

Dining and Lodging
$$$ ✕ **MacNean House & Bistro.** Tucked away on the Cavan-Fermanagh border, this simple guest house and bistro has become a place of pilgrimage for food lovers. The attraction is the inspired cuisine of Neven Maguire, a young Chef of the Year. Seafood dishes include steamed fillet of turbot with buttered spinach on a basil-butter sauce, and seasonal game such as saddle of hare stuffed with chicken and pesto mousse on a parsnip puree and rosemary jus. Desserts are Neven's specialty—try his hazelnut nougat glacé. Given the remoteness of Blacklion, you might want to book a room ($) when reserving a table. The

65-km (40-mi) detour makes sense if you are heading from Dublin to Sligo or Donegal. ⊠ *Blacklion,* ☎ *072/53022. MC, V.*

$$$$ ✕⊞ **Slieve Russell Hotel and Country Club.** This palatial modern coun-
★ try hotel on 300 acres 26 km (16 mi) west of Cavan makes a convenient break on the Dublin–Sligo journey. The luxurious bedrooms
have chunky, art deco–style furniture. The spa facilities are outstanding, but many guests come primarily for the golfing and the excellent
freshwater and trout fishing. White linens and wrought-iron chandeliers grace the formal Conall Cearnach restaurant, where the extensive menu includes traditionally prepared seafood dishes, such as black
sole on the bone or salmon hollandaise. The Brackley Buttery restaurant is more informal. ⊠ *Ballyconnell, Co. Cavan,* ☎ *049/952–6444,*
FAX *049/952–6474. 141 rooms with bath, 10 suites. 2 restaurants, 2
bars, 2 indoor pools, sauna, steam room, 9- and 18-hole golf courses,
4 tennis courts, health club, horseback riding, Ping-Pong, squash, fishing. AE, DC, MC, V.* 🐜

$$$ ✕⊞ **Cabra Castle.** This enormous, gray-stone castle with its crenelled
battlements and Gothic windows could have been designed in Holly-
wood. In fact, it was built in 1699 as the centerpiece of a 1,000-acre
estate, most of which now belongs to the Dun a Ri National Park. For
the full effect, ask for a "castle room," furnished with more elaborate
Victorian antiques than the others. The Victorian-Gothic theme is car-
ried through the bar and the restaurant with varying degrees of suc-
cess; don't miss the castle gallery, which has hand-painted ceilings and
leaded windows. ⊠ *Kingscourt, Co. Cavan,* ☎ *042/966–7030,* FAX *042/
966–7039. 29 rooms with bath. Restaurant, bar, 9-hole golf course,
horseback riding, fishing. AE, DC, MC, V.*

Outdoor Activities and Sports

Visitors are welcome at the 18-hole **County Cavan Golf Club** (⊠ Arn-
more House, ☎ 049/433–1283). There are two golf courses at the **Slieve
Russell Hotel** (⊠ Ballyconnell, ☎ 049/952–6444), a 9-hole, par-3,
parkland course and an 18-hole championship course.

Cootehill

🔟 *26 km (16 mi) northeast of Cavan.*

One of the most underestimated small towns in Ireland, Cootehill has
a lovely setting on a wooded hillside in the heart of County Cavan. Its
wide streets, with their intriguing old shops, are always busy without
being congested. Most of its visitors are anglers from Europe, the
United Kingdom, and the rest of Ireland.

★ Only pedestrians are allowed through the gates of **Bellamont Forest.**
After about a mile of woodlands, a trail leads to the exquisite, hilltop
Bellamont House, designed in 1728 by Edward Lovett Pearce, archi-
tect of Dublin's Bank of Ireland. Small but perfectly proportioned, it
has been virtually unaltered since it was built and is considered one of
Ireland's finest Palladian-style houses. It is now a private home but is
occasionally opened to the public. If you are interested, inquire locally
or at the Tourist Information Office (TIO) in Cavan (☞ *above*). Walk
up the main street of Cootehill to "the top of the town" (past the White
Horse hotel), and you will see the entrance to the forest.

Dining and Lodging

$ ✕⊞ **Riverside House.** The genuine, old-fashioned Irish hospitality at
Joe and Una Smith's farm is appreciated by both serious anglers and
nonsporting guests. The substantial Victorian house on 100 acres over-
looks the River Annalee. All rooms have peaceful views and are indi-
vidually decorated with modest antiques and family hand-me-downs.

Bring your boots if you want to explore around this working dairy farm. The lodging is signposted 1 km (½ mi) outside town off R188. ✉ *Co. Cavan,* ☎ *049/555–2150,* ⒻⒶⓍ *049/555–2150. 6 rooms, 5 with bath. Dining room, boating, fishing. MC, V.*

$ ✕🏨 **The White Horse.** This typical market-town hotel serves as a lively focal point for the community, and is particularly popular with visiting anglers. Some rooms in the rambling Victorian building are a bit small; all are plainly decorated, and the quieter ones are at the back. The restaurant, a softly lit, mahogany-furnished room in the interior of the hotel, is popular with town folk, who head here for generous portions and simply cooked dishes. ✉ *Market St., Co. Cavan,* ☎ *049/ 555–2124,* ⒻⒶⓍ *049/555–2407. 30 rooms, 24 with bath. Restaurant, 2 bars. AE, MC, V.*

Outdoor Activities and Sports

Rossmore Golf Club (✉ Rossmore Park, near Cootehill, ☎ 047/81316) is an 18-hole parkland course. (*See also* the 18-hole championship golf course at the **Nuremore Hotel,** *below.*)

Monaghan

⓫   *24 km (15 mi) north of Cootehill.*

A former British garrison town, Monaghan is built around a central square known as the Diamond. The town's old **Market House,** elegantly constructed of limestone in 1792, is now the tourist office (☞ Visitor Information *in* Midlands A to Z, *below*). The **County Museum** traces the history of Monaghan from earliest times to the present through archaeological finds, traditional crafts, artwork, and a variety of other historical artifacts. ✉ *Hill St.,* ☎ *047/82928.* 🎫 *Free.* ☉ *June–Sept., Tues.–Sat. 11–5; Oct.–May, Tues.–Sat. 11–1 and 2–5.*

OFF THE   **ROSSMORE FOREST PARK** – Outside town (on R189 Newbliss road),
BEATEN PATH you'll find fresh air in pleasant surroundings at this park with 691 acres of low hills, small lakes, and pleasant forest walks through rhododendron groves. Signposted nature trails are freely accessible.

Dining and Lodging

$$$ ✕🏨 **Nuremore Hotel and Country Club.** This Victorian country house
★   is now a luxury hotel with excellent sporting facilities, including its own trout lake. There are open fires in the large lounge, which is furnished with plump armchairs and Victorian tables. The bedrooms are decorated with mahogany Victorian furniture. The restaurant serves a hybrid French-Irish cuisine in formal surroundings. It is 80 km (50 mi) from both Dublin and Belfast, making it a popular weekend retreat for city dwellers. ✉ *Carrickmacross, Co. Monaghan,* ☎ *042/966–1438,* ⒻⒶⓍ *042/966–1853. 54 rooms with bath, 5 suites. Restaurant, bar, indoor pool, sauna, steam room, 18-hole golf course, 2 tennis courts, health club, horseback riding, squash, fishing. AE, DC, MC, V.* 🐾

Castle Leslie

⓬   *11 km (7 mi) northeast of Monaghan.*

Castle Leslie, originally a medieval stronghold, has been the seat of the Leslie family since 1664. The castle sits on the shores of deep, beautiful **Glaslough,** which means "green lake," whose waters are mirrorlike on sunny days. The present house was built around 1870 in a mix of Gothic and Italianate styles—Sir John Leslie, who built it, spent years in Italy and picked up many ideas there, including the colonnaded loggia, said to have been copied from Michelangelo's cloister at Santa Maria degli Angeli in Rome. The mildly eccentric Leslie family is known for its literary and artistic leanings—when Jonathan Swift stayed here, he wrote in the guest book: "Glaslough with rows of books upon its shelves/written by the Leslies about themselves." The family has many notable relations by marriage, including the Duke of Wellington and Sir Winston Churchill. Wellington's death mask is preserved at Castle Leslie, as is one of Churchill's baby dresses, along with an impressive collection of Italian works of art, including an Andrea della Robbia chimneypiece. There are 14 acres of gardens with miniature golf and croquet. Tea is served in the tearoom and conservatory. ⊠ *Glaslough,* ☎ *047/88109.* ▣ *£3, including tour.* ☉ *May–Aug., daily 2–6; tour on the hr and other times by appointment.*

Dining and Lodging

$$–$$$ ✗▣ **Castle Leslie.** Samantha Leslie herself is usually on hand to host a memorable country-house experience. All of the furniture is original, some of it going back to 1660. The large bedrooms are decked out in Victorian splendor with a wealth of antiques; most beds are either canopied, four-poster, or half-tester. Pre-dinner drinks are served next to a roaring log fire. A four-course dinner of Continental cuisine is served by candlelight in the dining room, with the waitresses wearing Victorian costumes. Entrées may include braised partridge in season, or salmon with sesame and ginger vinaigrette. ⊠ *Glaslough, Co. Monaghan,* ☎ *047/88109,* ℻ *047/88256. 14 rooms with bath. Dining room, boating, fishing. MC, V.* ✆

Clones

🔞　*24 km (15 mi) southwest of Monaghan.*

Clones (pronounced clo-*nez*) was the site, in early Christian times, of a monastery founded by St. Tighearnach, who died here in AD 458. An Augustinian abbey replaced the monastery in the 12th century, and its remains can still be seen near the 75-ft **round tower** on Abbey Street. In the central diamond of the town stands a 10th-century, Celtic **high cross,** with carved panels depicting scriptural scenes. Nowadays Clones, a small, agricultural market town 1 km (½ mi) from the Northern Ireland border, is one of two lace-making centers in County Monaghan (the other is Carrickmacross). In an attempt to bring in some income, local rectors' wives took up the craft, which was introduced in the 19th century. Crochetwork and small raised dots are two hallmarks of Clones lace. A varied selection is on display around the town and can be purchased at the **Clones Lace Centre.** ⊠ *Cara St.,* ☎ *047/52125.* ▣ *Free.* ☉ *Mon. and Wed.–Sat. 10–6.*

OFF THE　　**ANNAGHMAKERRIG –** This small forest park with a lake is the site of
BEATEN PATH　Annaghmakerrig House, home of the Shakespearian stage director Sir Tyrone Guthrie until his death in 1971. He left it to the nation as a residential center for writers, artists, and musicians. It is not officially open to the public, but anyone with a special interest in the arts or in its previous owner can ask to be shown around, and visitors can wander through and picnic on its grounds. ⊠ *5 km (3 mi) southeast of Newbliss,* ☎ *047/54003.*

Lodging

$$$ ▣ **Hilton Park.** To find this stately Georgian mansion, look for large
★ 　 black gates adorned with silver falcons 5 km (3 mi) outside Clones on R183 Ballyhaise road. The 500-acre grounds include three lakes, a working sheep farm, and an organic market garden. Next door is Clones

Golf Club (☞ Outdoor Activities and Sports, *below*). Johnny and Lucy Madden, the friendly hosts, run their house with stylish informality. All rooms are individually decorated with antiques and have lovely views; some have four-poster beds. Dinner of home-grown fruit and vegetables, combined with local meat and fish, is available for guests only. ⊠ *Clones, Co. Monaghan,* ☎ *047/56007,* FAX *047/56033. 6 rooms with bath. Dining room, lake, 9-hole golf course, croquet, boating, fishing. AE, MC, V. Closed Oct.–Mar..* ✎

Outdoor Activities and Sports

Clones Golf Club (⊠ Hilton Park, ☎ 047/56017) is a 9-hole course on limestone that is dry year-round.

NORTH TIPPERARY AND THE WEST MIDLANDS

This section covers the area's western fringe, picking up in the town of Boyle in County Roscommon. (If you do make it this far, be sure to consult Chapter 8; locales covered there are close to Boyle and environs.) It skirts the Lough Key, Lough Ree, Lough Derg, and the River Shannon and, depending on how you travel south, takes you through the hilly landscape of unspoiled County Leitrim—dappled with clean, cool lakes, the county is beloved of anglers for its peaceful, fish-filled waters; it is also almost uninhabited (though it has a liberal sprinkling of villages and is the home of one of Ireland's leading writers, John McGahern). Between the area's many bodies of water, much of the land is bog, a fragile ecosystem that rewards closer investigation. The towns are small and generally undistinguished, with the exceptions of Birr and Strokestown, both of which were laid out by architects and designed to complement the "big houses" that share their names. We then take you southward, to northern County Tipperary.

Boyle

⓮ *190 km (118 mi) northwest of Dublin.*

An old-fashioned town on the Boyle River midway between Lough Gara and Lough Key, Boyle makes a good starting point for visits to the nearby Curlew Mountains. A massive edifice in the center of town, **King House** was built about 1730 by the local King family, who moved 50 years later to larger quarters at Rockingham in what is now Lough Key Forest Park (☞ *below*); that house burned down in 1957. The King family originally came from Staffordshire, England, and aggressively worked to establish themselves as local nobility—Edward King, an ancestor of the Kings who settled here, drowned in the Irish Sea in 1636; he was the subject of Milton's poem "Lycidas." From 1788 to 1922 the house was owned by the British Army and used as a barracks for the Connaught Rangers, known as the fiercest regiment of the British Army (Wellington called them the "Devil's Own"). After extensive renovations, the house was opened to the public in 1995, with exhibits on the Connaught Rangers, the Kings of Connaught, and the history of the house. A coffee shop, popular with locals, serves traditional Irish breakfasts and hearty lunches, both with plenty of homemade baked goods on the menu. ☎ *079/63242.* ⊡ *£2.50.* ☉ *May–Sept., daily 10–6; Apr. and Oct., weekends 10–6; last tour at 5.*

Another reason to visit Boyle is the ruins of the **Cistercian abbey.** The church was founded in the late 12th century when the Romanesque style still prevailed, but as construction went on, the then-hot Gothic style made it to Ireland, evident in arches on the north side. A 16thto 17th-century gatehouse, through which you enter the abbey, has a small exhibition. ⊠ *On N4.* ⊙ *Freely accessible.*

OFF THE
BEATEN PATH

LOUGH KEY FOREST PARK – Part of what was once the massive Rockingham Estate, the park is now a popular base for campers, backpackers, walkers, and anglers. It consists of 840 acres on the shores of the lake and contains a bog garden, a deer enclosure, and a cypress grove. Ruins from Rockingham days, including the remains of a stable block, church, icehouse, and temple, are also found here. Boats can be hired on the lake, and there is also a restaurant. ⊠ *3 km (2 mi) northeast of Boyle off N4,* ☎ *079/62363.* ☜ *Parking £2, June–Sept.* ⊙ *Freely accessible.*

Lodging

$$ 🏨 **Royal Hotel.** The Royal has been at its town center location for over 250 years. Rooms vary in shape and size and are plainly but adequately furnished and well equipped. The chief reason for staying here, apart from the angling opportunities nearby, is to experience everyday life in the heart of an Irish small town. The restaurant overlooks a pretty stretch of river and serves simply prepared local produce. ⊠ *Bridge St., Co. Roscommon,* ☎ *079/62016,* ☒ *079/62016. 16 rooms with bath. Restaurant, bar, coffee shop. AE, DC, MC, V.*

Strokestown

🅖 *28 km (17 mi) south of Boyle.*

★ Strokestown has the widest main street in Ireland—laid out to rival the Ringstrasse in Vienna—which leads to three Gothic arches that mark the entrance to the grounds of **Strokestown Park House.** Home to the Pakenham Mahon family from 1660 to 1979, the house once sat on 27,000 acres and was the second-largest estate in Roscommon, after the King family's Rockingham (☜ *above*). The house has a complicated architectural history, which, to some degree, mirrors the histories of other Anglo-Irish houses. The oldest parts of the house date from 1696, Palladian wings were added in the 1730s to the original block, and the house was extended again in the early 19th century. Its contents are a rich trove specific to the site, as they were never liquidated in the auctions experienced by similar houses. The interior is full of curiosities, such as the gallery above the kitchen, which allowed the lady of the house to supervise domestic affairs from a safe distance. Menus were dropped from the balcony on Monday mornings with instructions to the cook for the week's meals. The 4-acre walled pleasure garden has the longest herbaceous border in Britain and Ireland. The **Irish Famine Museum,** in the stable yards, documents in detail the disastrous famine (1845–49) and the subsequent mass emigration. ☎ *078/33013.* ☜ *House £3.50; house, museum, and garden £8.50.* ⊙ *Apr.–Oct., daily 11–5:30; by appointment other times for groups.* ⊗

Roscommon

🅖 *43 km (27 mi) south of Boyle, 19 km (12 mi) south of Strokestown.*

Roscommon is the capital of County Roscommon, where sheep- and cattle-raising are the main occupations. It's a pleasant little town with many solid stone buildings, including the Bank of Ireland in the former courthouse and county jail. On the southern slopes of a hill in the lower part of town sit the remains of **Roscommon Abbey.** In the abbey's principal ruin, a church, are eight sculpted figures that represent gallowglasses (medieval Irish professional soldiers) and stand at the base of the choir. The ruins are freely accessible. To the north of Roscom-

mon town are the weathered remains of **Roscommon Castle,** a large
Norman stronghold first built in the 13th century.

Outdoor Activities and Sports

Bikes can be rented from **Brendan Sheerin** (⊠ Main St., Boyle, ☎ 079/
62010).

Athlone

⑰   *29 km (18 mi) southeast of Roscommon, 127 km (79 mi) west of Dublin,
121 km (75 mi) east of Limerick.*

Athlone is the main shopping hub for the surrounding area and an important road and rail junction. The introduction of a bypass has eased
traffic congestion, and a local initiative highlighting the attractions of
Athlone's "Left Bank" (behind the castle [☞ *below*]), where many of
the buildings date from at least 200 years ago, have combined to make
Athlone a more attractive destination.

Athlone Castle is the site most worth visiting in Athlone. Built in the
13th century, the castle lies beside the River Shannon, at the southern
end of Lough Ree. After their defeat at the Battle of the Boyne in 1691,
the Irish retreated to Athlone and made the river their first line of defense. The castle was extensively renovated in 1991 for its 300th anniversary. It remains an interesting example of a Norman stronghold
and houses a small museum of artifacts relating to Athlone's eventful
past. Admission includes access to an interpretative center depicting
the siege of Athlone in 1691, the flora and fauna of the Shannon, and
the life of the tenor John McCormack (1884–1945), an Athlone native and perhaps the finest lyric tenor Ireland has ever produced. ⊠
Town Bridge, ☎ *0902/72107.* ▭ *£2.50.* ⊙ *May–Sept., daily 10–5; Oct.–
Apr. by appointment.*

Dining and Lodging

$$$ ✕ **Le Château.** In Athlone's colorful Old Quarter, a former Presbyte-
rian church now houses this romantic restaurant. The furniture may
be ecclesiastical, but the decor strikes a nautical note. Candlelit tables
are set with large wineglasses and fine old bone china. Owner-chef
Stephen Linehan's menu may include medallions of veal with smoked
bacon, garlic, and herbs, or roast peppered monkfish with fresh herb
sauce. For dessert try the lemon tart or, in summer, fresh strawberry
vol-au-vents with homemade ice cream. ⊠ *Saint Peter's Port, The
Docks,* ☎ *0902/94517. AE, DC, MC, V. No lunch Mon.–Sat.*

$$$ ✕ **Wineport Restaurant.** About 5 km (3 mi) north of town on the shores
★   of Lough Ree is this pleasantly informal restaurant in a wooden
boathouse adorned with memorabilia from the original Lough Ree Yacht
Club. The menu changes every eight weeks, but roast organic venison
(from a nearby farm) served in a juniper marinade is a popular year-
round main course. New Irish cuisine, for example confit of salmon
with a black pudding champ (mashed potato), is also featured. ⊠ *Glasson,* ☎ *0902/85466. AE, DC, MC, V. Closed Mon.–Tues. Nov.–Feb.*

$$$ ✕▯ **Hodson Bay Hotel.** Head 4 km (2½ mi) out of town to this four-
★   story mansion on the shores of Lough Ree. Once an 18th-century
family home, the hotel is adjacent to Athlone's golf course (☞ Out-
door Activities and Sports, *below*) and has its own marina. All guest
rooms are coordinated in deep pastel shades with well-designed wooden
furniture. L'Escale restaurant, a romantic, candlelit room, overlooks
the lake. The menu offers imaginative Irish cooking with a French ac-
cent. To get to the hotel from Athlone, take the new Athlone by-
pass/ring road to the N61 Roscommon road, from where the hotel is
clearly signposted. ⊠ *Roscommon Rd., Athlone, Co. Westmeath,* ☎

0902/92444, ℻ 0902/92688. *93 rooms with bath, 7 suites. 2 restaurants, bar, indoor pool, sauna, 18-hole golf course, 2 tennis courts, health club, horseback riding, fishing. AE, DC, MC, V.* 🐾

Outdoor Activities and Sports

BICYCLING

Rent bikes from **M. R. Hardiman** (✉ Irishtown, ☎ 0902/78669).

BOATING

The Viking is a riverboat that travels up the Shannon to nearby Lough Ree. ✉ *The Strand*, ☎ *0902/73383.* 🎫 *£5.* ☼ *Sailings July–Sept., Thurs.–Tues. at 11, 2:30, and 4, Wed. at 4:30.*

A river cruiser for a floating holiday can be rented by the week from **Athlone Cruisers Ltd.** (✉ Jolly Mariner Marina, ☎ 0902/72892) or **S. G. S. Marine** (✉ Ballykeeran, ☎ 0902/85163).

GOLF

Athlone Golf Club (✉ Hodson Bay, ☎ 0902/92073 or 0902/92235) is a lakeside, 18-hole parkland course. **Glasson Golf & Country Club** (✉ Glasson, ☎ 0902/85120) is an 18-hole parkland course bordered on three sides by Lough Ree and the River Shannon. **Mount Temple Golf Club** (✉ Campfield Lodge, Moate, ☎ 0902/81545) is a 9-hole parkland course 19 km (12 mi) east of Athlone.

Clonmacnoise

★ ⑱ *20 km (13 mi) south of Athlone, 93 km (58 mi) east of Galway.*

Many ancient sites dot the River Shannon, but Clonmacnoise is early Christian Ireland's foremost monastic settlement and, like Chartres, a royal site. The monastery was founded by St. Ciaran between 543 and 549 at a location that was not as remote as it now appears to be— near the intersection of two of what were then Ireland's most vital routes: the Shannon River, running north–south, and the Eiscir Riada, running east–west. Like Glendalough, Celtic Ireland's other great monastic site, Clonmacnoise benefitted from isolation; surrounded by bog, it is accessible only via one road or the Shannon.

The monastery was founded on an esker (natural gravel ridge) overlooking the Shannon and a marshy area known as the Callows, which today is protected habitat for the corncrake, a wading bird. Numerous buildings and ruins remain. The small **cathedral** dates as far back as the 10th century but has additions dating from as recently as the 15th century. It was the burial place of kings of Connaught and of Tara, and of Rory O'Conor, the last High King of Ireland, buried here in 1198. The two round towers include **O'Rourke's Tower**, which was struck by lightning and subsequently rebuilt in the 12th century. There are **eight smaller churches.** The smallest is thought to be the burial place of St. Ciaran; the only one not built within the monastery walls is the Nun's Church, about 1 km (½ mi) east. The **high crosses** have been moved into the visitor center to protect them from the elements (copies stand in their original places); the best preserved of these are the **Cross of the Scriptures,** also known as **Flann's Cross.** Some of the treasures and manuscripts originating from Clonmacnoise are now housed in Dublin; most are at the National Museum, while the 12th-century *Book of the Dun Cow* is at the Royal Irish Academy Library (☞ Chapter 1).

Clonmacnoise survived raids by feuding Irish tribes, Vikings, and Normans for almost 1,000 years, until 1552, when the English garrison from Athlone reduced it to ruin. Since then it has remained a prestigious burial place. Among the ancient stones are many other graves of local people dating from the 17th to the mid-20th century, when a new graveyard was consecrated on adjoining land. ✉ *Near Shannon-bridge*, ☎ *0905/74195.* 🎫 *£3.50.* ⊙ *Mid-June–Sept., daily 9–7; Oct.–May, daily 10–6 or dusk.* 🕊

Bord na Mona Bog Rail Tour

★ ⑲ *10 km (6 mi) south of Clonmacnoise.*

As you pass through the small town of Shannonbridge, on either side of the road you'll notice vast stretches of chocolate-brown boglands and isolated industrial plants for processing this area's natural resource. Under the jurisdiction of Bord na Mona, the same government agency that makes commercial use of other boglands, the area is worth exploring. If you would like to have a close look at a bog, take a ride on the Bord na Mona Bog Rail Tour, which leaves from Uisce Dubh. A small, green-and-yellow diesel locomotive pulls one coach across the bog while the driver provides commentary on a landscape unchanged for millennia. There are more than 1,200 km (745 mi) of narrow-gauge bog railway, and the section on the tour, known as the Clonmacnoise and South Offaly Railway, is the only part accessible to the public. ✉ *Uisce Dubh, near Shannonbridge,* ☎ *0905/74114.* 🎫 *£3.50.* ⊙ *Tour Apr.–Oct., daily on the hr 10–5.* 🕊

Banagher

⑳ *21 km (13 mi) southeast of Shannonbridge.*

A small but lively village on the shores of the River Shannon, Banagher has a marina that makes the town a popular base for water-sports fans. Anthony Trollope, who came to Ireland as a post office surveyor in 1841, lived here while he wrote his first book, *The Macdermots of Ballycloran.* Charlotte Brontë spent her honeymoon here. **Flynn's** (✉ Main St., ☎ 0509/51312), a light and spacious Victorian-style bar in the center of town, has a lunch menu of generously filled sandwiches, salad platters, a roast meat of the day, and chicken, fish, or burgers with chips.

If you happen to be in Banagher on a Thursday or a Sunday, you can take a two-hour **Shannon cruise** on *The River Queen,* an enclosed launch that seats 54 passengers and has a full bar on board. ✉ *Silver Line Cruisers Ltd., The Marina,* ☎ *0509/51112.* 🎫 *£5.* ⊙ *Cruises June–mid-Sept., Thurs. at 3, Sun. at 2:30 and 4:30, weather permitting.*

Birr

㉑ *12 km (8 mi) southeast of Banagher, 130 km (80 mi) west of Dublin.*

Birr is a quiet, sleepy place with tree-lined malls and modest, Georgian houses. It was recently designated as a heritage town. The settlement's roots go back to the 6th century, but it was much later, in the mid-18th century, that Birr was given its modern-day appearance, as a Georgian building boom took hold.

★ All roads in Birr lead to the gates of **Birr Castle Demesne,** a Gothic Revival castle (built around an earlier 17th-century castle that was damaged by fire in 1823) that is still the home of the earls of Rosse. It is not open to the public, but you can visit the surrounding 150 acres of gardens. The present earl and countess of Rosse continue the family tradition of making botanical expeditions for specimens of rare trees, plants, and shrubs from all over the world. The formal gardens contain the tallest (32 ft) box hedges in the world and vine-sheltered hornbeam allees. In spring, you can see a wonderful display of flowering magnolias, cherries, crab apples, and naturalized narcissi; in autumn, the maples, chestnuts, and weeping beeches blaze red and gold. The grounds are laid out around a lake and along the banks of two adjacent rivers; above one of these stands the castle. The grounds also contain **Ireland's Historic Science Centre,** an exhibition on astronomy, photography, botany, and engineering housed in the stable block. The giant (72-inch) reflecting telescope, built in 1845, remained the largest in the world for the next 75 years and was recently restored. Allow at least two hours to see all that's here. ⊠ *Rosse Row,* ☎ *0509/20336.* 🎫 *£5.50.* ☉ *Apr.–Oct., daily 9–6.* 🐾

Dining and Lodging

$$$ ✕🏨 **Kinnitty Castle.** At the foot of the Slieve Bloom Mountains 16 km (10 mi) east of Birr, Kinnitty is an exuberant, turreted Gothic Revival edifice, rebuilt in 1927 of ashlar granite. Everything is on a large scale—bedrooms have large four-poster beds and intricately carved chairs, and heavy old beams are incorporated into the bathrooms in the old house. Accommodations in the new wing are smaller. The dining room has enormously tall windows and a dark wood floor. Typical main courses are panfried loin of lamb with its own sweetbreads or ragout of lobster from the tank, finished with sevruga caviar. ⊠ *Kinnitty, Birr, Co. Offaly,* ☎ *0509/37318,* ⨎ *0509/37284. 37 rooms with bath. Restaurant, bar, tennis court, horseback riding, Ping-Pong, fishing. AE, DC, MC, V.* 🐾

$$ ✕🏨 **Tullanisk House.** Set on 700 acres of woodland in its own deer
★ park, this 18th-century dower house for Birr Castle (☞ *above*) has been carefully restored into an elegant accommodation with the atmosphere of a private home. Rooms vary in size, but owner-hosts Susie and George Gossip have decorated each with character. Books and magazines are everywhere, and open fires, board games, and table tennis are available on wet days. Dinner (reservations essential) is served on family china and silverware by candlelight in the classic Georgian dining room. All guests sit at the host's table and share the same menu, which features fresh local produce, cooked usually by George, and game as a specialty during the winter. ⊠ *Co. Offaly,* ☎ *0509/20572,* ⨎ *0509/21783. 5 rooms with bath. Dining room, hiking, Ping-Pong. AE, MC, V.* 🐾

$ ✕🏨 **Dooly's.** This 250-year-old, black-and-white coaching inn is tucked away in a corner of Birr's central square. A log fire burns in the front lobby, decorated in the Georgian style. Rooms have pastel colors, floral drapes and bedspreads, and plain, dark-pastel walls. The relaxed bar and coffee shop are busy all day; a more formal dining experience is in the Emmet Restaurant. The five-course table-d'hôte dinner menu, an excellent value, may feature medallions of beef flambéd in whiskey and onions or fresh Corrib salmon steak poached in pink peppercorns and white wine. ⊠ *Emmet Sq., Co. Offaly,* ☎ *0509/20032,* ⨎ *0509/ 21332. 18 rooms with bath. Restaurant, bar, coffee shop, horseback riding, fishing. AE, DC, MC, V.* 🐾

$ ✕🏨 **The Maltings.** In a picturesque riverside setting near Birr Castle, this beautiful cut-stone and brick malt house is a family-run accommodation. Spacious rooms have small windows, country pine furniture, and simple matching floral drapes and spreads. The cheerful, low-ceiling restaurant overlooks the river and offers good value in plain cooking. ⊠ *Castle St., Co. Offaly,* ☎ ⨎ *0509/21345. 10 rooms with bath. Restaurant, sauna, exercise room. MC, V.*

Lough Derg

㉒ *16 km (10 mi) west of Birr on R489.*

Between Portland and Portumna the River Shannon widens into 32,000 acres of unpolluted water, known as Lough Derg, a popular center for water sports, including waterskiing, yachting, and motor cruising.

Fishermen flock here as well for pike- and coarse-angling. There are excellent woodland walks around the shore of the Lough. (Be sure not to confuse this Lough Derg with the lake of the same name in County Donegal, a well-known pilgrimage site, covered in Chapter 7.) The well-signposted, scenic **Lough Derg Drive,** approximately 90 km (54 mi), encircles the lake, passing through a number of pretty waterside villages, from Portumna in the north to Killaloe in the south. **Terryglass,** on the eastern shore of Lough Derg and well signposted on R439 from Birr, is particularly popular with water-sports enthusiasts and anglers, as well as regular vacationers seeking an away-from-it-all destination; it is considered one of the prettiest villages in Ireland.

Lodging

$ ▦ **Riverrun House.** Typical of the very best of the newer B&Bs around the country, this rambling farmhouse-style building in the middle of the village combines country stylishness with practicality. Clean, clutter-free rooms have duvet-covered king-size beds, framed botanical prints, one or two pieces of antique country pine, and throw rugs on stripped pine floors. Dinner isn't served, but the village has two pub-restaurants. A stream runs through the pretty, south-facing garden, and small children are made especially welcome. ⊠ *Terryglass, Nenagh, Co. Tipperary,* ☎ *067/22125,* ℻ *067/22187. 6 rooms with bath. Dining room, tennis court, bicycles. AE, MC, V.*

Outdoor Activities and Sports

The 18-hole parkland course at **Birr Golf Club** (⊠ The Glens, Birr, ☎ 0509/20082) is highly recommended by discerning golfers.

Roscrea

❷❸ *19 km (12 mi) south of Birr.*

The main Dublin–Limerick road (N7) passes through Roscrea, a charming town steeped in religious history, cutting right through a 7th-century monastery founded by St. Cronan. It also passes the west facade of a 12th-century Romanesque church that now forms an entrance gate to a modern Catholic church. Above the structure's round-headed doorway is a hood molding enclosing the figure of a bishop, probably St. Cronan.

With your back to St. Cronan's monastery, turn left and then right onto Castle Street to visit **Damer House,** a superb example of an early 18th-century town house on the grand scale. It was built in 1725 within the curtain walls of a Norman castle, at a time when homes were often constructed beside or attached to the strongholds they replaced. The house has a plain, symmetrical facade and a magnificent carved-pine staircase inside; on display are exhibits of local historical interest. The 13th-century stone castle is surrounded by a moat and consists of a gate tower, curtain walls, and two corner towers. The house is home to the **Roscrea Heritage Centre.** ⊠ *Castle St.,* ☎ *0505/21850.* ▦ *£2.50. ⊙ May–Sept., daily 9:30–6; Oct.–Apr., weekends 10–5.*

Outdoor Activities and Sports

Roscrea Golf Club (⊠ Demyrale, ☎ 0509/21130) is an 18-hole parkland course with views of the Slieve Bloom Mountains.

Nenagh

❷❹ *35 km (21 mi) west of Roscrea, 35 km (21 mi) east of Limerick.*

Nenagh was originally a Norman settlement; it grew to a market town in the 19th century. Standing right in the center of Nenagh, the **Castle Keep** is all that remains of the original town. Once one of five round towers linked by a curtain wall, and measuring 53 ft across the base, it rises to 100 ft, with 19th-century castellations at the top. The gatehouse and governor's house of Nenagh's old county jail now form the **Nenagh Heritage Centre,** which has permanent displays of rural life in the recent past before mechanization, as well as temporary painting and photography exhibits. ⊠ *Kickham St.,* ☎ *067/32633.* ⬚ *£2.* ☉ *Easter–Oct., weekdays 9:30–5, Sun. 2:30–5; Nov.–Easter, weekdays 9:30–5.*

Dining and Lodging

$ ✕ **Country Choice.** Food lovers from all over Ireland seek out this well-stocked delicatessen and sample the home-cooked fare in the simple coffee shop at the back of the store. Owner Peter Ward is known as one of the best suppliers of Irish farmhouse cheese, and locally made cheese features on his wife Mary's menus. Specialties include Cashel Blue, an Irish blue cheese, broccoli soup, as well as slow-cooked meat dishes like lamb ragout or beef in Guinness casserole. Home-baked bread and pastries are made with local flour. ⊠ *25 Kenyon St.,* ☎ *067/32596. No credit cards. Closed Sun.*

$$ ✕🏠 **Waterman's Lodge.** Perched on a hilltop with bay windows overlooking the Shannon and distant County Clare, this lovely lodge is an ideal rural retreat. Open fires, piles of books, high ceilings, and timber floors combine to create a relaxing, country-house atmosphere. Rooms have brass or cast-iron beds and modest antiques. Chef Thomas O'Leary's imaginative treatment of seasonal local produce is renowned. Try his roast rack of lamb with a parsley crust, sage-flavored couscous, and lamb jus. ⊠ *Ballina, Killaloe, Co. Tipperary,* ☎ *061/376333,* FAX *061/375445. 10 rooms with bath. Restaurant, horseback riding, fishing. DC, MC, V. Closed Dec. 22–mid-Mar..* ⊗

$ ✕🏠 **Ashley Park House.** Margaret and P. J. Mounsey invite guests to experience informal country-house living in their 18th-century fishing lodge overlooking Lough Ourna. Formal gardens and 76 acres of beech woodland surround the home, and abundant wildlife can be observed from a rowboat. High ceilings, country views, and an abundance of antiques are features of the large bedrooms. Dinners created from fresh local produce may include trout you've caught in the lake. ⊠ *Ardcroney, Co. Tipperary,* ☎ FAX *067/38223. 5 rooms, 2 with bath. Boating, fishing. No credit cards.*

Outdoor Activities and Sports

BOATING

Shannon Sailing (⊠ New Marina Complex, Dromineer, ☎ 067/24499) organizes cruises of scenic Lough Derg by water bus and also hires out cruisers and sailboards.

GOLF

Nenagh Golf Club (⊠ Beechwood, ☎ 067/31476), 8 km (5 mi) outside of town is a typical 18-hole, par-69 Midlands course: green, flat, and not too busy.

THE MIDLANDS A TO Z

Arriving and Departing

By Bus
Bus Éireann (☎ 01/836–6111) runs an express bus from Dublin to Mullingar in 1½ hours, with a round-trip fare of £9. Buses depart three times daily. A regular-speed bus, leaving twice daily, makes the trip in two hours.

By Car

Mullingar (the regional capital), Longford, and Boyle are on the main N4 route between Dublin and Sligo. It takes one hour to drive the 55 km (34 mi) from Dublin to Mullingar, and two hours from Mullingar to Sligo. To get from Mullingar to the southwest, a 150-km (94-mi) trip that takes about two hours, you can take N52 to Nenagh, where it meets N7, and follow that into Limerick. R390 from Mullingar leads you west to Athlone, where it connects with N6 to Galway. The 120-km (75-mi) drive takes about 2½ hours.

By Plane

The principal international airport serving the Midlands is **Dublin Airport** (☎ 01/844–4900). **Sligo Airport** (☎ 071/68280) has daily flights from Dublin on Aer Lingus. Car-rental facilities are available at Dublin Airport. For more information on these airports, *see* Arriving and Departing *in* Chapters 1 and 7.

By Train

A direct-rail service links Mullingar to Dublin (Connolly Station), with three trains every day making the 1½-hour journey. It costs £7.50 one-way and £12.50 round-trip. Contact **Irish Rail** (☎ 01/836–6222) for information.

Getting Around

By Bus

The express buses leaving Dublin (☞ Arriving and Departing by Bus, *above*) make stops at Mullingar (1½ hrs), Longford (2¼ hrs), Carrick-on-Shannon (3 hrs), Boyle (3¼ hrs), and Sligo (4¼ hrs). There is also a daily bus from Mullingar to Athlone and an express service connecting Galway, Athlone, Longford, Cavan, Clones, Monaghan, and Sligo. Details of all bus services are available from Bus Éireann depots at the following locations: **Athlone Railway Station** (☎ 0902/72651), **Cavan Bus Office** (☎ 049/433–1353), **Longford Railway Station** (☎ 043/45208), **Monaghan Bus Office** (☎ 047/82377), **Sligo Railway Station** (☎ 071/69888), and **Bus Éireann** (☎ 01/836–6111 in Dublin).

By Car

Most of the winding roads in the Midlands are uncongested, although you may encounter an occasional animal or agricultural machine crossing the road. In Mullingar, the cattle-trading town, roads can become badly crowded, however. If you're driving in the north of Counties Cavan and Monaghan, be sure to avoid "unapproved" roads crossing the border into Northern Ireland. The approved routes into Northern Ireland connect the towns of Monaghan and Aughnacloy, Castlefinn and Castlederg, Swalinbar and Enniskillen, Clones and Newtownbutler, and Monaghan and Rosslea. Those driving a rented car should make sure it has been cleared for cross-border journeys.

By Train

Trains from Mullingar, departing twice daily every weekday and Sunday, stop at Longford (35 mins), Carrick-on-Shannon (1 hr), Boyle (1¼ hrs), and Sligo (2 hrs).

Contacts and Resources

B&B Reservation Agencies

For a small fee, **Bord Fáilte** will book accommodations anywhere in Ireland through its central reservations system. B&Bs can be booked at local visitor information offices when they are open; however, even these reservations will go through the central system. For more information, *see* Lodging *in* Smart Travel Tips A to Z.

Car Rentals

There are a handful of car rental firms in the Midlands: **Hamill's Rent-a-Car** (⊠ Dublin Rd., Mullingar, ☎ 044/44500), **Gerry Mullin** (⊠ North Rd., Monaghan, ☎ 047/81396), **O'Reilly & Sons/Euromobil** (⊠ Dublin Rd., Longford, ☎ 043/46496).

Emergencies

Police, fire, and ambulance (☎ 999). For medical and ambulance service, contact Mullingar's **General Hospital** (☎ 044/40221).

PHARMACY

Weir's Chemist (⊠ Market Sq., Mullingar, ☎ 044/48462).

Outdoor Activities and Sports

FISHING

General information about fishing can be obtained in most hotels, B&Bs, and bars. Contact local TIOs (☞ *below*) or the Irish Tourist Board (☞ Visitor Information, *in* Smart Travel Tips A to Z) for more details on angling tournaments. For information on necessary licenses and permits, contact the **Eastern Regional Fisheries Board** (⊠ Balnagowan Mobhi Boreen, Dublin 9, ☎ 01/837–9209).

Visitor Information

Five Midlands Tourist Information Offices (TIOs) are open all year (not all have fax numbers): **Carrick-on-Shannon** (⊠ The Marina, Co. Leitrim, ☎ 078/20170), **Cavan** (⊠ Farnham St., Co. Cavan, ☎ 049/31942), **Monaghan** (⊠ Market House, Co. Monaghan, ☎ 047/81122), **Mullingar** (⊠ Dublin Rd., Co. Westmeath, ☎ 044/48650, FAX 044/40413), **Portlaoise** (⊠ James Fintan Lawlor Ave., ☎ 0502/21178). The Mullingar TIO (☞ *above*) has information on Counties Westmeath, Offaly, Monaghan, Cavan, and Laois.

Another nine Midlands TIOs are open seasonally: **Athlone** (⊠ Church St., ☎ 0902/94630), open April–October; **Birr** (⊠ Rosse Row, ☎ 0509/20110), open May–September; **Boyle** (⊠ Bridge St., ☎ 079/62145), open April–September; **Clonmacnoise** (⊠ Clonmacnoise, ☎ 0905/74134), open April–October; **Longford** (⊠ Main St., ☎ 043/46566), open June–September; **Nenagh** (⊠ Connolly St., ☎ 067/31610), open May–early September; **Roscommon** (⊠ The Square, ☎ 0903/26342), open mid-May–mid-September; **Tipperary** (⊠ James St., ☎ 062/51457), open May–October; **Tullamore** (⊠ Bridge St., ☎ 0506/52617), open mid-June–mid-September. For off-season inquiries about Boyle and Roscommon, consult the Sligo TIO (☞ Visitor Information *in* The Northwest A to Z *in* Chapter 7). For off-season inquiries about Tipperary, contact the Waterford TIO (☞ Visitor Information *in* The Southeast A to Z *in* Chapter 4).

4 THE SOUTHEAST

Counties Wexford, Carlow, Kilkenny, Tipperary, and Waterford

Although the Southeast doesn't have Ireland's wildest scenic landscape, it *does* have plenty to offer—things all Ireland, and the world, enjoy. Time-burnished Kilkenny glows with an old-world atmosphere, while Tipperary's Golden Vale is home to the country's most fertile farmland. Counties Wexford and Waterford are leading holiday destinations for natives in the know, with opera cognoscenti flocking to Wexford's famous festival. And long before Kleenex and Xerox turned their brand names into the thing itself, Waterford set a standard for cut crystal that all the world knows by name.

Updated by
Noeleen
McManus

T HE IRISH LIKE TO PUT LABELS ON AREAS, and "Ireland's sunny Southeast" is the tag they've taken to calling Counties Wexford, Carlow, Kilkenny, Tipperary, and Waterford. The moniker is by no means merely fanciful: the weather station on the coast at Rosslare reports that this region receives more hours of sunshine than anywhere else in the country. The Southeast, indeed, also has the driest weather in Ireland, with as little as 40 inches of rainfall per year—compared to an average of 80 inches on parts of the west coast. This is saying something in a country where seldom do more than three days pass without a shower of rain, which can vary from the finest light drizzle to a downpour that would convince Olympic swimmers they had never truly come to grips with the element of water. Little wonder the outdoor-loving Irish have made the Southeast's coast a popular vacation area. The whole area is Croesus-rich with natural beauty: not the rugged and wild wonders found to the north and west but an inland landscape of fertile river valleys and lush, undulating pastureland, with a coast that alternates between long, sandy beaches and rocky bays backed by low cliffs. Although the region is blessed with idyllic country sights and small and charming fishing villages, you'll find you never have to travel that far to find the bright lights—the cities of Kilkenny, Waterford, and Wexford.

The Southeast's coastal and inland areas both have a long, interesting history. The kings of Munster had their ceremonial center on the Rock of Cashel, which in the 7th century became an important monastic center and bishopric, and there were other thriving early Christian monasteries at Kilkenny, Ardmore, and Lismore. But the quiet life of early Christian Ireland was disrupted from the 9th century onward by a series of Viking invasions. The Vikings liked what they found here—a pleasant climate; rich, easily cultivated land; and a series of safe, sheltered harbors—so they stayed and founded the towns of Wexford and Waterford. (Waterford's name comes from the Norse Vadrefjord, Wexford's from Waesfjord.) Less than two centuries later, the same cities were conquered by Anglo-Norman barons and turned into walled strongholds. The Anglo-Normans and the Irish chieftains soon started to intermarry, but the process of integration came to a halt in 1366 with the Statutes of Kilkenny, based on English fears that if such intermingling continued they would lose whatever control over Ireland they had. The next great crisis was Oliver Cromwell's Irish campaign of 1650, which, in attempting to crush Catholic opposition to the English parliament, brought widespread woe.

Carlow Town, Kilkenny and Waterford cities, and Wexford Town together provide an introduction to Irish history. All have remnants of their successive waves of invaders—Celt, Viking, and Norman. The most beautiful is Kilkenny City, an important ecclesiastic and political center up to the 17th century and now a lively market town whose streets still contain many remains from medieval times, most notably St. Canice's Cathedral and a magnificent 12th-century castle that received in turn a sumptuous Victorian makeover. Wexford's narrow streets are built on one side of a wide estuary, and it has a delightful maritime atmosphere. Waterford, although less immediately attractive than Wexford, is also built on the confluence of two of the region's rivers, the Suir and the Barrow. It offers a rich selection of Viking and Norman remains, some attractive Georgian buildings, and also the world-renowned Waterford Glass Factory, open to visitors.

Beyond lies a tranquil countryside with more Edenic pleasures. The road between Rosslare and Ballyhack passes through quiet, atypical, flat countryside dotted with thatched cottages. Beyond Tramore, level, sandy beaches give way to rocky Helvick Head and the foothills of the Knockmealdown Mountains at Dungarvan. Among the inland riverside towns, Carrick-on-Suir and Clonmel each have a special, quiet charm. In the far southwest of County Waterford, near the Cork border, Ardmore presents early Christian remains on an exposed headland, while in the wooded splendor of the Blackwater Valley, the tiny cathedral town of Lismore has a hauntingly beautiful fairy-tale castle.

Anglers will scarcely believe the variety of fishing and scenery along the Rivers Barrow, Nore, and Suir, and especially in the Blackwater Valley area. County Tipperary is the location of the Rock of Cashel, a vast, cathedral-topped rock rising above the plain and one of Ireland's most stunning historic sights. The ancient seat of the kings of Munster, Cashel is also, according to legend, where St. Patrick converted the High King of Ireland to Christianity.

Pleasures and Pastimes

Dining

The restaurants in this region are generally small and informal. Seafood—especially Wexford mussels, crab, and locally caught salmon—appears on most menus, along with local lamb, beef, and game in season. Food is usually prepared in a simple, country-house style, but be ready for some pleasant surprises, as there are a number of ambitious Irish chefs at work in the area in both restaurants and hotels. For price ranges, *see* Dining *in* Smart Travel Tips A to Z.

Festivals and the Arts

There are two major arts festivals in the area: Kilkenny Arts Week, held in late August, features classical music, theater, and art exhibits, and the Wexford Opera Festival, where each year in late October and early November three rare operas are given full-scale productions with internationally renowned casts (☞ Nightlife and the Arts *in* Kilkenny City *and* Wexford Town, *below*).

Lodging

The coast is popular with Irish families during July and August, when it is advisable to book in advance, especially at places right on the coast. For price ranges, *see* Lodging *in* Smart Travel Tips A to Z.

Outdoor Activities and Sports

BICYCLING

The Southeast is a relatively unchallenging area for cyclists, with the only seriously hilly parts in the Knockmealdown and Comeragh mountains to the south of the region. If you enjoy bird life and sea vistas, try planning a coastal route—between Arklow and Wexford it is predominantly flat with expanses of sandy beaches. The Hook Peninsula between Wexford and Waterford has a network of small, quiet roads, many of them leading to tranquil fishing villages. Traveling from Waterford to Dungarvan via Dunmore East and Tramore offers a variety of scenery combining cliff-top rides with stretches of beachfront.

GOLF

Some of Ireland's best parkland courses can be found in the Southeast, and there is also a championship links course at Rosslare. Mount Juliet, near Kilkenny, has been publicly acclaimed by Nick Faldo as one of Europe's best. It is one of six 18-hole courses to open in the area in recent years. Expect to pay greens fees of around £18–£20 per day on weekdays and £22–£25 per day on weekends. *See* Chapter 9 for more details.

HIKING

Two hiking trails cross the region, and the scenery on both is interestingly varied with wooded hills, rich farmland, and several rivers. The South Leinster Way begins in the County Carlow town of Kildavin and makes its way southwest over Mt. Leinster and the River Barrow, terminating in Carrick-on-Suir. A second trail, the Munster Way, picks up where the first ends and leads through the Vee Gap in the Knockmealdown Mountains and on to Clogheen.

HORSEBACK RIDING

If you have any equestrian skills at all, you will probably want to ride some of the fine horses bred in this part of Ireland. Inland, the terrain is mainly arable farmland, while the long, sandy beaches of the coast are regularly used as gallops. Most establishments have riding for about £12 to £15 an hour—booking is generally essential—and many stables offer hunting packages to the more experienced rider; rates are available on request.

SPECTATOR SPORTS

The people of the Southeast are a sporting lot, and on any given day you're likely to find the stand at the races or the hurling matches overflowing. Greyhound racing is extremely popular here, and Irish dogs are considered to be among the best in the world. Races are held at night, and a bar and restaurant are usually within the stadium. Horse races are also held regularly in the area at small, informal meets. Ask locally about Gaelic football and hurling venues. These skillful and fast-moving games can often be watched for free, or for the nominal entrance price at one of the seven Gaelic Athletic Association (GAA) stadia in the area.

Exploring the Southeast

The Southeast is geographically a large region (a car is essential for getting around here), stretching from the town of Carlow near the border of County Wicklow (☞ Chapter 2) in the north to Ardmore near the border of County Cork (☞ Chapter 5) in the south. Outside of the months of July and August, when the Irish themselves head here for their own vacations, the region is relatively free of traffic, making it ideal for leisurely exploration. Wexford, Waterford, and Kilkenny all have compact town centers best explored on foot, and they also make good touring bases.

Numbers in the text correspond to numbers in the margin and on the Southeast, Kilkenny City, Wexford Town, and Waterford City maps.

Great Itineraries

IF YOU HAVE 3 DAYS

Three days is enough time for a greatest-hits itinerary of the Southeast, though it won't leave you much time for meandering along the back roads. Start in the south of the region by taking the main Cork–Wexford road (N25) and heading north to visit the popular seaside resort and cliff-top early Christian monuments at **Ardmore** ㊺. Stop in the famed pubs of **Dungarvan** ㊸ for a *ceilí* (Irish dance); then head on to **Lismore** ㊻, a small, pretty village on the Blackwater River, to tour the gardens of the Duke of Devonshire's spectacular castle. From Lismore drive north along a scenic route known as the Vee Gap to visit another great Irish castle at ⌘ **Cahir** ㊼. On the next day, spend the morning visiting that postcard icon, the awe-inspiring **Rock of Cashel** in the market town of **Cashel** ㊾. Drive via Urlingford on the main N8 to **Kilkenny City** ④–⑪, where you can wander the time-hallowed streets, explore its medieval cathedral, and visit its Victorian baronial castle

Castlecomer
R430
Ballyragget
N78
Dunmore
Cave
Old Leighlin 3 2
Kilkenny City
4 — 11
N10
Carlow Town 1
Tullow
R726
N9
R725
WICKLOW
Kildavin
Shillelagh
Kildare
Leighlinbridge
Muine Bheag
(Bagenalstown)
Woodenbridge
Arklow
R. Slaney
Bunclody
Gorey
ttsbridge
R700
N9
toneyford
R705
CARLOW
Borris
Ferns
nocktopher
Thomastown 12
Jerpoint
Abbey
Inistioge
R703
13 Graiguenamanagh
R729
St. Mullins
Clonroche
R. Barrow
15 Enniscorthy
R744
R741
R742
Blackwater
enny
KILKENNY
Mullinavat
R. Nore
N79
N25
WEXFORD
Oilgate
Curracloe
N11
R. Slaney
Irish
National
Heritage Park
Wexford Town
16 — 25
New Ross 14
N25
Wexford
Harbour
St. George's
Channel
John F. Kennedy
Arboretum
Dunganstown
Wellington
Bridge
Piercetown
Rosslare
26 Rosslare
Harbour
R24
R. Suir
N24
R733
Cheekpoint
28 Ballyhack
Carrick
R733
Duncormick
R736
Tomhaggard
TO WALES,
FRANCE
Waterford City
29 — 40
Passage
East
Duncannonfort
Fethard-
on-Sea
Lady's Island
R685
R675
42 41
Tramore Dunmore
East
Hook
Peninsula
Forlorn
Pt.
27 Kilmore Quay
R684
Waterford Harbour
Annestown
Churchtown
Saltee
Islands

Celtic Sea

N

KEY
Rail Lines
Ferry

0   20 miles
0   30 km

seat. Head to **Leighlinbridge** ② for a salmon steak at the Lord Bage-
nal Inn, then down to the unspoiled riverside village of ☷ **Graiguenamanagh** ⑬ and its Duiske Abbey. On the following morning head for
the coast again and have a look at the still vibrant old Viking port of
Wexford Town ⑯–㉕. Drive on down this pretty stretch of coast through
the picturesque waterside villages of **Kilmore Quay** ㉗ and **Ballyhack** ㉘
and cross by car ferry to ☷ **Waterford City** ㉙–㊵, another old Viking settlement on the estuary of the Rivers Suir and Nore-Barrow whose dazzling cut glass has carried the city's name to the banquet halls of the world.
Waterford is on the main Cork–Wexford road.

IF YOU HAVE 5 DAYS

Five days allows for a leisurely sampling of the different regions within
the Southeast, with time to get to know its three biggest towns,
Kilkenny, Wexford, and Waterford. Start in the north of the region,
approaching it through **Carlow Town** ①—a modern center but home
to several fascinating historical sights. Cross the River Barrow at **Leighlinbridge** ② and drive down to **Graiguenamanagh** ⑬, an unspoiled and
hilly riverside village with a nicely restored abbey. Continue on through
Thomastown ⑫, a stone-built village on the River Nore with a ruined
Cistercian monastery that had been a masterpiece of Irish Romanesque,
to ☷ **Kilkenny City** ④–⑪, a lovely town that features medieval coaching inns, Tudor almshouses, Georgian streets, and alleyway "slips." Next
morning explore the medieval city center with its castle and cathedral
on foot. Drive on through Urlingford to the spectacular **Rock of
Cashel**, symbol of both Celtic and Christian Ireland, in the market town
of **Cashel** ㊾. Continue to ☷ **Cahir** ㊼ at the foot of the Galtee Mountains where you can visit another kind of castle, this time of Norman
vintage, and inspect the town's numerous antiques shops.

Next day drive up through the scenic Vee Gap in the Knockmealdown
Mountains and detour to visit Mount Melleray Abbey, home to an order
of contemplative monks who welcome visitors. Continue to **Lismore** ㊻,
which has the Devonshire seat, one of Ireland's prettiest castles. Then
head for the coast and the main road south, which leads to **Ardmore** ㊺,
where the early Christians built a cliff-top monastery and round tower.
Spend the night either in ☷ **Dungarvan** ㊸—a cheerful little fishing
town—or inland among the sparsely populated Knockmealdown
Mountains in the ☷ **Nire Valley** ㊹. Next day drive through the unspoiled
scenery of the pretty market town **Clonmel** ㊿, and follow the River Suir
through **Carrick-on-Suir** ⑤① to the port of **Waterford City** ㉙–㊵. While
a commercial center, Waterford is luring travelers with pedestrian
malls and new historic exhibits, such as the large collection of recently
discovered Viking artifacts on display over the tourist office near the
Norman stronghold Reginald's Tower. Follow the River Nore north
to **New Ross** ⑭, a busy river port; signposts from here mark the way
to the **John F. Kennedy Arboretum**, which is near the cottage at Dunganstown where the president's great-grandfather was born. Then
pick up the main road to **Wexford Town** ⑯–㉕, a Viking settlement on
the estuary of the River Slaney. Outside town, at Ferrycarrig, is the **Irish
National Heritage Park**. If wildlife interests you, don't miss **Curracloe
Beach**, a 9-km (5½-mi) sandy beach to the north of the town.

On the next day, if you are heading north, take the N11 Dublin road
via **Enniscorthy** ⑮, a historic town on the banks of the River Slaney
dominated by its Norman castle. If you are heading south with time
to spare, take the small coastal road through **Kilmore Quay** ㉗, past
thatched cottages and narrow lanes, to **Ballyhack** ㉘, where you can
take a car ferry across the harbor back to Waterford and the road south.

When it Comes to Getting Local Currency at an ATM,

Same Thing.

Whether you're in Yosemite or Yemen, using your Visa® card or ATM card with the PLUS symbol is the easiest and most convenient way to get local currency.

For example, let's say you're in France. When you make a withdrawal, using your secured PIN, it's dispensed in francs, but is debited from your account in U.S. dollars. This makes it easy to take advantage of favorable exchange rates. And if you need help finding one of Visa's 627,000 ATMs in 127 countries worldwide, visit **visa.com/pd/atm**. We'll make finding an ATM as easy as finding the Eiffel Tower, the Pyramids or even the Grand Canyon.

It's Everywhere You Want To Be.

SEE THE WORLD IN FULL COLOR

Fodor's Exploring Guides bring all the great sights vividly to life with hundreds of photographs, fascinating historical background, and colorful anecdotes. Detailed maps and practical information keep you headed in the right direction.

Pair a **Fodor's** Exploring Guide with your trusted Gold Guide for a complete planning package.

Fodor's EXPLORING GUIDES

At bookstores everywhere.

When to Tour the Southeast

The Southeast is a good area of Ireland to visit off-season. Restaurants and accommodations are open between November and March, months when many places in the more touristy western regions are closed. Beware Christmas Eve to at least mid-January, though, when many restaurateurs take their own holidays, and some lodgings and restaurants refurbish for the following season. Drier weather in the Southeast also makes it a good choice if you're visiting in the spring and autumn. Remember that in July and August, the Irish themselves descend on the coastal resorts, so if you plan to head for the beaches of the Southeast in the summer, be sure to reserve accommodations well in advance.

ON THE ROAD TO KILKENNY CITY AND WEXFORD TOWN

Many sights in this region—notably rich in historical and maritime attractions—make a visit here memorably picturesque. From Carlow Town's small county seat you travel through the farmlands of the Barrow Valley to Kilkenny City—which, from an architectural point of view, is among the most pleasing towns of inland Ireland. The historic city center is endowed with an old-world atmosphere, thanks to the country gentry who made their headquarters here in the 18th century, building themselves fine town houses in the Georgian style. From Thomastown, just outside Kilkenny, another cross-country drive follows the River Nore to New Ross, where it meets the River Barrow, and proceeds to John F. Kennedy's ancestral home and the arboretum planted in his memory. You can then journey to the old Viking port of Wexford Town, now home to a celebrated opera festival, which presents rare works in the restored 18th-century Theatre Royal.

Carlow Town

❶ *83 km (52 mi) south of Dublin on N9.*

Carlow Town was established on the banks of the River Barrow by the Anglo-Normans in the 12th century. Its position on the border of the English Pale—the area around Dublin that was dominated by the English from Elizabethan times on—made it an important strategic center and hence the scene of many bloody battles and sieges. Today Carlow is a lively market town about an hour and a half from central Dublin. The presence of the large Institute of Technology here gives the town a lively buzz. It also has a thriving indigenous arts-and-crafts community.

The Roman Catholic **Cathedral of the Assumption** is one of Carlow Town's most prominent sights. Completed in 1883, the Gothic-style cathedral is notable for its stained-glass windows and a magnificently sculpted marble monument of its builder, Bishop James Doyle (1786–1834), a champion of Catholic emancipation; the monument was carved by the Irish sculptor John Hogan (1800–58). ⊠ *College St.,* ☎ *0503/31227.* ⊠ *Free.* ☉ *Daily 7:30–8.*

The ruins of the 13th-century **Carlow Castle,** a strategically important fortification held by the English on the southeastern corner of the Pale, still offers imposing views of the River Barrow. This castle withstood a siege by Cromwell's troops in 1650, only to be destroyed accidentally in 1814 when a Dr. Philip Middleton attempted to renovate the castle for use as a mental asylum. While setting off explosives to reduce the thickness of the walls, he managed to demolish all but the west-side curtain wall and its two flanking towers.

One of the most poignant sites in Carlow town is the **Croppies Grave** (⊠ 98 St., off of Maryborough St.), a small memorial garden where the bodies of 640 United Irishmen—called "Croppies" because they cropped their hair to mark their allegiance to a free, independent Ireland—were buried in a mass grave, following the Battle of Carlow during the 1798 rebellion against English rule. Two trees planted by a widowed mother of three young men still stand; the third fell in a storm in 1998, and its two halves are inscribed with a testimonial to the courage of the Croppies.

The **County Museum** has a series of reconstructed interiors depicting life in Carlow during the early 20th century. Its more prestigious exhibit is the Jackson Collection, some 10,000 documents on the Grand Juries and Petty Juries—consisting of landlords who, from the early 18th through late 19th century, carried out the functions of local government in Ireland under English rule—put together in the 19th century by the quartermaster at Carlow Military Barracks. The museum is in the town hall, accessed from the old butter market. ⊠ *Centaur St.,* ☎ *0503/40491.* ☜ *£1.* ⊙ *Tues.–Fri. 11–5, weekends 2–5.*

The famous **Browne's Hill Dolmen,** a stone monument dating from 2500 BC with a capstone weighing in at 100 tons, is one of the largest in Europe. The megalithic tomb, dating from the Stone Age (circa 3000–2000 BC), is thought to mark the burial place of a local king. The dolmen is reached via a pathway from the parking lot. ⊠ *3 km (2 mi) outside Carlow Town, on the Hacketstown Rd. (R726).* ☜ *Free.*

Dining and Lodging
☜ *following the text of a review is your signal that the property has a Web site, where you will find details and, usually, images; for a link, visit www.fodors.com/urls.*

$$$ ✕ **Cloisters Restaurant.** This 200-year-old house, owned by Michael and Patricia Hennessy, offers venison, guinea fowl, rack of lamb, and whatever fish is freshly available, prepared in unusual combinations by Patricia herself. A typical entrée is venison, beef, and chestnut stew with a venison sausage cracker, red onion marmalade, and wild mushroom cream. The wine list is limited but well balanced. ⊠ *29 Dublin St.,* ☎ *0503/40599. MC, V. Closed Sun.–Mon. No lunch.*

$ 🏠 **Barrowville Town House.** This elegant Regency-style house, minutes away from the center of Carlow Town, has been sensitively restored by its owners, Randal and Marie Dempsey, with a discreet blend of totally modern comfort and fine antique furnishings. The breakfast menu features smoked salmon, an Irish-cheese board, and Irish breakfast fry; it is served in a large conservatory, overlooking the garden, under a grapevine that enjoys rude good health, despite the Irish weather. ⊠ *Kilkenny Rd., Co. Carlow,* ☎ *0503/43324, FAX 0503/41953. 7 rooms with bath. Croquet. AE, MC, V.* ☜

Nightlife and the Arts
Founded in 1979 as a weekend event to bring together arts, literature, and the Irish language, **Éigse,** Carlow's annual festival, takes over the town in June each year for 10 days. Drama, classical and pop music, and street entertainment vie with impressive visual arts exhibitions around the town, including works by international artists. Irish music and dance play a prominent part in the celebrations. For information, contact the Éigse Festival Office (☎ 0503/40491) in the TIO (☞ Visitor Information *in* The Southeast A to Z, *below*).

Outdoor Activities and Sports

GOLF

Carlow Golf Club (✉ Deerpark, ☎ 0503/31695), 3 km (2 mi) north of town on the Dublin road, is set in a wild deer park; the 18-hole course remains open all year.

SPECTATOR SPORTS

Gaelic football and hurling are played at **Dr. Cullen Park GAA.**

Shopping

Carlow Craft Shop, in same space as the TIO (☞ Visitor Information *in* The Southeast A to Z, *below*), sells Ashling china made in Bagenalstown, as well as pottery, wood-turned pieces, and wrought-iron work, among other crafts.

Pembroke Studio (✉ Pembroke, ☎ 0503/41562) sells paintings, pottery, and bog-oak carvings by local artists.

Leighlinbridge

❷ *10 km (6 mi) south of Carlow Town on N9.*

In Leighlinbridge, the first bridge over the River Barrow was built in 1320 and is reputed to be one of the oldest functioning bridges in Europe. On the east bank of Leighlinbridge lie the ruins of **Black Castle,** built in 1181, one of the earliest Norman fortresses constructed in Ireland and the scene of countless battles and sieges over the centuries. A lone, ruined 400-year-old tower stands today.

Dining

$$$ ✕ **Lord Bagenal Inn.** This famous old family pub beside the River Barrow is full of cozy nooks and warm, open fires. It even has a small playroom for children (open until 7 PM). Besides being a wine buff, owner James Keogh is something of an art connoisseur, as the contemporary Irish art collection that lines the walls of Lord Bagenal testifies. The restaurant's seasonal menu is based on French country cooking and includes steak and poultry entrées, but it is renowned locally for its fresh seafood dishes. If you are interested in staying overnight in Leighlinbridge, inquire about the standard rooms (**$**) that were recently added. ✉ Main St., ☎ 0503/21668. DC, V.

Old Leighlin

❸ *5¾ km (3 mi) west of Leighlinbridge, signposted to the right off N9.*

Worth a quick stop, the tiny village of Old Leighlin is the site of a monastery, founded in the 7th century by St. Laserian, that once accommodated 1,500 monks. It hosted the church synod in AD 630 at which the Celtic Church initially accepted the Roman date for the celebration of Easter (the date was officially accepted at the Synod of Whitby in AD 664); this decision marked the beginning of a move away from old Brehon Law and the deliberalization of the Church. The building was rebuilt in the 12th century as St. Laserian's Cathedral and enlarged in the 16th century. Guided tours are available. Carey's, the village pub, is renowned for having been in the same family since 1542.

Kilkenny City

❹ *24 km (15 mi) southwest of Leighlinbridge on N10, 121 km (75 mi) southwest of Dublin.*

One of Ireland's most alluring destinations, Kilkenny City cries to be explored by foot or bicycle, thanks to its historic and easily circumnavigable town center. This is a lovely place where the centuries rub elbows with Georgian streets hard by Tudor stone houses—even the great town castle is a bewitching marriage of Gothic and Victorian styles. From a bird's-eye view, the city (population 22,000) is an impressively preserved, 900-year-old Norman citadel attractively situated on the River Nore, which forms the moat of its magnificently restored castle. In the 6th century, St. Canice (a.k.a. "the builder of churches") established a large monastic school here; the town's name reflects Canice's central role: Kil Cainneach means "Church of Canice." Kilkenny's medieval look wasn't established for another 400 years, when the Anglo-Normans fortified the city with a castle, gates, and a brawny wall.

Kilkenny holds a special place in the history of Anglo-Irish relations. The infamous 1366 Statutes of Kilkenny, intended to strengthen English authority in Ireland by keeping the heirs of the Anglo-Norman invaders from becoming absorbed into the Irish way of life, was an attempt at apartheid. Intermarriage became a crime punishable by death. Irish cattle were barred from grazing on English land. Anglo-Norman settlers could lose their estates for speaking Irish, for giving their children Irish names, or for dressing in Irish clothes. The native Irish were forced to live outside town walls in shantytowns. Ironically, the process of Irish and Anglo-Norman assimilation was well under way when the statutes went into effect; perhaps if this intermingling had been allowed to evolve, Anglo-Irish relations in the 20th century might have been more harmonious.

By the early 17th century, the Irish Catholics had grown impatient with such repression; they tried to bring about reforms with the Confederation of Kilkenny, which governed Ireland from 1642 to 1648, with Kilkenny as the capital. Pope Innocent X sent money and arms. Cromwell responded in 1650 by overrunning the town and sacking the cathedral, which he then used to stable his horses.

The center city is small, and despite the large number of historic sights and picturesque streets—in particular, Butter Slip and High Street—it can easily be covered in less than three hours. One of the most pleasant cities south of Dublin (and one of the most popular in summer, when it can be swamped with visitors), Kilkenny City is a center for well-designed crafts, especially ceramics and sweaters; the premier venue is the Kilkenny Design Centre. The city is also home to more than 60 pubs, many of them on Parliament and High streets, which also support a lively music scene. Many of the town's pubs and shops have old-fashioned, highly individualized, brightly painted facades, created as part of the town's 1980s revival of this Victorian tradition.

❺ In spite of Cromwell's defacements, **St. Canice's Cathedral** is still one of the finest cathedrals in Ireland, and it is the country's second-largest medieval church, after St. Patrick's Cathedral in Dublin (☞ Chapter 2). The bulk of the 13th-century structure (restored in 1866) was built in the early English style. Within the massive walls is an exuberant Gothic interior, given a somber grandeur by the extensive use of a locally quarried black marble. Many of the memorials and tombstone effigies represent distinguished descendants of the Normans, some depicted in full suits of armor. Look for a female effigy in the south aisle wearing the old Irish or Kinsale cloak; the 12th-century black marble font at the southwest end of the nave; and St. Ciaran's Chair in the north transept, also made of black marble, with 13th-century sculptures on the arms.

The biggest attraction on the grounds is the 102-ft **round tower**, which was built in 847 and is all that remains of the monastic development reputedly begun in the 6th century, around which the town arose. If

Kilkenny City

you have the energy to climb the tower's 167 steps, the 360-degree view from the top is tremendous. Next door is **St. Canice's Library**, containing some 3,000 16th- and 17th-century volumes. ⊠ *Dean St.,* ☎ *056/64971.* 🎫 *Cathedral £1.25 for prebooked groups, donations welcome from individuals; tower £1.* ☉ *Cathedral Easter–Oct., Mon.–Sat. 9–1 and 2–6, Sun. 2–6; Nov.–Apr., Mon.–Sat. 10–1 and 2–4, Sun. 2–4; tower access depends on weather.*

6 The 13th-century **Black Abbey** has been restored as a Dominican church by the order whose black capes gave the abbey its name. Nearby is the Black Freren Gate (14th century), the last remaining gateway to the medieval city. ⊠ *South of St. Canice's Cathedral.* 🎫 *Free.* ☉ *Daily 9–1 and 2–6.*

7 **Rothe House** is an example of a typical middle-class house of the Tudor period. Built by John Rothe between 1594 and 1610, it is owned by the **Kilkenny Archaeological Society** and houses a motley collection of Bronze Age artifacts, ogham stones, and period costumes. There's also a genealogical research facility that can help you trace your ancestors. ⊠ *Parliament St.,* ☎ *056/22893.* 🎫 *£2.* ☉ *Apr.–Oct., Mon.–Sat. 10:30–5, Sun. 2–5; Nov.–Feb., Mon.–Sat. 1–5, Sun. 3–5.*

8 **Kyteler's Inn** (⊠ *Kieran St.,* ☎ *056/21064*) the oldest in town, is notorious as the place where Dame Alice Kyteler, a member of a wealthy banking family and an alleged witch, was accused of poisoning her four husbands. The restaurant retains its medieval aura, thanks to its 14th-century stonework and exposed beams. Food and drink in this popular pub are as simple and plentiful as they would have been in Dame Alice's day—without her extra ingredients.

9 The **Tholsel,** or town hall, which was built in 1761 on Parliament Street, stands near the site of the medieval Market Cross.

⑩ The **Tourist Information Office (TIO)** is housed in the **Shee Alms House** (off the east side of High Street). The building was founded in 1582 by Sir Richard Shee as a hospital for the poor and served in that capacity until 1895. ⊠ *Rose Inn St.,* ☎ *056/51500.* ⊙ *Nov.–Mar., Mon.–Sat. 9–5; Apr., Mon.–Sat. 9–6; May–June, Mon.–Sat. 9–6, Sun. 11–1 and 2–5; July–Aug., Mon.–Sat. 9–7, Sun. 11–1 and 2–5; Sept., Mon.–Sat. 9–6, Sun. 11–1 and 2–5; Oct., Mon.–Sat. 9–6.*

★ ⑪ Founded in 1172 and dominating the south end of town, **Kilkenny Castle** served for more than 500 years, beginning in 1391, as the seat of the Butler family—later designated earls and dukes of Ormonde—one of the more powerful clans in Irish history. In 1967 the sixth Marquess of Ormonde handed over the present building, which dates largely from 1820, to the state; since then it's been through a series of restorations. The gray stone building, with two turreted wings and numerous chimneys poking over the battlements, stands amid rolling lawns beside the River Nore in 49 acres of landscaped parkland. Most impressive is the 150-ft-long, aptly named **Long Gallery,** a refined airy hall that contains a collection of family portraits, frayed tapestries, and a skylit, decorated ceiling of carved oak beams adjoined with Celtic lacework and adorned with brilliantly painted animal heads. The **Butler Gallery** houses a collection of modern art and frequently changing exhibitions. ⊠ *The Parade,* ☎ *056/21450.* ⊠ *Castle tour £3.50, grounds and Butler Gallery free.* ⊙ *Apr.–May, daily 10:30–5; June–Sept., daily 10–7; Oct.–Mar., Tues.–Sat. 10:30–12:45 and 2–5, Sun. 11–12:45 and 2–5.* ⊗

Dining and Lodging

$$$ ✕ **Cafe Sol.** Everything at this small, cheerful spot is homemade, except the pasta and baguettes, and all dishes, ranging from steak to pasta to fish of the day, are cooked to order. The roasted pepper-and-parsnip soup is an excellent starter, followed by roast organic goose with potato-and-apple stuffing, and date-and-orange cake. Oilcloths cover the tables during the day, while candles and linen dress up the mood for evening. ⊠ *William St.,* ☎ *056/64987. Reservations for Sat. dinner essential; reservations not accepted for lunch. MC, V. Closed Sun. No dinner Mon.–Tues. during winter months (variable).*

$$$ ✕ **Ristorante Rinuccini.** Kilkenny City's premier Irish-Italian restaurant is in the basement of a Georgian town house opposite Kilkenny Castle. Owner-chef Antonio Cavaliere is intensely involved in preparing luscious pasta dishes, like tortelloni stuffed with ricotta cheese and spinach, served in a creamy Gorgonzola cheese sauce; specialties of the house, such as organic Irish veal; and fresh seafood from Kilmore Quay. A splendid all-Italian wine list complements the menu, and there's a host of delicious homemade desserts. ⊠ *1 The Parade,* ☎ *056/61575. Reservations essential. AE, DC, MC, V. Closed last wk of Dec.*

$$$ ✕⌦ **Langton's.** One of Ireland's most famous "eating pubs," this family-run establishment, a landmark since the 1940s, is a labyrinthine collection of interconnected bars and restaurants. Most of the seating areas have open fires, but different ambiences, ranging from the leather-upholstered gentlemen's club in the Horseshoe Bar to an attempt at art deco in the spacious main dining room. Entrées include roast rack of lamb on eggplant and *capsicum frites* (fried peppers) with sauvignon jus, traditional Irish stew, as well as a big selection of steaks. ⊠ *69 John St., Co. Kilkenny,* ☎ *056/65133,* ℻ *056/63693. 24 rooms with bath, 2 suites. AE, DC, MC, V.*

$$
★ ⌦ **Butler House.** This elegant Georgian house, with its magnificent plastered ceilings and marble fireplaces, is an integral part of the Kilkenny Castle complex and once belonged to the Earls of Ormonde. All of the

rooms are beautifully decorated; ask for one with a bay window overlooking the secluded gardens and Kilkenny Castle. ⊠ *16 Patrick St.,
Co. Kilkenny,* ☎ *056/65707,* FAX *056/65626. 11 rooms with bath, 1
suite. Restaurant. AE, DC, MC, V.* 🍲

$–$$ 🏰 **Knocktopher Hall.** This characterful Georgian mansion 17½ km
(11 mi) south of Kilkenny on N10 makes a memorable touring base.
The house was built on the site of an earlier castle in 1740 and added
to over the years, ending up with romantic but unclassical gray stone
crenellations. Rooms are large, with 18th-century French beds and relaxing rural views. Golfers and equestrians often stay here and use the
sporting facilities at Mount Juliet (☞ Thomastown, *below*), only 8 km
(5 mi) away. The nightly five-course gourmet dinner is offered to residents only, who must book by noon. ⊠ *Knocktopher, Co. Kilkenny,*
☎ *056/68626,* FAX *056/68626. 4 rooms with bath. AE, MC, V.* 🍲

Nightlife and the Arts

The **Cat Laughs** is an early June festival with an international roster of
stand-up comedians. **Kilkenny Arts Week** (☎ 056/63663) runs for
nine days around the third week of August; classical music, film, theater, literary events, and visual-arts exhibits take place throughout
Kilkenny.

Outdoor Activities and Sports

BICYCLING

Bikes for exploring the quiet countryside around Kilkenny can be
rented through **J. J. Wall** (⊠ 88 Maudlin St., Co. Kilkenny, ☎ 056/
21236).

GOLF

Kilkenny Golf Club (⊠ Glendine, ☎ 056/65400), 2 km (1 mi) northeast of town, is an 18-hole, par-71, mainly flat course.

SPECTATOR SPORTS

The 1336 Statutes of Kilkenny expressly forbade the ancient Irish
game of hurling; today Kilkenny is considered one of the great hurling counties. Gaelic football and hurling matches are held at **Kilkenny
GAA Grounds** (⊠ Nowlan Park). At **Kilkenny Greyhound Racetrack**
(⊠ St. James's Park, Freshford Rd., ☎ 056/21214), evening meets are
held each Wednesday and Friday where betting is the main attraction.
Gowran Park (☎ 056/26126) holds horse races regularly.

Shopping

Kilkenny is a byword for attractive, original crafts that combine traditional arts with modern elements of design. You can see glass being
blown at the **Jerpoint Glass Studio** (⊠ Stoneyford, ☎ 056/24350), where
the glass is heavy, modern, uncut, and hand-finished. Their factory shop
is a good place to pick up a bargain. The town's leading outlet, the
Kilkenny Design Centre (⊠ Kilkenny Castle, ☎ 056/22118), in the old
stable yard opposite the castle, sells ceramics, jewelry, sweaters, and
handwoven textiles. **Murphy's Jewellers** (⊠ 85 High St., ☎ 056/
21127) specializes in heraldic jewelry. At **Nicholas Mosse Pottery** (⊠
Bennettsbridge, ☎ 056/27505) you can buy attractive hand-crafted and
decorated pottery—and see it made. **Rudolf Heltzel** (⊠ 10 Patrick St.,
☎ 056/21497) is known for its striking, modern designs of gold and
silver jewelry. **Stoneware Jackson Pottery** (⊠ Bennettsbridge, ☎ 056/
27175) makes distinctive, hand-thrown tableware and lamps. The
Sweater Shop (⊠ High St., ☎ 056/63405) carries a range of great
sweaters.

Thomastown

⑫ *14½ km (9 mi) south of Kilkenny on R700 and N9.*

Thomastown is a pretty, stone-built village on the River Nore. **Jerpoint Abbey,** near Thomastown, is one of the most notable Cistercian ruins in Ireland, dating from about 1160. The church, tombs, and the restored cloisters—decorated with affecting human figures and fantastical mythical creatures—are a must for all lovers of the Irish Romanesque. Guides are available from mid-June to mid-September. The last admission is 45 minutes before closing. ⊠ *2 km (1 mi) south of Thomastown,* ☎ *056/24623.* ⊡ *£2.* ⊗ *Mid-Mar.–May and Oct.– mid-Nov., daily 10–5; June–Sept., daily 9:30–6:30.*

Dining and Lodging

$$$$ ✕⊞ **Mount Juliet.** Within the walled 1,500-acre estate on the River Nore
   ★   lies this imposing, three-story Georgian mansion. Many of the house's original features are intact, including finely stuccoed ceilings and marble mantelpieces. Bedrooms are large and individually decorated, with mahogany furniture, super-king-size beds, and original fireplaces. Sixteen rooms are also available in Hunters Yard, their rustic decor proclaiming their conversion from the original stables. Eleven two-bedroom modern lodges complete Mount Juliet's accommodation. The two major activities here are horseback riding on the extensive trails within the estate and golfing on the Jack Nicklaus–designed parkland championship course. The Lady Helen McAlmont Restaurant, its tables adorned with crystal, silverware, and fine linen, serves haute cuisine with contemporary Irish touches. ⊠ *Co. Kilkenny,* ☎ *056/73000,* FAX *056/73019. 70 rooms with bath. 2 restaurants, 2 bars, indoor pool, sauna, 18-hole golf course, tennis court, archery, croquet, horseback riding, fishing. AE, DC, MC, V.* ✐

$$–$$$ ✕⊞ **Berryhill.** A charming, creeper-clad 1789 house perched high on
   ★   a ridge overlooking the River Nore and the picturesque village of Inistioge (southeast of Thomastown), this is a warm, comfortable family home on a working sheep farm. Guests can enjoy the bright, airy drawing room, with its baby grand piano and a drinks trolley with an "honesty book." Rooms are decorated in animal themes of an elephant, a pig, and a frog; the last has a veranda. Breakfast, served at the dining-room table in front of a big open fire, often includes fresh trout. Prebooking for dinner, country-house style, is essential. ⊠ *Inistioge, Co. Kilkenny,* ☎ FAX *056/58434. 3 suites. Croquet, fishing. MC, V. Closed Nov.–Apr.* ✐

Outdoor Activities and Sports

GOLF

For detailed information about **Mount Juliet Golf Course** (⊠ Co. Kilkenny, ☎ 056/73000), *see* Chapter 9.

HORSEBACK RIDING

The excellent facilities at **Mount Juliet** (⊠ Co. Kilkenny, ☎ 056/73000) are open to nonresidents.

Graiguenamanagh

⑬ *15 km (9 mi) northeast of Thomastown on R703.*

Graiguenamanagh (pronounced *Gray*-gun-a-manna) is a pretty, unspoiled village on the banks of the River Barrow at the foot of Brandon Hill. In the 13th century the early English-style church of **Duiske Abbey** was the largest Cistercian church in Ireland. The choir, the transept, and a section of the nave of the original abbey church are now part of a Catholic church. Purists will be disappointed by the modernization, carried out between 1974 and 1980, although various medieval building techniques were used. This is good walking country; ask locally for directions to the summit of **Brandon Hill** (1,694 ft), a 7-km (4½-mi) hike.

Dining and Lodging

$ ✕🏠 **Waterside.** All the rooms and the restaurant in this beautifully re-
★ stored 19th-century stone corn mill on the River Barrow have picturesque views of the water. The restaurant ($$$), which occupies the ground floor of the old mill building, has exposed pitch-pine beams and decorated windows; it serves Continental cuisine and has a good wine list. Located 27 km (17 mi) southeast of Kilkenny, Waterside is popular with hikers and those who value the nearby riding and golf. ⊠ *The Quay, Co. Kilkenny,* ☎ *0503/24246,* �📠 *0503/24733. 10 rooms with bath. Restaurant, bar, fishing. MC, V.* 🐾

New Ross

⑭ *17 km (11 mi) south of Graiguenamanagh on R705.*

New Ross is a busy inland port on the banks of the River Barrow. Even though it is one of the oldest towns in County Wexford, settled in the 13th century on an ancient monastic site, only the most dedicated history buffs will be tempted to stop and explore the steep, narrow streets above its unattractive docks. The major attraction in New Ross is a cruise up the River Barrow on the **Galley Cruising Restaurant** (☎ 051/ 421723). You can take in the peaceful farmlands along the riverbank while sampling lunch, afternoon tea, or dinner. The emphasis is on fresh local produce and seafood. The restaurant is open Easter–October only.

The **John F. Kennedy Arboretum** is clearly signposted from New Ross on R733, which follows the banks of the Barrow southward for about 5 km (3 mi). The cottage where the president's great-grandfather was born is in Dunganstown, and Kennedy relatives are still living in the house. About 2 km (1 mi) down the road at Slieve Coillte is the entrance to the arboretum, which has more than 600 acres of forest, nature trails, and gardens, as well as an ornamental lake. The grounds contain some 4,500 species of trees and shrubs and serve as a resource center for botanists and foresters. The top of the park offers fine panoramic views. ⊠ *Dunganstown,* ☎ *051/388171.* 🎫 *£2.* ⊙ *Daily 10–dusk.*

Ballylane Farm, a 200-acre working farm, supplies maps and information sheets to guide you along a nature walk, where you can observe local wildlife, farm animals, and crops. A coffee shop–restaurant serves lights meals when the nature walk is open to visitors. ⊠ *Signposted about 1 km (½ mi) past the turn to the Kennedy Arboretum (from Graiguenamanagh) on N25 New Ross–Wexford Rd.,* ☎ *051/425666.* 🎫 *£3.50.* ⊙ *Mid-Mar.–Apr., Sun. noon–5; May–Oct., daily 10–6; or by appointment.*

Enniscorthy

⑮ *32 km (20 mi) northeast of New Ross on N79.*

Enniscorthy, a thriving market town with a rich history, is on the main road between Dublin and Wexford, to the south of the popular resort of Gorey. Built on the steeply sloping banks of the River Slaney, the town is dominated by **Enniscorthy Castle,** built in the first quarter of the 13th century by the Prendergast family. The imposing Norman castle was the site of fierce battles against Oliver Cromwell in the 17th century and during the Uprising of 1798. Its square-towered keep now houses the **County Wexford Museum,** which contains thousands of historic items, including military memorabilia from the 1798 and 1916 uprisings. ✉ *Castle Hill,* ☎ *054/35926.* 🎫 *£3.* ☉ *May–Sept., Mon.– Sat. 10–6, Sun. 2–5:30.*

The **National 1798 Center** tells the tale of the United Irishmen and the ill-fated 1798 rebellion. ✉ *Arnold's Cross,* ☎ *054/37596.* 🎫 *£4.* ☉ *Mon.–Sat. 9:30–5, Sun. 11–5.*

St. Aidan's Cathedral stands on a commanding site overlooking the Slaney. This Gothic Revival structure was built in the mid-19th century under the direction of Augustus Welby Pugin, the architect of the Houses of Parliament in London. ✉ *Cathedral St.* 🎫 *Free.* ☉ *Daily 10–6.*

Outdoor Activities and Sports
GREYHOUND RACING

The **Showgrounds** (✉ Co. Wexford, ☎ 054/33172) have greyhound racing on Monday and Thursday at 8 PM, with bar and catering facilities available.

Shopping
Carley's Bridge Pottery (✉ Carley's Bridge, ☎ 054/33512), established in 1654, specializes in large terra-cotta pots. **Kiltrea Bridge Pottery** (✉ Kiltrea Bridge, Caime, ☎ 054/35107) stocks garden pots, plant pots, and country kitchen crocks.

Wexford Town

16 *24 km (15 mi) south of Enniscorthy on N11, 142 km (88 mi) south of Dublin.*

From its appearance today, you would barely realize that Wexford is an ancient place—in fact, it was defined on maps by the Greek cartographer Ptolemy as long ago as the 2nd century AD. Its Irish name is Loch Garman, but the Vikings called it Waesfjord—the harbor of the mud flats—which became Wexford in English. Wexford became an English garrison town after it was taken by Oliver Cromwell in 1649. (The Anglo-Norman conquest of Ireland began in County Wexford in 1169, so the British presence has deep roots, and Wexford has been an English-speaking county for centuries.)

The River Slaney empties into the sea at Wexford Town. The harbor has silted up since the days when the Viking longboats docked here; nowadays only a few small trawlers fish out of here. Wexford Town's compact center is set on the south bank of the Slaney, with its main street—the major shopping street of the town, with a pleasant mix of old-fashioned bakeries, butcher shops, stylish boutiques, and a share of Wexford's many pubs—running parallel to the quays on the riverfront. It can be explored on foot in an hour or two. Allow at least half a day in the area if you also intend to visit the Heritage Park at nearby Ferrycarrig, and a full day if you also want to take in Johnstown Castle Gardens and its agricultural museum, or walk in the nature reserve at Curracloe Beach to the north of the town. The town is at its best in late October and early November, when the Wexford Opera Festival (☞ Nightlife and the Arts, *below*) engenders a carnival atmosphere that affects all walks of life.

17 The **TIO** (✉ Crescent Quay, ☎ 053/23111) is a good place to start exploring Wexford Town on foot and to find out about guided walking tours organized by local historians.

Wexford Town

⓲ Standing in the center of Crescent Quay, a large bronze **statue of Commodore John Barry** (1745–1803) commemorates the man who came to be known as the "Father of the American Navy." Born in 1745 in nearby Ballysampson, Barry settled in Philadelphia at age 15, became a brilliant naval fighter during the War of Independence (thus avenging his Irish ancestors), and trained many young naval officers who went on to achieve fame for themselves.

Rising above the rooftops from most points in town are the graceful spires of two elegant examples of 19th-century Gothic architecture. These **twin churches** have identical exteriors, their foundation stones were laid on the same day, and their spires both reach a height of 230 ft. The **⓳ ⓴** **Church of the Immaculate Conception** is on Rowe Street. The **Church ㉑ of the Assumption** is on Bride Street. The **Franciscan Church** (⊠ School St.) has a ceiling worth noting for its fine, locally crafted stuccowork.

㉒ The **Wexford Bull Ring** (⊠ Quay St., back toward quays) was once the scene of bullbaiting, a cruel medieval sport that was popular among the Norman nobility. This arena was also the site of another, far more tragic event in 1649, when Cromwell's soldiers massacred 300 panic-stricken townspeople who had gathered here to pray as the army stormed their town.

㉓ The red sandstone **Westgate Tower** was the largest of five fortified gateways in the Norman and Viking town walls, and it is the only one remaining. The early 13th-century tower has been sensitively restored. Keep an eye out as you wander around this part of town for other preserved segments of the old town walls. ⊠ *Westgate,* ☎ *053/46506.* ⊡ *£1.50.* ☼ *Daily 9:30–4:40.*

㉔ The ruins of the 12th-century **Selskar Abbey** (⊠ Selskar St., south of Westgate Tower) still stand. Here the first treaty between the Irish and the Normans was signed in 1169.

㉕ The **Wexford Wildfowl Reserve** on the north bank of the Slaney is a short walk across the bridge from the main part of town. One-third of the world's Greenland white-fronted geese—as many as 10,000—spend their winters on the mud flats, known locally as slobs, which also draw ducks, swans, and other waterfowl. Hides are provided for bird-watchers, and an audiovisual show and exhibitions are available at the visitor center. ⊠ *North Slob, Wexford Harbour,* ☎ *053/23129.* ⊡ *Free.* ☼ *Mid-Apr.–Sept., daily 9–6; Oct.–Mid-Apr., daily 10–5.*

★ ☾ The **Irish National Heritage Park** is one of Ireland's most successful and enjoyable family attractions. This 35-acre, open-air theme park beside the River Slaney should not be missed. In about an hour and a half, a guide takes you through 9,000 years of Irish history—from the first evidence of humans on this island, at around 7000 BC, to the Norman settlements of the mid-12th century. Full-scale replicas of typical dwelling places illustrate the changes in beliefs and lifestyles. Highlights of the tour include a prehistoric homestead, a *crannóg* (lake dwelling), an early Christian *rath* (fortified farmstead), a Christian monastery, a horizontal water mill, a Viking longhouse, and a Norman castle. There are also examples of pre-Christian burial sites and a stone circle. Most of the exhibits are "inhabited" by students in appropriate dress who will answer questions. The unspoiled riverside site includes several nature trails. ⊠ *Ferrycarrig, 5 km (3 mi) north of Wexford Town on N11,* ☎ *053/20733.* ⊡ *£5.* ☼ *Mid-Mar.–Oct., daily 9:30–6:30; last admission at 5.* ⬗

OFF THE BEATEN PATH

CURRACLOE BEACH – This was the location used for the Normandy landing in Stephen Spielberg's film *Saving Private Ryan*. It is a popular swimming place in summer and is home to many migratory birds in the winter. It is 9 km (5½ mi) lomg, with a 1-km (½-mi) nature trail in the seashore sand dunes. ⊠ *11 km (7 mi) northeast of Wexford Town.*

Dining and Lodging

$$$ ✕ **Heavens Above.** This delightful evening restaurant is above a pub called the Sky and the Ground, and chef Liam Ford cooks up a storm in both. Main courses range from wild venison noisettes panfried in a juniper berry-and-cognac sauce to roast suckling pig, glazed with honey, and served with a lemon sauce. To feed the soul, you can listen to traditional music in the pub Monday through Wednesday. ⊠ *S. Main St.,* ☎ *053/21273. MC, V. Closed Sun.*

$$ ✕ **La Riva.** This is a characterful first-floor bistro, right in the center of town near the TIO. Informal is the word—tables have plain, unpolished wood tops and the daily specials are chalked up on a board. Charm enters the picture on Thursday, when a guitarist entertains by candlelight. The menu is light and eclectic, with many people opting for two or three starters in order to try as many of owner-chef Frank Chamberlaine's unusual combos as possible. Among the most popular dishes are crispy duck leg confit with mango and coriander salad, and rack of lamb with roast Mediterranean vegetables. ⊠ *Henrietta St.,* ☎ *053/24330. MC, V. Closed Jan. No lunch.*

$ ✕ **Oak Tavern.** About 2 km (1 mi) from Wexford Town and not far from the gates of the Irish National Heritage Park on the N11 Dublin road, the pub-restaurant in this family-run old-world inn on the River Slaney is a good place to stop on your way into town. In cold weather, warm yourself beside log fires that blaze in the lounge; in fair weather, relax on the riverside terrace. Steaks, local salmon, and plainly cooked seafood are on the menu. ⊠ *Enniscorthy Rd.,* ☎ *053/20922. AE, MC, V.*

$$$$ ✕🏨 **Ferrycarrig.** Overlooking the Slaney Estuary in rolling countryside 3 km (2 mi) from Wexford Town on N11, this is a favorite of regular, well-heeled visitors to Wexford; one of Ireland's not-so-numerous millionaires takes over the entire hotel for three weeks each year. Despite its very modern architecture, it blends well into its peaceful, riverside location, perhaps because of the owner's attention to detail: for instance, trees are placed just offshore to encourage birds to perch there. Choose between dining in the informal Boathouse Bistro or the more formal Tides Restaurant, the latter of which serves modern French cuisine. All the bedrooms have wonderful views of the river and green fields, and some also have balconies. ⊠ *Ferrycarrig Bridge, Co. Wexford,* ☎ *053/20999,* 🖷 *053/20982. 100 rooms with bath. 2 restaurants, bar, indoor pool, sauna, health club, fishing. AE, DC, MC, V.* ✍

$$ 🏨 **McMenamin's Town House.** Early breakfast by arrangement and an exceptional degree of comfort for its price range make this four-story Victorian villa, a short walk from the railway station in the town center, an ideal stopover en route to or from the Rosslare ferries. Book months rather than weeks in advance if you want a room here during the Opera Festival. The bedrooms are spacious, warm, and immaculately clean, with glorious, large pieces of highly polished Victorian furniture and antique beds, including a mahogany half-tester. There are about eight choices at breakfast, including fresh fish of the day or porridge (with rum!). Don't leave without tasting Kay and Seamus McMenamin's homemade whiskey marmalade. ⊠ *3 Auburn Terr., Redmond Rd., Co. Wexford,* ☎ 🖷 *053/46442. 6 rooms with bath. MC, V. Closed last 2 wks of Dec.* ✍

$$ ⛨ **White's Hotel.** Established in 1779, this redbrick hotel, fronted by a modern conservatory, is a friendly, convivial place in the heart of town. The guest rooms are a hodgepodge of different styles and levels of decor, albeit each with its own old-fashioned, comfortable charm. At press time, 40 additional, executive bedrooms were being built in the reclaimed Abbey Street wing. Live music is played in the Shelmalier Bar every Friday and Saturday. ⊠ *George's St., Co. Wexford,* ☎ *053/22311,* 𝔽𝔸𝕏 *053/45000. 82 rooms with bath. Restaurant, 2 bars, sauna, steam room, health club. AE, DC, MC, V.* ✍

Nightlife and the Arts

Touring companies and local productions can be seen in Wexford at the **Theatre Royal** (⊠ High St., ☎ 053/22400). Hands down, the **Wexford Opera Festival** (☎ 053/22144), held during the last two weeks of October and the very beginning of November, is the town's leading cultural event. A half century old, the festival puts on seldom-performed operas with top talent from all over the world. Along with an ever-expanding fringe, the festival supplies a feast of concerts and recitals that go from 11 AM until midnight.

Outdoor Activities and Sports

BICYCLING

If you'd like to explore the long, sandy coast of this area at a leisurely pace, bicycles can be rented at the **Bike Shop** (⊠ 9 Selskar St., ☎ 053/ 22514).

HORSEBACK RIDING

Curracloe House Equestrian Centre (⊠ Curracloe, ☎ 053/37129) will take you cantering on the spectacular Curracloe Beach (although local authority regulations are presently trying to ban beach riding) or trekking through the Wexford Sloblands. Facilities include a 25-jump cross-country course. **Horetown Equestrian Centre** (⊠ Horetown House, Foulksmills, ☎ 051/565786) specializes in residential riding holidays with cross-country riding across farmland and will teach you how to play polo-crosse. **Shelmalier Riding Stables** (⊠ Trinity, Forth Mountain, Taghmon, ☎ 053/39251) has cross-country riding across 3,000 acres of forest and mountain.

SPECTATOR SPORTS

Gaelic football and hurling can be seen at **Wexford Park GAA** (⊠ Clonard Rd.).Horse races are held regularly at the **Wexford Racecourse** (⊠ Bettyville, ☎ 053/42307) on the N25 at the outskirts of Wexford Town.

Shopping

At **Barker's** (⊠ 36–40 S. Main St., ☎ 053/23159) you can find Waterford crystal at factory prices, as well as local pottery and other crafts.

En Route The signpost for **Johnstown Castle Gardens** is reached by following N25 for 5 km (3 mi) toward Rosslare. The castle itself, a massive, Victorian-Gothic building in gray stone, is now an agricultural college, but the attractive and well-maintained grounds, with ornamental lakes and more than 200 different trees and shrubs, are open to the public. The main attraction is the **National Museum of Agriculture and Rural Life**, housed in the quadrangular stable yards, which shows what life was once like in rural Ireland. It also contains a 5,000-square-ft exhibition on the potato and the Great Famine (1845–1847). ☎ *053/ 42888.* ☔ *Gardens £1.50, May–Sept.; museum £2.50.* ☉ *Gardens daily 9:30–5:30; museum Apr.–May, weekdays 9–12:30 and 1:30–5, weekends 2–5; June–Aug., weekdays 9–5, weekends 11–5; Sept.–Nov., weekdays 9–12:30 and 1:30–5, weekends 2–5; Dec.–Mar., weekdays 9–12:30 and 1:30–5.*

ALONG THE COAST TO WATERFORD

This journey takes you along mainly minor roads through the prettiest parts of the coast in Counties Wexford and Waterford, pausing midway to explore Waterford City on foot.

Rosslare

26 *16 km (10 mi) southeast of Wexford Town on R470.*

Sometimes called Ireland's sunniest spot, the village of Rosslare is a seaside resort with an attractive beach, while Rosslare Harbour, 8 km (5 mi) south of the village, is one of Ireland's busiest ports and the terminus for car ferries from Fishguard and Pembroke in Wales and for Cherbourg and Roscoff in France. Vacationers head here to hike, golf, sun, and swim for the most part.

Dining and Lodging

$$$–$$$$ ✕⌂ **Kelly's.** This traditional seaside resort hotel has been owned and
★ run by the Kelly family since 1895. Its extensive recreational facilities are a big draw. Guest rooms are done in comfortable, rustic decor, and those facing the front have lovely sea views. Waterford glass chandeliers hang in the Ivy Room, where the menu includes fresh local produce served in classic French style. Casual bistro-style dining in La Marine features Irish produce in a rural, Mediterranean-style menu. ✉ *Co. Wexford,* ☎ *053/32114,* FAX *053/32222. 104 rooms with bath. 2 restaurants, beauty salon, 4 tennis courts, croquet, 18-hole golf course, squash, bicycles. AE, MC, V. Closed Dec.–Feb.* ✍

$ ⌂ **Tuskar House Hotel.** Found in a quiet area near the ferry port, this small, family-run hotel promises simple pleasures. Comfortable rooms, some with balconies, have good views of the sea, especially those in the rear; all are decorated with functional, modern furniture in a bright, cheery palette. Public rooms have lots of polished pine, glass, and greenery. Seafood is a specialty at the restaurant. ✉ *St. Martin's Rd., Rosslare Harbour, Co. Wexford,* ☎ *053/33363,* FAX *053/33033. 30 rooms with bath. Restaurant, bar. AE, DC, MC, V.* ✍

Nightlife and the Arts

Portholes bar at the **Hotel Rosslare** (✉ Rosslare Harbour, ☎ 053/33110) is a popular spot for lively, traditional Irish music twice a week during the summer.

Outdoor Activities and Sports

Rosslare Golf Club (✉ Rosslare Strand, ☎ 053/32203) is a 27-hole, par-72 championship links. A mixture of links and parkland can be found at the 18-hole, par-72 **St. Helen's Bay** (✉ Kilrane, ☎ 053/33669).

Kilmore Quay

27 *22 km (14 mi) south of Rosslare on R739.*

A quiet, old-fashioned seaside village of thatched and whitewashed cottages noted for its fishing industry, Kilmore Quay is also popular with recreational anglers and bird-watchers. From the harbor there is a pleasant view to the east over the flat coast that stretches for miles. **Kehoe's Pub** is the hub of village activity; its collection of maritime artifacts is as interesting as that of many museums. During two weeks in July (generally mid-July), the village hosts a lively **seafood festival** (☎ 053/29922) with a parade, seafood barbecues, and other events.

☼ The **Saltee Islands,** Ireland's largest bird sanctuary, are a popular off-shore day trip from Kilmore Quay. (From mid-May to mid-September, look for boats at the village waterfront or on the marina to take you to the islands, weather permitting.) In late spring and early summer, several million seabirds nest among the dunes and on the rocky scarp on the south of the islands. Even if you are not an ornithologist, it's worth making the trip at these times to observe the sheer numbers of gulls, kittiwakes, puffins, guillemots, cormorants, and petrels.

The **Kilmore Quay Maritime Museum** is onboard the lightship *Guillemot.* The boat, built in 1923, is the last Irish lightship to be preserved complete with cabins and engine room, and it contains models and artifacts relating to the maritime history of the area. ☎ 053/21572. ✆ £2. ⊙ May–Sept., daily noon–6; Apr. and Oct., weekends noon–6.

Dining and Lodging

$$ ✗ **Silver Fox.** Simplicity and freshness are the keynotes at this busy, family-run seafood restaurant. Chef and co-owner Nicky Cullen offers up to a dozen seafood options, including his very popular grilled lemon sole, topped with a creamy sauce of fresh prawns, scallops, mushrooms, and onions, plus a sprinkling of cheese. He also cooks up a few nonseafood options such as stuffed garlic mushrooms or deep-fried St. Killian (local Camembert-like) cheese. This place is popular, so reserve in advance. ⊠ *Kilmore Quay,* ☎ 053/29888. AE, MC, V. Closed Mid-Jan.–mid-Feb. No lunch Nov.–Mar.

$ ▥ **Quay House.** Originally the village post office, this whitewashed guest house is three minutes' walk from the pier. The solid old house has been carefully refurbished with Douglas fir pine floors throughout and country pine bedroom furniture. Guests, generally outdoor types, are encouraged to socialize in the lounge and the dining room. A room for drying and storing diving equipment is available. ⊠ *Kilmore Quay, Co. Wexford,* ☎ 053/29988, ℻ 053/29808. 10 rooms with bath. Restaurant, fishing. MC, V. ✍

Shopping
Country Crafts (⊠ Kilmore Quay, ☎ 053/29885) overlooks the harbor of Kilmore Quay and has a mixture of Irish-made crafts, antique pine furniture, and paintings by local artists.

En Route On leaving Kilmore Quay, make your way north to R736, and then head west through Duncormick and on to Wellington Bridge. Past the bridge, head toward Fethard-on-Sea on the **Ring of Hook** drive. This is a strange and atypical part of Ireland, where the land is exceptionally flat and the narrow roads are straight.

The Ring of Hook leads out to Hook Lighthouse and north again to **Duncannon,** a small resort with a sandy beach and a delightful nautical atmosphere, on the north side of Waterford Harbour. Its history is marked by the visits of two kings: James II beat a hasty retreat out of Ireland through Duncannon port after his defeat at the Battle of the Boyne in 1690, and his successor, William III, also spent some days here before leaving for England.

The imposing, star-shape stone **Duncannon Fort** was built in the 16th-century on the site of an Iron Age fortification; it was placed on the water's edge as a defense against a feared attack by the Spanish Armada. Restoration work was in progress at press time, to be completed by early 2002. ⊠ *Duncannon,* ☎ 051/389454. ✆ £2. ⊙ May–mid-Sept., daily 10–5:30.

Ballyhack

★ ㉘ *34 km (21 mi) west of Kilmore Quay.*

On the upper reaches of Waterford Harbour, the pretty village of Ballyhack, with its square castle keep, wooden buildings, thatched cottages, and green, hilly background, is admired by painters and photographers. A small car ferry makes the five-minute crossing to Passage East and Waterford. The gray stone keep of **Ballyhack Castle** dates from the 16th century. It was once owned by the Knights Templars of St. John of Jerusalem, who held the ferry rights by royal charter; traditionally, they were required to keep a boat at Ballyhack to transport injured knights to the King's Leper Hospital at Waterford. The first two floors have been renovated and house a number of local history exhibits. The last admission is 45 minutes before closing. ☎ *051/389468.* ☞ *£1.* ✆ *Mid-June–mid-Sept., daily 9:30–6:30.* ✎

Dining and Lodging

$$$ ✕ **Neptune Restaurant.** Pierce and Valerie McAuliffe's waterside restaurant—a ferry ride across the River Nore between Counties Waterford and Wexford—is a cookery school by day and a restaurant by night. The Neptune is renowned for its seafood, such as local salmon and hot crab *Behat* (white crabmeat oven-baked in vegetable sauce with French mustard and cheese), but also has excellent local meat and game dishes and a splendid wine list. If you're impressed by the cooking, you might like to check out the special "Taste of Ireland" cookery demonstrations for £12 a person, offered June through August on Wednesdays at lunchtime. ✉ *Ballyhack Harbour, New Ross,* ☎ *051/389284. Reservations essential. AE, DC, MC, V. Closed mid-Dec.–mid-Jan. No lunch except for groups by arrangement. No dinner Sun.; no dinner Mon.–Wed. mid-Jan.–Apr. and Oct.–mid-Dec.*

$$$–$$$$ ✕🏠 **Dunbrody Country House.** This historic country retreat is both stylish and pleasantly informal. Once the home of the seventh Marquess of Donegall, Dermot Chichester, the sprawling, two-story Georgian manor house is now owned and run as a small hotel by Kevin and Catherine Dundon. Kevin is a master chef with international experience, and Catherine oversees the ongoing restoration program. Rooms are spacious with peaceful country views, individually decorated, and furnished with Georgian antiques. The oak-floor dining room, serving contemporary Continental cuisine, overlooks a small sunken garden that is floodlit at night. ✉ *Arthurstown, New Ross, Co. Wexford,* ☎ *051/389600,* 🖷 *051/389601. 13 rooms with bath, 6 suites. Restaurant, bar, horseback riding. AE, DC, MC, V. Closed Mon.–Thurs. and last wk of Dec.–Feb.* ✎

Waterford City

㉙ *10 km (6 mi) west of Ballyhack by ferry and road (R683), 62 km (39 mi) southwest of Wexford Town, 158 km (98 mi) southwest of Dublin.*

The largest town in the Southeast and Ireland's oldest city, Waterford was founded by the Vikings in the 9th century and was taken over by Strongbow, the Norman invader, with much bloodshed in 1170. The city resisted Cromwell's 1649 attacks—his phrase "by Hook or by Crooke" refers to his two siege routes, one via Hook Head, the other via Crooke Village on the estuary—but fell the following year and did not prosper again until 1783, when George and William Penrose set out to create "plain and cut flint glass, useful and ornamental," and thereby set in motion a glass-manufacturing industry without equal. The best Waterford glass was produced from the late 1780s to the early 19th century. This early work, examples of which can be found in mu-

Waterford City

River Stair

John's R.

Adelphi Quay

William St.

Rose Lane

PEOPLE'S PARK

Court House

Fire Station

Catherine St.

Beau St.

The Mall

Bailey's New St.

Greytriar's St.

Henrietta St.

Colbeck St.

City Wall

Parnell St.

Spring Garden

The Quay

Custom House Parade

Olaf St.

High St.

Peter St.

Michael St.

New St.

Castle St.

Browne's Lane

City Wall

Barronstrand St.

Broad St.

Patrick St.

Alexander St.

Green

Health Centre

Meagher's Quay

Great George's St.

Ballybricken

Mayors Walk

Govt. Office

Merchants Quay

O'Connell St.

Granville Hotel

Arts Centre

Barker St.

Thomas St.

James St.

The Glen

Morgan St.

Lower Yellow Rd.

Bridge St.

Summer Hill

Military Rd.

220 yards

200 meters

0

0

N

Bishop's Palace ...**32**	Holy Trinity Cathedral **37**	Waterford Glass Factory **40**	
Blackfriars Abbey........**36**	Reginald's Tower **30**	Waterford Treasures/Tourist Information Office **39**	
Christ Church Cathedral **33**	St. Olaf's Church **35**		
City Hall **31**	Victorian Clock Tower **38**		
French Church **34**			

seums and public buildings all over the country, is characterized by a unique, slightly opaque cast that is absent from the modern product.

Waterford has better-preserved city walls than anywhere else in Ireland but Derry (☞ Chapter 8). Initially, the slightly run-down commercial center doesn't look too promising. You'll need to park your car and proceed on foot to discover the heritage that the city has made admirable efforts over the past decade to preserve. The compact town center can be visited in a couple of hours. Allow at least another hour if you intend to take the Waterford Crystal factory tour.

The **city quays**—at the corner of Custom House Parade and Peter Street—are a good place to begin a tour of Waterford City. (The TIO is also down there, at the Granary on Merchant's Quay.) The city quays stretch for nearly a mile along the River Suir and were described in the 18th century as the best in Europe.

㉚ **Reginald's Tower,** a waterside circular tower on the east end of Waterford's quays, marks the apex of a triangle containing the old walled city of Waterford. Built by the Vikings for the city's defense in 1003, it has 80-ft-high, 10-ft-thick walls; an interior stairway leads to the top. The tower served in turn as the residence for a succession of Anglo-Norman kings (including Henry II, John, and Richard II), a mint for silver coins, a prison, and an arsenal. It is said that Strongbow's marriage to Eva, the daughter of Dermot MacMurrough, took place here in the late 12th century, thus uniting the Norman invaders with the native Irish. It has been restored to its original medieval appearance and furnished with appropriate 11th- to 15th-century artifacts. ⊠ *The Quay,* ☎ *051/304220.* ⊡ *£1.50.* ☉ *Easter–May and Oct., daily 10–5; June–Sept., daily 9:30–6:30.*

㉛ One of Waterford's finer Georgian buildings, **City Hall,** on the Mall, dates from 1783 and was designed by John Roberts, a native of the city. On the way you'll pass some good examples of domestic Georgian architecture—tall, well-proportioned houses with typically Irish, semicircular fanlights above the doors. The arms of Waterford hang over City Hall's own entrance, which leads into a spacious foyer that originally was a town meeting place and merchants' exchange. The building contains two lovely theaters, an old Waterford dinner service, and an enormous 1802 Waterford glass chandelier, which hangs in the Council Chamber (a copy of the chandelier hangs in Independence Hall in Philadelphia). The Victorian horseshoe-shape **Theatre Royal** (☞ Nightlife and the Arts, *below*) is the setting for the annual Festival of Light Opera in September. ⊠ *The Mall,* ☎ *051/309900.* ⊡ *Free.* ☉ *Weekdays 10–5.*

㉜ The **Bishop's Palace** is among the most imposing of the remaining Georgian town houses. Only the foyer is open to the public. ⊠ *Alongside City Hall on The Mall.* ⊡ *Free.* ☉ *Weekdays 9–5.*

Off of Colbeck Street along Spring Garden Alley, you'll see one of the remaining portions of the **old city wall**; there are sections all around the town center.

㉝ The Church of Ireland **Christ Church Cathedral** is the only neoclassical Georgian Cathedral in Ireland. The story of Waterford City from the Norman invasion to the present day is told in an audiovisual presentation. ⊠ *Henrietta St.,* ☎ *051/858958.* ⊡ *£2.* ☉ *Audiovisual show Apr.–May and Sept.–Oct., weekdays 11:30, 2:30, and 4; June–Aug., Mon.–Sat. 9:30, 11:30, 2:30, and 4, Sun. 2:30 and 4; cathedral daily.*

㉞ Roofless ruins are all that's left of **French Church** (⊠ Greyfriar's St.), a 13th-century Franciscan abbey. The church, also known as Greyfriars, was given to a group of Huguenot refugees (hence the "French") in 1695. A splendid east window remains amid the ruins. The key is available at Reginald's Tower (☞ *above*).

35 **St. Olaf's Church** (⊠ St. Olaf's St.) was built, as the name implies, by the Vikings in the mid-11th century. All that remains of the old church is its original door, which has been incorporated into the wall of the existing building (a meeting hall).

36 The ruined tower of **Blackfriars Abbey** (⊠ High St.) belonged to a Dominican abbey founded in 1226 and returned to the crown in 1541 after the dissolution of the monasteries. It was used as a courthouse until Cromwellian forces destroyed it in the 17th century.

37 The Roman Catholic **Holy Trinity Cathedral** (⊠ Barronstrand St. between High St. and the clock tower on the quays) has a simple facade and a richly (some would say garishly) decorated interior with high, vaulted ceilings and ornate, Corinthian pillars. It was designed in neoclassic style by John Roberts (who also designed Christ Church Cathedral and City Hall [☞ *above*]). Surprisingly, it was built in the late 18th century, when Catholicism was barely tolerated, on land granted by the Protestant city fathers.

38 The **Victorian Clock Tower** (⊠ Merchant's Quay) was built in 1864 with public donations. Although it has no great architectural merit, it serves as a reminder of the days when Waterford was a thriving, bustling port.

39 **Waterford Treasures,** above the southeast's main TIO, uses interactive audiovisual technology to guide you through 1,000 years in the history of Waterford. Entertaining and educational, the exhibition displays Waterford's rich inheritance of rare and beautiful artifacts, from the Charter Roll 1372, a list of all charters granted to Waterford up to that time, written in Latin on vellum, to the sword of King Edward IV to 18th-century crystal. A restaurant and a shop are also on the premises. ⊠ *The Granary, Merchant's Quay,* ☎ *051/304500.* 💰 *£3.* ☉ *Sept.–May, daily 10–5; June–Aug., daily 9:30–9.*

If the weather is favorable, consider a **cruise** along Waterford's harbor and the wide, picturesque estuary of the River Suir. A luxury river cruiser departs from the quay beside Reginald's Tower. Tickets can be purchased at the TIO (☞ Visitor Information *in* The Southeast A to Z, *below*). ⊠ *Galley Cruises,* ☎ *051/421723.* ☉ *Tours June–Aug., daily at 3, weather permitting.*

40 The city's most popular attraction is the **Waterford Glass Factory,** about 2 km (1 mi) from the TIO. (Take the N25 Waterford–Cork road south from the quay, or ask at the tourist office about the regular bus service.) When the factory opened in 1783, it provided English royalty with a supply of ornate handcrafted flatware, chandeliers, and decorative pieces. Over the years, its clientele and product line diversified, and today the United States is the biggest market. The worthwhile tour of the factory takes you through the specialized crafts of blowing, cutting, and polishing glass—all carried out against a noisy background of glowing furnaces and ceaseless bustle. An extensive selection of crystal is on view (and for sale) in the showroom. To reserve a place in a 60-minute tour, which includes an optional 18-minute audiovisual show, call the factory or the tourist office. ⊠ *Cork Rd., Kilbarry,* ☎ *051/332500.* 💰 *£3:50.* ☉ *Nov.–Mar., weekday tours 9:30–3:15; Apr.–Oct., daily tours 8:30–4.*

Dining and Lodging

$$$ ✕ **Dwyers of Mary Street.** Walls painted in shades of gray and wine
★ and beech dressers displaying both antique and modern glass soften

and warm the interior of the old Royal Irish Constabulary barracks, now home to this French-influenced restaurant. The menu changes every four weeks; a typical meal might consist of a tartlet of Jerusalem artichokes and roast scallops, followed by a venison loin roast, carved on a bed of celeriac, and served with a port-and-orange sauce. ⊠ *8 Mary St.,* ☎ *051/877478. Reservations essential. AE, DC, MC, V. No lunch. No dinner Sun.*

$$$ ✕ **Wine Vault.** Yes, in the cellar of this Elizabeth town house, there really is a wine vault—and what a wine vault it is, with more than 350 labels. The ground floor is home to a busy and informal bistro with polished wooden tables where head chef Stephen Hartigan uses traditional Irish ingredients to produce intriguing dishes such as baked smoked haddock with colcannon and poached egg, or stuffed fillet of pork with black pudding and caramelized apple. ⊠ *High St.,* ☎ *051/853444. AE, MC, V. Closed Sun. No lunch Mon.*

$$$$ ✕🏨 **Waterford Castle.** If coming to the Emerald Isle didn't take you far enough away from your real life, this 17th-century stone castle (with 19th-century additions) on its own 310-acre island in the River Suir may do the trick. The island is 3 km (2 mi) outside Waterford City and can be reached only by car ferry. The Great Hall and the drawing room have fine oak paneling, ornate antique furniture, and tapestries. The luxuriously decorated guest rooms have four-poster beds. Some bathrooms have original tile work and all have reproduction claw-foot tubs. Plush is the word in the Munster Room restaurant, with its detailed plastered ceiling, oak furniture, and deep-burgundy Donegal carpet, where the fare tends to country-style dishes like poached salmon, asparagus served in puff pastry, and bread-and-butter pudding. ⊠ *The Island, Ballinakill, Co. Waterford,* ☎ *051/878203,* FAX *051/879316. 14 rooms with bath, 5 suites. Restaurant, indoor pool, 18-hole golf course, 2 tennis courts, croquet, fishing. AE, DC, MC, V.*🐾

$$$ 🏨 **Granville Hotel.** In the heart of Waterford, this floodlit landmark overlooking the River Suir is one of Ireland's oldest hotels, with many historical connections. The patriot Thomas Francis Meagher was a previous owner, and Charles Stuart Parnell addressed mass meetings from its balcony when campaigning for Home Rule. The public rooms have an old-world Georgian character; bedrooms are decorated in 18th-century style. Ask for a room at the back if traffic disturbs you. ⊠ *Meagher Quay, Co. Waterford,* ☎ *051/305555,* FAX *051/305502. 98 rooms with bath. 2 restaurants, bar. AE, DC, MC, V.*🐾

$ 🏨 **Foxmount Farm & Country House.** For a pleasant change of pace, you can stay on a working dairy farm in the peaceful countryside. This elegant 17th-century house on its own extensive grounds is about 5 km (3 mi) outside town on the road to the Passage East ferry. The creeper-clad farmhouse has an informal style, with welcoming log fires and intriguing antiques. Your host, Margaret Kent, is renowned for her evening meals ($$$, residents only), using much of the farm's own produce, as well as fruit and herbs from her own garden. You are invited to bring your own wine, and enjoy a glass or two around the hearth after dinner. ⊠ *Passage East Rd., Co. Waterford,* ☎ *051/874308,* FAX *051/854906. 6 rooms, 4 with bath. Dining room, tennis court. No credit cards. Closed Nov.–mid-Mar.* 🐾

Nightlife and the Arts

Interesting work by contemporary artists can be seen at the **Dyehouse Gallery and Waterford Pottery** (⊠ Dyehouse La., ☎ 051/878166). Culture buffs won't want to miss the **Garter Lane Arts Centre** (⊠ 22A O'-Connell St., ☎ 051/855038). Call ahead for a schedule of upcoming concerts, exhibits, and theater productions at the center. **T&H Doolan's Bar** (⊠ 32 George's St., ☎ 051/872764) hosts traditional Irish music most summer nights and on Monday and Tuesday year-round. **Waterford International Festival of Light Opera** (☎ 051/874402), the only competitive event of its kind, is a great draw for amateur musical societies from throughout Ireland and Great Britain. The festival runs for 17 nights every September at the **Theatre Royal** (✉ City Hall, The Mall, ☎ 051/874402). The **Waterford Show** tells the story of Waterford's culture and heritage through music, song, and dance. Book at Waterford Crystal or the Tourist Information Office (☎ 051/875788). The show takes place at City Hall, 9 PM Thursday, Saturday, and Sunday, May–September. The admission cost of £8 includes a preshow drink and a glass of wine during the show.

Outdoor Activities and Sports

GOLF

Faithlegg Golf Club (✉ Faithlegg House, Checkpoint, ☎ 051/382241) is an 18-hole, par-72 course set in mature landscape on the banks of the River Suir. **Waterford Castle Golf Club** (✉ The Island, Ballinakill, ☎ 051/871633) is an 18-hole, par-72 course that claims to be Ireland's only true island course.

HORSEBACK RIDING

Horses are available by the hour at **Kilotteran Equitation Centre** (✉ Kilotteran, ☎ 051/384158).

SPECTATOR SPORTS

Gaelic football and hurling can be seen at the **Waterford GAA Grounds** (✉ Walsh Park).

Shopping

The best selection of crystal in Waterford City itself is on show at **Joseph Knox** (✉ 3 Barronstrand St., ☎ 051/875307). The **Waterford Design Centre** (✉ 44 The Quay, ☎ 051/856666) has two floors devoted to Irish crafts, gifts, and fashion.

While in Waterford, definitely pay a visit to the world-famous **Waterford Glass Factory** (✉ Cork Rd., Kilbarry, ☎ 051/332500 [☞ Waterford City, *above*]). The showroom displays an extensive selection of Waterford crystal and Wedgwood china.

Dunmore East

❹❶ *16 km (10 mi) southeast of Waterford City via R683 and R684.*

Home to an attractive lighthouse, Dunmore East is a quaint, one-street fishing village of thatched cottages at the head of Waterford Harbour. It's also home to many colorful, but noisy, kittiwakes, who nest in the steep cliffs overlooking the harbor. Plenty of small beaches and cliff walks are nearby, and you get a wonderful view of the estuary from the hill behind the village.

Dining

$$$ ✗ **Ship Restaurant.** Fresh, local seafood is the emphasis at this simply furnished restaurant on the ground floor of a 19th-century house overlooking the bay. Chef Billy Fitzpatrick's food is a mixture of French and Irish influences. Start with an arrangement of pickled seafood with a brunoise of ratatouille enhanced by gazpacho sauce. Entrées include grilled or panfried black sole and roulade of Dover sole filled with saffron mousse. ☎ *051/383141 or 051/383144. DC, MC, V. Closed Mon. No dinner Sun. No lunch Sept.–Apr.*

Tramore

❹❷ *11 km (7 mi) south of Waterford City on R675, 4 km (2½ mi) west of Dunmore East.*

☾ Tramore has a 5-km-long (3-mi-long) **beach** that is a popular escape for families from Waterford and other parts of the Southeast, as the many vacation homes and camper parks show. It is Ireland's biggest seaside resort and a dream-come-true for young children, but it is not to everybody's taste. Part of the seafront is overshadowed by a 50-acre amusement park, a miniature railway, and new vacation home developments, although the upper half of town is more quiet and reserved. At the western end of the beach, the sand gives way to rocky cliffs guarded by the Metal Man, a giant cast-iron figure who stands atop a great pillar. It's said that if a young woman hops on one foot around the base of the pillar three times, she will be married within a year. This custom, which is still observed in a lighthearted way, can be traced back to a stone that stood on the spot centuries ago and was used in ancient Celtic fertility rites.

Dining and Lodging

$ ✕ **Esquire.** Originally built in 1932 as a gentlemen's bar, the upstairs restaurant of the Esquire retains the air of a gentleman's club. Patron and chef Paul Horan applies his skills to fresh local produce. A full à la carte menu with such dishes as smoked salmon, Irish peppered steak with brandy, and vegetarian specials is served in the restaurant, while a simpler—and faster—bar-food menu is also available. ⊠ *Cross Market St.,* ☎ *051/381324. MC, V. No lunch Mon.–Sat.*

$–$$ ✕🖬 **Annestown House.** This large, white Victorian house is romantically perched above the sea and has its own private path down to Annestown Cove, one of many secluded coves along this breathtakingly beautiful stretch of coast between Tramore and Dungarvan. It has been in the family of John Galloway since 1820. With his wife, Pippa, John welcomes guests into a home full of nooks and crannies, lots of books, and a large billiard table. Bedrooms are generally large and full of character, with wonderful sea views at the front of the house. Dinner is served at 7:45 PM; book by noon. ⊠ *Annestown, Co. Waterford,* ☎ *051/396160,* 🗚 *051/396474. 5 rooms with bath. Tennis court, croquet, billiards. AE, MC, V. Closed Dec.–mid-Feb.*

Outdoor Activities and Sports

GOLF

Tramore Golf Club (⊠ Newtown Hill, ☎ 051/386170) is an 18-hole championship parkland course overlooked by the Comeragh Mountains.

SPECTATOR SPORTS

Horse races are held regularly at **Tramore Racecourse** (⊠ signposted on R675 from Waterford, ☎ 051/381425).

En Route West of Tramore on R675 you'll find **Annestown,** a smaller, quieter resort town with a good, sandy beach. The former copper-mining center of **Bunmahon,** now a fishing village popular with vacationers, is 8 km (5 mi) from here. A scenic footpath, signposted from Bunmahon, follows the Mahon River as it tumbles down from the Comeragh Mountains. This pleasant coastal drive offers views of unusual rock formations in the cliffs interspersed with sand dunes, as well as various rare flowers and birds. Attractive, easily accessible beaches are at **Stradbally** and **Clonea.**

Dungarvan

➃➌ *42 km (26 mi) southwest of Tramore on R675.*

Gradually the lowlands of Wexford and eastern Waterford, with their covering of soft grasses, give way to heath and moorland; the bog is created and maintained by the wetter climate of the hillier western Waterford countryside. You will see the mountains responsible for this change in climate rising up behind Dungarvan, the largest coastal town in County Waterford. This bustling fishing and resort spot is situated at the mouth of River Colligan, which empties into Dungarvan Bay here. It is a popular base for climbers and hikers.

OFF THE
BEATEN PATH

RING (AN RINNE) – In this Gaeltacht area on Dungarvan Bay, the Irish language is still in daily use, unusual in the south and east of the country. In Colaiste na Rinne, a language college, courses have been provided in the Irish since 1909. ✉ *7 km (4¼ mi) from Dungarvan, off N674.*

Dining and Lodging

$$–$$$$ ✕ **The Tannery.** Mediterranean and Asian influences, in the form of spices, occasionally surface in the cooking of chef-owner Paul Flynn. The secret, he says, is knowing when to meddle in what is otherwise classic French and Italian cuisine. Quiet mainstream jazz provides sophisticated background music in the high-ceiling room with tall windows in an old waterside tannery. ✉ *10 Quay St.,* ☎ *058/45420. AE, DC, MC, V. Closed Mon. No dinner Sun., Sept.–June, and 2 wks in Jan.*

$$ ⛴ **The Gold Coast Golf Hotel.** With great views of Dungarvan Bay, the hotel is one of the newest parts of a family-run and family-friendly property, including 16 self-catering holiday cottages (built around the 37-bedroom hotel), and 10 golf villas on the edge of its woodland course on a links setting. Rooms are bright, comfortable, and spacious. Guests are entitled to use the facilities of the Gold Coast's sister hotel, the Clonea Strand, just 2½ km (1½ mi) away; they include a games room, leisure complex, and Clonea's 3-km (2-mi) sandy beach. ✉ *Co. Waterford,* ☎ *058/42249 or 058/42416,* ℻ *058/43378. 37 rooms with bath. Restaurant, bar, indoor pool, 18-hole golf course, tennis court, exercise room, fishing, playground. AE, DC, MC, V.* 🐾

Nightlife and the Arts

A *ceili* (Irish dance) is held nightly during the summer at **Colaiste na Rinne** (✉ Ring, ☎ 058/46104). The **Seanachie Pub** (✉ Ballymacart, Ring, ☎ 058/46285) features traditional music and dancing in the courtyard on Sunday during the summer.

Outdoor Activities and Sports

BICYCLING

If you are tempted to explore the coast of the Dungarvan area and the nearby Nire Valley on two wheels, bicycles can be rented at **Tony O'Mahony** (✉ 14 Sexton St., Abbeyside, ☎ 058/43346).

GOLF

West Waterford Golf Club (✉ Coolcormack, ☎ 058/43216) is an 18-hole, par-72 parkland course open year-round.

SPECTATOR SPORTS

Hurling and football are played at **Fraher Field GAA.**

THE NIRE VALLEY, THE BLACKWATER VALLEY, AND COUNTY TIPPERARY

"It's a long way to Tipperary . . ." so run the words of that famed song sung all over the world since World War I. Actually, Tipperary is *not* so far to go, considering that, as Ireland's biggest inland county, it's within easy striking distance of Waterford and Cork. Moving in from the coastline, you can travel through some of Ireland's most lush pasturelands and to some of its most romantic sites, such as Lismore Castle. The Nire Valley, in the mountains between Dungarvan and Clonmel, is a popular area for hiking and pursuing other outdoor pleasures. The Blackwater Valley is renowned for its beauty, peacefulness, and excellent fishing. Some of the finest racehorses in the world are raised in the fields of Tipperary, which is also the county in where you'll find the Rock of Cashel—the greatest group of monastic ruins in all Ireland.

The Nire Valley

④ *29 km (18 mi) northwest of Dungarvan on R672.*

A visit to the Nire Valley is worthwhile only if you have time to take a walk in this remote but enchanting spot. The valley of the River Nire starts in the village of **Ballymacarbry** and runs along the base of the Comeragh Mountains. Both forest and mountain walks pass through quiet country where sheep far outnumber people. **Knocknagriffin,** the highest peak in the Comeraghs at 2,476 ft, with views back to Waterford on the coast andinland to Tipperary Town, is easily accessible to a moderately fit walker. Walking instructions and maps are provided locally by **Nire Valley Tourist Information** (☎ 052/36455).

Dining and Lodging

$$-$$$ ✕⌂ **Hanora's Cottage.** This is one of Ireland's premier B&Bs, built in
★ the heart of the Nire Valley by owner Seamus Wall's great-grandparents in the late 19th century. The guest rooms are a generous size by cottage standards and are prettily decorated with chintz curtains and spreads; six have hot tubs and three have double hot tubs, particularly welcome if you take part in the main activities here—nearby golf, riding, and walking. (Guided walks are offered every Saturday.) The less energetic simply unwind in front of the open fire and wait to be fed dishes like fillet of salmon in prawn and Chablis sauce or medallions of fillet steak with onions, mushrooms, and mustard. Packed lunches are provided using Seamus's famous home-baked brown bread. ✉ *Ballymacarbery, Co. Waterford,* ☎ *052/36134,* ℻ *052/36540. 11 rooms with bath. Dining room, hot tub. MC, V.*

Outdoor Activities and Sports

Explore the Nire Valley on horseback by joining a guided hack from **Melody's Riding Stables** (✉ Ballymacarbry, ☎ 052/36147).

Ardmore

④ *24 km (15 mi) south of Dungarvan on N25.*

Ardmore is a delightful village, with ancient roots, on its own peninsula at the base of a tall cliff. In the 5th century, St. Declan is reputed to have disembarked here from Wales and founded a monastery, 30 years before St. Patrick arrived in Ireland. Ardmore's monastic remains are found on the top of the cliff. The ruined, 12th-century **Cathedral of St. Declan** has some ogham stones inside and weathered but interesting biblical scenes carved on its west front. The saint is said to be buried in **St. Declan's Oratory,** a small early Christian church that has
★ been partially reconstructed. The 97-ft-high **round tower,** one of 70 round towers remaining in Ireland, is in exceptionally good condition. Round towers were built by the early Christian monks as watchtowers and belfries but came to be used as places of refuge for the monks and their valuables during Viking raids. This is the reason the doorway is 15 ft above ground level—once inside, the monks could pull the ladder into the tower with them.

Lismore

⑯ *40 km (25 mi) northwest of Ardmore on N72 and R671.*

The enchanting little town of Lismore is built on the banks of the Blackwater, a river famous for its trout and salmon. Popular with both anglers and romantics, from the 7th to the 12th century it was an important monastic center, founded by St. Carthac (or Carthage), and it had one of the most renowned universities of its time. The village has two cathedrals, a Roman Catholic one from the late 19th century and the Church of Ireland St. Carthage's, which dates from 1633 and incorporates fragments of an earlier church. The latter cathedral also has interesting tombs and effigies.

★ As you cross the bridge entering Lismore, you will be struck by a dramatic view of the magnificent **Lismore Castle**, a vast, turreted gray stone building atop a rock that overhangs River Blackwater. There has been a castle here since the 12th century, but the present structure, built by the sixth Duke of Devonshire, dates from the mid-19th century. The house is not open to the public, unlike the upper and lower gardens, which consist of woodland walks, including an unusual yew walk said to be more than 800 years old, and an impressive display of magnolias, camellias, and shrubs. ☎ *058/54424.* ☞ *£3.* ☉ *End of Apr.–mid-Oct., daily 1:45–4:45.*

En Route Leaving Lismore, heading east on N72 for 6½ km (4 mi) toward Cappoquin, a well-known coarse-angling center, you can pick up R669 north into the **Knockmealdown Mountains.** Your route is signposted as the Vee Gap road, the Vee Gap being its summit, from where you'll have superb views of the Tipperary plain, the Galtee Mountains in the northwest, and a peak called Slievenamon in the northeast. If the day is clear, you should be able to see the Rock of Cashel, ancient seat of the kings of Munster, some 32 km (20 mi) away. Just before you enter the Vee Gap, look for a 6-ft-high mound of stones on the left side of the road. It marks the grave of Colonel Grubb, a local landowner who liked the view so much that he arranged to be buried here standing up so that he could look out over the scene for all eternity.

You might like to break your journey and visit **Mount Melleray Abbey.** This was the first post-Reformation monastery, founded in 1832 by the Cistercian Order in what was then a barren mountainside wilderness. Over the years the order has transformed the site into more than 600 acres of fertile farmland. The monks maintain strict vows of silence, but visitors are welcome to join in services throughout the day and are permitted into most areas of the abbey. It is also possible to stay in the guest lodge by prior arrangement, but booking ahead is essential. ✉ *Cappoquin, just south of the Vee Gap, signposted off R669, 13 km (8 mi) from Lismore,* ☎ *058/54404,* 🖷 *058/52140.* ☞ *Free.* ☉ *Daily 7:45 AM–8 PM.*

Dining and Lodging

$$–$$$ ✕🛏 **Richmond House.** This handsome three-story Georgian country house is set deep in the countryside just outside Cappoquin. The atmosphere is informal, unpretentious, and very relaxing, under the personal supervision of owners Claire and Paul Deevy. The public rooms, with their log fires and traditional rust-and-cream decor, retain characterful echoes of the old-world country hotel. Paul is a talented chef who uses local produce whenever possible to create dishes like his cassoulet of local seafood (scallops, monkfish, salmon, dover sole, and prawns) with saffron cream sauce. ✉ *Cappoquin, Co. Waterford,* ☎ *058/54278,* 🖷 *058/54988. 9 rooms with bath. Restaurant, bar, horseback riding, fishing. MC, V. Closed last wk of Dec.–mid-Feb.* ✍

Cahir

47 *37 km (23 mi) north of Lismore, at crossroads of R668, N24, and N8.*

Cahir Castle is situated on a rocky island on the River Suir, in the middle of the town, and is one of Ireland's largest and best-preserved castles, retaining its dramatic keep, tower, and much of its original defensive structure. An audiovisual show is available, as are guided tours (upon request). ☎ 052/41011. ⌷ £2. ☉ *Mid-Mar.–mid-June and mid-Sept.–mid-Oct., daily 9:30–5:30; mid-June–mid-Sept., daily 9–7:30; mid-Oct.–mid-Mar., daily 9:30–4:30; last admission 45 mins before closing.*

Dining and Lodging

$ ✕⌷ **Bansha Castle.** In the heart of quiet, wooded country backed by the Glen of Aherlow, about 8 km (5 mi) from Cahir on the N24 Tipperary road, sits this 18th-century stone house with a Norman-style round tower. It has been in John Russell's family for more than half a century and has a relaxed, inviting atmosphere: the family cat occupies the best fireside armchair in the chintz-strewn but unfussy drawing room. Large rooms, all with great views, are simply furnished with plain carpets and mahogany reproduction pieces, but walls are decorated in strong, vibrant colors. John's wife, Teresa, uses locally grown organic produce in her good home cooking. A plethora of activities, such as walking, golfing, salmon and trout fishing, and horseback riding, are nearby. ⌷ *Bansha, Co. Tipperary,* ☎ *062/54187,* FAX *062/54294. 6 rooms, 4 with bath. Dining room. No credit cards.*

Outdoor Activities and Sports

Explore the Galtee mountains and the Glen of Aherlow on horseback with **Bansha House Stables** (⌷ Bansha, ☎ 062/54194).

En Route To your left as you drive from Cahir to Tipperary Town on N24 is the **Glen of Aherlow,** a lovely 16-km-long (10-mi-long) wooded stretch skirting the River Aherlow and its tributaries between the Galtee Mountains to the south and the Slievenamuck Hills to the north. The highest summit in the Galtees is the 3,018-ft Galtymore Mountain.

Tipperary Town

48 *22 km (14 mi) northwest of Cahir on N24.*

Tipperary Town, a dairy-farming center at the head of a fertile plain known as the Golden Vale, is a good starting point for climbing and walking in the hills around the Glen of Aherlow, but the small country town, on the River Ara, is worth visiting in its own right, too. In **New Tipperary,** a neighborhood built by local tenants during Ireland's Land War (1890–1891), old buildings, like Dalton's Heritage House, have been restored; you can visit the Heritage House by calling the offices of Clann na hEireann (☞ *below*). You can also visit the old **Butter Market** on Dillon Street; the **Churchwell** at the junction of Church, Emmet, and Dillon streets; and the grave of the grandfather of Robert Emmett—one of the most famous Irish patriots—in the graveyard at St. Mary's Church. A statue of Charles Kickham, whose novel *The Homes of Tipperary* chronicled the devastation of this county through forced emigration, has a place of honor in the center of town. Adjacent to **St. Michael's Church,** with its stained-glass window of a soldier killed during World War I, is Bridewell Jail; housed in one of the cell blocks is Tipperary's **Family History Research Centre** (⌷ The Bridewell, St. Michael St., ☎ 062/52725), which traces people's Tipperary roots. The **headquarters of Clann na hEireann** (⌷ 45 Main St., ☎ 062/33188) researches the origins and history of surnames throughout Ireland and promotes clan gatherings.

Nightlife and the Arts

Tipperary is famous for its traditional music and dancing which happen when the mood strikes. Ask locals to recommend a good pub for a session.

Outdoor Activities and Sports

Tipperary Racecourse (✉ Limerick Junction, ☎ 062/51357) is situated 5 km (3 mi) northwest of town.

Cashel

49 *17 km (11 mi) northeast of Tipperary Town on N74.*

Cashel is a market town on the busy Cork–Dublin road, with a lengthy history as a center of royal and religious power. From roughly AD 370 until 1101, it was the seat of the kings of Munster, and it was probably at one time a center of Druidic worship. Here, according to legend, St. Patrick arrived in about AD 432 and baptized King Aengus, who became Ireland's first Christian ruler. One of the many legends associated with this event is that St. Patrick plucked a shamrock to explain the mystery of the Trinity, thus giving a new emblem to Christian Ireland.

★ The awe-inspiring, oft-mist-shrouded **Rock of Cashel** is one of Ireland's most visited sites. The rock itself, a short walk to the north of the town, rises as a giant, circular mound 200 ft above the surrounding plain; it is crowned by a tall cluster of gray monastic remains. Legend has it that St. Patrick baptized King Aengus here and that the devil, flying over Ireland in a hurry, took a bite out of the Slieve Bloom Mountains to clear his path (the gap, known as the Devil's Bit, can be seen to the north of the rock) and spat it out in the Golden Vale.

The best approach to the rock is along the **Bishop's Walk,** a 10-minute hike that begins outside the drawing room of the Cashel Palace hotel (☞ Dining and Lodging, *below*) on Main Street.

The **museum** in the vicar's choral across from the entrance to the Rock provides a 15-minute audiovisual display, as well as enthusiastic young guides who will ensure that you do not miss the many interesting features of the buildings atop the Rock of Cashel.

The shell of **St. Patrick's Cathedral** is the largest building on the summit. The 13th-century cathedral was originally built in a flamboyant variation on Romanesque style, but it was destroyed by fire in 1495. The restored building was desecrated during the 16th century in a ugly incident in which hundreds of townspeople who had sought sanctuary in the cathedral were burned to death when Cromwell's forces surrounded the building with turf and set it afire. A series of sculptures in the north transept represent the apostles, other saints, and the Beasts of the Apocalypse. Look for the octagonal staircase turret that ascends beside the **Central Tower** to a series of defensive passages built into the thick walls. From the top of the Central Tower, you'll have a wonderful view of the surrounding plains and mountains. Another passage gives access to the **round tower,** a well-preserved, 92-ft-high building.

The entrance to **Cormac's Chapel,** the best-preserved building on top of the Rock, is behind the south transept of the cathedral. The chapel was built in 1127 by Cormac Macarthy, king of Desmond and bishop of Cashel (combination bishop-kings were not unusual in the early Irish church). Note the high corbeled roof, modeled on the traditional covering of early saints' cells (as at Glendalough [☞ Chapter 2] and Dingle [☞ Chapter 5]); the typically Romanesque, twisted columns around the altar; and the unique carvings around the south entrance. ✉ *Rock* *of Cashel,* ☎ *062/61437.* ☜ *£3.* ⊘ *Mid-Mar.–mid-June, daily 9:30–5:30; mid-June–mid-Sept., daily 9–7:30; mid-Sept.–mid-Mar., daily 9:30–4:30.* ✍

In the same building as the TIO, the **Cashel of the Kings Heritage Center** explains the historic relationship between the town and the Rock and includes a scale model of Cashel as it looked during the 1600s. ✉ *City Hall,* ☎ *062/62511.* ☜ *£1.* ⊘ *Sept.–Mar., weekdays 9:30–5:30; Apr.–June, daily 9:30–5:30; July–Aug., daily 9:30–8.*

The **G. P. A. Bolton Library,** on the grounds of the St. John the Baptist Church of Ireland Cathedral, has a particularly fine collection of rare books, manuscripts, and maps, some dating from the beginning of the age of printing in Europe. ✉ *John St.,* ☎ *062/61944.* ☜ *£2.* ⊘ *June–Sept., daily 11–4:30.*

Dining and Lodging

$$$$ ✕ **Chez Hans.** This small, converted Victorian church at the foot of
★   the Rock of Cashel oozes old-world charm. Dark wood and tapestries provide an elegant background for tables dressed in white linen. Traditional French cuisine with a hint of nouvelle takes advantage of fresh Irish ingredients. Specialties include roast rack of Tipperary spring lamb with a fresh herb crust, and a selection of seafood, like salmon, hake, and mussels, served in a light chive velouté. ✉ *Rockside,* ☎ *062/61177. Reservations essential. MC, V. Closed Sun.–Mon. and 1st 3 wks of Jan. No lunch.*

$$ ✕ **Spearman Restaurant.** This small, family-run restaurant is tucked away in the center of Cashel, near the TIO. Stained-glass windows and tall-back chairs make a statement against the vibrant lemons and limes of the decor. It's a pleasant backdrop for the cuisine of chef John Spearman, who has a reputation for creating imaginative, affordable food based on the best of fresh local produce. ✉ *97 Main St.,* ☎ *062/61143. AE, DC, MC, V. Closed Nov. No lunch Dec.–Apr., no dinner Sun.–Mon., Oct.–May.*

$$$$ ✕▥ **Cashel Palace.** Dramatically set at the foot of the Rock of Cashel,
★   this 1730s redbrick-and-limestone bishop's palace is an exquisite accommodation. The pine-paneled entrance hall is dominated by twin marble fireplaces and Corinthian columns; a striking, intricately carved red-pine staircase sweeps upstairs. Antiques and spacious bathrooms characterize the luxurious guest rooms on the first floor of the main house, while the rooms on the second floor, ex-servants quarters, and in the Mews have a cozier decor. The menu at the elegant Three Sisters Restaurant relies on game in season, local lamb and beef, and fresh fish creatively prepared, while the bistro-style basement Bishop's Buttery serves simple, light meals all day. Don't miss the lovely gardens to the rear of the house, where you can see the descendants of the original hop plants used by Richard Guinis to brew the first "Wine of Ireland." Guinis went on, with his son, Arthur, to found the famous Guinness Brewery in Dublin (☞ Chapter 2). ✉ *Main St., Co. Tipperary,* ☎ *062/62707,* ℻ *062/61521. 13 rooms with bath. 2 restaurants, bar, fishing. AE, DC, MC, V.* ✍

$$$ ▤ **Dundrum House Hotel.** Nestled beside the River Multeen, 12 km (7½ mi) outside busy Cashel, is this magnificent, four-story Georgian house. Sixteen high-ceiling bedrooms take up the main house; the rest are in a three-story wing built during the house's previous incarnation as a convent and in a recently added wing. All the older rooms have large pieces of early Victorian furniture and lovely views of the surrounding parkland. The old convent chapel, stained-glass windows intact, is now a cocktail bar. Elaborate plaster ceilings, attractive period furniture, and open fires make the spacious dining room and lounge inviting. ✉ *Dundrum, Co. Tipperary,* ☎ 062/71116, FAX 062/71366. *61 rooms with bath. 2 restaurants, 2 bars, pool, sauna, steam room, 18-hole golf course, tennis court, fishing. AE, DC, MC, V.* 🐾

Nightlife and the Arts

Folksinging, storytelling, and dancing are enjoyed evenings from June through September, Tuesday through Saturday, at the **Bru Boru Heritage Center** (☎ 062/61122) at the foot of the Rock of Cashel. Entertainment usually begins at 9 PM and costs £8, £25 with dinner.

Outdoor Activities and Sports

GOLF

The natural features of the mature Georgian estate at Dundrum House Hotel (☞ Dining and Lodging, *above*) have been incorporated into an 18-hole, par-72 course for the **County Tipperary Golf and Country Club** (✉ Dundrum House Hotel, Dundrum, ☎ 062/71717).

SPECTATOR SPORTS

About 20 km (12 mi) north of Cashel, **Semple GAA Stadium** (✉ Thurles, ☎ 0504/22702) is where major hurling and football championships in the Southeast take place, as well as many exciting minor contests.

Clonmel

🔟 *24 km (15 mi) southeast of Cashel on R688.*

As the county seat of Tipperary, Clonmel is set on the prettiest part of the River Suir, with wooded islands and riverside walks. It is one of Ireland's largest and most prosperous inland towns. There has been a settlement here since Viking days; in the 14th century the town was walled and fortified as a stronghold of the Butler family. At one end of town is the **West Gate**, built in 1831 on the site of the medieval one. Among other notable buildings are the **Main Guard**, built in 1695 to house the courts of the Palatinate, a separate jurisdiction ruled by the Butlers, and the **Franciscan friary** and **St. Mary's Church of Ireland**, both of which incorporate remains of earlier churches and some interesting tombs and monuments.

Dining and Lodging

$$$ ✕ **Mulcahy's of Clonmel.** This superb series of interconnecting bars and restaurant areas serves a wide selection of food, from the East Lane Cafe's à la carte to the daily carvery lunch to the Kitchen Grill menu of good pub grub, like deep-fried scampi. Mulcahy's has recently added 10 modern bedrooms over the pub. ✉ *47 Gladstone St.,* ☎ 052/22825. AE, DC, MC, V.

$$–$$$ ✕🏨 **Minella Hotel.** This granite-faced Georgian manor hotel is in a quiet neighborhood on the bank of the River Suir. The bedrooms afford fine views of the river, particularly those in the front and in the east wing. Three of the eight suites have four-poster beds and private steam rooms, while the remaining five have hot tubs. The Victorian furnishings in the main house are comfortable; walls are decorated with hunting prints. The dining room is oak-paneled and has a good reputation for freshly prepared classic cuisine. ✉ *Coleville Rd., Co. Tipperary,* ☎ 052/22388, FAX 052/24381. *62 rooms with bath, 8 suites. Restaurant, bar, health club, fishing. AE, DC, MC, V.*

Outdoor Activities and Sports

GOLF

Clonmel Golf Club (✉ Lyreanearla, ☎ 052/24050) is an 18-hole course on the slopes of the Comeragh Mountains, 5 km (3 mi) from Clonmel.

Hurling and Gaelic football are played at the **Clonmel GAA Grounds** (✉ Western Rd.). Horse races are held regularly at **Clonmel Racecourse** (✉ Powerstown Park, ☎ 052/25719).

Carrick-on-Suir

51 *20 km (12 mi) east of Clonmel on N24.*

Carrick-on-Suir lies partly in County Tipperary and partly in County Waterford. The beautifully restored **Ormonde Castle** is the town's main attraction. The castle, dating from 1450, is fronted by the 16th-century Ormonde Manor House, an interesting and well-preserved Tudor mansion. The town is one of several claiming to be the birthplace of Anne Boleyn, and the house is said to have been built in order to entertain her daughter, Queen Elizabeth I, who never visited here. It contains some good, early stuccowork, especially in the 100-ft Long Room, and many arms and busts of the English queen. ☎ *051/640787.* ✉ *£2.* ◷ *Mid-June–Sept., daily 9:30–6:30.*

Shopping
The **Tipperary Crystal Factory Shop** (✉ Ballynoran, ☎ 051/641188), a factory outlet that offers free tours of the glass-cutting facility weekdays between 10 and 3:30, has a showroom in a replica thatched cottage, open daily.

THE SOUTHEAST A TO Z

Arriving and Departing

By Car
Waterford City, the regional capital, is easily accessible from all parts of Ireland. From Dublin, take N7 southwest, change to N9 in Naas, and continue along this highway through Carlow Town and Thomastown until it terminates in Waterford. N25 travels east–west through Waterford City, connecting it with Cork in the west and Wexford Town in the east. From Limerick and Tipperary Town, N24 stretches southeast until it, too, ends in Waterford City.

By Ferry
The region's primary ferry terminal is found just south of Wexford Town at Rosslare. **Stena Sealink** (☎ 053/33115) sails directly between Rosslare Ferryport and Fishguard, Wales. Pembroke, Wales, and France's Cherbourg and Roscoff can be reached on **Irish Ferries** (☎ 053/33158).

By Plane
Waterford Regional Airport (☎ 051/875589) is on the Waterford–Ballymacaw road in Killowen. Waterford City is 9½ km (6 mi) from the airport. A hackney cab from the airport into Waterford City costs approximately £10. **British Airways** (☎ 051/875589 or 800/626747) schedules flights out of this small regional airport daily to Stanstead, England.

Getting Around

By Bus
Bus Éireann (☎ 01/836–6111 in Dublin, 051/873401 in Waterford) makes the Waterford–Dublin journey six times daily for about £7 one-way. There are five buses daily between Waterford City and Limerick and four between Waterford City and Rosslare. The Cork–Waterford journey is made eight times daily. In Waterford City, the terminal is Waterford Bus Station.

By Car
For the most part, the main roads in the Southeast are of good quality and are free of congestion. Side roads are generally narrow and twisting, and drivers should keep an eye out for farm machinery and animals on country roads.

By Train
Waterford City is linked by **Irish Rail** (☎ 01/836–6222 in Dublin, 051/873401 in Waterford) service to Dublin. Trains run from Plunkett Station in Waterford City to Dublin four times daily, making stops at Thomastown, Kilkenny, Bagenalstown, and Carlow Town. The daily train between Waterford City and Limerick makes stops at Carrick-on-Suir, Clonmel, Cahir, and Tipperary Town. The train between Rosslare and Waterford City runs twice daily.

Contacts and Resources

B&B Reservation Agencies
For a small fee, **Bord Fáilte** will book accommodations anywhere in Ireland through its central reservations system. B&Bs can be booked at local visitor information offices as well when they are open. For more information, *see* Lodging *in* Smart Travel Tips A to Z.

Car Rentals
The major car-rental companies have offices at Rosslare Ferryport, and in most large towns rental information can be found through the local tourism office. Typical car-rental prices start at about £40 per day with unlimited mileage, and they usually include insurance and all taxes. **Budget** has offices in Rosslare Harbour (⊠ The Ferryport, ☎ 053/33318) and Waterford Airport (☎ 051/421670). **Hertz** has offices in Rosslare Harbour (☎ 053/33238) and Waterford City (☎ 051/878737).

Emergencies
Police, fire, and **ambulance** (☎ 112 or 999). **Waterford Regional Hospital** (⊠ Ardkeen, ☎ 051/873321).

Guided Tours
Kilkenny: Irish City Tours (☎ 01/458–0054) operates open-top coach tours from the castle gate Easter through September, daily 10:30–5. Walking tours of Kilkenny are arranged by **Tynan Tours** and operate March to October, Monday through Saturday, from the Kilkenny TIO (☎ 056/65929).

Waterford City: Burtchaell Tours (☎ 051/873711) leads a Waterford walk at noon and 2 PM daily from March through September. It leaves from the Granville Hotel.

Wexford Town: Walking tours of historic Wexford Town can be pre-booked for groups by contacting Seamus P. Molloy (☎ 053/22663).

Outdoor Activities and Sports
FISHING
For further information on angling activities in the region, contact the **Southern Regional Fisheries Board** (⊠ Anglesea St., Clonmel, Co. Tipperary, ☎ 052/80055).

SPECTATOR SPORTS
Tickets to major Gaelic football and hurling matches are usually taken up by members, but for smaller venues, or for some of the less fiercely contested matches, inquire at local TIOs.

Visitor Information
Ten Tourist Information Offices (TIOs) in the Southeast are open all year (not all have fax numbers): **Carlow Town** (⊠ Bridewell La., Co.

Carlow, ☎ 0503/31554, FAX 0503/30065). **Carrick-on-Suir** (✉ Heritage Centre, Main St., Co. Tipperary, ☎ 051/640200). **Clonmel** (✉ Community Office, 8 Sarsfield St., Co. Tipperary, ☎ 052/22960, FAX 052/26378). **Dungarvan** (✉ The Courthouse, Co. Waterford, ☎ 058/41741, FAX 058/45020). **Enniscorthy** (✉ Wexford Museum, The Castle, Co. Wexford, ☎ 054/34699). **Gorey** (✉ Markethouse, Main St., Co. Wexford, ☎ 055/21248, FAX 055/22521). **Kilkenny** (✉ Shee Alms House, Rose Inn St., ☎ 056/51500, FAX 056/63955). **Lismore** (✉ Heritage Centre, Co. Waterford, ☎ 058/54975, FAX 058/53009). **Waterford City** (✉ 41 The Quay, Co. Waterford, ☎ 051/875823, FAX 051/876720). **Wexford Town** (✉ Crescent Quay, Co. Wexford, ☎ 053/23111, FAX 053/41743).

Another seven TIOs are open seasonally: **Ardmore** (✉ Seafront Car Park, Co. Waterford, ☎ 024/94444, FAX 024/94056), open June–mid-September. **Cahir** (✉ Castle Car Park, Co. Tipperary, ☎ 052/41453), open May–September. **Cashel** (✉ Cashel Heritage Centre, Co. Tipperary, ☎ 062/61333, FAX 062/61789), open April–September. **New Ross** (✉ Harbour Centre, The Quay, Co. Wexford, ☎ 051/421857), open May–September. **Rosslare** (✉ Rosslare Ferry Terminal, Kilrane, Rosslare Harbour, Co. Wexford, ☎ 053/33232, FAX 053/33421), open April–September. **Tipperary Town** (✉ 3 James St., Co. Tipperary, ☎ 062/51457), open May–October. **Tramore** (✉ Town Centre, Co. Waterford, ☎ 051/281572), open June–August.

5 THE SOUTHWEST

In and Around Cork and Killarney,
the Ring of Kerry, the Dingle Peninsula,
and Shannonside

Spectacular is the word for the Southwest, where superlatives flow as continuously as the Rivers Lee and Blackwater. Five-star scenery is everywhere, from Kinsale along the coast west to Mizen Head in the far southwest corner to the glorious mountains and lakes of Killarney. And the food! Thanks to its accomplished chefs and the bounty of farms, fields, lakes, and coast, County Cork has become to the Irish food world what California is to America's. You'll also find a mild climate, the nation's second- and third-largest cities, and extensive Irish-speaking areas: what more could you ask for?

Updated by
Alannah
Hopkin

C ORK, KERRY, LIMERICK, AND CLARE—the sound of these Southwest Ireland county names has an undeniably evocative Irish
lilt. A varied coastline, spectacular scenery (especially around
the famous lakes of Killarney), and a mild climate have long attracted
visitors to this region. Although the Southwest contains Cork and
Limerick—Ireland's second- and third-largest cities—its most notable
attractions are rural: miles and miles of pretty country lanes meandering
through rich but sparsely populated farmland. Even in the two main
cities the pace of life is perceptibly slower than in Dublin. To be in a
hurry in this region is being ill-mannered. It was probably a Kerryman
who first remarked that when God made time, he made plenty of it.

As you look over thick, fuchsia hedges at thriving dairy farms or stop
off at a wayside restaurant to sample the region's seafood or locally
raised meat, it is hard to imagine that some 150 years ago this area
was decimated by famine. Thousands perished in the fields and the work-
houses, and thousands more took "coffin ships" from Cobh in Cork
Harbour to the New World. Between 1845 and 1849 the population
of Ireland fell by more than a million, or roughly 30% (according to
the 1841 census, the Irish population was 8,175,124). Many small villages in the Southwest were wiped out. The region was battered again
in the War for Independence and the Civil War that was fought with
intensity in and around "Rebel Cork" between 1919 and 1921. Economic recovery only began in the late 1960s, which led to a boom in
hotel construction and renovation—not always, alas, done in the appropriate style.

Outside of Killarney and Shannon, tourist development remains fairly
low-key. The area is trying to absorb more visitors without losing too
much of what attracts them in the first place: uncrowded roads, pol-
lution-free beaches and rivers, easy access to golf and fishing, and unspoiled scenery where wildflowers, untamed animals, and rare birds
(which have all but disappeared in more industrialized European countries) still thrive.

South of the city of Cork, the main business and shopping town of the
region, the resort town of Kinsale is the gateway to a relatively unspoiled
coastline containing Roaring Water Bay, with its main islands, and the
magnificent, natural harbor, Bantry Bay. The southwest coast of the
region is formed by three peninsulas: the Beara, the Iveragh, and the
Dingle; the road known as the Ring of Kerry makes a complete circuit
of the Iveragh Peninsula. Killarney's sparkling blue lakes and magnificent sandstone mountains, inland from the peninsulas, have a unique
and romantic splendor, immortalized in the 19th century by the writings of William Thackeray and Sir Walter Scott. Around the Shannon
estuary you enter "castle country," an area littered with ruined castles
and abbeys as a result of Elizabeth I's attempt to subdue the old Irish
province of Munster in the 16th century. Limerick City, too, bears the
scars of history from a different confrontation with the English, the
Siege of Limerick, which took place in 1691. Today, it is Limerick's
other "scars"—described so memorably in Frank McCourt's noted best-
seller *Angela's Ashes*—that now lure travelers to discover (or rediscover)
the city (☞ Close Up: Risen from the Ashes: Frank McCourt's Limerick).

Although the Southwest has several sumptuous country-house hotels,
it is basically an easygoing, unpretentious region, where informality
and simplicity are the keynotes of hospitality. As in the rest of Ireland,
social life revolves around the pub, and a visit to your "local" is the

best way to find out what's going on. Local residents have not lost their natural curiosity about "strangers," as visitors are called. You will frequently be asked, "Are you enjoying your holiday?" "Yes" is not a good enough answer—what the locals are really after is your life story.

Pleasures and Pastimes

Dining
The Southwest—especially County Cork—rivals Dublin as Ireland's food-culture epicenter. Cork has astonishing resources: sparkling waters full of a wide array of fish, acre after acre of potato fields, cows galore, wild mushrooms and berries, and much more. Cork's dedicated, inventive chefs turn this bounty into a feast in food markets (Cork City's English Market, most notably), bakeries, cafés, restaurants, B&Bs, and country houses. In tiny Shanagarry, Darina and Tim Allen train hundreds of chefs every year at their Ballymaloe Cookery School. Outstanding restaurants and the International Gourmet Festival in October draw crowds to Kinsale, the "Gourmet Capital of Ireland." Whether trained at home or abroad, area chefs put a premium on fresh, local (often organically grown) produce. Restaurants outside main cities tend to be seasonal, and choice will be limited between November and mid-March. To sample the region's best cuisine, consult our five-day gastronomic tour (☞ Great Itineraries, *below*). For price ranges, *see* Dining *in* Smart Travel Tips A to Z.

Lodging
Some of the most sumptuous country-house hotels in Ireland are in the Southwest. You'll also find more modest establishments, many in spectacular seaside locations. Though some country houses appear grand, their main aim is to provide a relaxed stay in beautiful surroundings. A good pair of walking boots and a sensible raincoat are more useful here than a formal wardrobe. If you want to dress for dinner, as some people do, feel free. By and large, however, informality is the order of the day. Keep in mind that facilities may be minimal—only expensive hotels have fitness centers, for instance. At the least, most hotels can organize golf, deep-sea fishing, freshwater angling, and horseback riding. Most B&Bs have introduced private bathrooms and, in the larger towns, televisions and direct-dial phones in rooms. Accommodations in West Cork, Killarney, and Dingle are seasonal; between November and March, many places close down, but outside these months—especially from July to mid-October—hotels are busy, so book well in advance. If your first choice for a hotel is full, ask for a recommendation to similar lodgings nearby. For price ranges, ☞ Lodging *in* Smart Travel Tips A to Z.

Nightlife and the Arts
Mid-June through September, you'll find musical entertainment in pubs on most nights; in other seasons, Thursday through Sunday are the busiest times. Dingle is the best place for traditional Irish music; elsewhere, pubs and clubs offer a mix of traditional, country, rock, and jazz. Spontaneous music "seisuns" are common, especially on the Dingle Peninsula; elsewhere, performances usually begin around 9. Nightclubs are usually attached to hotels or bars; they are open from 10:30 PM until 1 or 2 AM. Expect to pay a £5–£8 cover fee.

Outdoor Activities and Sports
BICYCLING
You'll find some of the most spectacular scenery in the country around Glengarriff, Killarney, and Dingle. The length of the hills—rather than their steepness—is the challenge here, but without the hills there would-

n't be such great views. A less-strenuous option, equally scenic but on a smaller scale, is the coast of West Cork between Kinsale and Glengarriff. The Beara Peninsula proves very popular with cyclists, who enjoy its varied coastal scenery and relative lack of vehicles. Traffic can be a problem in July and August on the Ring of Kerry, where there is a lack of alternative routes to the one main circuit. Because of the various mountain ranges in the area, rain is never far off, except on the hottest summer days, so always carry a light, waterproof jacket. For bicycle rentals, expect to pay about £6 per day, or £25 for seven days, with a £40 refundable deposit. Book well in advance between May and September, as demand is high and availability is limited.

FISHING

Besides having an abundance of facilities for sea angling and a wealth of salmon and trout rivers, the Southwest enjoys the bonus of scenic surroundings—be it the black-slate cliffs of the coast or the lush vegetation of Killarney and the Ring of Kerry. Shore fishing is available all along the coast, from Cobh in the east to Foynes in the west. The whole region offers excellent opportunities for lake and river fishing, although most anglers head for Waterville or Killarney. Coarse anglers will find pike at Macroom and coarse-angling facilities at Mallow and Fermoy. The deep-sea fishing season runs from April to October. Boat rentals cost about £20 per person per day. Boats can be rented at Ballycotton, Cork Harbour in Cobh, Midleton, Passage West, Crosshaven, Kinsale, Courtmacsherry, Clonakilty, Castletownshend, Valentia Island, Fenit, and Dingle.

GOLF

Many of the Southwest's 18-hole courses are world-famous, championship clubs set amid wonderful scenery. The leading courses in the region—Cork Golf Club, the Old Head Golf Links, Waterville Golf Links, Killarney Golf and Fishing Club, and Tralee Golf Club—are all covered in depth in Chapter 9.

HIKING

The far southwest around Killarney and Dingle is classic hiking country, with spectacular scenery and a feeling of wilderness—even though you're never more than 3 or 4 km (2 or 3 mi) from civilization. On higher ground, fog can come down very quickly, so follow local advice on weather conditions and adjust your schedule accordingly. Two signposted, long-distance walking trails wind through the region: the 214-km (134-mi) Kerry Way begins in Killarney and loops around the Ring of Kerry, and the 153-km (95-mi) Dingle Way loops from Tralee around the Dingle Peninsula. Both routes consist of paths and "green (unsurfaced) roads," with some stretches linked by surfaced roads. In general, these routes, although rough underfoot, are suitable for families, particularly in summer. The 209-km (130-mi) Beara Way mainly is an off-road walk around the rugged Beara Peninsula in West Cork.The Blackwater Way is a 168-km (104-mi) trail that follows the lower slopes of the Knockmealdown Mountains to the rich farms and woodlands of the Blackwater Valley. The Sheep's Head Way encircles the Sheep's Head Peninsula and has glorious views of Bantry Bay along its 88-km (55-mi) route. Additional walks can be found in Killarney National Park; Gougane Barra, northeast of Ballylickey off R584 in County Cork; Farran, off N22 about 16 km (10 mi) west of Cork City in County Cork; the Ballyhoura Mountains on the Cork-Limerick border, off N20 at Ballyhea about 16 km (10 mi) north of Buttevant; and Currachase Forest Park, east of Askeaton off N69 in County Limerick.

Exploring the Southwest

Our coverage of the Southwest is organized into seven sections: Cork City (which includes a side trip to the ever-popular Blarney Castle, home of the Blarney Stone); East Cork and the Blackwater Valley (covering Youghal and Ballymaloe); Kinsale to Glengarriff via Bantry Bay (Mizen Head, Cape Clear, and other points in the far Southwest); the Ring of Kerry; In and Around Killarney; the Dingle Peninsula; and North Kerry and Shannonside. We begin in Cork (under the assumption that you'll approach from points east) and make a clockwise sweep of the area. We end on the northern fringe, crossing over the border from County Kerry into County Limerick and then briefly dipping into the very southeastern reaches of County Clare in the area immediately around Shannon Airport. If you fly into Shannon, you can easily travel the entire sequence in reverse, or pick and choose from those places that interest you.

Among the most notable attractions in the Southwest are the Lakes of Killarney, which require a day or more; you simply must explore these wonders partly on foot to enjoy them fully. Killarney also makes a good base for discovering the Ring of Kerry and the Dingle Peninsula. The main cities in the area—Cork, Tralee, and Limerick—have quiet charm, but they cannot compete with the magnificent scenery farther west. Kinsale is a favorite starting point for a leisurely drive through the coast west to Bantry, which can take one day or three, depending on your appetite for unscheduled stops and impromptu exploration. Two national parks, Glengarriff near the sea and Gougane Barra in the mountains, are also worth visiting.

Numbers in the text correspond to numbers in the margin and on the Southwest, Cork City, and Killarney and Environs maps.

Great Itineraries

IF YOU HAVE 3 DAYS

Base yourself in ⊞ **Killarney** ㊸ for both nights, and reserve one day for a leisurely exploration of Killarney's famous lakes and mountains. Visit the **Gap of Dunloe** ㊿ on an organized tour and walk or ride horseback through the gap itself, crossing the lake beyond by rowboat. The next day head for the Ring of Kerry via **Killorglin** ㊷ and enjoy the mix of subtropical vegetation caused by the nearby Gulf Stream and rugged cliffs. Follow the granite-walled Pass of Keimaneigh to **Bantry** ㉝. A cliff-top road runs between Bantry and Glengarriff, with wonderful sea views along the 24-km (15-mi) Bantry Bay inlet. The stretch of road between **Glengarriff** ㉞ and Killarney, known as the tunnel road, is one of Ireland's most famous scenic routes. It comes into Killarney past the **Ladies' View** �51, little changed since it impressed Queen Victoria's ladies-in-waiting almost 150 years ago.

IF YOU HAVE 5 DAYS FOR A GASTRONOMIC TOUR

Apart from the innovative chefs working in the kitchens of some of Dublin's finest restaurants, Cork is indisputably Ireland's leading food region (☞ Dining *in* Pleasures and Pastimes, *above*)—with superlative country-house hotels serving food prepared from the freshest local ingredients; the country's leading cooking school; and its self-proclaimed "gourmet capital." If you're a dedicated foodie or you've already done a wider sweep through the country and you want to focus on one region, our five-day itinerary, taking in the Southwest's best food, may be for you. Begin in **Cork City** ①–⑲ and stop in at the not-to-be-missed **English Market** ⑭. Stay overnight and sample the classic French cuisine at ⊞ **Fleming's,** an elegant Georgian house on its own grounds. On the next day head out to ⊞ **Ballymaloe House** in **Shanagarry** ㉔, for 50 years the Allen family farm and today run by three generations of the family. The decor is simple but elegant country-style, and the emphasis is on fresh local produce and fish from nearby Ballycotton. If you plan carefully, you may be able to fit in a one-day cooking class at the **Ballymaloe Cookery School and Gardens,** 2 km (1 mi) away, also run by the Allen family. At the least, the gardens, with their wide variety of herbs and edible plants, are a pleasant way to see food before it hits the table. Next drive northwest to **Mallow** ㉗ in the Blackwater Valley to ✴ **Longueville House,** another family-run operation, albeit on a grander scale. Proprietor William O'Callaghan's President's Restaurant earns raves as one of the finest in Ireland; he also runs one of Ireland's only vineyards. From here, head to **Kenmare** ㉟, where the ✴ **Sheen Falls Lodge** has 300 acres of semitropical gardens beside the fall of the River Sheen; stroll in the gardens before dining in La Cascade restaurant. The following day drive back toward the pretty waterfront village of **Kinsale** ㉙, where spots like the **Vintage** and the ✴ **Blue Haven Hotel** have helped earn the town the title "Gourmet Capital of Ireland." Return to Cork City the next day.

IF YOU HAVE 7 DAYS

Start at **Bunratty Castle** ㊹, the nearest attraction to Shannon Airport and a must-see for first-time visitors. Continue on to ✴ **Limerick City** ㊸ and take a look at either the restored **King John's Castle** or the Celtic and medieval treasures at the **Hunt Museum.** Spend the night in Limerick; the following day, head south for Blarney, where you can kiss the Blarney Stone at **Blarney Castle** ⑳, and browse through Ireland's largest selection of crafts shops. Then proceed to ✴ **Cork City** ①–⑲, where you can make an overnight stop. Take a walk around the city center and enjoy the city's lively nightlife, including pubs, restaurants, and theater. The next day head east to Cork Harbour to visit **Cobh** ㉒, where the Queenstown Heritage Centre documents the history of Irish emigration. Cross the harbor by ferry and visit ✴ **Kinsale** ㉙, a historic little port built on hilly slopes, with a star-shape fort dating from 1620 on its large, natural harbor. The town is a fashionable resort with gourmet restaurants, crafts shops, and art galleries. The following day, drive through scenic West Cork around Bantry Bay and into **Glengarriff** ㉞, where you can take a boat to the subtropical gardens of **Garnish Island,** a few minutes offshore. Continue on to **Kenmare** ㉟, a pretty village on a river estuary, and then go on to ✴ **Killarney** ㊳ via a scenic road known as the Windy Gap. Spend the night here and make an early start the next day, either taking a half-day tour of the **Gap of Dunloe** ㊿ or viewing the splendid scenery in the park around **Muckross House** ㊻. In the afternoon, leave for the Ring of Kerry, driving past **Sneem** ㊱ through subtropical vegetation to ✴ **Waterville** ㊲ or ✴ **Caragh Lake** on the west side of the Ring. From Cahirciveen you can see the Dingle Peninsula across the water and the stretch of road that you will take to reach ✴ **Dingle Town** ㊽, the next overnight stop and the best base for exploring the peninsula. A short drive outside town, you'll find the spectacular cliffs and early Christian remains beyond **Slea Head** ㊾. On the final day, drive across the Connor Pass and up to **Tralee** ㊼, which has a lively museum devoted to County Kerry's past and a steam railway running from nearby **Blennerville** ㊺. From Tralee, return to Limerick City and Shannon Airport on the Adare road (N21) or take N69 to Tarbert and the ferry into County Clare to reach Galway and the west of Ireland.

When to Tour the Southwest

The weather is most likely to be warm and sunny in July and August, but there is no guarantee against rain. July and August are the busiest months with Irish, British, and Continental tourists heading for the area

ATLANTIC OCEAN

CLARE

Kilkee

Kilrush

Killimer
Tarbert

N67

N68

N69

61 Glin

Ballybunion

Mouth of
the Shannon

R523

Listowel
60

Abbeyfeale

N69

Ardfert

*Brandon
Bay*

*Tralee
Bay*

Tralee

N21

Castleisland

Kilmakedar Church
Gallarus Oratory

Mt. Brandon

Kilcummin

R559

Blennerville

58 **59**

N70

R577

R578

Ballydavid

Connor
Pass

DINGLE PENINSULA

Castlemaine

Castlegregory

R557

Ballyferriter **57**

R561 **52**

Inch

Killorglin

N22

**Killarney
Area**

N72

Dunquin **56** **54**

**Dingle
Town** **53**

Annascaul

42

R562

43 **51**

Slea Head **55**

Dunbeg

Ventry

Rossbeigh

Inch

*Blasket
Islands*

Dingle Bay

Glenbeigh **41**

Kerry

*Caragh
Lake*

*Lake
Leane*

Muckross

KERRY

*Upper
Lake*

KILLARNEY
NATIONAL
PARK

N22

Cahirciveen

Ring

N70

of

IVERAGH PENINSULA

R568

**Valentia
Island** **38**

40

Staigue
Fort

N70

35

Kenmare

R569

R584

*Ballinskelligs
Bay*

Kerry

Sneem **36**

Tahilla

R571

Gougane Barra
National Park

Ballinskelligs

Waterville **37**

N70

Ring

of

Parknasilla

N71

**Skellig
Islands**

39

Kenmare River

Eyenes

BEARA PENINSULA

34 **Glengarriff**

Ballylickey

Garnish
Island

R586

Allihies

Castletownbere

R572

Bantry Bay

33 **Bantry**

Bere Island

Durrus

N71

*Dursey
Island*

Ballydehob

N71

Skibbereen

N71

Schull

R592

Liss Ard
Foundation

31 R596

Uni

Castletownshend

Mizen Head
Signal Station

Goleen

R595

Crookhaven

Roaring Water Bay

32 **Baltimore**

Sherkin
Island

*Cape Clear
Island*

Ennis
Tuamgraney
Nenagh
Quin
66 Craggaunowen
Project
Killaloe
65 Knappogue
Castle
Bunratty Castle
and Folk Park
TIPPERARY
Shannon
64
Thurles
N75
River Shannon
63 Limerick
City
Plassey
Foynes
Askeaton
R518
LIMERICK
N20
N24
R497
N8
62 Adare
Croom
Holycross
N74
Cashel
Rathkeale
Ballingarry
Tipperary
Newcastle
West
N21
N20
Kilmallock
Milford
Kilfinnane
N8
Cahir
N24
Clogheen
Mitchelstown
R576
R579
WATERFORD
8
Castletownroche
N8
Lismore
Kanturk
28
N72
27
Mallow
N72
26 Fermoy
River Blackwater
Dungarvan
N72
CORK
Rathcormac
N20
Blarney
Castle
N8
Youghal
20
23
Blarney
Cork City
Fota
Island
Midleton
N25
1 — 19
R579
R617
21
25
Macroom
R629
24 Shanagarry
N22
N71
N27
N28
22 Cobh
Cloyne
Ballycotton
R600
Cork
Harbour
Dunmanway
N71
Bandon
ra
k
Kilbrittain
29 Kinsale
R600
Charles Fort
Timoleague
30
N71
R597
N71
Clonakilly
Courtmachsherry
Rosscarbery
Glandore
Union Hall
end
Celtic Sea
N

0 _____ 20 miles

0 _____ 30 km

in large numbers. Visiting in high season means the bars and restaurants of the area will be lively but also crowded. The best time to visit the Southwest is in the "shoulder seasons"—May through June and September through October, when the weather will still be mild; most if not quite all accommodations and attractions will be open, and crowds can be avoided. It may be wet, but it seldom gets cold in this part of the world.

CORK CITY

❶ *254 km (158 mi) south of Dublin, 105 km (65 mi) south of Limerick City.*

The major metropolis of the south, Cork is Ireland's second-largest city (population 175,000), but put this in perspective—roughly half of Ireland's 3.6 million people live in and around Dublin, a city 10 times the size. Though small relative to the capital, Cork is a spirited, lively place, with a formidable pub scene, some of the country's best traditional music, a respected and progressive university, attractive art galleries, and offbeat cafés.

The city received its first charter in 1185 from Prince John of Norman England, and it takes its name from the Irish word *corcaigh,* meaning "marshy place." The original 6th-century settlement was spread over 13 small islands in the River Lee. Major development occurred during the 17th and 18th centuries with the expansion of the butter trade, and many attractive Georgian-design buildings with wide bowfront windows were constructed during this time. As late as 1770, Cork's present main streets—Grand Parade, Patrick Street, and the South Mall—were submerged under the Lee. Around 1800, when the Lee was partially dammed, the river divided into two streams that now flow through the city, leaving the main business and commercial center on an island, not unlike Paris's Ile de la Cité. As a result, the city features a number of bridges and quays, which, although initially confusing, add greatly to the port's unique character.

"Rebel Cork" emerged as a center of the Nationalist Fenian movement in the 19th century. The city suffered great damage during the War of Independence in 1919–21, when much of its center was burned. Cork is now regaining some of its former glory as a result of sensitive commercial development and an ongoing program of inner-city renewal. In late summer and early autumn, the city hosts some of Ireland's premier festivals, including October's huge **Cork Jazz Festival**, which draws about 50,000 visitors from around the world; the **Cork Film Festival**, also in October; and a number of others. *See* Nightlife and the Arts, *below,* for more information.

Exploring Cork City

"Cork is the loveliest city in the world. Anyone who does not agree with me either was not born there or is prejudiced." Whether or not Cork merits this accolade of native poet and writer Robert Gibbings, the city does have plenty to recommend it, including several noteworthy historic sites. These, though spread out, are still best visited on foot. Patrick Street is the center city's main thoroughfare.

A Good Walk

Start your walk on Grand Parade, the geographical center of the city and home to the **Tourist Information Office** ②. **Bishop Lucey Park** ③, a green space opposite the TIO, leads to the **Triskel Arts Centre** ④, where you can see arts exhibitions and films, and find out about arts events around town. From here, take Washington Street to the corner of Grattan Street, where you'll find the newly restored 18th-century **Court House** ⑤. Backtrack to North Main Street and take it to the **Cork Vision Centre** ⑥, housed in a once-derelict 18th-century church, where a helpful scale model of the city can be seen. Continue down North Main Street to the River Lee. If churches appeal to you, cross Shandon Bridge and climb the hill (a serious hike) to St. Mary's Pro-Cathedral. Halfway up the hill on the right is Shandon, a maze of tiny terraced houses, in the midst of which is **St. Anne's Church** ⑦, and Cork's old butter market, the Firkin Crane. Leaving the Firkin Crane at your back, return to the river by Upper Street. Cross the river on the modern Christy Ring Bridge, which leads to **Cork Opera House** ⑧, where touring productions and variety acts perform, and **Crawford Municipal Art Gallery** ⑨. Beside the gallery is **Paul Street** ⑩, Cork's liveliest shopping area, containing boutiques, bookstores, and cafés. Take one of the narrow left hand lanes to reach **Patrick Street** ⑪, Cork's main, pedestrianized shopping street. Following it to your left, you'll come upon **Patrick's Bridge** ⑫, from where you'll have a view of the steep north side of the city. Take Winthrop Street, off Patrick Street, to Oliver Plunkett Street, and admire the neoclassical **General Post Office** ⑬; browse, if you wish, at the shops nearby. Return, via Oliver Plunkett Street, to the Grande Parade, where you'll find the **English Market** ⑭, a covered food market, on your right. A left will take you to a pedestrian footbridge across the river; go right, following the quays westward, until you reach Bishop Street and the 19th-century Gothic **St. Finbarre's Cathedral** ⑮.

If you want to extend your walk by about 3 km (2 mi), turn left on leaving the cathedral, taking the small road downhill on the right. Go left where it meets the river and cross the bridge to Lancaster Quay. Follow the street, which turns into Western Road, making a left for the architecturally noteworthy campus of **University College, Cork** ⑯. Across Western Road is the **Mardyke** ⑰, a riverside walk that leads to the well-tended **Fitzgerald's Park** ⑱ and the **Cork Public Museum**, where you can soak up interesting tidbits about Cork's history. Turn left out of the museum, and take Daly Bridge, which will lead you to Sunday's Well, a hilly residential area with the castlelike **Cork City Gaol** ⑲. Return to the city center along Sunday's Well Road and North Mall, where you can enjoy the sight of several recently restored Georgian houses.

TIMING

You could easily complete the first part of this walk, from the TIO to St. Finbarre's Cathedral, in a morning or an afternoon, depending on how seriously you intend to take advantage of shopping opportunities along the way. However, if you plan to visit everything, then allow a full day, with a break for lunch at the English Market (☞ Farmgate Café *in* Dining, *below*).

Sights to See

✎ *following the text of a review is your signal that the property has a Web site, where you will find details and, usually, images; for a link, visit www.fodors.com/urls.*

❸ **Bishop Lucey Park.** This tiny green oasis in the heart of the city was opened in 1985 in celebration of the 800th anniversary of Cork's Norman charter. During its excavation, workers unearthed portions of the city's original fortified walls, now preserved just inside the arched entranceway. Sculptures by contemporary Cork artists are scattered throughout the park. ⊠ *Grand Parade.* ☒ *Free.*

⑲ Cork City Gaol. This castlelike building contains an austere, 19th-century prison, where inmates lived in wretched conditions. Life-size figures occupy the cells, and sound effects illustrate the appalling conditions that prevailed in the gaol from the early 19th century through the founding of the Free State after the 1916 Uprising. A **Radio Museum** in the Governor's House tells the history of broadcasting in Cork. ⊠ *Sunday's Well,* ☎ *021/430–5022.* 🎫 *£3.* ☉ *Oct.–Easter, daily 10–4; Easter–Sept. daily 9:30–5.*✍

❽ Cork Opera House. This unattractive concrete hulk went up in 1965 to replace the much-loved, ornate old opera house that was ruined in a fire. Recent attempts to integrate the Opera House with its neighbor, the Crawford Municipal Art Gallery (☞ *below*), have softened its grim facade. A piazza area with pavement cafés and street performers was to be completed by 2001. ⊠ *Lavitt's Quay,* ☎ *021/427–0022.*

❻ Cork Vision Centre. In an area that was once the bustling heart of medieval Cork, the center provides an excellent introduction to the city's geography and history. The centerpiece is a detailed 1:500 scale model of Cork, showing how it has grown and changed over the ages. ⊠ *N. Main St.,* ☎ *021/427–9925.* 🎫 *£1.* ☉ *Tues.–Sat. 10–5. Guided tours of city model on request.*

❺ Court House. A landmark in the very center of Cork, this magnificent classical building has an imposing Corinthian portico and is still in use as the district's main court house. The exterior was cleaned and fully restored in 2000, and looks every bit as good as when it was built in 1835. ⊠ *Washington St.,* ☎ *021/427–2706.* ☉ *Weekdays 9–5.*

★ ❾ Crawford Municipal Art Gallery. The large redbrick building, dressed with limestone, was built in 1724 as the Custom House. It is now Ireland's leading provincial art gallery. An imaginative expansion, completed in 2000, gave it an extra 10,000 square ft of gallery space, to be used in displaying visiting exhibitions, as well as adventurous shows of modern Irish artists, mounted by the gallery itself. Its permanent collection includes a number of landscape paintings depicting Cork in the 18th and 19th centuries. Take special note of works by Irish painters William Leech (1881–1968), Daniel Maclise (1806–70), James Barry (1741–1806), and Nathanial Grogan (1740–1807). The café, run by the Allen family of Ballymaloe (☞ *Shanagarry, below*), is a good place for a light lunch or a homemade sweet. ⊠ *Emmet Pl.,* ☎ *021/427–3377.* 🎫 *Free.* ☉ *Weekdays 9–5, Sat. 9–1.*✍

★ ⑭ English Market. Food lovers should head for one of the misleadingly small entrances to this large covered market, housed in an elaborate, red-and-brown-brick and cast-iron Victorian building. (Its official name is the Princes Street Market, and it's also known locally as the Covered Market.) A turn-of-the-century predecessor to today's urban farmers' markets, this is a great place to get a sense of Cork's thriving food scene. Among the 140 stalls, keep an eye out for the **Alternative Bread Co.,** which produces more than 40 varieties of handmade bread every day. **Iago,** Sean Calder-Potts's deli, features fresh pasta and a wide range of cheeses and charcuterie. Olive oil, olive-oil soap, and olives from Greece, Spain, France, and Italy are all found at the **Olive Stall. Kay O'Connell's Fish Stall,** in the market's legendary fresh-fish alley, sells local smoked salmon. **O'Reilly's Tripe and Drisheen** is the last existing retailer of a Cork specialty, tripe (cow's intestines) and *drisheen* (blood sausage). Upstairs is the Farmgate, an excellent café (☞ Dining and Lodging, *below*). ⊠ *Entrances on Grand Parade and Princes St.* ☉ *Mon.–Sat. 9–5:30.*

⑱ Fitzgerald's Park. Beside the north channel of the River Lee in the west of the city, this small, well-tended park contains the **Cork Public Museum,** a Georgian mansion that houses a well-planned exhibit of Cork's history from ancient times to the present, with a strong emphasis on the city's Republican history. ☎ *021/427–0679.* ☜ *Free.* ☉ *Weekdays 11–1 and 2:15–5, Sun. 3–5.*

⑬ General Post Office. This neoclassic building with an elegant colonnaded facade was once Cork's Opera House. It dominates a street otherwise occupied by fashion boutiques, jewelry stores, and antiques shops. ✉ *Oliver Plunkett St.,* ☎ *021/427–2000.* ☉ *Weekdays 9–5:30, Sat. 9–5.*

NEED A
BREAK?

The friendly, old **Long Valley** (✉ Winthrop St., ☎ 021/427–2144), popular with artists, writers, students, and eccentrics, serves tea, coffee, and pints, as well as oversize sandwiches.

⑰ Mardyke. This is a popular riverside walk where cricket, very much a minority sport in Ireland, is played on summer weekends.

⑪ Patrick Street. Extending from Grand Parade in the south to Patrick's Bridge (☞ *below*) in the north, Panna (as it is known locally) runs in a graceful curve. If you look above some of the standardized plate-glass and plastic shop facades here, you'll see examples of the bowfront Georgian windows that are emblematic of old Cork. The street saw some of the city's worst fighting in the years 1919–21, during the War of Independence. This is Cork's main shopping thoroughfare, a pedestrian priority area, containing a mainstream mix of department stores, clothes shops, pharmacies, and bookshops. Most stores are open Monday through Saturday 9 to 5:30 and sometimes Sunday 2 to 5.

⑫ Patrick's Bridge. From this vantage point on the River Lee you can look back past the statue of Father Mathew (1790–1861), Cork's temperance apostle, down the curve of Patrick Street, and north across the river to St. Patrick's Hill, where tall Georgian houses have been converted to professional use, mostly as doctors' offices. The hill is so steep that steps are cut into the pavement. Tall ships that once served the butter trade used to load up beside the bridge at Merchant's Quay before heading downstream to the open sea. The design of the large, red-brick shopping center on the site today evokes the warehouses of old. ✉ *Patrick St.* ☉ *Freely accessible.*

⑩ Paul Street. A narrow street between the River Lee and Patrick Street and parallel to both, Paul Street is the backbone of the trendy shopping area that now occupies Cork's old French Quarter. The area was first settled by Huguenots fleeing religious persecution in France. The Paul Street Piazza is a popular place for street theater and entertainment. The shops here offer the best in modern Irish design—from locally made fashion items to handblown glass—and, in an alley north of the piazza, a good selection of antiques.

❼ St. Anne's Church. The church's pepper-pot Shandon Steeple, which has a four-sided clock and is topped with a golden, salmon-shape weather vane, is visible from most vantage points in the city and is the chief reason why St. Anne's is so frequently visited. The Bells of Shandon were immortalized in an atrocious but popular 19th-century ballad of that name. If you climb the 120-ft tower, your reward is being able to ring the bells, with the assistance of sheet tune cards, out over Cork. Beside the church, Firkin Crane, Cork's former 18th-century butter market, houses two small performing spaces. Adjacent is the Shandon Craft Market. ✉ *Church St.,* ☜ *£1; with bell tower £1.50.* ☉ *May–Oct., Mon.–Sat. 9:30–5; Nov.–Apr., Mon.–Sat. 10–3:30.*

ST. MARY'S PRO-CATHEDRAL – Dating from 1808, it is architecturally undistinguished, and chiefly worth the uphill hike only if you are interested in tracing your Cork ancestors—its presbytery has records of births and marriages dating from 1784. ⊠ *Cathedral Walk.* ▨ *Free.* ☉ *Daily 9–6.*

⑮ **St. Finbarre's Cathedral.** This was once the entrance to medieval Cork. According to tradition, St. Finbarre established a monastery on this site around AD 650 and is credited as the founder of Cork. The present, three-spire Gothic cathedral, which was completed in 1879 and underwent major restorations in 1999, belongs to the Church of Ireland and houses a 3,000-pipe organ. ⊠ *Bishop St.,* ☎ 021/496–3387. ▨ *Free.* ☉ *Daily 9–6.*

❷ **Tourist Information Office (TIO).** This is the place to make reservations and find out about happenings in and around the Cork–Kerry region. ⊠ *Grand Parade,* ☎ 021/427–3251. ☉ *Weekdays 9–6, Sat. 9–1.*

❹ **Triskel Arts Centre.** In a converted pair of town houses, the center has exhibitions of contemporary arts and crafts, a coffee shop, and a small auditorium that shows films and live theater. It's a good place to get the pulse of artsy goings-on about town. ⊠ *Tobin St.,* ☎ 021/427–2022. ▨ *Free.* ☉ *Weekdays 11–6, Sat. 11–5, and during advertised performances.*

★ ⑯ **University College, Cork.** The Doric porticoed gates of U.C.C. stand about 2 km (1 mi) from the center of the city in a westerly direction. The college, with a campus population of about 10,000, is a constituent of the National University of Ireland. The main quadrangle is a fine example of 19th-century university architecture in the Tudor-Gothic style, reminiscent of many Oxford and Cambridge colleges. Several ancient ogham stones are on display here, as are occasional exhibitions of archival material from the old library. The **Honan Collegiate Chapel,** to the east of the quadrangle, was built in 1916 and modeled on the 12th-century, Hiberno-Romanesque style, which is best exemplified by the remains of **Cormac's Chapel** at Cashel (☞ Chapter 4). Most noteworthy about the chapel is its collection of arts and crafts, altar furnishings, and textiles in the Celtic Revival style, and its stained-glass windows. Three large modern buildings have been successfully integrated with the old, including the **Boole Library,** named for mathematician George Boole (1815–64), a past alumnus, whose Boolean algebra laid the foundation for modern computing. Both indoors and out the campus is enhanced by works from its collection of contemporary Irish art, one of the best in the country. A pleasant landscaped walk through the grounds has recently been renovated. ⊠ *Western Rd.,* ☎ 021/490–3000. ▨ *Free.* ☉ *Weekdays 9–5, but tel. to confirm Easter week, July–Aug., and mid-Dec.–mid-Jan.*

Dining and Lodging

$$$ ✗ **Cafe Paradiso.** This simple, café-style restaurant near the university and across from Jurys Hotel (☞ *below*) serves Mediterranean-style food, which is so tasty that even dedicated meat-eaters forget it's vegetarian. The room is basic, with assorted tables and spindly chairs; the daily special is chalked up on a board, and the food is served on enormous platters. Chef Denis Cotter garners raves for his risottos with seasonal vegetables (such as pumpkin and radicchio), his gougères-choux pastry rings with savory fillings, and his excellent, homemade desserts. ⊠ *16 Lancaster Quay, Western Rd.,* ☎ 021/427–7939. *MC, V. Closed Sun. and last 2 wks in Aug.*

$$$ ✗ **Ivory Tower.** Seamus O'Connell is the adventurous, young owner-chef of this small town-center restaurant. Bare wooden floors and stick-back chairs in the first-floor Georgian dining room are warmed

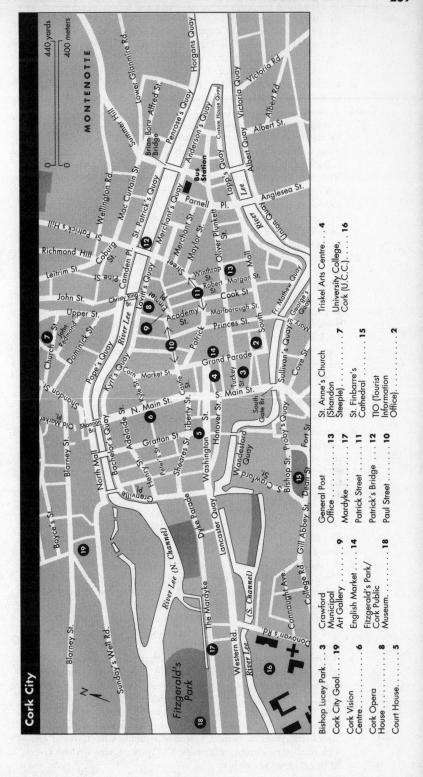

Cork City

MONTENOTTE

Bishop Lucey Park . . . **3**
Cork City Gaol **19**
Cork Vision
Centre **6**
Cork Opera
House **8**
Court House **5**

Crawford
Municipal
Art Gallery **9**
English Market **14**
Fitzgerald's Park/
Cork Public
Museum **18**

General Post
Office **13**
Mardyke **17**
Patrick Street **11**
Patrick's Bridge . . . **12**
Paul Street **10**

St. Anne's Church
(Shandon
Steeple) **7**
St. Finbarre's
Cathedral **15**
TIO (Tourist
Information
Office) **2**

Triskel Arts Centre . . . **4**
University College,
Cork (U.C.C.) **16**

by the original artwork on display, but the real star here is the brilliantly eclectic menu. O'Connell has cooked in Mexico and Japan and describes his approach as "trans-ethnic fusion." Tagliatelle of flashed squid, wild pheasant tamale, and Cajun blackened swordfish with banana ketchup are just some of the surprising—and very accomplished—combinations offered. ✉ *35 Princes St.,* ☎ *021/427–4665. MC, V. Closed Sun.–Mon.*

$–$$$ ✕ **Lovett's.** The Lovett family has been setting high standards on the Cork gastronomic scene since 1977. Their Georgian house, surrounded by mature grounds in a prosperous suburb, has a formal dining room lined with portraits of 18th-century Cork society. The establishment is known for its extensive wine list, which focuses on vineyards with Irish origins, making it strong on Bordeaux. As for food, start with hot black-and-white pudding terrine with onion and raisin confit, followed perhaps by black sole on the bone with citrus butter. The brasserie ($) is more informal. ✉ *Churchyard La., off Well Rd., Douglas,* ☎ *021/429–4909. AE, DC, MC, V. Closed Sun.–Mon. and 1 wk at Christmas. No lunch Sat.*

$$ ✕ **Jacobs on the Mall.** The imaginative cooking of a well-traveled young chef, Mercy Fenton, is one of the attractions here; the other is its location in what was once a Victorian Turkish bath. The high-ceilinged room has an enormous skylight, and is held up by cast-iron pillars. Modern art adorns the cream-color walls, and a tall blue banquette forms a bold room divider. Typical starters include tartare of smoked haddock and cucumber with a tomato vinaigrette, or oysters with ginger and lime relish. Main courses may feature steamed brill with crisp vegetable parcels or roast rump of lamb with *mash* (mashed potatoes), vegetables, and a thyme jus. For dessert try the baked vanilla cheesecake with poached fruit compote. ✉ *30A South Mall,* ☎ *021/425–1530. AE, MC, V. Closed Sun.*

$ ✕ **Farmgate Café.** On a terrace above the fountain at the Princes Street
★ entrance to Cork's English Market (☞ *above*), this is one of the best lunch spots in town. One side of the terrace is open to the market and operates as self-service; the other side is glassed in and served by waiters (reservations advised). Tripe and drisheen are always on the menu, while daily specials include less challenging but no less traditional dishes such as corned beef with *colcannon* (potatoes and cabbage mashed together with butter and seasonings) and loin of smoked bacon with *champ* (potato mashed with scallions or leeks). ✉ *English Market,* ☎ *021/427–8134. MC, V. Closed Sun. No dinner. Last food orders 4 PM.*

$ ✕ **Isaac's.** This popular brasserie-style restaurant is north of the river (cross at Patrick's Bridge and turn right) in a converted warehouse. High ceilings, well-spaced tables covered in oilcloth, modern art, and jazz music create an eclectic, energetic atmosphere. The East-meets-Mediterranean menu has many tempting options, including warm salads with Clonakilty black pudding and king prawns in spicy tomato sauce. ✉ *MacCurtain St.,* ☎ *021/450–3805. AE, MC, V. No lunch Sun.*

$ ✕ **Proby's Bistro.** In a striking and stylish modern building with patio tables and sun umbrellas optimistically placed on the terrace, this riverside bistro near St. Finbarre's Cathedral is a short walk from the main shopping area. The spacious ground-floor restaurant has an open fire, oilcloth-covered tables, and a bold Mediterranean decor that suits the light, flavorsome food. The menu is mainly rustic Italian—bruschetta, polenta, risotto, mixed-leaf salads with flavored oils—with occasional Eastern influences. ✉ *Proby's Quay, Crosses Green,* ☎ *021/431–6531. MC, V.*

$$$ ╳🖬 **Clarion Hotel & Suites, Morrison's Island.** This luxury hotel on the urban riverside is a two-minute walk from Patrick Street. Spacious, modern one- and two-bedroom suites with kitchen are furnished with handcrafted light-oak furniture. Regular rooms are large, with a similar style of furniture, and half of them have river views. Polished marble floors and warm terra-cotta–color walls enhance the stylish, mezzanine-level bar and Morrison's Bistro, overlooking the river. The lunch menu has a choice of substantial baguettes and sandwiches, while the evening menu has entrées ranging from sole on the bone with garlic butter to bacon-wrapped fillet of chicken in red wine sauce. Four penthouses have terrace views of the city and the river. ⊠ *Morrison's Quay, Co. Cork,* ☎ *021/427–5858,* 𝔽𝔸𝕏 *021/427–5833. 30 rooms with bath, 26 suites. Restaurant, bar. AE, DC, MC, V.* ✎

$$$ ╳🖬 **Jurys.** Beside the River Lee, a five-minute walk from the city center, is this modern, two- and three-story structure made of smoked glass and steel. Its large, open lobby-restaurant area has a waterfall and hanging greenery (some of it plastic). Cork's Bar is popular with the locals at lunch and in the early evening. The mezzanine-level Fastnet Restaurant serves an à la carte international menu with an emphasis on fresh local produce. Bedrooms, plain yet spacious, have quilted spreads, small sofas, and floor-to-ceiling picture windows. The most desirable rooms overlook the interior patio garden and pool. ⊠ *Western Rd., Co. Cork,* ☎ *021/427–6622,* 𝔽𝔸𝕏 *021/427–4477. 185 rooms with bath. 2 restaurants, 2 bars, indoor-outdoor pool, sauna, 2 tennis courts, health club, squash. AE, DC, MC, V.* ✎

$$ ╳🖬 **Hotel Isaac's.** This city-center hotel was stylishly renovated from an old warehouse into a busy restaurant and accommodation complex. Rooms are bright and cheerful, with polished wood floors and rustic pine furniture. The restaurant and some of the rooms overlook a tiny courtyard garden with a waterfall cascading down one side. The dining room also operates as Greene's Restaurant, where fresh produce is prepared in a mix of Irish and Mediterranean styles. ⊠ *48 MacCurtain St., Co. Cork,* ☎ *021/450–0011,* 𝔽𝔸𝕏 *021/450–6355. 36 rooms with bath. Restaurant, cafeteria, Ping-Pong. MC, V.* ✎

$ ╳🖬 **Flemings.** This detached three-story Georgian house has a double dining room ($$$) with plush, Louis XV–style padded chairs, gilt-framed portraits, and crystal chandeliers. Owner-chef Michael Fleming applies French expertise to local produce, some of which comes from the garden. Starters may include *foie gras de canard* or hot oysters, while typical main courses are pot roast of guinea fowl, or symphony of seafood in a champagne sauce. For dessert, try the beautifully presented tasting plate. Rooms have brocade bedspreads and curtains, and are quiet as well as spacious. Ask about the special value "dine and stay" package. Flemings is on the edge of the city, signposted off Lower Glanmire Road (the main road out of town in the Dublin–Waterford direction). ⊠ *Silver Grange House, Tivoli, Co. Cork,* ☎ *021/482–1621,* 𝔽𝔸𝕏 *021/482–1178. 4 rooms with bath. Restaurant, bar. AE, DC, MC, V.*

$$$$ 🖬 **Hayfield Manor.** Built in 1996 in a surprisingly successful pastiche
★ of the country-house style, the manor sits beside the university campus, five minutes' drive from the city center. The marble-floor lobby is dominated by a splendid, carved-wood double staircase, while a wood-paneled library overlooks the walled patio and garden. Rooms are spacious, with unobtrusive decor in a vaguely Louis XV style. The Victorian-style bar serves lunch, and then bar food until 7 PM, when the Manor Room restaurant opens for dinner. The fitness center is exclusively for the hotel's patrons. ⊠ *College Rd., Co. Cork,* ☎ *021/431–5600,* 𝔽𝔸𝕏 *021/431–6839. 53 rooms with bath. Restaurant, bar, indoor pool, sauna, health club. AE, DC, MC, V.* ✎

$$ 🏨 **Rochestown Park.** Set in 7 acres of mature gardens in the fashionable suburb of Douglas, 5 km (3 mi) south of the city, Rochestown was built around a Victorian manor house that overlooks the estuary of Cork Harbour. However, the four-lane ring road to the cross-river tunnel runs between the hotel grounds and the estuary, so it is less romantic than it sounds. All the rooms are decorated in a modern style with cotton spreads, wool carpets, and light-oak fixtures. The large health center specializes in thalassotherapy—seaweed wraps and baths. ✉ *Rochestown Rd., Douglas, Co. Cork,* ☎ *021/489–2233,* FAX *021/489–2178. 115 rooms with bath. Restaurant, bar, indoor pool, sauna, health club. AE, DC, MC, V.* 🐾

$ 🏨 **Island House.** Young, independent travelers will appreciate the central location and budget rates at this five-story riverside hostel. On the ground floor is a café–cum–steak house, while a large self-catering kitchen is available on the fourth floor. Rooms—single, double, triple, or four-bunk—are laid out on corridors accessed by an open terrace. Ask for a river view, as the others overlook neighboring buildings. Pine beds have brightly colored spreads with matching curtains, and all rooms have TV. ✉ *Morrison's Quay, Co. Cork,* ☎ *021/427–1716,* FAX *021/427–1719. 51 rooms, 43 with bath. Restaurant, free parking. MC, V. Closed 1 wk at Christmas.*

$ 🏨 **Jurys Cork Inn.** This modern budget hotel pursues the same policy as its Dublin and Galway counterparts, charging per room, each of which sleeps three adults or two adults and two children. Beside a busy bridge over the River Lee, the inn is a short walk from the city center and bus and rail stations. Rooms are well appointed for the price range: bright and airy with light-wood trim and matching drapes and spreads. ✉ *Anderson's Quay, Co. Cork,* ☎ *021/427–6444,* FAX *021/427–6144. 133 rooms with bath. Restaurant, bar. AE, DC, MC, V.* 🐾

$ 🏨 **Victoria Lodge.** This exceptionally well appointed B&B, built in the early 20th century as a Capuchin monastery, is a five-minute drive from the town center; it is also accessible by several bus routes. Breakfast is served in the spacious old refectory with its intact polished benches and paneled walls; the common room is now a television lounge. The simple, comfortable bedrooms have pastel-color chenille spreads, cotton curtains, and mahogany bureaus. ✉ *Victoria Cross, Co. Cork,* ☎ *021/454–2233,* FAX *021/454–2572. 30 rooms with bath. AE, MC, V.*

Nightlife and the Arts

FESTIVALS AND SEASONAL EVENTS

Ireland's oldest film festival, the **Cork Film Festival** (☎ 021/427–1711) was established in 1956 and has evolved into one of the country's most important cinema events. New feature-length films and documentaries from Ireland and abroad share the bill with short films, a particular specialty of this festival. It's usually held the second week of October. Near the end of every October, the **Cork Jazz Festival** (☎ 021/427–0463) brings major national and international performers to venues throughout the city.

GALLERIES

The **Lavit Gallery** (✉ 5 Father Mathew St., off South Mall, ☎ 021/427–7749) has a representative selection of oils and watercolors by members of the Cork Arts Society and other Irish artists, all of which are for sale. Offbeat exhibits can be found at the **Triskel Arts Centre** (✉ Tobin St., off S. Main St., ☎ 021/427–2022). The **Vangard Gallery** (✉ Carey's La., Paul St., ☎ 021/427–8718) has exhibitions of prints, paintings, and sculpture by leading contemporary Irish artists.

Cork Opera House (⊠ Lavitt's Quay, ☎ 021/427–0022) is the city's major hall for touring productions and variety acts. Smaller productions are staged at the **Everyman Palace** (⊠ MacCurtain St., ☎ 021/450–1673), where the ornate Victorian interior has been lovingly restored.

PUBS AND NIGHTCLUBS
La Bodega (⊠ Cornmarket St., ☎ 021/427–2878), a converted wine warehouse, is the hippest—and loudest—spot in town. Night owls will appreciate the late-night music club at the Cork Opera House, the **Half Moon** (⊠ Half Moon St., ☎ 021/427–0022), which features live jazz and blues from up-and-coming local bands most weekends from 11 PM. See *The Examiner* or *The Evening Echo* for details. The bar at the **Metropole Hotel** (⊠ MacCurtain St., ☎ 021/450–8122) is one of the best places for jazz. **Pavilion** (⊠ Carey's La., ☎ 021/427–6228) has late-night disco Wednesday through Monday nights. Traditional musicians occasionally gather at **An Spailpin Fanach** (⊠ 28 S. Main St., ☎ 021/427–7949).

Outdoor Activities and Sports
BICYCLES
Rent a bike to explore the city and its environs at **Rothar Cycle Tours** (⊠ 2 Bandon Rd., at Barrack St., ☎ 021/431–3133).

FISHING
Fishing tackle, bait, and licenses, as well as friendly advice on local resources, can be obtained at **T. W. Murray** (⊠ 87 Patrick St., ☎ 021/427–1089).

GOLF
Cork Golf Club (⊠ Little Island, ☎ 021/435–3451 [☞ Chapter 9]). **Douglas Golf Club** (⊠ Douglas, ☎ 021/489–1086) is a tree-lined, parkland, 18-hole course in the southern suburbs of the city. **Lee Valley Golf Club** (⊠ Clashanure, Ovens, ☎ 021/733–1721) is a par-72, 18-hole, championship course 15 minutes west of the city. **Monkstown Golf Club** (⊠ Parkgarriffe, Monkstown, ☎ 021/484–1376) is an 18-hole, par-70, strategically bunkered, parkland course 11 km (7 mi) southeast of the city.

HORSEBACK RIDING
Hitchmough Riding School (⊠ Highland Lodge, Monkstown, ☎ 021/437–1267) has an indoor arena for all-weather riding. **Pinegrove Riding School** (⊠ White's Cross, ☎ 021/430–3857) will provide one- and two-hour hacks in the countryside north of the city.

Shopping
ANTIQUES
Irene's (⊠ 22 Marlboro St., ☎ 021/427–0642) sells antique jewelry. **Mills Antiques** (⊠ 3 Paul's La., ☎ 021/427–3528) carries Irish, English, and European paintings, printings, silver, porcelain, and small furniture. For furniture, paintings, and other large decorative objects try **O'Regan's Antiques** (⊠ 21 Lavitt's Quay, ☎ 021/427–2902). **Pinnacle** (⊠ 44A MacCurtain St., ☎ 021/450–1319) stocks antique pine, glass, porcelain, paintings, and prints. **Victoria's** (⊠ 2 Oliver Plunkett St., ☎ 021/427–2752) carries interesting jewelry, Victoriana, and period clothes.

BOOKS
Mercier Bookshop (⊠ 18 Academy St., ☎ 021/427–5040), off Patrick Street, sells new books and publishes its own list of Irish and local-interest titles.

CLOTHING

Fashion lovers will find a choice of internationally famous designer labels at the tiny but elegant boutique called the **Dressing Room** (⌧ 8 Emmet Pl., ☎ 021/427–0117), opposite the entrance to the Cork Opera House. **Monica John** (⌧ French Church St., ☎ 021/427–1399) sells locally designed high-fashion ladies' wear, as well as some imported lines. **Quills** (⌧ 107 Patrick St., ☎ 021/427–1717) has a good selection of Irish-made fashion and casual wear for both women and men. For casual weatherproof clothing, try the **Tack Room** (⌧ Unit 3, Academy St., ☎ 021/427–2704).

DEPARTMENT STORE

Brown Thomas (⌧ 18 Patrick St., ☎ 021/427–6771) is Cork's leading department store. The fashion floor is well worth a visit to check out items by Irish and international designers. Refuel at the coffee shop, where healthful open sandwiches and homemade soup are available. The ground floor has an excellent cosmetics hall and a good selection of Irish crystal and designer menswear.

MUSIC

Fans of Irish music should visit the **Living Tradition** (⌧ 40 MacCurtain St., ☎ 021/450–2040).

SHOPPING CENTER

The **Merchant's Quay Shopping Centre** (⌧ Merchant's Quay, ☎ 021/427–5466) is the largest indoor mall in downtown Cork.

SPORTING GOODS

The **Golf Addict** (⌧ 6 Emmet Pl., ☎ 021/427–3393) stocks everything the serious golfer could need, as well as an amusing range of nonessential golf paraphernalia and gifts. **Great Outdoors** (⌧ 23 Paul St., ☎ 021/427–6382) caters to most outdoor sports needs. **Matthews** (⌧ Academy St., ☎ 021/427–7633) has a wide selection of sporting gear. For inexpensive rainwear, go to **Penney's** (⌧ 27 Patrick St., ☎ 021/427–1935).

Side Trips From Cork City

Blarney, 10 km (6 mi) northwest of Cork City on R617, and Cork Harbour, 16 km (10 mi) east of the city, make perfect day trips. Blarney's main attractions are Blarney Castle and the famous Blarney Stone, while Cork Harbour's draws include Fota Island, with an arboretum and wildlife park, and the lovely fishing port of Cobh.

Blarney

"On Galway sands they kiss your hands, they kiss your lips at Carney, but by the Lee they drink strong tea, and kiss the stone at Blarney." This famous rhyme celebrates one of Ireland's most noted icons—the Blarney Stone, which is the main reason most people journey to Blarney, a small community built around a village green. In the center of Blarney is **Blarney Castle,** or what remains of it: the ruined central keep is all that's left of this mid-15th-century stronghold. The castle contains the famed **Blarney Stone,** set in a wall below the castle's battlements; kissing the stone, it is said, endows the kisser with the fabled "gift of gab." It's 127 steep steps to the battlements. To kiss the stone, you must lie down on the battlements, hold on to a guardrail, and lean your head way back. It's good fun and not at all dangerous. Expect a line from mid-June to September 1; while you wait, you can admire the views of the thickly wooded River Lee valley below and chuckle over how the word "blarney" came to mean what it does. As the story goes, Queen Elizabeth I wanted Cormac MacCarthy, Lord of Blarney, to will his castle to the crown, but he consistently refused her request with eloquent excuses and soothing compliments. Exhausted by his comments, the queen reportedly exclaimed, "This is all Blarney. What he says he rarely means."

Visitors can also take pleasant walks around the castle grounds; **Rock Close** contains oddly shaped limestone rocks landscaped in the 18th century and a grove of ancient yew trees that is said to have been the center of Druid worship. ☎ *021/438–5252.* ☞ *£3.50.* ☉ *May and Sept., Mon.–Sat. 9–6:30, Sun. 9–5:30; June–Aug., Mon.–Sat. 9–7, Sun. 9–5:30; Oct.–Apr., Mon.–Sat. 9–sundown, Sun. 9–5:30.*

Two hundred yards from the castle, **Blarney Castle House** was built in 1784 in the style of a Scottish baronial mansion. The three-story, gray stone building has picture-book turrets and fancy, stepped gables. The interior features Elizabethan and Victorian antiques, a fine stairwell, and numerous family portraits. ☎ *021/438–5252.* ☞ *£3.* ☉ *June–mid-Sept., Mon.–Sat. noon–5.*

$ ✕ **Blair's Inn.** This traditional country inn is just five minutes' drive from Blarney on R578 and is a perfect haven from the tour-bus culture that prevails in the village. It has a wooded riverside location and is famed for its exuberant window-box displays. In summer, enjoy the beer garden; in winter warm wood fires flicker in the cozy interior. Freshly prepared local produce is served in generous portions: favorites include Irish stew with lamb, carrots, and potatoes, as well as corned beef. Live entertainment is booked every Sunday from 9 PM, plus Monday from May to October. ✉ *Cloghroe,* ☎ *021/438–1470. MC, V.*

OUTDOOR ACTIVITIES AND SPORTS

Muskerry Golf Club (✉ Carrigrohane, near Blarney, ☎ 021/438–5297) is an 18-hole, par-71 parkland course.

SHOPPING

Blarney has more crafts shops than anyplace else in Ireland. Most of these stores are concentrated south and west of the village green, a two-minute walk from the castle. A shopping visit here can be profitably used for price comparison and bargain hunting; in spite of appearances, these shops, in general, will not rip you off. **Blarney Woolen Mills** (☎ 021/438–5280) has the largest stock and the highest turnover. The mills sell everything from Irish-made high fashion to Aran hand-knit items to leprechaun key rings.

Cork Harbour

To explore Cork Harbour, follow the signposts for Waterford on N25 along the northern banks of the River Lee. Alternatively, a suburban rail service from **Kent Station** (☎ 021/450–6766 for timetable) has stops at Fota Island and Cobh (pronounced cove), and it offers better harbor views than the road.

☞ ㉑ **Fota Island** encompasses a magnificent arboretum and the 70-acre wildlife park, an important breeding center for cheetahs and wallabies. It also contains free-ranging monkeys, zebras, giraffes, ostriches, flamingos, emus, and kangaroos. ✉ *On R624, 19 km (12 mi) from Cork City,* ☎ *021/481–2678.* ☞ *Wildlife park £4.40, arboretum and gardens free, parking £1.* ☉ *Mid-Mar.–Sept., Mon.–Sat. 10–6, Sun. 11–6.*

★ ㉒ Many generations who departed the port of Cork on immigrant ships for the New World left from **Cobh,** a pretty fishing port and seaside resort with a considerable 19th-century presence and maritime history. The **Queenstown Project,** in the old Cobh railway station, re-creates the experience of the million emigrants who left the town between 1750 and the mid-20th century. It also tells the stories of the great transatlantic liners, including the *Titanic,* whose last port of call was Cobh, and the *Lusitania,* which was sunk by a German submarine off this coast on May 7, 1915, with the loss of 1,198 lives. Many of the *Lusitania*'s victims are buried in Cobh, which has a memorial to them on the local quay. ⊠ *Great Island, 24 km (15 mi) from Cork City on R624,* ☎ *021/481–3591.* ☒ *£3.50.* ☉ *Feb.–Nov., daily 10–6.* ✑

The best view of Cobh is from **St. Colman's Cathedral,** an exuberant neo-Gothic granite church designed by Pugin in 1868. Inside are granite niches that portray scenes of the Roman Catholic Church's history in Ireland, beginning with the arrival of St. Patrick.

Cork Harbour opens to the sea some 8 km (5 mi) from Cobh at **Roches Point.** One-hour harbor tours from Marine Transport are a splendid way to take in Cobh's glorious watery environs. ⊠ *Kennedy Pier,* ☎ *021/481–1485.* ☒ *£3.50.* ☉ *Tours May–Sept., daily at 10, 11, noon, 1:30, and 2:30.*

OUTDOOR ACTIVITIES AND SPORTS

Fota Island Golf Club (⊠ Carrigtwohill, ☎ 021/488–3700) is a par-72, 18-hole course.Explore Cork Harbour from the water by renting a sailing dinghy from **International Sailing Center** (⊠ 5 E. Beach, Cobh, ☎ 021/481–1237).

EAST CORK AND THE BLACKWATER VALLEY

Although most visitors to Cork head west out of the city for the scenic coastal areas between Cork and Glengarriff, the east and the north of the county are also worth exploring. East Cork, Youghal in particular, is popular with Irish tourists for its long, sandy beaches. The main attraction in North Cork is the Blackwater River, which crosses the county from east to west. It is famous for its trout and salmon fishing and its scenery. This section starts in the far corner of the county at Youghal and works its way west toward the Kerry border.

Youghal

㉓ *48 km (30 mi) east of Cork City on N25, 74 km (46 mi) south of Waterford.*

Situated on the mouth of the Blackwater River, on the border between Counties Cork and Waterford, Youghal (pronounced yawl) is an ancient walled seaport with a fine, natural harbor. The town was included in a 40,000-acre land grant given to Sir Walter Raleigh by Elizabeth I in the late 16th century. Local legend states that Sir Walter Raleigh planted the first potatoes in Ireland here, a claim disputed by several other locations (and by all accounts he spent little time here). Its long, sandy beach makes it a popular summer day-trip destination for Corkonians. The town itself is in the throes of some major investment, aimed at updating its appeal.

The **clock tower** (⊠ Main St.), Youghal's main landmark, dates from 1776 and was originally built as a jail. A set of steps beside the clock tower leads up to a well-preserved stretch of the old town walls. From here there is a magnificent panorama of the town and the estuary. The **Youghal Heritage Centre** relates the town's history through an audio-visual presentation. If this whets your appetite, trained guides are available to show you the town; a walking tour takes about an hour and a half. ⊠ *Market Sq.,* ☎ *024/92390.* ☒ *£1, tour £2.50.* ☉ *June–mid-Sept., daily 9:30–7; mid-Sept.–May, weekdays 9:30–5:30.*

At the Youghal **quays,** you may see today's catch being unloaded from one of the small, brightly painted trawlers that fish these waters. The **Moby Dick Lounge Bar** (⊠ Market Sq., ☎ 024/92756) contains memorabilia of the filming here of John Huston's version of Melville's *Moby-Dick,* in which Youghal masqueraded as New Bedford, Massachusetts. **St. Mary's Collegiate Church** (on top of the town walls) dates from the 13th century and contains many interesting monuments, including the tomb of Richard Boyle (1566–1643), who succeeded Sir Walter Raleigh as Mayor of Youghal and became the first earl of Cork. The brightly painted monument commemorates his three wives and 16 children and is similar to the monument in St. Patrick's' Cathedral in Dublin, which Sir Richard ordered because he was not sure whether he would die in Dublin or Youghal. ⊠ *Emmet Pl.,* ☎ *024/92350.* ☜ *Free.* ⊙ *Key available from adjacent lodge.*

Dining and Lodging

$$$ ✕▥ **Aherne's.** In the Fitzgibbon family since 1923, Aherne's has a highly
★ regarded seafood restaurant and bar that draw food lovers from Cork City (it's under an hour's drive). Popular main courses include hot buttered lobster, grilled salmon with fresh fennel, and more elaborate creations such as plaice stuffed with oysters in a red-wine sauce. The inexpensive bar food includes seafood pie topped with mashed potatoes. In their own modern wing, the 12 bedrooms are furnished with Victorian and Georgian antiques. ⊠ *163 N. Main St., Co. Cork,* ☎ *024/92424,* ℻ *024/93633. 12 rooms with bath. Restaurant, bar, fishing. AE, DC, MC, V.* ⊛

$ ✕▥ **Ballymakeigh House.** Signposted off N25 9½ km (6 mi) west of
★ Youghal, this is the Irish farmhouse of your dreams. From the conservatory behind the creeper-clad house you can breakfast on one of Margaret Browne's fresh strawberry muffins while watching the cows amble home. Reserve by 5 PM for her legendary six-course dinners, which have a set menu of the best local produce available that day; herbs and edible flowers from the Ballymakeigh garden add color to many dishes. The impeccably kept, cozy rooms show attention to detail. This is the kind of place where most people end up staying much longer than just one night. ⊠ *Killeagh, Co. Cork,* ☎ *024/95184,* ℻ *024/95370. 7 rooms with bath. Dining room, tennis court, Ping-Pong, bicycles. MC, V.*

Outdoor Activities and Sports

Youghal Golf Club (⊠ Knockavery, Co. Cork, ☎ 024/92787) is a scenic, 18-hole, par-70 course that overlooks the bay.

Shanagarry

㉔ *27 km (17 mi) southwest of Youghal via N25 and R632.*

Until recently, Shanagarry was a quiet farming village well off the beaten track, chiefly known for its Quaker connections. The most famous Shanagarry Quaker was William Penn (1644–1718), the founder of the Pennsylvania colony, who grew up in **Shanagarry House,** still a private residence in the center of the village. The entry gates are across from **Shanagarry Castle,** now owned and being restored by the potter and entrepreneur Stephen Pearce (☞ Shopping, *below*). The house's most famous tenant since William Penn was Marlon Brando, who stayed here in the summer of 1995 while filming *Divine Rapture* in nearby Ballycotton.

Ballymaloe House (☞ Dining and Lodging, *below*), one of Ireland's first country-house hotels, on the eastern edge of the village, has brought a stream of visitors to the area. On the other side of Shanagarry, **Ballymaloe Cookery School and Gardens,** run by Darina and Tim

Allen (daughter-in-law and son of Ballymaloe House original founders Myrtle and the late Ivan Allen), attracts budding chefs from all over Ireland and, increasingly, from points beyond, to its wealth of cooking classes and programs, which range from one day to 12 weeks. (Its graduates can be found in the kitchens of many Irish restaurants, which often promote the connection.) Darina Allen, one of Ireland's best-known chefs, tends formal herb, fruit, and vegetable gardens, as well as a Celtic maze (about knee-high). A meal or a snack at the Garden Café, serving the famous Ballymaloe-style fresh food as well as pizzas from a wood-burning oven, adds greatly to the visit. ⊠ *Kinoith House,* ☎ *021/464–6785.* ⌘ *Gardens £3.* ☉ *May–Sept., daily 9–6.*

OFF THE BEATEN PATH	**BALLYCOTTON –** Five kilometers (3 miles) beyond Shanagarry on R629, this pretty fishing village is built on the top of a cliff overlooking an island where large colonies of seabirds breed. There are pleasant cliff walks and a nearby beach.

Dining and Lodging

$$$ ✕▥ **Ballymaloe House.** One of Ireland's best-known country houses,
★   Ballymaloe has been the home of Myrtle and the late Ivan Allen (who died in 1998) for nearly 50 years. Gentle hills rise up behind the house, while farmland surrounds it as far as the eye can see. Each color-theme guest room is elegantly, if simply, decorated (rooms do not have TVs). Myrtle, the doyenne of Irish cooking, presides over the dining room (jacket and tie required), the walls of which are hung with Ivan's notable Irish art collection. Chef Rory O'Connell presents a daily changing, six-course, haute Irish menu that relies on fresh fish from nearby Ballycotton, local lamb and beef, and homegrown herbs and vegetables. The superb, mostly local cheeses exemplify Myrtle's long-standing practice of supporting small food purveyors. ⊠ *Midleton, Co. Cork,* ☎ *021/465–2531,* ℻ *021/465–2021. 32 rooms with bath. Restaurant, bar, pool, tennis court. AE, DC, MC, V.* ✍

Shopping

The ceramicist Stephen Pearce makes tableware and bowls in four signature styles—the newest is a gold porcelain—that are available in many Irish crafts shops. He sells a wide selection at his own **Stephen Pearce Emporium** (⊠ near Cloyne, ☎ 021/464–6262), where he also stocks an interesting range of Irish-made crafts.

Midleton

㉕ *12 km (8 mi) east of Cork City on N25, 15 km (9 mi) northwest of Shanagarry on R629.*

Midleton is a pleasant market town at the head of the Owenacurra estuary, near the northeast corner of Cork Harbour. Its gray stone buildings date mainly from the early 19th century. Midleton is famous for its school, Midleton College, founded in 1696, and its distillery, founded in 1825 and modernized in 1975, which manufactures spirits—including Irish whiskey—for distribution worldwide.

The **Jameson Heritage Centre** has tours of the Old Midleton Distillery, to show you how Irish whiskey—*uisce beatha,* "the water of life"—was made in the old days. The old stone buildings are excellent examples of 19th-century industrial architecture, and an impressively large old waterwheel is still in operation. The biggest pot still in the world, a copper dome capable of holding 32,000 imperial gallons of whiskey, is also found here. Early in the tour, requests are made for a volunteer "whiskey taster"—so be alert if this option appeals. The tours end with a complimentary glass of Jameson's Irish whiskey (or a soft drink). A crafts center and café are also on the premises. ⊠ ☎ 021/461–3594. 🎫 £3.95. ⊘ Mar.–Oct., daily 9–4:30; Nov.–Feb., tours only, weekdays at 12:30 and 3, weekends at 2 and 4.

Fermoy

㉖ 35 km (22 mi) north of Cork City on N8, 43 km (27 mi) west of Youghal on R634 (Tallow Rd.), which adjoins N72.

An army town dating mainly from the mid-19th century, Fermoy is a major crossroads on the Dublin–Cork road (N8); the east–west road that passes through town (N72) is an attractive 98-km (61-mi) alternative route to Killarney. Its bridge spanning the Blackwater is flanked by two weirs dating from 1689. The town is popular with fishers.

Dining and Lodging

$$ ✕🏠 **Ballyvolane House.** An informal country-house atmosphere pervades this imposing 1728 stone mansion surrounded by extensive gardens, beyond which is a 100-acre dairy farm. Dinner is served at a large table in the elegant dining room; family silver is set on white linens. The rooms are exceptionally big, sitting areas are generous, and decor consists of a rich assortment of antiques and family heirlooms. Both dinner and accommodation must be booked at least 24 hours in advance, but the preplanning is well worth it. The village of Castlelyons is signposted off N8 in Rathcormac, just south of Fermoy. ⊠ Castlelyons, Co. Cork, ☎ 025/36349, 𝖥𝖠𝖷 025/36781. 6 rooms with bath. Dining room, horseback riding, fishing. MC, V. ✍

Outdoor Activities and Sports

For local information on salmon and trout angling contact the **Salmon Angler's Association** (Liam McGarry, ⊠ Moorepark, Co. Cork, ☎ 025/31422).

Mallow

㉗ 30 km (19 mi) west of Fermoy on N72.

In the 18th century, Mallow was a popular spa, often mentioned in the same breath as Bath. Today it is an angling center and market town. (It's at the intersection of the Cork–Limerick and Waterford–Killarney roads, within an hour's drive of all four towns.) At the bottom of Mallow's Main Street, the **Clock House** is a half-timber building dating from 1855. It shares the site with the Rakes of Mallow Club, the headquarters of the notorious 18th-century gamblers, drinkers, and fortune hunters remembered in the song "The Rakes of Mallow." Not much remains today of Mallow's glory, but the old **Spa Well** can still be seen in the town center, and there are several interesting facades with overhanging bay windows on Main Street dating from the 18th and early 19th centuries. The English novelist Anthony Trollope lived at No. 139 for a time, and he rode with the Duhallow Hunt, enhancing the fame of the local pack. The ruins of **Mallow Castle,** which dates from the late 16th century, are at the bottom of the main street behind (freely accessible) ornamental gates. The castle was burned by the Jacobites in 1689, and its stables were later converted into a house, which is still in use as a private home. From here you can view the white, fallow deer that are unique to Mallow and were originally presented by Elizabeth I.

OFF THE BEATEN PATH   **ANNE'S GROVE GARDENS –** These gardens were inspired by the ideas of William Robinson, a 19th-century gardener who favored naturalistic planting. Exotic foliage borders paths winding down to the Blackwater; magnificent spring magnolias and primulas summer hydrangeas are among the plants on view in the rolling countryside. ✉ *Castletown-roche, 12 km (7 mi) east of Mallow,* ☎ *022/26145.* ☜ *£3.* ☉ *Mid-Mar.–Sept., Mon.–Sat. 10–5, Sun. 1–6.*

Dining and Lodging

$$$ ✗🏨 **Longueville House.** The Southwest of Ireland has no shortage of
★   outstanding country-house hotels, but by many accounts Longueville wins highest honors. Limestone quoins frame the facade of the imposing Georgian mansion. The three-story central block is flanked by two wings, while a Victorian-era, glass-and-iron conservatory punctuates the east end. The stately drawing rooms, decorated with large, gilt-framed mirrors, overlook the tranquil 500-acre estate, which rolls down to the Blackwater. Bedrooms are comfortable and filled with antiques. At the Presidents' Restaurant (named for the portraits of the Republic's presidents on the walls), William O'Callaghan, son of founding proprietors Michael and Jane O'Callaghan, serves an outstanding and elegant Irish-French–style menu prepared largely using produce from the houses's own farm, garden, and river. ✉ *Co. Cork,* ☎ *022/47156,* ﬀ *022/47459. 20 rooms with bath. Restaurant, bar, fishing. AE, DC, MC, V. Closed end of Dec.–mid-Feb.* ☙

Outdoor Activities and Sports

Mallow Golf Club (✉ Ballyellis, Co. Cork, ☎ 022/21145) is an 18-hole, par-72 parkland course with excellent views of the Blackwater Valley.

Kanturk

㉘   *15 km (9 mi) west of Mallow on N72 and R579.*

Kanturk lies at the meeting of two rivers, the Allow and the Dalua. It is more of a village than a town, but its interesting Victorian shopfronts bear witness to its past importance as a market town. The freely accessible **Kanturk Castle** (✉ 2 km [1 mi] outside town on the R579 Banteer Rd.) was built by a local Macarthy chieftain in 1601, but its completion was prevented by English neighbors complaining it was too large for an Irishman. Ornate stone fireplaces and mullioned windows in the five-story shell give some idea of the scope of Macarthy's ambitions.

Dining and Lodging

$$$$ ✗🏨 **Assolas Country House.** This ivy-covered 17th-century manor
★   possesses the air of a dignified family home, and hosts Joe and Hazel Bourke have perfected the picture by furnishing the house and its bedrooms with period antiques. Dinner begins in front of the blazing log fire in the drawing room, where guests peruse the night's menu over aperitifs. Old Bourke family silver is on the tables in the red Queen Anne dining room. Hazel's refined culinary skills, as well as the well-manicured gardens, are renowned. ✉ *Co. Cork,* ☎ *029/50015,* ﬀ *029/50795. 9 rooms with bath. Restaurant, tennis court, boating, fishing. AE, MC, V. Closed Nov.–mid-Mar.* ☙

KINSALE TO GLENGARRIFF VIA BANTRY BAY

This section takes you on a scenic drive of about 136 km (85 mi) around the unspoiled coast of West County Cork. We begin at the historic old port—and now booming seaside town—of Kinsale and meander through a variety of seascapes to the lush vegetation of Glengarriff. The drive from Kinsale to Glengarriff can take under two hours nonstop, but the whole point of making this journey is to linger anywhere that tickles your fancy.

Kinsale

★ ㉙ *29 km (18 mi) southwest of Cork City on R600.*

At the tip of the wide, fjordlike harbor opening out from the River Bandon, Kinsale's town center consists of small streets lined by upscale shops and eateries with colorful, pastel facades. Its steep, narrow streets climb up the slopes of Compass Hill. Tall, slate-roof and unusual slate-front houses have an unmistakable Spanish influence, which can be traced back to the Battle of Kinsale in 1601, when the Irish and Spanish joined forces to fight the English—and lost. The loss was a serious one for the Irish aristocracy, and they soon took off for Europe, leaving behind their lands to English settlers. Kinsale went on to become an important fishing port as well as a British army and naval base.

Today Kinsale has a number of fine restaurants—it is often referred to as "the Gourmet Capital of Ireland," a billing it especially lives up to during the first week in October, when it hosts its annual **Gourmet Festival** (☞ Festivals and Seasonal Events *in* Smart Travel Tips A to Z). But foodies alone can't claim Kinsale; yacht owners and deep-sea anglers are also a big presence here. A signposted walking tour of the town, with an accompanying booklet (£1 from the Kinsale TIO or Boland's on Pearse Street), will familiarize you with its history.

Cuttings and memorabilia from the wreck of the *Lusitania* (☞ Cobh, *above*) are among the best artifacts in Kinsale's local **museum,** housed in the town's 17th-century, Dutch-style courthouse. The 1915 inquest into the *Lusitania*'s sinking took place in the **courtroom,** briefly making it the focus of the world's attention; it has been preserved as a memorial. ⊠ *Old Courthouse, Market Pl.,* ☎ *021/477–2044.* ☜ *£2.* ◷ *Mon.–Sat. 11–5, Sun. 3–5.*

On the harbor shore on the east side of the Bandon's estuary, the
★ British built **Charles Fort** in the late 17th century, in the wake of their defeat of the Spanish and Irish forces. One of the best-preserved "star forts" in Europe, it encloses some 12 acres on a cliff top (it's similar to Fort Ticonderoga in New York State). If the sun is shining, take the footpath signposted **Scilly Walk;** it winds along the edge of the harbor under tall, overhanging trees and then through the village of Summer Cove. ⊠ *3 km (2 mi) east of town,* ☎ *021/477–2684.* ☜ *£2.50.* ◷ *Mid-Mar.–Oct., daily 10–6; Nov.–mid-Mar., weekends 10–5.* ✍

The **Spaniard Inn** (⊠ Scilly, ☎ 021/477–2436) looks over the town and harbor from a hairpin bend on the road to Charles Fort. Inside, sawdust-covered floors and a big open fire make this onetime fishermen's bar a cozy spot in the winter. In the summer, you can take a pint to the sunny veranda and watch the world go by on land and sea.

Dining and Lodging

$$$$ ✕ **The Vintage.** One of Ireland's original front-parlor, cottage-style restau-
★ rants, this is the place for a special occasion, even though the atmosphere is informal and welcoming. The cozy, low-beamed interior is enhanced by Swiss owner Raoul de Gendre's art collection. Tables are beautifully appointed with specially designed glassware, linen cloths, and tall glass candleholders. Up to four chefs toil over an ambitious à la carte menu. The classic Continental cuisine absorbs Irish influences, such as Lobster Dublin Lawyer (whole lobster with mustard-whiskey sauce). Appetizers include caviar and sautéed fresh duck foie gras. The wine list has more than 150 primarily European wines. ⊠ *50 Main St.,* ☎ *021/477–2502. AE, DC, MC, V. Closed Jan.–mid-Mar. No lunch.*

$$$ ✗ **The Cottage Loft.** The hand-painted purple and yellow traditional wooden shopfront sets the tone for this cozy town-center eatery that manages to be consistently different from everyone else on the block. Owner-chef Michael Buckley's menu is small but interesting. Possible starters include breast of pigeon marinated in red wine and served with a dark-chocolate sauce, and for a main course you might have a kebab of local seafood with a lightly curried fruit sauce. Steaks, with optional pepper or Irish whiskey sauce, are a strong point. There are six rooms with bath above the restaurant. ✉ *6 Main St.,* ☎ *021/477–2803. AE, MC, V. No lunch.*

$$$ ✗ **Man Friday.** The name refers to Kinsale's alleged connection with the original Robinson Crusoe, Alexander Selkirk (Kinsale was reputedly his last port of call before shipwreck). Man Friday occupies a series of interconnecting rooms and has a terrace for drinks in fine weather. Steaks and seafood, prepared in an unpretentious Continental style, are the main business here. The generous portions, along with the bustling atmosphere, make it the sort of place that locals and visitors alike return to again and again. On a hilltop overlooking Kinsale Harbour, it's about 1 km (½ mi) outside town. ✉ *Scilly,* ☎ *021/477–2260. AE, DC, MC, V. Closed Sun.*

$$$ ✗ **Restaurant Antibes.** The smallish dining room has a plaster-decorated ceiling, Art Deco posters of its namesake, elegant blue-and-white napery, and a good buzz. Antibes is known for such traditional seafood dishes as sole on the bone and Dublin Bay prawns with herb butter. It also serves rack of lamb and generously sized steaks with optional brandy and pepper sauce, as well as some vegetarian dishes. Desserts are substantial affairs: profiteroles come with chocolate and butterscotch sauces, and homemade ice creams are served in a brandy snap basket. ✉ *Pearse St. and The Glen,* ☎ *021/477–2125. AE, DC, MC, V. Closed Nov.–Feb. No lunch.*

$$ ✗ **Max's Wine Bar.** One of Kinsale's original gourmet restaurants, Max's is now run by enthusiastic French owner-chef Olivier Queva and his partner, Anne Marie Galvin. The L-shape front parlor of a low-beamed town house creates an atmospheric setting. This is the place for a light lunch, especially if you are keen on salads. At dinner Olivier's classical French background is evident in his treatment of the daily catch and in his clever ways with unusual cuts, like oxtail and pig's trotters. ✉ *Main St.,* ☎ *021/477–2443. MC, V. Closed Nov.–mid-Mar.*

$–$$ ✗ **The Bulman.** Kinsale has other pub-restaurants, but none can boast the idyllic waterside location of this ever-popular bar. At lunchtime simple pub grub—mussels steamed in white wine, perhaps, or a meaty burger and chips—is served at the bar. In the evening the first-floor restaurant has tables with romantic views of the sunset over the harbor. The menu includes freshly made pasta, Thai chicken curry, local salmon with lemon-herb butter sauce, and steaks. ✉ *Summercove,* ☎ *021/477–2131. MC, V. No lunch Sun.*

$ ✗ **Crackpots.** The food in Kinsale is great but can be tough on the budget. At Carole Norman's "ceramic café" you can sample the light, eclectic menu without fear of bankruptcy. An old grocery shop has been transformed into a simple but elegant eatery with warm yellow walls and two cozy dining areas, one of which has a small open fire. Behind the restaurant is Carole's pottery workshop; if you like your dinner plate, you can buy it. ✉ *3 Cork St.,* ☎ *021/477–2847, MC, V. Closed Mon.–Wed. Nov.–Mar.*

$$$ ✗🛏 **Blue Haven.** This attractive, yellow-stucco, blue-trim town house combines an acclaimed seafood restaurant with a small hotel. Rooms are both in the main house and in the house next door. New rooms have custom-designed dark-oak furniture, canopied antique beds, and spacious baths; those in the main house, though generally smaller, are cheerfully decorated with paintings by local artists. Inexpensive bar food is served until 9:30 PM in the lounge bar, the patio, and the conservatory, which all have swagged curtains, hanging plants, and nautical brass. The quiet, pastel-color restaurant overlooks a floodlit garden with a fountain adorned by cherubs. ⊠ *3 Pearse St., Co. Cork,* ☎ *021/477–2209,* FAX *021/477–4268. 18 rooms with bath. Restaurant, bar, fishing. AE, DC, MC, V.*

$ ✕🏨 **The White House.** One of the oldest inns in Kinsale, the White House has managed to retain the traditional warm Irish welcome in spite of greatly increased visitor numbers. Food is served both in the bar and in a connecting room known as Chelsea's Bistro. The best options are the traditional Irish dishes, like boiled bacon and cabbage, which come with enormous boiled potatoes in their skins. The fish of the day is often a sophisticated combination, due to the fact that the pub shares a kitchen with Restaurant Antibes (☞ *above*). The bedrooms vary in size, but all have fully tiled, good-sized bathrooms and are decorated in pastel colors; the quietest ones are on the upper floors. ⊠ *Pearse St. and The Glen, Co. Cork,* ☎ *021/477–2125,* FAX *021/477–2045. 12 rooms with bath. Restaurant, bar. AE, DC, MC, V.* ✎

$$$$ 🏨 **Perryville House.** By far the most luxurious—and most expensive—
★ accommodation in town, this double-fronted 19th-century house with an attractive wrought-iron balcony overlooks the inner harbor. The public rooms are beautifully decorated, giving the impression of a private home. Front bedrooms have sea views, but ones at the rear are quieter: an important factor in July and August. All rooms, imaginatively furnished with Victorian antiques, have extralarge beds, fresh flowers, robes, and all the extras you would expect at a top-grade hotel. ⊠ *Long Quay, Co. Cork,* ☎ *021/477–2731,* FAX *021/477–2298. 15 rooms with bath, 7 suites. AE, DC, MC, V. Closed Nov.–mid Mar.*

$$ 🏨 **The Moorings.** Only yards from the water's edge in the fishing village of Scilly, this hotel has a panoramic view across Kinsale Harbor and yet is only a few minutes' walk from Kinsale's town center. Hosts Pat and Irene Jones are full of friendly advice and won't discourage you if you're tempted to install yourself in the sunny conservatory and simply watch the boats go by. Nicely sized guest rooms have large tiled bathrooms, patchwork-quilt spreads, and paintings by local artists. ⊠ *Scilly, Co. Cork,* ☎ *021/477–2376,* FAX *021/477–2675. 9 rooms with bath. MC, V.*

$$ 🏨 **Old Bank House.** This tall, narrow Georgian town house is owned
★ and managed with sophisticated flair by Michael and Marie Riese, a Swiss-Irish couple. The large, high-ceilinged rooms have tall windows, double-glazed against traffic noise. Pretty touches like dried flower arrangements and modern prints add to the elegance. The higher the room the better the view, so regulars will be glad to hear that an elevator has been installed. Michael was previously chef-owner of Vintage restaurant (☞ *above*), and his breakfasts are memorable. ⊠ *Pearse St., Co. Cork,* ☎ *021/477–4075,* FAX *021/477–4296. 17 rooms with bath. AE, MC, V.* ✎

$$ 🏨 **Sovereign House.** If you're looking for history in this heritage town, here is the real thing. Built in 1708 as the home of the Sovereign (Lord Mayor) of Kinsale, this imposing Queen Anne town house has a symmetrical stone facade and a quiet, central location. The interior is furnished in the baronial style with heavy family heirlooms, exposed stonework, stone-flagged floors, and original fireplaces. Rooms are large and luxurious, with many original features, including some massive exposed beams and Victorian-style bathrooms. There is a warm welcome from your host James McKeown, who will advise on local golf, fishing, and dining. ⊠ *Newman's Mall, Co. Cork,* ☎ *021/477–2850,* FAX *021/477–4723. 4 rooms with bath. Billiards. MC, V.*

$ ▣ **Kilcaw House.** Value for the money and off-road parking make this guest house a good choice. On busy weekends when the town can be buzzing into the small hours, Kilcaw's location—2 km (1 mi) outside town on the Cork side of the R600—guarantees peace and quiet. An open fire in the lobby, polished pine floors, and striking colors add character to the farmhouse-style building. Rooms are well equipped, spacious, and uncluttered, with country pine furniture and throw rugs on the wooden floors. ⊠ *Pewter Hole Cross, Co. Cork,* ☎ *021/477–4155,* FAX *021/477–4755. 7 rooms with bath. AE, MC, V.*

Nightlife and the Arts

The **Bacchus Brasserie** (⊠ Guardwell, ☎ 021/477–2382) has late-night dancing for the over-25s. The **Shanakee** (⊠ Market St., ☎ 021/477–4472) is renowned for traditional Irish music. Check out the **Spaniard Inn** (⊠ Scilly, ☎ 021/477–2436) for live rock and folk groups.

Outdoor Activities and Sports

BICYCLES

Rent a bike from **D&C Cycles** (⊠ 18 Main St., Co. Cork, ☎ 021/477–4884) to explore the picturesque hinterland of Kinsale.

DIVING

Kinsale Dive Centre (⊠ Castlepark Marina Centre, Co. Cork, ☎ 021/477–4959) will take you on a guided wreck dive and rents all necessary equipment.

FISHING

For deep-sea angling contact **Ireland Southwest Angling Ltd.** (⊠ Castlepark Marina Centre, Co. Cork, ☎ 021/477–4959).

WATER SPORTS

The **Oysterhaven Holiday and Activity Center** (⊠ Oysterhaven, ☎ 021/477–0738) offers rental of all sailboarding equipment, including wet suits.

Shopping

Boland's (⊠ Pearse St., ☎ 021/477–2161) features some unusual items, including exclusive sweaters, designer rainwear, and linen shirts. **Giles Norman Photography Gallery** (⊠ 44 Main St., ☎ 021/477–4373) sells unusual black-and-white photographs of Irish scenes. The **Keane on Ceramics** (⊠ Pier Rd., ☎ 021/477–2085) gallery represents the best of Ireland's ceramics artists. **Kinsale Crystal** (⊠ Market St., ☎ 021/477–4463) is a master cutter's studio that sells 100% Irish, hand-blown, hand-cut crystal. **Victoria Murphy** (⊠ Market Quay, ☎ 021/477–4317) has an interesting selection of small antiques and antique jewelry.

En Route Leaving Kinsale through its center, following the quays and driving west along the Bandon River toward the bridge on R600, takes you through **Garretstown Woods** (signposts for Clonakilty on R600), carpeted with wild bluebells in April. You'll then travel past the edge of Courtmacsherry Bay, running alongside a wide, saltwater inlet that teems with curlew, plover, and other waders.

Timoleague

➌ *19 km (12 mi) west of Kinsale on R600.*

The small town of Timoleague marks the eastern end of the Seven Heads Peninsula, which stretches around to Clonakilty. A mid-13th-century **Franciscan abbey** at the water's edge is Timoleague's most striking monument. (Walk around the back to find the entrance gate.) The abbey was sacked by the English in 1642 but, like many other ruins of its kind, was used as a burial place until recent times. A tower and walls with Gothic-arched windows still stand, and you can trace the ground plan of the old friary—chapel, refectory, cloisters, and wine cellar (at one time the friars were well-known wine importers).

Timoleague Castle Gardens are right in the village. Although the castle is now a picturesque ruin adjoining a modest early 20th-century house in gray stone, the original gardens have survived. Palm trees and other frost-tender plants flourish in the mature shrubbery. There are two large, old-fashioned walled gardens, one for flowers and one for fruits and vegetables. ☎ *023/46116.* ⊡ *£2.* ☉ *Easter weekend and June–Aug., daily noon–6.*

Courtmacsherry, the pretty village of multicolor cottages glimpsed across the water, has sandy beaches that make it a popular holiday resort. It can be reached by following the signposts from Timoleague.

Dining and Lodging

$$$ ✕ **Casino House.** Midway between Kinsale and Timoleague on the
★ coastal R600, this traditional farmhouse was converted to an informal restaurant by owner-chefs Michael and Kerrin Relja. The home is decorated in an uncluttered style, and two small dining rooms—one blue and one green—have private sitting rooms for pre-dinner drinks next to an open fire. Menu highlights include starters of garlic prawn salad and lobster risotto; such main courses as roast loin of lamb served with Roman gnocchi; and summer fruits with sabayon as a seasonal dessert. ⊠ *Coolmaine, Kilbrittain,* ☎ *023/49944. MC, V. Closed Wed. mid-Jan.–mid-Mar.; Easter–Oct.; Mon.–Thurs. Nov.–early Jan.*

$ ✕🏠 **Lettercollum House.** This rambling country-manor house dating from 1861 is 2 km (1 mi) outside the village and looks back across the estuary to Courtmacsherry Bay. Chef-proprietors Con McLoughlin and Karen Austin create an informal but welcoming atmosphere; rooms are large, bright, and airy, with wonderful views. Organic herbs, salads, and soft fruit for the table are grown in a walled garden, and pigs are raised on-site. The restaurant is in the chapel—Lettercollum was once a convent—which retains its stained-glass windows and confessional. ⊠ *Timoleague, Co. Cork,* ☎ *023/46251,* ℻ *023/46270. 9 rooms with bath. Restaurant, lounge. MC, V. Closed Nov.–mid-Mar.* ✎

En Route Many of the shops and businesses in the small market town of **Clonakilty,** 9½ km (6 mi) from Timoleague on R600/N71, have abandoned chrome and plastic materials for traditional, hand-painted signs and wooden facades—to very charming effect. The best of the several traditional music pubs in town is **De Barra's** (⊠ 55 Pearse St., ☎ 023/33381). Many fine, sandy beaches are near Clonakilty; the best are at **Inchydoney,** 3 km (2 mi) outside of town.

The **birthplace of Michael Collins** (1890–1922) is signposted about 5 km (3 mi) west of Clonakilty off N71 (just past the tiny village of Lissavaird). The ground plan of the simple homestead where the controversial founder of the modern Irish Army was born was reinstated by his late nephew, and there is a bronze memorial (it's freely accessible). There is another memorial in the nearest village, **Woodfield,** opposite the pub where Collins is said to have had his last drink on the day he was shot in an ambush.

The road briefly joins the sea again at **Rosscarbery,** where you leave the main road by turning left at the signpost for Glandore at the end of the causeway. Glandore and Union Hall are twin fishing villages on either side of the landlocked Glandore Harbour. With its steep hill and pretty church, **Glandore** is a popular spot for visitors from the United Kingdom and Germany. Glandore's influx of affluent visitors and expensive yachts has not been shared in **Union Hall,** where simple fishing trawlers still tie up at the quay. In the area hereabouts, you are truly in the back of beyond, where tiny roads are without route numbers.

Castletownshend (clearly signposted from Union Hall via Rineen) has an unusual number of graciously designed, large stone houses, mostly dating from the mid-18th century, when it was an important trading center. Its main street runs steeply down a hill to the sea. The sleepy town awakens in July and August, when its sheltered harbor bustles. Sparkling views await from the cliff-top perch of St. Barrahane's Church, which has a medieval oak altarpiece and three stained-glass windows by the early 20th-century Irish artist Harry Clarke. The low-beamed interior of **Mary Ann's** (☎ 028/36146), one of the oldest bars in the country, is frequented by a very friendly mix of visitors and locals and is a good place for a pint and a bite of bar food. Writer Edna O'Brien claims that it is her favorite pub in the whole world.

Skibbereen

③ *85 km (53 mi) west of Kinsale, 35 km (22 mi) west of Timoleague.*

Skibbereen is the main market town in this neck of southwest Cork, and it's a good base for the sights nearby. The weekly cattle market (Wednesday) and country market (Friday)—not to mention the plethora of pubs punctuated by bustling shops and coffeehouses—keep the place jumping year-round.

Garden lovers, take note: still partially under construction but well worth visiting is the **Liss Ard Foundation.** More than 40 acres are planted with various lakeside gardens designed to highlight the natural beauty of the landscape in an ecologically sound way. Particularly worthwhile is the 10-acre **Sky Garden,** designed by American artist James Turrell to celebrate the beauty of the sky. Allow two to three hours. An optional guided tour is included in the admission price. ⊠ *On Castletownshend road out of Skibbereen,* ☎ *028/22368.* 🎫 *£5.* ☽ *May–Oct., daily 10–dusk; call for hrs Nov.–Apr.*

Dining and Lodging

$$$ ✕ **Island Cottage.** This unlikely venture has become a pilgrimage spot
★   for food lovers, who praise the high standard of cooking and the beautiful wilderness location on Heir Island. Your hosts John Desmond and Ellmary Fenton are internationally trained chefs, and prepare a set five-course menu utilizing local produce, some of it picked in the wild on the island and appearing in such dishes as Cape Clear turbot on a bed of sea spinach, or such desserts as terrine of vanilla ice cream with meringue in a blackberry sauce. Cookery courses and demonstrations can be arranged, as can lunch or private dinner parties for groups of 20 or more. Advance booking is necessary; when you call, John and Ellmary will give you details of the ferry that takes you to the island (£4 for a four-minute ride). ⊠ *Heir Island,* ☎ *028/38102. No credit cards. Closed Oct.–May, Mon.–Tues. June–Sept. No lunch..* 🕮

$ ✕🏨 **Heron's Cove.** You really will see herons outside your window at Sue Hill's idyllic harborside retreat. This modern house, built on the edge of a secluded sea inlet, is only a few minutes' walk from Goleen's appealing village center. The exceptionally well equipped rooms, furnished in part with antiques, have excellent views from every window. During summer, fresh local seafood stars on the menu, which also includes lamb, duck, and steak. Fresh herb sauces and homemade mayonnaise make subtle accompaniments, and there's a terrific wine list. Off-season (November–March), evening meals are prepared on request for guests only. It is 29 km (18 mi) west of Skibbereen on R591. ✉ *The Harbour, Goleen, Co. Cork,* ☎ *028/35225,* FAX *028/35422. 5 rooms with bath. Restaurant, fishing. AE, DC, MC V.* ✍

$ ✕⌂ **West Cork Hotel.** This family-run hotel in a large Victorian building on the River Ilen has a stylish old colonial ambience. Refurbished rooms are comfortable as well as a good value for the price range. The restaurant, famous for its steaks, serves fashionable dishes like Louisiana crab cakes as well as traditional favorites. ✉ *Bridge St., Co. Cork,* ☎ *028/21277,* FAX *028/22333. 36 rooms with bath. Restaurant, bar, horseback riding, fishing. AE, DC, MC, V.*

Nightlife and the Arts

The **West Cork Arts Center** (North St., ☎ 028/22090) has regular exhibits of work by local artists. The on-site crafts shop also sells items made by area artisans.

Outdoor Activities and Sports

Bicycles to explore West Cork's coast and country can be rented from **N. W. Roycroft** (✉ Ilen St., ☎ 028/21235).

Baltimore

32 *13 km (8 mi) southwest of Skibbereen on R595.*

The beautiful, crescent-shape fishing village of Baltimore is a popular sailing center and attracts its share of vacationing families from Ireland and abroad, especially during the peak summer months. The village was sacked in 1631 by a band of Algerian sailors; as a result, watchtowers were installed at the harbor mouth to protect the town.

Sherkin Island, one of Baltimore's two famous attractions, is 1 km (½ mi) off the coast, only a 10-minute ferry ride away. Seven ferries are scheduled daily (☎ 028/20125 for times). On the island, you'll find the ruins of **Dún Na Long Castle** and **Sherkin Abbey,** both built around 1470 by the O'Driscolls, a seafaring clan known as the "scourge of the Irish seas." The island's population today is 90, and there are several safe, sandy beaches and abundant wildlife.

Even more impressive than Sherkin Island is **Cape Clear Island,** a 2- by 5-km (1- by 3-mi) island that is part of the West Cork Gaeltacht, or Irish-speaking area. The ferry to the island, which is 6 km (4 mi) offshore, takes about an hour from Baltimore (£9 round-trip; ☎ 028/39119 for sailing times). It's exciting to watch the skipper thread his way through the many rocks and tiny islands of Roaring Water Bay. You have excellent views of the **Fastnet Rock Lighthouse,** focus of a renowned yachting race. Sparsely populated (about 200 residents), the island has one pub and a few simple B&Bs, but it is otherwise rugged and unblemished (electricity from the mainland was not brought over, via an underground cable, until April 1997), and it can be explored on foot in about an hour. Bird-watchers may want to schedule more time: Cape Clear is the southernmost point of Irish territory, and its observatory, the oldest in the Republic, has racked up all kinds of sightings of rare songbird migrants. Whales, dolphins, and large flocks of oceangoing birds can be seen offshore in the summer.

Outdoor Activities and Sports

Sailing dinghies and sailboards can be rented by the hour or the day from **Baltimore Sailing School** (✉ The Pier, ☎ 028/20141).

Bantry

③③ *25 km (16 mi) northwest of Skibbereen on N71.*

★ Bantry is an unprepossessing town with a large market square at the head of Bantry Bay, where a long plaza attracts artisans, craftspeople, and musicians in summer. As you enter Bantry, on the right-hand side of the road you'll see the porticoed entrance to **Bantry House,** one of Ireland's most magnificent houses, beautifully situated overlooking the sea. First built in the early 1700s, then subsequently altered and expanded later that century, the house as it looks today is largely the vision of Richard White, the second earl of Bantry, who also created the Italianate gardens that surround it. On his European grand tours, Richard gobbled up fine art, furniture, and other antiques, including Aubusson tapestries said to have been ordered by Louis XV for the marriage of Marie Antoinette to the Dauphin. Some of the rooms are now a little shabby, but the beauty of the location compensates for the lack of polish. The long climb to the top of the rear garden pays off with what has been called "one of the great views in Ireland." Next to the house is the **Bantry 1796 French Armada Exhibition Center,** a small but worthwhile museum illustrating the abortive attempt by Irish Nationalist Wolfe Tone and his French ally General Hoche to land 14,000 troops in Bantry Bay to effect an uprising. ☎ 027/50047. 🖾 *Gardens £2, house £4, museum £3.* ⊙ *Mar.–Oct., daily 9–6.*

Dining and Lodging

$$$$ ✕ **Blair's Cove House.** In the converted stables of a Georgian mansion overlooking Dunmanus Bay, gleaming silverware, pink tablecloths, and a large crystal chandelier are set off, jewel-in-the-rough style, against stone walls and exposed beams. A covered, heated terrace overlooks the rose-filled courtyard and fountain and is used in summer. The cuisine is French-Irish (the owners are French) with an emphasis on fresh local produce. 🖾 *Blair's Cove, Durrus,* ☎ *027/61041. MC, V. Closed Sun. No lunch Mon.*

$$$$ ✕ **Shiro Japanese Dinner House.** One of the biggest surprises of West ★ Cork's culinary world has been the success of this tiny, 20-seat restaurant, serving authentic Japanese cuisine in an Edwardian house surrounded by palm trees. The room is decorated with watercolors by the hostess, Tokyo-born Kei Pilz. 🖾 *Ahakista, Durrus,* ☎ *027/67030. Reservations essential. AE, DC, MC, V. Closed Jan.–Feb. No lunch.*

$$ ✕🍽 **Sea View House.** Set in its own wooded grounds overlooking Bantry ★ Bay, this large, three-story, 19th-century country-house hotel offers excellent value for the money. Owner-manager Kathleen O'Sullivan keeps an eagle eye on what was, until 1980, her private home. Inlaid antique furniture, polished brass, and ornate curtains set a tone of luxury. Bedrooms with sea views have small sofas in the bay windows; others have views of the wooded gardens. Polished tables in the elegant dining room are set with crocheted mats and linen napkins; service is friendly and informal. 🖾 *Ballylickey, Co. Cork,* ☎ *027/50073,* 📠 *027/51555. 17 rooms with bath. Restaurant, bar, horseback riding, fishing. AE, DC, MC, V. Closed mid-Nov.–mid Mar.*

Nightlife and the Arts

During the **West Cork Chamber Music Festival,** roughly 20 concerts are held from the last weekend in June through the first in July in the library at exquisite Bantry House. For information on themes and international guest artists for the 2001 event, or for news of other chamber music concerts held at Bantry House throughout the year, contact the West Cork music office (🖾 1 Bridge St., ☎ 027/52788).

Outdoor Activities and Sports

Bantry Park Golf Club (✉ Donemark, Co. Cork, ☎ 027/50579) is an 18-hole, par-71 course overlooking Bantry Bay.

Shopping

One of the Southwest's larger independents, **Bantry Bookstore** (✉ New St., ☎ 027/50064) has six rooms full of new, antiquarian, and secondhand books. **Manning's Emporium** (✉ Ballylickey, ☎ 027/51049) is a showcase for locally made farmhouse cheeses, pâtés, and salamis—an excellent place to put together a picnic or just to browse.

En Route   The glorious sweep of **Bantry Bay** is on your left as you climb out of Bantry past Ballylickey on N71.

Glengarriff

❸❹   *14 km (8 mi) northwest of Bantry on N71, 21 km (13 mi) south of Kenmare.*

One of the jewels of Bantry Bay is Glengarriff, the "rugged glen" much loved by Thackeray and Sir Walter Scott. The descent into wooded, sheltered Glengarriff reveals yet another kind of landscape: thanks to the Gulf Stream, it is mild enough down here for subtropical plants to thrive. Trails along the shore are covered with rhododendrons, and they afford beautiful views of the nearby inlets, loughs, and lounging seals. You are back on the beaten path, with crafts shops, tour buses, and boatmen soliciting your business by the roadside.

Garnish Island, about 10 minutes offshore, features beautiful, formal Italian gardens; shrubberies with rare subtropical plants; and excellent views from the Grecian temple. From the island's Martello tower, built at the end of the 18th century, the British watched for attempted landings by Napoleonic forces, including Hoche's ill-fated one. (The price for the boat ride is fixed at £5 round-trip.) ☎ 027/63040. 🖭 £2.50. ⊙ July–Aug., Mon.–Sat. 9:30–6:30, Sun. 11–7; Apr.–June and Sept., Mon.–Sat. 10–6:30, Sun. 1–7; Mar. and Oct., Mon.–Sat. 10–4:30, Sun. 1–5; last landing 1 hr before closing.

En Route   Glengarriff is the gateway to the **Ring of Beara,** a 137-km (85-mi) scenic drive that encircles the Beara Peninsula on R572. Just beyond the busy fishing port of Castletownbere lie the ruins of Dunboy Castle and House (freely accessible). **Dursey Island,** at the tip of the peninsula, is a birdwatcher's paradise accessible only by cable car. From Dursey Island, head for tiny **Allihies,** the former site of a huge copper mine, and detour along a precipitous and breathtaking coastal road to Eyeries—a ghost town–like village overlooking Coulagh Bay—and then up the south side of the Kenmare River to Kenmare. If you have extra time, you might want to backtrack to R584 and visit **Gougane Barra National Park,** where the hermit St. Finbarr had his mountain retreat. It is the source of the River Lee, and has nature trails.

THE RING OF KERRY

Running along the perimeter of the Iveragh Peninsula, the dramatic Ring of Kerry is probably the single most popular tourist route in Ireland. Stunning mountain and coastal views are around almost every turn of the road. The only drawback: on a sunny day, it seems like half the tourists in Ireland are there, packed into buses, on bikes, or backpacking along the same two-lane road. Because tour buses ply the Ring counterclockwise, we recommend that independent travelers take it clockwise, starting at Kenmare. This is equally convenient whether you're approaching from Glengarriff (on N71) or Killarney (also on N71), which is the traditional starting point. The trip covers 176 km (110 mi) on N70 (and briefly R562) if you start and finish in Killarney; the journey will be 40 km (25 mi) shorter if you only venture between Kenmare and Killorglin. Allow at least one full day to circumnavigate the Ring. And because rain blocks views across the water to the Beara Peninsula in the east and the Dingle Peninsula in the west, pray for sunshine. It makes all the difference.

Kenmare

㉟ *21 km (13 mi) north of Glengarriff, 34 km (21 mi) south of Killarney on N71.*

A small market town at the head of the sheltered Kenmare River estuary, Kenmare was founded in 1670 by Sir William Petty (Cromwell's surveyor general, a multitasking entrepreneur) and today is a lively touring base with an unusually wide selection of restaurants and accommodations for such a small place. Most of its buildings date from the 19th century, when it was part of the enormous Lansdowne Estate, itself assembled by Petty. The **Kenmare Heritage Centre** explains the history of the town and supplies a walking route pointing out places of interest. ☎ *064/41233.* ☞ *£2.* ☉ *Easter–Sept., Mon.–Sat. 9:30–5:30.*

Dining and Lodging

$$ ✕ **An Leath Phingin.** The name means "The Half Penny," and this stylish little place with exposed stone walls and modern pine tables specializes in northern Italian cuisine. Never let it be said that Kerry is predictable! The explanation lies in owner-chef Con Guerin's links with Bologna, where he learned the art of making fresh pasta. The combination of Irish and Italian is epitomized by a starter of baked aubergine with olive oil, tomato, local goat's cheese, and basil, or a 12-inch Quattro Formaggi pizza featuring four Irish cheeses—Milleens, Cashel Blue, local goat's, and Gubeen. ⊠ *35 Main St.,* ☎ *064/41559. MC, V. Closed Nov.*

$$ ✕ **Cafe Indigo.** Although the theme color of the minimalistic decor is a predictable indigo, the menu features eclectic international combinations. Crispy spring rolls with sweet pepper sauce, seared scallops with celeriac puree and mango vanilla-bean salsa, and bitter chocolate lemon torte with vanilla sauce are recommendations. The Square Pint pub serves tempting bar food downstairs: spiced lentil soup, seafood pie, Irish stew, and imaginative sandwiches. ⊠ *The Square,* ☎ *064/42356. AE, DC, MC, V.*

$–$$ ✕ **Packies.** Owner-chef Maura O'Connell Foley established Kenmare's original first-class restaurant, the Lime Tree, but she has since opted for a quieter life at Packies. The small room has a flagstone floor, an exposed-stone fireplace, and paintings by local artists. The delicious bistro-style menu includes wild smoked salmon with red onion and caper salsa as well as crab claws with garlic butter or olive oil. ⊠ *Henry St.,* ☎ *064/41508. MC, V. Closed Sun. and Nov.–Easter.*

$$$$ ✕🖫 **Park Hotel.** This sprawling, 1897 stone château is one of Ireland's
★ premier country-house hotels. A two-minute walk to town, the 11-acre property has views of the Caha Mountains and terraced lawns that sweep down to the bay. A marble fireplace and a tall grandfather clock preside over the thickly carpeted lobby. Owner-manager Francis Brennan is a stickler for authenticity and has made great efforts to recapture the hotel's heyday. The bedrooms are individually designed with late-Victorian furniture faithful to the house's original period; walnut or mahogany bedroom suites have matching wardrobes, chests of drawers, and headboards. Be sure to sample the modern Irish cuisine of the renowned restaurant, which uses local ingredients in a mélange of

Asian and Continental styles. ⊠ *Co. Kerry,* ☎ *064/41200,* FAX *064/41402. 49 rooms with bath. Restaurant, bar, 18-hole golf course, tennis court, croquet, Ping-Pong, fishing, bicycles. AE, DC, MC, V. Closed Jan.– mid-Apr.* ✍

$$$$ ✕⬚ **Sheen Falls Lodge.** The magnificent setting—300 secluded acres of lawns, semitropical gardens, and forest between Kenmare Bay and the falls of the River Sheen—is easily matched by this rambling, bright-yellow, slate-roof manor house, built by the descendants of Sir William Petty, and the former seat of the earls of Kerry. The public rooms, decorated in warm orange tones, include a mahogany-paneled library with more than 1,000 books, mainly of Irish interest, and a billiards room adjacent to the bar. The bedrooms all offer stunning bay or river views. The restaurant, La Cascade (it overlooks the falls), serves classic French cuisine. ⊠ *Co. Kerry,* ☎ *064/41600,* FAX *064/41386. 45 rooms with bath, 8 suites, 8 superior-deluxe rooms. Restaurant, bar, indoor pool, sauna, steam room, tennis court, croquet, health club, horseback riding, fishing, billiards, library. AE, DC, MC, V. Closed first 3 wks in Dec.* ✍

$ ⬚ **Muxnaw Lodge.** A romantic black-and-white house with steep gables, the lodge was built in 1801 and has a magical view over Kenmare Bay. It is surrounded by mature gardens and trees and is only a short walk from town. Rooms are spacious and cozy, individually decorated with interesting antique furniture but also boasting up-to-the-minute conveniences like television and tea- and coffee-making facilities. The atmosphere in general is genteel, old-world, as if the 20th century had passed the place by. Dinner, featuring local produce and plain home cooking, must be booked by noon. Bring your own wine. ⊠ *Castletownbere Rd., Co. Kerry,* ☎ *064/41252. 5 rooms with bath. Tennis court, fishing. No credit cards.*

$ ⬚ **Sallyport House.** Across the bridge on the way into Kenmare, this substantial, 1932 family home has been enlarged to serve as a comfortable B&B. The spotless rooms, all with harbor or mountain views, are furnished with a variety of Victorian and Edwardian antiques. Janey Arthur has placed family heirlooms in all rooms; if you are interested in old Irish furniture, ask for a tour. ⊠ *Glengariff Rd., Co. Kerry,* ☎ *064/42066,* FAX *064/42067. 5 rooms with bath. No credit cards. Closed mid-Nov.–Mar.* ✍

Nightlife

Try **O Donnabhainós** (⊠ Henry St., ☎ 064/41361) for traditional music.

Outdoor Activities and Sports

Seafari (⊠ Kenmare Pier, ☎ 064/83171) has two-hour, eco-nature and seal-watching cruises and also runs the Marine Activities Centre (May–October, weather permitting), which offers sea fishing, sailboat day trips, sailboarding, canoeing, waterskiing, and tube rides.

Shopping

Avoca Handweavers (⊠ Moll's Gap, ☎ 064/34720) sells wool clothing and mohair rugs and throws in a wide range of colors and weaves. **Black Abbey Crafts** (⊠ 28 Main St., ☎ 064/42115) specializes in fine Irish-made crafts. **Cleo's** (⊠ 2 Shelbourne St., ☎ 064/41410) stocks Irish-made wool and linen, and Irish hand knits, which have striking designs, often drawn from Ireland's past.

Sneem

36 *27 km (17 mi) southwest of Kenmare on N70.*

This is one of the prettiest villages in Ireland—and, it can seem, one of the most popular. Sneem (from the Irish for "knot") is settled around an English-style green on the estuary of the Ardsheelaun River, its streets filled with houses washed in different colors. Also, look for "the pyramids" (as they are known locally) beside the parish church. These 12-ft-tall, traditional stone structures with stained-glass insets look as though they have been here forever. In fact, the sculpture park was completed in 1990 to the design of the Kerry-born artist James Scanlon, who has won international awards for his work in stained glass.

Staigue Fort, signposted 4 km (2½) mi inland at Castlecove, is one of the finest examples of an Iron Age stone fort in Ireland. Approximately 2,500 years old, this structure, made from local stone, is almost circular and about 75 ft in diameter, with only one entrance, on the south side. From the Iron Age (from 500 BC to the 5th century AD) and early Christian times (6th century AD), such "forts" were, in fact, the fortified homesteads for several families of one clan and also where their cattle lived. The walls at Staigue Fort are almost 13 ft wide at the base and 7 ft wide at the top; they still stand at 18 ft on the north and west sides. Within the walls stairs lead to narrow platforms on which the lookouts stood. (Private land must be crossed to reach the fort, and a nominal "compensation for trespass" of 50p–£1 is often requested by the landowner.)

Lodging

$$$$ 🏨 **Parknasilla Great Southern.** A porter in a frock coat and striped gray pants typifies the elegant and slightly stuffy early 20th-century atmosphere of this grand old hotel. Previous guests include General de Gaulle, Princess Grace, and George Bernard Shaw, who wrote much of *Saint Joan* while staying here. Although some rooms are a bit plain, they are tastefully decorated in soft pinks and blues. Continental cuisine is served in the Pygmalion Restaurant. The sheltered coastal location, 3 km (2 mi) south of Sneem, and excellent sporting facilities make it an ideal retreat. ⊠ *Parknasilla, Co. Kerry,* ☎ 064/45122, FAX *064/45323. 84 rooms with bath, 1 suite. Restaurant, bar, indoor pool, sauna, 9-hole golf course, tennis court, horseback riding, windsurfing, boating, fishing. AE, DC, MC, V.* 🏷

$ 🏨 **Tahilla Cove Country House.** The house itself is modern and much-added-to over the years—the attraction is its idyllic location, with its own stone jetty in a sheltered private cove. Guests can enjoy the plump, chintz armchairs and open log fire in the large sitting room or laze on the terrace overlooking 14 acres of subtropical gardens and the cove. Rooms are of varying sizes, comfortably furnished in a homey way, and all but two have sea views. ⊠ *Tahilla Cove, Co. Kerry,* ☎ 064/ 45204, FAX 064/45104. 9 rooms with bath. Restaurant, bar, fishing. AE, DC, MC, V. Closed mid-Oct.–Mar.* 🏷

En Route   **Derrynane House** was once the home of Daniel O'Connell (1775–1847), "The Liberator," who campaigned for Catholic Emancipation (the granting of full rights of citizenship for Catholics), which became a reality in 1828. The house with its lovely garden and 320-acre estate now forms **Derrynane National Park.** The south and east wings of the house (which O'Connell himself remodeled) are open to visitors and contain much of the original furniture and other items associated with O'Connell. ⊠ *Near Caherdaniel, 30 km (18½ mi) west of Sneem off N70,* ☎ *066/947-5113.* 🎫 *House £2, parking free.* 🕐 *Jan.–Mar. and Nov.–Dec., weekends 1–5; Apr. and Oct., Tues.–Sun. 1–5; May–Sept., Mon.–Sat. 9–6, Sun. 11–7.*

Waterville, Valentia Island, and the Skelligs

Waterville: 35 km (22 mi) west of Sneem, 5 km (3 mi) north of Caherdaniel on N70; Valentia Island: 21 km (13 mi) northwest of Waterville; Skellig Islands: 40 km (25 mi) west of Waterville.

③ Like many other villages on the Ring of Kerry, **Waterville** has a few restaurants and pubs, but little else. It *is* famous for game-fishing opportunities, its 18-hole championship golf course (adopted as a warming-up spot for the British Open by Tiger Woods, who was a big hit with the local community), and for the fact that Charlie Chaplin and Charles de Gaulle once spent their summers here. Salmon and trout fishing are excellent at nearby Lough Currane.

OFF THE
BEATEN PATH

BALLINSKELLIGS – Outside Waterville, a scenic detour is signposted from the main Ring to this small, Irish-speaking fishing village with an old monastery, a pub, and a fine sandy beach.

③ In the far northwestern corner of the Ring, **Valentia Island** lies across Portmagee Channel. Some of the romance of visiting an island has been lost since Valentia was connected to the mainland by a road bridge in 1971. The island still gives its name to weather reports, but the station that monitors the Atlantic weather systems has now moved onto the nearby mainland.

★ ③ The **Skelligs**—Little Skellig, Great Skellig, and the **Washerwoman's Rock**—are distinctive conical-shape rock islands visible from Valentia Island on a clear day. The largest rock, the Great Skellig, or **Skellig Michael,** rises 700 ft out of the Atlantic. It has the remains of a settlement of early Christian monks, reached by climbing 600 increasingly precipitous steps. In spite of 1,000 years of battering by Atlantic storms, the church, oratory, and beehive-shape living cells are surprisingly well preserved.

The **Skellig Experience,** where the road bridge joins Valentia Island, contains exhibits on local bird life, the history of the lighthouse and keepers, and the life and work of the early Christian monks. There is also a 15-minute audiovisual show that allows you to "tour" the monastery on Skellig Michael without leaving dry land. If, however, you'd like to see the Skelligs up close (landing is prohibited without a special permit), you can take a 1½-hour guided cruise. Little Skellig is the breeding ground of more than 22,000 pairs of gannets, while **Puffin Island** to the north has a large population of shearwaters, storm petrel, and puffins. Photographers will love the boat trip, but take note that the waters are choppy at the best of times. ⊠ *Valentia,* ☎ *066/947–6306.* ⌷ *Center £3, cruise £15 (includes admission to center).* ۩ *Apr.–June and Sept., daily 9:30–5; July–Aug., daily 9:30–7; call to confirm weather-dependent cruise times.* ֎

Dining and Lodging

$ ✕⌷ **Smuggler's Inn.** On a 2-km-long (1-mi-long) sandy beach, Lucille and Harry Hunt's small, family-run guest house has a restaurant with renowned seafood. It's an ideal spot for a leisurely lunch or a quick pint and a sandwich. Bedrooms are individually decorated with chintz spreads and curtains. Seven of them offer great sea views. ⊠ *Cliff Rd., Waterville, Co. Kerry,* ☎ *066/947–4330.* ﬀ︎ *066/947–4422. 10 rooms with bath. AE, DC, MC, V. Closed Dec.–Feb.*

$$ ⌷ **Butler Arms.** The white, castellated towers at the corners of this hotel provide a familiar landmark on the Ring. The building has been in the same family for three generations; it has a regular clientele, predominantly male, who come back year after year for the excellent fishing and golf facilities nearby. It was a favorite base for Charlie Chaplin. Although the accommodations are neither smart nor chic, the rambling old lounges with open turf fires are comfortable places to relax and converse. ⊠ *Waterville, Co. Kerry,* ☎ *066/947–4144,* ﬀ︎ *066/947–4520.*

30 rooms with bath. Restaurant, 2 bars, tennis court, horseback riding, fishing. AE, DC, MC, V. Closed mid-Oct.–Mar.. ✍

Nightlife
Head for the **Inny Tavern** (✉ Inny Bridge, Waterville, ☎ 066/947–4512) for live Irish music.

Outdoor Activities and Sports
Waterville Golf Links (✉ Co. Kerry, ☎ 066/947–4102), an 18-hole, par-72 course, is one of the toughest and most scenic in Ireland or Britain (☞ Chapter 9).

Cahirciveen

40 *18 km (11) mi north of Waterville on N70, 27½ km (17 mi) southwest of Glenbeigh.*

Cahirciveen (pronounced cah-her-sigh-*veen*) is the gateway to the western side of the Ring of Kerry, and it is the main market town and shopping center for South Kerry, at the foot of Bentee Mountain. The **O'Connell Memorial Church** (✉ Main Rd.), a large and elaborate neo-Gothic church that dominates the main street, was built in 1888 of Newry granite and local black limestone to honor the local hero, Daniel O'Connell (☞ En Route *in* Sneem *above*); it is the only church in Ireland named for a layman. Following the tradition in this part of the world, the town's modest, terraced houses are painted in different colors—the brighter the better. The **Cahirciveen Heritage Centre** is housed in the converted former barracks of the Royal Irish Constabulary, an imposing, castlelike structure built after the Fenian Rising of 1867 to suppress any further revolts. The community-funded center has well-designed displays depicting scenes from times of famine in the locality, the life of Daniel O'Connell, and the restoration of this fine building from a blackened ruin. ✉ *Barracks*, ☎ 066/947–2777. 🎫 £2.50. ☉ *June–Sept., Mon.–Sat. 10–6, Sun. 2–6; Mar.–May and Oct., weekdays 9:30–5:30.*

En Route The road from Cahirciveen to Glenbeigh is one of the highlights of the Ring. To the north is Dingle Bay and the jagged peaks of the Dingle Peninsula, which will, in all probability, be shrouded in mist. If they are not, the gods have indeed blessed your journey. The road runs close to the water here, and beyond the small village of Kells, it climbs high above the bay, hugging the steep side of Drung Hill before descending to Glenbeigh. Note how different the stark character of this stretch of the Ring is from the gentle, woody Kenmare Bay side.

Glenbeigh

41 *27 km (17 mi) northeast of Cahirciveen on N70, 11½ km (7 mi) west of Killorglin.*

On a boggy plateau by the sea, the block-long town of Glenbeigh is a popular holiday base, offering excellent hiking in the **Glenbeigh Horseshoe**, as the surrounding mountains are known, and exceptionally good trout fishing on Lough Coomasaharn.

Worth a quick look, the **Kerry Bog Village Museum** is a cluster of reconstructed, fully furnished cottages, which gives a vivid portrayal of the daily life of the region's working class in the early 1800s. ✉ *Beside Red Fox Bar*, ☎ 066/976–9184. 🎫 £2.50. ☉ *Mar.–Nov., daily 8:30–7; Jan.–Feb. by request.*

A signpost to the right outside Glenbeigh points to **Caragh Lake,** a tempting excursion to a beautiful expanse of water set among gorse- and heather-covered hills and majestic mountains. The road encircles the lake, hugging the shoreline much of the way.

ROSSBEIGH – North of Glenbeigh, this beach consists of about 3 km (2 mi) of soft, sandy coastline backed by high dunes. It faces Inch Strand, a similar formation across the water on the Dingle Peninsula (☞ The Dingle Peninsula, *below*).

Dining and Lodging

$$$ ✕🏨 **Caragh Lodge.** Built in the mid-19th century as a fishing lodge, this charming old house by Caragh Lake sits in 9 acres of spectacular gardens filled with azaleas, camellias, and magnolias. Two large rooms in the main house are furnished with Victorian and Georgian antiques; rooms in the courtyard and the garden annex are smaller; and another block has six larger rooms and one suite. Comfortable sitting rooms overlook the lake, as does the dining room. Owner Mary Gaunt supervises the four-course, set dinner menu (nonguests should book in advance). ⊠ *Caragh Lake, Killorglin, Co. Kerry,* ☎ *066/976–9115,* 𝖥𝖠𝖷 *066/976–9316. 14 rooms with bath, 1 suite. Restaurant, sauna, tennis court, boating, fishing. AE, DC, MC, V. Closed mid-Oct.–mid-Apr. No lunch.*

$$$ 🏨 **Ard na Sidhe.** Sidhe (pronounced sheen) means "Hill of the Fairies,"
★ and this secluded, gabled Edwardian mansion certainly fits a fairy-tale story. The house is built of stone walls, now ivy-covered, and is punctuated by casement windows set in stone mullions. Attractive, large rooms have coordinated carpets and spreads as well as lovely floral drapes on the bay windows; those in the main building are the nicest. Antiques and open fires adorn the traditionally furnished lobby and lounges. The hotel also has delightful, lakeside gardens. ⊠ *Caragh Lake, near Killorglin, Co. Kerry,* ☎ *066/976–9105,* 𝖥𝖠𝖷 *066/976–9282. 20 rooms with bath. Restaurant, bar, boating, fishing. AE, DC, MC, V. Closed Oct.–3rd wk in Apr.*🏖

Outdoor Activities and Sports

Dooks Golf Club (☎ 066/976–8205) is a challenging traditional links on the shore of Dingle Bay (☞ Chapter 9).

Killorglin

㊷ *14 km (9 mi) east of Glenbeigh, 22 km (14 mi) west of Killarney.*

The last stop on the Ring before Killarney (or the first, if you're going counterclockwise), the hilltop town of Killorglin is the scene of the **Puck Fair,** three days of merrymaking during the second weekend in August. A large billy goat with beribboned horns, installed on a high pedestal, presides over the fair. The origins of the tradition of King Puck are lost in time. Though some horse, sheep, and cattle dealing still occurs at the fair, the main attractions these days are free outdoor concerts and extended drinking hours. The crowd is predominantly young and invariably noisy, so avoid Killorglin at fair time if you've come for peace and quiet. On the other hand, if you intend joining in the festivities, be sure to book accommodations well in advance.

Dining

$$$ ✕ **Nick's Seafood and Steak.** Owner-chef Nick Foley trained as a veterinary surgeon but prefers life in the kitchen. The old, stone town house has a bar–cum–dining room at street level and a quieter dining room on the floor above. Foley is known for his wide choice of local seafood and his steaks. In winter, sample the haunch of Kerry venison in red-wine and juniper sauce. ⊠ *Main St.,* ☎ *066/976–1219. AE, DC, MC, V. Closed Nov. and Mon.–Tues. Dec.–Easter.*

IN AND AROUND KILLARNEY

One of southwest Ireland's most attractive locales, Killarney is also the most heavily visited city in the region (its proximity to the Ring of Kerry and to Shannon Airport helps to ensure this). Light rain is typical of the area around Killarney, but because of the region's topography, it seldom lasts long. Indeed, the clouds' approach over the lakes and the subsequent showers can actually add to the spectacle of the ever-changing scenery. The rain is often followed within minutes by brilliant sunshine and, yes, even a rainbow.

Exploring Killarney and Environs

Killarney: 87 km (54 mi) west of Cork City on N22, 19 km (12 mi) southeast of Killorglin, 24 km (15 mi) north of Glengarriff.

If writers like Sir Walter Scott and William Thackeray had to struggle finding the superlatives to describe the lakes and mountains of Killarney, it is not surprising that they remain among the most celebrated—and indisputably the most commercialized—attractions in Ireland. Killarney's heather-clad mountains, lush subtropical vegetation, and deep-blue lakes dotted with wooded isles have left a lasting impression on a long stream of visitors, beginning in the 18th century with the English travelers Arthur Young and Bishop Berkeley. Visitors in search of the natural beauty so beloved by the Romantic movement began to flock to the Southwest. By the mid-19th century, Killarney's stunning scenery was considered as exhilarating and awe-inspiring as anything in Switzerland or England's Lake District. The influx of affluent visitors that followed the 1854 arrival of the railway transformed the lives of Kerry's impoverished natives and set in motion a snowball of commercialization that continues today.

But the beauty of the surrounding area—an unbeatable combination of wild mountain scenery and lush foliage—persists. The air smells of damp woods and heather moors. Amazingly, the vegetation is splendid at any time of year. The red fruits of the Mediterranean strawberry tree (*Arbutus unedo*) are at their height in October and November. Also at that time, the bracken turns rust, contrasting with the many evergreens. In late April and early May, the purple flowers of the rhododendron *ponticum* put on a spectacular display. (This Turkish import has adapted so well to the climate that its vigorous growth threatens native oak woods, and many of the purple plants are being dug up by volunteers in an effort to control their spread.)

Much of the Killarney environs is encompassed by Killarney National Park, over 24,700 acres of lake and mountain scenery, a good portion of it wilderness. It is famous for its native natural habitats and species, including oak holly woods, yew woods, and red deer. Signposted self-guiding trails within the park introduce these habitats (☞ Hiking, *below*). At the heart of the National Park is Muckross Demesne, whose entrance is 4 km (2½ mi) from Killarney on N71. The National Park visitor center is at Muckross House (☞ *below*). Cars are not allowed in Muckross Demesne; you can either walk, hire a bicycle, or take the traditional Killarney option and use a jaunting car, a pony, and trap (☞ Guided Tours in the Southwest A to Z, *below*).

43 You may want to limit time spent in **Killarney** itself if discos, Irish cabarets, and singing pubs—the last a local specialty with a strong Irish-American flavor—aren't your thing. Killarney's nightlife is at its liveliest from May to September; Irish and European visitors pack the town in July and August, while peak season for Americans follows in Septem-

Killarney and Environs

ber and October. At other times of the year, particularly from November to mid-March, when many of the hotels are closed, the town is quiet to the point of being eerie. Given the choice, go to Killarney in April, May, or early October.

★ **④④ Aghadoe** (⊠ 5 km/3 mi west of Killarney on the R562 Beaufort–Killorglin road) is an outstanding place to preview some of the sights in the area. Standing beside Aghadoe's 12th-century ruined church and round tower, be sure to remember to breathe as you watch the shadows creep across the Lower Lake, with Innisfallen Island (☞ *below*) in the distance and the Gap of Dunloe (☞ *below*) away to the west.

④⑤ Torc Waterfall (⊠ Killarney National Park, N71 , 8 km/5 mi south of Killarney), is reached by a footpath that begins in the parking lot outside the gates of the Muckross Demesne. After your first view of the roaring cascade, which will appear after about 10 minutes' walk, it's worth the climb up a long flight of stone steps to the second, less-frequented clearing.

④⑥ Muckross House, a 19th-century, Elizabethan-style manor, now houses the **Kerry Folklife Centre,** where bookbinders, potters, and weavers demonstrate their crafts. The elegantly furnished rooms portray the lifestyle of the landed gentry in the 1800s, while downstairs in the basement you can experience the conditions of servants employed in the house. Inside you'll also find the **Killarney National Park Visitor Centre.** The informal grounds are noted for their rhododendrons and azaleas, the water garden, and the outstanding limestone rock garden. In the park beside the house, the **Muckross Traditional Farms** comprise reconstructed farm buildings and outhouses, a blacksmith's forge, a carpenter's workshop, and a selection of farm animals, including poultry and cattle. It is a reminder of the way things were done on the farm before the advent of electricity and the mechanization of farming.

Meet and chat with the farmers and their wives as they go about their work. ⊠ *Killarney National Park, Muckross Demesne, Muckross Rd. (N71), 6½ km (4 mi) south of Killarney,* ☎ *064/31440.* ⊠ *Visitor center free, farms or house £4, farms and house £6.* ☉ *House Sept.–June, daily 9–5:30. Visitor center Nov.–mid-Mar., on request; mid-Mar.–June, Sept.–Oct., daily 9–6; July–Aug., daily 9–7. Farms mid-Mar.–Apr., weekends 2–6; May, daily 1–6; June–Sept., daily 10–7; Oct., daily 2–6.*

47 The 15th-century Franciscan **Muckross Friary** is amazingly complete, although roofless. The monks were driven out by Oliver Cromwell's army in 1652. An ancient yew tree rises above the cloisters and breaks out over the abbey walls. Three flights of stone steps allow access to the upper floors and living quarters, where you can visit the cloisters and what was once the dormitory, kitchen, and refectory. ⊠ *Killarney National Park, Muckross Demesne, Muckross Rd. (N71), 4 km (2½ mi) south of Killarney.* ⊠ *Free.* ☉ *Mid–June–early Sept., daily 10–5.*

48 **Ross Castle,** a fully restored 14th-century stronghold, was the last place in the province of Munster to fall to Oliver Cromwell's forces in 1652. A later dwelling has 16th- and 17th-century furniture. ⊠ *Knockreer Estate, off Muckross Rd. (N71), 2 km (1 mi) south of Killarney,* ☎ *064/35851.* ⊠ *£3.* ☉ *Apr. and Oct., daily 10–5; May and Sept., daily 9–6; June–Aug., daily 9–6:30.*

49 The romantic ruins on **Innisfallen Island** date from the 6th or 7th century. Between 950 and 1350 the *Annals of Innisfallen* were compiled here by monks. (The book survives in the Bodleian Library in Oxford.) To get to the island, which is on Lough Leane, you can rent a rowboat at Ross Castle (£2 per hour), or you can join a cruise (£6) in a covered, heated launch.

★ **50** Massive, glacial rocks form the side of the **Gap of Dunloe,** one of Killarney's primary sights. The Gap is a narrow mountain pass that stretches for 6½ km (4 mi) between MacGillicuddy's Reeks, Ireland's highest mountains to the west, and the Purple Mountains. Five small lakes are strung out beside the road. (The rocks create strange echoes: give a shout to test it out.) Cars are banned from the gap, but in summer the first 3 km (2 mi) are busy with horse and foot traffic, much of which turns back at the halfway point. For information on guided tours of the gap, *see* Guided Tours *in* Southwest A to Z, *below.*

At the entrance to the Gap of Dunloe, **Kate Kearney's Cottage** (⊠ 19 km/12 mi west of Killarney, ☎ 064/44116) is a good place to rent a jaunting car or pony. Kate was a famous beauty who sold illegal *poteen* (moonshine) to visitors from her home, contributing greatly, one suspects, to their enthusiasm for the scenery. Appropriately enough, it's now a pub and a good place to pause for a glass of Irish coffee.

The southern end of the Gap is marked by **Lord Brandon's Cottage** a tea shop serving soup and sandwiches. From here, a path leads to the edge of the Upper Lake, where you can journey onward by rowboat. It is an old tradition for the boatman to carry a bugle and illustrate the echoes. The boat passes under Brickeen Bridge and into the Middle Lake, where 30 islands are steeped in legends, many of which your boatman is likely to recount. Look out for caves on the left-hand side on this narrow stretch of water. ⊠ *7 km (4½ mi) west of Killarney.* ☉ *Easter–Sept., 10 AM–dusk.*

★ **51** If the weather is fine, head southwest 19 km (12 mi) out of Killarney on N71 to **Ladies' View,** a panorama of the three lakes and the surrounding mountains. The name goes back to 1905, when Queen Victoria was a guest at Muckross House (☞ *above*). Upon seeing the view, her ladies-in-waiting were said to have been dumbfounded by its beauty.

Dining and Lodging

$$$$ ✕ **Fredrick's.** Breathtaking views of Killarney's lakes from the rooftop
★ restaurant of the Aghadoe Heights hotel (☞ *below*) make this the ultimate romantic venue. And, as if that weren't enough, the food is outstanding. Silver candelabra, white linen, and fully upholstered chairs beckon from the tables (ask for one at the front when you book). The English chef prepares a classic French menu, which varies according to season. Main courses include classics such as black sole grilled or meunière or more unusual dishes like medallions of veal with crab soufflé. This is one of the most expensive restaurants in Ireland, but it will provide an unforgettable culinary experience. ☒ *Aghadoe Heights,* ☎ *064/31766. Jacket and tie. AE, DC, MC, V.*

$$$ ✕ **Gaby's Seafood.** The best seafood in Killarney packs Gaby's small
★ dining room, with its tiled floors, pine booths, and red-gingham cloths with matching lamp shades. Try the seafood mosaic (seven or eight kinds of fresh fish in a cream-and-wine sauce) or lobster Gaby (shelled, simmered in a cream-and-cognac sauce, and served back in the shell). ☒ *17 High St.,* ☎ *064/32519. AE, DC, MC, V. Closed Sun. and mid-Feb.–mid-Mar. No lunch.*

$$ ✕ **Dingles.** If you want to feel more like a local than a visitor, then Gerry and Marie Cunningham's relaxed Killarney town-center restaurant is the place to go. Open fires, old church pews, and interesting bric-a-brac create a characterful ambience, while Gerry supplies the warm welcome that keeps the locals coming back. Marie's cooking uses the best local ingredients in simple, unshowy dishes like roast rack of Kerry lamb, or baked crab and prawns au gratin. ☒ *40 New St.,* ☎ *064/31079. AE, DC, MC, V. Closed Nov.–Mar. No lunch.*

$ ✕ **Sheila's.** Simply furnished with stripped-pine tables and red paper place mats, Sheila's has fed the people of Killarney and its visitors for more than 30 years—it was recently handed down from mother to daughter. The unpretentious menu features such Irish specials as corned beef with cabbage and Irish stew (Kerry lamb stewed with barley, carrots, onion, and potatoes). In a town bedeviled by tourist traps, this friendly spot is an excellent value. The restaurant is licensed to serve wine only. ☒ *75 High St.,* ☎ *064/31270. AE, DC, MC, V.*

$$$$ ✕🏨 **Aghadoe Heights.** Its location on a bluff 4 km (2½ mi) outside Killarney (on the Tralee side, signposted off N22) translates into unforgettable lake views that will long remain with you—especially if enjoyed from the aerie of the famous hotel restaurant, Fredrick's (☞ *above*), one of Ireland's best. Eight acres of grounds ensure absolute peace and quiet. The luxurious interior was fully revamped for the 2000 season, and is a pleasant combination of antique and modern styles. Most bedrooms have lake views, and all are relatively large, with good-size bathrooms, matching floral drapes and spreads, lace-covered cushions, and fitted natural wood furniture. ☒ *Aghadoe Heights, Co. Kerry,* ☎ *064/31766,* 🖷 *064/31345. 72 rooms with bath, 3 suites. Restaurant, bar, indoor pool, sauna, tennis court, fishing. AE, DC, MC, V.* ☕

$$ ✕🏨 **Foley's.** Inside this 19th-century former coaching inn in the center of Killarney, chef-owner Carol Hartnett does the cooking and makes use of local ingredients, including superior Irish cream and butter. Roulade of trout stuffed with prawn mousse and grilled T-bone steak with garlic butter are two typical main dishes. The wine list offers more than 200 selections, and a pianist entertains in summer. All rooms are decorated with Victorian antiques and old country furniture, including sofas and chaises lounges; windows are double-glazed, so the rooms are quieter than you would expect. ☒ *23 High St., Co. Kerry,*

☎ *064/31217,* ℻ *064/34683. 32 rooms with bath. Restaurant. AE, DC, MC, V. Closed Nov.–Mar.*

$$ ✕⌂ **The Mills Inn.** If you wince at the idea of Killarney's tour-bus crowds, consider staying 15 minutes' drive from town in this old coaching inn. Ballyvourney is a small, Irish-speaking village on the main Cork–Killarney road, distinguished only by the rapid-flowing River Sullane. But hosts Denis and Mary Scannell rightly claim the inn is "where you meet the real Ireland." The inn incorporates an old castle ruin, as well as a stable yard and pretty gardens. Rooms, well insulated from bar and traffic noise, have cozy cottage furnishings. The restaurant serves generous portions of local beef and seafood from Kenmare; the main bar, which often hosts live music, has simple, hearty fare such as Irish stew. ✉ *Ballyvourney, Macroom, Co. Cork,* ☎ *026/45237,* ℻ *026/45454. 12 rooms with bath. Restaurant, 2 bars. MC, V.* ❧

$ ✕⌂ **Climber's Inn.** The name says it all: this place is primarily for walkers and climbers. Its location, 30 km (18 mi) from Killarney in a tiny village at the base of Ireland's highest mountain, Carrantouhill, is an inspiration in itself. Rooms are simple, with sturdy pine beds, brightly colored duvet covers and curtains, and power showers. The bar serves excellent pub grub, including local sea trout from Caragh Lake (a real delicacy, quite unlike commercially reared trout), and the famous Irish stew—Highland lamb casserole. Guided wilderness walks, which could be the most memorable adventures you have in Ireland, can be pre-booked. ✉ *Glencar, Co. Kerry,* ☎ *066/976–0101,* ℻ *066/976–0104. 10 rooms with bath, 1 dorm with 10 bunks. Bar, fishing. AE, DC, MC, V. Closed Mon.–Thurs. Nov.–mid Mar.* ❧

$$$ ⌂ **Europe.** A secluded lakeside location (a five-minute drive from Killarney) and luxurious but unfussy decor give this modern, five-story hotel the edge over its competitors. Most bedrooms have solid-pine trim, a lake view, and a private balcony. The spacious lounges and lobbies, although a bit impersonal, have picture windows overlooking the lake and mountains, an imaginative display of old carved timber, and antiques. The sports facilities, including an Olympic-size pool, are among the best and most up-to-date in the area. ✉ *Killorglin Rd., Fossa, Co. Kerry,* ☎ *064/31900,* ℻ *064/32118. 205 rooms with bath. 2 restaurants, 2 bars, indoor pool, sauna, tennis court, horseback riding, fishing, bicycles. AE, DC, MC, V. Closed Nov.–mid-Mar.* ❧

$$ ⌂ **Beaufort House.** This secluded Georgian house, set in 40 acres of woodland and situated 9 km (5½ mi) outside Killarney on the R562 Killorglin road, is convenient for both Killarney and the Ring of Kerry. Donald and Rachel Cameron like to warn their guests that while they offer peace and privacy, two small children and a dog are also in residence. The hall, library, and drawing room all have open fires. The large, uncluttered rooms are furnished with a variety of antiques. The evening meal, often featuring local lamb or home-caught fish, must be booked 24 hours ahead. Three kilometers (2 miles) of private salmon and trout fishing are nearby on the River Laune. ✉ *Co. Kerry,* ☎ *064/ 44764,* ℻ *064/44764. 4 rooms with bath. Fishing. MC, V. Closed Nov.– Easter, except by arrangement.* ❧

$$ ⌂ **Glencar House.** Hikers, anglers, and wilderness lovers will be happy out here in the Kerry Highlands, about 20 minutes' drive from Killarney and 10 minutes' drive from Killorglin. (From Killarney, turn off the N72 Killorglin road at the sign for Beaufort, and turn right at the first T-junction.) The rambling two-story house was originally built as a hunting lodge in 1670 by the Earl of Lansdowne. Today it is a small, unpretentious country house, with huge elk antlers over the fireplace and stuffed birds and animals at every turn. Rooms are relatively spacious, with country pine furniture and breathtaking views of Killarney's famous mountain range, the MacGillicuddy's Reeks. ✉ *Glencar, Co. Kerry,*

☎ 066/976–0102, FAX 066/976–60167. *18 rooms with bath. Restaurant, bar, fishing. MC, V.* 🐾

$ 🏨 **Arbutus.** Run by the friendly Buckley family since it was built more than 60 years ago, this is a good budget hotel in Killarney's town-center—a short step from the bus and train station and a three-minute walk from the main shopping and dining area. The lobby has an open fire, and the quiet, oak-paneled bar is popular with locals. The rooms in the second-story section are recommended for their roominess and updated furnishings. ✉ *College St., Co. Kerry,* ☎ *064/31037,* FAX *064/ 34033. 44 rooms with bath. Restaurant, bar. AE, DC, MC, V.*

$ 🏨 **Earls Court House.** In a quiet suburb within walking distance of Killarney's center, this comfortable guest house is furnished with interesting antiques collected by Emer Moynihan, who likes to greet her guests with tea or coffee and scones. Bedrooms are spacious, with large bathrooms and an elegant mix of antique and reproduction Victorian furniture. Breakfast is served at mahogany tables in a large, sunny, wooden-floored room; menu choices include pancakes and kippers. ✉ *Woodlawn Junction, Muckross Rd. (N71), Co. Kerry,* ☎ *064/34009,* FAX *064/34366. 11 rooms with bath. MC, V.* 🐾

$ 🏨 **Lime Court.** Budget accommodations have been springing up along the Muckross road between Killarney and the national park; this one is only a five-minute walk from the town center. The modern building has two large bay windows at the front, with the rooms in an extension behind it, away from the road. Antiques and large potted plants adorn the reception area, while a baby grand piano anchors the spacious lounge. The relatively large guest rooms overlook green fields and are light, airy, and plainly but comfortably furnished with small sitting areas. ✉ *Muckross Rd. (N71), Co. Kerry,* ☎ *064/34547,* FAX *064/ 34121. 16 rooms with bath. Ping-Pong. MC, V.* 🐾

Medieval Banquets

The **Killarney Manor Banquet** is a five-course meal hosted by "Lord and Lady Killarney" in their 1860, castellated manor house. The food, with a choice of poached salmon or roast Kerry lamb for the main course, is served by waitresses in 19th-century costume. The entertainment is excellent by any standards, with a team of professional singers and dancers presenting favorite Irish tunes. ✉ *Loreto Rd.,* ☎ *064/31551.* 🎟 *Entertainment plus 5-course meal and mulled-wine reception £29, entertainment £11.* ☉ *Apr.–Oct., daily 8 PM; entertainment 8:45– 10:45.*

Nightlife and the Arts

Singing bars are popular in Killarney, where a professional leads the songs and encourages audience participation and solos. Try the **Laurels** (✉ Main St., ☎ 064/31149). **Buckley's Bar** (✉ College St., ☎ 064/ 31037) in the Arbutus Hotel has traditional entertainment nightly from June to September. The **Crypt Nightclub** (✉ College Sq., ☎ 064/ 31038) is a spook-themed late-night venue for the over-23s. **Gleneagles** (✉ Muckross Rd., ☎ 064/31870) is the place for big-name cabaret—from Sharon Shannon to the Wolfe Tones—and also has a late-night disco.

Outdoor Activities and Sports

FISHING

Killarney's lakes and rivers have salmon and brown trout. To improve your technique contact **Angler's Paradise** (✉ Loreto Rd., Muckross, ☎ 064/33818), where the Michael O'Brien International Fishing School organizes game, coarse, and deep-sea fishing trips by day or by night. **O'Neill's** (✉ Plunkett St., ☎ 064/31970) provides fishing tackle, bait, and licenses.

GOLF

Beaufort Golf Course (⊠ Churchtown, Beaufort, ☎ 064/44440) has an 18-hole, par-71 course surrounded by magnificent scenery, and unlike most other Irish golf clubs, it has buggy-, trolley-, and club-rental facilities. For many people, the two courses at the legendary **Killarney Golf and Fishing Club** (⊠ Mahony's Point, ☎ 064/31034) are the chief reason they're in town; for details *see* Chapter 9.

HIKING AND WALKING

The **Kerry Way,** a long-distance walking route, passes through the **Killarney National Park** on its way to Glenbeigh (detailed leaflet from the TIO). For the less adventurous, four safe and well-signposted nature trails of varying lengths are at hand in the national park. Try the 4-km (2½-mi) Arthur Young's Walk, which passes through old yew and oak woods frequented by Sika deer. The **Mangerton walking trail** is reached by turning left off N71 midway between Muckross Friary and Muckross House (following signposts). The summit of **Mangerton Mountain** (2,756 ft) can be reached on foot in about two hours—less should you choose to rent a pony (☞ Horseback Riding, *below*). **Torc Mountain** (1,764 ft) can be reached off Route N71; it is a satisfying 1½-hour climb. Do not attempt mountain climbing in the area in misty weather, since visibility can quickly drop to zero.

HORSEBACK RIDING

Killarney Riding Stables Ltd. (⊠ Ballydowney, ☎ 064/31686) organizes four- and seven-day treks in Killarney National Park, with accommodation.

Shopping

Shopping in Killarney means crafts and souvenirs, and the most reliable crafts stores are on Main Street and High Street; they all carry a standard range of crystal, hand knits, T-shirts, sweatshirts, and tweed hats. **Blarney Woolen Mills** (⊠ 10–11 Main St., ☎ 064/33222) has a large selection of crafts, clothing, and souvenirs. **Bricín Craft Shop** (⊠ 26 High St., ☎ 064/34902) has an interesting collection of handmade crafts including candles, ceramics, and handwoven wool. Visit the **Frank Lewis Gallery** (⊠ 6 Bridewell La., beside General Post Office, ☎ 064/34843) for original paintings and sculptures. **MacBee's** (⊠ New St., ☎ 064/33622) is a stylish modern boutique stocking the best of Irish high fashion. The **Sweater Company** (⊠ 3 New St., ☎ 064/35406) carries classic and designer knitwear.

THE DINGLE PENINSULA

The Dingle Peninsula stretches for some 48 km (30 mi) between Tralee (pronounced tra-*lee*) in the east and Slea Head in the west. Small in size yet topographically diverse and brazenly scenic, Dingle's peninsula is composed of rugged mountains and cliffs, interspersed with softly molded glacial valleys and lakes. Along its coast stretch long, sandy beaches and rocky cliffs pounded by the Atlantic Ocean. On the coastal plains, drystone walls enclose small, irregular fields, while exceptional prehistoric and early Christian remains are scattered throughout the peninsula. Dingle is notorious for its heavy rainfall and an impenetrable sea mist, which can strike at any time of year. (If it does, sit it out in Dingle Town or the village of Dunquin, and enjoy the friendly bars, cafés, and crafts shops.) At its far western end, west of Dingle Town, the peninsula, like parts of County Kerry, is Gaeltacht: Irish is still spoken on a daily basis, although like most other Gaeltacht communities, it is bilingual nowadays, with English as the second language.

The peninsula can be covered in a long day trip of about 160 km (99 mi). (If mist or continuous rain is forecast, postpone your trip until visibility improves.) From Killarney, Killorglin, or Tralee, head for Castlemaine, and take the coast road (R561 and R559) to the town of Dingle. You'll pass through the sheltered seaside resort of Inch, 19 km (12 mi) west of Castlemaine and 45 km (28 mi) northwest of Killarney, where the head of Dingle Bay is cut off by two sand spits that enclose Castlemaine Harbour. Inch has a 6½-km (4-mi) sandy beach backed by dunes that are home to a large colony of natterjack toads.

Annascaul

52 *7 km (4½ mi) west of Inch.*

Near the junction of the Castlemaine and Tralee roads, Annascaul was an important livestock center until the 1930s. This explains why such a small village has such a wide road—cattle trading was carried out in the streets—and also why it boasts so many pubs for so few residents. Photographers will be tempted to snap **Dan Foley's** (☎ 066/915–7252) flamboyantly painted pub. Wander in for a pint; the legendary Dan Foley, who was a magician, a farmer, and an expert on local history, is no longer with us, but tales about him are still told in Annascaul.

Dingle Town

53 *18 km (11 mi) west of Annascaul, 67 km (42 mi) west of Killarney, 45 km (28 mi) west of Killorglin on R561.*

Backed by mountains and facing a sheltered harbor, Dingle, the chief town of its eponymous peninsula, has a year-round population of 1,400 that more than doubles in the summer months. Although many expect Dingle to be a quaint and undeveloped Gaeltacht village, Dingle in fact offers a wide choice of crafts shops, seafood restaurants, and pubs; still, its main streets—the Mall, Main and Strand streets, and The Wood—can be covered in less than an hour. Celebrity hawks, take note: off-season Dingle is favored as a hideaway by several celebrities, including Julia Roberts, Paul Simon, and Dolly Parton. These and others have their visits commemorated on Green Street's "path of stars."

Dingle's pubs are well known for their music, but among them **O'Flaherty's** (⊠ Bridge St., at the entrance to town, ☎ 066/915–1983), a simple, stone-floored bar, is something special and a mecca for traditional musicians. Spontaneous sessions occur most nights in July and August, less frequently at other times. Even without music, this pub provides a good spot to compare notes with fellow travelers.

Since 1985 Dingle's central attraction, apart from its music scene, has been a winsome bottle-nosed dolphin who has taken up residence in the harbor. The Dingle dolphin, or **Fungie,** as he has been named, will play for hours with swimmers (a wet suit is essential) and scuba divers, and he follows local boats in and out of the harbor. It is impossible to predict whether he will stay, but boatmen have become so confident of a sighting that they offer trippers their money back if Fungie does not appear. Boat trips (£5) leave the pier hourly in July and August between 11 and 6, weather permitting. At other times, call Jimmy Flannery Sr. (☎ 066/915–1163).

Dining and Lodging

$$ ✕ **Beginish.** Dingle is an oasis in a culinary desert, although this spot
★ is outstanding by any standard. Muted classical music floats through the small rooms, carpeted in pale green, with fresh flowers on the blue-linen tablecloths. The food imaginatively interprets French nouvelle cui-

sine; specialties include beef with Roquefort polenta, roast loin of Kerry lamb with phyllo-wrapped lambs' kidneys, and local crabmeat served with avocado and a chili mayonnaise. The wine list, with about 100 choices, includes a good selection of half-bottles. ⊠ *Green St.,* ☎ *066/915–1588. AE, DC, MC, V. Closed Mon. and mid-Nov.–mid-Mar. No lunch.*

$$ ✕ **The Chart House.** This square, sparsely furnished room on the eastern edge of town has nautical decor that complements its name. Fresh local produce is given a light and imaginative treatment by owner-chef Jim McCarthy and his team. Black pudding from Annascaul may be paired with ginger-spiced apples, wrapped in phyllo pastry, and served with a bacon jus as a starter, or you may get smoked salmon, served with a wasabi-like spiced horseradish cream. Locally caught John Dory is panfried, served with mussel risotto and a mustard grain sauce. Fillet of beef is a perennial favorite, seared and served on a bed of bubble and squeak (fried cabbage and potato) with a peppercorn sauce. For dessert, try the American-style pancakes with homemade vanilla ice cream and butterscotch sauce. ⊠ *The Mall,* ☎ *066/915–2255. MC, V. Closed Jan.–mid-Feb.*

$ ✕ **Fenton's.** Step beyond the yellow door of this town house to find a cozy, cottage-style restaurant with quarry-tile floors and local art for sale on the walls. The candlelit tables are covered in oilcloth, but the napkins are linen. The bistro-style menu is straightforward and unfussy, allowing for a quick turnover during Dingle's hectic high season. Some dishes, like the cassoulet of mussels in a garlic cream sauce, are available in starter or main-course portions. Sirloin steak is served with caramelized onions and a red-wine sauce. ⊠ *Green St.,* ☎ *066/915– 1209, AE, DC, MC, V. Closed mid-Nov.–mid-Mar.*

$$$ ✕▥ **Dingle Skellig.** A five-minute walk from town center, this is a showcase of Irish craft, art, and design. The light-wood-framed, octagonal reception area has specially commissioned stained-glass doors, and original paintings hang in the corridors. The spacious rooms have modern, pale-wood furniture and drapes and spreads with bold prints; more than half have sea views (if you want one, say so when reserving). Floor-to-ceiling windows in the Coastguard Restaurant look out over Dingle Bay; this is the town's only eatery right at the water's edge, and, as you'd expect, the specialty is seafood. ⊠ *Co. Kerry,* ☎ *066/915– 1144, ℻ 066/915–1501. 110 rooms with bath. Restaurant, bar, indoor pool, steam room, exercise room. AE, DC, MC, V. Closed Jan.– mid-Mar.*

$ ▥ **Alpine House.** The landmark Alpine is neither spanking new nor old-world. In fact, this plain, family-run, three-story establishment is one of the original guest houses in Dingle, dating from 1963. The location, at the entrance to the town with views over Dingle Bay, is superb. It is quiet, yet Dingle's harbor, pubs, and restaurants are only a two-minute walk away, and private parking is also available. Rooms are bright and cheerful, with pine furnishings, and well equipped for the price range. This value-for-money lodging has many fans, so book well ahead year-round. ⊠ *Mail Rd., Co. Kerry,* ☎ *066/915–1250, ℻ 066/915–1966. 10 rooms with bath. MC, V.*

$ ▥ **Greenmount House.** Wonderful views of the town and harbor await at this modern B&B, a short walk uphill from the town center (turn right at the roundabout at the entrance to Dingle and right again when you come to the first T-junction). A modern bungalow connects to an extension, where six suites each have a sitting room and balcony. Rooms in the original house, though smaller, are impeccable and comfortably decorated with pine beds and floral drapes and spreads. An outstanding breakfast is served in the conservatory, which connects the two buildings. ✉ *Gortanora, Co. Kerry,* ☎ *066/915–1414,* FAX *066/915–1974. 12 rooms with bath. Lobby lounge. MC, V.* 🐾

$ 🏨 **Pax House.** A kilometer (½ mile) from the town center, this solid modern bungalow has a panorama of Dingle Harbour. Stand on the balcony and watch the fishing boats return with their catch while the sun sets slowly in the west. Rooms are simple but well equipped. Breakfast is a generous affair, with fresh seafood on the menu and a selection of Irish cheeses on the buffet. ✉ *Upper John St., Co. Kerry,* ☎ *066/915–1518,* FAX *066/915–2461. 7 rooms with bath. MC, V.*

Nightlife

Nearly every bar on the Dingle Peninsula, particularly in the town of Dingle, offers music nightly in July and August. **O'Flaherty's** (☞ *above*) is a fine place for traditional music. For sing-along and dance, try **An Reált—The Star Bar** (✉ The Pier, ☎ no phone).

Outdoor Activities and Sports

BICYCLES

You're likely to remember a bike ride around Slea Head (☞ *below*) for a long time to come. Bicycles may be rented at **Dingle Bicycle Hire** (✉ The Tracks, ☎ 066/915–2166).

Shopping

Don't miss Dingle's café-bookshop, one of the first in the world. Visit **An Cafe Liteartha** (☎ 066/915–1388), for new and secondhand books of local interest, and friendly conversation. **Leác a Ré** (✉ Strand St., ☎ 066/915–1138) sells a variety of handmade Irish crafts. Lisbeth Mulcahy at the **Weaver's Shop** (✉ Green St., ☎ 066/915–1688) sells outstanding handwoven, vegetable-dyed woolen wraps, mufflers, and fabric for making skirts.

Ventry

54 *8 km (5 mi) west of Dingle Town on R561.*

The next town after Dingle along the coast, Ventry has a small outcrop of pubs and newsagents and a long, sandy beach with safe bathing and ponies for rent. Between Ventry and Dunquin, you'll find several interesting archaeological sites on the spectacular, cliff-top road along Slea Head.

En Route **Dunbeg,** an Iron Age promontory fort, can be seen on the left below the road, after you pass between two tall hedges of fuchsia bushes about 6 km (4 mi) west of Ventry (it's freely accessible; follow the signposts across fields). A fortified stone wall cuts off the promontory, and the landward side is protected by an elaborate system of earthworks and trenches. Within the enclosure is a ruined circular building, with walls up to 22 ft wide. Unlike Staigue Fort on the Ring of Kerry (☞ *above*), this was not a homestead but most probably a refuge in times of danger.

If you continue west along the coast road beyond Dunbeg, you'll see signs indicating "Prehistoric Beehive Huts"—*clocháns* in Irish. Built of unmortared stone on the southern slopes of Mt. Eagle, these cells were used by hermit monks in the early Christian period; some 414 exist between Slea Head and Dunquin. Due to the increase in traffic, some local farmers, on whose land these monuments stand, are charging a "trespass fee" of 50p to £1 from visitors.

Slea Head

★ **55** *16 km (10 mi) west of Dingle Town on R561, 8 km (5 mi) west of Ventry.*

From the top of the towering cliffs of Slea Head at the southwest extremity of the Dingle peninsula the view of the Blasket Islands and the Atlantic Ocean is unforgettable—guaranteed to stop you in your tracks. Alas, Slea Head has become so popular that tour buses, barely able to negotiate the narrow road, are causing traffic jams, particularly in July and August. **Coumenole,** the long, sandy strand below, looks beautiful and sheltered, but swimming here is dangerous. This treacherous stretch of coast has claimed many lives in shipwrecks—most recently in 1982, when a large cargo boat, the *Ranga,* foundered on the rocks and sank. In 1588, four ships of the Spanish Armada were driven through the Blasket Sound; two made it to shelter, and two sank. One of these, the *Santa Maria de la Rosa,* was found only recently and is currently being excavated by divers during the summer months.

The largest of the **Blasket Islands** visible from Slea Head, the **Great Blasket** was inhabited until 1953. The Blasket islanders were great storytellers and were encouraged by Irish linguists to write their memoirs. *The Islandman,* by Tomás O Crohán, gives a vivid picture of a hard way of life. "Their likes will not be seen again," O Crohán poignantly observed. The **Blasket Centre** explains the heritage of these islanders and celebrates their use of the Irish language with videos and exhibitions. ⊠ *Dunquin,* ☎ *066/915–6371.* ⊠ *£2.50.* ☉ *Easter–June and Sept., daily 10–6; July–Aug., daily 10–7.* ✍

Dunquin

⑤⑥ *13 km (8 mi) west of Ventry on R559, 5 km (3 mi) north of Slea Head.*

Once the mainland harbor for the Blasket islanders, Dunquin is at the center of the Gaeltacht, and it attracts many students of Irish language and folklore. David Lean shot *Ryan's Daughter* hereabouts in 1969. The movie gave the area its first major boost in tourism, though it was lambasted by critics—"Gush made respectable by millions of dollars tastefully wasted," lamented Pauline Kael—sending Lean into a dry spell he didn't come out of until 1984's *A Passage to India.* **Kruger's Pub** (☎ 066/915–6127), Dunquin's main social center, has long been frequented by artists and writers—including Brendan Behan—and it still is; it's also the only eatery for miles and a good place to stop for a bite.

Dunquin's pier (signposted from the main road) is surrounded by cliffs of colored Silurian rock, more than 400 million years old and rich in fossils. Down at the pier you'll see *curraghs* (open fishing boats traditionally made of animal hide stretched over wooden laths and tarred) stored upside down, usually covered in canvas. Three or four men walk the curraghs out to the sea, holding them aloft over their heads. Similar boats are used in the Aran Islands (☞ Chapter 6), and, when properly handled, they prove extraordinarily seaworthy. If you're interested in going out to the Blaskets, inquire at the pier in June, July, and August for boats heading to Great Blasket during the day, depending on the weather. (There's no scheduled ferry service, nor a phone.)

En Route **Clogher Strand,** a dramatic, windswept stretch of rocks and sand, is not a safe spot to swim, but a good place to watch the ocean dramatically pounding the rocks when a storm is approaching or a gale is blowing. Overlooking the beach is **Louis Mulcahy's pottery studio.** One of Ireland's leading ceramic artists, Mulcahy produces large pots and urns that are both decorative and functional. He has trained several local people to work in the studio, and visitors are welcome to watch the work in progress and to buy items at workshop prices. ⊠ *Clogher Strand,* ☎ *066/915–6229.* ☉ *Daily 9:30–6.*

Ballyferriter

⁵⁷ *5 km (3 mi) northeast of Dunquin, 14 km (9 mi) west of Dingle on R559.*

Like the other towns at this end of the Dingle peninsula, Ballyferriter is a Gaeltacht village, and mainly a holiday spot for vacationers with RVs, many of them German or Dutch. The area around here is great for walking.

One of the best-preserved, early Christian churches in all of Ireland, **Gallarus Oratory** dates from the 7th or 8th century and ingeniously makes use of corbeling—successive levels of stone projecting inward from both side walls until they meet at the top to form an unmortared roof. The structure is still watertight after more than 1,000 years. ⊠ *8 km (5 mi) notheast of Ballyferriter on R559.* ▨ *Free.*

Kilmakedar Church is one of the finest examples of Romanesque (early Irish) architecture surviving. Although the Christian settlement dates from the 7th century, the present structure was built in the 12th century. Native builders integrated foreign influences with their own local traditions, keeping the blank arcades and round-headed windows but using stone roofs, sloping doorway jambs, and weirdly sculpted heads. Ogham stones and other interestingly carved, possibly pre-Christian stones are on display in the churchyard. ⊠ *8 km (5 mi) northeast of Ballyferriter on R559.* ▨ *Free.*

En Route   The **Connor Pass** is a mountain route that passes from south to north over the center of the peninsula and offers magnificent views of **Brandon Bay, Tralee Bay,** and the beaches of North Kerry, leaving **Dingle Bay** in the south. The road is narrow, and the drops on the hairpin bends are precipitous; be sure to nominate a confident driver who is not scared of heights, especially in misty weather. It was from Brandon Bay that Brendan the Navigator (AD 487–577) is believed to have set off on his famous voyages in a specially constructed curragh. On his third trip it is possible that he reached Newfoundland or Labrador, then Florida. Brendan was the inspiration for many voyagers, including Christopher Columbus.

The summit of **Mt. Brandon** (3,127 ft) is on the left as you cross the Connor Pass from south to north and is accessible only to hikers. Do not attempt the climb in misty weather. The easiest way to make the climb is to follow the old pilgrims' path, Saint's Road; it starts at Kilmakedar Church (☞ above) and rises to the summit from Ballybrack, which is the end of the road for cars. At the summit, you'll reach the ruins of an early Christian settlement. The top can also be approached from a path that starts just beyond Cloghane (signposted left on descending the Connor Pass); the latter climb is longer and more strenuous.

Blennerville

⁵⁸ *60 km (37 mi) east of Ballyferriter, 5 km (3 mi) west of Tralee on R560.*

The five-story **windmill** with black and white sails is the main attraction in Blennerville, a village on the western edge of Tralee. The surrounding buildings have been turned into a visitor center, with crafts workshops and an exhibition recalling Blennerville's past as County Kerry's main point of emigration during the Great Famine (1845–49). ☎ *066/712–7777.* ▨ *£2.50.* ☉ *Apr.–Oct., daily 10–5.*

The **Jeanie Johnston Visitor Shipyard** has a recently built replica of a famous 19th-century emigrant vessel, a tall ship named the *Jeanie Johnston* (1847–58). After her inaugural voyage, she returns to

Blennerville in 2001, where she is to form the centerpiece of a visitor experience that includes audiovisual displays on ship building and Ireland's marine heritage, and a computerized index of Irish emigrants to North America from the 1800s to the present day. ☎ *066/712–9999.* 🖼 *£4.* ⊙ *Daily 9:30–5:30.*

A very popular **steam railway** shuttles back and forth along the 3 km (1½ mi) of tracks between Blennerville and Tralee, with departures from each terminus every half hour May through September. ☎ *066/712–7444.* 🖼 *£2.50.*

Tralee

59 *5 km (3 mi) northeast of Blennerville, 50 km (31 mi) northeast of Dingle on R559.*

County Kerry's capital and its largest town, Tralee (population 21,000) has neither ruins nor quaint architecture, yet it makes a go at attracting visitors without them. Tralee has long been associated with the popular Irish song "The Rose of Tralee," the inspiration for the annual **Rose of Tralee International Festival.** The last week of August, Irish communities from around the world send young women to join native Irish competitors; one of them is chosen as the "Rose of Tralee." Visitors, musicians, and entertainers pack the town; a horse race run at the same time contributes to the crowds. Tralee is also the home of **Siamsa Tíre**—the National Folk Theatre of Ireland, which stages dances and plays based on Irish folklore (☞ Nightlife and the Arts, *below*).

The **Kerry County Museum,** Tralee's major cultural attraction, traces the history of Kerry's people from 5000 BC to the present using dioramas and an entertaining audiovisual show; there's also a streetcar ride through a life-size reconstruction of Tralee in the Middle Ages. ⊠ *Ashe Memorial Hall, Denny St.,* ☎ *066/712–7777.* 🖼 *£5.50.* ⊙ *Sept.–July, Mon.–Sat. 10–6; Aug., Mon.–Sat. 10–8.*

♨ Ireland's biggest water complex, **AquaDome** has sky-high water slides, a wave pool, raging rapids, water cannons, and other thrills; adults can seek refuge in the Sauna Dome. ⊠ *Dingle Rd.,* ☎ *066/712–8899.* 🖼 *£5.* ⊙ *Mid-May–Aug., daily 10–10; Sept.–mid-May, weekdays 2–10, weekends 11–8.*

Lodging

$$$ 🏨 **Ballyseede Castle.** Golfers, take note: the former Fitzgerald Castle
★ is within easy reach of five of the best courses in the region. Victorian additions complement this 15th-century, three-story building. Individually decorated rooms are generously furnished with antiques, and two magnificent drawing rooms with ornamental plasterwork and marble fireplaces complete the picture. Try the Yeats room, which is one of the fanciest. Ballyseede is 3 km (2 mi) east of Tralee on the main Limerick road (N21). ⊠ *Co. Kerry,* ☎ *066/712–5799,* ☎ *066/712–5287. 12 rooms with bath. Restaurant, bar, horseback riding, fishing. MC, V.*

$$ 🏨 **Abbeygate.** Built in 1995 on the site of Tralee's old marketplace (virtually in the town center, though on a quiet spot behind today's main shopping street), this is an attractive addition to the town's hotels. Nicely sized rooms have country-style wood furniture and large, tiled bathrooms. The Old Market Place Pub, a rambling, imaginatively designed bar, seats 500 people and is built in the traditional style with wood floors, open fireplaces, and a cozy atmosphere. There is bar food at lunchtime and music and dancing nightly from June to September and at least three nights a week at other times. ⊠ *Maine St., Co. Kerry,* ☎

066/712–9888, ℻ 066/712–9821. 100 rooms with bath. Restaurant, 2 bars. AE, DC, MC, V.

$$ ☎ **Brandon.** A modern, five-story hotel in the center of town, the Brandon is not especially exciting, but it is the only place in Tralee with a pool and a fitness center. The decent-size rooms are furnished plainly with chunky pine and have uninspiring urban views. The restaurant is reputable. Rates shoot up during the Rose of Tralee Festival (late August) and the Listowel races (third week in September). ⊠ Princes St., Co. Kerry, ☎ 066/712–3333, ℻ 066/712–5019. 182 rooms with bath. Restaurant, 2 bars, indoor pool, sauna, steam room, health club, horseback riding, fishing. AE, DC, MC, V.

Nightlife and the Arts

Ballad sessions are more popular here than is traditional Irish music. **Horan's Hotel** (⊠ Clash St., ☎ 066/712–1933) has disco music and cabaret acts nightly during July and August and on weekends only during the off-season.

Try to catch the **National Folk Theater of Ireland** (Siamsa Tíre). Language is no barrier to this colorful entertainment, which re-creates traditional rural life through music, mime, and dance. ⊠ Godfrey Pl., ☎ 066/712–3055. ☎ £10. ☉ Shows July–Aug., Mon.–Sat. at 8:30; May–June and Sept., Tues. and Thurs. at 8:30.

Outdoor Activities and Sports

BICYCLES

Bicycles can be rented from **Tralee Bicycle Supplies** (⊠ Strand St., ☎ 066/712–2018).

GOLF

You are in the heart of great golfing country in Tralee. For detailed descriptions of **Ballybunion Golf Club (Old Course)** (⊠ Ballybunion, ☎ 068/27146) and **Tralee Golf Club** (⊠ West Barrow, Ardfert, ☎ 066/713–6379), see Chapter 9.

HORSEBACK RIDING

El Rancho Farmhouse and Riding Stables (⊠ Ballyard, ☎ 066/712–1840) specializes in residential trekking holidays on the Dingle trail between Tralee and the Dingle Peninsula.

OFF THE BEATEN PATH
BALLYBUNION – A detour 41 km (25 mi) northwest of Tralee on N69 and R553 will take you to this seaside resort, famous for its long, sandy beach and championship golf course (☞ Chapter 9). A large bronze statue of President Clinton commemorates a round he played in 1998.

NORTH KERRY AND SHANNONSIDE

Until several decades ago, Shannon meant little more to most people—if it meant anything at all, that is—than the name of the longest river in the British Isles, running for 273 km (170 mi) from County Cavan to Limerick City in County Clare. But mention Shannon nowadays and people think immediately of the major airport, which has become the principal gateway to western Ireland. In turn, what also comes to mind are many of the glorious sights of North Kerry and Shannonside: a slew of historic castles, including Bunratty, Glin, and Knappogue (several feature wonderful medieval banquets); Adare, sometimes called "Ireland's Prettiest Village," and the neighboring Adare Manor, one of Ireland's grandest country-house hotels; and Limerick City, which now attracts visitors tracing the memories so movingly captured in Frank McCourt's international best-seller Angela's Ashes. Picking up where the Dingle Peninsula route left off, this section begins in Listowel, in the northwest of County Kerry, and then jumps across the Kerry-Limerick border, where the first stop is in Glin, on the south side of the Shannon estuary. Limerick City, the Republic's third largest, and those parts of County Clare on the north side of the Shannon round it out. A hint to travelers arriving at Shannon Airport: if you plan to focus on the Southwest, follow the trips outlined in this chapter from back to front.

Listowel

⑩ *27 km (16 mi) northeast of Tralee on N69.*

A small, sleepy market town, Listowel only really comes alive for its annual horse race during the third week of September. You reach the town from the west by driving along a plain at the base of Stack's Mountain.

Dining

$–$$$ ✕ **Allo's Bar and Bistro.** Just off Listowel's main square, this traditional-style rustic bar dates from 1859 and serves the best local produce, freshly prepared. Chef Armel Whyte and his partner, Helen Mullane, prepare local beef and lamb but are best known for their imaginative fish recipes, which often include oysters and lobster, not otherwise widely available hereabouts. ⊠ *41 Church St.,* ☎ *068/22880. AE, MC, V. Closed Sun. No dinner Feb.*

En Route   From Listowel, head north on N69 18 km (11 mi) to **Tarbert,** the terminus for the **ferry to Killimer** in West Clare, a convenient 20-minute shortcut if you're heading for the west of Ireland. The **Shannon,** with a length of 273 km (170 mi), is the longest river in Ireland or Britain. The magnificent estuary stretches westward for a further 96 km (60 mi) before reaching the sea.

Glin

⑪ *6½ km (4 mi) east of Tarbert on N69, 51 km (32 mi) north of Tralee on N69.*

The Fitzgerald family has held the title of Knight of Glin since the 14th century. While the family has built numerous structures in the area, ★ the present **Glin Castle,** situated on the banks of the Shannon, dates only from 1785. Between 1820 and 1836 the 25th knight added crenellations and Gothic details to make the house look more like an ancestral home. A delicate plasterwork ceiling, painted in the original red and green, graces the neoclassic hall, which opens onto a splendid "flying" staircase: two risers that join to a single central tongue. The present Knight of Glin (the 29th), Desmond Fitzgerald, a Harvard-educated art historian, is an expert on Irish decorative arts (and an outspoken arts advocate), so it's fitting that the house has an exceptional collection of Irish 18th-century mahogany and walnut furniture. ☎ *068/34173.* 🖾 *£3.50.* ☉ *May–June, daily 10–noon and 2–4; other times by appointment.* 🖎

Dining and Lodging

$$$$ ✕🏨 **Glin Castle.** You can experience Irish castle living here at the Fitzgerald family home, one of the outstanding private houses of the world. The house sits on 500 acres encompassing formal gardens, parkland, and a dairy farm. Ballybunion is the nearest golf course (☞ Chapter 9). The large rooms, elegantly furnished with the outstanding Irish pieces for which Glin is renowned, are both intimate and comfortable. Country-house cuisine is served in the dining room, where portraits of Fitzgerald ancestors hang on the red walls. The menu makes use of locally produced meat and poultry and freshly caught fish, as well as vegetables and fruit from the walled garden. ✉ *Co. Limerick,* ☎ *068/34112,* FAX *068/34364. 6 rooms with bath. Tennis court, croquet, horseback riding, boating, fishing. AE, MC, V.* ✎

En Route Nine kilometers (5½ miles) east of Glin on N69, **Foynes** was the landing place for transatlantic air traffic in the 1930s and '40s. Flying boats used to land here to refuel before heading on to their European destinations. The **Flying Boat Museum,** in the terminal of the original Shannon Airport, celebrates Foynes's aviation history; it's a must for devoted flying buffs. ☎ *069/65416.* ▣ *£3.* ⊙ *Apr.–Oct., daily 10–5.*

The N69 continues to Limerick through **Askeaton,** where the ruins of a 15th-century Desmond stronghold almost cover a rocky islet on the River Deel. On the bank of the river are the well-preserved ruins of a (freely accessible) 15th-century Franciscan friary.

Castle Matrix, in Rathkeale on R518, dates from 1440, when it was in possession of the earls of Desmond. Confiscated by Elizabeth I, the castle served as a meeting place for the young poets Edmund Spenser and Walter Raleigh in 1589. Raleigh subsequently brought the first potato tubers from North Carolina to Castle Matrix, from where they were distributed throughout south Munster (the old provincial name for the region). In 1962, the late Colonel Sean O'Driscoll, an American architect, bought Castle Matrix and restored it. The library, which serves as the headquarters of the **Irish Heraldry Society,** has an important collection of documents relating to the "Wild Geese," Irish mercenaries who served in European armies in the 17th and 18th centuries. ✉ *Rathkeale,* ☎ *069/64284.* ▣ *£3.50.* ⊙ *Mid-May–mid-Sept., Sat.–Tues. 11–5.*

Adare

★ ⑥ *19 km (12 mi) southwest of Limerick City on N21, 82 km (51 mi) northeast of Tralee on N21, 40 km (25 mi) east of Glin.*

A picture-book village with several thatched cottages amid wooded surroundings on the banks of the River Maigue, Adare is rich in ruins; on foot, you can locate the remains of two 13th-century abbeys, a 15th-century friary, and the keep of a 13th-century Desmond castle. Providing that once-upon-a-time allure that has helped make this famous as one of Ireland's prettiest villages, the many stone-built cottages, often adorned with colorful, flower-filled window boxes, have a centuries-old look; they were, in fact, built in the mid-19th century by the third Earl of Dunraven, a popular landlord, for the tenants on his estate. Nowadays they house various boutiques selling traditional Irish crafts and antiques and also a gourmet restaurant (☞ Wild Geese *in* Dining and Lodging, *below*). Adare Manor, an imposing Tudor–Gothic Revival mansion, which was once the grand house of the Dunraven peerage, is now a celebrated luxury hotel (☞ Adare Manor *in* Dining and Lodging, *below*).

Dining and Lodging

$$$ ✕ **Wild Geese.** This low-ceiling thatched cottage opposite the Dunraven Arms (☞ *below*) houses a cozy, characterful series of small dining rooms in which the cooking is seriously good. Co-owner and chef Serge Coustrain trained in classical French cuisine but is not averse to adventurous combinations. Main courses include light seafood combinations such as panfried fillet of red mullet with vegetable risotto and coriander pesto. Game is a popular option in the winter months. The Wild Geese dessert platter for two features a sample of all desserts, includ-

ing fantastic homemade ice cream. ⊠ *Rose Cottage,* ☎ *061/396451. AE, DC, MC, V. Closed Sun.–Mon. and 3 wks in Jan.*

$$$$ ✕⛫ **Mustard Seed at Echo Lodge.** In 1996, after 10 years in the vil-
★ lage of Adare, owner-chef Dan Mullane moved his highly regarded restaurant 13 km (8 mi) southwest to the village of Ballingarry. Its new home, an 1884 former convent on 6 acres, has a series of themed guest rooms—black-and-white, carnival, Chinese, and so on—all of which have views over rolling countryside. Head chef Owen Sherry uses only the best local produce, plus herbs and vegetables from Echo Lodge's own organic garden. Shark is a regular among the seafood in summer, while a more typical main course is honey-glazed lamb shank with a cassoulet of beans and homegrown baby vegetables. Fruits from the garden are used in such desserts as hot crunchy apple-and-black-currant crumble with a quenelle of Calvados, cream, and caramel sauce. ⊠ *Ballingarry, Co. Limerick,* ☎ *09/68508,* FAX *069/68511. 12 rooms with bath. Restaurant, bar. AE, MC, V. Closed Sun.–Mon. Oct.–Apr.*

$$$ ✕⛫ **Dunraven Arms.** This two-story inn in Adare's picturesque village center, established in 1792, oozes old-world charm. Little wonder, then, that it is sometimes the very first port of call with visitors arriving at Shannon Airport, about 40 km (25 mi) northwest; in fact, Charles Lindbergh stayed in the inn's Room 6 while he advised on the design of the airport. The dark walls of the cozy bar and lounges are hung with paintings and prints of horseback riders. The bedrooms are comfortably and tastefully decorated with antiques. Junior suites in the newer wing are furnished with antique four-poster beds. The elegant Maigue Restaurant specializes in modern Irish cuisine, while informal dining is offered in the pretty bar area. ⊠ *Main St., Co. Limerick,* ☎ *061/396633,* FAX *061/396541. 76 rooms with bath, 6 executive suites, 14 junior suites. Restaurant, bar, indoor pool, steam room, health club, horseback riding, fishing. AE, DC, MC, V.*

$$ ✕⛫ **Fitzgeralds Woodlands House Hotel.** Under the energetic owner-management of the Fitzgerald family, the business has grown from a small B&B to a thriving modern hotel set in 44 acres of grounds on the Limerick side of the village. Rooms are relatively spacious, individually decorated in various modern styles, and well maintained. Ask for one with a view of the pretty gardens. Timmy Mac's bar is a popular meeting place for locals. The Brennan Rooms serves a traditional Irish table d'hôte menu featuring local lamb, pork, and beef. More adventurous cooking will be found in the bistro-style coffee shop in Timmy Mac's, which features a range of locally grown organic food. ⊠ *Knockanes, Co. Limerick,* ☎ *061/396118,* FAX *061/396073. 84 rooms with bath, 8 suites. 2 restaurants, bar, indoor pool, sauna, health club, horseback riding, fishing. AE, DC, MC, V.* ⚘

$$$$ ⛫ **Adare Manor.** Until 1988, this Victorian Gothic mansion was the home of the earls of Dunraven. Today it is a grand hotel owned by New Jersey business executive Tom Kane and his wife, Judy. Vast stone arches, heavy Flemish wood carvings, and an elaborately decorated ceiling adorn the lordly central hall, off which are a library and drawing and dining rooms. The glorious 36-ft-high, 100-ft-long gallery, wainscoted in oak, is the architectural highlight, though it is used only for special events. The eight "staterooms" in the original house are the most sumptuous, with huge marble bathrooms, comfortable seating areas, and stone-mullioned windows. Most rooms have super-king-size beds and non-working fireplaces; all have heavy drapes and thick carpets and overlook either the 840 acres of grounds or the River Maigue, which runs right beside the hotel. Adare's golf course, designed by Robert Trent Jones, is considered one of the best courses in Ireland (☞ Chapter 9). ⊠ *Co. Limerick,* ☎ *061/396566,* FAX *061/396124. 63 rooms with bath. Restau-*

rant, 2 bars, indoor pool, sauna, 18-hole golf course, horseback riding, fishing. AE, DC, MC, V.

Outdoor Activities and Sports

GOLF

Adare Manor Golf Club (☎ 061/396204) is an 18-hole, par-69 parkland course (☞ Chapter 9).

HORSEBACK RIDING

The **Clonshire Equestrian Center** (☎ 061/396770) has all-weather riding facilities and will also organize trail riding and residential holidays.

Shopping

Adare Gallery (⊠ Main St., ☎ 061/396898) sells Irish-made jewelry, porcelain, and woodwork, as well as original paintings. **Carol's Antiques** (⊠ Main St., ☎ 061/396977) sells antique furniture, silver, china, and objects of art from one of Adare's tiny cottages. **George Stacpoole** (⊠ Main St., ☎ 061/396409) sells a combination of antiques and books.

Limerick City

⑥ *19 km (12 mi) northeast of Adare, 198 km (123 mi) southwest of Dublin.*

At the head of the Shannon estuary and the intersection of a number of major crossroads, Limerick is an industrial port and the fourth-largest city in the Republic (population 75,000). The area around the cathedral and the castle is the old part of the city, dominated by mid-18th-century buildings with fine Georgian proportions. Economic investment is helping to spiff up its former image as an unattractive city marked by high unemployment and a higher crime rate than elsewhere in the Republic. Frank McCourt's 1996 memoir, *Angela's Ashes*—set in Limerick, where McCourt grew up desperately poor—has also helped to pique interest in the city's fortunes today (☞ Close-Up: Risen from the Ashes: Frank McCourt's Limerick, *below*). If you fly into or out of Shannon Airport, you may well pass through here; if you have a few hours to spare, check out the revitalization firsthand. (The answer to the question everyone asks—no, a direct connection is not thought to exist between the city and the facetious five-line verse form known as a limerick, which was first popularized by the English writer Edward Lear in his 1846 *Book of Nonsense*.)

Like most other Irish coastal towns, Limerick was originally a 9th-century Danish settlement, and in 1197 Richard I granted the city's charter. In 1691, after the Battle of the Boyne, the Irish retreated to the walled city, where they were besieged by William of Orange, who made three unsuccessful attempts to storm the city but then raised the siege and marched away. A year later, another of William's armies overtook the city for two months, and the Irish opened negotiations. The resulting Treaty of Limerick—which guaranteed religious tolerance—was never ratified, and 11,000 men of the Limerick garrison joined the French Army rather than fight in a Protestant "Irish" army.

★ In the Old Customs House on the banks of the Shannon in the city center, the **Hunt Museum** has the finest collection of Celtic and medieval treasures outside the National Museum in Dublin. Ancient Irish metalwork, European objets d'art, and a selection of 20th-century European and Irish paintings—including works by Jack B. Yeats—are on view. A café overlooks the river. ⊠ *Rutland St.,* ☎ *061/312833.* £4. ⊙ *Oct.–Apr., Tues.–Sat. 10–5, Sun. 2–5; May–Sept., Mon.–Sat. 10–5, Sun. 2–5.*

Limerick is a predominantly Catholic city, but the Protestant **St. Mary's Cathedral** is the city's oldest religious building. Once a 12th-century

CLOSE UP: RISEN FROM THE ASHES: FRANK MCCOURT'S LIMERICK

THE ALCOHOLIC PA. The starving, shivering brood of children. The sheep's head for Christmas. The rags for diapers. The little white coffin. And the long-suffering, abused ma. These are some of the elements that rivet the reader of *Angela's Ashes* (1996, Scribners), Frank McCourt's memoir of his impoverished childhood in Limerick—a rags-to-riches story, with the riches always being more spiritual than material. Called by *Newsweek* "the publishing event of the decade," and compared by some to the *Grapes of Wrath* in its power, pain, and joy, *Angela's Ashes* has a few million hardcover copies, won the Pulitzer, and gone Hollywood. The book seems to speak to the Irish in everyone's soul if best-seller lists, from Japan to Germany, are any indication. Not surprisingly, the city of Limerick—the rain-sodden setting of this 1930–1940s hard-luck saga—has become a new pilgrimage place for readers eager to partake of the tearfulness of it all. Busloads of McCarthys and O'Dwyers now clamber over the sites described in the book, ending up at South's pub to raise a pint in Frank's honor and to count their blessings.

In the memoir narrated from a child's perspective, Limerick looms as "a gray place with a river that kills." Many children, including McCourt's twin brothers, succumb to tuberculosis, with the rest to run an obstacle course—in shoes with flapping soles—of flea-ridden bedcovers, cane-wielding teachers, doomsday-spouting priests, and fathers who drink their paycheck, beat their wives, and tell their sons to search the skies for the Angel of the Seventh Step, bringer of new babies. Yes, Limerick has its historic sights—King John's Castle, St. Mary's Cathedral, and other landmarks of the town's medieval district—but now the down-and-out addresses of McCourt's childhood draw as much attention from visitors.

As it turns out, the slums described so unflinchingly in the book have long been torn down; in fact, Limerick today is flush with new money, renovated 19th-century Georgian row houses, prosperous shopping malls, and restaurants with fancy names like Quenelles. Even the dread River Shannon has undergone a makeover—swans, not refuse, now navigate its flowing stream. Nevertheless, plenty of *Angela's Ashes* sites remain: Leamy's National School on Hartstonge Street, where "Hoppy" O'Halloran and other schoolmasters used to beat any charges who couldn't add 19 to 47; the St. Vincent de Paul Society, where Angela once went begging for furniture and other assistance; People's Park, where Frank once took his younger brothers to make them forget their empty stomachs; plus many other emotional landmarks.

LIKE THE IRISH *SHANACHIE*—storyteller—still spouting tales at many a local pub, Frank McCourt has dug deep into the communal wellspring of Irish memory. The fact that his story has nothing to do with leprechauns and Celtic queens and everything to do with a family history that most families would wish to hide, let alone hang out in the sun to dry, says a good deal about the new Ireland and its people's wish for closure. McCourt's childhood experiences may not have been the happiest, but they are surely worth reading about, remembering, and revisiting, as so many travelers are now making a point of doing.

palace—pilasters and a rounded Romanesque entrance were part of the original structure—it dates mostly from the 15th century (the black-oak carvings on misericords in the choir stalls are from this period). The cathedral underwent a major restoration program in 2000. ⊠ *Bridge St.,* ☎ *061/416238.* ⊙ *Daily 9–6.*

The office of the **Limerick Regional Archives** (⊠ Michael St., ☎ 061/410777) is in the Granary, built in 1774 for grain storage. For a small fee, the archives provides a genealogical research service.

First built by the Normans in the early 1200s, **King John's Castle** still bears traces on its north side of the 1691 bombardment. If you climb the drum towers (the oldest section), you'll have a good view of the town and the Shannon. Inside, a 22-minute audiovisual show illustrates the history of Limerick and Ireland; an archaeology center has three excavated, pre-Norman houses; and two exhibition centers display models of Limerick's history from its founding in AD 922. ⊠ *Castle St.,* ☎ *061/411201.* 🎫 *£4.20.* ⊙ *Apr.–Sept., daily 9:30–5; Oct.–Mar., weekends 9:30–5.*

On **O'Connell Street,** you'll find the main shopping area, which consists mostly of modest chain stores. However, the street lies one block inland from (east of) the Arthur's Quay Shopping Centre, a shopping mall, which, along with the futuristic Tourist Information Center, is one of the first fruits of a civic campaign to develop Limerick's Shannonside quays. **Cruises Street,** a pedestrian thoroughfare, has Limerick's most chic shops (even though they are chiefly high-street multiples) and an inviting atmosphere (with occasional street entertainers); it is on the opposite side of O'Connell Street from the Arthur's Quay Shopping Centre.

Plassey, 5–10 minutes from Limerick on the Ring road (signposted Dublin N7), is the setting for the University of Limerick, which has a small, nicely landscaped campus.

Dining and Lodging
For lodging convenient to Shannon Airport, *see* Adare, *above,* and Ennis and Newmarket-on-Fergus *in* Chapter 6.

$$ ✕ **Freddy's Bistro.** Tucked away into a quiet lane between busy O'Connell and Henry streets, this informal two-story restaurant fills an atmospheric 18th-century coach house. Old brick walls are complemented by the warm color scheme, which glows in candlelight. Pasta with smoked chicken and seafood tagliatelle are popular main courses; for dessert try the hot, sticky toffee pudding. ⊠ *Theatre La., off Lower Glentworth St.,* ☎ *061/316141. MC, V. Closed Sun.–Mon. No lunch.*

$$ ✕ **Green Onion Café.** There's a great buzz in this hip young eatery just across the road from the Hunt Museum. The large room, which used to be the town hall, is divided into intimate spaces through judicious use of booths and two floors. Owner-chef Donal O'Callaghan creates a witty, stylish menu. Typical dishes include smoked Irish cheese (Gubbeen) and spinach tartlet, pork fillet coated in pistachio nuts with herb butter, jerk chicken with jalapeño salsa, and salmon with basil beurre blanc. For dessert, try the prune and toffee pudding with roasted nutty butterscotch. ⊠ *Old Town Hall Building, Rutland St.,* ☎ *061/400710. AE, DC, MC, V.*

$$ ✕ **Roo's Bistro Bar.** Kieran Pollard and his wife, Sindy Magner, run this restaurant in the stylish riverfront development near Jurys Inn (☞ *below*). The decor is modern, with strong colors, polished timber floors, and Aboriginal art. Kieran was a chef in Australia, as is reflected by the

eclectic cuisine. Starters may include seafood fettuccine, Caesar salad, or oysters au naturel. Fillet of beef is panfried and topped with a potato tarragon cake, and lobster comes grilled, boiled, or Thermidor. ✉ *Unit Four, Steamboat Quay,* ☎ *061/411111. MC, V. No lunch.*

$–$$ ✕ **Jasmine Palace.** Gourmet dining never really caught on in Limerick, but the city abounds in Chinese restaurants. Of several reasonably elegant ones in the town center, this second-floor eatery on the main street (opposite the Royal George Hotel) has been there longest, and many would claim that it's the best. Irish steak is served on a sizzling platter with black bean sauce; the duck and prawn pot is an individual stewpot with pieces of duck and whole king prawns in a rich, spicy sauce. ✉ *37 O'Connell St.,* ☎ *061/412484. AE, DC, MC, V. No lunch Mon.–Sat.*

$ ✕ **Mortell's.** This simple daytime restaurant decked out in bright pink and mahogany is in the main shopping area. It is both a general café, serving full Irish breakfasts and baked goods, and a seafood restaurant. It has been in the family for more than 40 years, and everything, from the doughnuts to the brown bread to the mayo, is made on the premises. Only the freshest local seafood is served. If you've never tried fish-and-chips, this is the place to start. ✉ *49 Roches St.,* ☎ *061/415457. AE, DC, MC, V. Closed Sun. No dinner.*

$$$ ✕ ⊞ **Castletroy Park.** Sitting grandly atop a hill on the outskirts of town
★ (follow signs for the N7 Dublin road), with views of the university campus and the surrounding countryside, this large, three-story, redbrick-and-stone hotel is a real gem. The lobby, with its polished wood and Oriental rugs, leads to a large conservatory–cum–coffee shop overlooking an Italian-style courtyard. The guest rooms, scented with potpourri, are decorated with solid wood furniture, muted floral drapes and spreads, and rag-rolled walls. The fitness center, one of the best around, has a large pool. You can mix with the locals in the Merry Pedlar Pub and Bistro or enjoy a formal meal in MacLaughlin's restaurant. ✉ *Dublin Rd., Co. Limerick,* ☎ *061/335566,* ℻ *061/331117. 78 rooms with bath, 7 suites, 22 executive rooms. 2 restaurants, bar, in-room data ports, indoor pool, sauna, steam room, health club. AE, DC, MC, V.* ⌖

$$ ⊞ **Greenhills.** This friendly, family-run hotel is a modern low-rise in a quiet, suburban area where N18 meets the city-center route. Twenty minutes from Shannon and five minutes from the city center, it makes an excellent touring base. The best and newest rooms are in a quiet wing above the fitness center and are big enough to have a small couch, tables, and chairs. All the rooms are color-coordinated in various styles with dark-wood furniture and tiled bathrooms. Children will love the pool, and in high season they can take part in the hotel's children's club. ✉ *Ennis Rd., Co. Limerick,* ☎ *061/453033,* ℻ *061/ 453307. 55 rooms with bath. Restaurant, bar, coffee shop, indoor pool, sauna, steam room, tennis court, children's programs (ages 4–12). AE, DC, MC, V.*

$ ⊞ **Jurys Inn.** Clean, airy, and in good shape, unlike some of Limerick's other budget spots, this hotel is part of the Jurys chain, which rents per room rather than per person. (The "inn," though, is something of a misnomer, as the hotel is large and relatively anonymous.) Rooms are a good size for the price bracket and have light-wood furnishings. It overlooks an urban stretch of the Shannon being converted from industrial to leisure use and is a short step from the main shopping and business district. ✉ *Lower Mallow St., Mount Kennett Pl., Co. Limerick,* ☎ *061/207000,* ℻ *061/400966. 151 rooms with bath. Restaurant, bar. AE, DC, MC, V.* ⌖

Nightlife and the Arts

ART GALLERIES

The **Belltable Arts Center** (✉ 69 O'Connell St., ☎ 061/319866) has a small auditorium for touring productions and exhibition space. The **Dolmen Gallery** (✉ Honan's Quay, ☎ 061/417929) shows work by contemporary artists and has an excellent café. The **Limerick City Gallery** (✉ Pery Sq., ☎ 061/310633) has a small, permanent collection of Irish art and mounts exhibits of contemporary art.

PUBS, CABARET, AND DISCOS

The Officer's Club upstairs at the **Castle Lane Tavern** (✉ Nicholas St., King's Island, ☎ 061/318044) has live dinner entertainment Tuesday through Saturday in the form of an Irish cabaret, culminating in a "hooley" with audience participation. Sessions often take place in the downstairs bar. **Hogan's** (✉ 20–24 Old Clare St., ☎ 061/411279) has a traditional "seisun" every Tuesday and Friday year-round. The **Locke Bar** (✉ 3 George's Quay, ☎ 061/413733), a riverside pub, is one of Limerick's oldest bars, dating from 1724, and has traditional music Sunday, Monday, and Tuesday nights. Traditional music is also featured at **Nancy Blake's Pub** (✉ 19 Denmark St., ☎ 061/416443) year-round Sunday–Wednesday from 9 PM.

Outdoor Activities and Sports

BICYCLES

Bicycles can be rented from **The Bike Shop** (✉ O'Connell Ave., ☎ 061/315900).

FISHING

Jim Robinson's Angling Centre (✉ St. Bridget's, Farranshone, ☎ 061/453–3808) will make arrangements for either boat or river-bank pike fishing. Fishing tackle, bait, and licenses can be obtained at **Steve's Fishing Tackle** (✉ 19 Catherine St., ☎ 061/413484).

GOLF

Castletroy Golf Club (✉ Golf Links Rd., Castletroy, ☎ 061/335753) is a challenging 18-hole, par-71 parkland course in the city suburbs. **Limerick Golf and Country Club** (✉ Ballyneety, ☎ 061/351881) is an 18-hole, par-72 parkland course.

HORSEBACK RIDING

Clarina Riding Center (✉ Clarina, near Limerick City, ☎ 061/353087) has riding by the hour.

Shopping

The **Arthur's Quay Shopping Centre** (✉ Arthur's Quay, ☎ 061/419888) near the TIO is the city's biggest indoor mall. **Celtic Bookshop** (✉ 2 Rutland St., ☎ 061/401155) specializes in books of Irish interest. **Lane Antiques** (✉ 45 Catherine St., ☎ 061/339307) is an old-world gallery selling antiques, prints, paintings, collectibles, and antiquarian books.

Bunratty Castle and Folk Park

★ ⓒ 64 *18 km (10 mi) west of Limerick City on N18 (the road to Shannon Airport).*

Bunratty Castle and Folk Park are two of those rare attractions that appeal to all age groups and manage to be both educational and fun. The castle, built in 1460, has been fully restored and decorated with 15th- to 17th-century furniture and furnishings. It gives a wonderful insight into the life of those times. As you pass under the walls of Bunratty, look for the three "murder holes," which allowed defenders to pour boiling oil on attackers below. On the castle grounds, and every bit as quaint as some first-time visitors expect all of modern Ireland to be, **Bunratty Folk Park** re-creates a 19th-century village street and has examples of the traditional rural housing of the region. Exhibits include a working blacksmith's forge; demonstrations of flour milling, bread making, candle making, thatching, and other traditional skills; and a variety of farm animals in reconstructed small holdings. An adjacent museum of agricultural machinery cannot compete with the furry and feathered live exhibits. Medieval banquets are held at the castle twice nightly (☞ Knappogue Castle, *below*) for those who want to dine on Roast Beast and quaff mead made from fermented honey, apple juice, clover, and heather. ☎ 061/361511. ☜ £5.50. ⊙ Sept.–May, daily 9:30–5:30 (last entry 4:15); June–Aug., daily 9:30–7 (last entry 6).

A *céilí* at Bunratty Folk Park is the next-best thing if you can't get a reservation for a banquet; this program features traditional Irish dance and song and a meal of Irish stew, soda bread, and apple pie. ☎ 061/360788. ☜ £27 including wine. ⊙ May–Sept., daily 5:45 and 9.

No visit to Bunratty is complete without a drink in **Durty Nelly's** (☎ 061/364072), an old-world (but touristy) pub with a fanciful decor that has inspired imitations around the world.

Knappogue Castle and Craggaunowen Project

21 km (13 mi) and 27 km (17 mi) north of Bunratty.

65 A 15th-century MacNamara stronghold, **Knappogue Castle** has been extensively restored and furnished in 15th-century style. Its name means the "Hill of the Kiss," and, like Bunratty, it's a venue for medieval-style banquets. The castle looks spectacular at night when floodlit. ✉ 5 km (3 mi) southeast of Quin on R649, ☎ 061/368103. ☜ £3.50. ⊙ May–Sept., daily 9:30–4:30.

66 The **Craggaunowen Project** includes **Craggaunowen Castle**, a 16th-century tower house restored with furnishings from the period. Particularly worth seeing are the two replicas of early Celtic-style dwellings that have been constructed on the castle grounds. On an island in the lake, reached by a narrow footbridge, is a clay-and-wattle *crannóg*, a fortified lake dwelling; it resembles what might have been built in the 6th or 7th century when Celtic influence still predominated in Ireland. The reconstruction of a small ring fort shows how an ordinary farmer would have lived in the 5th or 6th century, at the time Christianity was being established. Characters from the past explain their Iron Age (500 BC–AD 450) lifestyle; show you around their small holding, stocked with animals; and demonstrate crafts skills from bygone ages. It is a strange experience to walk across the little wooden bridge above reeds rippling in the lake into Ireland's Celtic past as a jumbo jet passes overhead on its way into Shannon Airport—1,500 years of history compressed into an instant. ✉ Kilmurry, Sixmilebridge, signposted off the road to Sixmilebridge about 10 km (6 mi) east of Quin, ☎ 061/367178. ☜ £4. ⊙ Mid-Mar.–mid-Apr., Fri.–Sun. 10–5; mid-Apr.–mid-May and mid-Sept.–mid-Oct., daily 10–6; mid-May–mid-Sept., daily 9–6.

Medieval Banquets

If you're a first-time visitor, you may not want to miss the **medieval banquets** held at the Bunratty and Knappogue castles. Do note, though, that both events cater largely to overseas visitors, many of them on organized tours, and they're likely to have little appeal for independent travelers in search of "the real Ireland." But if you're up for it, a warmhearted evening of Irish hospitality should be taken in the lighthearted spirit in which it is offered. Medieval banqueting may not be authentic, but it is fun. At Bunratty, you'll be welcomed by Irish colleens in 15th-century dress, who bear the traditional bread of friendship, then led off to a honey-and-mead reception. Before sitting down at the long tables in the candlelit great hall, you don a bib. You'll need it, because you'll be eating the four-course meal medieval-style—with your fingers! Serving "wenches" take time out to sing a few ballads or pluck the strings of a harp. Because the banquets are so popular, book as far in advance as possible. *Bunratty and Knappogue:* ☎ 061/360788. ⌘ *4-course meal, wine, mead, and entertainment £32.* ☉ *Daily, subject to demand, 5:45 and 8:45.*

THE SOUTHWEST A TO Z

Arriving and Departing

By Bus

Bus Éireann operates Expressway services from Dublin to Limerick City, Cork City, and Tralee. Add approximately one hour to the journey time by train. Most towns in the region are served by the provincial Bus Éireann network (☎ 01/836–6111 in Dublin, 061/313333 in Limerick, 021/450–8188 in Cork, 066/712–3566 in Tralee).

By Car

The main driving access route from Dublin is N7, which goes 192 km (120 mi) directly to Limerick City; from Dublin, pick up N8 in Portlaoise and drive 257 km (160 mi) to Cork City. The journey time between Dublin and Limerick runs just under 3 hours; between Dublin and Cork it takes about 3½ hours.

By Ferry/Bus

Train connections between Rosslare Harbour and Cork City, Limerick City, and Tralee all involve changing at Limerick Junction, so the journey time is usually longer than by car or bus. It is quicker and cheaper, if less comfortable, to use the long-distance buses that service the ferries. **International Express Supabus** leaves London's Victoria Coach Station daily and travels overnight via Bristol to Fishguard, then on to Cork, Killarney, and Tralee. Timetables can be obtained from any National Express Coach Station or by calling Supabus in Luton, England (☎ 1582/404511). An Irish company, **Slattery's** (☎ 020/7482–1604), runs a bus service from London to Cork and Tralee. The journey to Cork via Rosslare is by bus and ferry, and, at about 14 hours, arduous. (A note about both these phone numbers: since they are U.K. numbers, if you dial from Ireland, first dial 00 [access code] and 44 [the U.K. country code].)

Swansea–Cork Ferries (☎ 1792/456116, which can also be accessed from the U.K.) operates a 10-hour crossing between the two ports on a comfortable, well-equipped boat. Supabus (☞ *above*) will get you to the Swansea ferry from anywhere in the United Kingdom.

By Ferry/Car

From the United Kingdom, the Southwest has two ports of entry: Rosslare (in County Wexford) and Cork City. (*See* The Southeast A to Z *in* Chapter 4, for Rosslare ferry details.) From Rosslare Harbour by car, take N25 208 km (129 mi) to Cork; allow 3½ hours for the journey. You can pick up N24 in Waterford for the 211-km (131-mi) drive to Limerick City, which also takes about 3½ hours.

By Plane

The Southwest has two international airports: Cork on the Southwest coast, and Shannon in the West. **Cork Airport** (☎ 021/431–3131), 5 km (3 mi) south of Cork City on the Kinsale road, is used primarily for flights to and from the United Kingdom. Regular 30-minute internal flights are scheduled between Shannon and Dublin, Shannon and Cork, and Cork and Dublin. **Shannon Airport** (☎ 061/471444), 26 km (16 mi) west of Limerick City, is the point of arrival for all transatlantic flights; it also serves some flights from the United Kingdom and Europe. **Kerry County Airport** (☎ 066/976–4644) at Farranfore, 16 km (10 mi) from Killarney, mainly services small planes, but it is gradually increasing its commercial traffic with at least one daily flight from London. *See* Air Travel *in* Smart Travel Tips A to Z for specific information about airlines.

BETWEEN AIRPORTS AND MAJOR CITIES

By Bus from Cork Airport. Bus service runs between the airport and the **Cork City Bus Terminal** (✉ Parnell Pl., ☎ 021/450–6066) every 30 minutes, on the hour and the half hour. The ride takes about 10 minutes and costs about £2.

By Bus from Shannon Airport. Bus Éireann (☎ 061/474311) runs a regular bus service to Limerick City between 8 AM and midnight. The ride takes about 40 minutes and costs £3.50.

By Taxi. Taxis can be found outside the main terminal building at Shannon and Cork airports. The ride from Shannon Airport to Limerick City costs about £18; from Cork Airport to Cork City costs about £5.

By Train

From **Dublin Heuston Station** (☎ 01/836–6222), the region is served by three direct rail links to Limerick City, Tralee, and Cork City. Journey time from Dublin to Limerick is 2½ hours; to Cork, 2¾; to Tralee, 3¾. For passenger inquiries: ☎ 061/315555 in Limerick, 021/450–6766 in Cork, 066/712–3522 in Tralee.

Getting Around

By Bus

The provincial bus service, cheaper and more flexible than the train, covers all the region's main centers. Express services are available between Cork City and Limerick City (twice a day); Cork and Tralee (once a day, high season only); and Killarney, Tralee, Limerick, and Shannon (once a day, twice in peak season).

If you plan to travel extensively by bus, a copy of the Bus Éireann timetable (£1 from bus terminals) is essential. As a general rule, the smaller the town, and the more remote, the less frequent its bus service. For example, Kinsale, a well-developed resort 29 km (18 mi) from Cork, is served by at least five buses a day, both arriving and departing; Castlegregory, a small village on the remote Dingle Peninsula, has bus service only on Friday.

The main bus terminals are at **Cork** (✉ Parnell Pl., ☎ 021/450–8188); **Limerick** (✉ Colbert Station, ☎ 061/313333); and **Tralee** (✉ Casement Station, ☎ 066/712–3566).

By Car

A car is the ideal way to explore this region, packed as it is with scenic routes, attractive but remote towns, and a host of out-of-the-way restaurants and hotels that deserve a detour. Roads are generally small, with two lanes (one in each direction). You will find a few miles of two-lane highway on the outskirts of Cork City, Limerick City, and Killarney, but much of your time will be spent on roads so narrow and twisty that it is not advisable to exceed 64 kph (40 mph).

Getting around the Southwest is every bit as enjoyable as arriving, provided you set out in the right frame of mind—a relaxed one. There is no point in imposing a rigid timetable on your journey when you are visiting one of the last places in Western Europe where you are as likely to be held up by a donkey cart, a herd of cows, or a flock of sheep as by road construction or heavy trucks.

By Train

The rail network, which covers only the inner ring of the region, is mainly useful for moving from one touring base to another. Except during the peak season of July and August, only four trains a day run between Cork (or Limerick) and Tralee. More frequent service is offered between Cork City and Limerick City, but the ride involves changing at Limerick Junction—as does the journey from Limerick to Tralee—to wait for a connecting train. Be sure to ascertain the delay involved in the connection. (For passenger inquiries, *see* Arriving and Departing by Train, *above*.) The journey from Cork to Tralee takes about 2 hours; from Cork to Limerick, about 1¼ hours; from Limerick to Tralee, about 3 hours.

Contacts and Resources

B&B Reservation Agencies

For a small fee, **Bord Fáilte** (the Irish Tourist Board) will book accommodations anywhere in Ireland through its central reservations system. B&Bs can be booked at local visitor information offices when they are open; however, even these reservations will go through the central reservations system. For more information, *see* Lodging *in* Smart Travel Tips A to Z.

Car Rentals

All the major car-rental companies have desks at Shannon and Cork airports.

Shannon Airport: Avis (☎ 061/471094). **Budget** (☎ 061/471361). **Dan Dooley** (☎ 061/471098). **Hertz** (☎ 061/471369). **Murray's Europcar** (☎ 061/701200). **Payless Bunratty** (☎ 061/475549).

Cork Airport: Avis (☎ 021/428–1111). **Budget** (☎ 021/431–4000). **Enterprise** (☎ 021/434–7388). **Hertz** (☎ 021/496–5849). **Johnson & Perrott** (☎ 021/428–1169). **Murray's Europcar** (☎ 021/491–7300).

Killarney: Avis (☎ 064/36655). **Budget** (☎ 064/34341). **Murray's Europcar** (☎ 064/31237). **Randles** (☎ 064/31237).

Emergencies

Police, fire, and **ambulance** (☎ 999).

DOCTORS AND DENTISTS
Southern Health Board (✉ Dennehy's Cross, Cork, ☎ 021/454–5011).

PHARMACIES
Cork: Phelan's (✉ 9 Patrick St., ☎ 021/427–2511). **Killarney: P. O'-Donoghue** (✉ Main St., ☎ 064/31813). **Limerick: Roberts** (✉ 105 O'-Connell St., ☎ 061/414414).

Guided Tours

Bus Éireann, part of the state-run public-transport network, offers a range of day and half-day guided tours from June to September. They can be booked at the bus stations in Cork or Limerick or at any TIO (☞ Visitor Information, *below*). A full-day tour costs £12, half-day £7.50, both exclusive of meals and refreshments. Bus Éireann also offers open-top bus tours of Cork City on Tuesday and Saturday in July and August for £4.

Tourist Trails, which allow the visitor to follow a signposted route while reading an accompanying booklet (£1), have been set up in Cork City, Limerick City, Youghal, Kinsale, and Killarney. Booklets can be purchased at local TIOs. History buffs should inquire at TIOs for details of guided walking tours, which are organized during the summer by local volunteers.

TOUR OPERATORS

Gerry Coughlan of **Arrangements Unlimited** (⊠ 1 Woolhara Park, Douglas, Cork City, Co. Cork, ☎ 021/429–3873, ℻ 021/429–2488) can prearrange special-interest group tours of the region. Half-day and full-day tours are individually planned for groups of 10 or more to satisfy each visitor's needs.

Country House Tours (⊠ 71 Waterloo Rd., Dublin 4, ☎ 01/668–6463, ℻ 01/668–6578) organizes self-driven or chauffeur-driven group tours with accommodations in private country houses and castles. It also conducts special-interest tours, including gardens, architecture, ghosts, and golf.

Into the Wilderness (⊠ Climber's Inn, Glencar, Killarney, Co. Kerry, ☎ 066/976–0101) organizes guided walking, climbing, and cycling tours in the Kerry Highlands and Killarney National Park.

Limerick City Tours (⊠ Noel Curtin, Rhebogue, Co. Limerick, ☎ 061/ 311935) provides inexpensive walking tours of Limerick from June to September (and by arrangement other months).

Shannon Castle Tours (⊠ Bunratty Folk Park, Bunratty, Co. Clare, ☎ 061/360788) will escort you to an "Irish Night" in Bunratty Folk Park or take you to a medieval banquet at Bunratty or Knappogue Castle (☞ *above*); although the banquets aren't authentic, they are a boisterous occasion and full of goodwill.

St. Mary's Action Centre (⊠ 44 Nicholas St., Limerick, Co. Limerick, ☎ 061/318106) has a walking tour of Limerick's historic center and of locations highlighted in Frank McCourt's *Angela's Ashes.*

KILLARNEY AREA

Destination Killarney (⊠ Scott's Gardens, Killarney, Co. Kerry, ☎ ℻ 064/32638) is the foremost Killarney tour operator. Besides offering full-day and half-day tours of Killarney and Kerry by coach or taxi, the group will prearrange your visit, lining up accommodations, entertainment, special-interest tours, and sporting activities in one package. A full-day (10:30–5) tour costs from £10 to £14 per person, excluding lunch and refreshments. The Killarney Local Circuit tour is an excellent half-day 10:30–12:30 orientation. The memorable Gap of Dunloe tour at £14 includes a coach and boat trip. Add £12 for a horseback ride through the gap. More conventional day trips can also be made to the Ring of Kerry, the Loo Valley, and Glengarriff; the city of Cork and Blarney Castle; Dingle and Slea Head; and Caragh Lake and Rossbeigh.

Gray Line Shannonway Tours (⊠ Limerick TIO, Arthur's Quay, Limerick, Co. Limerick, ☎ 061/413088) organizes full-day and half-day coach tours of Killarney and the Shannon region from mid-June through September.

Jaunting cars (pony and trap) that carry up to four people can be rented at a stand outside Killarney TIOs. They can also be found at the entrance to Muckross Estate and at the Gap of Dunloe. A ride costs between £12 and £24, negotiable with the driver, depending on duration (one–two hours) and route. **Tangney Tours** (⊠ Kinvara House, Muckross Rd., Killarney, Co. Kerry, ☎ 064/33358) is the leading jaunting-car company and will also organize tours by coach or water bus, and entertainment.

The following companies will organize full-day and half-day trips by coach or taxi around Killarney and the Ring of Kerry: **Dero's Tours** (⊠ 22 Main St., Killarney, Co. Kerry, ☎ 064/31251), **Corcoran's Tours** (⊠ 10 College St., Killarney, Co. Kerry, ☎ 064/36666), **Killarney & Kerry Tours** (⊠ Innisfallon, 15 Main St., Killarney, Co. Kerry, ☎ 064/33880).

Outdoor Activities and Sports

FISHING

Your hotel or the local TIO can suggest places that rent boats. The latter will also recommend locations for coarse and game fishing, or contact the **South Western Regional Fisheries Board** (⊠ 1 Nevilles Terr., Macroom, Co. Cork, ☎ 026/41221).

HIKING

Details about the Southwest's eight long-distance hiking trails, related maps, and guides are contained in the Irish Tourist Board publication *Walking Ireland,* available from Tourist Information Offices (☞ Visitor Information, *below*).

WATER SPORTS

Because of the demands of Irish insurance laws, boat charter is still in its infancy here, with only one company in business for bareboat charter. For the same reason, dinghy rentals are not widespread, and you will need to demonstrate your competence. Sailboards, on the other hand, are relatively easy to rent. Wet suits (also rentable) are essential for sailboarding except on the hottest days in July and August. Rental of sailboarding equipment, including wet suits, starts at about £10 an hour. Sailing dinghies, as well as sailboards, can be rented by the hour (from about £6) or by the day (from about £20). Dinghy- and sailboard-rental contacts are listed under the towns that provide them.

The average cost of a six-berth yacht between 28 and 35 ft ranges from £120 per person per week (low season) to £200 (high season).

For details of residential dinghy sailing courses in the Southwest, contact **Glenans Irish Sailing Club** (⊠ 28 Merrion Sq., Dublin 2, ☎ 01/661–1481). Contact **Sail Ireland Charters** (⊠ Trident Hotel, Kinsale, Co. Cork, ☎ 021/772927, ℻ 021/774170) for bareboat charters.

Visitor Information

Bord Fáilte provides a free information service; its TIOs also sell a selection of tourist literature. For a small fee it will book accommodations anywhere in Ireland.

SEASONAL OFFICES

TIOs in the following towns are open Monday through Saturday 9–6; in July and August they are also open Sunday 9–6: **Bantry** (⊠ Co. Cork, ☎ 027/50229), open May–October. **Clonakilty** (⊠ Co. Cork, ☎ 023/33226), open May–October. **Dingle** (⊠ Co. Kerry, ☎ 066/915–1188), open March–November. **Kenmare** (⊠ Co. Kerry, ☎ 064/41233), open April–October. **Kinsale** (⊠ Pier Rd., Co. Cork, ☎ 021/477–2234, 021/477–4417 off-season, ℻ 021/774438), open March–November. **Youghal** (⊠ Co. Cork, ☎ 024/92390), open May–mid-September.

YEAR-ROUND OFFICES

The following TIOs are open Monday through Saturday 9–6; in July and August they are also open Sunday 9–6: **Blarney** (⊠ Co. Cork, ☎

021/438–1624). **Cork City** (✉ Grand Parade, Co. Cork, ☎ 021/427–3251, FAX 021/427–3504). **Killarney** (✉ Aras Fáilte, Beech Rd., Co. Kerry, ☎ 064/31633, FAX 064/34506). **Limerick** (✉ Arthur's Quay, Co. Limerick, ☎ 061/317522, FAX 061/317939). **Shannon Airport** (✉ Co. Clare, ☎ 061/471664, FAX 061/471661. **Skibbereen** (✉ North St., Co. Cork, ☎ 028/21766, FAX 028/21353). **Tralee** (✉ Ashe Memorial Hall, Denny St., Co. Kerry, ☎ 066/712–1288, FAX 066/712–1700).

6 THE WEST

*Cliffs of Moher, the Burren,
Galway City, the Aran Islands,
Connemara, County Mayo*

With the most westerly seaboard in Europe, the West remains a place apart—the most Irish part of Ireland. Nature's magnificence awaits: the majestic Cliffs of Moher, the eerie expanse of the Burren, the "hidden kingdom" of Connemara, and the Aran Islands, which do constant battle with the stormy Atlantic. But there are also grand baronial houses to visit—Ashford Castle and Kylemore Abbey—and Galway, the city that loves to celebrate. As one of Europe's fastest-growing metropolises, it has much to be happy about.

A**S ANY DUBLINER WILL TELL YOU,** the West is distinctively different from the rest of Ireland. Within Ireland, the West refers
to the region that lies west of the River Shannon; most of this
area falls within the old Irish province of Connaught. The coast of this
region lies at the far western extremity of Europe, facing its nearest
neighbors in North America across 3,200 km (2,000 mi) of Atlantic
ocean. While the East, the Southwest, and the North were influenced
by either Norman, Scots, or English settlers, the West escaped systematic
resettlement and, with the exception of the walled town of Galway,
remained purely Irish in language, social organization, and general outlook far longer than the rest of the country. The land in the West, predominantly mountains and bogs, did not immediately tempt the
conquering barons. Oliver Cromwell was among those who found the
place thoroughly unattractive, and he gave the Irish chieftains who would
not conform to English rule the choice of going "to Hell or Connaught."

Updated by
Alannah
Hopkin

It wasn't until the late 18th century, when better transport improved
communications, that the West started to experience the so-called foreign influences that had already Europeanized the rest of the country.
The West was, in effect, propelled from the 16th century into the 19th.
Virtually every significant building in the region dates either from before the 17th century or from the late 18th century onward. As in the
Southwest, the population of the West was decimated by the Great
Famine (1845–49) and by the waves of mass emigration that persisted
until the 1950s. Towns were unknown in pre-Christian Irish society,
and even today, 150 years after the famine, many residents still live on
small farms rather than in towns and villages. Especially during the
wet, wintry months, you can still walk out of your country house, hotel,
or B&B in the morning and smell the nearby turf fires.

Today, the West is, for many, the most typically Irish part of the country. Particularly in western County Galway, you'll find the highest
concentration of Gaeltacht (Irish-speaking communities) in all of Ireland, with roughly 40,000 native Irish speakers making their homes
here. When the first entirely Irish-language TV station began broadcasting in late 1996, it was from the tiny village of Spiddle, on the north
shore of Galway Bay in the heart of the Gaeltacht. Throughout this
area, you'll see plenty of signs that are in Irish only. Who would suspect that Gaillimh is the Irish for Galway? (*See* Getting Around by Car
in The West A to Z, *below,* for the Irish names of a few major locales.)
But wherever you go in the West, you'll not only see, but more importantly *hear,* the most vital way in which traditional Irish culture survives here—musicians play in pubs all over the West, and they are
recognized as being the best in the Republic (☞ Close Up: A Year-Round
Fleadh, *below*).

A major factor in the region's recovery from economic depression has
been the lure of its spectacular scenery to visitors. By and large, though,
the development that has come with the cultivation of tourism in the
West has been mercifully low-key and unobtrusive. Yes, residents of
the West have encouraged the revival of such cottage industries as knitting, weaving, and woodworking. But apart from a seaside promenade
and fun palace at Salthill, just outside Galway, the area has seen no
major investment in public amenities. Alas, this relative unconcern with
development cuts both ways—the 5,000-acre Connemara National Park
is among the few protected areas in one of Ireland's most important
bogland areas. Much of the bogland in Connemara and County Mayo
has already been farmed for its peat, leaving bereft swaths of land

lamented by environmentalists. However, in recent years the lobby for peatland protection has succeeded in getting large areas of bog set aside for conservation.

There may be no better sign of the West's aspiration both to move forward *and* still remain tied to its traditions than thatched cottages, which are popular hereabouts as holiday homes. Some of the traditional whitewashed cottages are truly old, while others have been built *to resemble* the old. Of course, there's nothing new about the West's greatest virtue for visitors, apart from its glorious scenery and high-flying capital city: its people. No matter how many times you get out of the car for a photo-op—and we guarantee that you're going to *fly* through rolls of film out here—the stories that you're going to tell when you show your friends and family those pictures are going to be about the *seisún*, or session (informal performance of traditional music), you stumbled upon in a small pub; the tiny, far-from-the-madding-crowds lake near Connemara that you made your own; and the great *craic* ("crack," or good conversation and fun) you're likely to discover wherever you go.

Pleasures and Pastimes

The Arts, Festivals, and Seasonal Events

The Irish in the West love their festivals, and they certainly know how to put on a full celebration. The Cúirt Literary Festival and the Galway Oyster Festival are but two of many annual events hosted by Galwegians; however, the highlight of the annual festival calendar is the Galway Arts Festival. During the second two weeks in July the town—already ordinarily abuzz—hosts theater, film, rock, jazz, traditional music, poetry readings, comedy acts, and visual arts exhibitions, plus a joyous parade by the street theater company Macnas, one of several local troupes to gain international recognition through the festival. Throughout the year, Galway's renovated Town Hall Theater lights up its stage for performances by, among many other groups, the 26-year-old Druid Theatre, whose adventurous productions regularly travel to Dublin and London. Not to be outdone by their neighbor to the south, a smaller but very lively festival in Connemara, the Clifden Community Arts Week, is held in mid-September, while the Westport Arts Festival takes place in the last week of September.

Dining

Because the West has a brief high season—from mid-June to early September—and a quiet off-season, it doesn't have as big a choice of small, owner-operated restaurants as other parts of Ireland. Often the best place to eat is a local hotel—Sheedy's Restaurant and Country Inn in Lisdoonvarna, for example, which has one of the few excellent chefs in County Clare, or Rosleague Manor in Letterfrack. The dominant style of cuisine in the West might be called "country-house cooking," with an emphasis on classic, but lovingly prepared, dinner-party fare: homemade pâté, a seafood cocktail, tournedos or salmon hollandaise, and chocolate mousse for dessert. Galway and Clifden boast a handful of restaurants showcasing adventurous contemporary Irish cooking, including Kirwan's Lane Creative Cuisine and K.C. Blake's in Galway, and Destry's and Erriseask House in Clifden. For price ranges, *see* Dining *in* Smart Travel Tips A to Z.

Lodging

Some of Ireland's finest country-house and castle hotels, distinguished old and new hotels, and a good choice of inexpensive B&Bs are found in the West. Ashford and Dromoland castles are undoubtedly the stars of the region, but less over-the-top places such as Ballynahinch Castle and Cashel House Hotel, both in Connemara, offer similar comfort on a smaller, more intimate scale. The region is short on moderately priced hotels (particularly Galway City), but to compensate, there are wonderful places to stay in the lower price range. One of the great attractions of staying in the West, however much you pay for the night, is the restful atmosphere of many of the hotels and guest houses, often situated in the middle of a large private estate beside a lake or river, overlooking the sea or distant mountains. Accommodations are busy in July and August, and the best places are also filled in May, June, and September, particularly on weekends, so reserve well in advance. As wonderful as many properties are, facilities like tennis courts and indoor pools are scarce, as are television sets in bedrooms, even in upscale hotels. For price ranges, *see* Lodging *in* Smart Travel Tips A to Z.

Outdoor Activities and Sports

FISHING

Some of the best angling in Europe is on the West's rivers, lakes, and seas. Game fishing for wild Atlantic salmon, wild brown trout, and sea trout is one of the main attractions of the West. The salmon and brown trout season runs from March through September, closing earlier in some waters. Generally, fishing is at its best between mid-May and mid-June. The sea trout season starts in late May and runs through September; it has been disappointing in some places in recent years due to the infestation of sea lice. Some improvement was reported in 2000, and strenuous efforts are being made to ensure a good season in 2001. Shore fishing is available all along the coast. Boats can be hired from April to October for deep-sea fishing (about £20 per person per day) from the following ports: Doonbeg, Liscannor, and Ballyvaughan in County Clare; Roundstone, Spiddle, Clifden, Cleggan, and Inishbofin Island in County Galway; and Westport, Ballina, Belmullet, and Killala in County Mayo.

HIKING AND WALKING

If you like challenging hills and relatively rough terrain, the West is excellent hiking country. The unusual, almost lunar landscape of the Burren in County Clare is less demanding than the terrain in Connemara. Here, and in the country to the north of Connemara in South County Mayo, the countryside is sparsely populated and subject to sudden changes in weather—usually a portent of rain. There are four signposted trails in the area. The Burren Way runs from Lahinch Promenade to Ballyvaughan on the shores of Galway Bay, a distance of 35 km (22 mi). The trail runs through the heart of the Burren's limestone landscape, with ever-changing views of the Aran Islands and Galway Bay. The Western Way's County Galway section extends from Oughterard on Lough Corrib through the mountains of Connemara to Leenane on Killary Harbour, a distance of 50 km (30 mi). Its 177-km (110-mi) County Mayo section known as the Western Way (Mayo) and the Foxford Way continues past Killary Harbour to Westport on Clew Bay, inland to Newport and across the boglands of north County Mayo to the Ox Mountains east of Ballina; this trail includes some of the finest mountain and coastal scenery in Ireland. The Newport Bangor Trail runs for 48 km (30 mi) through the Nephin Mountain range in northwest Mayo, connecting the two towns, Newport and Bangor. A 387-km (240-mi) hiking route though Irish-speaking Connemara stretches along the shores of Galway Bay from Spiddle to Carraroe, Carna, Letterfrack, and Clonbur, on the northern shore of Lough Corrib.

SPECTATOR SPORTS: SAILING AND HORSE RACING

Galway hookers, solid, heavy, broad-beamed sailing boats with distinctive, gaff-rigged, brownish-red sails, can still be seen on the waters of Galway Bay. Enthusiasts maintain a small fleet and hold frequent races on the bay in July and August (☞ Kinvara, *below*). Many small horse races are held throughout the year in the West, including trotting races, pony races, beach derbies, and the like. Local Tourist Information Offices (TIOs) can provide details. The main event is the Galway Races, beginning immediately following the end of the Galway Arts Festival, at the end of July and beginning of August. This boisterous, full-scale festival attracts a massive crowd and all manner of sideshows, with cardsharps, fortune-tellers, rifle ranges, and open-air concerts.

Pubs and Live Traditional Music
No matter how you choose to spend your time in the West, be sure to visit at least one pub. For whether or not you drink a pint of Guinness or any other alcohol, pubs here are more than just bars—they're the area's vital social centers, places to connect with natives and other travelers, to pick up leads about current and local activities, and, above all, to hear Irish traditional music played live (☞ Close Up: A Year-Round Fleadh, *below*).

Shopping
Galway City and Ennis are the West's major shopping areas. Their most interesting shops carry crafts, Irish-made clothing, jewelry, books, and antiques. Connemara has a large concentration of crafts shops; it is the best place in Ireland to buy an Aran sweater—either the traditional, off-white designs or the plain, linen and cotton Aran-style knits in jewel-tone red, green, or blue. Galway City is the place to buy a Claddagh ring. On the Aran Islands, sally rods are woven into attractive baskets (once used for potatoes or turf), and colorful woven belts, known as *críoses,* are hand-plaited from strands of wool. Handwoven woolen or mohair shawls or rugs provide an affordable touch of luxury. Musical instruments, traditionally made furniture, Connemara marble jewelry, modern lead crystal, batik, handmade beeswax candles, and dried flower arrangements are among the West's many other goods—in addition to tweeds and sweaters, of course.

Exploring the West

Our coverage of the West is organized into five parts, which cover this territory from south to north. Our first section, the Burren and Beyond—West Clare to South Galway, picks up minutes from Shannon Airport and not far from Ennis, the gateway to coastal County Clare. Our second section shows you the very best of buzzing, bustling Galway City, and our third takes you out to the three Aran Islands, standing guard at the mouth of Galway Bay. Our fourth section, Through Connemara and County Mayo, brings you north of Galway Bay and west of Galway City into the fabled "hidden kingdom" of Connemara and beyond to the highlights of County Mayo: monumental Croagh Patrick, the pretty town of Westport, and the breathtaking Achill Island. Our fifth section gives a brief overview of some of the highlights along the North Mayo Coast. Allow at least four days for exploring the region, seven days if you aim to visit the Aran Islands and Achill Island. Although distances between sites are not great, you may want to take scenic—and slower—national secondary routes. Covering 80 km–112 km (50 mi–70 mi) per day on these roads is a comfortable target.

Numbers in the text correspond to numbers in the margin and on the West and Galway City maps.

Great Itineraries
IF YOU HAVE 4 DAYS

Assuming you're arriving in the West via Shannon Airport or by crossing into County Clare via the Killimer–Tarbert ferry, you'll first pass through either **Ennis** ② or **Kilrush** ③. If the weather's good, head for the beach town of **Kilkee** ④. If not, head right for the **Cliffs of Moher** ⑥. Next stop should be the heart of the **Burren** ⑨, though you might want to stop at the **Burren Display Centre** in Kilfenora first to pick up more information about Ireland's strangest landscape. Both **Doolin** ⑦ and ☷ **Lisdoonvarna** ⑧ are within the Burren and famous for their traditional music. Spend the night in Lisdoonvarna, or in ☷ **Kinvara** ⑭ or ☷ **Ballyvaughan** ⑩, both on Galway Bay.

On your second day, head right for ☷ **Galway City** ⑮–㉙. Spend the morning exploring Galway on foot, poking around its shops, and finding out whether any theater or other performing arts events are on that night. In the afternoon, take a cruise up the River Corrib or drive out along the north shore of Galway Bay to **Salthill** ㉙ and beyond into the Gaeltacht. Eat an early dinner right in Galway before taking in some theater, or drive to one of the restaurants outside town for a leisurely dinner. Whether or not you go to the theater, try to get to a pub in town for some traditional live music and good *craic* before heading off to bed.

On your third day, you can kick around Galway—easily the liveliest city in Ireland after Dublin and the only large city in the West, so be sure you've had your fill of its buzz before you depart. There are plenty of special events to keep you busy, particularly if you're here during a festival. You also might want either to take the ferry out to the **Aran Islands** ㉚–㉜ for the day or make the quick trip south to **Coole Park** ⑫ and **Thoor Ballylee** ⑬, the two southernmost sites in the west of Ireland important to W. B. Yeats (most of the rest are in County Sligo [☞ Chapter 7]). Either way, again spend the night in Galway or at one of the country houses outside town (or perhaps even in a B&B on the Aran Islands, if you make it out there). Alternatively, if you're ready for scenery and a smaller town, head out through the moorlands of Connemara through **Oughterard** ㉝ to the Alpine-like coastal village of ☷ **Clifden** ㉟, where you'll find gorgeous scenery and a surprisingly good selection of pubs and restaurants. Spend the night here or in a country house, hotel, or B&B in or around ☷ **Cashel** ㉟ or ☷ **Letterfrack** ㊳.

If you've spent your third night in Galway, follow the alternative day-three itinerary above, but don't linger too long in Clifden. Push on, as should those who stayed the night in or near Clifden, first to **Connemara National Park**, just outside **Letterfrack** ㊳, then just beyond to the **Kylemore Valley**'s ㊴ much-photographed Kylemore Abbey, which has a breathtaking lakeside location and a better-than-average crafts shop. Continue through **Leenane** ㊵ to ☷ **Westport** ㊶, the prettiest village in County Mayo and a good place to spend the night. On the way, you won't be able to miss the distinctive conical shape of **Croagh Patrick**, the penitential mountain that was a refuge of St. Patrick during his years spent converting Ireland to Christianity. Try to be in Westport on Thursday, when its old-fashioned farmers' market is held. On your fourth day, make the walk up Croagh Patrick or stroll around Clew Bay seeing how many islands you can count. If the weather cooperates, you might want to venture out to **Achill Island** ㊷. At the end of the day, continue on north to Sligo (☞ Chapter 7) or head for a Midlands destination (☞ Chapter 3).

The West

Achill Island 42
Doogort
Keel
Achill Sound
Clare
Mulrany
Lough Peeagh
R319
N59

TO BANGOR
Nephin Beg Range
Céide Fields 45
Cross-molina
Ballina 44
Lough Conn
TO KILLALA
Foxford
N5
River Moy
Swinford
N58

Newport
Clew Bay
MAYO
Pontoon
Ballyvary
N5
N5

Castlebar 43
N60

Westport 41
R335
N60
Claremorris
N17

Louisburg
Croagh Patrick
Sheffry Hills
N59
Lough Mask
Ballinrobe
Tuam
N17

Inishturk
Mweelrea Mtns.
Delphi
N59
Leenane 40
Cong 34
N84
TO CRAUGHWELL

Inishbofin Island
Killary Harbour
Kylemore Valley 39
Kylemore Abbey
Renvyle
Letterfrack 38
Connemara Nat'l Park
N59
GALWAY

Clifden 37
Ballynahinch 36
R341
R341
Cashel 35
Recess
N59
Maam Cross
Lough Corrib
Oughterard 33
Rosscahill
N59
Athenry
N6

Ballyconneely
Bertraghboy Bay
R340
R340
R336
R336
Galway City 15 29
N6
Oranmore
N18

Ros an Mhil (Rossaveal)
R336
Spiddle
Barna
Salthill
Galway Bay
Clarinbridge
Kilcolgan
Kinvara 14
Thoor Ballylee 13

ATLANTIC OCEAN
Inishmore 30
Dun Aengus Fort
Kilronan
Inishmaan 31
Aran Islands
32 **Inisheer**
Conor Fort
Doolin 7
Ballyvaughan
10
Ailwee Cave
The Burren 9
Coole Pk. 12
Gort
N66
Lough Cutra
CLARE

The Cliffs of Moher 6
R478
Burren Centre
8 **Lisdoonvarna**
R476
R480
R460
N18

Lahinch 5
Kilfenora
Ennistymon
Corofin 11
Mal Bay
N67
R474
N85
Ennis 2
Clarecastle

Milltown Malbay
Newmarket-on-Fergus 1
Shannon

Kilkee 4
R487
Kilrush 3
Killimer
N68
River Shannon
Askeaton

Loop Head
Mouth of Shannon
Tarbert
Glin
N69
LIMERICK
Rathkeale

KERRY

0 — 10 miles
0 — 15 km

N

Our four-day itinerary can easily be expanded into a seven-day trip, with the following modifications: spend a full two days exploring western County Clare, staying one night in the seaside town of **Lahinch** ⑤ (especially if you're a golfer or are traveling with one) and another in any of the towns noted above. Depending on how much time you want to spend in Galway, you might want to make it to **Coole Park** ⑫ and **Thoor Ballylee** ⑬ on one of your first two days in the West, rather than taking a bite out of the time you have for Galway and the Aran Islands. Begin your third (rather than your second) day by heading to 🆃 **Galway City** ⑮–㉙. Plan on spending three full days based either right in or just outside Galway. Spend two of these days in Galway itself and one on a day trip out to the **Aran Islands** ㉚–㉜. On your sixth day, follow our alternative day-three itinerary above, ending up either in 🆃 **Cashel** ㉟, 🆃 **Clifden** ㊲, or 🆃 **Letterfrack** ㊳ for the night. Then follow our day-four itinerary above for your seventh day.

When to Tour the West

"Soft weather," as the Irish call on-again, off-again rainy days, is almost always a possibility in the West, but the months of May and October are likelier to be drier than the rest of the year. The Burren is at its best in May, when the wildflowers are in season. April, May, and October are good times for an off-peak visit. In July and August, expect to rub elbows with Irish families taking their holidays here; these are also the best months to hear traditional music. It doesn't take many visitors to overwhelm Galway City's narrow streets, so if you don't love crowds, steer clear in late July, when the Arts Festival and Galway Race take place back-to-back. Many restaurants and accommodations in Connemara and the Burren are seasonal and close from October to Easter, although thanks to a steady rise in demand, the season is definitely extending slightly each year. If you do choose to visit the West between November and March, your choice of places to stay and to eat will be limited, but you do get to feel as though you have the place to yourself. A word of warning, though: during the winter, the weather in the West can be harsh, with gales and rain sweeping in day after day from the Atlantic.

THE BURREN AND BEYOND—WEST CLARE TO SOUTH GALWAY

County Clare claims two of Ireland's unique natural sites: the awesome Cliffs of Moher and the stark, mournful landscape of the Burren, which hugs the coast from Black Head in the north to Doolin and the Cliffs of Moher in the south. Yet western County Clare is widely beloved among native Irish for a natural phenomenon significantly less unique than these: its beaches. Though just another Irish beach town to some, Kilkee, to name just one, is a favorite summer getaway. So whether you're looking for inimitable scenery or just a lovely beach to plunk down on for a few hours and relax in the sun (if you're lucky!), this section will introduce you to the natural wonders of the West.

This journey begins at Newmarket-on-Fergus, within minutes of Shannon Airport, and it makes a good jumping-off point for a trip through the West if you've just arrived in Ireland and are planning to head for Galway. It also follows directly from the end of Chapter 5, which concludes 10 km (6 mi) down the road, at Bunratty Castle and Folk Park (and the Knappogue Castle and Craggaunowen Prolect, also nearby), so be sure to take a moment to glance at those sights to decide whether to include them as you get under way. This area is also the connecting link between County Limerick (and other points in the Southwest) and Galway City. If you're approaching it from the Southwest and you're not going into Limerick City itself, it's easy to begin exploring the region from Killimer, reached via the ferry from Tarbert (☞ Arriving and Departing *in* The West A to Z, *below*).

Newmarket-on-Fergus

❶ *13 km (8 mi) north of Shannon Airport on N18.*

A small town in County Clare, Newmarket-on-Fergus is chiefly remarkable nowadays as the town nearest to Dromoland Castle, formerly the home of Lord Inchiquin, chief of the O'Brien clan.

Dining and Lodging

✍ *following the text of a review is your signal that the property has a Web site, where you will find details and, usually, images; for a link, visit www.fodors.com/urls.*

$$$$ ✕🏠 Dromoland Castle. Dromoland is the ancestral home of the
★ O'Briens, the descendants of Brian Boru, High King of Ireland. The massive, turreted, neo-Gothic castle—dating from the 19th century, when it replaced its 16th-century predecessor—looks the part, standing regally beside a scenic lake, surrounded by tidily landscaped formal gardens, discreetly landscaped private homes, and a golf course. Inside, the grand, plushly carpeted rooms are graced with large ancestral portraits, crystal chandeliers, and oak paneling. Bedrooms overlook the old Queen Anne stable yard and feature Regency-style furniture. The vast suites have ruched drapes on the tall windows, great views over the park, and antiques, many of them Irish-Georgian. Outstanding Continental cuisine is served in the formal, oak-wainscoted Earl of Thomond Restaurant, while a less formal atmosphere prevails at the Fig Tree restaurant in the Dromoland Golf and Country Club. ⊠ *Co. Clare,* ☎ *061/ 368144,* 𝔽𝔸𝕏 *061/363355. 74 rooms with bath. Restaurant, bar, 18-hole golf course, 2 tennis courts, Ping-Pong, fishing, bicycles. AE, DC, MC, V.* ✍

$ ✕🏠 Hunter's Lodge. A comfortable, unpretentious village pub, the lodge makes an ideal first or last stop for visitors to the West who are traveling via Shannon Airport, 12 km (8 mi) down the road. The pub has an old-world style, with an open fire and a quiet local trade. Well-equipped rooms have timber floors with scatter rugs and are attractively decorated with select pieces of old oak furniture. The restaurant, known for its cheerful service and simply prepared surf and turf, is a good value. ⊠ *The Square, Co. Clare,* ☎ *061/368577,* 𝔽𝔸𝕏 *061/368057. 6 rooms with bath. Restaurant, bar, free parking. AE, DC, MC, V.*

Outdoor Activities and Sports

Dromoland Golf Course (☎ 061/368444) is one of the most scenic in the country, set in a 700-acre estate of rich woodland on the grounds of Dromoland Castle. The 18-hole, par-71 course has a natural lake that leaves little room for error on a number of holes.

Ennis

❷ *9½ km (6 mi) north of Newmarket-on-Fergus on N18, 37 km (23 mi) northwest of Limerick, 142 km (88 mi) north of Tralee.*

A major crossroads and a convenient stop between the West and the Southwest, Ennis is the county town of County Clare, a pleasant market town with an attractively renovated, pedestrianized center. While the quaint wooden shopfronts and brightly painted premises may look old, the majority of them date only from the 1990s. Ennis has always fostered traditional arts, especially fiddle playing and step-dancing (a kind of square dance). The **Fleadh Nua** (pronounced fla-*nooa*) festival at the end of May attracts both performers and students of Irish music. Two statues in Ennis bear witness to the role its citizens have played in Irish democracy. On a tall limestone column above a massive pediment in the town center stands a **statue of Daniel O'Connell** (1775–1847), "The Liberator" (☞ En Route *under* Sneem *in* Chapter 5), who was a member of Parliament for County Clare between 1828 and 1831 and instrumental in bringing about Catholic Emancipation. Outside the courthouse (in the town park, beside the River Fergus, on the west side of Ennis) stands a larger-than-life bronze **statue of Eamon De Valera** (1882–1975), who successfully contested the election here in 1917, thus launching a long political career. Although De Valera was born in the United States, his maternal forebears were from County Clare. He was the dominant figure in Irish politics during the 20th century, serving as prime minister for most of the years from 1937 until 1959, when he resigned as leader of Fianna Fáil, the party he founded, and went on to serve as president of Ireland until 1973.

Dining and Lodging

$–$$ ✕ **The Cloister.** The restaurant is built into the walls and garden of Ennis's 13th-century abbey beside the river in the heart of town. Stone walls and floors and open fires give a robust character to the main rooms, while there is a conservatory for lighter, brighter dining. The bar food menu features old reliables such as Irish stew (lamb, potato, onion, and carrots) and fish pie with mashed potato topping, while more classic Continental cuisine is offered on the restaurant menu. Local, traditional musicians, who are among the best in the country, hold sessions almost every night at the bar. ⊠ *Club Bridge, Abbey St.,* ☎ *065/682–9521. MC, V. Closed lunch Sun.*

$$ ✕▥ **West County.** This lively modern hostelry, affiliated with Best Western, is a popular stopping point on the Limerick–Galway road (N18), and five minutes' walk from Ennis's lively town center. It caters successfully to both the visitor and the business traveler and has a large fitness center, unusual in the West. Rooms are good-size, and while most overlook the car park, they are at least quiet. Service is helpful and friendly in spite of the relatively large size of the hotel. In July and August there is nightly Irish cabaret-style entertainment at the bar. Boru's Porterhouse serves traditional Irish fare including local steak and seafood. ⊠ *Co. Clare,* ☎ *065/682–8421,* ℻ *065/682–8801. 152 rooms with bath. 3 indoor pools, sauna, health club, fishing. AE, DC, MC, V.* ✧

$$$$ ▥ **Carnelly House.** This 250-year-old Queen Anne–style, redbrick house is an elegant, convenient base for exploring the West, 5 km (3 mi) south of Ennis and 16 km (10 mi) from Shannon Airport. The perfectly proportioned drawing room has elaborate plasterwork decorations. The large, comfortable bedrooms have canopied or four-poster beds and bucolic views over the 100-acre estate. Hosts Dermot and Rosemarie Gleeson will fill you in on the beguiling house's colorful history. ⊠ *Clarecastle, Co. Clare,* ☎ *065/682–8442,* ℻ *065/682–9222. 5 rooms with bath. Horseback riding, fishing. MC, V. Closed Dec.– Feb..* ✧

Nightlife

Although Ennis is not as fashionable as, say, Galway, it is one of the West's traditional music hot spots. Below are the pubs where you're likeliest to hear sessions, but keep in mind they don't necessarily take place every night and the scene is constantly changing. Phone ahead to check whether a session is happening.

Cruise's (✉ Abbey St., ☎ 065/684–1800). Fawl's (✉ The Railway Bar, 69 O'Connell St., ☎ 065/682–4463). Kerins' (✉ Lifford, ☎ 065/682–0582). Knox's (✉ Abbey St., ☎ 065/682–9264). O'Halloran's Bar (✉ 8 High St., ☎ 065/682–3090). Poet's Corner Bar (✉ Old Ground Hotel, O'Connell St., ☎ 065/682–8167). The Temple Gate (✉ The Square, ☎ 065/682–3300).

Outdoor Activities and Sports

BICYCLING

Cycle into the Burren on a bike rented from M.F. Tierney Cycles & Fishing (✉ 17 Abbey St., ☎ 065/682–9433).

GOLF

Ennis Golf Club (✉ Drumbiggle Rd., ☎ 065/682–4074) is an 18-hole, par-70 parkland course overlooking the town.

HORSEBACK RIDING

Ballyshannon Riding Establishment (✉ Ballyshannon House, Quin, ☎ 065/682–5645) has woodland trail riding and beginners' lessons and will provide riding equipment.

Shopping

Stop in at the Antique Loft (✉ Clarecastle, ☎ 065/684–1969) for collectibles and pine and mahogany antiques. The Belleek Shop (✉ 36 Abbey St., ☎ 065/682–9607) carries Belleek china, Waterford crystal, and Donegal Parian china, as well as Lladró, Hummel, and other collectible china. Carraig Donn (✉ 29 O'Connell St., ☎ 065/682–8188) stocks Waterford glass and other Irish crystal, Belleek and other fine china, and its own array of knitwear. At Clare Business Center (✉ Francis St., ☎ 065/682–0166) you'll find a variety of crafts workshops that sell to the public. The Inis Gallery (✉ 11 Chapel La., ☎ 065/682–1559) sells Irish fine art prints and maps. Shannon Crystal (✉ Sandfield Center, Galway Rd., ☎ 065/682–1250) is a factory outlet that displays the craft of hand-cutting lead crystal.

Kilrush

❸ *43 km (27 mi) southwest of Ennis on N68.*

Like most other mid-19th-century towns in West Clare, Kilrush was laid out with a large central square radiating out into the town's main streets. The widest of these leads to the harbor and the docks. This plan makes the small market town (population 3,000) seem bigger than it actually is. An exhibition entitled "Kilrush in Landlord Times" explains the history of the town from its beginnings in the late 18th century; it's also the starting point for a heritage walk through the town's streets that takes you back to the 19th century. ✉ *Town Sq.,* ☎ *065/ 905–1577.* ⚏ *£1.* ☉ *May–Sept., Mon.–Sat. 9:30–5:30, Sun. noon–4.*

Outdoor Activities and Sports

Kilrush Golf & Sports Club (✉ Parknamoney, Ennis Rd., ☎ 065/905–1138) is an 18-hole, par-70 course that overlooks the Shannon estuary.

Scattery Island Ferries (✉ Kilrush Marina, Co. Clare, ☎ 065/905–1327) run a 20-minute boat trip to Scattery Island, a picturesque destination that has a ruined 6th-century monastic settlement complete with round tower. From May to early September, two-hour dolphin-watching trips (£10) run out to the Shannon Estuary, where a school of 40 or so bottle-nosed dolphins regularly plays. Trips are weather permitting and subject to demand; phone ahead to confirm.

Kilkee

❹ *12 km (8 mi) west of Kilrush on N68.*

Kilkee is one of the most beloved west-coast beach resorts among native Irish people, many of whom have summered here for generations. Its major draw is its safe bathing—both in the waters along its magnificent long, sandy beach and in deep rock pools known as Pollock holes, which remain full at low tide (they attract scuba divers as well as swimmers). From Kilkee, you can take an excursion to **Loop Head Lighthouse** on R487, about a 38-km (24-mi) round-trip. Loop Head is the westernmost point of County Clare, situated at the northern tip of the mouth of the Shannon, the very end of its long estuary.

Outdoor Activities and Sports

Kilkee Golf and Country Club (✉ East End, ☎ 065/905–6048) overlooks the sea and has spectacular, cliff-edge holes. Founded in 1896, it was expanded in 1994 to an 18-hole, par-72 course.

En Route The main route heads north up the coast on N67. Sandy beaches and more Pollock holes can be found by taking a left off the main road at any sign that indicates STRAND and traveling for about 2½ km (1½ mi).

Lahinch

❺ *47 km (30 mi) north of Kilkee on N67, 30 km (18 mi) west of Ennis on N85.*

Lahinch is a busy resort village beside a long, sandy beach backed by dunes, best known for its links golf courses and—believe it or not—its surfing. In 1972, the European Surfing Finals were held here, putting Lahinch on the world surfing map. Today Tom and Rosemary Buckley's **Lahinch Surf Shop** (✉ The Promenade, ☎ 065/708–1543), Ireland's oldest (open since 1990), is ground-zero for County Clare surfers.

Dining and Lodging

$ ✗ **Egan's.** For all appearances, this is a normal Victorian pub with an open fire and orange lightbulbs casting a romantic glow. The difference is the wine list—good Bordeaux is sold by the case to customers all over Ireland, but Cru Bourgeois and other less-expensive wines are also sold by the bottle at supermarket prices (less than 10% markup compared to the standard 33%) and can be sampled for £2 a glass. Sandwiches and light snacks are served until 9 PM. ✉ *Liscannor,* ☎ *065/708–1430. No credit cards.*

$$ ✗▣ **Aberdeen Arms.** This beautifully refurbished Victorian seaside hotel
★ is a model of its kind, offering elegance and comfort in a friendly, easygoing setting. Humorous golfing prints hanging on the dark-paneled walls of the bar and grill room appeal to the many golfers who stay here. The newest rooms face the sea and have spectacular skylights and windows. All rooms are large and tastefully decorated with built-in, cream-color melamine closets; plain carpets; and matching cream-floral drapes and spreads. Some rooms have Georgian-style tables and chairs. The main dining room offers a varied menu of French-Irish cuisine. ✉ *Co. Clare,* ☎ *065/708–1100, FAX 065/708–1228. 55 rooms with bath. 2 restaurants, 2 bars, sauna, 10 tennis courts, health club, fishing, bicycles. AE, DC, MC, V.* ✎

Nightlife

For traditional music try the **19th** (☎ 065/708–1440).

Outdoor Activities and Sports

The 6,613-yard, 18-hole, par-72 championship course at **Lahinch Golf Club** (☎ 065/708–1003), which opened in 1892, has challenging links following the natural contours of the dunes. The **Castle Course** (☎ 065/708–1003), the newer 18-hole, par-72 Lahinch course, offers a more carefree round of seaside golf, with shorter holes than the championship course (☞ Chapter 9).

Shopping

The **Design Lodge** (☎ 068/708–1744) is a small shop that carries Irish-made goods, including sweaters, linen, tweed, and other fine gift items.

The Cliffs of Moher

★ ❻ *10 km (6 mi) northwest of Lahinch on R478.*

One of Ireland's most breathtaking natural sites, the majestic Cliffs of Moher rise vertically out of the sea in a wall that stretches over a long, 8-km (5-mi) swath and as high as 710 ft. You can see stratified deposits of five different rock layers in the cliff face. Numerous seabirds, including a large colony of puffins, make their home in the shelves of rock on the cliffs. On a clear day you can see the Aran Islands and the mountains of Connemara to the north, as well as the lighthouse on Loop Head and the mountains of Kerry to the south. **O'Brien's Tower** is a defiant, broody sentinel built at the cliffs' highest point. The parking area is a favorite spot of performers; in the high season, there's likely to be free entertainment—step dancers, fiddle players, or even a one-man band. The **visitor center,** a good refuge from passing rainsqualls, has a gift shop and tearoom. ☎ *065/708–1171.* ⌨ *Free.* ☉ *Cliffs and O'Brien's Tower freely accessible; visitor center mid-Feb.–Apr., daily 10–5; May–June and Sept., daily 10–6; July–Aug., daily 9:30–6:30.* ❧

Doolin

❼ *6 km (4 mi) north of the Cliffs of Moher on R479.*

A tiny village consisting almost entirely of B&Bs, hostels, pubs, and restaurants, Doolin is widely said to have three of the best pubs in Ireland for traditional music (☞ Nightlife *and* Close Up: A Year-Round Fleadh, *below*). But with the worldwide surge of interest in Irish music during the last decade, the village is more of a magnet for European musicians than it is for young, or even established, Irish artists. On **Doolin Pier,** about 1½ km (1 mi) outside the village, local fishermen sell their catch fresh off the boat—lobster, crayfish, salmon, and mackerel. From spring until early fall (weather permitting), a regular ferry service takes visitors for a 30-minute ride to Inisheer, the smallest of the Aran Islands (☞ Getting Around *in* The West A to Z, *below.*).

Dining and Lodging

$$$ ✕ **Bruach na Haille.** The name means "the bank of the river Aille," and the river can be seen from the side windows of this charming cottage restaurant, owned by John and Helen Browne for 20 years. The low-beamed, cozy rooms have flagstone floors; old dressers laden with colorful delft china; and open turf fires. Lobster from Doolin Pier is usually on the menu, as is a renowned sirloin steak with Irish whiskey sauce. ⌧ *Roadford,* ☎ *065/707–4120. AE, DC, MC, V. Closed Nov.–mid-Mar. No lunch.*

$$ ✕⌸ **Aran View House.** On the coast road in the Fanore direction, about 10 minutes' walk from Doolin village, this hotel commands magnificent views of the Aran Islands in the west, Doolin Pier and the Cliffs of Moher in the south, and the gray limestone rocks of the Burren to the north. The 1736 house has been modernized, with lovely antique touches such as four-poster beds and Georgian reproduction furniture. Bay windows in the ambitious restaurant let you savor the views, while the decor impresses with Regency chairs and dusky pink napery.

✉ *Co. Clare,* ☎ *065/707–4061,* FAX *065/707–4540. 19 rooms with bath. Restaurant, bar, fishing. AE, DC, MC, V. Closed Nov.–Mar.*

Nightlife

Doolin's three pubs famous for their traditional music sessions are **Gus O'Connor's** (☎ 065/707–4168), **McDermott's** (☎ no phone), and **Mc-Gann's** (☎ 065/707–4133). Gus O'Connor's also serves excellent bar food.

Outdoor Activities and Sports

Cycle along the coast on a bike rented from **Patrick Moloney, Doolin Hostel** (☎ 065/707–4006).

Shopping

Doolin Crafts Gallery (☎ 065/707–4309), beside the cemetery and the church, carries only Irish-made goods, including sweaters, modern lead crystal, linen, lace, and tweed. A jeweler's workshop and a resident batik maker are also on the premises. Don't miss the 1-acre garden, which has more than 600 plants from all over the world. The garden and the Flagship Restaurant are open daily Easter–September.

Lisdoonvarna

❽ *5 km (3 mi) east of Doolin on R478.*

One of only two spa towns in Ireland (the other is Enniscrone, in western County Sligo), Lisdoonvarna has several sulfurous and iron-bearing springs with radioactive properties, all containing iodine. The town grew up in the late 19th century to accommodate visitors who wished to "take the waters." Its buildings reflect a mishmash of mock-architectural styles: Scottish baronial, Swiss chalet, Spanish hacienda, and American motel. Depending on your taste, it's either lovably kitschy or unappealingly tacky. If you're curious about health cures, the **Lisdoonvarna Spa and Bath House** is worth a visit. Iron and magnesia elements make the drinking water taste terrible (as does most spa water). In comparison, the bathing water is pleasant, if enervating. Electric sulfur baths, massage, wax baths, a sauna, and a solarium are available at the spa complex, which sits on the edge of town in an attractive parkland setting. ☎ *065/707–4023.* ✍ *Complex free, sulfur baths £5 (book in advance).* ⊙ *Early June–early Oct., daily 10–6.*

In July and August, Lisdoonvarna is a favorite getaway for Irish under-30s. It's also the traditional vacationing spot for the West's bachelor farmers, who used to congregate here at harvest time in late September with the vague intention of finding wives. (Irish farmers are notoriously shy with women and reluctant to marry, often postponing the event until their mid- or late-fifties, if ever.) This tradition is now formalized in the **Matchmaking Festival,** held during late September. Middle-aged singles dance to the strains of country-and-western bands, and a talent contest is held to name the most eligible bachelor.

Dining and Lodging

$ ✕▦ **Ballinalacken Castle.** On a hill 4 km (2½ mi) outside Lisdoonvarna, this sprawling Victorian lodge is on 100 acres of wildflower meadows beside the 16th-century ruins of an O'Brien stronghold. Its bow windows take advantage of glorious panoramic views of the Atlantic, the Aran Islands, and the Connemara hills. Guest rooms come in all different shapes and sizes; some have marble fireplaces and high ceilings. Six large rooms are in a recently built wing; all have sea views and dark-wood furniture. The public rooms are a haphazard mix of hand-me-downs, modern items, lovely old Irish oak, and sumptuous, inlaid bureaus. Local chef Frank Sheedy, formerly of Sheedy's Inn, who has cooked in some of Ireland's best restaurants, serves an imaginative and surprisingly sophisticated menu using local seafood, lamb, and beef. ✉ *Co. Clare,* ☎ *065/707–4025,* FAX *065/707–4025. 12 rooms with bath. Restaurant, bar. MC, V. Closed early Oct.–Mar.* ✎

$ ✗🍴 **Carrigann.** Settled into prettily landscaped gardens and just two minutes' walk from the village center, this small, friendly hotel is popular with hikers, who come for the guided walks and independent exploration. Hosts Mary and Gerard Howard keep a library of special-interest books on the Burren beside the turf fire in the sitting room; their maps and notes are also available. Rooms are modestly furnished but well equipped for the price range. Gerard also runs his own butcher shop, guaranteeing top-quality meat on the hotel's menu. Meals are supplemented by herbs from the garden and fresh local fish. ✉ *Co. Clare,* ☎ *065/707–4036,* FAX *065/707–4567. 20 rooms with bath. Fishing. MC, V. Closed Nov.–Feb.* ✎

$ ✗🍴 **Sheedy's Restaurant and Country Inn.** Originally a 17th-century
★ farmhouse, this small, friendly hotel is only a short walk from the town center and the spa wells. It's been in the hands of the Sheedy family since 1855, and was recently passed on to a new generation, John and Martina. The rooms are simple, spotlessly clean, and well cared for. John Sheedy was Chef de Cuisine at Ashford Castle (☞ *Cong, below*) until moving back home, and makes creative use of local produce in contemporary French-Irish–style fare. The informal Seafood Bar in the foyer serves simple dishes like crab claws in garlic butter, local smoked salmon, and seafood platters. ✉ *Co. Clare,* ☎ *065/707–4026,* FAX *065/707–4555. 11 rooms with bath. Restaurant, bar, tennis court. AE, MC, V. Closed Oct.–Mar.*

Nightlife
Country music and ballad singing are popular in the bars of Lisdoonvarna. For traditional music try the **Roadside Tavern** (☎ 065/707–4084).

Shopping
To see an audiovisual presentation on smoking Atlantic salmon, plus live demonstrations of the oak-smoking process, visit the **Burren Smokehouse Ltd.** (☎ 065/707–4432). You can also buy neatly packaged whole sides of salmon to take home.

The Burren

★ ❾ *Extending throughout western County Clare from the Cliffs of Moher in the south to Black Head in the north, as far southeast as Corofin.*

As you travel north toward Ballyvaughan, the landscape becomes rockier and stranger. Instead of the seemingly ubiquitous Irish green, gray becomes the prevailing color. You're now in the heart of the Burren, a 300-square-km (116-square-mi) expanse that is one of Ireland's fiercest landscapes. The Burren is aptly named: it's an Anglicization of the Irish word *bhoireann* ("a rocky place"). Stretching off in all directions, as far as the eye can see, are vast, irregular slabs of fissured limestone (known as karst) with deep cracks between them. From a distance, it looks like a lunar landscape, so dry that nothing could possibly grow on it. In the spring (especially from mid-May to mid-June), the Burren becomes a wild rock garden, as an astonishing variety of wildflowers bloom between the cracks in the rocks, among them at least 23 native species of orchid. The Burren also supports an incredible variety of wildlife, including frogs, newts, lizards, badgers, stoats, sparrow hawks, kestrels, and dozens of other birds and animals. The wildflowers and other plants are given life from the spectacular caves, streams, and potholes that lie beneath the rough, scarred pavements. With the advent of spring, *turloughs* (seasonal lakes that disappear in dry weather) appear on the plateau's surface. Botanists are particularly intrigued by the cohabitation of Arctic and Mediterranean plants, many so tiny (and rare, so please do not pick any) you can't see them from your car window; make a point of exploring some of this rocky terrain on foot. Numerous signposted walks run through both coastal and inland areas. For a private guided tour, contact Mary Angela Keane (☎ 065/707–4003; £25 per hour) or Shane Connolly (☎ 065/707–7168; £10 per person); May and June are peak months for flora, but a tour is worthwhile at any time of year.

The tiny **Burren Centre** has a modest audiovisual display and other exhibits that explain the Burren's geology, flora, and archaeology. ⊠ *Kilfenora, 8 km (5 mi) southeast of Lisdoonvarna on R476,* ☎ *065/708–8030.* ◻ *£2.50.* ☉ *June–Aug., daily 9:30–6; mid-Mar.–May and Sept.–Oct., daily 10–5.*

Beside the Burren Centre in Kilfenora, the ruins of a small 12th-century church, once the **Cathedral of St. Fachan,** have been partially restored as a parish church. There are some interesting carvings in the roofless choir, including an unusual, life-size human skeleton. In a field about 165 ft west of the ruins is an elaborately sculpted **high cross** that is worth examining, even though parts of it are badly weathered.

Nightlife
Vaughan's Pub (☎ 065/708–8004) in Kilfenora is known for its traditional music sessions.

Ballyvaughan

⑩ *16 km (10 mi) north of Lisdoonvarna on N67.*

A pretty little waterside village and a good base for exploring the Burren, Ballyvaughan attracts walkers and artists who enjoy the views of Galway Bay and access to the Burren. Outside Ballyvaughan, you'll see a signpost to the right for **Ailwee Cave,** the only such chamber in the region accessible to those who aren't spelunkers. This vast, 2-million-year-old cave is illuminated for about 3,300 ft and contains an underground river and waterfall. ☎ *065/707–7036.* ◻ *£4.75.* ☉ *Early Mar.–June and Sept.–early Nov., daily 10–6 (last tour at 5:30); July–Aug., daily 10–7 (last tour at 6:30).*

Dining and Lodging

$$$ ✕🏨 **Gregan's Castle Hotel.** The Haden family runs this quiet, meticu-
★   lous, large Victorian country house, at the base of the aptly named Corkscrew Hill (on N67, midway between Ballyvaughan and Lisdoonvarna). The house is surrounded by gardens and overlooks Galway Bay and the gray mountains of the Burren. All bedrooms are individually furnished with Georgian and Victorian antiques and William Morris wallpaper. The spacious rooms on the ground floor have private patio gardens but lack the splendid views of the rooms upstairs. The restaurant, rather formal for this part of the world (jacket and tie are required), serves updated French cuisine. ⊠ *Co. Clare,* ☎ *065/707–7005,* ℻ *065/707–7111. 18 rooms with bath, 4 suites. Restaurant, bar, croquet, fishing, bicycles. AE, MC, V. Closed Nov.–Mar..* ✆

$$ ✕🏨 **Hyland's Hotel.** In the heart of the Burren, this family-run, yellow-and-red coaching inn dates back to the early 18th century. A turf fire greets you in the lobby. Rooms vary in size and shape, but all have pine furniture and fresh-looking color-coordinated drapes and spreads. If you like mountain views, ask for a room with a skylight looking out over the Burren. The restaurant, cheerfully decorated in country pine with red tablecloths, specializes in simply prepared local produce. There is live music in the bar most nights from June to mid-September and Irish storytelling once a week. ⊠ *Co. Clare,* ☎ *065/707–7037,*

FAX *065/707–7131. 30 rooms with bath. Restaurant, bar. AE, MC, V. Closed 2nd week of Jan.–Feb..*

$ ×🖼 **Admiral's Rest.** You can guess from the nautical bric-a-brac on view that this place belongs to a retired naval man—John Macnamara, who is an expert on the Burren's wildlife. In a modernized cottage on the coast road between Lisdoonvarna and Ballyvaughan, the restaurant is across the road from the sea, which is visible through the large windows. Varnished stone floors, stone-topped tables, *súgán* (rope-seated) chairs, an open wood-and-turf fire, and posies of wildflowers on the tables make up the rugged decor. Seafood is the mainstay of the tasty menu. Nine inexpensive B&B rooms with shared baths are in the bungalow next door. ⊠ *Fanore, Co. Clare,* ☎ *065/707–6105,* FAX *065/ 707–6161. 9 rooms. AE, MC, V. Closed Nov.–Easter.*

Nightlife

The **Monk's Pub** (☎ 065/707–7059), near the waterfront, has great music sessions and a friendly ambience.

En Route From Ballyvaughan, it's a 48-km (30-mi) trip circumnavigating Galway Bay to Galway City. If you're eager to get there, skip the next two towns and head there directly, first passing through Kinvara (☞ *below*). If you're on a more leisurely pace, head back south through the Burren on R480 and R476 to Corofin.

Corofin

⑪ *23 km (14½ mi) south of Ballyvaughan, 16 km (10 mi) east of Kilfenora on the R476.*

If you're searching for your Irish roots, Corofin's **Clare Heritage Center** has a genealogical service and advice for do-it-yourselfers. Its displays on the history of the West of Ireland in the 19th century cover culture, traditions, emigration, and famine, as it exposes some grim statistics. In 1841, for example, the population of County Clare was 286,394. Fifty years later, famine and emigration had reduced this number to 112,334, and the population continued to decline, reaching an all-time low of 73,597 in 1956. (It is now heading back to the 90,000 mark.) ☎ *065/683–7955.* 🎟 *£2.* ☉ *Apr.–Oct., daily 10–6; Nov.–Mar. (genealogy service only), weekdays 9–5; Heritage Center by appointment.*

In a 15th-century castle on the edge of Corofin, the **Dysert O'Dea Castle Archaeology Centre** has an exhibition on the antiquities of the Burren. Twenty-five monuments stand within a 1½-km (1-mi) radius of the castle; these date from the Bronze Age to the 19th century, and all are described at the center. ☎ *065/683–7722.* 🎟 *£2.50.* ☉ *May–Sept., daily 10–6.*

Coole Park and Thoor Ballylee

Coole Park: 24 km (15 mi) northeast of Corofin on N18; Thoor Ballylee: 5 km (3 mi) north of Coole Park, signposted from N66.

⑫ On the left side north of the little town of Gort is **Coole Park,** once home to Lady Augusta Gregory (1859–1932), W. B. Yeats's patron and his cofounder of Dublin's Abbey Theatre (☞ Chapter 1). Yeats visited here often, as did almost all of the other writers who contributed to the Irish literary revival in the first half of the 20th century, including George Bernard Shaw and Sean O'Casey. Douglas Hyde, the first president of Ireland, was also a visitor. The house fell derelict after Lady Gregory's death and was demolished in 1941; the grounds are now a national forest and wildlife park. The only reminder of its literary past is the **Autograph Tree,** a copper beech on which many of Lady Gregory's famous guests carved their initials. Picnic tables make this a lovely alfresco lunch spot. ☎ *091/631804.* ✉ *Visitor center £2, park free.* ☉ *Visitor center mid-Apr.–mid-June, Tues.–Sun. 10–5; mid-June–Aug., daily 9:30–6:30; Sept., daily 10–5; park daily 10–dusk.*

⑬ Thoor Ballylee is a sight Yeats fans won't want to miss. This is one of the only major sites in the West of Ireland associated with the Nobel Prize–winning poet that is *not* in County Sligo (☞ Chapter 7). In his fifties and newly married, Yeats bought this 14th-century Norman tower as a ruin in 1916 for £35. The tower is located beside a whitewashed, thatched-roof cottage, with a tranquil stream running alongside it. Its proximity to Lady Gregory's house at Coole Park made it a desirable location, though it required significant work on Yeats's part to make it livable. He stayed here intermittently until 1929 and penned some of his more mystical works here, including *The Tower* and *The Winding Stair.* It's now fully restored with his original decor and furniture. The audiovisual display is a useful introduction to the poet and his times. ☎ *091/631436.* ✉ *£3.* ☉ *Easter–Sept., daily 10–6.*

Kinvara

⑭ *13½ km (8½ mi) east of Ballyvaughan, 15 km (9 mi) northwest of Gort on N67, 25 km (15½ mi) south of Galway City.*

Whether you're coming from Ballyvaughan or from Gort, Kinvara is worth a visit. The picture-perfect village is a growing holiday base, thanks to its gorgeous bay-side locale, great walking and sea angling, and numerous pubs. Kinvara is best known for its long-standing early August sailing event, **Cruinniú na mBád** (Festival of the Gathering of the Boats), in which traditional brown-sailed Galway hookers laden with turf race across the bay. (Hookers were used until the early part of this century to carry turf, provisions, and cattle across Galway Bay and out to the Aran Islands. A sculpture in Galway's Eyre Square [☞ *below*] honors their local significance.)

On a rock to the north of Kinvara Bay, the 16th-century **Dunguaire Castle** commands all the approaches from Galway Bay. It is said to be on the site of a 7th-century castle built by the King of Connaught. One of its previous owners, Oliver St. John Gogarty, was a surgeon, man of letters, and model for James Joyce's Buck Mulligan, a character in *Ulysses.* Today Dunguaire is used for a literarily themed medieval banquet that honors local writers and others with ties to the West, including Lady Gregory, W. B. Yeats, Sean O'Casey, and Pádraic Ó'Conaire (☞ Eyre Square *in* Galway, *below*). ☎ *091/637108.* ✉ *Castle £2.50, banquets £32.* ☉ *May–Sept., daily 9:30–5; banquets at 5:30 and 8:30.*

Dining and Lodging

$ ✕ **Moran's of the Weir.** Signposted off the main road on the south side of Clarinbridge, this waterside thatched cottage, the home of the Moran family since 1760, houses a simply furnished restaurant at the back that serves only seafood. It's *the* place to stop to sample the local oysters, grown on a bed in front of the restaurant—but only when there is an "r" in the name of the month of your travels! ✉ *The Weir, Kilcolgan,* ☎ *091/796113. AE, MC, V.*

$$ ✕🏨 **Merriman Inn.** This whitewashed, thatched inn on the shores of Galway Bay may look traditional, but, in fact, it's a midsize hotel. The Merriman is decorated with locally made, well-designed furniture, as well as original crafts, paintings, and sculpture. The bar and lounge both have open fires and a relaxed, friendly atmosphere. Guest rooms are quiet and well equipped. The Quilty Room is a large, airy restaurant adorned with mood-enhancing landscape paintings. Local seafood—

such as tournedos of salmon pan-seared with a confit of fennel and a sharp, spicy jus—is featured on the French-influenced menu, but you can also try succulent local lamb. ✉ *Co. Galway,* ☎ *091/638222,* ꜰꜰ *091/637686. 32 rooms with bath. Restaurant, bar, meeting room. AE, DC, MC, V. Closed Jan.*

$ 🏠 **Burren View Farm.** On the edge of Galway Bay, 5 km (3 mi) west of Kinvara, this simple B&B is relatively isolated on a working sheep and cattle farm and has a million-dollar view. Stone-walled fields dotted with sheep surround the yellow two-story house. The breakfast room, sun lounge, and front bedrooms look out across a wide sea inlet to the gray expanse of the Burren. Rooms are plain and homey but clean and well maintained. Wholesome evening meals, Irish or Continental style, are cooked on request, while food is also available in the local pub, a five-minute walk away. ✉ *Doorus, Kinvara, Co. Galway,* ☎ *091/ 637142,* ꜰꜰ *091/638131. 5 rooms, 2 with bath. Dining room, tennis court, fishing. AE, DC, MC, V. Closed Nov.–Mar.*

Nightlife and the Arts

The first weekend in May, Kinvara hosts the annual **Cuckoo Fleadh** (☎ 091/637145). You can hear traditional music most nights at the **Winkles Hotel** (✉ The Square, ☎ 91/637137).

GALWAY CITY

⑮ *27 km (12½ mi) north of Kinvara, 219 km (136 mi) west of Dublin, 105 km (65 mi) north of Limerick.*

Galway is often said to be a state of mind as much as it is a specific place. The largest city in the West today (population 60,000) and the ancient capital of the province of Connaught, Galway is also one of the fastest-growing cities in Europe. It's an astonishing fact, and you have to wonder where this city can possibly grow. For even though Galway is the largest city in the West, its heart is *tiny*—a warren of streets so compact that if you spend more than a few hours here, you'll soon be strolling along with the sort of easy familiarity you'd feel in your hometown.

For many Irish people, Galway is a favorite weekend getaway, the liveliest place in the Republic, and the city of festivals. It's also a university town: University College Galway (or UCG as it's locally known) is a center for Gaelic culture (Galway marks the eastern gateway to the West's large Gaeltacht). A fair share of UCG's 9,000 students pursue their studies in the Irish language. Galway is, in fact, permeated by youth culture. On festival weekends, you'll see as many pierced and tattooed teenagers and twentysomethings here as you'd find at a rock concert.

But its students aren't its only avant-garde, as Galway has long attracted writers, artists, and musicians. The last keep the traditional music pubs lively year-round. Its two small but internationally acclaimed theater companies draw a steady stream of theater people.

Although you're not conscious of it when you're in the center of town, Galway is spectacularly situated, on the north shore of Galway Bay, where the River Corrib flows from Lough Corrib out into the sea. The seaside suburb of Salthill, on the south-facing shore of Galway Bay, has spectacular vistas across the vividly blue bay to Black Head on the opposite shore.

Galway's founders were Anglo-Normans who arrived in the mid-13th century and fortified their settlement against "the native Irish," as local chieftains were called. Galway became known as "the City of the Tribes" because of the dominant role in public and commercial life of the 14 families who founded it. Their names are still common in Galway and elsewhere in Ireland: Athy, Blake, Bodkin, Browne, D'Arcy, Dean, Font, French, Kirwan, Joyce, Lynch, Morris, Martin, and Skerret. The city's medieval heritage, a fusion of Gaelic and Norman influences, is apparent in the intimate two- and three-story stucco buildings, the windy streets, the narrow passageways, and the cobblestones underfoot.

Galway's growth and popularity mean that at its busiest moments, pedestrians jam-pack its narrow, one-way streets, while cars are gridlocked. If there's a city that doesn't sleep in Ireland, this is it. In fact, if you want to be guaranteed a quiet night's sleep, either ask for a room in the back of your center-city hotel or simply stay outside of town.

Exploring Galway City

Most of the city's sights, aside from the cathedral and the university campus, can be found in a narrow sector of the medieval town center that runs from Eyre Square in a southwesterly direction to the River Corrib. Eyre Square is easily recognizable, as it is the only green space in central Galway. It only takes five minutes to walk straight down Galway's main shopping street, the continuation of the north side of Eyre Square, to the River Corrib, where it ends. Not only is the city center compact, it is also largely pedestrianized, so there is really only one way to see it: on foot. Even the farthest point, the university campus, is less than a 15-minute walk from Eyre Square. A walk to Galway's seaside suburb, Salthill, 3 km (2 mi) west of Galway, and its long seaside promenade, is a favorite local occupation, traditionally undertaken on a Sunday afternoon; for this excursion you may prefer to take the car.

A Good Walk

Orient yourself at **Eyre Square** ⑯, part of which is occupied by **Kennedy Park.** Before you really get going, you may want to stop in at the **Tourist Information Office** ⑰ off the southeast corner of the square. At the top (north side) of Eyre Square, turn left down Williamsgate Street. This is the spine of old Galway. Its name changes four times before it reaches the River Corrib, successively called **William Street, Shop Street, High Street,** and **Quay Street.** If you have any postcards to mail, you may want to stop at the General Post Office, on the left side of Eglinton Street, the first right off Williamsgate Street. At the corner of William and Shop streets, **Lynch's Castle** ⑱ is one of Galway's oldest buildings. Continue down Shop Street to the pedestrian way just beyond Abbeygate Street; here **Lynch Memorial Window** ⑲ and **Collegiate Church of St. Nicholas** ⑳ are adjacent to one another. James Joyce fans might want to make the 30-second detour across Lombard and Market streets to Bowling Green, site of the **Nora Barnacle House** ㉑.

It's a minute's walk from the church to **Tig Neachtain** ㉒ (Naughton's in English, pronounced *knock*-tons), a pub (popular with locals) at the corner of Cross Street and Quay/High Street. This corner is the very heart of old Galway's main historic and commercial district: nearly all the city's best restaurants, bars, boutiques, art galleries, and crafts, antiques, and bookstores line the narrow, winding streets and alleys in this vicinity. Nothing is more than a five-minute walk from anything else. If this area is bursting at the seams, one block to the east of Shop/High Street, between Abbeygate and Cross streets, the quieter Middle Street has a number of worthwhile stores and restaurants, as well as the national Irish-language theater.

The **Spanish Arch** ㉓ and the **Galway City Museum** ㉔ are adjacent, right on the river's east bank, across from the Jurys Galway Inn parking lot.

Just beyond Jurys (☞ Dining and Lodging, *below*) but before crossing the Wolfe Tone Bridge, turn right onto the pedestrian path that parallels the river. Follow it past the William O'Brien Bridge to the **Salmon Weir Bridge** ㉕ (you'll need to jog off the path onto Abbeygate Street just short of the bridge to gain access to it). As you cross the bridge, look ahead to the **Cathedral of Our Lady Assumed into Heaven and St. Nicholas** ㉖ (known locally simply as "the cathedral"). A five-minute walk down University Road brings you to **University College Galway** ㉗. For a pretty stroll back to the center of town, turn right onto Canal Road and follow it back to the intersection of Dominick Street, Fairhill, and Raven Terrace. From here it's a brief jog to Claddagh Quay, which will take you out to the **Claddagh** ㉘. If you're out this far, you may want to continue on to **Salthill** ㉙; otherwise, head back to the center of town.

TIMING

You could easily take this walk in a morning or afternoon (minus the walk out to Salthill), although if you browse in stores, chat with locals, or stop off for a pint or a cup of tea, you could stretch it out into a *very* leisurely all-day excursion. You may want to plan your day so you hit only what most interests you, leaving time to explore along the bay, get out to Salthill, or take a bay cruise.

Sights to See

㉖ **Cathedral of Our Lady Assumed into Heaven and St. Nicholas.** On an island forming the west bank of the River Corrib beside the Salmon Weir Bridge, Galway's largest Catholic church was dedicated by Cardinal Cushing of Boston in 1965. The cathedral was built on the site of the old Galway jail; a white cross embedded into the pavement of the adjacent parking lot marks the site of the cemetery that stood beside the prison. ☒ *Free.* ☺ *Freely accessible.*

㉘ **Claddagh.** On the west bank of the Corrib estuary, this district was once an Irish-speaking fishing village outside the walls of the old town. The name is an Anglicization of the Irish *cladach,* which means "marshy ground." It retained a strong, separate identity until the 1930s, when its traditional thatched cottages were replaced by a conventional housing plan and its unique character and traditions were largely lost. One thing has survived: the Claddagh ring, composed of two hands clasped around a heart with a crown above it (symbolizing love, friendship, and loyalty), is still used by many Irish people as a wedding ring. Traditionally, the ring is worn with the heart facing into you if you're married or otherwise unavailable and with the heart facing outward (indicating your heart is open) if you're still looking for Mr. or Ms. Right. Reproductions in gold or silver are favorite souvenirs of Galway.

⑳ **Collegiate Church of St. Nicholas.** Built by the Anglo-Normans in 1320 and enlarged in 1486 and again in the 16th century, the church contains many fine carvings and gargoyles dating from the late Middle Ages, and it is one of the best-preserved medieval churches in Ireland. Legend has it that Columbus prayed here on his last stop before setting off on his voyage to the New World. On Saturday mornings, a **street market,** held in the pedestrian way beside the church, attracts two dozen or so vendors and hundreds of shoppers. ☒ *Lombard St.* ☒ *Free.* ☺ *Daily 8–dusk.*

⑯ **Eyre Square.** The largest open space in central Galway on the east side of the Corrib, Eyre Square encompasses a hodgepodge of monuments and concrete and grassy areas. In the center is **Kennedy Park,** a patch of lawn named in honor of John F. Kennedy, who spoke from here when he visited the city in June 1963. At the north end of the park, a 20-ft-

Galway City

River Corrib

Newcastle Rd.

27

University Rd.

Eglinton Canal

Nuns Island

26

Goal Rd.

Newcastle Rd.

Mill St.

New Rd. St.

St. Helens St.

Henry St.

Raleigh Row

Sea Rd.

Munster Ave.

Fr. Griffin Rd.

Fairhill

St. Nicholas Rd.

Nuns Island St.

Dominick St.

Dominick St. Upper

Wolfe Tone Bridge

Claddagh Quay

Grattan Rd.

Waterside

Wood Quay

St. Vincents Ave.

Headford Rd.

St. Bridget's Pl.

Brendan's Ave.

Eyre St.

Prospect Hill

25

River Corrib

Abbeygate St.

Eglinton St.

Williamsgate St.

Post Office

Bowling Green

21

Market St.

19

20

Shop St.

18

William St.

Lwr. Abbeygate St.

EYRE SQUARE

Kennedy Park

Eyre Square

16

Eyre Square Shopping Centre

Victoria Pl.

17

Forster St.

Station Rd.

Train Station

Lombard St.

Guard St.

High St.

Middle St.

St. Augustine St.

Merchants Rd.

Queen St.

Bridge St.

22

Wm. O'Brien Bridge

Cross St.

The Cornstore

Quay

Flood St.

New Dock St.

Dock Rd.

Dock Rd.

Commercial Dock

24

23

The Long Walk

Old Dock

N

0 — 330 yards

0 — 300 meters

To Salthill

29

Nimmo's Pier

28

CLADDAGH

SOUTH PARK

high steel **sculpture** standing in the pool of a fountain represents the brown sails seen on Galway hookers, the area's traditional sailing boats (☞ Kinvara, *above*). Seated beside this sculpture is the genial stone **figure of Pádraic Ó'Conaire,** a pioneer of the Irish-language revival at the turn of the last century who was born in Galway (his birthplace fronting on the docks is marked with a plaque). When he died in a Dublin hospital in 1928, his only possessions were his pipe (a replica of which he holds here), his tobacco, and an apple. Now the entrance to Kennedy Park, the **Browne Doorway** was taken in 1905 from the Browne family's town house on Upper Abbeygate Street; it has the 17th-century coats of arms of both the Browne and Lynch families, called a "marriage stone," because when the families were joined in marriage their coats of arms were, too. Keep an eye out for similar if less elaborate versions of the entranceway as you walk around the old part of town. The **bronze cannons** were presented at the end of the Crimean War to the Connaught Rangers, a legendary regiment of the British Army made up of Irish men recruited from the West of Ireland (☞ King House *in* Boyle *in* Chapter 3).

㉔ Galway City Museum. Next door to the Spanish Arch (☞ *below*), the city's civic museum contains an array of materials relating to local history: old photographs, antiquities (the oldest is a stone axe head carbon-dated to 3500 BC), and other historical gewgaws. ⊠ *Spanish Arch,* ☎ *091/567641.* 🎫 *£1.* ⊙ *Mid-Mar.–Sept., daily 10–1 and 2:15–5:15; Oct.–mid-Mar., Wed.–Fri. 10–1 and 2:15–5:15.*

⑲ Lynch Memorial Window. Embedded in a stone wall above a built-up Gothic doorway off Market Street, the window marks the spot where, according to legend, James Lynch FitzStephen, mayor of Galway in the early 16th century, condemned his son to death after he confessed to murdering a Spanish sailor who had stolen his girlfriend. When no one could be found to carry out the execution, Judge Lynch hanged his son himself, ensuring that justice prevailed, before retiring into seclusion.

⑱ Lynch's Castle. Now a branch of the Allied Irish Banks, this is the finest remaining example in Galway of a 16th-century fortified house—fortified because neighboring Irish tribes persistently raided the village, whose commercial life excluded them. Decorative details on its stone lintels are usually found only in southern Spain. Like the Spanish Arch (☞ *below*), it serves as a reminder of the close trading links that once existed between Galway and Spain. ⊠ *Shop St.*

㉑ Nora Barnacle House. On June 16, 1904, James Joyce (1882–1941) had his first date with Nora Barnacle, who would later become his wife. He subsequently chose to set *Ulysses* on this day, now known universally as Bloomsday (☞ Close Up: ReJoyce! A Walk through *Ulysses* and James Joyce's Dublin *in* Chapter 1)—"a recognition of the determining effect upon his life of his attachment to her," as Joyce's biographer Richard Ellman has said. Nora was born here, the daughter of a poor baker; today it has a modest collection of photographs, letters, and memorabilia, and a small gift shop. ⊠ *4 Bowling Green,* ☎ *091/ 564743.* 🎫 *£1.* ⊙ *Mid-May–mid-Sept., Mon.–Sat. 2–5; off-season by appointment.*

★ ㉕ Salmon Weir Bridge. The bridge itself is nothing special, but in season—from mid-April to early July—shoals of salmon are visible from its deck as they lie in the clear river water before making their way upstream to the spawning grounds of Lough Corrib. It is a memorable sight.

㉙ Salthill. Three kilometers (2 miles) west of Galway, Salthill is a lively, hugely popular seaside resort with its own fun palace. Its promenade is the traditional place "to sit and watch the moon rise over Claddagh, and see the sun go down on Galway Bay"—as Bing Crosby used to croon in the city's most famous song.

🄷 **Spanish Arch.** Built in 1584 to protect the quays where Spanish ships unloaded cargoes of wines and brandies, the arch now stands in the parking lot opposite Jurys Galway Inn (☞ Dining and Lodging, *below*). It's easily (and often) mistaken for a pile of weathered stones, yet it's another reminder of Galway's—and Ireland's—past links with Spain (☞ Kinsale *in* Chapter 5).

🄢 **Tíg Neachtain (Naughton's Pub).** You can hear traditional music every night at this popular pub, which stands at a busy little crossroads in the heart of the old town. Grab a spot at one of its old-fashioned partitioned snugs at lunchtime for an inexpensive selection of imaginative bar food. It's a good place to mingle with local actors, writers, artists, musicians, and students, although it can get sardine-can crowded. ⊠ *17 Cross St.,* ☎ *091/566172.*

🄸 **Tourist Information Office.** Just off Eyre Square, around the corner from the bus and train station and the Great Southern Hotel (☞ Dining and Lodging, *below*), this is the place to make reservations and find out about the latest happenings around town. ⊠ *1 Victoria Pl.,* ☎ *091/ 563081.* ☉ *Weekdays 9–6, Sat. 9–1.*

🄬 **University College Galway (UCG).** Across the River Corrib, in the northwestern corner of the city, UCG was opened in 1846 to promote the development of local industry and agriculture, but today it's a center for Irish-language and Celtic studies. The Tudor-Gothic–style quadrangle, completed in 1848, is worth a visit, though much of the rest of the campus is architecturally undistinguished. Its library boasts an important archive of Celtic-language materials, and in July and August, it also hosts courses in Irish studies for overseas students.

Dining and Lodging

$$$ ✕ **Kirwan's Lane Creative Cuisine.** A revamped alley at the river end of Quay Street is home to Mike O'Grady's stylish modern restaurant. Blue-stained wooden tables, narrow floor-to-ceiling windows, and a quarry-tile floor set the stage for a sophisticated menu. Fresh prawn cocktail is served with sauce Marie-Rose and a passion-fruit mayo, while confit of duck leg comes with braised red cabbage, star anise, and balsamic oil. Main courses have similarly unpredictable twists—rack of lamb is served with sweet potato mash, basil oil, and apricots, while monkfish tails come with a simple lemon and coriander dressing. ⊠ *Kirwan's La.,* ☎ *091/568266. AE, DC, MC, V. Closed Sun.*

$$$ ✕ **Nimmo's.** Swiss chef Stephan Zeltner, who established himself on the Galway scene with a small restaurant above Naughton's Pub (☞ *above*), is now at this riverside location in an old stone building with a separately run wine bar downstairs. The long, spacious second-floor room has original paintings on the walls and well-spaced tables set with white linen. Zeltner prepares robust food, exemplified by panfried chicken breast with duck foie gras or noisettes of venison with apple and Calvados. ⊠ *Spanish Arch,* ☎ *091/563565. AE, DC, MC, V. Closed Sun. No lunch.*

$$ ✕ **Malt House.** Hidden away in an alley off High Street in the center of old Galway, Barry and Therese Cunningham's bustling pub-restaurant has long been popular with both locals and visitors for good food served in informal surroundings. You can either eat in the bar itself or in the fancier main room (beamed ceilings; white, rough-cast walls; and chintz curtains) just off the bar. Fresh prawns panfried in garlic butter is a popular seafood option, while the sirloin steak with green pep-

percorn sauce and the rack of lamb with a parsley crust should please landlubbers. ✉ *Old Malte Arcade, High St.,* ☎ *091/563993. AE, DC, MC, V. Closed Sun. Oct.–Apr.*

$–$$ ✗ **K.C. Blakes.** K.C. stands for Casey, as in owner-chef John Casey, who turned a medieval stone town house once associated with city founders the Blake family into a dark, ultramodern eatery. Dishes range from traditional Irish beef-and-Guinness stew to contemporary combinations like black pudding croquettes with pear and cranberry sauce; everything is prepared with fresh ingredients. ✉ *10 Quay St.,* ☎ *091/ 561826. AE, MC, V.*

$–$$ ✗ **McDonagh's Seafood Bar.** The McDonaghs are one of Galway's most entrepreneurial families, in charge of several hotels and this spot, a longtime town landmark. After a major renovation, it's now partly a fish-and-chips bar and partly a "real" fish restaurant. If you've yet to try fish-and-chips, this is the place to start: cod, whiting, mackerel, haddock, or hake is deep-fried in a light batter while you watch, and served with a heap of freshly cooked chips (French fries). Or try Galway oysters au naturel, or a bowl of mussels steamed in wine and garlic. ✉ *22 Quay St.,* ☎ *091/565001. DC, MC, V. No lunch Sun. Oct.–Apr.*

$ ✗ **Bridge Mills.** Renovations have altered this 400-year-old former grain mill beside the River Corrib into a restaurant and minimall. You can even sit outdoors beside a bubbling stream and watch local fishermen pulling salmon out of the river. Lunch fare includes fresh salads, sandwiches, and hot specials. The dinner menu is more substantial, with large steaks and vegetarian choices, such as spinach and ricotta cannelloni. ✉ *O'Brien's Bridge,* ☎ *091/566231. AE, MC, V. No dinner Oct.–mid-May.*

$$$$ ✗🏨 **Glenlo Abbey.** Five minutes outside the city on N59 Clifden road, Glenlo Abbey is surrounded by its own golf course and has views over Lough Corrib. Built in 1740, it was previously a private home (not a monastery, as the name implies). The lobby resembles a gentlemen's club, with its solid parquet floors, leather chesterfield sofas, and old, leather-bound books. The spacious bedrooms are in a newer wing and have Georgian-style furniture and super-king-size beds. The bathrooms have marble walls and, some, whirlpool baths. The Pullman Restaurant, two *Orient Express* carriages installed in the grounds, offers a novelty dining experience; informal bar food is served in the Oak Cellar Bar. In the oddly spelled Ffrench Room, Irish and international cuisine is served in formal, Regency-style surroundings. ✉ *Bushy Park, Co. Galway,* ☎ *091/526666,* 🖷 *091/527800. 38 rooms with bath, 6 suites. 2 restaurants, bar, sauna, 9-hole golf course, tennis court, fishing. AE, DC, MC, V.*

$$$$ ✗🏨 **St. Cleran's.** This gorgeous graystone Georgian mansion (35 km/21 mi east of Galway on the N6 Dublin road) was the home of director John Huston in the 1960s and has been lovingly restored by its present owner, entertainer Merv Griffin. Subtlety is not Merv's strong point, and some visitors are overwhelmed by snow-white deep-pile carpets, ubiquitous crystal chandeliers, and loud check sofas, while others find the exuberance of the decor, and the hedonistic luxury it creates, highly enjoyable. Rooms are individually decorated with top-quality antiques. Views over the rolling countryside are superb and country sports opportunities are excellent. Japanese chef Hisashi Kumagai presides over the elegant, formal restaurant (reservations essential for nonresidents), offering unusual specialties such as sea scallops in coriander broth with onion confit as well as noisette of venison with woodland mushroom ragout and Madeira sauce. ✉ *Craughwell, Co. Galway,* ☎ *091/846555,* 🖷 *091/846600. 12 rooms with bath. Restaurant, bar, miniature golf, horseback riding, fishing. AE, MC, V.* ✦

$ ✕⌂ Cregg Castle. On a 165-acre wildlife preserve about 15 km (9 mi) north of Galway on N17 (turn left for Corrandulla just beyond Clare-galway), this 17th-century castle is pleasantly informal. The Broder-icks, the owners, all play instruments, and traditional sessions often take place around the huge log-and-turf fire in the Great Hall. Bedrooms vary in shape and size and are decorated mainly with sturdy Victorian bygones. Breakfast is served until noon around an antique dining table that seats 18 people. The restaurant is licensed to serve wine only; reservations for dinner should be made by 12 noon. ✉ *Corrandulla, Co. Galway,* ☎ FAX *091/791434. 8 rooms, 7 with bath. Restaurant. AE, MC, V. Closed Nov.–Feb..* ✑

$$$ ⌂ Ardilaun House. This lovely 19th-century house lies at the end of a
 ★   tree-lined avenue in a quiet suburb, midway between the city center and the Salthill promenade—about five minutes' drive from both. Open fires, fresh flower arrangements, and Regency-style furniture characterize the quiet public rooms overlooking the gardens. The individually designed bedrooms are decorated with a pink, gray, or green color scheme and Irish-made mahogany furniture with brass trim. For views of the bay, book an even-numbered room on the top floor. Other rooms, which are just as pleasant, overlook the flower garden, shrubberies, and a fountain. ✉ *Taylor's Hill, Co. Galway,* ☎ *091/521433,* FAX *091/521546. 81 rooms with bath, 7 suites. Restaurant, 2 bars, indoor pool, sauna, health club. AE, DC, MC, V.* ✑

$$$ ⌂ Galway Bay. It's big and modern, but it's also restful and comfortable, with a panoramic view of Galway Bay. The facade of this yellow-painted giant at the quiet end of Salthill is divided into small-scale sections with peaked gables. The beach and the 1-km (½-mi) promenade, popular with joggers, are right across the road. About 70% of the rooms have a sea view; the rest overlook a quiet residential area. Color-coordinated rooms are a generous size and have large windows and all modern facilities, from minibars to in-room data ports (on request). Advantages of staying 3 km (2 mi) outside town include hassle-free car parking and quiet nights. ✉ *The Promenade, Salthill, Co. Galway,* ☎ *091/ 520520,* FAX *091/520530. 148 rooms with bath, 2 suites. Restaurant, bar, coffee shop, indoor pool, sauna, steam room, health club, fishing. AE, DC, MC, V.* ✑

$$$ ⌂ Galway Great Southern. Built in 1845 to coincide with the arrival of the railway, and grandly situated on the southeastern side of Eyre Square, this is still the best address in town. A pianist tickles the ivories in the large lobby, which, like the two bars, is a popular gathering spot. All the guest rooms are decorated in tastefully muted, color-coordinated schemes, with Georgian-style tables and chairs. The large, deluxe rooms in the original building have tall ceilings and windows and are particularly elegant, though those at the front directly above the bar can be noisy late into the night. Rooms at the back are newer; those in the back on the fifth floor have views of Galway Bay, as does the swimming pool. French-Irish cuisine is served at the formal Oyster Room. ✉ *Eyre Sq., Co. Galway,* ☎ *091/564041,* FAX *091/566704. 112 rooms with bath, 3 suites. Restaurant, 2 bars, indoor pool, sauna. AE, DC, MC, V.* ✑

$ ⌂ Jurys Galway Inn. At the foot of Galway's busy Quay Street, right on the banks of the Corrib, this four-story hotel offers good-quality budget accommodation. Each room is big enough for three adults, or two adults and two children, and the Jurys fixed-price policy applies to all of them. The light, airy rooms have modern pine fittings, plain carpets and walls, double-glazed windows, and fully equipped bathrooms. Those overlooking the river are quieter than those in front. The atmosphere unavoidably tends toward anonymous-international, but it's centrally located and the level of comfort is high for the price range. ✉ *Quay St., Co. Galway,* ☎ *091/566444,* ℻ *091/568415. 128 rooms with bath. Restaurant, bar, parking (fee). AE, DC, MC, V.*

$ 🏠 **Norman Villa.** Dee and Mark Keogh's Victorian town house, mid-
★   way between the city center and the seaside promenade of Salthill, is
ideally located, away from the bustle but within easy walking distance
of both places. Brightly painted walls, Victorian brass beds with Irish
linen sheets, varnished floorboards, wooden shutters, and fun, offbeat
paintings and artifacts make for a lively, pleasant decor. ✉ *86 Lower
Salthill, Co. Galway,* ☎ ℻ *091/521131. 5 rooms with bath. Free
parking. MC, V. Closed last 2 wks. in Jan.*

Nightlife and the Arts

Because of its small size and concentration of pubs and restaurants,
Galway can seem even livelier at 11 PM than it is at 11 AM. On week-
ends, when there are a lot of students and other revelers in town, Eyre
Square and environs can be rowdy late at night after pub-closing time.
On the plus side, if you've been staying out in the countryside and you're
ready for a little nightlife, you're certain to find plenty of it here.

FESTIVALS AND SEASONAL EVENTS

Mid-April's **Cuirt Literary Festival** (☎ 091/565886) brings in leading
Irish and international writers for a week of readings and other events.
The **Galway Arts Festival** (☎ 091/583800), the city's premier annual
event, spans the last two weeks in July and includes drama, film,
music, children's events, and a huge parade. At the end of September,
the **Galway International Oyster Festival** (☎ 091/527282) indulges vis-
itors with the "food of the gods." The **Galway Races** at Ballybrit Race
Course (to the north of town off N17) start the day after the Galway
Arts Festival ends for a week of mad revelry.

PUBS AND OTHER NIGHTSPOTS

The best area for traditional music is the Quay/Shop Street area be-
tween Eyre Square and the Spanish Arch. You will usually find a ses-
sion after about 9 PM at **Cottage Bar** (✉ Lower Salthill, ☎ 091/
526754), **Tiġ Neaċhtain's** (✉ 17 Cross St., ☎ 091/568820), **Paddy's**
(✉ Prospect Hill, ☎ 091/567843), the **Quays** (✉ Quay St., ☎ 091/
561777), and **Taaffe's** (✉ 19 Shop St., ☎ 091/564066). **Aras na Gael**
(✉ 45 Lower Dominick St., ☎ 091/526509) is one of the few Irish-
speaking pubs in the city center. **Cuba** (✉ Eyre Sq., ☎ 091/565991),
on three floors, draws diners and salsa lovers for Cuban cocktails and
cigars to the beat of Latin music from DJs and live bands. **Le Graal** (✉
38 Lower Dominick St., ☎ 091/567614), licensed to sell wine only, is
a bar-brasserie that metamorphoses into a lively late-night spot.

THEATER

An Taibhdhearc (✉ Middle St., ☎ 091/562024), pronounced awn *tie*-
vark, was founded in 1928 by Hilton Edwards and Micháel
Macliammóir as the national Irish-language theater. It continues to pro-
duce first-class shows, mainly of Irish works in both the English and
the Irish languages.

The **Druid Theatre** company (✉ Chapel La., ☎ 091/568617) is respected
for its adventurous and accomplished productions, mainly of 20th-cen-
tury Irish and European plays. The players perform at the Royal
Court's small stage in London; when they're home, they usually ap-
pear at the Town Hall: this is where they eventually brought their 1997–
98 success, Martin McDonagh's *Leenane Trilogy,* which opened in Lon-
don and later traveled to Sydney, Australia, and off-Broadway.

Macnas (✉ Fisheries Field, Salmon Weir Bridge, ☎ 091/561462) is an
internationally renowned, Galway-based troupe of performance artists

CLOSE-UP: A YEAR-ROUND FLEADH

DUBLIN MAY BE THE POLITICAL capital of Ireland, but Galway is the center of its traditional-music universe, a place where you can hear this music all through the year, whether or not there's a *fleadh,* or traditional music festival, going on. ☞ **Galway City** and its environs have given birth to some of the most durable names in Irish music: De Danann, Arcady, singers Dolores and Seán Keane, and the mercurial accordion genius Mairtín O'Connor. Seán Ryan, acknowledged master of the tin whistle, has been playing every Sunday at **Crane's** for nearly 20 years. The hottest sessions these days take place at the ☞ **Cottage Bar** in Lower Salthill, where up-and-coming young musicians are drawn by the cozy atmosphere and the fine acoustics. In the city itself, there's still plenty of music to be found at old reliables such as ☞ **Tíg Neachtain's,** ☞ **Taaffe's,** and ☞ **Aras na Gael.**

South of Galway the fishing village of ☞ **Kinvara** hosts the annual **Cuckoo Fleadh,** a small but growing festival that will turn 10 years old in 2003. Resident musicians like De Danann alumni Jackie Daly and Charlie Piggott play regularly at **Winkles Hotel,** where, in 1989, a very young and relatively unknown accordion player got together with a few friends for a casual recording session. The resulting album, *Sharon Shannon,* went platinum virtually overnight, becoming the most suc-cessful traditional-music recording ever released. Today, Shannon, who grew up on a farm outside Corofin, County Clare, and played her first accordion when she was 11, is one of Ireland's leading traditional Irish musicians.

Down the road, the lively market town of ☞ **Ennis** (where Shannon took lessons from local maestro Frank Custy) has come into its own, attracting a growing cadre of musicians: the Custys, Siobhán and Tommy Peoples, Josephine Marsh, P. J. King, flute player Kevin Crawford, and, most recently, accordion whiz kid Murt Ryan, from Tipperary. Sessions take place at an ever-changing roster of pubs; ☞ **O'Halloran's Bar,** ☞ **Knox's** and, most notably, ☞ **Cruise's** are all hot venues. This last pub boasts an adjacent concert venue where a few years ago a group of local musicians recorded a lovely live album, *The Sanctuary Sessions.* Still available through stores specializing in traditional music, the album is an excellent introduction to Irish music, with the featured artists including most of the above-mentioned musicians as well as banjo player Mary Shannon and the wonderful Galway singer Seán Tyrrell. In May, Ennis is home to the ☞ **Fleadh Nua** festival—which celebrated its 25th year in 1998—with concerts, competitions, workshops, and *céilís* (Irish dancing and song).

—By Sarah McQuaid

who have raised street theater to new levels. Their participation in the Galway Arts Festival's annual parade is always much anticipated.

The **Town Hall Theatre** (✉ Courthouse Sq., Woodquay, ☎ 091/569777), opened in 1995 in the city's former town hall, is lit virtually every night.

VISUAL ARTS AND GALLERIES
Art Euro Gallery (✉ The Bridge Mills, O'Brien's Bridge, ☎ 091/562884) has a collection of free-blown glass and unusual handmade ceramics by Irish and other European artists. High-quality work by local artists can be found at **Kenny's Bookshop & Art Galleries** (☞ Shopping, *below*). The art gallery at **University College Galway** (☎ 091/524411) has a number of exhibits each year.

Outdoor Activities and Sports

BICYCLING
Set off to explore the Galway area, especially its coast, by renting a bike from **Mountain Trail Bike Shop** (✉ The Cornstore, Middle St., ☎ 091/569888).

FISHING
You can get fishing licenses, tackle, and bait and arrange to hire a traditional fly-fishing guide or book a sea angling trip at **Freeny's Sports** (✉ 19–23 High St., ☎ 091/562609). **Murt's** (✉ 7 Daly's Pl., Woodquay, ☎ 091/561018) can also handle your fishing needs.

GOLF
Galway Bay Golf and Country Club (✉ Renville, Oranmore, ☎ 091/790500) is an 18-hole, par-72 parkland course designed by Christy O'-Connor Jr. on the shores of Galway Bay. The **Galway Golf Club** (✉ Blackrock, Salthill, ☎ 091/522033) is an 18-hole, par-71 course with excellent views of Galway Bay, the Burren, and the Aran Islands. Some of the fairways run close to the ocean.

RIVER CRUISING
A **Corrib Cruise** from Wood Quay (behind the Town Hall Theatre at the Rowing Club) is a lovely way to spend a fine afternoon; it lasts 1½ hours and travels 8 km (5 mi) up the River Corrib and about 6 km (4 mi) around Lough Corrib. You can also rent the boat for an evening. ☎ 091/592447. ⊡ £6. ☉ May–Sept., daily 2:30 and 4:30; July–Aug., daily 12:30.

TENNIS
There are nine courts at the **Galway Lawn Tennis Club** (✉ Threadneedle St., Salthill, ☎ 091/522353) available to nonmembers at £4 per hour.

WATER SPORTS
Bow Waves (✉ 11 Ashleigh Grove, Knockacarra, ☎ 091/591481) schedules individually tailored trips around Galway Bay on high-performance inflatables. Life jackets and wet gear are included in the price. Ride the waves for thrills, or take it easy on a seal and dolphin watch. **Galway Bay Sailing Club** (✉ Renville, Oranmore, ☎ 091/794527) offers dinghy sailing and board sailing on Lough Corrib or on coastal waters. Instruction is also available.

Shopping
For a brief overview of Galway's shopping scene, *see* A Good Walk, *above*.

BOOKSTORES
Charlie Byrne's Bookshop (✉ The Cornstore, Middle St., ☎ 091/561766) sells a large, varied selection of used books and remainders. **Kenny's Bookshop & Art Galleries** (✉ High St., ☎ 091/562739) has

five floors of books of Irish topics, mainly secondhand and antiquarian, as well as prints, maps, and a small art gallery.

CLOTHING, CRAFTS, AND GIFTS

Don't miss **Design Concourse Ireland** (✉ Kirwan's La., ☎ 091/566016), a spectacular one-stop shop for the best in Irish handcrafted design. **Design Ireland Plus** (✉ The Cornstore, Middle St., ☎ 091/567716; The Grainstore, Lower Abbeygate St., ☎ 091/566620) has an excellent range of contemporary Irish-made crafts and clothing. **Faller's Sweater Shop** (✉ 25 High St., ☎ 091/564833; 35 Eyre Sq., ☎ 091/561255) has the choicest selection of Irish-made sweaters, competitively priced. **Meadows & Byrne** (✉ Castle St., ☎ 091/567776) sells the best in modern household items. **O'Máille's** (✉ 16 High St., ☎ 091/562696) carries Aran sweaters, handwoven tweeds, and classically tailored clothing. Browse in **Treasure Chest** (✉ William St., ☎ 091/563862) for china, crystal, gifts, and classic clothing.

JEWELRY

The **Claddagh Jewellers** (✉ Eyre Sq., ☎ 091/562310) has a wide selection of traditional Claddagh rings and other jewelry.

MALLS

Slightly off the beaten path, the **Cornstore** (✉ Middle St.) has some stylish shops that tend to be less crowded than their competitors on the main streets. On the southwest side of Eyre Square and imaginatively designed to incorporate parts of the old town walls, the **Eyre Square Shopping Centre** (✉ Eyre Sq.) offers a wide range of moderately priced clothing and household goods.

MUSIC

Back2Music (✉ 30 Upper Abbeygate St., ☎ 091/565272) specializes in traditional Irish musical instruments, including the hand-held drum, the *bohdran* (pronounced bau-rawn). **Mulligan** (✉ 5 Middle St. Court, ☎ 091/564961) carries more than 6,000 CDs, records, and cassettes, with a large collection of traditional Irish music.

VINTAGE GOODS

Twice as Nice (✉ 5 Quay St., ☎ 091/566332) sells a mix of new and vintage men's and women's clothing, linens, lace, and jewelry at reasonable prices.

THE ARAN ISLANDS

The Aran Islands—Inishmore, Inishmaan, and Inisheer—are remote western outposts of the ancient province of Connaught (though they are not the country's westernmost points; that honor belongs to the Blasket Islands [☞ Chapter 5]). These three islands were once as barren as the limestone pavements of the Burren, of which they are a continuation. Today, the land is parceled into small, man-made fields surrounded by stone walls. The views from here are spectacular. Witness the uninterrupted expanse of the Atlantic on the western horizon; to the northeast, the Connemara coast and its Twelve Bens; and, to the southeast, County Clare's Burren and the Cliffs of Moher.

The islands have been populated for thousands of years. Nowadays the Irish-speaking inhabitants enjoy a daily air service to Galway (subsidized by the government), motorized curraghs, multichannel TVs, and all the usual modern home conveniences. Yet they have retained a distinctness from mainlanders, preferring simple home decor, very plain food, and tightly knit communities, like the hardy fisher and farming folk from whom they are descended. Crime is virtually unknown in these parts; at your B&B, you'll find no locks on the guest-room doors, and the front-door latch will be left open.

Many islanders have sampled life in Dublin or cities abroad but have returned to raise families, keeping the population stable at around 1,500. Through the years, the islands have also attracted writers and artists, including J. M. Synge (1871–1909), who learned Irish on Inishmaan and wrote about its people in his play *Riders to the Sea*. The film *Man of Aran*, made on Inishmore in 1932 by the American director Robert Flaherty, is a classic documentary recording the islanders' dramatic battles with sea and storm. (The film is shown in the Community Hall in Kilronan, Inishmore, every afternoon during July, August, and early September.)

The best time to visit the islands is May and early June while the unusual, Burren-like flora is at its best and before the bulk of the approximately 200,000 annual visitors arrive. (For details on getting to the Aran Islands, *see* Getting Around *in* The West A to Z, *below*.)

Inis Mór (Inishmore)

③⓪ *24 km (15 mi) south of Ros an Mhil (Rossaveal), 48 km (30 mi) west of Galway Docks.*

With a population of 900, Inishmore is the largest of the islands and the closest to the Connemara coast. It's also the most commercialized, its appeal slightly diminished by road traffic. In the summer, ferries arriving at **Kilronan,** Inishmore's main village and port, are met by minibuses and pony and cart drivers, all eager to show visitors "the sights." More than 8 km (5 mi) long and about 3 km (2 mi) wide at most points, with an area of 7,640 acres, the island is just a little too large to explore comfortably on foot in a day. The best way to see it is really by bicycle; bring your own or rent one from one of the three vendors right near the quay (☞ below). The **Aran Heritage Centre** explains the history and culture of the islanders, who for many years lived in virtual isolation from the mainland. ☎ 099/61355. ☑ £2. ☉ Apr.–Oct., daily 10–7.

★ The main attraction on Inishmore is **Dún Aengus,** one of the finest prehistoric monuments in Europe, dating from about 2000 BC. Spectacularly set on the edge of a 300-ft cliff overlooking a sheer drop, the fort has defenses consisting of three rows of concentric circles. Who the builders were defending themselves against is a matter of conjecture. From the innermost rampart there's a great view of the island and the Connemara coast. In order to protect this fragile monument from erosion, visitors are asked to approach it only through the **visitor cen**ter, which gives access to a 1-km (½-mi) uphill walk over uneven terrain, so wear sturdy footwear. ☒ *Kilmurvey, 7 km (4 mi) west of Kilronan,* ☎ 099/61010. ☑ £1. ☉ Mar.–Oct., daily 10–6; Nov.–Feb. daily 11:30–3:30. ✍

Lodging
The only hotel on the islands is on Inis Oirr, but there's no shortage of B&Bs, mostly in simple family homes. The best way to book is through the **Galway City TIO** (☞ Galway, *above*). Each island has at least one wine-licensed restaurant serving plain home cooking. Most B&Bs will provide a packed lunch and an evening meal (called high tea) on request.

$ ⊡ **Kilmurvey House.** At the foot of Dún Aengus fort, about 6½ km (4 mi) from the quay and the airport (accessible by minibus), this rambling 200-year-old stone farmhouse is the first choice of many visitors to the island—about 60% of them American. ☒ *Kilmurvey, Co. Galway,* ☎ 099/61218, ℻ 099/61397. *12 rooms with bath. Dining room. MC, V. Closed Nov.–Feb.*

Nightlife

The place to go for traditional music is the **American Bar** (✉ Kilronan, ☎ 099/61130).

Outdoor Activities and Sports

Bicycles can be rented May through October from **Aran Bicycle Hire** (☎ 099/61132), **Burke and Mullin** (☎ 099/61402), and **Costello's** (☎ 099/61241).

Inis Meáin (Inishmaan)

③ *3 km (2 mi) east of Inishmore.*

The middle island in both size and location, Inishmaan has a population of about 300 and can be comfortably explored on foot. In fact, you have no alternative if you want to reach the island's major antiquities: Conor Fort, a smaller version of Dún Aengus; the ruins of two early Christian churches; and a chamber tomb known as the Bed of Diarmuid and Grainne, dating from about 2000 BC. You can also take wonderful cliff walks above secluded coves. It's on Inishmaan that the traditional Aran lifestyle is most evident. Until the mid-1930s or so, Aran women dressed in thick, red-woolen skirts to keep out the Atlantic gales, while the men wore collarless jackets, baggy trousers made of homespun tweed with *pampooties* (hide shoes without heels, suitable for walking on rocks), and a wide, hand-plaited belt called a *críos* (pronounced krish). Most islanders still don hand-knitted Aran sweaters, though nowadays they accompany them with jeans and sneakers.

Inis Oirr (Inisheer)

③ *4 km (2½ mi) east of Inishmaan, 8 km (5 mi) northwest of Doolin.*

The smallest and flattest of the islands, Inisheer can be explored on foot in an afternoon, though if the weather is fine, you may be tempted to linger on the long, sandy beach between the quay and the airfield. In the summer, Inisheer's population of 300 is augmented by high school students from all over Ireland attending the Gaeltacht, or Irish-language, school. Only one stretch of road, about 500 yards long, links the airfield and the village. The **Church of Kevin,** signposted to the southeast of the quay, is a small, early Christian church that gets buried in sand by storms every winter. Every year the islanders dig it out of the sand for the celebration of St. Kevin's Day on June 14. A pleasant walk through the village takes you up to **O'Brien's Castle,** a ruined 15th-century tower that sits on top of a rocky hill—the only hill on the island.

It's worth making a circuit of the island to get a sense of its utter tranquillity. A maze of footpaths runs between the high stone walls that divide the fields, which are so small that they can support only one cow each, or two to three sheep. Those that are not cultivated or grazed turn into natural wildflower meadows between June and August, overrun with harebells, scabious, red clover, oxeye daisies, saxifrage, and tall grasses. It seems almost a crime to walk here—but how can you resist taking a rest in the corner of a sweet-smelling meadow on a sunny afternoon, sheltered by high stone walls with no sound but the larks above and the wind as it sifts through the stones? "The back of the island," as Inisheer's uninhabited side facing the Atlantic is called, has no beaches, but people still swim off the rocks.

Lodging

$ 🏨 **Hotel Inisheer.** A pleasant, modern low-rise in the middle of the island's only village, a few minutes' walk from the quay and the airstrip, this simple, whitewashed building with a slate roof and half-slated walls has bright, plainly furnished rooms. The five newer rooms are slightly larger than the other 10. The restaurant (open to nonguests) is the best bet on the island, although much of the food is imported frozen. ⊠ *Lurgan Village, Co. Galway,* ☎ *099/75020,* ℻ *099/75099. 15 rooms, 12 with bath. Restaurant, bar, bicycles. AE, DC, MC, V. Closed Oct.–Mar.*

THROUGH CONNEMARA AND COUNTY MAYO

Bordered by the long expanse of Lough Corrib on the east and the deeply indented, jagged coast of the Atlantic on the west, rugged, desolate western County Galway is known as Connemara. Like the American West, it's an area of spectacular, almost myth-making geography—of glacial lakes; gorgeous, silent mountains; lonely roads; and hushed, uninhabited boglands. The Twelve Bens, "the central glory of Connemara," as author Brendan Lehane has called them, together with the Maamturk Mountains to their north, lord proudly over the area's sepia boglands. More surprisingly, stands of Scotch pine, Norwegian spruce, Douglas fir, and Japanese Sitka grow in Connemara's valleys and up hillsides—the result of a concerted national project that has so far reforested 9% of Ireland. In the midst of this wilderness, you'll find few people, for Connemara's population is sparse even by Irish standards. Especially in the off-season, you're far more likely to come across sheep strolling its roads than another car.

Two main routes—one inland, the other coastal—lead through Connemara. To take the inland route described below, leave Galway City on the well-signposted outer-ring road and follow signs for N59—Moycullen, Oughterard, and Clifden. If you choose to go the coastal route, you'll travel due west from Galway City to Rossaveal on R336 through Salthill, Barna, and Spiddle—all in the heart of the West's strong Gaeltacht, home to roughly 40,000 Irish speakers. Although this is one of the most impressive and unspoiled coastal roads in Ireland, it has been scarred by modern one-story concrete homes—a sort of faux-Spanish hacienda style favored by locals. (Most of the traditional thatched houses in the West are now used as vacation homes.) You can continue north on R336 from Rossaveal to Maam Cross and then head for coastal points west, or pick up R340 and putter along the coast.

Oughterard

🌑 *27 km (17 mi) northwest of Galway City on N59.*

Small and pretty Oughterard (pronounced *ook*-ter-ard) is the main village on the western shores of **Lough Corrib** and one of Ireland's leading angling resorts. The lough is signposted to the right in the village center, less than 1½ km (1 mi) up the road. From mid-June to early September, local boatmen offer trips on the lough, which has several islands. It is also possible to take a boat trip to Cong (☞ *below*), at the north shore of the lough. Midway between Oughterard and Cong, **Inchagoill Island** (the Island of the Stranger), a popular destination for a half-day trip, has several early Christian church remains. The cost of boat rides is negotiable; expect to pay about £6 per person.

Lodging

$$$ 🏨 **Connemara Gateway.** This adventurously designed, modern low-rise with traditional, gray-slate roofs above whitewashed walls combines the best of the old and the new. With a nod to the classic Irish cottage, the lobby and bar are decorated with wooden and cast-iron artifacts and chintz sofas. Guest rooms have modern furniture, floral wall panels with matching drapes, and fluffy mohair coverlets. All have sitting areas beside the large teak-framed windows, which overlook the gardens and the distant hills. There's a strong tour-bus trade, but it doesn't spoil the charming atmosphere. The hotel is about 1 km (½ mi) outside the village on the Galway side of N59. ⊠ *Co. Galway,* ☎ *091/ 552328,* FAX *091/552332. 62 rooms with bath. Restaurant, bar, indoor pool, sauna, tennis court, fishing. AE, DC, MC, V. Closed Dec.–mid-Feb.* ✍

$$ ☒ **Ross Lake House.** Five kilometers (3 miles) from Oughterard and well off the beaten track, this Georgian house is a low-key country hide-away. Managed by an enthusiastic couple, Henry and Elaine Reid, the house is set near a stream and within 5 acres of colorful gardens. (In spite of the name there is no lake on the grounds, but there are plenty of them nearby.) The interior is comfortably furnished with Victorian antiques and welcoming open fires. Guest rooms in the converted stables are sim-pler and a little smaller than those in the house, but all have peaceful garden views. A table d'hôte dinner menu offers good-quality, plain coun-try-house cooking. ⊠ *Rosscahill, Co. Galway,* ☎ *091/550109,* FAX *091/550109. 13 rooms with bath. Restaurant, bar, tennis court, horse-back riding, fishing. AE, DC, MC, V. Closed Nov.–mid-Mar.* ✍

Nightlife
For good music try **Faherty's** (☎ 091/552194).

Outdoor Activities and Sports
Oughterard Golf Club (☎ 091/552131) has an 18-hole, par-70 park-land course suitable for novices and those who wish to improve their games.

En Route   As you continue northwest from Oughterard on N59, you'll soon pass a string of small lakes on your left; their shining blue waters reflect-ing the blue sky are a typical Connemara sight on a sunny day. Six-teen kilometers (10 miles) northwest of Oughterard, the continuation of the coast road (R336) meets N59 at **Maam Cross** in the shadow of Leckavrea Mountain. Once an important meeting place for the peo-ple of north and south Connemara, it's still the location of a large monthly cattle fair. Walkers will find wonderful views of Connemara by heading for any of the local peaks visible from the road. Beyond Maam Cross, some of the best scenery in Connemara awaits on the road to **Recess,** 16 km (10 mi) west of Maam Cross on N59. At many points on this drive, a short walk away from either side of the main road will lead you to the shores of one of the area's many small loughs. Stop and linger if the sun is out—even intermittently—for the light filtering through the clouds gives splendor to the distant, dark-gray mountains and creates patterns on the brown-green moorland below. In June and July, it stays light until 11 PM or so, and it is worth taking a late-evening stroll to see the sun's reluctance to set. In Recess, **Joyce's** (☎ 095/34604) carries a good selection of contemporary ceramics, handwoven shawls, books of Irish interest, original paintings, and small sculptures.

Cong

③④ *23 km (14 mi) northeast of Maam Cross on N59.*

Resting on a narrow isthmus between Lough Corrib and Lough Mask on the County Mayo border, the pretty, old-world village of Cong, which can be detoured to from Maam Cross, is dotted with ivy-covered thatched cottages and dilapidated farmhouses. Cong is surrounded by many stone circles and burial mounds, but its most notable ruins are those of the **Augustine Abbey** (⊠ Abbey St., ☎ no phone), dating from the early 13th century and still exhibiting some finely carved details.

It can be seen overlooking a river near fabulous Ashford Castle (☞ Lodging, *below*). Cong's 15 minutes of fame came in 1952, when John Ford filmed *The Quiet Man*, one of his most popular films, here; John Wayne plays a prizefighter who goes home to Ireland to court the fiery Maureen O'Hara. (Pauline Kael called the film "fearfully Irish and green and hearty.") The **Quiet Man Heritage Cottage,** in the village center, is an exact replica of the cottage used in the film, with reproductions of the furniture and costumes, a few original artifacts, and pictures of Barry Fitzgerald and Maureen O'Hara on location. ☎ 092/ 46089. ✆ £2.50. ⊙ *Mar.–Nov., daily 10–6.*

Lodging

$$$$ ⊞ **Ashford Castle.** Perched at the head of Lough Corrib, surrounded
★ by neatly manicured lawns and gardens, this massive, flamboyantly turreted and crenellated castle was built in 1870 for the Guinness family in a mock-Gothic baronial style, incorporating an earlier 1228 structure built by the De Burgos family. Now American owned, Ashford is one of Ireland's most luxurious castle-hotels. Large oil paintings in gilt frames hang from the castle's carved stone walls above polished-wood paneling, illuminated by crystal chandeliers. Deluxe rooms have generous sitting areas, heavily carved antique furniture, and extralarge bathrooms. The suites are vast and faultless, furnished with Georgian antiques and blissfully comfortable. The bedrooms in the discreetly added wing are all individually designed and furnished with selected Victorian antiques. ⊠ *Co. Mayo,* ☎ *092/46003,* ℻ *092/46260. 72 rooms with bath, 11 suites. 2 restaurants, 2 bars, sauna, steam room, 9-hole golf course, 2 tennis courts, health club, horseback riding, boating, fishing, bicycles. AE, DC, MC, V.* ✍

Cashel

㉟ *8 km (5 mi) south of Recess on R340, 49½ km (31 mi) west of Cong.*

Cashel is a quiet, extremely sheltered angling center at the head of Bertraghboy Bay. General de Gaulle is among the many people who have sought seclusion here. A word of caution in this area: stray sheep, bolting Connemara ponies, cyclists, and reckless local drivers are all regular hazards on the narrow mountain roads hereabouts.

Dining and Lodging

$$$ ✕⊞ **Cashel House.** Quietly secluded on 40 acres of woodlands at the
★ head of Cashel Bay—with exotic shrubs flowering and Connemara ponies grazing out back—Kay and Dermot McEvilly's luxurious country house has possibly more antiques and curios per square foot than any other hotel in Ireland. Intricately carved oak tables, Biedermeier bureaus, gilt mirrors, Georgian bookcases, ormolu clocks, and other knickknacks are liberally scattered around the lobby, lounge, library, and downstairs corridors. More antiques and curios turn up in the bedrooms, which have king-size beds (canopied in the 13 minisuites), pink-and-green drapes and spreads, and brass bedside lamps. For a view of the sea rather than the garden, ask for a front room. In the dining room, the table d'hôte menu, with more choices than at many other country houses, is particularly strong on fresh local seafood. ⊠ *Co. Galway,* ☎ *095/31001,* ℻ *095/31077. 19 rooms with bath, 13 suites. Restaurant, tennis court, horseback riding, beach, boating, fishing, bicycles. AE, DC, MC, V. Closed mid-Jan.–mid-Feb.* ✍

$$$ ⊞ **Zetland Country House.** Built for the Earl of Zetland on a hill overlooking secluded Cashel Bay, John and Mona Prendergast's mid-Victorian hunting lodge is an unforgettable experience within the wilderness beauty of Connemara. Mature grounds and flowering shrubs are surrounded by views of the rocky, heather-covered shores and the jewel-like waters of Cashel Bay. A dining room with massive antique side-boards adorned with family silver overlooks the bay, as does the large and blissfully quiet sitting room. Bedrooms are large and many have sea views, but those with garden views are also attractive. The comfortable quarters are elegantly furnished with Georgian and Victorian antiques of polished mahogany. ⊠ *Co. Galway,* ☎ *095/31111,* 𝔽𝔸𝕏 *095/ 31117. 19 rooms with bath. Restaurant, bar, tennis court, fishing. AE, DC, MC, V. Closed Nov.–mid-Apr.* ⊛

Outdoor Activities and Sports

Cashel Equestrian Center (⊠ Cashel House, ☎ 095/31001) offers scenic treks and the chance to ride a Connemara pony on its home ground.

Ballynahinch

③⑥ *10 km (6 mi) west of Cashel on R341.*

Along the shores of Ballynahinch Lake you'll enter more forested country. Woodland in this part of Ireland indicates the proximity of a "big house" whose owner can afford to plant trees for pleasure and prevent their being cut down for fuel.

Lodging

$$$ 🏨 **Ballynahinch Castle.** Built in the late 18th century on the Owenmore
★ River amid 40 walkable wooded acres, Ballynahinch was once the home of Richard Martin (1754–1834), who was known as "Humanity Dick," the founder of the Royal Society for the Prevention of Cruelty to Animals. Comfort without ostentation is the hallmark here. The tiled lobby with Persian rugs has two inviting leather chesterfields in front of an open fire. The biggest bedrooms, in the discreetly added ground-floor wing, have four-poster beds, Georgian-style mahogany furniture, and floor-to-ceiling windows overlooking the river. Rooms in the old house are equally comfortable and quiet. The castle is signposted off N59 between Recess and Clifden. ⊠ *Recess, Co. Galway,* ☎ *095/ 31006,* 𝔽𝔸𝕏 *095/31085. 20 rooms with bath, 10 suites. Restaurant, bar, tennis court, croquet, fishing, horseback riding. AE, DC, MC, V. Closed Feb. and last wk of Dec.* ⊛

Clifden

★ **③⑦** *23 km (14 mi) west of Recess, 79 km (49 mi) northwest of Galway City on N59.*

With roughly 1,100 residents, Clifden would be called a village by most, but in these parts it is looked on as something of a metropolis. It is far and away the prettiest town in Connemara, as well as its unrivaled "capital." Clifden's first attraction is its location—perched high above Clifden Bay on a forested plateau, its back to the spectacular Twelve Ben Mountains. The tapering spires of the town's two churches add to its alpine feel. A selection of small restaurants, lively bars with music most nights in the summer, pleasant accommodations, and excellent walks make the town a popular base. It's quiet out of season, but in July and August crowds flock here, especially for August's world-famous **Connemara Pony Show.** Horse breeders come from around the world to check out Ireland's finest yearlings and stallions. Clifden's popularity, which has led to a chaotic one-way traffic system and loud techno music blasting out of certain bars, means that if you're over 25 and value your peace and quiet, you'd best choose a base outside town.

A 2-km (1-mi) walk along the beach road through the grounds of the ruined **Clifden Castle** is the best way to explore the seashore. It was built in 1815 by John D'Arcy, the town's founder, who laid out the town's wide main street on a long ridge with a parallel street below it. D'Arcy was High Sheriff of Galway, and his greatest wish was to establish a center of law and order in what he saw as the lawless wilderness of Connemara. Before the founding of Clifden, the interior of Connemara was largely uninhabited, with most of its population clinging to the seashore. Take the aptly named **Sky Road** to really appreciate Clifden's breathtakingly scenic setting. Signposted at the west end of town, this high, narrow circuit of about 5 km (3 mi) heads west to Kingstown, skirting Clifden Bay's precipitous shores.

Dining and Lodging

$$ ✕ **Destry's.** Owned by Paddy and Julia Foyle of Quay House (☞ *below*), this upbeat, extrovert town-center eatery on two floors is named for the Marlene Dietrich film *Destry Rides Again*. The decor combines film memorabilia with local bric-a-brac—look for the skull that sits on top of a Georgian fanlight. The menu is similarly unpredictable, eclectic with a strong Mediterranean influence, making use of good-quality olive oil and fresh herbs. The signature dessert is Lethal Chocolate Pud, made with a carefully guarded secret recipe. ⊠ *The Square,* ☎ *095/21722. MC, V. Closed Mon. and Nov.–mid-Mar.*

$$ ✕ **O'Grady's Seafood.** A Clifden institution, this intimate, town-center restaurant serves fresh local produce, primarily seafood, more modishly than you might expect in the wilds of Connemara. Once a shop, the small main room is decorated in dark pinks and reds with wrought-iron dividers between the tables. Typical main courses might include a duo of monkfish and blackened scallops on a cilantro duxelles with two sauces, or crisp breast of duckling in its own juice with sweet caramelized onions. ⊠ *Market St.,* ☎ *095/21450. MC, V. Closed Sun. and Nov.–Apr.*

$$$ ✕🎦 **Rock Glen Manor House.** Cross the bridge at the west end of
★ town and walk ⅘ km (½ mi) down the R341 Roundstone road to find John and Evangeline Roche's beautifully converted shooting lodge, built in 1815. Riding boots and tennis rackets in the hall make this feel more like a private home than a top-class hotel. A turf fire warms the large, sunny drawing room, with plump white armchairs, magazines, books, and board games. Guest rooms are nicely furnished with Georgian pieces, with fluffy mohair or chintz bedspreads and fully tiled bathrooms. In the Victorian-style restaurant, you might enjoy such dishes as roasted rack of lamb with an herb crust and mushroom duxelles. ⊠ *Co. Galway,* ☎ *095/21035,* 🗷 *095/21737. 29 rooms with bath. Restaurant, bar, tennis court, horseback riding, fishing. AE, DC, MC, V. Closed Nov.–mid-Mar. No lunch.* ✧

$$ ✕🎦 **Erriseask House.** The rambling, two-story modern house is on its
★ own private beach along the rocky shore of Mannin Bay. Warm wooden floors, well-crafted furniture, and an admirable lack of clutter combine to create a restful and very comfortable interior. Chef Stefan Matz has won many awards for his fine cooking, which is planned daily. Freshly turf-smoked fillet of beef is a house specialty. ⊠ *Ballyconneely, Co. Galway,* ☎ *095/23553,* 🗷 *095/23639. 8 rooms with bath, 5 suites. Restaurant. AE, DC, MC, V. Closed Nov.–Mar.* ✧

$$ 🎦 **Quay House.** A roaring turf fire in the sitting room greets visitors to this three-story Georgian house, Clifden's oldest building (1820). It's a short walk from the busy town center, and an oasis of calm beside the harbor quay. Rooms are unusually spacious, and those in the main house are imaginatively decorated with deep-color walls and witty bygones; all but one have sea views. There are also seven studio rooms with tiny kitchens and balconies overlooking the harbor. Proprietors Julia and Patrick Foyle tucked in homey touches such as books and

model boats. The excellent restaurant, Destry's (☞ *above*), has moved
to the town center. ⊠ *Connemara, Co. Galway,* ☎ *095/21369,* FAX *095/
21608. 14 rooms with bath. Fishing. MC, V. Closed Nov.–mid-Mar.
except by arrangement.* ⊛

Nightlife

The best place in town for music is the **Abbeyglen Castle** (⊠ Sky Rd.,
☎ 095/21201), which has sessions in the bar most nights from June
to September and occasional visits by big-name acts.

Outdoor Activities and Sports

BICYCLING

Explore Connemara by renting a bike from **John Mannion & Son** (⊠
Railway View, ☎ 095/21160).

GOLF

On a dramatic stretch of Atlantic coastline, the 18-hole, par-72 course
at the **Connemara Golf Club** (⊠ Ballyconneely, south of Clifden, ☎ 095/
23502) measures 7,174 yards (☞ Chapter 9).

HORSEBACK RIDING

Errislannan Manor Connemara Pony Stud and Riding Center (☎ 095/
21134) provides mountain treks, instruction, and courses for children.

Shopping

Millar's Connemara Tweeds (⊠ Main St., ☎ 095/21038) is a general
art-and-crafts gallery with a good selection of traditional tweeds and
hand knits. The **Station House Courtyard** (⊠ Old Railway Station, ☎
095/21699) is a newly restored cobbled courtyard with crafts studios
and top designer-wear outlets.

En Route   Continue toward Letterfrack through the **Inagh Valley,** which is flanked
by two impressive mountain ranges with distinctive, conical-shape
peaks, rising almost directly—without any foothills—to over 1,968 ft.

Letterfrack

🟤 *14 km (9 mi) north of Clifden on the N59.*

The 5,000-acre **Connemara National Park** lies southeast of the village
of Letterfrack. Its **visitor center** covers the area's history and ecology,
particularly the origins and growth of peat—and presents the de-
pressing statistic that more than 80% of Ireland's peat, 5,000 years in
the making, has been destroyed in the last 90 years. You can also get
details on the many excellent walks and beaches in the area. ☎ *095/
41054.* ⊠ *Park free, visitor center £2.* ☉ *Park freely accessible; visitor center Apr.–May and Sept.–mid. Oct., daily 10–5:30; June, daily
10–6:30; July–Aug., daily 9:30–6:30.*

Dining and Lodging

$$$ ✕🏨 **Renvyle House.** A lake at its front door, the Atlantic Ocean at its
back door, and the mountains of Connemara as a backdrop make for
an enthralling setting for this hotel 8 km (5 mi) north of Letterfrack.
Once the retreat of the man of letters Oliver St. John Gogarty, Ren-
vyle's has a rustic, informal ambience, with exposed beams and brick-
work and numerous open turf fires. All the comfortable guest rooms,
elegantly decorated in a floral country-house style, have breathtaking
views. The softly lit restaurant's table d'hôte menu is based on the tra-
ditional country-house style. ⊠ *Renvyle, Co. Galway,* ☎ *095/43511,*
FAX *095/43515. 65 rooms with bath. Restaurant, bar, pool, 9-hole golf
course, 2 tennis courts, horseback riding, fishing. AE, DC, MC, V. Closed
Jan.–Feb.* ⊛

$$$ ✕⊞ **Rosleague Manor.** Anne and Patrick Foyle's pink, creeper-clad,
★ two-story Georgian house sits on 30 lovely acres of wooded grounds
overlooking Ballinakill Bay and the mountains of County Mayo and
Connemara. Inside, the clutter of walking and shooting sticks beneath
the grandfather clock in the hall sets the tone, which is fairly informal.
The solidly comfortable bedrooms are furnished with well-used Vic-
torian and Georgian antiques, four-poster or large brass bedsteads, and
drapes that match the William Morris wallpaper. The best rooms are
at the front on the first floor, overlooking the bay. At dinner in the su-
perb restaurant, baked monkfish with crispy capers and balsamic vine-
gar is a typical entrée. ✉ *Co. Galway,* ☎ *095/41101,* ℻ *095/41168.
19 rooms with bath. Restaurant, bar, sauna, tennis court, horseback
riding. AE, MC, V. Closed Nov.–Mar..* ✎

Nightlife
For traditional music, try the **Bards' Den** (☎ 095/41042).

Outdoor Activities and Sports
Little Killary Adventure Center (✉ Salruck, Renvyle, Co. Galway, ☎
095/43411) provides sailing and windsurfing instruction on sheltered,
coastal waters.

Shopping
Connemara Handcrafts (☎ 095/41058) carries an extensive selection
of crafts and women's fashions made by the stellar Avoca Handweavers
(☞ Chapter 2); there's also an above-average coffee shop.

Kylemore Valley

③⑨ *6½ km (4 mi) between Letterfrack and the intersection of N59 and R344.*

One of the more conventionally beautiful stretches of road in Connemara
passes through Kylemore Valley, which lies between the Twelve Bens
to the south and the naturally forested Dorruagh Mountains to the north.
Kylemore (the name is derived from Coill Mór, Irish for "big wood")
looks "as though some colossal giant had slashed it out with a couple
of strokes from his mammoth sword," as John FitzMaurice Mills has
★ written. **Kylemore Abbey,** one of the most photographed castles in all
of Ireland, is visible across a reedy lake with a backdrop of wooded
hillside. The vast Gothic Revival, turreted, gray stone castle was built
as a private home between 1861 and 1868 by Mitchell Henry, a mem-
ber of Parliament for County Galway, and his wife, Margaret, who had
fallen in love with the spot during a carriage ride while on their hon-
eymoon. The Henrys spared no expense—the final bill for their house
is said to have come to £1.5 million—and employed mostly local la-
borers, thereby abetting the famine relief effort (this area was among
the worst hit in all of Ireland). In 1920, nuns from the Irish Abbey of
the Nuns of St. Benedict, fleeing their abbey in Belgium during World
War I, eventually sought refuge in Kylemore, which had been through
a number of owners and decades of decline after the Henrys. Still in
residence today, the Benedictine nuns now run a girls' boarding school
here. Three reception rooms and the main hall are open to the public,
as are a crafts center and simple cafeteria. An exhibition and video ex-
plaining the history of the house can be viewed year-round at the
abbey, and the grounds are freely accessible most of the year. A newly
restored 6-acre walled Victorian garden opened in 1999. Ask at the
crafts shop for directions to the **Gothic Chapel** (a five-minute walk from
the abbey), a tiny replica of Norwich Cathedral built by the Henrys.
(Norwich was built by the English Benedictines, in a felicitous antici-
pation of Kylemore's fate.) ✉ *About ¾ km (½ mi) back from the Kyle-
more Valley road,* ☎ *095/41146.* ▣ *Chapel free, exhibition £3, garden*

£3. ⊘ *Crafts shop Mar. 17–Nov., daily 10–6; cafeteria Easter–Nov., daily 9:30–6; grounds Easter–Nov., daily 9–dusk; exhibition and garden Easter–Nov., daily 9–5:30.* ❧

En Route Beyond Kylemore, N59 travels for some miles alongside **Killary Harbour,** a narrow fjord (the only one in Ireland) that runs for 16 km (10 mi) between County Mayo's Mweelrea Mountains to the north and County Galway's Dorruagh Mountains to the south. The harbor has an extremely safe anchorage, 13 fathoms (78 ft) deep for almost its entire length and sheltered from storms by mountain walls. The rafts floating in Killary Harbour belong to fish-farming consortia who artificially raise salmon and trout in cages beneath the water. This is a matter of some controversy all over the West. Although some people welcome the employment opportunities, others bemoan the visual blight of the rafts. **Sea Cruise Connemara** (✉ Nancy's Point, 2 km/1 mi west of Leenane on the N59 Clifden road, ☎ 091/566736) runs 1½-hour trips around Killary Harbour in an enclosed launch with seating for 120 passengers, plus a bar and restaurant, from mid-April through mid-October.

Leenane

⓵ *18 km (12 mi) east of Letterfrack on N59.*

Nestled idyllically at the foot of the Maamturk Mountains and overlooking the tranquil waters of Killary Harbour, Leenane is a tiny village noted for its role as the setting for the 1990 film *The Field,* which starred Richard Harris. Its name appears in Martin McDonagh's *Leenane Trilogy,* an unflattering view of rural Irish life featuring a cast of tragi-comic grotesques. However, although it was an international hit for Galway's Druid Theatre Company in 1997, it brought a renown that the people of Leenane presumably could have done without. Leenane's **Cultural Centre** illustrates the traditional industry of North Connemara and West Mayo. More than 20 breeds of sheep graze around the house, and there are live demonstrations of carding, spinning, weaving, and the dyeing of wool with natural plant dyes. ☎ 095/42323. ☜ *£2.50.* ⊘ *Apr.– June and Oct., daily 9:30–7; July–Aug., daily 9 AM–7 PM.*

Lodging

$$ ⚷ **Delphi Lodge.** In the heart of what is arguably Mayo's most spec-
★ tacular mountain and lake scenery, 6 km (4 mi) northwest of Leenane, this attractive Georgian sporting lodge with a lovely lakeside setting is heavily stocked with fishing paraphernalia. Owners Peter and Jane Mantle are gracious hosts and valuable storehouses of information and stories. The bright, spacious bedrooms, some of which have lake views, feature pine furniture, floral curtains, and wonderfully comfortable beds. Guests dine together; there is an excellent wine list and a self-service bar. ✉ *Leenane, Co. Mayo,* ☎ *095/42211,* ℻ *095/42296. 12 rooms with bath. AE, MC, V. Closed Mid-Dec.–mid-Jan.* ❧

En Route You have two options for traveling onward to Westport. The first is to take the direct route on N59. The second is to detour through the **Doolough Valley** between the Mweelrea Mountains (to the west) and the Sheeffry Hills (to the east) and on to Westport via Louisburgh (on the southern shore of Clew Bay). This latter route adds about 24 km (15 mi) to the trip, but devotees of this part of the West claim that it'll take you through the region's most impressive, unspoiled stretch of scenery. If you opt for the longer route, turn left onto R335 1½ km (1 mi) beyond Leenane. Just after this turn, you'll hear the powerful rush of the Aasleagh Falls. You can park over the bridge, stroll along the river's shore, and soak in the splendor of the surrounding mountains.

Look out as you travel north for the great bulk of 2,500-ft **Croagh Patrick**; its size and conical shape make it one of the West's most distinctive landmarks. On clear days a small, white building is visible at its summit (it stands on a ½-acre plateau), as is the wide path that ascends to it. The latter is the **Pilgrim's Path,** which about 25,000 people, many of them barefoot, follow each year to St. Patrick in the oratory on its peak. St. Patrick spent the 40 days and nights of Lent here during the period he was converting Ireland to Christianity. The traditional date for the pilgrimage is the last Sunday in July; in the past, the walk was made at night, with pilgrims carrying burning torches, but that practice has been discontinued. The climb can be made in about three hours (round-trip) on any fine day and is well worth it for the magnificent views of the islands of Clew Bay, the Sheeffry Hills to the south (with the Bens visible behind them), and the peaks of Mayo to the north. The climb starts at Murrisk, a village about 8 km (5 mi) before Westport on the R335 Louisburgh road.

Westport

★ ④ *32 km (20 mi) north of Leenane on R335.*

By far the most attractive town in County Mayo, Westport is on an inlet of Clew Bay, a wide expanse of sea dotted with islands and framed by mountain ranges. The architect James Wyatt planned the town in the late 18th century when he was employed to finish nearby Westport House (☞ *below*). Westport's streets radiate from its central **Octagon,** where an old-fashioned farmers' market is held on Thursday mornings; look for work clothes, harnesses, tools, and children's toys for sale. Traditional shops—ironmongers, drapers, and the like—dot the streets that lead to the Octagon, while a riverside mall is lined with tall lime trees. The town is a popular fishing center and has several good beaches close by.

At Westport's Quay, about 2 km (1 mi) outside town, a large warehouse has been attractively restored as holiday apartments, and there are some good bars and decent restaurants; its central attraction, however, is **Westport House,** a stately home built on the site of an earlier castle. The house was originally begun in 1730 to the designs of Richard Castle (☞ Leinster House *in* Chapter 1 and Powerscourt and Russborough Houses *in* Chapter 2), added to in 1778, and completed in 1788 by architect James Wyatt for the marquess of Sligo. The rectangular, three-story house is furnished with late-Georgian and Victorian pieces. Family portraits by Opie and Reynolds, old Irish silver, and a collection of old Waterford glass are all on display. The home is superbly situated beside a lake with a small formal garden; additional gardens are undergoing restoration. A word of caution: Westport isn't your usual staid country house. The old dungeons, which belonged to the earlier castle (believed to have been the home of the 16th-century warrior queen, Grace O'Malley), now house video games, and the grounds have given way to a small amusement park for children and a children's zoo. If these elements don't sound like a draw, arrive early when it's less likely to be busy. ⊠ *Off N59 south of Westport turn-off, clearly signposted from the Octagon,* ☎ *098/25430.* ☞ *House £6.50, family day ticket for all attractions £30.* ☉ *House May and Sept., weekends 2–5; grounds and house June, daily 2–6; July–Aug. 21, Mon.–Sat. 11:30–6, Sun. 2–6; Aug. 22–31, daily 2–6.*

Dining and Lodging

$$ ✕ **Quay Cottage.** Fishing nets, glass floats, lobster pots, and greenery hang from the high-pitched, exposed-beam roof of this tiny waterside cottage at the entrance to Westport House. Both an informal wine bar

and a shellfish restaurant, it attracts a youngish crowd in search of a good time and good food. Rush-seated chairs, polished-oak tables, and an open fire in the evenings add to the comfortable, none-too-formal atmosphere. Try the chowder special (a thick vegetable and mussel soup), garlic-butter crab claws, or a half-pound steak fillet, and be sure to sample the homemade brown bread. The restaurant serves wine only. ⊠ *The Quay,* ☎ *098/26412. AE, MC, V. Closed Jan.*

$$$ ✕🏠 **Newport House.** This handsome, creeper-covered Georgian house beside the Newport River dominates the village of Newport, 12 km (7 mi) north of Westport on N59. Kieran and Thelma Thompson's grand and elegant private home has spacious public rooms furnished with gilt-framed family portraits, Regency mirrors and chairs, handwoven Donegal carpeting, and crystal chandeliers hanging from ornate stucco ceilings. In the dining room, oysters, smoked salmon, roast breast of duck, and similar local delicacies are served, along with homemade ice creams for dessert. The sweeping staircase, lighted by a lantern and a glass dome, leads to an airy gallery and the bedrooms. Bright and less elaborate than the public rooms, these are decorated with pretty chintz drapes and a mix of Victorian antiques and old furniture. Most bedrooms have sitting areas and good views of the river and gardens. ⊠ *Newport, Co. Mayo,* ☎ *098/41222,* 🆁🆇 *098/41613. 19 rooms with bath. Restaurant, bar, fishing. AE, DC, MC, V. Closed Oct.–mid-Mar.* ✺

$$ ✕🏠 **Olde Railway Hotel.** By far the best bet in Westport's town center, this Victorian railway hotel offers both character and comfort. Fishing trophies, Victorian plates, framed prints, and watercolors brighten up the lobby and lounge. A mix of Victorian and older pieces decorate the sunny bedrooms, which have double-glazed Georgian sash windows. Two top picks: Room 209 has a heavy Victorian bed and a river view; and Room 114 has a Victorian chaise lounge and a large Georgian wardrobe. Overlooking the landscaped gardens, the Conservatory Restaurant serves fresh local produce and game specialties. ⊠ *The Mall, Co. Mayo,* ☎ *098/25605,* 🆁🆇 *098/25090. 24 rooms with bath. Restaurant, 2 bars, fishing. AE, MC, V. Closed mid-Jan.–mid-Feb.* ✺

Nightlife

A good spot to try for traditional music is the **Ardmore Pub** (⊠ The Quay, ☎ 098/25994). In Westport's town center try **Matt Molloy's** (⊠ Bridge St., ☎ 098/26655), owned by a member of the Chieftains, where traditional music is of course the main attraction.

Outdoor Activities and Sports

BICYCLING

Enjoy the spectacular scenery of Clew Bay at a leisurely pace on a rented bike from **J. P. Breheny & Sons** (⊠ Castlebar St., ☎ 098/25020).

FISHING

Fishing tackle, bait, and licenses can be obtained at **Patrick Kelly** (⊠ Bridge St., ☎ 098/25982).

GOLF

Westport Golf Club (⊠ Carrowholly, ☎ 098/28262), beneath Croagh Patrick, overlooks Clew Bay. Designed by Fred Hawtree in the early 1970s, the 18-hole, par-73 course has twice been the venue for the Irish Amateur Championship (☞ Chapter 9).

HORSEBACK RIDING

Drummindoo Stud and Equitation Center (⊠ Castlebar Rd., ☎ 098/25616) will take you on the Clew Bay Trail, a three-day trek riding on the superb beaches around Clew Bay staying in farmhouses along the route. Alternatively, you can rent a horse by the hour.

Shopping

Carraig Donn (✉ Bridge St., ☎ 098/26287) has its own range of knitwear and a good selection of crystal, jewelry, and ceramics. **Mc-Cormack's** (✉ Bridge St., ☎ 098/25619) has a traditional butcher shop downstairs, but upstairs it's an attractive gallery and café with work by local artists for sale. **Satch Kiely** (✉ Westport Quay, ☎ 098/25775) carries fine antique furniture and decorative pieces. **Westport Crystal** (✉ The Quay, ☎ 098/27780) is a factory outlet with a range of exclusive stemware and giftware.

Achill Island

★ ⓐ *16 km (10 mi) west of Mulrany, 58 km (36 mi) northwest of Westport.*

Heaven on earth in good weather, when its splendid scenery can be fully appreciated, Achill Island is a destination you'll probably want to head for—but only if you'll be able to *see* its cliff walks and sandy beaches. At 147 square km (57 square mi) and only 20 ft away from the mainland, this mass of bogs and wild heather is the largest island off Ireland's coast. A short causeway leads from the mainland to **Achill Sound,** the first village on the island. The main road runs through rhododendron plantations to **Keel,** which has a 3-km (2-mi) beach with spectacular cathedral-like rock formations in the cliffs at its east end. There's a longer scenic route signposted ATLANTIC DRIVE. **Dugoort,** on the north shore of the island, is a small village with a beautiful golden strand. Nearby is the cottage used by Heinrich Böll, German writer and Nobel Prize winner, whose *Irish Diary,* written in the 1950s, has introduced many visitors to this part of Ireland. The cottage today is part of a center for German-Irish cultural exchanges. On Achill's north coast above Dugoort, 2,204-ft **Slievemore** is the island's highest summit. Until just a few years ago, the people of Achill made a very poor living. Tourism has improved things, as has the establishment of cottage industries (mainly knitting) and shark fishing, which is popular from April to July. Alas, Achill's popularity has led to a rash of new, not always appropriate development, most noticeably clusters (or "villages") of bleak concrete vacation cottages that stand empty for 10 months out of 12.

Lodging

$ 🏨 **Ostan Gob A'Choire.** In the first village you approach arriving from the mainland, this small, waterside, two-story town house (its name means "Achill Sound Hotel") has a brick-and-plate-glass bedroom extension. All bedrooms have sea views, but the nicer ones, with tweed curtains and reproductions of Georgian furniture, are in the old building. The smaller rooms are already a little worn, but they are spotlessly clean and have pleasant views of the sound. ✉ *Achill Sound, Co. Mayo,* ☎ *098/45245,* 🅵🅰🆇 *098/45621. 36 rooms with bath. Restaurant, bar, bicycles. MC, V. Closed Oct.–Mar.* ☕

Outdoor Activities and Sports

Tour the cliffs of Achill on a bike from the **Ostan Gob A'Choire** (☎ 098/45245; ☞ Lodging, *above*). Bikes can also be rented from **O'Malley's Island Sports** (✉ Keel P.O., ☎ 098/43125).

En Route The shortest route to Ballina (N59 via Bangor and Crossmolina) runs for about 24 km (15 mi) across desolate, almost uninhabited bog, some of which has had its turf cut down to rock level by successive generations searching for fuel. If you intend to visit the Mullet peninsula, take this route. If you are heading directly for Ballina, we suggest you take the longer but more interesting route by backtracking to Newport and continuing through Castlebar, Pontoon, and Foxford.

Castlebar

㊸ *40 km (26 mi) east of Achill Island, 18 km (11 mi) east of Westport on N5.*

The administrative capital of Mayo, Castlebar is a tidy little town with an attractive, tree-bordered green. In 1879 Michael Davitt founded the Land League here, in the **Imperial Hotel** (⊠ The Green, ☎ 094/21961); it's worth a visit to check out the Gothic-style dining room, where the simply prepared country food is probably unchanged since Davitt's day. Hatred of landlords ran high in the area, due to the ruthless, battering-ram evictions ordered by the Earl of Lucan. The disappearance in the 1960s of his high-living successor, the seventh earl, after the violent death in London of his children's nanny, is said to have given today's tenants a perfect pretext for withholding their rents. Although coffee making isn't a strong point around here, the **Linen Hall Arts Centre** (⊠ Linenhall St., ☎ 094/23733) serves espresso and cappuccino in its café; grab a cup after viewing the art exhibitions and performances often scheduled here.

En Route As you travel from Castlebar northeast to Ballina, there is a choice of two routes. The longer and more scenic is via the tiny, wooded village of Pontoon, skirting the western shore of Lough Conn and passing through the rough bogland of the Glen of Nephin, beneath the dramatic heather-clad slopes of Nephin Mountain (2,653 ft). The shorter route follows N5 and N58 to Foxford, a pretty village with several crafts and antiques shops. A good place for a break is at the **Foxford Woollen Mills Visitor Center,** where you can explore the crafts shop and grab a bite at the restaurant. The **"Foxford Experience"** tells the story of the wool mill (famous for its tweeds and blankets) from the time of the famine—when it was founded by the Sisters of Charity to combat poverty—to the present day. ⊠ Foxford, ☎ 094/56756. ☑ £3. ☉ Sept.–June, Mon.–Sat. 10–6, Sun. 2–6; July–Aug., Sun. noon–6; tour every 20 mins.

Ballina

㊹ *40 km (25 mi) northeast of Castlebar.*

Ballina's chief attraction is fishing for salmon and trout in the River Moy and nearby Lough Conn. Although it is the largest town in County Mayo (population 7,500), to some eyes, Ballina's town center may appear run-down; however, its unspoiled, old-fashioned shops and pubs contain many treasures. Try the bar food at **Gaughan's** (⊠ O'Rahilly St., ☎ 096/21151), where the classic wooden interior dates back to the mid-19th century. On the same street, **McGrath's Foodland Delicatessen** (☎ 096/21198) is an old-fashioned grocery handy for picnic materials.

Dining and Lodging

$$ ✕🏠 **Enniscoe House.** A pink Georgian mansion on the shores of Lough Conn, 4½ km (3 mi) south of Crossmolina and 20 km (13 mi) west of Ballina, Enniscoe sits on 150 acres crisscrossed with pleasant walks and 3¼ km (2 mi) of peaceful lakeshore. Owner Susan Kellett inherited the house, and she has been preserving and enhancing the property. She's converted many of the farm buildings into offices, which now house a number of independent organizations, including a Mayo genealogy center and the Cloonamoyne Fishery. The formal ornamental garden is also undergoing renovations. Colorful corridors, fishing motifs, and quirky, slightly crooked stairways make this a wonderfully appealing spot. Meals include fruits grown in the organic garden. ⊠ *Castlehill, Ballina, Co. Mayo,* ☎ *096/31112,* ℻ *096/31773. 6 rooms with bath. Restaurant, fishing. AE, MC, V. Closed mid-Oct.–Mar.* ✍

$$ ✕⬚ **Mount Falcon Castle.** Owner-manager Constance Aldridge's rambling Victorian-Gothic country house 5 km (3 mi) outside Ballina is within easy reach of several beautiful, small beaches. Aldridge is renowned for putting guests at ease and encouraging them to mingle, and she makes children especially welcome. You can salmon fish on the River Moy right on the hotel's extensive grounds; horseback riding, sea fishing, and golf are nearby. Rooms are furnished comfortably with a mix of antiques and heirlooms, and they overlook the wooded grounds. In the dining room, the country-style home cooking, which takes advantage of local produce, has a fine reputation. ⊠ *Ballina, Co. Mayo,* ☎ *096/70811,* ℻ *096/71517. 10 rooms with bath. Restaurant, tennis court, fishing. AE, DC, MC, V. Closed Feb.–Mar.* ✍

$$$ ⬚ **Downhill Hotel.** Delightfully situated on 40 wooded acres beside a gushing tributary of the River Moy (just off the N59 Sligo road), this hotel is a popular spot with anglers and outdoor types. The late-Victorian main house feels a little gloomy downstairs, but it is comfortable. Rooms in the new wing tend to be smaller than those in the main house, but the former have good views of the river across the garden. Rooms in the main house are decorated with Georgian-style furniture and tastefully coordinated quilts and drapes. There's music in the bar on weekends and midweek in July and August. ⊠ *Co. Mayo,* ☎ *096/ 21033,* ℻ *096/21338. 50 rooms with bath. Restaurant, 2 bars, indoor pool, hot tub, sauna, steam room, 3 tennis courts, exercise room, squash, fishing. AE, DC, MC, V.* ✍

Outdoor Activities and Sports

BICYCLING

Head for the coast north of Ballina on a bike from **Gerry's Cycle Center** (⊠ 6 Lord Edward St., ☎ 096/70455).

FISHING

Fishing bait, tackle, and licenses can be obtained from **John Walkin** (⊠ Tone St., ☎ 096/22442).

GOLF

The **Carne Golf Links** at Belmullet Golf Club (⊠ Belmullet, ☎ 097/ 82292), 72 km (45 mi) west of Ballina, is one of Ireland's renowned links courses (☞ Chapter 9). **Enniscrone Golf Club** (⊠ Enniscrone, ☎ 096/36297), 13 km (8 mi) north of Ballina, is an 18-hole, par-72 course (☞ Chapter 9).

THE NORTH MAYO COAST

Killala, 12 km (7½) mi north of Ballina, is a pleasant little seaside town overlooking Killala Bay. This was the scene of the unsuccessful French invasion of Ireland, led by Wolfe Tone in 1798. The history of this tiny bishopric goes back much further, though, as evidenced by its round, 12th-century tower.

Killala is the gateway to the north Mayo coast, a dramatic, windswept stretch of cliffs continuing to Erris Head on the Mullet peninsula in the far west of the county. The sparsely inhabited landscape beneath an ever-changing sky consists of small farms and open moorland. The small roads and stunning views are attractive to cyclists, but be warned: the wind howls in across the Atlantic directly from Iceland, the nearest land mass. Although there are no signposted trails on this coast, there are plenty of cliff footpaths and small roads for walkers to explore. Don't miss the blowholes on Downpatrick Head, great gaps in the rocks through which plumes of water spew in rough weather.

★ ④⑤ Nowadays, the chief reason for visiting this coast is the **Céide Fields.** Widely recognized as one of Europe's most significant megalithic sites, the fields consist of rows and patterns of stones that have been preserved under a 5,000-year-old bog. These stones are the remnants of dwelling places and stone-walled fields built by a peaceful, well-organized farming community. A striking glass-and-steel pyramid houses the visitor center, where displays and an audiovisual show bring this strange landscape to life. Admission includes an optional guided walk through an excavated section of the stones; wet-weather gear is provided when necessary. ⊠ *R314, 5 km (3 mi) west of Ballycastle,* ☎ *096/43325.* ⚑ *£2.50.* ☉ *Mid-Mar.–May and Oct., daily 10–5; June–Sept., daily 9:30–6:30; Nov., daily 10–4:30.* 🐾

Shopping
Hackett & Turpin (⊠ Carrowteige, Ballina, ☎ 097/88925) is a factory outlet for Irish sweaters. From R314 beyond the Céide Fields, follow signs for Benwee Head.

THE WEST A TO Z

Arriving and Departing

By Bus
Bus Éireann (☎ 01/836–6111 in Dublin, 061/313333 in Limerick, 021/508188 in Cork) operates a variety of expressway services into the region from Dublin, Cork City, and Limerick City to Ennis, Galway City, Westport, and Ballina, the principal depots in the region. Expect bus rides to last about one hour longer than the time by car.

By Car
The 219-km (136-mi) Dublin–Galway trip takes about three hours. From Cork City take N20 through Mallow and N21 to Limerick City, picking up the N18 Ennis–Galway road in Limerick. The 209-km (130-mi) drive from Cork to Galway takes about three hours. From Killarney the shortest and most pleasant route to cover the 193 km (120 mi) to Galway (three hrs) is N22 to Tralee, then N69 through Listowel to Tarbert and the ferry across the Shannon Estuary to Killimer in County Clare, joining N68 in Kilrush, and then picking up N18 in Ennis. The ferry leaves Tarbert every hour on the half hour and takes 20 minutes, avoiding a 104-km (65-mi) detour through Limerick City. It costs £8 one-way, £12 round-trip. (Ferries return from Killimer every hour on the hour.)

By Plane
The West's most convenient international airport is **Shannon** (☎ 061/471444), 25 km (16 mi) east of Ennis in the Southwest (☞ The Southwest A to Z *in* Chapter 5). **Galway Airport** (☎ 091/752874), near Galway City, is used mainly for internal flights, with steadily increasing U.K. traffic. **Knock International Airport** (☎ 094/67222), at Charlestown—near Knock, in County Mayo—is also used for internal flights and has direct daily services to London's Stansted, Manchester, and Birmingham. A small airport for internal traffic only is also located at **Knockrowen,** Castlebar, in County Mayo (☎ 094/22853). Flying time from Dublin is 25–30 minutes to all airports. No scheduled flights run from the United States to Galway or Knock; use Shannon Airport (☞ The Southwest A to Z *in* Chapter 5).

Aer Lingus has daily flights from London's Heathrow Airport to Galway and Knock via Dublin; the trip takes about two hours. **Ryanair** flies to Knock daily from London's Luton Airport; flying time is 80 minutes. **Loganair** flies to Knock from Birmingham, Manchester, and Glasgow.

BETWEEN THE AIRPORT AND THE CITIES

Galway: Galway Airport is 6½ km (4 mi) from Galway City. No regular bus service is available from the airport to Galway, but most flight arrivals are taken to Galway Rail Station in the city center by an airline courtesy coach. Inquire when you book. A taxi from the airport to the city center costs about £7.

Knock: If you're flying to Knock International Airport, you can pick up your rental car at the airport. Otherwise, inquire at the time of booking about transport to your final destination. No regular bus service is available from the airport.

By Train

Galway City, Westport, and Ballina are the main rail stations in the region. For County Clare, travel from Cork City, Killarney, or Dublin's Heuston Station to **Limerick City** (☎ 061/315555) and continue the journey by bus. Trains for Galway, Westport, and Ballina leave from Dublin's **Heuston Station** (☎ 01/836–6222). The journey time to Galway is 3 hours; to Ballina 3¾ hours; and to Westport 3½ hours. Train passengers can call for information in Galway (☎ 091/564222), Ballina (☎ 096/71818), and Westport (☎ 098/25253).

Getting Around

By Bus

In July and August, the provincial bus service is augmented by daily services to most resort towns. Outside these months, many coastal towns receive only one or two buses per week. Bus routes are often slow and circuitous, and service can be erratic. A copy of the Bus Éireann timetable (75p from any station) is essential. The main bus stations are located at **Ennis** (☎ 065/682–4177), **Galway City** (✉ Ceannt Station, ☎ 091/562000), **Westport** (✉ Railway station, ☎ 098/25711), and **Ballina** (☎ 096/71800).

By Car

A car is essential in the West, especially from September through June. Although the main cities of the area are easily reached from the rest of Ireland by rail or bus, transport within the region is sparse and badly coordinated. If a rental car is out of the question, your best option is to make Galway your base and take day tours (available mid-June through September) west to Connemara and south to the Burren, and a day or overnight trip to the Aran Islands. It *is* possible to explore the region by local and intercity bus services, but you will need plenty of time.

The West has good, wide main roads (National Primary Routes) and better-than-average local roads (National Secondary Routes), both known as "N" routes. If you stray off the beaten track on the smaller Regional ("R") or unnumbered routes, particularly in Connemara and County Mayo, you may encounter some hazardous mountain roads. Narrow, steep, and twisty, they are also frequented by untended sheep, cows, and ponies grazing "the long acre" (as the strip of grass beside the road is called) or simply straying in search of greener pastures. If you find a sheep in your path, just sound the horn, and it should scramble away. A good maxim for these roads is "You never know what's around the next corner." Bear this in mind, and adjust your speed accordingly. Hikers and cyclists constitute an additional hazard on narrow roads in the summer.

Within the Connemara Irish-speaking area, signs are in Irish only. The main signs to recognize are Gaillimh (Galway), Ros an Mhíl (Rossaveal), An Teach Doite (Maam Cross), and Sraith Salach (Recess). A good map, available through newsagents and TIOs, gives Irish and English names where needed.

By Ferry to the Aran Islands

Aran Ferries (⊠ TIO, Victoria Pl., Eyre Sq., ☎ 091/568903 or 091/592447) runs a boat from Rossaveal, 32 km (20 mi) west of Galway City, which makes the crossing in 20 minutes and costs about £19 round-trip, including the shuttle bus from Galway.

Island Ferries (☎ 091/565352), which has a booking office on Victoria Place opposite the TIO in Galway City, has a one-hour crossing from Rossaveal for £18 round-trip, with up to five sailings a day in summer, weather permitting. Bicycles are transported free off-season, but there may be a charge in July and August: inquire when booking. Discounts are available for families, students, and groups of four or more. If you stay a night or two on the islands, ask about accommodations when booking your ferry, as there are some very competitive deals.

Between June and September, **O'Brien Ferries** (New Docks, ☎ 091/567676) has sailings from Galway Docks, a five-minute walk from Eyre Square. The ferries run three times a week in June and September (usually Tuesday, Thursday, and Saturday), daily in July and August. The crossing takes 90 minutes and costs £14 round-trip.

If you are heading for **Inisheer,** the smallest island, the shortest crossing is from Doolin in County Clare (☞ The Burren and Beyond—West Clare to South Galway, *above*). A ferry leaves from Doolin Pier, with up to 12 sailings daily, from the middle of March through the end of September. The crossing takes about 30 minutes and costs £16 round-trip.

BY FERRY BETWEEN THE ISLANDS
Frequent **interisland ferries** are available in summer months, but tickets are nontransferable, so ask the captain of your ferry about his interisland schedule if you plan to visit more than one island; otherwise, your trip can become expensive.

By Plane to the Aran Islands

Aer Arann (☎ 091/593034) has four flights daily on weekdays and two flights on weekends. During July and August planes leave every half hour. The flights call at all three of the Aran Islands and leave from **Connemara Airport** (☎ 091/593034) at Inver, 29 km (18 mi) west of Galway, accessible by shuttle bus. The journey takes about six minutes and costs about £36 round-trip, or about £44 including one night's bed-and-breakfast. For about £25 you can fly one-way and travel one-way by boat from Rossaveal. Ask about other special offers at the time of booking.

By Train

Rail transportation is not good within the West. The major destinations of Galway City and Westport/Ballina are on different branch lines. Connections can only be made between Galway and the other two cities by traveling inland for about an hour to Athlone (☞ Arriving and Departing by Train, *above*, and Chapter 3).

Contacts and Resources

B&B Reservation Agencies

For a small fee, **Bord Fáilte** will book accommodations anywhere in Ireland through its central reservations system. B&Bs can be booked at local TIOs (☞ Visitor Information, *below*) when they are open; however, even these reservations will go through the central reservations system. For more information, *see* Lodging *in* Smart Travel Tips A to Z.

Car Rentals

If you haven't already picked up a rental car at Shannon Airport (☞ The Southwest A to Z *in* Chapter 5), try the following:

Galway City and Vicinity: Avis (☎ 091/568886). **Budget** (☎ 091/566376). **Enterprise** (☎ 091/771200). **Euro Mobil** (☎ 091/753037). **Hertz Rent A Car** (☎ 091/752502). **Johnson & Perrot** (☎ 091/568886). **National** (☎ 091/771929).

Knock International Airport, Charlestown, Co. Mayo: Casey's Auto Rentals (☎ 094/24618). **Diplomat Rent A Car** (☎ 094/67252).

Emergencies

Police, fire, and **ambulance** (☎ 999).

DOCTORS AND DENTISTS

County Clare: Mid-Western Health Board (⊠ Catherine St., Limerick, Co. Limerick, ☎ 061/316655). **Counties Galway and Mayo: Western Health Board** (⊠ Merlin Park, Galway City, ☎ 091/751131).

PHARMACIES

Galway: Matt O'Flaherty (⊠ 39 Eyre Sq., ☎ 091/562927). **Westport: O'Donnell's** (⊠ Bridge St., ☎ 098/25163).

Guided Tours

Galway City's **TIO** (☞ Visitor Information, *below*) has details of walking tours of Galway, which are organized by request.

The only full- and half-day guided bus tours in the region start from Galway. **Bus Éireann** (☎ 091/562000) coordinates two full-day tours, one covering Connemara and the other the Burren (each £12). Tours run from early June to mid-October only, with the widest choice available between mid-July and mid-August. Book in advance at the Galway City TIO (☞ Visitor Information, *below*) or at **Ceannt Railway Station** (☎ 091/562000) or the **Salthill TIO** (☎ 091/520500), which also serve as departure points.

Lally Tours (☎ 091/562905) runs a day tour through Connemara and County Mayo and another to the Burren. It also operates a vintage double-decker bus, departing from Eyre Square, which runs hourly city tours from 10:30 AM until 4:30 PM.

O'Neachtian Day Tours (☎ 091/553188)) operates full-day tours of Connemara and the Burren. Tickets, £13 each, can be purchased from the Galway City TIO (☞ Visitor Information, *below*); tours depart across the street.

Outdoor Activities and Sports

BICYCLING

All TIOs (☞ Visitor Information, *below*) in the West provide lists of suggested cycle tours.

BOARD AND DINGHY SAILING

One- and two-week courses in sailing and board sailing are available at the **Glénans Center,** based on an otherwise uninhabited island in Clew Bay near Westport. Contact the center's head office (⊠ 28 Merrion Sq., Dublin, ☎ 01/661–1481).

FISHING

Details of the numerous fisheries in the area are available from the local TIOs (☞ Visitor Information, *below*), or consult the Irish Tourist

Board leaflet "Angling Ireland" (£2). Similar leaflets are available on coarse-angling (angling for freshwater fish) and sea-angling.

HIKING

For backcountry walking, consult "Irish Walk Guides—The West," a pamphlet available at local TIOs (☞ Visitor Information, *below*), and take local advice on weather conditions.

Visitor Information

Bord Fáilte provides free information service, tourist literature, and an accommodations booking service at its TIOs.

MAIN OFFICES

The following offices are open all year, generally weekdays 9–6, daily during high season: **Aran Islands (Inishmore)** (⊠ Co. Galway, ☎ 099/61263, FAX 099/61420). **Ennis** (⊠ Arthur's Row, Town Center, Co. Clare, ☎ 065/682–8366). **Galway City** (⊠ 1 Victoria Pl., Eyre Sq., Co. Galway, ☎ 091/563081, FAX 091/565201). **Oughterard** (⊠ Main St., Co. Galway, ☎ 091/552808, FAX 091/552811). **Westport** (⊠ The Mall, Co. Mayo, ☎ 098/25711, FAX 098/26709).

SEASONAL OFFICES

These offices are open as indicated, generally weekdays 9–6 and Saturday 9–1: **Achill** (⊠ Co. Mayo, ☎ 098/45384), open June–August. **Ballina** (⊠ Co. Mayo, ☎ 096/70848), open April–October. **Castlebar** (⊠ Co. Mayo, ☎ 094/21207), open May–mid-September. **Clifden** (⊠ Co. Galway, ☎ 095/21163), open March–October. **Cliffs of Moher** (⊠ Co. Clare, ☎ 065/708–1171), open April–October. **Kilkee** (⊠ Co. Clare, ☎ 065/905–6112), open May–August. **Kilrush** (⊠ Co. Clare, ☎ 065/905–1047), open June–August. **Salthill** (⊠ Salthill, Co. Galway, ☎ 091/520500), open May–September. **Thoor Ballylee** (⊠ Near Gort, Co. Clare, ☎ 091/631436), open April–mid-October.

7 THE NORTHWEST

Yeats Country, Donegal Bay, the Northern Peninsulas

On an island where there's no shortage of majestic scenery, the Northwest claims its fair share. Cool, clean waters from the roaring Atlantic Ocean shape the landscape into long peninsulas—a raw, sensual landscape that looks like Earth is still under construction, above which soar breezy, rocky crests. Clouds and rain linger over proud mountains, soft glens, jagged cliffs, sandy beaches, and heathered bogs, to be chased within minutes by sunshine and rainbows. Two brothers, the writer William Butler Yeats and the painter Jack, immortalized this land in their work. Walk in their footsteps, and you'll be struck anew by the dance of nature and art.

Updated by
Aoife
Fitzpatrick

GLANCE AT A MAP OF IRELAND THAT HAS scenic roads marked in green, and chances are your eye will quickly be drawn to the far-flung peninsulas of the Northwest. At virtually every bend in the roads of counties Donegal, Leitrim, and Sligo there's something to justify all those green ribbons. But what that something is *now* may not be what it is an hour from now. As they say, if you don't like the weather, just wait five minutes. The air, the light, and the colors of the countryside change as though with a turn of a kaleidoscope. Look once, and see scattered, snow-white clouds flying above tawny slopes. Look again, and suddenly the sun has brilliantly illuminated magnificent reds and purples in the undergrowth. The fickle skies brighten and darken at will, tempting a spectrum of subtle shades from the unkempt gorse and heather, then washing the grassy meadows greener than any green you've ever seen.

The Northwest covers the most northerly part of Ireland's Atlantic coastline, running from Sligo in the south along Donegal's remote, windswept peninsulas to Malin Head in the far north. These maritime landscapes are said to have given their colors to the most famous local product, handwoven tweed, which reflects the browns of the peaty heathland and the purples of the heather. Donegal, a sparsely populated rural county of small farms and fishing boats, shares its inland border with Northern Ireland; the border is partly formed by the River Foyle. Inland from Sligo is Leitrim, a county best known for its numerous lakes and loughs, some of which join up with the River Shannon, on the easterly border of this region (and which is covered with greater depth in Chapter 3).

County Donegal was part of the near-indomitable ancient kingdom of Ulster, which was not conquered by the English until the 17th century. By the time the English withdrew in the 1920s, they had still not eradicated rural Donegal's Celtic inheritance. It thus shouldn't come as a surprise that County Donegal contains Ireland's largest Gaeltacht (Irish-speaking area). Driving in this part of the country, you'll either be frustrated or amused whenever you come to a crossroads. Signposts show only the Irish place-names, often so unlike the English versions as to be completely unrecognizable. All is not lost, however, as maps generally give both the Irish and the English names, and locals are usually more than happy to help out with directions (in English)—usually with a yarn thrown in.

Tucked into the folds of the Northwest's hills, modest little market towns and unpretentious villages with muddy streets go about their business quietly. In the squelchy peat bogs, cutters working with long shovels pause to watch and wave as you drive past. Remember to drive slowly along the country lanes, for around any corner you may find a whitewashed thatched cottage with children playing outside its scarlet door, a shepherd leading his flock, a wayward sheep or two looking philosophical about having strayed from their field, or a farmer wobbling along in the middle of the road on his old faithful sit-up-and-beg bicycle.

A raw and sensual landscape—it almost seems as if Earth were still under construction here—the Northwest is overwhelmingly rural and underpopulated. That's not to say there isn't a bit of hurly-burly here. The Northwest's boomtown, Sligo Town, is in the throes of a major renaissance—on a typical weekday, its little winding streets are as busy as those of Galway and it seems to be giving Dublin's Temple Bar a run for its money when it comes to stylish restaurants and trendy people—an amazing feat for a town of only 19,000 souls. Sligo Town pulses not only in the present but with the charge of history, for it was the childhood home of W. B. and Jack Yeats, the place that, more than any other, gave rise to their particular geniuses—or, as Jack put it: "Sligo was my school and the sky above it." More bright lights are found in Letterkenny, which boasts the longest main street of any town in Ireland. Glenveagh National Park exemplifies the surprising alliance between nature and culture you'll find in the Northwest. Here, perched on the edge of a glorious lake in the midst of 24,000 acres of some of Ireland's most thrilling wilderness, sits a fairy-tale castle. The castle reflects the life and times of the man who owned it for 50 years: Henry McIlhenny, the millionaire American philanthropist and art collector whose Impressionist paintings now hang in one of the finest art museums in America.

Keep in mind, though, that the whole region—and County Donegal in particular—attracts plenty of visitors during July and August; this is a favorite vacation area for people who live in neighboring Northern Ireland. To be frank, a few places are quite spoiled by popularity with tourists and careless development. The Rosses Peninsula on Donegal's west coast, still sometimes described as beautiful, is marred by too much building. Bundoran, on the coast between Sligo Town and Donegal Town, a cheap and cheerful family beach resort full of so-called "Irish gift shops" and "amusement arcades," is another place to pass through rather than visit. On the whole, though, the Northwest is big enough, untamed enough, and grand enough to be able to absorb all of its summer (and weekend) tourists without too much harm.

Pleasures and Pastimes

Dining

Although the Northwest has not been considered a great gastronomic center, in the last few years Sligo Town has established itself as a sort of last stop for food lovers, with a number of food-related shops worth visiting. On the dining front, here and there, newcomers are serving up well-above-average food in memorable settings, though overall, the majority of restaurants offer plain and simple fare such as traditional Irish lamb stew or bacon and cabbage served with generous helpings of potatoes (often prepared in at least two ways on the same plate), washed down with creamy, lip-smacking pints of Guinness. You're likely to find the finest food at the higher-quality country houses, where chefs elegantly prepare local meat, fish, and produce in a hybrid Irish-French haute cuisine. Another new trend: several of the area's more successful restaurants have recently added accommodations, making them good overnight destinations. For price ranges, *see* Dining *in* Smart Travel Tips A to Z.

Lodging

True, it's the farthest-flung corner of Ireland, but the Northwest has a steady stream of arrivals—especially in July and August, when visitors seek out its joys. Residents of Northern Ireland are particularly apt to use the Northwest as a nearby weekend getaway. As a result, good bed-and-breakfasts and small hotels can be found throughout the region. In the Northwest's two major towns—Sligo Town and Donegal Town—as well as the small coastal resorts in between, traditional provincial hotels have been modernized (albeit not always elegantly), yet they retain some of the charm that comes with older buildings and personalized service. Away from these areas, your options are more restricted, and your best overnight choice, with some exceptions, is usually a modest guest house offering bed, breakfast, and an evening meal. Because of its large Gaeltacht population, you should consider staying in an Irish-speaking home; the local Tourist Information Office (TIO) can be helpful in making a booking with an Irish-speaking family. The Northwest is also home to a number of first-class country-house hotels where you can expect the gracious professionalism you'll find in comparable properties elsewhere in Ireland. For price ranges, *see* Lodging *in* Smart Travel Tips A to Z.

Nightlife

As in other regions in Ireland where there are few large towns, the pub in the Northwest is the center of nightlife. Always ask locally or at your hotel if there is a nearby pub with a weekly *seisun,* or an informal performance of traditional folk music. Many hotels or large pubs, particularly at resort towns in season, put on some form of entertainment—a disco or live music—most nights of the week. Discos (often called "dances") are usually full of local and visiting teenagers and twentysomethings. These discos are far from sophisticated but are often a lot of fun (and great for meeting people). When there isn't a disco, you will find some kind of live music, usually a local traveling band that plays rock-and-roll standards and country-and-western music. These appeal to an older crowd, often the parents of the kids who danced the night away in the same place the night before.

Outdoor Activities and Sports

BICYCLING

Steep hills, winding and poorly kept roads, occasionally strong winds, and the frequent possibility of cold weather and rain make the Northwest one of Ireland's most challenging areas for cyclists. Now the good news: plenty of low-cost accommodations, astonishing scenery, empty roads, and a chance to stop and chat with the locals can make either serious touring throughout all of the region or gentle meandering around a small area an immensely rewarding experience.

FISHING

The angling in Ireland's Northwest is of the highest class, attracting enthusiasts and connoisseurs from the world over. Yet there's so much space and so much water that it can feel as if you have the whole place to yourself. There are a dozen sea-fishing festivals during the season, open to visiting anglers. Anglers will find that the best area for brown trout is around Bundoran, including Lough Melvin. In western County Donegal, you'll have good opportunities for catching sea trout. Plenty of salmon and brown trout live in the rivers of southern County Donegal and northern County Sligo. More brown trout can be found in the loughs near Dunfanaghy in northern County Donegal, near Bundoran on the border of Donegal and Sligo counties, and in the border area of Sligo and Leitrim counties. Pike and coarse anglers can cast their lines in the abundant County Leitrim lakes. For more information, *see* Fishing *in* Contacts and Resources *in* The Northwest A to Z, *below.*

GOLF

The Northwest has a large number of 9- and 18-hole courses, most in seaside locations, and several of them are world-class. The Northwest's best 18-hole courses all welcome visitors; *see* Chapter 9 for the three best courses in the region. Expect to pay greens fees of around £25–£40 a day.

HIKING AND WALKING

Trails in the Northwest provide the experienced walker with challenging opportunities. It helps to be able to read a map, and on high ground you're wise not to take any chances with the weather, which can suddenly turn wet and misty. The mountain districts (such as the Blue Stacks, near Donegal Town) offer rough walks with dramatic views. Long-distance footpaths may be found across County Donegal, in County Leitrim, and around Lough Gill in County Sligo. Good shorter trails are also accessible within Glenveagh National Park.

SURFING

There's great surfing along the Atlantic shores of Counties Donegal and Sligo. Head to Strandhill, Rossnowlagh, and Bundoran on the Sligo and south County Donegal coasts or to Marble Strand and Rosapenna in north County Donegal. These areas have excellent conditions for world-class surfing. Take note that, in Ireland, a surf shop can only rent surfing equipment to individuals taking lessons. Establishments recommended by the European Surf Federation and Irish Surfing Association have approved, qualified instructors and are insured to give surfing instruction. For more information, *see* Surfing *in* Contacts and Resources *in* The Northwest A to Z, *below.*

Sweaters, Tweeds, and China

Most of the Aran sweaters you'll see throughout Ireland are made in County Donegal, the area most associated today with high-quality, hand-woven tweeds and hand-knit items. Made of plain, undyed wool and knit with distinctive crisscross patterns, Aran sweaters are durable, soft, and often weatherproof and can be astonishingly warm. Not so long ago, these pullovers were worn by every County Donegal fisherman, usually made to a design belonging exclusively to his own family. Today there's a greater variety in patterns, but most of the sweaters still have that unmistakable Aran look. High-quality machine-made tweeds, especially tweed jackets, also have a long history in the area and are widely available. Locally made Parian china is a thin, fine, and pale product of very high quality and workmanship. Elaborate flower motifs and a basket-weave design are two distinctive features of this china, which has been a specialty of Belleek, on the Donegal-Fermanagh border, for more than 100 years. In recent years, it has also developed in and around Ballyshannon.

Exploring the Northwest

Our coverage of the Northwest is organized into three autonomous routes, although they can easily be linked if you want to poke around the area over five or so days. The first journey begins in Sligo Town and covers its immediate environs—all the major sights within a roughly 24-km (15-mi) radius, many of which have strong associations with Yeats. The second trip skirts the entirety of Donegal Bay, from Mullaghmore in the south to Glencolumbkille to the far north and west, before heading inland as far as Ardara. The last route begins at the other end of Donegal, in Letterkenny, and covers the far northwest corner of County Donegal before swinging you back around to the Inishowen Peninsula, the tip-top of Ireland, delicately balanced between the Republic and Northern Ireland. If you decide to explore this chapter from back to front (this makes sense if you're arriving in the Northwest from Northern Ireland), begin with the last itinerary, in Letterkenny; skip the trip to the Inishowen Peninsula; and pick up the middle tour from either Gratan Lough or Burtonport.

Numbers in the text correspond to numbers in the margin and on the Yeats Country and Around Donegal Bay, Sligo Town, and the Northern Peninsulas maps.

Great Itineraries

IF YOU HAVE 2 DAYS

Start your tour in **Sligo Town** ①–⑧, the cozy heart of County Sligo. The settlement is dominated by the stark outline of the hill that rears up to the north of the town—Yeats's "bare Ben Bulben," in whose shadow he asked to be buried. To whet your appetite for the works of Sligo's most famous poet, have a look at the memorabilia in the **Model and Niland Centre** ③, where there are also some of the starkly atmospheric oils painted by his brother, Jack. Take along a volume of Yeats's poetry (or at the least his poem "The Lake Isle of Innisfree") as you follow the signposted Yeats Trail around woody, gorgeously scenic **Lough Gill** ⑩, where you'll begin to understand why this land inspired some of Yeats's finest poems. After the road north passes Yeats's simple grave in **Drumcliff** ⑭ churchyard, take a detour to **Lissadell House** ⑮, the home of the beautiful, aristocratic Gore-Booth sisters, where Yeats was a frequent visitor, and then head on to **Creevykeel** ⑰, an important court tomb dating from 3000 BC. Drive through **Ballyshannon** ⑲, where the River Erne empties into Donegal Bay, and continue on to the large village of 🏨 **Donegal Town** ⑳, a good place to stay the night, for this is where the roads of the area meet and then go their own ways to the north and west.

On the next day take the road to the thriving fishing port of **Killybegs** ㉒, beyond which point the views of Donegal Bay improve as the road twists and turns before descending into Kilcar, a village (like others hereabouts) known for its tweed making. The road then crosses a stretch of barren moorland and reaches **Glencolumbkille** ㉓, a scenic hamlet spread out around the rocky harbor of Glen Bay; it has associations with the reclusive and controversial early Christian missionary St. Columba. On the far side of the Glengesh Pass, the small village of **Ardara** ㉔ is the center of the region's tweed heritage and also a good spot to hear traditional music. Return from here southward to Donegal Town and either to Dublin (☞ Chapter 1) via Ballyshannon or to Galway (☞ Chapter 6) via Sligo.

IF YOU HAVE 5 DAYS

For your first two days, follow the first day of the two-day itinerary above, but take *two* whole days to do it. You may want to push on at the end of your second day to 🏨 **Ardara** ㉔ and visit the tweed heritage center there rather than stop at 🏨 **Donegal Town** ⑳, though both have a range of accommodations and some nightlife. On your third day, follow the coast road from Ardara up to Dungloe. Your rate of progress from here on will depend much on the weather and your pace, as the heathery headlands offer innumerable side excursions. North of Dungloe is a large Irish-speaking parish known as the **Rosses** ㉞, which has a wild Atlantic coast off which is the island of **Aranmore**, accessible from Burtonport. Working northward around this peninsula brings you to Bun Beag (Benbeg). From here another optional circuit can be made of the **Gweedore Headland** ㉝, with its bleak dramatic terrain (somewhat marred by modern bungalow development), which will bring you to Bloody Foreland Head, named for the vivid reds that appear on the rock face during the long western sunsets. Meenlaragh, east along the same headland, is the departure point for **Tory Island** ㉜, a rocky, inaccessible place that has nevertheless been inhabited since prehistoric times. Some of the Tory Island fishermen have developed a sideline producing naive art.

🏨 **Dun Fionnachaid** ㉛ is a pleasant village built in the Plantation era on the shores of Sheephaven Bay, within easy reach of **Ards Forest Park** ㉚, which has trails leading to prehistoric sites. Near **Creeslough** ㉙, you'll find **Doe Castle**, romantic and dramatically perched on the edge of the southern end of Sheephaven Bay. **Carraig Airt** ㉘, a small village with some enjoyable old-fashioned pubs, gives access to a signposted Atlantic Drive around the Rosguill Peninsula. From here either head

Yeats Country and Around Donegal Bay

south through attractively sleepy Milford to **Ramelton** ㉘, a hilly little town on the edge of Lough Swilly, one of the loveliest of Donegal's big fjordlike inlets, and on to 🏨 **Letterkenny** ㉕, a convenient base for exploring the rest of the county; or head north to 🏨 **Rathmullan** ㉗, where a number of hotels are right on the shores of Lough Swilly. If you enjoy modern and contemporary art, on your next day head for the **Glebe House and Gallery**, on the northwest shore of **Gartan Lough** ㊲, which exhibits works by major Impressionists, Picasso, Jack Yeats, and the art of the Tory Islanders. If the outdoors beckons, head northwest for **Glenveagh National Park** ㊱, which also boasts a delightful Victorian-castle country house; if archaeology is your passion, then head east to the dramatic fort of **Grianan Ailigh** ㊳, which provides a spectacular panorama of Donegal, Derry, and the Inishowen Peninsula. From Letterkenny head northeast across the border into Northern Ireland and the city of Derry (☞ Chapter 8) or south for Sligo Town and Galway (☞ Chapter 6).

When to Tour the Northwest

In July and August, the Northwest gets busy with families from Northern Ireland, Dublin, and Great Britain. Musicians play most nights at village pubs, and the weather may be warm enough for hardy folk to swim in the sea, but accommodations may be hard to come by. Between November and February, in contrast, the area is empty of tourists, and with good reason—gales bring cold, lashing rain in from the Atlantic, shrouding the wild, lonely scenery that is the Northwest's greatest asset. What's more, because so many of the area's hotels are seasonal, you'll have a limited choice. The best months to visit here are easily April, May, June, September, and October.

YEATS COUNTRY— SLIGO TOWN AND ENVIRONS

Just as James Joyce made Dublin his own through his novels and stories, Sligo and environs are bound to the work of William Butler Yeats (1865–1939), Ireland's first of four Nobel laureates, and, no less, his brother, Jack B. (1871–1957), one of Ireland's most important 20th-century painters, whose expressionistic landscapes and portraits are as emotionally fraught as his brother's poems are lyrical and plangent. The brothers Yeats intimately knew and eloquently celebrated in their art not only Sligo Town itself but the surrounding countryside with its lakes, farms, woodland, and dramatic mountains that rise up not far from the center of town. Often on this route, you'll have glimpses of "bare Ben Bulben's head," as the poet Yeats called flat-topped Ben Bulben Mountain, which looms over the western end of the Dartry range. The areas covered here are the most accessible parts of the Northwest, easily reached from Galway.

Sligo Town

★ ❶ *60 km (37 mi) northeast of Ballina, 138 km (86 mi) northeast of Galway, 217 km (135 mi) northwest of Dublin.*

The only sizable town in the whole of the Northwest, Sligo (population 19,000) is the best place to begin a tour of Yeats Country. It retains all the charm of smaller, sleepier villages, all the while in the throes of an economic boom—Europe's largest videotape factory is just outside of town, it's the center of Ireland's plastics industry, and the streets ring with the bite of buzz saws and the tang of resin as new apartments, shopping malls, and cinema complexes are tastefully erected behind traditional facades. By day Sligo's as lively and crowded as Galway, its considerably larger neighbor to the southwest. Locals, students from the town's college, and visitors bustle past its historic buildings and along its narrow sidewalks and winding streets and crowd its one-of-a-kind shops, eateries, and traditional pubs. More than any other town in the Northwest, Sligo has a buzz and energy that come as a surprise to anyone who hasn't visited recently.

Squeezed onto a patch of land between Sligo Bay and Lough Gill, Sligo is clustered on the south shore between two bridges that span the River Garavogue, just east of where the river opens into the bay. The new pedestrian zone along the south shore of the river between the two bridges means that you can now enjoy vistas of the river right in the center of town.

Sligo was often a battleground in its earlier days. It was attacked by Viking invaders in 807 and, later, by a succession of rival Irish and Anglo-Norman conquerors. In 1642, the British soldiers of Sir Frederick Hamilton fell upon Sligo, killing every visible inhabitant, burning the town, and destroying the interior of the beautiful medieval abbey. Then, between 1845 and 1849, more than a million inhabitants died in the potato famine or fled to escape it—an event poignantly captured in the words of a letter from local father Owen Larkin to his son in America in 1850, inscribed on a brass plaque down by the river: "I am now I may say alone in the world all my brothers and sisters are dead and children but yourself. We are all ejected out of Lord Ardilaun's ground, the times was so bad and all Ireland in such a state of poverty that no person could pay rent. My only hope now rests with you, as I am without one shilling and I must either beg or go to the poorhouse." Stand there a moment by the river, then turn again to the bustling heart of Sligo today, and marvel at humanity's capacity to reinvent itself.

❷ At the **Yeats Memorial Building** the annual Yeats International Summer School is conducted every August (☞ Seasonal Events *in* Nightlife and Arts, *below*). The **Sligo Art Gallery** shows rotating exhibits of contemporary art: call ahead to see if there will be an exhibition during your visit. Across the street is Rohan Gillespie's innovative **sculpture of the poet**, draped in a flowing coat overlaid with excerpts from his work. It was unveiled in 1989 by Michael Yeats, W. B.'s son, in commemoration of the 50th anniversary of his father's death. ⊠ *Hyde Bridge,* ☎ *071/45847.* ☞ *Free.* ☾ *Mon.–Sat. 10–5:30.*

❸ The **Model and Niland Centre,** previously the Model Arts Centre, contains works by contemporary artists from Ireland and abroad. It is also the new home of the **Niland Collection,** one of Ireland's largest collections of works by Jack B. Yeats, who once said, "I never did a painting without putting a thought of Sligo in it (Beckett once wrote that Yeats painted "desperately immediate images"). Among his works here are the *Island Funeral* (1923), *Sailor Home from the Sea* (1912), and *Leaving the Far Point* (1946). The collection, previously housed in the town library building, also includes paintings by John Yeats (father of Jack and W. B.), who had a considerable reputation as a portraitist, as well as Sean Keating, Paul Henry, and other leading Irish artists of the 20th century. Other items in the collection are first editions by W. B. and such intriguing memorabilia as the author's personal letters and the Irish tricolor flag that draped his coffin when he was buried at nearby **Drumcliff** (☞ *below*). The center has performance and workshop spaces and hosts various literature, music, and film programs. There's also a café. ⊠ *The Mall,* ☎ *071/41405.* ☞ *Small fee for some programs.* ☾ *Daily 11–5 and during performances.*

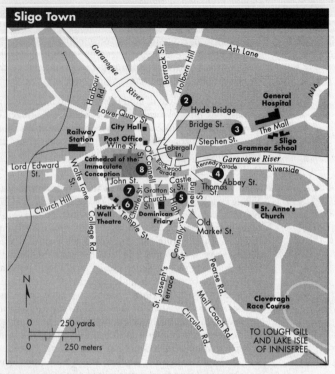

④ The **Sligo Abbey,** the town's only existing relic of the Middle Ages, was built for the Dominicans by Maurice FitzGerald in 1253. After a fire in 1414, it was extensively rebuilt, only to be destroyed again by Cromwell's Puritans under the command of Sir Frederick Hamilton in 1642. Today the abbey consists of a ruined nave, aisle, transept, and tower. Some fine stonework remains, especially in the 15th-century cloisters. ⊠ *Abbey St.,* ☎ *071/46406.* ⊑ *£1.50.* ☉ *June–Sept., daily 9:30–6:30.*

⑤ The **Courthouse** (⊠ Teeling St.), built in 1878 in the Victorian Gothic style, has a flamboyant, turreted sandstone exterior; it is not open to casual visitors. After it was built, the structure became a symbol for English power. The Courthouse takes its inspiration from the much larger Law Courts in London. Just north of the Courthouse on the east side of Teeling Street, look for the window designating the law firm of **Argue and Phibbs,** one of Sligo's most popular photo-ops.

The **Dominican Friary,** still a functioning church, is on High Street. Along this street, as well as Church and Charles streets, you'll notice that Sligo has numerous churches of all denominations. Presbyterians, Methodists, and even Plymouth Brethren are represented, as well as Anglicans (Church of Ireland) and, of course, Roman Catholics. According to the Irish writer Sean O'Faolain, "The best Protestant stock in all Ireland is in Sligo." The Yeats family was part of that stock.

⑥ County Sligo's **TIO** (Tourist Information Office) is useful for the whole of the Northwest. It's in the same building as the **Hawk's Well Theatre** (☞ Theater, *below*). The TIO sells an excellent "Tourist Trail" walking map of Sligo and information about bus tours of Yeats Country. It will also give you details of boat tours of Lough Gill, complete with recitals of Yeats's poetry—an excellent way to see the lough. ⊠ *Temple and Charles Sts.,* ☎ *071/61201.* ⊑ *Free.* ☉ *Sept.–mid-Mar., week-*

days 9–1 and 2–5; mid-Mar.–mid-June, weekdays 9–6, Sat. 10–2; mid-June–Aug., Mon.–Sat. 9–8, Sun. 10–6.

❼ Designed in 1730 by Richard Castle, who designed Powerscourt and Russborough Houses in County Wicklow (☞ Chapter 2), little **St. John's Cathedral** (Church of Ireland) has a handsome square tower and fortifications. In the north transept you'll find a memorial to Susan Mary Yeats, mother of W. B. and Jack. Next door is the larger and newer Roman Catholic **Cathedral of the Immaculate Conception** (with an entrance on Temple Street), consecrated in 1874. ⊠ *John St.* 🎟 *Free.* ☉ *Freely accessible.*

❽ Sligo's most famous pub is **Hargadon's** (⊠ 4 O'Connell St., ☎ 071/70933), a dark, old-style public house with cozy, private, wood-paneled snugs (cubicles); stone and wood floors; rust-red interior walls; and a handsome golden-oak and green-painted facade. It's a good place for a bowl of stew and a creamy pint of Guinness. Around the corner from Hargadon's on Wine Street are the offices of the local weekly newspaper, the *Sligo Champion,* whose editor grandly declared in its first issue in 1836: "Let no one think the *Champion* will be a vehicle of slander—we are determined never to sully our pages with personalities."

Dining and Lodging

✎ *following the text of a review is your signal that the property has a Web site, where you will find details and, usually, images; for a link, visit www.fodors.com/urls.*

$ ✕ **Bistro Bianconi.** The all-white decor—blond wood and white-tile floors—lives up to the name. But the minimalism ends there. The menu is a virtual display of fireworks, with a page-long selection of gourmet pizzas baked in the wood-burning oven, with toppings both traditional and innovative. Baked cannelloni and ravioli are other Italian favorites. ⊠ *44 O'Connell St.,* ☎ *071/41744. AE, MC, V.*

$$$$ ✕🏨 **Cromleach Lodge.** This small country hotel, on a hillside overlooking
★ Lough Arrow, has a pleasant, country-style interior; bedrooms are spacious, decorated in relaxing pastel shades, and have views out over the lough. The restaurant (reservations required) is particularly notable; all the tables in the three small dining rooms offer panoramic views. Fillet of turbot on a julienne of fennel with Pernod cream and a warm salad of marinaded lamb fillet with organic lentils are two typical and delicious entrées. The hotel is off N4 at Castlebaldwin, 27 km (17 mi) east of Sligo and 8 km (5 mi) east of Ballymote. ⊠ *Lough Arrow, Castlebaldwin, Co. Sligo,* ☎ *071/65155,* ℻ *071/65455. 10 rooms with bath. Restaurant, bar, fishing. AE, DC, MC, V. Closed Nov.–Jan.*

$$$$ ✕🏨 **Markree Castle.** From the front, this fortresslike 1640 castle looks slightly forbidding and cold, but seen from the garden in the back, it is spare and elegant. The ancestral home of Charles Cooper, who now owns and manages it with his wife, Mary, Markree is Sligo's oldest inhabited castle. The public rooms include the oak-paneled entry hall, with a large stained-glass window at the top of the grand staircase; a skylit gallery that doubles as the bar; and a formal dining room with ornate, Louis XIV plasterwork. Bedrooms (somewhat haphazardly furnished) are spread over a number of floors and wings, with modernized bathrooms. The kitchen offers up an excellent table d'hôte menu, and on Sunday a traditional lunch attracts a sizable, family-oriented crowd. The castle sits on a 1,000-acre estate 11 km (7 mi) south of Sligo Town just off N4. ⊠ *Collooney, Co. Sligo,* ☎ *071/67800,* ℻ *071/67840. 30 rooms with bath. Restaurant, bar, horseback riding. AE, DC, MC, V.*

$$$ ✕🎦 **Coopershill.** Seven generations of the O'Hara family have lived
★   in this three-story Georgian farmhouse since it was built in 1774. Be-
yond the elegant, symmetrical stone facade, with its central Palladian
window, the large public rooms are furnished with appealing period
antiques and overstuffed furniture. The spacious, beautifully furnished
bedrooms have pretty floral wallpaper, and most have four-poster or
canopy beds. In the tranquil dining room overlooking the woods,
meals made with fresh Irish ingredients and a wide choice of wines are
served by candlelight from a grand sideboard set with family silver and
crystal. Coopershill is signposted from Drumfin crossroads, 17 km (11
mi) southeast of Sligo off N4. ✉ *Riverstown, Co. Sligo,* ☎ *071/65108,*
℻ *071/65466. 6 rooms with bath. Dining room, tennis court, boat-
ing, fishing, billiards. AE, DC, MC, V. Closed Nov.–mid-Mar..* ❧

$$ ✕🎦 **Temple House.** This vast Georgian mansion on more than 1,000
acres, with a working farm and organic garden, has been in owners
Sandy and Deb Perceval's family since 1665. Rooms are furnished with
Georgian and Victorian furniture, including highly polished mahogany
tables and sideboards and the original rugs. Guests can visit formal terraced gardens and a private lake with waterside footpaths. Deb prepares the evening meal (book by noon), using farm-fresh produce
accompanied by fine wines. Typical entrées include herbed leg of lamb
with roast potatoes, tomato fondue and glazed carrots, and poached
wild salmon with hollandaise and cucumber sauce. Children can sleep
in an annex to your room and high tea is served for younger visitors
at 6:30 PM daily. Because of Sandy's allergies, guests are asked to avoid
using perfumes, deodorants, and aerosols. The house is about 19 km
(12 mi) south of Sligo, signposted off N17. ✉ *Ballymote, Co. Sligo,*
☎ *071/83329,* ℻ *071/83808. 5 rooms with bath. Dining room, boating, fishing. AE, MC, V. Closed Dec.–Mar..* ❧

$$$ 🎦 **Silver Swan Hotel.** Standing in the center of Sligo Town on the Hyde
Bridge, this comfortable, mid-range hotel has a wonderful view of the
Garavogue River rushing beneath the bridge. Although the 1960s-style
exterior will disturb style purists, the interior has been redecorated and
the bedrooms refurbished with dark-wood, modern decor. Noise can
be a problem when the hotel is hosting live music sessions, so ask for
a room away from the louder public rooms below. ✉ *Hyde Bridge,
Co. Sligo,* ☎ *071/43231,* ℻ *071/42232. 29 rooms with bath. Restau-
rant, bar. AE, DC, MC, V.*

$$$ 🎦 **Sligo Park Hotel.** Two kilometers (1 mile) out of Sligo Town on N4,
this is a modern, well-designed, and extremely comfortable establish-
ment with a friendly staff, an excellent restaurant with a well-chosen
wine list, and a first-rate fitness center. Dancing and piano entertainment take place on some evenings. Although its predictable, reliable
comforts appeal to business travelers, it makes a reasonable base for
visitors to Yeats Country. ✉ *Pearse Rd., Co. Sligo,* ☎ *071/60291,* ℻
*071/69556. 110 rooms with bath. Restaurant, bar, indoor pool, 2 ten-
nis courts, health club. AE, DC, MC, V.* ❧

Nightlife and the Arts

PUBS AND CLUBS

A few miles south of town, a popular spot with the locals, the **Thatch**
pub (✉ Thatch, Ballysadare, ☎ 071/67288), has traditional music sessions on Thursday and Sunday. Open later than most other pubs, **Toffs**
(✉ Kennedy Parade, ☎ 071/61250) has a sizable dance floor that teems
with Sligo's younger set bopping to a mix of contemporary dance
music and older favorites.

SEASONAL EVENTS

Established in 1959, the **Yeats International Summer School** takes
place during the first two weeks of August. Scholarly lectures, poetry

readings, and various side events are open to the public. For details contact the Yeats Society (⊠ Yeats Memorial Building, Hyde Bridge, ☎ 071/42693).

Dozens of high-profile and local performers take part in the **Sligo Arts Festival** (☎ 071/69802), held during late May and early June.

THEATER

Sligo Town's **Hawk's Well Theatre** hosts amateur and professional companies from all over Ireland (and occasionally from Britain) in a variety of shows. ⊠ *Temple St.,* ☎ *071/61526.* ⊡ *£2–£15.* ⊙ *Box office Mon.–Sat. 10–6; call for show times.*

Outdoor Activities and Sports

BICYCLING

Explore Lough Gill, Rosses Point, and other areas of scenic beauty by renting a bicycle from **Gary's Cycles** (⊠ Quay St., ☎ 071/45418; fees are £7 per day, £40 per week).

GOLF

County Sligo Golf Club (⊠ Rosses Point, ☎ 071/77186), also known as Rosses Point, is one of Ireland's great championship links (☞ Chapter 9).

HORSEBACK RIDING

For riding in the countryside around Sligo contact the **Sligo Riding Centre** (⊠ Carramore, ☎ 071/61353).

Shopping

Sligo Town has the Northwest's most thriving shopping scene, with a nice variety of food-related, crafts, and hand-knits shops, many with colorful storefronts. In addition to stylish sweaters, **Carraig Donn** (⊠ 41 O'Connell St., ☎ 071/44158) carries a selection of pottery, glassware, linens, and children's Aran knits. The **Cat & the Moon** (⊠ 4 Castle St., ☎ 071/43686) specializes in an eclectic and stylish mix of Irish-made crafts, jewelry, pottery, ironwork, and scarves. The gourmet deli **Cosgrove and Son** (⊠ 32 Market St., ☎ 071/42809), selling everything from Parma ham to Carageen moss boiled in milk, a local cure for stomach upsets, is a good place to stock up for a picnic or food for the road. **Cross Sections** (⊠ 2 Grattan St., ☎ 071/42265) sells lovely tableware, glassware, and kitchenware. **Tír na nóg** (⊠ Grattan St., ☎ 071/62752), Irish for "Land of the Ever-young," sells organic foods, including local cheeses and honeys, and other health-oriented items; a sister store across the street sells cards and posters.

Knocknarea

⑨ *8 km (5 mi) southwest of Sligo Town on R292 Strandhill Rd.*

Knocknarea is the "cairn-heaped grassy hill," as Yeats called it, rising 1,083 ft to the southwest of Sligo Town on a promontory that juts into Sligo Bay. The mountain is also memorably depicted in W. B.'s brother Jack's painting *Knocknarea and the Flowing Tide.* A car park on R292 gives pedestrian access (a 45-minute walk) to the summit, where there's a tremendous view of the mountains of Counties Donegal and Sligo. At its summit, and visible from a huge distance, sits a huge cairn—a heaped-stone monument made with 40,000 tons of rock. The cairn is traditionally associated with "passionate Maeve," as Yeats called her, the 1st-century AD Celtic queen of Connaught who went to war with the men of Ulster in a bid to win the mighty Bull of Cuailgne, and was subsequently killed while bathing in a lake. The story is told in the *Táin,* the greatest of all the Irish heroic legends. Romantics like to think that Maeve is buried in this massive cairn, although archaeologists suspect

that it more likely covers a 3,000-year-old passage grave—and who's
to say both aren't right? Either way, it's a pleasant climb on a summer
day. There are tremendous views from the cairn, and nature has installed a handy stream for washing your boots as you take the laneway
back down.

Strandhill, a seaside resort with a touch of charm, is 3 km (2 mi)
northwest of Knocknarea, off R292. It has a good, sandy beach,
stretches of which are favored by surfers, and a center complete with
seaweed baths scheduled to open in early 2001. The **Perfect Day Surf
Club** (✉ Strandhill, ☎ 071/68464) offers 1½ hrs of instruction plus
equipment for £15. It caters to surfing novices and aficionados alike
and is approved by the European Surf Federation and Irish Surfing Association.

Dining

$–$$ ✕ **Strand Restaurant.** This casual spot serves appealing bar food from
noon to 5; dinner service begins at 6. Among the items on the restaurant's à la carte menu are avocado pear with goat's cheese and monkfish with Pernod sauce, followed by hazelnut meringue with brown-bread
ice cream and Irish cheeses. The restaurant is also popular for its traditional Irish Sunday lunch. Light paneling, cozy booths, and a peat
fire make the Strand's pub an equally comfortable place to relax on a
breezy Sligo evening. ✉ *Shore Rd., Strandhill,* ☎ *071/68641. MC, V.
Closed Mon.*

En Route   A short drive southeast of Knocknarea (on the minor road back to Sligo
Town), **Carrowmore** is the largest group of megalithic tombs in all of
the British Isles. The oldest of the 60 tombs, dolmens, and other ruins
here predate those at Newgrange (☞ Chapter 2) by roughly 700 years;
most are communal tombs dating from 4800 BC, though, unfortunately,
more than 100 have been badly damaged, leaving around 40. A restored cottage houses a small exhibition about the tombs. ✉ *Carrowmore,* ☎ *071/61534.* 🎫 *£1.50.* ⊘ *May–Oct., daily 9:30–6:30.*

Lough Gill

★ ❿   *1½ km (1 mi) east of Sligo Town on R286, 17 ½ km (11 mi) east of
Knocknarea.*

Beautiful, gentle Lough Gill means simply "Lake Beauty" in Irish.
When the soldiers of Sir Frederick Hamilton sacked Sligo in 1642, legend has it that they flung the silver bell of the abbey into the depths
of Lough Gill, where today it is said that only the pure can hear it ring.
In fine weather the lough is serenity itself: sunlight on the meadows
all around, a gossamer of telegraph wire draped over the woods down
to a loughside cottage, the lap of water, a salmon leaping, a yacht sailing by. To get to the Lough from Sligo Town, take Stephen Street, which
turns into N16 (signposted to Manorhamilton and Enniskillen). Turn
right almost at once onto R286. Within minutes you will find gorgeous
views of the lake so adored by the young Yeats.

On the eastern shore of Lough Gill, **Parke's Castle** is a sturdy, fortified house built in the 17th century by an English planter (a colonist
settling on Irish lands confiscated from Catholic owners) who needed
the strong fortifications to defend himself against a hostile populace.
His relations with the people were made worse by the fact that he obtained his building materials mainly by dismantling a historic fortress
on the site, formerly belonging to the clan leaders of the O'Rourkes
of Breffni (once the name of the district). The entrance fee includes a
short video show on the castle and local history. There's also a snack
bar. In the summer, boat trips of the lough leave from here. Times vary,

but the Sligo TIO (☞ Visitor Information, *below*) has up-to-date information. ⊠ *Fivemile Bourne, on R288,* ☎ *071/64149.* ⊡ *£2.* ☉ *Mar. 13–17, daily 10–5; Apr.–May, Tues.–Sun., 10–5; June–Sept., daily 9:30–6:30; Oct., daily 10–5.*

A few minutes' walk along a footpath south of Parke's Castle (☞ *above*) lie the handsome remains of **Creevelea Abbey.** In fact not an abbey but a friary, Creevelea was founded for the Franciscans in 1508 by a later generation of O'Rourkes. It was the last Franciscan community to be founded before the suppression of the monasteries by England's King Henry VIII. Like many other such ruined abbeys, the place still has religious meaning for the local people, who treat it with reverence. One curiosity of this abbey is the especially large south transept; notice, too, its endearing little cloisters, with well-executed carvings on the pillars of St. Francis of Assisi. ⊠ *Signposted at Dromahair on R288.* ⊡ *Free.* ☉ *Freely accessible.*

Dining and Lodging

$–$$ ✕⊞ **Stanford Village Inn.** This stone-fronted inn is one of the only stops where you can gain sustenance before exploring Lough Gill. It has six newly refurbished, country-style rooms. A hearty meal, an open fire, and, if your timing is good, an impromptu session of traditional Irish music await you. The inn is off of R288, 19 km (12 mi) outside of Sligo Town. ⊠ *Dromahair, Co. Letrim,* ☎ *071/64140,* ℻ *071/64770. 6 rooms with bath. Restaurant, bar. MC, V.*

Lake Isle of Innisfree

⑪ *15 km (9 mi) south of Sligo Town via Dromahair on N4 and R287.*

In 1890 William Butler Yeats was walking through the West End of London when, seeing in a shop window a ball dancing on a jet of water, he was suddenly overcome with nostalgia for the lakes of his Sligo home. It was the moment, and the feeling, that shaped itself into his most famous poem, "The Lake Isle of Innisfree":

I will arise and go now, and go to Innisfree,
And a small cabin build there, of clay and wattles made:
Nine bean-rows will I have there, a hive for the honey-bee,
And live alone in the bee-loud glade . . .
I hear lake water lapping with low sounds by the shore;
While I stand on the roadway, or on the pavements grey,
I hear it in the deep heart's core.

Though there is nothing particularly visually exceptional about Innisfree (pronounced *innish*-free), the "Lake Isle" is a must-see if you're a Yeats fan. To reach Innisfree from Dromahair, take R287, the minor road that heads back along the south side of Lough Gill, toward Sligo Town. Turn right at a small crossroads, after 4 or 5 km (2 or 3 mi), where signposts point to Innisfree. A little road leads another couple of miles down to the lakeside, where you can see the island just offshore.

OFF THE BEATEN PATH
DOONEY ROCK – On the southwestern end of Lough Gill, a little beyond the Innisfree turnoff, a tranquil nature walk takes you to this rock, from the top of which is a picturesque panorama of the lake and of Cottage Island; this is where Yeats daydreamed, contemplated the lake's islands, and imagined a fiddler on the rock who made "folk dance like a wave of the sea." A brochure from the wooden box in the parking lot gives the particulars of the area's diverse flora, as well as a few interesting historical tidbits.

Manorhamilton

⑫ *25 km (15 mi) east of Sligo Town.*

The small rural town of Manorhamilton was built in the 17th century for the Scottish planter Sir Frederick Hamilton, who had been given the local manor house by Charles I of England (hence the town's name). The manor itself is now an ivy-covered ruin, and there's not much to see here. The surrounding scenery, however, is spectacular.

En Route   On your way to Rosses Point, stop at **Glencar Lough,** where you'll find waterfalls; a parking lot and footpath lead to one of the highest. The lake is fed by the River Drumcliff and streams at the foot of the Dartry Mountains: "Where the wandering water gushes/From the hills above Glencar/In pools among the rushes/That scarce could bathe a star," as Yeats put it in his poem "The Stolen Child." ⊠ *16 km (10 mi) west of Manorhamilton on N16; right at waterfall signpost.*

Rosses Point

⑬ *8 km (5 mi) northwest of Sligo Town on R291, 38½ km (24 mi) west of Manorhamilton.*

Yeats and his brother, Jack, often stayed at Rosses Point during their summer vacations, and it is obvious why they returned. Glorious pink and gold summer sunsets wash over the seemingly endless stretch of sandy beach. **Coney Island** lies just off Rosses Point. Local lore has it that the captain of the ship *Arathusa* christened Brooklyn's Coney Island after this island, but there's probably more legend than truth to this, as it is widely agreed that New York's Coney Island was named after the *konijn* ("wild rabbits" in Dutch) that abounded there during the 17th century. Two popular sportsmen's havens, the **County Sligo Golf Club** (☞ Sligo Town, Outdoor Activities and Sports, *above,* and Chapter 9), which has magnificent views of the sea and Ben Bulben, and the Sligo Yacht Club, are also here.

Drumcliff

⑭ *7 km (4½ mi) north of Sligo Town on N15, 15 km (9½ mi) northeast of Rosses Point.*

W. B. Yeats lies buried with his wife, Georgie, in an unpretentious grave in the cemetery of Drumcliff's simple Protestant church, where his grandfather was rector for many years. Yeats actually died on the French Riviera in 1939, but it took almost a full decade for his body to be brought back here—to the place that more than any other might be called his soul-land. In the poem "Under Ben Bulben," he spelled out not only where he was to be buried but also what should be written on the tombstone: "Cast a cold eye/On life, on death./Horseman, pass by!" It is easy to see why the majestic Ben Bulben (1,730 ft), with its sawn-off peak (not unlike Yosemite's Half-Dome), made such an impression on the poet: the mountain gazes calmly down upon the small church, as it does on all of the surrounding landscape—and at the same time stands as a sentinel facing the mighty Atlantic.

In addition to its significance as a Yeats site, Drumcliff is where St. Columba, a recluse and missionary who established Christian churches and religious communities in Northwest Ireland, is thought to have founded a monastic settlement around AD 575. The monastery that he founded before sailing off to the Scottish isle of Iona flourished for many centuries, but all that is left of it now is the base of a **round tower** and a carved **high cross** (both across N15 from the church) dating from around AD 1000, with scenes from the Old and New Testaments, including Adam and Eve with the serpent and Cain slaying Abel.

The **Old Stables Tea House and Craft Shop** (✉ next to the Protestant church, ☎ 071/44956) is a good place to stop for a snack and to pick up some Yeats poetry and books about him; it's open March through October.

Lissadell House

⓯ *14½ km (9 mi) northwest of Sligo Town, 3½ km (2 mi) west of Drumcliff, signposted from N15.*

Beside the Atlantic waters of Drumcliff Bay, on the peninsula that juts out between Donegal and Sligo bays, Lissadell is an austere but classic Georgian residence built in 1834 by Sir Robert Gore-Booth. An enlightened landlord, he mortgaged the house to help his poverty-stricken tenants during the famine years. His descendants still own Lissadell, which is filled with all manner of artifacts brought back from every corner of the globe by the family, who were great travelers. Aficionados of all things Yeatsian will appreciate the house, for the family became good friends of William Butler Yeats, who recalled seeing the house often as a child from his grandmother's carriage. On a visit to the house in 1894, he met the two Gore-Booth daughters, Eva and Constance, and subsequently recalled their meeting in verse: "The light of evening, Lissadell,/Great windows open to the south,/Two girls in silk kimonos." Eva became a poet, while sister Constance Markievicz led a dramatic political life as a fiery Irish nationalist, taking a leading role in the 1916 Easter Uprising against the British. She survived the uprising, going on to become the first woman member of the Dáil (Irish Parliament).

"That old Georgian mansion," as Yeats called it, was designed by the London architect Francis Goodwin. Its two most notable features are a dramatic 33-ft-high gallery, with 24-ft-tall Doric columns, clerestory windows, and skylights; and the dining room, where Constance's husband, Count Markievicz, painted portraits of members of the family and household employees on the pilasters. A copy of Yeats's poem "In Memory of Eva Gore-Booth and Con Markievicz" is displayed in the house. The woods of the Lissadell estate have become a forestry and wildlife reserve; they serve as a home to Ireland's largest colony of barnacle geese, along with several other species of wildfowl, and are a fine place for bird-watchers. ☎ *071/63150.* ✐ *£3.* ☉ *June–mid-Sept., Mon.–Sat. 10:30–12:30 and 2–4:30.*

AROUND DONEGAL BAY

As you drive north from Sligo Town to Donegal Town, the glens of the Dartry Mountains (home of Ben Bulben) gloriously roll by to the east, while coastal fields break open here and there to give startling views across the waters of Donegal Bay to the west. On the distant horizon the Donegal hills beckon. This stretch is dotted with numerous prehistoric sites, and it has become the Northwest's most popular vacation area. You'll pass a few small and unremarkable seashore resorts, and, in some places, you may find that haphazard and fairly tasteless construction detracts from the scenery. In between these minor resort developments, you'll find wide-open spaces free of traffic and full of fresh air. The most interesting part of this area lies on the north side of the bay—all that rocky indented coastline due west of Donegal Town. Here you enter the heart of away-from-it-all County Donegal.

Mullaghmore

🔟 *20 km (13 mi) northeast of Lissadell House, 37 km (24 mi) north of Sligo Town.*

In the high season, the picturesque, usually sleepy fishing village of Mullaghmore becomes congested with tourists. Its main attractions: a 3¼-km-long (2-mi-long) sandy beach; the turreted, fairy-tale Classie Bawn, the late Lord Louis Mountbatten's home (he, his grandson, and a local boy were killed when the IRA blew up his boat in the bay in 1979); and Ben Bulben, rising up off in the distance. A short drive along the headland is punctuated by unobstructed views beyond the rocky coastline out over Donegal Bay. When the weather is fair, you can see all the way across to St. John's Point and Drumanoo Head in Donegal.

Dining and Lodging

$ ✕▣ **Beach Hotel.** If there's a chill in the air, you can warm up at the roaring fires in the restaurant and residents' lounge of this large harborside Victorian hotel. The pale peach building is decorated in a nautical theme to commemorate the loss of three galleons of the Spanish Armada in the bay in September 1588. Enjoy wonderful views of the pier and the bay from the hotel bars, or tuck into the de'Cuellar Restaurant's acclaimed seafood menu. Top starters include hot crab claws with garlic, while favorite main courses are dressed lobster and the house seafood platter. Save room for the homemade brown bread ice cream. ⊠ *Co. Sligo,* ☎ *071/66103,* 🖷 *071/66448. 28 rooms with bath. Restaurant, 2 bars, indoor pool, hot tub, sauna, steam room, exercise room, horseback riding. AE, MC, V.*

Creevykeel

🔟 *3 km (2 mi) southeast of Mullaghmore, 16 km (10 mi) north of Drumcliff signposted from N15.*

Creevykeel is one of Ireland's best megalithic court-tombs. The site (signposted) lies off the road, just beyond the edge of the village of Cliffony. You'll see a burial area and an enclosed open-air "court" where rituals were performed around 3000 BC. Bronze artifacts found here are now in the National Museum in Dublin (☞ Exploring Dublin *in* Chapter 1).

Bundoran

🔟 *12 km (8 mi) northeast of Creevykeel on N15.*

Resting on the south coast of County Donegal, Bundroan is one of Ireland's most popular seaside resorts, a favorite haunt of the Irish from both the North and the South. If souvenir shops and amusement arcades aren't your thing, north of the town center is a handsome beach at **Tullan Strand,** washed by good surfing waves. Between the main beach and Tullan, the Atlantic has sculpted cliff-side rock formations that the locals have christened with whimsical names such as the Fairy Bridges, the Wishing Chair, and the Puffing Hole (this last one blows wind and water from the waves pounding below).

Outdoor Activities and Sports

FISHING

Good fishing is 6½ km (4 mi) away from Bundoran at **Lough Melvin.** Ask locally for **Pat Barrett's Tackle Shop** (⊠ Main St., ☎ 072/41504) for bait, tackle, and local information.

Bundoran Golf Club (☎ 072/41302) is an 18-hole, par-70 course on the cliffs above Bundoran beach.

Ballyshannon

🔞 *6½ km (4 mi) north of Bundoran on N15.*

The former garrison town of Ballyshannon rises gently from the banks of the River Erne and has good views of Donegal Bay and the surrounding mountains. The town is a typical hodgepodge of shops, arcades, and hotels, but its triangular central area has several bars and places to grab a snack. The biggest and most popular pub is the green-shuttered **Seán Óg's** (⊠ Market St., ☎ 072/51585), which serves light Irish meals all day and features traditional music in the evenings. The town was also the birthplace of the prolific Irish poet William Allingham. Each year in early August, the normally quiet village springs to life with a grand festival of folk and traditional music (☞ Nightlife and the Arts, *below*).

Exquisite chinaware and porcelain are made at the **Donegal Irish Parian China Factory** (☞ Shopping, *below*), the Republic's largest manufacturer of Parian china (so named because it resembles the clear, white marble from the Greek island of Paros). There's a free 15-minute tour, a 10-minute video, and a showroom, shop, and tearoom.

OFF THE BEATEN PATH **LOUGH DERG** – From Whitsunday to the Feast of the Assumption (that is, from June to mid-August), tens of thousands determinedly beat a path to this lonely, out-of-the-way lake, ringed by heather-clad slopes. In the center of the lough, Station Island—known as St. Patrick's Purgatory—is one of Ireland's most popular pilgrimage sites, even though it is also the most rigorous and austere of such sites in the country. Pilgrims stay on the island for three days without sleeping, and eat only black tea and dry toast. They walk barefoot around the island, on its flinty stones, to pray at a succession of shrines. The pilgrimage has been followed since time immemorial; during the Middle Ages, it attracted large numbers of devotees from foreign lands. To reach the shores of Lough Derg, turn off the main N15 Sligo–Donegal road in the village of Laghy onto the minor R232 Pettigo road, which hauls itself over the Black Gap and descends sharply into the border village of Pettigo, about 21 km (13 mi) from N15. From here, take the Lough Derg access road for 8 km (5 mi). Note: nonpilgrims may not visit the island from June to mid-August. If you wish to know more about St. Patrick's Purgatory in order to become a pilgrim, write to Reverend Prior. ⊠ *Lough Derg, Pettigo, Co. Donegal.*

Dining and Lodging

$$$ ✕🏨 **Sand House Hotel.** Behind the mock manor-house exterior of this 19th-century former fishing lodge lies a large, modern hotel. Right on Donegal Bay, about 8 km (5 mi) northwest of Ballyshannon and 16 km (10 mi) south of Donegal Town, this makes a peaceful, well-positioned base for sightseeing along the coastline; the hotel has access to 3 km (2 mi) of beach. Renovated, well-kept bedrooms are beautifully decorated with antiques and overlook either the sea or the Donegal hills. The restaurant caters to the plain, hearty appetites of Irish vacationers looking for something a bit special. Fresh seafood, including Donegal Bay oysters and mussels, is the daily specialty. ⊠ *Rossnowlagh, Co. Donegal,* ☎ *072/51777,* ℻ *072/52100. 45 rooms with bath. Restaurant, bar, tennis court, horseback riding, Ping-Pong, surfing, fishing. AE, DC, MC, V. Closed Nov.–Easter.* 🍲

Nightlife and the Arts

In early June, during the **Ballyshannon Drama Festival** (☎ 072/52109), the town hosts different drama companies for a program of mainly Irish plays. Held on the bank holiday weekend at the beginning of August, the **Ballyshannon Music Festival** (☎ 072/51088) is one of Ireland's largest, longest-running, and best folk-music events. Visitors can hear both well-known and unknown folk and traditional musicians, while impromptu sessions pop up at pubs. A party atmosphere prevails, attracting up to 12,000 visitors annually.

Shopping

The goods of the best-known producer of Belleek chinaware, **Belleek Pottery** (⊠ 6½ km/4 mi away, on the border between the Republic and the North, ☎ 028/6865–8501 in Northern Ireland), can be found in the shops of Donegal and Sligo. For more information on the factory, *see* Chapter 8.

About 1½ km (1 mi) west of Belleek, before the border to Northern Ireland, you'll find **Celtic Weave China** (⊠ on R230, Cloghore, ☎ 072/51844). This small family business specializes in the basket-weave design and in elaborate floral decoration, and they can make a single piece of china to your specifications. Prices range from £6 to £1,500, but most pieces cost less than £100.

Donegal Irish Parian China Factory (⊠ on N15 south of Ballyshannon, ☎ 072/51826, ☞ *above*) makes delicate, cream-color pottery by traditional methods, to a large degree by hand. The factory sells its wares at lower prices than you'll see in retail stores. The least-expensive items (spoons or thimbles) cost around £5. A full tea set starts at about £250.

En Route   On your way to Donegal Town, a sign on the right points to **Donegal Craft Village** (☞ Shopping *in* Donegal Town, *below*).

Donegal Town

⑳ *21 km (13 mi) north of Ballyshannon, 66 km (41 mi) northeast of Sligo Town.*

With a population of about 3,000, Donegal is Northwest Ireland's largest small village—marking the entry into the back-of-the-beyond of the wilds of County Donegal. The town is centered on the triangular Diamond, where three roads converge (N56 to the west, and N15 to the south and the northeast) and the mouth of the River Eske pours gently into Donegal Bay. You should have your bearings in five minutes, and seeing the historical sights takes less than an hour; if you stick around any longer, it'll probably be to do some shopping—arguably Donegal's top attraction.

Donegal was previously known in Irish as Dun na nGall, "Fort of the Foreigners." The foreigners being referred to were Vikings, who set up camp here in the 9th century to facilitate their pillaging and looting. They were driven out by the powerful O'Donnell clan (originally Cinel Conail), who made it the capital of Tyrconail, their extensive Ulster territories. Donegal was rebuilt in the early 17th century, during the Plantation period, when Protestant colonists were planted on Irish property confiscated from their Catholic owners. The **Diamond**, like that of many other Irish villages, dates from this period. Once a marketplace, it has a 20-ft obelisk monument to the Four Masters (☞ *below*).

Donegal Castle was built by clan leader Hugh O'Donnell in the 1470s. More than a century later, this structure was the home of his descendant Hugh Roe O'Donnell, who faced the might of the invading English and was the last clan chief of Tyrconail. In 1602 he died on a trip to Spain while trying to rally reinforcements from his allies. In 1610, its new English owner, Sir Basil Brooke, reconstructed the little castle, adding the fine Jacobean fortified mansion with towers and turrets that can still be seen today (he was responsible for the Diamond, as well). The small enclosed grounds are pleasant; inside, there are only a few rooms to see, including the garderobe (the rest room) and a great hall with an exceptional vaulted wood-beam roof. ⊠ *Tirchonaill St., near north corner of the Diamond,* ☎ *073/22405.* ⊡ *£3.* ☉ *Easter–Oct., daily 9:30–6:30.*

The ruins of the **Franciscan abbey,** founded in 1474 by Hugh O'Donnell, are a five-minute walk south of town at a spectacular site perched above the Eske, where it begins to open up into Donegal Bay. The complex was burned to the ground in 1593, razed by the English in 1601, and ransacked again in 1607; the ruins include the choir, south transept, and two sides of the cloisters, between which lie hundreds of graves dating back to the 18th century. The abbey was probably where the *Annals of the Four Masters* was written from 1632 to 1636. The *Annals* chronicles the whole of Celtic history and mythology of Ireland from earliest times up to the year 1618. The **Four Masters** were four monks who believed (correctly, as it turned out) that Celtic culture was doomed after the English conquest, and they wanted to preserve as much of it as they could. At the National Library in Dublin, you can see facsimile pages of the monks' work (☞ Exploring Dublin *in* Chapter 1); the original is kept under lock and key. ⊠ *Off N15, behind Hyland Central Hotel.* ⊡ *Free.* ☉ *Freely accessible.*

Dining and Lodging

$ ✕ **Blueberry Tea Room.** This pleasant, ground-floor restaurant and café is across the street from Donegal Castle. Proprietors Brian and Ruperta Gallagher serve breakfast, lunch, afternoon tea, and a light evening meal. Daily specials—such as Irish lamb stew, a variety of pasta dishes, and quiche—are served from 8 AM to 8 PM. Soups, sandwiches, salads, and fruit are on the regular menu, along with homemade desserts, breads, scones, and jams. ⊠ *Castle St.,* ☎ *073/22933. V. Closed Sun.*

$$$$ ✕🏠 **St. Ernan's House.** On its own wooded tidal island in Donegal Bay,
★ a five-minute drive from town, St. Ernan's is one of the most spectacularly situated country houses in Ireland. The two-story house was built by a nephew of the Duke of Wellington in 1826. Today Brian and Carmel O'Dowd, the meticulous owner-managers, foster a relaxed, serene atmosphere. Guest rooms are simple but elegant, with antiques and views of the bay. Dinner, from a light meal ($$) to a leisurely five-course meal ($$$$), is served in the intimate and elegant dining room (open to nonguests). The menu, which changes nightly, draws upon fresh local produce, prepared in the Irish country-house style. Pigeon and quail with oyster mushrooms is a typical starter; lamb in a rich red wine sauce or wild salmon with a green herb sauce might follow. A stroll around the island is a perfect way to finish off the evening. ⊠ *St. Ernan's Island, Co. Donegal,* ☎ *073/21065,* ℻ *073/22098. 10 rooms with bath, 1 suite. Dining room. MC, V. Closed Nov.–Easter.* 🐾

$$$ ✕🏠 **Harvey's Point.** At the foot of the Blue Stack Mountains, nestled beside Lough Eske, this Swiss-owned hotel has spacious, well-equipped bedrooms, where you will be greeted with a complimentary decanter of brandy. The split-level dining room, which has spirit-lifting lake views, sets the scene for a meal of wild Irish smoked salmon (in generous helpings), monkfish, duck, and a host of other fresh Irish fare served with a French twist. ⊠ *Lough Eske, Co. Donegal,* ☎ *073/22208,* ℻ *073/ 22352. 20 rooms with bath. Restaurant, bar, tennis court, boating, bicycles. AE, DC, MC, V.* 🐾

$$$ 🏨 **Hyland Central.** Right on Donegal's central square, this family-run hotel is affiliated with Best Western. The slightly shopworn public areas have a touch of old-world style. Although some of the bedrooms are spacious, their decor—simple built-ins and imitation black-leather and teak furniture—is nothing to write home about. On the plus side, rooms in the back have huge picture windows with lovely views of Donegal Bay. The efficient staff serves good, filling food in the large dining room. ⊠ *The Diamond, Co. Donegal,* ☎ *073/21027,* 𝖥𝖠𝖷 *073/22295. 90 rooms with bath. Dining room, indoor pool, steam room, health club. AE, DC, MC, V.*

Nightlife and the Arts

The **Abbey Hotel** (⊠ The Diamond, ☎ 073/21014) has music every night in July and August and a disco every Sunday night throughout the year. During the summer, people pack **McGroarty's Bar** (⊠ north side of the Diamond, ☎ 073/21049) for traditional music each Thursday night; it's also a good place to stop for a casual bite.

Outdoor Activities and Sports

About 8 km (5 mi) from Donegal Town lies **Donegal Golf Club** (⊠ Murvagh, Laghey, Co. Donegal, ☎ 073/34054), with one of Ireland's great championship courses (☞ Chapter 9).

Shopping

Browse a While (⊠ Main St., ☎ 074/22783) is a good place to stop off if you're in the mood for some light reading. Stocked with a startling range of magazines, the shop also carries a small range of pulp fiction. Long the principal marketplace for the region's wool products, Donegal Town has several smaller shops with local hand weaving, knits, and crafts. The main store in town, **Magee's** (⊠ The Diamond, ☎ 073/21100), carries renowned private-label tweeds for both men and women (jackets, hats, scarves, suits, and more), as well as pottery, linen, and crystal. **Simple Simon's** (⊠ The Diamond, ☎ 073/22687), the local health-food store, has crafts, cards, essential oils, and other whole-Earth items. The shop also carries a range of breads and cakes from the kitchen on the premises and a good smattering of local foods. About 1½ km (1 mi) south of town, beside the main N15, the **Donegal Craft Village** is a complex of workshops where you can buy pottery, handwoven goods, and ceramics from local young craftspeople and watch the items being made.

En Route As you travel west on N56, which runs slightly inland from a magnificent shoreline of rocky inlets with great sea views, it's worthwhile turning off the road from time to time to catch a better view of the coast. About 6½ km (4 mi) out of Donegal Town, N56 skirts **Mountcharles,** a bleak hillside village that looks back across the bay.

Bruckless

㉑ *19 km (12 mi) west of Donegal Town on N56.*

Don't be fooled by the round tower in the churchyard at Bruckless—it's a 19th-century belfry, not an authentic medieval structure. Soon after Bruckless, N56 turns inland across the bogs toward Ardara. The road now becomes R263, which runs through attractive heathland and wooded hills down to Killybegs.

Dining and Lodging

$ ✕🏨 **Castle Murray House Hotel.** Panoramas of distant mountains, the sapphire-blue waters of MacSwyne's Bay, and the long, narrow unspoiled peninsula, punctuated at its tip by a lighthouse, await visitors to this hotel 1½ km (1 mi) out on the 9½-km-long (6-mi-long) St. John's Point Peninsula. The original house has been extended and modernized;

rooms are basic but comfortable. Natives trek here for the restaurant ($$), where Thierry Delcros, the French-born owner-chef, prepares superb French cuisine. Selections might include phyllo-wrapped parcel of duck or the specialty of the house, prawns and monkfish in garlic butter. The hotel is 21 km (13 mi) west of Donegal Town. ✉ *St. John's Point, Dunkineely, Co. Donegal,* ☎ *073/37022,* FAX *073/37330. 10 rooms with bath. Restaurant, bar. MC, V. Closed mid-Jan.–mid-Feb. and Mon.–Tues. mid-Feb.–Easter and Oct.–mid-Jan.*

$ 🏠 **Bruckless House.** A two-story, 18th-century farmhouse on the north side of Donegal Bay, 8 km (5 mi) outside Killybegs and within an easy drive of Glencolumbkille, Ardara, and Donegal Town, this unusual bed-and-breakfast stands on 19 acres, comprising woods, gardens, and a meadow where Irish draft horses and Connemara ponies roam. Public rooms in the main building have a fine view of Bruckless Bay; their decor has an Asian flavor reflecting years spent in Hong Kong by the owners, Clive and Joan Evans. Upstairs, the bedrooms are conventional but comfortable. A separate two-bedroom, self-catering gate lodge, the former servants quarters, is at the entrance to the estate. Wholesome breakfasts are prepared with fruit from the Evanses' prizewinning garden, freshly laid eggs from their hens, and milk and cream from the resident cow. ✉ *Co. Donegal,* ☎ *073/37071,* FAX *073/37070. 4 rooms, 2 with bath; one 2-bedroom gate lodge. Dining room. AE, MC, V. Closed Oct.–Mar.* 🐾

Killybegs

② *6½ km (4 mi) west of Bruckless, 28 km (17 mi) west of Donegal Town on R263.*

Trawlers from Spain and France are moored in the harbor at Killybegs, one of Ireland's busiest fishing ports. Though it's one of the most industrialized places along this coast, it's not without some charm, thanks to its waterfront location. Killybegs once served as a center for the manufacture of Donegal hand-tufted carpets, which can be found in the White House and the Vatican. The **Harbour Store** (✉ Main St., ☎ 073/32122), right on the wharf, has plenty to make both fishermen and landlubbers happy, including boots and rain gear, competitively priced sweaters, and unusual bright yellow or orange fiberglass-covered gloves (made in Taiwan!).

Dining and Lodging

$$ ✕🏠 **Bay View Hotel.** Directly across from Killybegs's harbor, the Bay View is the town's most bustling spot. The hotel is spare and modish, nicely paneled in light wood, and the modern, functional bedrooms are pleasantly decorated in pale colors. The Irish table d'hôte menu changes daily, with Bruckless mussels in a white wine and garlic sauce and braised young duckling served with market vegetables and an orange and cherry coulis typifying the fare. The hotel has extensive fitness facilities and is well placed for seeing the glorious north shore of Donegal Bay. Special rates include greens fees for Portnoo (outside Ardara) and Murvagh (outside Donegal) for golfers. ✉ *Main St., Co. Donegal,* ☎ *073/31950,* FAX *073/31856. 40 rooms with bath. Restaurant, bar, indoor pool, sauna, health club. AE, MC, V.* 🐾

En Route   The narrows, climbs, and twists of R263 afford terrific views of Donegal Bay before descending into pretty **Kilcar,** a traditional center of tweed making. The next village, signposted by its Irish name, An Charraig (Carrick), clings to the foot of the **Slieve League Mountains,** whose dramatic, color-streaked ocean cliffs are, at 2,000 ft, the highest in Ireland and among the most spectacular. To see them, take the little road to the Irish-speaking village of Teelin, 1½ km (1 mi) south from Carrick. Then take the narrow lane (signposted to Bunglass) that climbs steeply to the top of the cliffs. For an even more thrilling perspective, some hardy folk walk on the difficult coastal path from Teelin.

Glencolumbkille (Gleann Cholm Cille)

㉓ *8 km (5 mi) west of Carrick, 27 km (17 mi) west of Killybegs on R263.*

At the far end of a stretch of barren moorland, the tiny hamlet of Glencolumbkille (pronounced glen-colm-*kill*) clings dramatically to the rockbound harbor of Glen Bay. Because it is at the heart of County Donegal's shrinking Gaeltacht, or Irish-speaking region, it has a strong, rural Irish flavor, as do its pubs and brightly painted row houses. Its name means St. Columba's Glen (or, alternatively, Columba's Glen Church); the legend goes that St. Columba, the Christian missionary (☞ Drumcliff *in* Yeats Country, *above*), lived here during the 6th century with a group of followers. Some 40 prehistoric cairns, scattered around the village, have become connected locally with the St. Columba myths. The **House of St. Columba,** on the cliff top rising north of the village, is a small oratory said to have been used by the saint himself. Inside, stone constructions are thought to have been his bed and chair. Every year on June 9, starting at midnight, local people make a 3-km (2-mi) barefoot procession called "An Turas" (the journey) around 15 medieval crosses and ancient cairns, collectively called the stations of the cross. Near the beach in Glencolumbkille is the **Folk Village,** an imaginative museum of rural life. Three small cottages, with bare-earth floors, represent the very basic living conditions of the 1720s, 1820s, and 1920s. The complex, built after local priest Father McDyer imaginatively started a cooperative to help combat rural depopulation, includes an interpretative center, 1881 schoolhouse, nature walk, tea shop, and crafts shop selling local handmade products, including, intriguingly, wines made from fuchsias and bluebells. ☎ *073/30017.* ☜ *£2.* ☉ *Easter–Sept., Mon.–Sat. 10–6, Sun. noon–6.*

Ardara

★ ㉔ *28 km (17 mi) northeast of Glencolumbkille, 40 km (25 mi) northwest of Donegal Town.*

Fortuitously situated at the head of a lovely ocean inlet, the unpretentious, old-fashioned hamlet of Ardara (pronounced ar-dar-*ah*) is built around the L-shape intersection of its two main streets. (If you come from Glencolumbkille, expect a scenic drive full of hairpin curves and steep hills as you cross over Glengesh Pass.) Ardara has been an important wooltrading center for centuries. Great cloth fairs were once held on the first of every month, and cottage workers in the surrounding countryside still provide Ardara (and County Donegal) with high-quality, handwoven cloths and hand knits. If you're looking for a chunky Aran sweater, "Ireland's capital of handwoven tweeds and knitwear," as Ardara bills itself, has several stores to choose from (☞ Shopping, *below*). The **Ardara Heritage Centre** celebrates Donegal's history of producing tweed and knitwear. A weaver works at a traditional loom, while photographs and displays provide a historical overview; there's also an audiovisual show. ⊠ *Main St.,* ☎ *075/41704.* ☜ *Free.* ☉ *Daily 9:30–6.*

There are a number of pubs where you can hear traditional music yearround (☞ Nightlife and the Arts, *below*). The long-established **Nesbitt Arms** (⊠ Main St., ☎ 075/41103) is a good place for a reasonably priced drink and snack. It can get very crowded during the high season.

Dining and Lodging

$$ ✗⛳ **Woodhill House.** John and Nancy Yates's spacious home stands
★ on 4 acres of wooded grounds only ½ km (¼ mi) from Ardara. The cream-
color exterior is Victorian, but parts of the interior and the coach house
date from the 17th century. High ceilings and marble fireplaces are in
the fine public rooms; the hall has a lovely round table and stained-
glass window. Bedrooms are less grand but large, with superb views
of the Donegal highlands. Visitors and locals alike enjoy frequent Irish
folk music sessions presented in the bar. The 40-seat restaurant uses
fresh, local ingredients on its Cordon Bleu à la carte and table d'hôte
menus, with meals prepared in a French-Irish style. Entrées might in-
clude duck in port wine sauce, wild local salmon with garlic and
spinach sauce, or rack of lamb with herbs picked from the 18th-cen-
tury walled garden. The elaborate desserts are all homemade. ✉ *Done-
gal Rd., Co. Donegal,* ☎ *075/41112,* 🆑 *075/41516. 9 rooms with bath.
Restaurant, bar, horseback riding, fishing. AE, DC, MC, V. Closed 1
wk at Christmas.* 🐾

$ ⛳ **Green Gate.** If you're looking for an alternative to country houses
and village hotels, Frenchman Paul Chatenoud's remote cottage over-
looking Ardara, the Atlantic, and spectacular Donegal scenery is one of
the most beautiful little guest houses in Ireland. The four spare rooms
are in a converted stone outbuilding with a thatched roof. Chatenoud,
even more charming than his hideaway, is eager to point guests toward
Donegal's best-kept secrets. It's worth visiting here for a peek at the glow-
ing compliments in the guest book. To reach the hotel from Ardara, fol-
low the sign for Donegal and turn right after 200 yards. ✉ *Ardvally,
Co. Donegal,* ☎ *075/41546. 4 rooms with bath. No credit cards.*

$ ⛳ **Greenhaven House.** Only a few minutes from the village, Eileen Mol-
loy's modern, one-story home has its own gardens and marvelous
views of the nearby mountains and bay. You'll be warmed by a peat
fire in the lounge and wake up to a hearty breakfast (included). Eileen
can also advise you on shopping for hand knits and other items. ✉
Portnoo Rd., Co. Donegal, ☎ *075/41129,* 🆑 *075/41129. 6 rooms with
bath. Dining room, lounge. No credit cards. Closed Dec.*

Nightlife and the Arts

For a small, old-fashioned village, Ardara has a surprising number of
pubs, many of them offering evenings of traditional music. The **Cen-
tral Bar** (✉ Main St., ☎ 075/41311) has music almost every night dur-
ing the summer and on weekends the rest of the year. One of the
smallest bars in the Republic, **Nancy's Pub** (✉ Front St., ☎ 075/
41187) has some corners that make you wonder if you've wandered
into the owners' sitting room; it finds space for a folk group several
nights a week in the high season.

Outdoor Activities and Sports

Rent a bike (£7 per day, £30 per week) from **Donal Byrne** (✉ West
End, ☎ 075/41156).

Shopping

Many handwoven and locally made knitwear items are on sale here;
some stores commission goods directly from knitters, and prices are
about as low as you'll find anywhere. Handsome, chunky Aran hand-
knit sweaters (£60–£100), cardigans (similar prices), and scarves (£16)
are all widely available. Stores like **Campbells Tweed Shop** (✉ Front
St., ☎ 075/41128) carry ready-to-wear tweeds—sports jackets for
women run up to about £120; for men, up to about £150. **C. Bonner
& Son** (✉ Front St., ☎ 075/41303) and **E. Doherty (Ardara) Ltd.** (✉
Front St., ☎ 075/41304) stock a selection of traditional Irish prod-
ucts, such as glassware and linen, from other parts of the country.

NORTHERN DONEGAL

Traveling on northern County Donegal's country roads, you'll feel that you have escaped at last from the world's hurry and hassle. There's almost nothing up here but scenery, and plenty of it: broad, island-studded loughs of deep, dark tranquillity; unkempt, windswept, sheep-grazed grasses on mountain slopes; ribbons of luminous greenery following sparkling streams; and the mellow hues of wide bog lands, all under shifting and changing cloudscapes. This trip—apart from Inishowen Peninsula, which is included as a separate excursion at the end—could take anywhere from one day to a week, depending on how low a gear you slip into after a few breaths of Donegal air. It begins in Letterkenny, the largest town in the county (population 6,500), but if you want to pick up the journey from Ardara, then follow the itinerary in reverse. If you choose to abbreviate the trip, try at least to catch the rewarding Fanad and Rosguill peninsulas and the drive around Sheephaven Bay. Just one word of warning—don't be a bit surprised if you find a sheep standing in the middle of a mountain road looking as though you, rather than it, are in the wrong place.

Letterkenny

㉕ *55 km (34 mi) northeast of Ardara, 51 km (32 mi) northeast of Donegal Town, 35 km (21 mi) west of Derry.*

One of the fastest-growing towns in all of Ireland, Letterkenny, like Donegal to the south, is at the gateway to the far Northwest; you're likely to come through here if you're driving west out of Northern Ireland. Letterkenny's claim to fame has been that it has the longest main street in the whole country. Another distinctive feature is its towering neo-Gothic Victorian **St. Eunan's Cathedral.** None of Letterkenny's shops or pubs are particularly special, but lots of locals bustling around make it an interesting place to get a feel for what it's like to live in a modest-size Irish town today. If you're here in the middle of August you could catch the **Letterkenny Folk Festival,** which attracts musicians from all over Europe. The main County Donegal **TIO,** loaded with maps, literature, and advice, is 1½ km (1 mi) south on the Derry road, N13. ☎ 074/21160. ⊘ *Sept.–May, weekdays 9–5; June, Mon.–Sat. 9–6; July–Aug., Mon.–Sat. 9–8, Sun. 10–2.*

Dining and Lodging

$$ ✕🏠 **Mount Errigal Hotel.** One of County Donegal's smartest and most modern hotels, although not at all posh, this property appeals to both business and family-vacation visitors. Service is friendly and professional. The clean and comfortable bedrooms are efficiently arranged with pale-color furnishings. The Glengesh, the hotel's softly lit restaurant, decorated in the Roman style, serves popular Irish cooking. The bar buzzes with locals seeking a relaxed night out, and folk music, jazz, or dancing is frequently scheduled on weekends. ⊠ *Ballyraine, Co. Donegal,* ☎ *074/22700,* ⊠ *074/25085. 105 rooms with bath, 2 suites. Restaurant, 2 bars, indoor pool, sauna, health club. AE, DC, MC, V.* ❧

Ramelton

㉖ *13 km (8 mi) northeast of Letterkenny on R245.*

A small, handsome former Plantation town built by the prosperous Stewart family, Ramelton (or Rathmelton, though the pronunciation is the same) climbs uphill from a river harbor close to **Lough Swilly,** one of the loveliest of Donegal's big, fjordlike ocean inlets. The village was the birthplace of Francis Makemie (1658–1708), who preached here

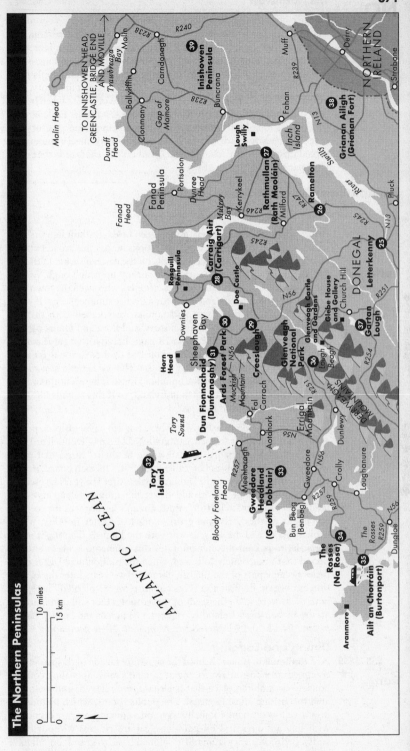

The Northern Peninsulas

ATLANTIC OCEAN

10 miles

15 km

N

Malin Head

TO INNISHOWEN HEAD, GREENCASTLE, BRIDGE END AND MOVILLE

R238

R240

R239

Malin

Traubreaga Bay

Ballyliffin

Carndonagh

Clonmany

Gap of Mamore

Dunaff Head

Inishowen Peninsula

Buncrana

Muff

Derry

NORTHERN IRELAND

Strabane

39

38

Grianan Ailigh (Grianan Fort)

Fahan

Inch Island

N13

R239

Lough Swilly

27

Rathmullan (Rath Maoláin)

Milford

Kerrykeel

R246

R245

Portsalon

Dunree Head

Fanad Head

Fanad Peninsula

Mulroy Bay

Carraig Airt (Carrigart)

28

Doe Castle

Ramelton

26

R247

R245

Pluck

R245

N13

25

Letterkenny

R251

DONEGAL

Church Hill

Gartan Lough

37

Glebe House and Gallery

Glenveagh Castle and Gardens

Lough Beagh

36

Glenveagh National Park

R254

Rosguill Peninsula

Downies

Sheephaven Bay

30

29

Creeslough

N56

Horn Head

Ards Forest Park

31

Dun Fionnachaid (Dunfanaghy)

Muckish Mountain

Fal

Carrach

Errigal Mountain

R251

Dunlewy

DERRYVEAGH MOUNTAINS

N56

Aghahork

N56

R254

N56

Tory Sound

Tory Island

32

Bloody Foreland Head

Meenlaragh

R257

Gweedore Headland (Gaoth Dobhair)

33

Gweedore

R257

Crolly

Loughanure

N56

R259

R259

Dungloe

Bun Beag (Bunbeg)

The Rosses

The Rosses (Na Rosa)

34

Aranmore

Ailt an Chorráin (Burtonport)

35

before emigrating and founding the American Presbyterian church. In the 18th century it was an important port that exported salmon, butter, grain, linen, and iodine (made from the local seaweed). Houses of wealthy merchants of the time lined the Mall, but the coming of the railway to nearby Letterkenny heralded the end of Ramelton's prosperity. However, Lough Swilly continued to play its part in history, sheltering vast fleets of British ships during the First World War, when Ireland was still part of the Empire. The **Bridge Bar** (✉ Bridge End, ☎ 074/51119) has long been favored by locals and summertime visitors as a place to meet for a drink. Enjoy a good, hearty meal (dinners are served upstairs, away from the bar), and take in the bands that regularly pack the place at night.

Rathmullan (Rath Maoláin)

㉗ *11 km (7 mi) northeast of Ramelton on R247.*

An ancient harbor village set among green fields, Rathmullan (its Irish name means "ring fort of Maoláin") looks across the broad expanse of Lough Swilly to the Inishowen hills on the eastern shore. In the last five years or so, holiday homes have sprung up near Lough Swilly's sandy shores, bringing with them vacationers who swell the town's ordinarily tiny population and make for a livelier summer scene. If you'd like to take an hour or two and familiarize yourself with this unspoiled little town's main sights, history, and flora and fauna, pick up "Rathmullan: A Walking Tour," a 28-page, handwritten guide penned by resident Margaret Carton and published by the National Trust for Ireland. It's available at the County Donegal TIO (☞ Letterkenny, *above*), Letterkenny bookshops, or Rathmullan House. There's nothing quite comparable for any other town in Ireland, so if this sounds like your cup of tea, don't pass it up.

Rathmullan's modest harbor was where English naval officers, posing as ordinary merchant seamen, captured Red Hugh O'Donnell in 1587. They invited him aboard to taste some of their "cargo of foreign wines," and the sociable clan leader fell for it. Once on board, he was shipped to imprisonment in Dublin Castle. After six years he escaped and returned to Donegal with added determination to defend his homeland—but to no avail. In 1607, Rathmullan's harbor was the scene of the Flight of the Earls, the great exodus of Ulster nobility, which brought to an end the 13-year war with the English. The **Flight of the Earls Heritage Centre** commemorates this momentous event and the period that immediately followed, when the million-acre Ulster territories became part of the English domain. Two years later the Plantation era began: English and Scots colonists were "planted" here, and with them were sown the seeds of the Troubles that still dominate the affairs of Northern Ireland (☞ Chapter 8) across the border. ☎ *No phone.* ▨ *£1.50.* ☉ *Easter–Sept., Mon.–Sat. 10–6, Sun. noon–6:30.*

Dining and Lodging

$$$–$$$$ ✕▨ **Rathmullan House.** Behind the signature facade of this two-story, ★   cream-color mansion awaits one of Ireland's most appealing country houses—a rambling place that is elegant *and* relaxed, and well situated for visiting all of Donegal. The public rooms, which include the bright-yellow drawing room, library, and a coffee room, are decorated with fine antiques and oil paintings; all are elegant without being stuffy. Bedrooms vary from old-fashioned basic to grand, but all have antiques, well-appointed bathrooms, elegant wallpaper, and fine fabrics. Rooms in the front overlook Lough Swilly, whose long, sandy, deserted beach lies steps from Rathmullan's front door. In a pavilion with a tented ceiling and floor-to-ceiling windows, the dining room has views

of the gardens and the lake, as well as a delicious menu, which changes nightly. Breakfast (included) is a feast. ⊠ *Co. Donegal,* ☎ *074/58188,* 🖷 *074/58200. 23 rooms with bath. Dining room, bar, indoor pool, steam room, tennis court, croquet, beach. AE, DC, MC, V. Closed Jan.*

$$$ 🔟 **Fort Royal Hotel.** On 18 acres of verdant grounds beside Lough Swilly, Ann and Robin Fletcher's spacious, comfortable hotel, once an aristocratic private home, is a decent alternative to the Rathmullan House (☞ *above*). It attracts a regular clientele, who enjoy its relaxed professionalism and marvelous location. Rooms are clean, and resident chef Tim, Ann and Robin's son, has several hotelier awards to his credit. ⊠ *Co. Donegal,* ☎ *074/58100,* 🖷 *074/58103. 15 rooms with bath. Restaurant, bar, 9-hole golf course, tennis court, squash, beach. AE, DC, MC, V. Closed Nov.–Mar.*

En Route Extending north from here is the barren and rock-strewn **Fanad Peninsula.** The signposted Fanad Scenic Drive takes you 27 km (17 mi) up along the west shore of Lough Swilly to low-lying Fanad Head at its northern tip, then down again through the tiny resort village of Kerrykeel, with views of long, narrow Mulroy Bay twisting and turning to your right. If you want to cut the journey short, you can take the back road directly from Rathmullan to Kerrykeel for 9½ km (6 mi).

Carraig Airt (Carrigart)

28 *14 km (9 mi) north of Ramelton on R245, 35 km (22 mi) northwest of Rathmullan.*

A small village with a lot of charm and many old-fashioned pubs, Carraig Airt (Carrigart) is at the base of a slender isthmus. This is the neck of the extremely beautiful **Rosguill Peninsula,** which has a rocky heart and a fringe of sand dunes and beaches and is encircled by the signposted 15 km (9 mi) **Atlantic Drive.** It's not as far off the beaten track as you might think; you'll see several caravan sites and housekeeping cottages, popular with visitors from Northern Ireland. The little nearby resort town of **Downings** (Na Dúnaibh) has a long, sandy beach and good fishing; tweeds can be bought from **John McNutt Homespun Tweeds Factory** (☎ 074/55158) and linens from **McNutts of Donegal Ltd.** (☎ 074/55643).

Outdoor Activities and Sports

Horses for hacking or trekking on the Rosguill Peninsula can be rented at **Carrigart Riding School** (⊠ Co. Donegal, ☎ 074/53583).

Creeslough

29 *16 km (10 mi) southwest of Carraig Airt on N56.*

To the southwest of the Rosguill Peninsula and across Sheephaven Bay lies this small town at the foot of Muckish Mountain. Nearby, on the southern end of Sheephaven Bay, stands **Doe Castle,** protected on three sides by the sea and by a moat on its fourth side. The tall, weather-beaten tower is at the center of a complex structure enclosed within sturdy defenses. Described by attacking English forces in 1587 as "the strongest fortress in all the province," the impressive edifice dates from at least 1440, when it became the home of MacSweeney Doe, one of the "gallowglasses" (from the Irish *gall o glach*)—foreign mercenaries employed by the O'Donnell clan. Despite the castle's present poor condition, it was still occupied by his descendants until 1890. MacSweeney Doe's curiously carved tombstone is fixed to the southwest tower of the outer wall. ⊠ *5½km (3½ mi) off N56, signposted south of Creeslough.* 🖻 *Free.* ☉ *Usually open; if locked, inquire at caretaker's cottage on approach path.*

Ards Forest Park

30 *9½ km (5 mi) north of Creeslough on N56.*

Clinging to Sheephaven Bay's southwest shore, the 1,188-acre Ards Forest Park (reached by passing through adjacent Creeslough [pronounced *creesh*-la]) is the former wooded estate of a Capuchin friary; the friary itself is still occupied by the Capuchins. Four prehistoric, fortified sites and one dolmen lie within the grounds, which offer some of the most varied landscape of any of Ireland's national forest parks, including rivers, loughs, salt marshes, valleys, and, of course, the bay. If the weather is fine, the park's forest trails and picnic sites are great places to enjoy the scrubbed sea air. ☎ *074/21139.* 🎫 *Free; parking £2 weekends Easter–June and July–Sept.* ☉ *Daily 8 AM–9 PM.*

Dun Fionnachaid (Dunfanaghy)

31 *8 km (5 mi) northwest of Ards Forest Park.*

On the very edge of Sheephaven Bay, Dun Fionnachaid (Dunfanaghy) is a tidy, former Plantation village. If you're ready for a short break, the hotel noted below serves decent, unpretentious local fare for about £8 for lunch. When the tide goes out, the vast sand flats of **Killyhoey Beach** are uncovered and the sea recedes into the far distance, but as it rises again, the sands are submerged in double-quick time. On the west side of Dunfanaghy, the signpost to **McSwyne's Gun** (McSwyne is the old spelling of MacSweeney) leads to a huge, natural blowhole that gives out a deafening bang when the tide rushes in during rough weather.

★ A little back road runs from Dunfanaghy up to **Horn Head,** the most spectacular of County Donegal's Atlantic headlands. From its sheer 600-ft cliffs, the views along the coast to the other headlands ranged one behind the other are spectacular. Bird-watchers should note that the cliffs are home to hundreds of seabirds, including puffin and guillemot.

Dining and Lodging

$$ ✕🏨 **Arnold's Hotel.** Right at the entrance to the village, this friendly hotel has been run by three generations of the Arnold family and is a favorite with Irish vacationers. Rooms are unassuming and relaxed; the best overlook the landscaped garden. Guests have the option of eating the generous, traditional Irish meals in the dining room or in the more casual Garden Bistro. Special-interest classes, such as photography, writing, bridge, wine-tasting, and bird-watching, are available for guests on the weekends. ✉ *Main St., Co. Donegal,* ☎ *074/36208,* FAX *074/36352. 30 rooms with bath. Bar, dining room, tennis court, horseback riding, baby-sitting. AE, DC, MC, V. Closed Dec.–mid-Mar. and weekdays Nov.*

En Route West of Dunfanaghy the terrain is rougher, wilder, and rockier; you're also likely to hear the Irish language being spoken. The N56 reaches round 11 km (7 mi) to **Fal Carrach** (Falcarragh), the site of an Irish-language college. Another 13 km (8 mi) around the rugged seashore, in good weather, you can catch a ferry from **Meenlaragh** (near Gortahork) to Tory Island.

Tory Island

32 *14½ km (9 mi) offshore.*

Harsh weather and difficult currents make Tory Island fairly inaccessible. (The boat trip lasts more than an hour on seas that are rough even on the best days; be prepared to get soaked, too.) Despite being rocky, ocean-battered, and barren (not even a single tree), the island has been inhabited since prehistoric times. Islanders speak their own dialect and refer to the mainland as "Ireland." Prehistoric and medieval relics are scattered about the landscape. Poised on the cliffs is the partly ruined, pink-granite **round tower** with its conical cap still intact. At Tory Island's eastern end, the prehistoric ruin, **Balor's Fort,** was purportedly the residence of Balor, the terrifying, one-eyed Celtic god of night and darkness. At the northeastern tip, the **Wishing Stone** has the power, it is said, to destroy enemies. Still talked about is the time (1884) when the stone's powers were invoked against the British gunboat *Wasp,* whose passengers (mainly policemen) had come to collect taxes—something the islanders were unaccustomed to paying. The ship sank, and all but six of the crew were lost.

Most of the islanders live the simple life of fisherfolk, though quite a few have unexpected sidelines as artists. In 1968, the well-known Irish painter Derek Hill met islander James Dixon, who felt that he could do a better job of painting than Hill. Many other Tory Island residents thought they could, too, and today the Tory Island artists, depicting their own life and landscape in a naive style using nothing more than standard house paints, are widely acclaimed and have exhibited elsewhere in Ireland (☞ Glebe House and Gallery *in* Gartan Lough, *below*) and abroad. **Dixon's Gallery** (☞ Tory Island Hotel *in* Dining and Lodging, *below*) sells the work of the Tory islanders; prices range from £50 to £200.

Dining and Lodging

$ ✕🏨 **Tory Island Hotel (Ostan Thoraig).** After living and working in England for 10 years, native islander Pat Doohan returned with his wife, Berney, to build and run the Tory Island Hotel. (He also watches over the nearby Dixon's Gallery [☞ *above*].) The comfortable guest rooms are large, sunny, and nicely decorated in a peach, blue, and green palette, with matching curtains and bedspreads; all have TVs and phones. A fireplace warms the bar, which is a popular local hangout. Traditional music sessions and *céilí* dancing regularly liven things up. The restaurant overlooks the sea. ⊠ *Co. Donegal,* ☎ *074/35920,* ⅏ *074/35613. 14 rooms with bath. Restaurant, bar. MC, V. Closed Dec.–Mar.*

Gweedore Headland (Gaoth Dobhair)

🟤 *27 km (17 mi) east of Meenlaragh on R257.*

When you return from Tory Island to Meenlaragh, you're on the edge of the Gweedore Headland, which can be circumnavigated on the coast road (R257). Gweedore is rocky, sparsely covered with heather and gorse, and low-lying until you reach its northernmost point, **Bloody Foreland Head.** This dramatic name for once does not recall the slaughter of some historic battle, describing instead the vivid red hues of the gaunt rock face when illuminated at sunset.

The Rosses (Na Rosa)

🟤 *13 km (8 mi) south of Bloody Foreland Head on R259.*

The next distinctive headland south of Gweedore (on the road south after you pass through Bun Beag [Benbeg] and Croithli [Crolly]) is the Rosses (Na Rosa in Irish, meaning "the headlands")—even more beautiful than Gweedore. The bleak but dramatic terrain here, as at Gweedore, has not benefited from a liberal sprinkling of modern bungalows. The coast road (R259) struggles over the inhospitable, stony landscape, crisscrossed with water channels and strewn with more than 100 lakes. Yet quite a number of people manage to survive here, many of them

Irish speakers (this is the heart of the Donegal Gaeltacht). The decline of population and living standards was reversed by Patrick Gallagher (1873–1964), who became known as Paddy the Cope. Son of a poor local family, he left school at 10, went to Scotland as a farmhand, and saved enough money to return home in the 1950s and buy a small holding of his own. Gallagher, affectionately remembered throughout the area, persuaded the citizens around the Rosses to set up cooperatives to bring in new farming methods and machinery, as well as cooperatively owned stores to keep prices down.

Ailt an Chorráin (Burtonport)

㉟ *16 km (10 mi) southwest of Crolly on R259.*

This village of Ailt an Chorráin (Burtonport), which claims to land more salmon and lobster than any other fishing port in Ireland, is the departure point for a trip over to **Aranmore,** 6½ km (4 mi) offshore. Aranmore means "big island," and it is indeed the largest and most populous of County Donegal's rocky offshore fragments. The ride out takes 25 minutes, but although it's fairly accessible, the island still feels remote and ungoverned. It has been inhabited for thousands of years (about 1,000 people live on it today), and it offers good fishing as well as striking cliff scenery and views back onto the Rosses; there's a prehistoric fort on its south side. ⛴ *Ferry £2.* ⊘ *7 crossings daily.*

Back on the mainland, if you follow the coast another 6½ km (4 mi) southeast, R259 rejoins N56 at **An Clochan Liath** (Dungloe), a pleasant little fishing town regarded as the capital of the Rosses, though there's little to do or see here.

En Route   Traveling on N56 north from Dungloe, go a couple of miles beyond Gaoth Dobhair (Gweedore) village, on the little River Clady, and take R251 to skirt the south side of **Errigal Mountain** to the village of Dunlewy, 26 km (16 mi) east of Dungloe. This whole drive passes through some of the best scenery in all of County Donegal. Serene Errigal looks especially grand from Dunlewy. On the edge of Dunlewy Lough, the **Dunlewy Centre** is an interesting spot to pause for a look at a reconstructed 19th-century weaver's home where you can watch a demonstration of old-style weaving and an audiovisual show, then have a guided tour of the cottage. Half-hour boat trips on the lake include storytelling and a history of the area. A café and crafts shop are also on the premises. ✉ *Dunlewy,* ☎ *075/31699.* ⛴ *Weaving demonstration, show, and tour £3; boat trip £3.* ⊘ *Mid Mar.–Oct., Mon.–Sat. 10:30–6, Sun. 11–7.*

Glenveagh National Park

★ **㊱** *45 km (28 mi) east of Ailt an Chorráin (Burtonport) on R251, 27 km (17 mi) northwest of Letterkenny.*

Bordered by the Derryveagh Mountains (Derryveagh means "forest of oak and birch"), Glenveagh National Park encompasses 24,000 acres of wilderness—mountain, moorland, lakes, and woods—that has been called "the largest and most dramatic tract in the wildest part of Donegal." Within its borders, a thick carpet of russet-color heath and dense woodland rolls down the Derryveagh slopes into the broad, open valley of the River Veagh (or Owenbeagh), which opens out into Glenveagh's spine: long and narrow, dark and clear **Lough Beagh.**

The Glenveagh lands have long been recognized as a remote and beautiful region. Between 1857 and 1859, John George Adair, a ruthless gentleman farmer, assembled the estate that now makes up the park.

In 1861, he evicted the estate's hundreds of poor tenants without compensation and destroyed their cottages. Nine years later, Adair began to build **Glenveagh Castle** on the eastern shore of Lough Veagh, but he soon departed for Texas. He died in 1885 without returning to Ireland, but his widow, Cornelia, moved back to make Glenveagh her home. She created the four different **gardens** covering 27 acres, planted the luxuriant rhododendrons here, and began the job of making this flamboyantly turreted and battlemented 19th-century folly livable.

The gardens and castle as they appear today are almost entirely an American invention—the product of the loving attentions of Glenveagh's last owner. U.S. millionaire Henry P. McIlhenny bought the estate in 1937 and, beginning in 1947, lived here for part of every year for almost 40 years. An avid art collector and philanthropist, McIlhenny decorated every inch of the house himself and entertained lavishly. The house has been maintained just as it was on his last occupancy in 1983; later that year, he made a gift of the house to the nation. He had sold the government the surrounding land in 1975, which it opened to the public in 1984 as Ireland's third national park.

Beyond the castle, footpaths lead into more remote sections of the park, including the **Derrylahan Nature Trail,** a 1½-km (1-mi) signposted trail where you may suddenly catch sight of a soaring falcon or chance upon a shy red deer. The park is home to one of Ireland's two largest herds; the other is at Killarney (☞ Chapter 5). Guided walks are held May through October. The visitor center at the park's entrance has a permanent exhibition on the local way of life and on the influence of climate on the park's flora and fauna. Skip the sleep-inducing audiovisual and instead have a bite to eat in the cafeteria. ✉ *Church Hill,* ☎ *074/37090.* ✑ *£2, guided tour of castle £2.* ☉ *Easter–Oct., daily 10–6:30.*

Gartan Lough

❸ *13 km (8 mi) southeast of Glenveagh on R251, 17 km (11 mi) northwest of Letterkenny.*

Close to Church Hill village, Gartan Lough is technically within the national park and is administered partly by the park authorities. The lake and the surrounding mountainous country are astonishingly beautiful. St. Columba was supposedly born here in AD 521, and the legendary event is marked by a huge cross at the beginning of a footpath into the national park. Nearby are other dubious "relics" of the saint, which are popularly believed to possess magical powers: the Natal Stone, where the saint is thought to have first opened his eyes, and the Stone of Loneliness, where he is said to have slept. However, the superstitions do rub off—the soil of Gartan was carried by soldiers from the area to the trenches of the First World War as a protective relic.

On the northwest shore of Gartan Lough, just off R251, sits **Glebe House and Gallery,** a fine Regency manor with 25 acres of gardens. For 30 years, Glebe House was the home of the distinguished landscape and portrait artist Derek Hill, who furnished the house in a mix of styles with art from around the world; in 1981 he gave the house and its contents, including his outstanding art collection, to the nation. Highlights include paintings by Renoir and Bonnard, lithographs by Kokoschka, ceramics and etchings by Picasso, and the paintings *Whippet Racing* and *The Ferry, Early Morning* by Jack B. Yeats, as well as Donegal folk art produced by the Tory islanders (☞ *above*). The decoration and furnishings of the house, including original William Morris wallpaper, are

worth a look as well. ✉ *Church Hill*, ☎ *074/37071.* 🎫 *£2.* ⊙ *Easter
and mid-May–Sept., Sat.–Thurs. 11–6:30.*

At the **Colmcille Heritage Centre** you can learn more about St. Columba
and his times. Return to R251 and turn right almost at once onto R254
in Church Hill; straightaway you'll arrive at the exhibition and inter-
pretation center, which features medieval manuscripts, stained glass,
and displays tracing the decline of the Celtic religion and the rise of
Irish Christianity. Audiovisual displays and interactive computer pre-
sentations enhance your historical journey. ✉ *Gartan, Church Hill*, ☎
074/37306. 🎫 *£1.50.* ⊙ *May and Sept.–Oct., Mon.–Sat. 10:30–6:30,
Sun. 1–6:30; June–Aug., Mon.–Sat. 10–6:30, Sun. noon–6:30.*

Grianan Ailigh (Grianan Fort)

★ ㊳ *29 km (18 mi) northeast of Letterkenny on N13.*

A circular stone Celtic fort, the Grianan Ailigh (Grianan Fort) definitely
merits a visit, although it is, like the Inishowen Peninsula (☞ *below*),
northeast of Letterkenny and thus closer to Northern Ireland (☞
Chapter 8) than the majority of Donegal sites covered here. The fortress
sits on top of an 810-ft hill; on a fine day, the panorama of the rolling
Donegal and Derry landscape is breathtaking. To the north lies the Swilly
estuary, flowing around Inch Island into Lough Swilly. On either side
rise the hills of the Fanad and Inishowen peninsulas, though they're often
partly veiled by mists. As for the fort, what you'll see is a circular stone
enclosure with a diameter of about 76 ft, which you can enter through
a gate (it's open most of the year). Inside, earth ramparts and concentric defenses punctured by passages surround a sturdy central structure.
No one knows when Grianan Fort was built, but it was probably an Iron
Age fortress. Its position was accurately recorded in the 2nd century AD
by the geographer Ptolemy of Alexandria. In the 5th century it became
the seat of Ulster's O'Neill chieftains and remained so until the 12th century, despite serious attempts by their enemies to destroy it, especially
in the year 674 and again in 1101. The present-day fortress, however,
owes a good deal to overzealous "restoration" in the 1870s by Dr. Walter Bernard, a Derry historian; before that, it was in ruins. If you're
traveling north on N13, look for signs to Buncrana, because the easy-
to-miss sign for the fort is opposite. Instead of turning to Buncrana,
take the narrow lane that climbs and turns for more than 2 km (1 mi)
to the top of the hill. The fort is freely accessible.

Inishowen Peninsula

㊴ *Peninsula circuit from Fahan to Muff via Malin Head and Inishowen
Head: 161 km (100 mi).*

The most northerly point in all of Ireland, the huge Inishowen Peninsula is a grandly green, wild piece of land with a solid, mountainous
interior. It is enclosed by Lough Swilly on one side, Lough Foyle on
another, and the battering Atlantic to the north. Despite a string of small
and untempting coastal resorts, it remains unspoiled and less traveled
than most other parts of the country. If you decide to make the Inishowen
circuit (known as the "Inishowen 100," for its length in miles) plus
the 64-km (40-mi) round-trip to reach it from Letterkenny, you'll need
to allow at least one whole day, though it is possible to make an abbreviated visit in less time.

Just off of R238, as you head toward Buncrana, is **Fahan** (pronounced
fawn), which has monastic ruins that include the early Christian **St.
Mura cross slab.** A popular, downscale beach resort favored by Derry
denizens, **Buncrana** has a 14th-century O'Doherty tower that gradu-

ally became part of an 18th-century mansion. Shortly after you pass Buncrana, turn left at the fork in the road away from R238 onto the coast road, which will take you past the 19th-century fort on Dunree Head, up and over the spectacular viewpoint of the **Gap of Mamore**, where the 1,250-ft Croaghcarragh rises up on one side and the 1,361-ft Mamor Hill echoes it on the other. The road heads north toward **Dunaff Head**, where Lough Swilly opens into the ocean. Rejoin R238 at Clonmany and take it through **Ballyliffin,** another small resort town with an O'Doherty tower on the beach, and a convenient place for a snack or meal.

By the junction of R238 and R240, you'll see a church with a curious remnant of early Christianity against one wall—the decorated, 7th-century **Donagh Cross,** accompanied by a couple of pillar stones. The strange carvings on the stones clearly date from a pre-Christian period. Around the corner from the Donagh Cross, **Carndonagh,** the area's main market town, has several more medieval monastic remains; **Slieve Snaght,** Inishowen's highest peak, at 2,019 ft, lies just southwest of town. As it runs up beside Trawbreaga Bay, R238 turns into R242 shortly before the picturesque village of **Malin**; it's another 16 km (10 mi) up to **Malin Head,** the most northerly point in all of Ireland and an important spot for birds migrating south in autumn. Although it has good views, Malin Head is not as dramatic a spot as some of the other headlands.

From Malin Head, take the signposted route across the peninsula to **Moville,** a sleepy waterside resort on the Lough Foyle side. From here, it's 8 km (5 mi) to **Inishowen Head,** the peninsula's rocky eastern tip. On the way to the head, at **Greencastle,** you'll see the fortifications of foreigners who tried to control the nine counties of Ulster: a 14th-century Anglo-Norman fortress and an English fort built five centuries later to defend against French support for the Irish. The drive along the lough shore toward Derry (☞ Chapter 8), though attractive, is punctuated by small, uninteresting villages whose modernized pubs cater to visitors from Derry. If you want to turn away from Derry toward Letterkenny before reaching the border, take R239 from Muff to **Bridge End,** home to one of the most attractive of Ireland's many new Catholic churches.

Dining and Lodging

$–$$ ✕ **Corncrake Restaurant.** Five years ago, Bríd McCartney and Noreen Lynch gave up the Dublin rat race to open the most stylish little restaurant between Derry and New York. They grow all their own herbs and specialize in seafood and lamb. Standouts include salmon *coulibiac* (mélange of fresh salmon, rice, hard-cooked eggs, mushrooms, shallots, and dill, enclosed in a hot pastry envelope) as a main course and fallen chocolate soufflé with prunes and Armagnac for dessert. The two also run excellent weekend cooking courses for £200, which includes all meals, instruction, and accommodation at the nearby Rossaor House. ⊠ *Carndonagh,* ☎ *077/74534. No credit cards.*

$$–$$$ ✕🖼 **St. John's Country House and Restaurant.** A cozy, old-fashioned ★ atmosphere prevails at this restored lakeside Georgian house. Homemade bread is baked daily to serve with the fresh garden soups and pâtés. The six-course table d'hôte menu changes monthly and offers appetizers such as seafood chowder or a terrine of salmon and monkfish wrapped in spinach. Fillets of brill with herbs and fennel sauce, and Donegal rack of lamb served with mascarpone risotto and rosemary, are typical main courses. Desserts include homemade ice creams and carrageen moss with fruit coulis. Dining in the new conservatory area of the restaurant adds an extra touch of romance to those long summer nights. With comfortable, elegant rooms, the hotel is a relaxing oasis, enhanced by the exceptional hospitality of its host, Reggie

Ryan. ✉ *Fahan, Co. Donegal*, ☎ *077/60289*, FAX *077/60612. 4 rooms with bath, 1 suite. AE, MC, V. Closed mid-Feb.–mid-Mar.*

Outdoor Activities and Sports

For hacking and trekking on the Inishowen Peninsula contact **Lenamore Stables** (✉ Muff, ☎ 077/84022), which offers excellent rates for bed-and-breakfast, with riding included.

Shopping

National Knitting Centre (✉ Lisfannon, near Buncrana, ☎ 077/62355) sells hand-knit goods and offers residential courses in traditional Irish hand knitting.

THE NORTHWEST A TO Z

Arriving and Departing

By Bus

Bus Éireann (☎ 01/836–6111 in Dublin, 071/60066 locally) can get you from Dublin to Sligo Town in four hours for £9 one-way, £13 round-trip. Three buses a day from Dublin are available. Another bus route, four times a day from Dublin (five on Friday), goes to Letterkenny, in the heart of County Donegal, in 4¼ hours, via a short trip across the Northern Ireland border; it's £10 one-way, £14.50 round-trip. Other Bus Éireann services connect Sligo Town to towns all over Ireland.

By Car

Sligo, the largest town in the Northwest, is relatively accessible on the main routes. The N4 travels the 224 km (140 mi) directly from Dublin to Sligo, but you need to allow at least four hours for this journey. The N15 continues from Sligo Town to Donegal Town and proceeds from Donegal Town to Derry City, just over the border in the province of Northern Ireland. The fastest approach for anyone driving up from the West and the Southwest is on N17, connecting Sligo to Galway, though the landscape is undistinguished.

By Plane

The principal international air-arrival point to the Northwest is the tiny airport at Charlestown, **Knock International Airport** (☎ 094/67222), 54½ km (34 mi) south of Sligo Town. **City of Derry Airport** (☎ 028/7181–0784), a few miles over the border, receives flights from Manchester and Glasgow. City of Derry (also called Eglinton) is a particularly convenient airport for reaching northern County Donegal. **Donegal Airport** (☎ 075/48232), in Carrickfinn, is not far from Dungloe and typically receives flights from Dublin. **Sligo Airport** (☎ 071/68280 or 071/68318) at Strandhill, 8 km (5 mi) west of Sligo Town, is the other area airport.

Aer Arann has direct, daily flights between Donegal Airport and Dublin, and Sligo Airport and Dublin. **British Airways Express** flies to Eglinton (Derry) Airport from Manchester and Glasgow. **Ryanair** has flights to Knock Airport from London Stansted daily.

BETWEEN THE AIRPORTS AND YOUR DESTINATION

By Bus. If you aren't driving, Knock Airport becomes less attractive, as you'll have no easy public transportation link to your destination, except the once-a-day (in season) local bus to Charlestown, 11 km (7 mi) away. Nor can you rely on catching a bus at the smaller airports, except at Sligo Airport, where buses run from Sligo Town to meet all flights.

By Car. Knock Airport has a convenient car-rental desk. You can also pick up rental cars at Sligo and Eglinton (Derry) airports.

By Taxi. Cabs sometimes wait outside Knock Airport to meet incoming flights, but passengers arriving at the other airports may have to phone a local taxi company. Phone numbers of taxi companies are available from airport information desks and are also displayed beside pay phones inside the airport terminals.

By Train

Sligo Town is the northernmost direct rail link to Dublin. From Dublin three trains a day are available, and the journey takes 3 hours and 20 minutes. The fare is £14.50 one-way or day-return, £19 round-trip. If you want to get to Sligo Town by rail from other provincial towns, you'll be forced to make some inconvenient connections and take roundabout routes. The rest of the region has no railway services. Contact **Irish Rail** (☎ 01/836–6222).

Getting Around

By Bus

Bus Éireann services operate out of Sligo Town (☎ 071/60066 or 074/21309) and Letterkenny (☎ 071/60066 or 074/21309) to destinations all over the region, as well as to other parts of Ireland. From Sligo Town, you can reach almost any point in the region for less than £10. **McGeehans** (☎ 075/46150) is one of several local bus companies linking towns and villages in the Northwest.

By Car

Roads are uncongested, but in some places they are in a poor state of repair (French bus drivers refused to take their buses into County Donegal some summers back, as a gesture of protest about the state of the roads). In the Irish-speaking areas, signposts are written only in the Irish (Gaelic) language, which can be confusing. You need to prepare beforehand for this by checking the Irish place names on your route.

Contacts and Resources

B&B Reservation Agencies

For a small fee, **Bord Fáilte** will book accommodations anywhere in Ireland through its central reservations system. B&Bs can be booked at local visitor information offices when they are open; however, even these reservations will go through the central reservations system. For more information, *see* Lodging *in* Smart Travel Tips A to Z.

Car Rentals

You can rent a car in Sligo Town from **Euro Mobil** (☎ 071/67291). **Murray's Europcar** (☎ 071/68400) rents cars from Sligo Airport. **Murray's Europcar** (☎ 078/33013) also has a branch at Knock Airport. A medium-size four-door costs around £50 per day with unlimited mileage (inclusive of insurance and taxes), or around £220 per week. If you're planning to tour mostly northern County Donegal, you may find it more convenient to rent a car in Derry from **Ford** (☎ 01504/360420). If you're planning to drive a rental car across the border to Northern Ireland, inform the company in advance and check the insurance policy.

Emergencies

Police, fire, and **ambulance** (☎ 999).

HOSPITALS

Letterkenny General Hospital (✉ High Rd., Letterkenny, Co. Donegal, ☎ 074/25888). **Sligo General Hospital** (✉ Dromahair Rd., Sligo Town, Co. Sligo, ☎ 071/71111).

Guided Tours

Walking tours of Sligo Town usually depart twice daily in July and August from the TIO. They are free and last about 1 to 1½ hours. However, the guides are generally students, so a tip of £1 or £2 is welcome. Check details with the TIO (☎ 071/61201). For a friendly, relaxed minibus tour of the area in July and August, call **John Houze** (☎ 071/42747 or 086/833–9084). He is a knowledgeable guide who leads popular tours to Lough Gill (£6.50 morning tour, £7.50 afternoon) and north of Sligo Town to Drumcliff, Lissadell House, and Glencar lake and waterfall (£6.50). He also does a full-day tour, including a boat trip to the Lake Isle of Innisfree (£20). **Bus Éireann** (☎ 071/60066 or 074/21309) has budget-priced, guided, one-day bus tours of the Donegal Highlands and to Glenveagh National Park, which start from Bundoran, Sligo Town, Ballyshannon, and Donegal Town.

Nightlife and the Arts

Outside Sligo Town, the Northwest features few serious arts activities and events, though there are a number of festivals and seasonal events. The local press, including the *Donegal Democrat,* the *Leitrim Observer,* and *Sligo Champion,* has useful events listings.

Outdoor Activities and Sports

BIRD-WATCHING

For more information, contact the **Irish Wild Bird Conservancy** (✉ 8 Longford Pl., Monkstown, Co. Dublin, ☎ 01/280–4322).

FISHING

A **fishing license** is not needed for sea fishing or for coarse and pike angling. For game fishing (salmon and sea trout), the license costs £3 for one day, £10 for 21 days, or £25 for a full season. The full-season license is valid throughout the whole country; there's also a local annual license, valid only in the Northwest, for £12. Senior citizens are exempt from these costs. You can obtain licenses for County Donegal from the **Northern Regional Fisheries Board** (✉ Ballyshannon, Co. Donegal, ☎ 072/51435). Please note that you must purchase share certificates if you intend to do coarse fishing or angling for brown trout in County Donegal; the rates are £3 for one day, £5 for 21 days, or £12 for a season. For licenses in Counties Sligo and Leitrim, contact the **North-Western Regional Fisheries Board** (✉ Ballina, Co. Mayo, ☎ 096/22623). Some tackle shops are also permitted to sell licenses.

For complete information on fishing in the Northwest waters, suitable accommodations, details of boat rentals, and so on, ask the Irish Tourist Board (☞ Visitor Information *in* Smart Travel Tips A to Z) for the annual *Anglers' Guide.*

Bait, tackle, and local information can be found at the following places:

County Donegal: John McGill (✉ Main St., Ardara, ☎ no phone); O'-Doherty's (✉ Main St., Donegal Town, ☎ no phone); and Pat Barrett (✉ Finner Rd., Bundoran, ☎ 072/41504).

County Leitrim: Geraghty's (✉ Main St., Carrick-on-Shannon, ☎ 078/21316) and Aodh Flynn (✉ Deerpark, Manorhamilton, ☎ no phone).

County Sligo: Barton Smith (✉ Hyde Bridge, Sligo Town, ☎ 071/42356).

GOLF

For a full list of golf courses in the region, contact the Irish Tourist Board (☞ Visitor Information *in* Smart Travel Tips A to Z) or local TIOs (☞ Visitor Information, *below*). For detailed information about the Northwest's championship courses, including Donegal Golf Club, County Sligo Golf Club, and Enniscrone Golf Club, *see* Chapter 9.

HIKING

Contact **Field Officer, Long Distance Walking Routes Committee** (⊠ Irish Sports Council, 21 Fitzwilliam Sq., Dublin 2, ☎ 01/676–3837) to learn about Northwest walking routes.

HORSEBACK RIDING

Ask the **Association of Irish Riding Establishments** (⊠ Mespil Hall, Kill, Co. Kildare, ☎ 045/877208) for information on recognized establishments that offer full riding vacations including lodging.

SURFING

Ask the **Irish Surfing Association** (⊠ Tigh-na-Mara, Rossnowlagh, Co. Donegal, ☎ 073/25013) for specific information on surfing in the region.

Visitor Information

The TIO in **Sligo Town** (in the extreme south of the region) is the main visitor information center for the whole Northwest. ⊠ *Temple and Charles Sts., Co. Donegal,* ☎ *071/61201,* FAX *071/60360.* ☉ *Sept.–mid-Mar., weekdays 9–1 and 2–5; mid-Mar.–mid June, weekdays 9–6, Sat. 10–2; mid June–Aug., Mon.–Sat. 9–8, Sun. 10–6.*

If you are traveling in County Donegal in the North, try the TIO at **Letterkenny,** about 1½ km (1 mi) out of town. ⊠ *Derry Rd., Co. Donegal,* ☎ *074/21160,* FAX *074/25180.* ☉ *Sept.–May, weekdays 9–1 and 2–5; June, Mon.–Sat. 9–1 and 2–6; July–Aug., Mon.–Sat. 9–8, Sun. 10–2.*

SEASONAL OFFICES

These offices are open only during the summer months (usually the first week in June to the second week in September):

Bundoran (⊠ Main St., Co. Donegal, ☎ 072/41350). **Donegal Town** (⊠ Quay St., Co. Donegal, ☎ 073/21148, FAX 073/22762). **Dungloe** (⊠ Village Center, Co. Donegal, ☎ 075/21297).

8 NORTHERN IRELAND

Belfast, the Antrim Coast, Derry, Lough Erne, and the Mountains of Mourne

With peace—precious peace—abiding, it's a fine time to discover this overlooked corner of Europe. Northern Ireland offers a great bounty of treasures, including Palladian stately houses, the Giant's Causeway, and two rapidly changing cities—Derry and Belfast, both noted for Victorian architecture and other irresistible pleasures. Now that significant progress has been made toward an end to the long-standing, headline-making conflict known as the Troubles, why not discover this heritage-rich array of delights?

Updated by
Aoife
Fitzpatrick

LEGEND HAS IT THAT WELL OVER A MILLENNIUM ago a marauding chieftain caught sight of the shores of Northern Ireland from the deck of his boat and offered this green fertile land to whichever of his two sons could first lay hand on it. As the two rival sons rowed for the shore in their separate boats, one began to draw ahead—whereupon the other drew his sword, cut off his own hand, and threw it onto the beach—and so, by blood and sacrifice, won this new province. To this day the arms of Northern Ireland feature this same severed limb: the celebrated "Red Hand of Ulster."

From this bardic tale to the "Troubles" of today, Northern Ireland has had a long and often ferocious history. But come here and you'll find any thoughts of violence vanishing in the face of the country's outstanding natural beauty; its magnificent, stately houses; and the genuine, open hospitality of its inhabitants. The Six Counties, or Ulster (as Northern Ireland is often called), cover less than 14,245 square km (5,500 square mi) in all, but within their boundaries they contain some of the most unspoiled scenery you could hope to find—the granite Mountains of Mourne; the Giant's Causeway, made of extraordinary volcanic rock; more than 320 km (200 mi) of coastline with long, unspoiled beaches and hidden coves; and rivers and island-strewn lakes that provide fabled fishing grounds, among them the largest freshwater lake in Europe, Lough Neagh. Ancient castles and Palladian-perfect 18th-century treasure houses are as numerous here as almost anywhere else in Europe, and each has its own tale of heroic deeds, dastardly treachery, or lovelorn ghosts. Northern Ireland not only shelters this great heritage in stone, but it also holds an even greater legacy in its celebrated descendants. Nearly one in six of the more than 4½ million Irish who made the fateful journey across the Atlantic to seek their fortune in the New World was from Ulster, and of this group (and from their family stock), more than a few left their mark in America: Davy Crockett, President Andrew Jackson, General Ulysses S. Grant, President Woodrow Wilson, General Stonewall Jackson, financier Thomas Mellon, merchant Paul Getty, and writer Edgar Allen Poe.

Present-day Northern Ireland, a province under the rule of the United Kingdom, includes six of the old Ulster's nine counties and retains its sense of separation, both in the vernacular of the landscape and (some say) in the character of the people. The hardheaded and industrious Scots-Presbyterians, imported to make Ulster a bulwark against Ireland's Catholicism, have had a profound and ineradicable effect on the place. The North appears to boast more factories, neater-looking farms, better roads, and—in its cities—more of the two-story redbrick houses typical of Great Britain than does the Republic. For all that, the border between North and South is of little consequence to visitors.

Ireland's ancient history truly began in the North when settlers came to the banks of the River Bann 9,000 years ago. Five thousand years later Bronze Age settlers built the great stone circles idiomatic in the North to Counties Down and Tyrone, and later the Iron Age brought the Celts. St. Patrick, son of a Roman official and once a slave in County Antrim, returned to spread Christianity in the 5th century. But from the first Norman incursions in the 12th century onward, the English made greater and greater inroads into Ireland, endeavoring to subdue what they believed was a potential enemy. Ulster proved the hardest part to conquer, but in 1607 Ulster's beaten Irish nobility fled their homeland forever, many of them going to France and Spain, in the great exodus known as the Flight of the Earls. Their abandoned lands were distributed by the English to "the Planters"—staunch Protestants from England and Scotland.

After three centuries of smoldering tensions and religious strife, 1916 saw the Easter Uprising and then, in the parliamentary elections of 1918, an overwhelming Nationalist vote across Ireland for Sinn Féin ("We Ourselves"), the party that believed in independence for all of Ireland. In the five northeastern counties of Ulster, however, only seven seats went to the Nationalists, and 22 to the Unionists, who wanted to remain an integral part of the United Kingdom. At 2:10 AM on December 6, 1921, in the British prime minister's residence at 10 Downing Street, Michael Collins signed the Anglo-Irish Treaty, designating a six-county North to remain in British hands, in exchange for complete independence for Ireland's 26 counties as the Irish Free State.

Fast-forward to 1968, when, in the spirit of the student protesters in Paris and Washington, and after 40 years of living with an apparently permanent and sectarian Unionist majority, students in Belfast's Queen's University launched a civil rights movement, claiming equal rights in jobs, housing, and opportunity. The brutality with which these marches were suppressed in front of the world's press led to worldwide revulsion, riots, and counter-riots. The Irish Republican Army (IRA), which had lain dormant for decades, hijacked what was left of the shattered civil rights movement, which once had a smattering of Protestant students among its ranks. Armed British troops who had at first been welcomed by many in the Catholic ghettos as protectors from Protestant paramilitaries now found themselves welcomed by neither side. Britain imposed Direct Rule. No one was happy, and the decades of guerrilla conflict that ensued between the IRA, the UDA/UVF (Protestant/Loyalist paramilitaries), and the British government continued in a mix of lulls and terrors—apart from the IRA's annual Christmas "truce"— until the summer of 1994, when the "Provos," as they are colloquially known, called an ongoing cease-fire, confirmed in July 1997.

Belfast reveled in its new peace. New hotels, shopping malls, and restaurants came off dusty drawing boards. People who had not seen the city's center for a quarter of a century gazed at its bright lights. Today, the IRA and Loyalist cease-fires are still in place, but major divisions remain. The various shades of Unionism are closely identified with the "planted" Protestant population, while Nationalists and Republicans are inextricably associated with the "native" Irish community, which traces its genetic inheritance back to the Iron Age Celtic invaders and which is almost entirely Catholic. Today, in blue-collar Protestant areas you'll see curbstones and lampposts painted in the British colors of red, white, and blue; entwined British and Red Hand Ulster flags fluttering from tall poles raised in pocket-handkerchief front yards; and countless signs and crests declaring proud devotion to Ulster and the Queen. By contrast, in Irish Republican and Nationalist Catholic districts, you'll note the green, white, and gold of the Irish Republic's Tricolor flickering in the breeze.

Don't worry if this all seems impossibly complex. Even locals say wryly, "If you understand Northern Ireland politics, you're missing the point." In any case, the province's turbulent history cannot mask the fact that it is a region incredibly rich in natural beauty and artistic treasures, such as the great Georgian estates and Belfast's Victorian architecture. For overseas travelers, Northern Ireland remains one of the increasingly rare forgotten spots of Europe.

Pleasures and Pastimes

Dining

While it has nowhere near the number of innovative restaurants as Dublin (which is five times more populous), Belfast has witnessed an influx of international influences with new restaurants, bistros, wine bars, and—as in Dublin—European-style café-bars where you can get good food *and* linger over a drink.

By and large, though, hearty, unpretentious cooking predominates, with good-quality, fresh local fish and meat simply prepared. You're virtually guaranteed to find certain traditional dishes on menus here, such as Guinness and beef pie; champ (creamy, buttery mashed potatoes with scallions); oysters from Strangford Lough; Ardglass herring; mussels from Dundrum; and smoked salmon from Glenarm. A widespread favorite is the Ulster fry, an inexpensive pub plate of bacon, black pudding, mushrooms, sausages, tomatoes, and eggs, served with potato or soda bread—one of the reasons Northern Ireland has one of the highest rates of heart disease in the world. The delights of ethnic restaurants, including Chinese, Japanese, Indian, Persian, and Thai, are now found in Belfast, and even beyond.

Casual dress is quite acceptable at most establishments, though jeans are usually discouraged. As for the cost of a meal here, by the standards of the Republic or the United States, or even the rest of the United Kingdom, restaurant prices are surprisingly moderate. A service charge of 10% may be indicated on the bill; it is customary to pay this, unless the service was bad. For price ranges, *see* Dining *in* Smart Travel Tips A to Z.

Festivals

Festivals, marches, and other excuses to gather fill the calendar in Ulster—certainly as much as in the South, and possibly more so than. Every village in Nationalist areas has its own annual celebration; such *fleadhs* (festivals, pronounced flahs) are especially common in June and July. If you're interested in the Troubles, you may want to see the often-controversial Orangemen's (Unionist) March on July 12 and the Ancient Order of Hibernians (Nationalist) marches of August 15, but be aware that in recent years some Orange marches have led to ugly confrontations as they've traversed Nationalist/Republican areas. The Belfast Folk Festival in September is a weekend of traditional Irish music and dance at downtown locations. The Belfast Festival at Queen's University, which lasts three weeks each November, is the North's cultural high point of the year. Its heady mix of drama, music, dance, and film is centered on the Queen's University campus—the most pleasant area of town. *See* The Arts, *below,* for more detailed information about these and other festivals.

Lodging

Since the advent of the 1994 cease-fire, major hotel chains both in the Republic and abroad have been investing in the North. In Belfast's environs visitors can choose from the humblest terraced town houses or farm cottages to the grandest country houses. Dining rooms of country-house lodgings frequently reach the standard of top-quality restaurants. All accommodations in the province are inspected and categorized by the Northern Ireland Tourist Board, which publishes all names, addresses, and ratings in the handbook *Where to Stay* (U.K.£4.99). The tourist board can also give you information about the hundreds of excellent-value special offers available in the low season from October to March—single nights to weekend deals, the most intimate B&Bs to

Belfast's finest hotels. For price ranges, *see* Lodging *in* Smart Travel Tips A to Z.

Outdoor Activities and Sports

BICYCLING

Roads are good and fairly traffic-free, so cycling is popular. Once in the countryside you will often have the run of long, winding roads, but be prepared for the changeable weather. There's no need to have a bike of your own—many towns offer places to rent them.

BIRD-WATCHING

The province has an unexpectedly wide range of habitats and bird species for such a tiny area. The best time to come is winter, but even in summer visitors can participate in first-class bird-watching, especially on the Antrim uplands, all down the Antrim coast, and on the nearby islands.

FISHING

With a 606-km (466-mi) coastline, part on the Atlantic and part on the Irish Sea, as well as major lakes and an abundance of unpolluted rivers, the North is a great place for anglers. Set your rod for salmon on the Bann, Bush, and Foyle rivers and for brown trout in their tributaries. There are bigger lake trout in Loughs Neagh, Melvin, and Erne, while pike and other coarse (white) fish abound in the Erne. Turbot and plaice are taken off the north coast, where sea bass may be caught from the shore. For further information, *see* Fishing *in* Contacts and Resources *in* Northern Ireland A to Z, *below*.

HIKING AND WALKING

Northern Ireland is magnificent walking country. Ask at tourist offices for details of their local walking and cycling trails, 14 of which spring off the Ulster Way, an 896-km (560-mi) trek for serious hikers that runs around the six counties and links up with marked trails on the other side of the border. The terrain never demands more than a pair of sturdy walking shoes. Many cities and towns have their own historic and scenic trails, including a multitude of serene walks within striking distance of Belfast; for further information, *see* Hiking and Walking *in* Contacts and Resources *in* Northern Ireland A to Z, *below*.

OUTDOOR ACTIVITIES AND SPORTS

Sitting on the back of a horse or pony is a great way to travel into places that are out of bounds to motorists. Woodland, beaches, and rough country become accessible on guided rides, some suitable for complete beginners. There are some 35 riding and trekking centers around the province, and several of them offer accommodations.

SPECTATOR SPORTS

As on the rest of the island, people in Ulster take their sport seriously, particularly Saturday's soccer and rugby and Sunday's hurling and Gaelic football events. Dates of local matches are listed in local newspapers. Greyhound racing has roots deep in the Celtic psyche. During the summer, you'll come across the very English sport of cricket being played throughout the province. There are two horse racing tracks—the one at Downpatrick is particularly atmospheric. One oddity is the ancient precursor of bowls, called bullets, which is still played in County Armagh. It involves throwing bowls (originally they were cannonballs, hence the name) along a narrow, winding country lane; the first to cover 3 km (2 mi) is the winner. The All-Ireland Championship for this sport is held in early August in Armagh. Tourist offices carry details of local and province-wide events.

Shopping

The best of the North's traditional products, many made according to time-honored methods, include the exquisite linen and superior handmade woolen garments that you might associate only with the Republic of Ireland. Handmade lacework also remains a handicraft from the countrywomen of some Northern Ireland districts. Visitors should keep an eye out for hand-cut crystal from County Tyrone and for the mellow, cream-color Parian china of Belleek. Traditional music CDs and the unadorned blackthorn walking stick are two good choices at the other end of the price scale.

Exploring Northern Ireland

With as fine a setting as you'll find anywhere in Britain, the city of Belfast is Northern Ireland's main gateway. A naturally lively, friendly city, Belfast has plenty of distinguished hotels and restaurants, fascinating museums, Victorian architecture, and strong maritime connections. It is testimony to the spirit of Belfast that the long years of sectarian violence have not dimmed its vivacity. Northern Ireland's second city, Derry, is also looking to the future and has an appealing personality all its own—beautiful rows of Georgian houses are being restored, and new museums, tourist attractions, and crafts shops are opening apace in the small city center, which is still enclosed by its medieval walls and one of Europe's best-preserved examples of a fortified town.

Along the shores of the North's coasts and lakes, green, gentle slopes descend majestically into hazy, dark-blue water against a background of more slopes, more water, and huge, cloud-scattered skies. The Antrim Coast is among the most scenic in all of Ireland, while Dunluce Castle, the Giant's Causeway, and the small towns along the east coast give the traveler a choice of sites along the excellent roads. Enniskillen, in County Fermanagh, is bright and bustling, and the surrounding Lough Erne has magnificent lake views, as well as one of Ireland's most impressive round towers, on Devenish Island. On the other side of Enniskillen stand Castle Coole and Florence Court, two graceful mansions of the 18th-century Anglo-Irish nobility.

Numbers in the text correspond to numbers in the margin and on the Northern Ireland and Belfast maps.

Great Itineraries

IF YOU HAVE 2 DAYS

The first day leave the bustling Victorian industrial metropolis of **Belfast** ①–⑰, the starting and ending point of your itinerary, and head north to the remarkable natural formations of the **Giant's Causeway** ㉕ and the teetering cliff-top remains of **Dunluce Castle** ㉗ via the breathtaking **Glens of Antrim** ㉒, ending the day in the dramatically rejuvenated city of ⛏ **Derry** ㉛–㊵. The next day head south to the tranquil beauty of **Lough Erne** with visits to the ancient monastic site of **Devenish Island** ㊺, the historic town of **Enniskillen** ㊻, and the exquisite neoclassic beauty of **Castle Coole** ㊼. Finish your second day back in ⛏ **Belfast.**

IF YOU HAVE 4 DAYS

Leave **Belfast** ①–⑰ and head north to the **Glens of Antrim** ㉒ with a look at the characteristic twin towns of rugged **Cushendall** and pretty Cushendun before heading for the **Giant's Causeway** ㉕ and **Dunluce Castle** ㉗. Then follow the coast road via Downhill as far as ⛏ **Derry** ㉛–㊵, where you'll spend the night. The following day head south for **Belleek** ㊸, home of the famous pottery, via the emotive **Ulster-American Folk Park** ㊶ and the reconstructed dwellings of the **Ulster History**

Malin Head

Tory Island

Fanad Head

Horn Head

Malin

Culdaff

Carndonagh

Inishowen Head

Du C

Moville

Creeslough

Rathmullan

Milford

Carrowkeel

Lough Foyle

Blackhill

Aghadowey

Ramelton

Muff

Derry
31 — 40

Campsie

A2

30

Limavady

B66

Letterkenny

B190

Dungiven

A6

Claudy

SPERRIN MOUNTAINS

DERRY

Tobermore

Lifford

B48

Glenties

Stranorlar

Castlefin

Strabane

Sion Mills

Ballybofey

BLUE STACK MOUNTAINS

A5

Newtownstewart

A505

Cookstown

Ulster-American Folk Park

41

42

Ulster-History Park

Pomeroy

Donegal Town

Omagh

B46

TYRONE

A29

Dungannon

A47

B4

Kesh

A32

Dromore

A32

Fintona

A4

Ballygawley

Lower Lough Erne

44

Castle Archdale Country Park

B122

Clogher

Augher

A28

Aughnacloy

43

White Island

A46

B82

Fivemiletown

Belleek

Lough Melvin

FERMANAGH

Devenish Island

Ballinamallard

B80

45

46

47

Castle Coole

A4

Enniskillen

Lisbellaw

Florence Court

A32

Lisnaskea

Rosslea

Upper Lough Erne

Newtown Butler

R. Finn

Kintyre
(Scotland)

Rathlin
Island

**Giant's
Causeway**

Carrick
-a-Rede

To Campbeltown, Scotland

25

**Dunluce
Castle**

A2

B15

Fair Head

27 **26**

Portstewart

B17

Bushmills

24

Ballycastle

Cushendun

A44

Armoy

28 **Coleraine**

A29

Cushendall

Red Bay

A54

Ballymoney

A26

Glenariff

A2

**Glens of
Antrim** **22**

North Channel

shill

owey

Garvagh

R. Bann

A29

Kilrea

ANTRIM MOUNTAINS

Carnlough **23**

Carnlough Bay

Carnlough

To Cairnryan, Scotland

29 **Upperlands**

Maghera

A43

A42

ANTRIM

**Bellaghy
Bawn**

ore

Bellaghy

A6

Ballymena

A36

Ballygally

Larne

To Stranraer

Toome

A26

Randalstown

A8

Ballyclare

Whitehead

To Heysham

Magherafelt

Antrim

To Isle of Man

Newtownabbey

A2

Eden

To Liverpool

Stewartstown

A26

Carrickfergus **21**

Belfast Lough

Bangor

*Lough
Neagh*

Crumlin

A52

**Belfast
Castle** **18**

**Ulster Folk and
Transport Museum** **20**

Ardboe

Belfast

1 — 17

Holywood

Newtownards

Mount Stewart **52**

Comber

A20

Greyabbey

*Ards
Peninsula*

Lisburn

**Irish Linen Centre
and Lisburn Museum** **19**

*Strangford
Lough*

A21

A1

Hillsborough

A24

Saintfield

Cragavon

Lurgan

Killyleagh

A20

Portadown

A3

Ballynahinch

Strangford

Portaferry **51**

A29

A1

Armagh **48**

Car Ferry

A3

Banbridge

DOWN

A25

Downpatrick **50**

Markethill

R. Bann

Castlewellan

Ardglass

ARMAGH

A28

A25

Dundrum

Keady

B133

Dundrum Bay

Bessbrook

Newry

A2

Newcastle

Camlough

*Slieve Donard
Mountain*

49

**The Mountains
of Mourne**

Warrenpoint

A2

Carlingford Lough

Kilkeel

N

0 _____ 10 miles

0 _____ 15 km

Park ㊷; don't miss the holy islands of **White** ㊹ and **Devenish** ㊺. Spend the night in or around the historic town of ⊟ **Enniskillen** ㊻. The next day follow the road to leafy **Armagh** ㊽, Ireland's ecclesiastical capital, and **Navan Centre**, on the site of the legendary fort of the Red Branch Knights. Travel southeast to the magnificent **Mountains of Mourne** ㊾ via Bessbrook, a pretty Quaker model village that also happens to be home to the busiest military helicopter base in Europe. Pass through Newry and Kilkeel, finishing the day in ⊟ **Portaferry** ㊿. The last day make your way to Belfast along the shores of Strangford Lough to the fairy-tale gardens of **Mount Stewart** ㊽ and the brilliantly designed **Ulster Folk and Transport Museum** ⑳. Return to Belfast.

When to Tour Northern Ireland

The best time to visit the area is from May to September, when the weather is a little friendlier to travelers, especially in coastal and lake areas. Apart from holiday weekends there should be no trouble getting accommodation anywhere outside Belfast. If heading for Belfast, book in advance. Most of the city's cultural events—except early August's lively West Belfast Festival—take place in the autumn.

BELFAST

❶ *167 km (104) mi north of Dublin.*

Belfast was a great Victorian success story, an industrial boomtown whose prosperity was built on trade—especially linen and shipbuilding (the *Titanic* was built here, giving Belfast the nickname "Titanic Town"). The key word here, of course, is *was*—linen is no longer a major industry, and shipbuilding has severely suffered. For two decades, news about Belfast was news about the Troubles—until the 1994 cease-fire. Since then, the North's capital city has benefited from major hotel investment, gentrified quaysides, a heralded performing arts center, and heartfelt efforts on the part of the tourist board to claim for the North its share of the visitors pouring into the Euro-buzzing Emerald Isle. Although the 1996 bombing of offices at the Canary Wharf in London disrupted the 1994 peace agreement, cease-fire was officially reestablished on July 20, 1997, and this embattled city began its quest for a newfound identity. This is a fascinating place in the throes of a major historical transition, a city with some of the warmest, wryest people in all of Ireland; a fair amount of new construction; and, most of all, a palpable will to move forward.

Before English and Scottish settlers arrived in the 1600s, Belfast was a tiny village called Béal Feirste (Sandbank Ford) belonging to Ulster's ancient O'Neill clan. With the advent of the Plantation period, Sir Arthur Chichester, from Devon in southwest England, received the city, and his son was made Earl of Donegall. Protestant French Huguenots fleeing persecution settled near here, bringing their valuable linen work skills. In the 18th century, Belfast saw a phenomenal expansion—its population doubled in size every 10 years, despite an ever-present sectarian divide. Although the Anglican gentry despised the Presbyterian artisans—who, in turn, distrusted native Catholics—Belfast's growth continued at a dizzying speed. Having laid the foundation stone of the city's university in 1845, Queen Victoria returned to Belfast in 1849 (she is recalled in the names of buildings, streets, bars, monuments, and other places around the city), and in the same year, the university opened and took the name Queen's College. Nearly 40 years later, in 1888, Victoria granted Belfast its city charter. Today its population is 300,000—one-quarter of all Northern Ireland's citizens.

Belfast is a fairly compact city, its center made up of roughly three contiguous areas that are easy to navigate on foot; from the south end to the north it's about an hour's leisurely walk.

Golden Mile

This arrowhead-shape area extending from Howard Street in the north to Shaftesbury Square at the southern tip, bordered on the west by Great Victoria Street and on the east by Bedford Street and Dublin Road, is a great area to begin an exploration of Belfast. Although it doesn't quite glow the way the name suggests, bustling Golden Mile and its immediate environs harbor some of Belfast's most noteworthy historic buildings. In addition, the area is filled with hotels, major civic and office buildings, as well as some restaurants, cafés, and stores. Even if you don't end up staying here, you're likely to pass through it often.

A Good Walk

Begin your stroll at the centrally located **Europa Hotel** ② and the **Grand Opera House** ③ next door. Even if you're just starting out, at least poke your head in the glorious **Crown Liquor Saloon** ④, a restored Victorian gin palace across the street from the Europa. From the Crown, turn right along Great Victoria Street and then right again onto Howard Street to reach Belfast's Donegall Square, dominated by its columned and domed **City Hall** ⑤. Walk away from Donegall Square and up May Street, taking an almost immediate right onto Alfred Street. When you come to the junction with Clarence Street, the Tudor-Gothic **St. Malachy's Church** ⑥ will be on your left-hand side. Stop in to gaze awhile at the beautiful fan-vaulted ceiling. From here, walk to the end of Clarence Street, and turn right onto Bedford Street into the Golden Mile proper, where you will come upon **Ulster Hall** ⑦.

TIMING
You'll need about 1½ hours to enjoy the offerings on this route—you can extend this time depending on how long you would like to spend soaking up the atmosphere of places like the Crown Liquor Saloon on your way.

Sights to See

✎ following the text of a review is your signal that the property has a Web site, where you will find details and, usually, images; for a link, visit www.fodors.com/urls.

★ ⑤ **City Hall.** Built between 1898 and 1906, the massive, exuberant Renaissance Revival City Hall dominates Donegall Square. Modeled on St. Paul's Cathedral in London, it was designed by Brumwell Thomas, who was knighted but had to sue to get his fee. Before you enter, take a stroll around Donegall Square, where you'll find statues of Queen Victoria; a monument commemorating the *Titanic* (built in Belfast); and a column honoring the U.S. Expeditionary Force, which landed in the city on January 26, 1942—the first contingent of the U.S. Army to land in Europe. When U.S. president Bill Clinton visited in November 1995, a huge reception was held on the green front lawn; it included a performance by hometown boy Van Morrison, whose "Days Like This" had become an unofficial anthem of the 1994 cease-fire. Head inside under the porte cochere at the front of the building. From the entrance hall (the base of which is a **whispering gallery**), the view up to the heights of the 173-ft **Great Dome** is a feast for the eyes. With its complicated series of arches and openings, stained-glass windows, Italian marble inlays, decorative plasterwork, and paintings, this is Belfast's most ornate public space—homage to the might of the British empire. The guided tour gives access to the Council Chamber, Great

Hall, and Reception Room, all upstairs. ✉ *Donegall Sq.,* ☎ *028/
9032–0202.* 🎫 *Free.* ⊙ *Mon.–Sat. 9–5; guided tours June–Sept., weekdays 10:30, 11:30, and 2:30, Sat. 2:30; Oct.–May, Mon.–Sat. 2:30.*

★ ❹ **Crown Liquor Saloon.** Opposite the Europa Hotel on Great Victoria
Street and now owned by the National Trust (the U.K.'s official conservation organization), the Crown is one of Belfast's glories: built in
1894, the bar has richly carved woodwork around cozy snugs (cubicles), leather seats, colored tile work, and abundant mirrors. It's been
kept immaculate, is still lit by gas, and is the perfect setting for a pint
of Guinness and a plate of oysters. When you settle in your snug, note
the little gunmetal plates used by the Victorians for lighting their
matches. ✉ *46 Great Victoria St.,* ☎ *028/9027–9901.* ⊙ *Daily 11:30
AM–midnight.*

❷ **Europa Hotel.** A landmark in Belfast, the Europa is a monument to the
resilience of the city in the face of the Troubles. The most bombed hotel
in western Europe, it has been targeted 11 times by the IRA since the
early 1970s and refurbished every time. Today, owned by affable Ulster
millionaire hotel magnate Billy Hastings, it shows no signs of its explo-
sive history. ✉ *Great Victoria St. at Glengall St.,* ☎ *028/9032–7000.*

★ ❸ **Grand Opera House.** Designed in 1894 by the famous theater architect Frank Matcham, this reveals the Victorian age's fascination with
the East. Beautifully restored in the 1970s, the Grand Opera House
(☞ Nightlife and the Arts, *below*) is worth a visit, even if you don't
go to a show, for a chance to admire the opulence of the gilt moldings,
ornamental plasterwork, and exquisite ceiling fresco by contemporary
Irish artist Cherith McKinstry. It was the site of Van Morrison's 1984
album *Live at the Grand Opera House, Belfast.* By far the best way
to see and enjoy the place is to attend a show; musicals, operas, and
conventional theater all share billing. ✉ *Great Victoria St.,* ☎ *028/
9024–1919.* 🎭

❻ **St. Malachy's Church.** Just inside the doors to St. Malachy's Cathedral
is a memorial to its chief benefactor, Captain Thomas Griffiths. The
church, designed by Thomas Jackson, was built in 1844. Its interior
is well worth a viewing, paying particular attention to its fan-vaulted
ceiling. While many of the original fixtures and fitting have succumbed
to the ravages of time, this swirling masterpiece of plasterwork survives in wonderful decorative order. Inspiration for the design was taken
from the chapel of Henry VII at Westminster Abbey in London. Note
the church organ, which has survived for 150 years. ✉ *Alfred St.,* ☎
028/9032–1713. 🎫 *Free.* ⊙ *No set hrs.*

❼ **Ulster Hall.** Home to the Ulster Orchestra, and host to occasional rock
concerts (one of the most famous being Led Zepplin's world stage debut
of the song "Stairway to Heaven" in March 1971), Ulster Hall was
originally built as a ballroom in 1862. The hall was the venue for the
political rallying of Nationalist politicians such as Charles Stewart Parnell (1846–91) and Patrick Henry Pearse (1879–1916), before the
Irish Republic was formed in 1921. It also houses a splendid Mulhol-
land Organ, a Victorian instrument of considerable size. ✉ *Bedford
St.,* ☎ *028/9032–3900.* ⊙ *No set hrs.*

Central District

Immediately north of the Golden Mile, extending from Donegall Square
north almost to St. Anne's Cathedral, is Belfast's Central District. Although not geographically the center of the city, this area is the old heart
of Belfast and has the highest concentration of retail outlets that Belfast
has to offer. It's a frenetic place—the equivalent of Dublin's Grafton

and Henry streets in one—where both locals *and* visitors shop. Cafés, pubs, offices, and stores of all kinds, from department stores to the Gap and Waterstone's (there's even a Disney store), occupy the red-brick and white-Portland-stone buildings and modern architecture that line its narrow streets. A leisurely stroll around the many pedestrianized streets will allow you to take in a mix of commercial offerings and historical sites.

A Good Walk

Begin at the **Linenhall Library,** ⑧ the gray building on Donegall Square's northwest corner. Walk north up Donegall Place, Belfast's main shopping street, which turns into Royal Avenue, taking a right at North Street; here you'll find the main **Northern Ireland Tourist Board Information Centre** ⑨. Backtrack to Church Street, at the end of which is **St. Anne's Cathedral** ⑩. Take Dongeall Street to North Street and go east down **High Street** to busy Victoria Street and the leaning **Albert Memorial Clock Tower** ⑪. From here, walk up Queen's Square to the river and Donegall Quay. You'll be able to see parts of Belfast's historic shipyards and two of the world's largest cranes in the Harland and Wolff shipyard, which built the *Titanic*. Vere left at the river to the **Lagan Lookout Visitor Centre** ⑫. Perched on the river, the center is opposite the back of the **Custom House** ⑬. Walking south down Oxford Street will bring you to the new Waterfront Hall (☞ Nightlife and the Arts, *below*) on the river at the end of the street. From here, you can return to the city center via busy Chichester Street. Or, if you're so inclined, wander north behind St. Anne's to the Cathedral Quarter, a maze of cobbled streets that the city fathers plan to transform over the next few years into a combination of Temple Bar in Dublin and the Left Bank in Paris.

TIMING

It is easy to get waylaid shopping and investigating new developments along the river when taking this walk, so allow yourself at least two hours to cover the area comfortably.

Sights to See

⑪ **Albert Memorial Clock Tower.** Tilting a little to one side, not unlike Pisa's more notorious leaning landmark, the clock tower was named for Queen Victoria's husband, Prince Albert. The dilapidated square on which it stands underwent a face-lift for 2001. The tower itself is not open to the public. ⊠ *Victoria Sq.*

⑬ **Custom House.** The 19th-century architect Charles Lanyon was responsible for the design of the Custom House. This building and many others in Belfast, including the unusual **Sinclair Seaman's Church** (☞ Churches Around the City, *below*), bear the hallmarks of his skill. While it is not open to the public, it is worth circling the house to view the lofty pediment of Brittania, Mercury, and Neptune on the front, carved by acclaimed stonemason Thomas Fitzpatrick. ⊠ *Donegall Quay.*

★ **High Street.** Off High Street, especially down to Ann Street (parallel to the south), run narrow lanes and alleyways called entries. Though mostly cleaned up and turned into chic shopping lanes, they still hang on to something of their former raffish character, including distinctive pubs with little-altered Victorian interiors. Among the most notable are the following: the **Morning Star** (⊠ Pottinger's Entry off High St.), with its large windows and fine curving bar; **White's Tavern** (⊠ wine-cellar entry off High St.), Belfast's oldest pub, founded in 1630, which, although considerably updated, still has a warm and comfortable ambience, with plush seats and a big, open fire; **Magennis's Whiskey Café** (⊠ 84 May St.), in splendid counterpoint to the Waterfront Hall's space-age ambience; and **McHugh's** (⊠ Queen's Sq.), in what is reckoned to be the city's oldest extant building, dating from 1710.

☞ ⑫ **Lagan Lookout Visitor Centre.** Situated right at the edge of Lagan Weir, this center delves into the history of the River Lagan and the weir by means of interactive exhibits. It is a good venue for children to learn about the river's history and surroundings. At night, the exterior of the building is flooded with blue light, adding to the feel that the riverside developments in Belfast have been inspired by the Southbank in London. The shipyard cranes visible beyond—Samson and Goliath—are two of the world's largest. ⊠ *Lagan Weir, Donegall Quay,* ☎ 028/9031–5444. ☜ *U.K.£2.* ☉ *Apr.–Sept., weekdays 11–5, Sat. noon–5, Sun. 2–5; Oct.–Mar., Tues.–Fri. 11–3:30, Sat. 1–4:30, Sun. 2–4:30.*

❽ **Linenhall Library.** This gray building on Donegall Square's northwest corner is in fact a comfortable private library, founded in 1788 and designed by Charles Lanyon. The library, significantly expanded in 1998, has an unparalleled collection of 80,000 documents relating to the Troubles; it is also a perfect hideaway for relaxing with a newspaper, or soaking up the old-world atmosphere in the library's café. An early librarian, Thomas Russell, was hanged in 1803 for supporting an Irish uprising. On the walls are paintings and prints that show Belfast views and landmarks. Much of this artwork is for sale and makes excellent and original souvenirs or gifts. ⊠ *17 Donegall Sq. N,* ☎ 028/9032–1707. ☜ *Free.* ☉ *Weekdays 9:30–5:30, Sat. 9:30–4.*

❾ **Northern Ireland Tourist Board Information Centre.** This is the main point for picking up maps and details for travel in Northern Ireland. The office incorporates the plush, comprehensive Belfast Welcome Centre. ⊠ *St. Anne's Court, 59 North St.,* ☎ 028/9024–6609, ℻ 028/9031–2424. ☉ *Sept.–June, Mon. 9:30–5:15, Tues.–Sat. 9–5:15; July–Aug., Mon. 9:30–7, Tues.–Sat. 9–7, Sun. noon–4.*

❿ **St. Anne's Cathedral.** A somber heaviness and deep, rounded arches are the hallmarks of the Irish neo-Romanesque style, and both elements dominate this large edifice, which is basilican in plan and was built at the turn of the 20th century. Lord Carson (1854–1935), who was largely responsible for keeping the six counties inside the United Kingdom, is buried here beneath a suitably austere gray slab. New landscaping around the cathedral provides a place to rest your legs in good weather. ⊠ *Donegall St.,* ☎ 028/9032–8332. ☜ *Free.* ☉ *Weekdays 9:15–4:45, Sat. 9:15–4.*

NEED A
BREAK?
At the start of Royal Avenue, turn left into Bank Street to find **Kelly's Cellars** (⊠ 30–32 Bank St., ☎ 028/9032–4835), a traditional bar with character. Specialties include Ulster fry as well as champ and sausages. Two centuries ago, Kelly's Cellars was the regular meeting place of a militant Nationalist group, the Society of United Irishmen, whose leader, Wolfe Tone (who was a Protestant), is remembered as the founder of Irish Republicanism.

University Area

At Belfast's southern end, this part of the city around Queen's University is by far the most appealing place for a casual stroll. Dotted with parks, botanic gardens, and leafy streets of fine, intact 19th-century, two- and three-story buildings, the area evokes an older, more leisurely pace of life. The many pubs and excellent restaurants make this the center of the city's nightlife.

Belfast

A Good Walk

From the southern tip of Shaftesbury Square, head farther south down **Botanic Avenue** and watch the cityscape of the Golden Mile quickly transform into the more peaceful and residential university area. Take note of the **Lower Crescent**, with its range of bars and restaurants, on your right. Continue, crossing University Street, and you will soon find the **Union Theological College** ⑭ on your left. To your right, you will see the side of **Queen's University** ⑮; walk around the campus via University Square and University Road to the **Stranmillis** area of the city and Stranmillis Road. In to the left are the **Botanic Gardens** ⑯; enclosed in the Gardens is the **Ulster Museum** ⑰.

TIMING

Allow a leisurely morning or afternoon to visit the sights, taking your time at the Botanic Gardens and Ulster Museum.

Sights to See

★ ⑯ **Botanic Gardens.** Laid out in 1827 on land that slopes down to the River Lagan, tucked between **Queen's University** (☞ *below*) and the **Ulster Museum** (☞ *below*), these gardens are a glorious haven of grass, trees, flowers, curving walks, and wrought-iron benches where it was not unusual, in their Victorian heyday, to find 10,000 of Belfast's citizens strolling on a Saturday afternoon. Begun in 1839 and completed in 1852, the **Palm House,** constructed of curved iron and glass, is the oldest curvilinear greenhouse in the world—a technical marvel designed by Charles Lanyon in 1839. The **Tropical Ravine House,** though not architecturally distinguished, has an outstanding collection of tropical flora. If you stay in the university area, this is easily the nicest place in Belfast for an early morning stroll or jog—and if it's cold and rainy you can always take shelter in the steamy jungles of the Tropical Ravine. ⊠ *Stranmillis Rd.,* ☎ *028/9032–4902.* ☞ *Free except during concerts.* ☉ *Gardens daily dawn–dusk. Palm House and Tropical Ravine House, Apr.–Sept., weekdays 10–5, weekends 1–5; Oct.–Mar., weekdays 10–4, weekends 2–4.*

⑮ **Queen's University.** Dominating University Road is Queen's University itself. The main university buildings, modeled on Oxford's Magdalen College and designed by the ubiquitous Charles Lanyon, were constructed in 1849 in a Tudor Revival style. The long, handsome red-brick-and-sandstone facade of the main building has large leaded windows, with three square towers and crenellations galore. **University Square,** really a terrace, is another treasure from the same era. There is a Seamus Heaney library, named after the Ulster-born 1997 Nobel Prize–winning poet. ⊠ *University Rd.,* ☎ *028/9033–5252.* ☉ *May–Sept., Mon.–Sat. 10–4; Oct.–Apr., weekdays 10–4.*

Stranmillis. Once its own village, now the off-campus quarter, Stranmillis is one of Belfast's more appealing neighborhoods, filled with tree-lined residential streets on which you'll see scurrying academics and find a wide choice of ethnic eateries. Reached via Stranmillis Road (near the **Ulster Museum** [☞ *below*]), the neighborhood is home to "Little Paris," a stretch of shops and cafés. The community reaches down to the riverside towpath along the Lagan. **Malone Road** joins the river farther south, close to the out-of-town **Giant's Ring** (off Ballyleeson Road), a large, Neolithic earthwork focused on an impressive dolmen. To get this far, unless you're a vigorous walker (it's possible to come all the way on the Lagan towpath), you'll be happier driving in a car or taking a bus: Ulsterbus 13 passes close to the site, and on the return journey it will take you back to Donegall Square.

★ ⑰ **Ulster Museum.** In the southwest corner of the **Botanic Gardens** (☞ *above*), the museum has three floors devoted to the history and prehistory of Ireland and, in particular, Northern Ireland, together with a considerable collection of 19th- and 20th-century fine art. A skeleton of the now-extinct Irish giant deer is a highlight of the natural history section. Other major holdings are the trove of jewelry and gold ornaments—as well as a cannon and other armaments—recovered from the Spanish Armada vessel *Girona* and two sister galleons sunk off the Antrim coast in 1588. Perhaps the most imaginative, user-friendly sections are on the first floor; one colorfully traces the rise of Belfast's crafts, trade, and industry; the other tells the story of the Nationalist movement and explains the separation of the North from the rest of the country. A small café is on level three, and a free guidebook is available at the reception desk. ⊠ *Stranmillis Rd.,* ☎ *028/9038–3000.* ☜ *Free.* ⊙ *Weekdays 10–5, Sat. 1–5, Sun. 2–5.*

⑭ **Union Theological College.** Like Queen's University (☞ *above*) on the opposite side of the street, the Union Theological College, with its colonnaded, Doric facade, owes the charm of its appearance to architect Charles Lanyon. The building's other claim to fame is that, before the completion of the parliament buildings at Stormont, Northern Ireland's House of Commons was convened in the library, and the college's chapel played host to the Senate. ⊠ *108 Botanic Ave.,* ☎ *028/9020–5080.* ☜ *Free.* ⊙ *No set hrs; tours by appointment.*

OFF THE BEATEN PATH

CHURCHES AROUND THE CITY – Belfast has so many churches you could visit a different one nearly every day of the year and still not make it to all of them. The oldest house of worship is the Church of Ireland **Knockbreda Parish Church** (⊠ Church Rd. off A24 on the south side of city). This dark, sturdy, and atmospheric structure was built in 1737 by Richard Cassels, who designed many of Ireland's finest mansions. It quickly became *the* place to be buried—witness the vast 18th-century tombs in the churchyard. Closer to the city center, the **First Presbyterian Church** (⊠ Rosemary St.) dates from 1783 and has an interesting elliptical interior. It also hosts lunchtime concerts. The Church of Ireland's **St. George's** (⊠ High St.), built in 1816, has a tremendous Georgian portico and pretty box pews. By the riverfront is one of the most appealing churches, Presbyterian **Sinclair Seamen's Church** (⊠ Corporation Sq. off Donegall Quay). It was designed by—guess who—Charles Lanyon, the architect of Queen's University (☞ *above*), and has served the seafaring community since 1857. A maritime theme pervades the building: the pulpit is shaped like a ship's prow; the bell is from HMS *Hood,* sunk in 1916; and even the collection plates are shaped like lifeboats.

Dining

Cooking in Belfast is experiencing the same development and rejuvenation as the city itself. The choice of restaurants is more limited than in Dublin, but two or three of the best kitchens are a match for anything else in Ireland. The best chefs—Michael Deane, the Rankins, and Robbie Millar—have worked abroad and have brought back a sophisticated awareness of international cooking styles. Beyond the top-tier places, there are many other spots where you'll find good-quality, fresh local fish or meat prepared in a simple style.

$$$ ✕ **Cayenne.** Celebrity TV chefs Paul and Jeanne Rankin, innovative cooks who travel widely, run this Golden Mile spot. The Rankins' previous venture on the same premises was the renowned Roscoff. Less formal than its predecessor, Cayenne serves fusion cuisine with an

Asian twist; for an appetizer, you might get eggplant spring rolls or miso-glazed cod, with main dishes ranging from char-grilled rib eye, served with red onion and mushroom *bruschetta* (a type of Italian garlic bread), to wok-smoked salmon with bombay potatoes and fresh coriander. The dessert menu includes mouthwatering temptations like white chocolate cheesecake tart and lemongrass crème brûlée. This is an excellent choice for a late meal after taking in an opera or concert in Waterfront Hall. ⊠ *Shaftesbury Sq. at end of Great Victoria St.,* ☎ *028/ 9033–1532. AE, DC, MC, V. Closed Sun. No lunch Fri.*

$$$ ✕ **Deane's.** Chef Michael Deane became a celebrity for his accomplished
★ food in a tiny open kitchen in an equally tiny Victorian railroad station a few miles outside Belfast. Now he has a much larger two-story room—a brasserie downstairs and formal restaurant upstairs—in the center of Belfast, close to City Hall. Deane's tastes are eclectic; he has worked in Bangkok, and Thai influences particularly shine in his subtle way with spices. Squab is a Deane specialty, served in a light lasagna with celeriac leaves, spinach, and foie gras for a starter. For a main dish Deane dry-marinates a squab with cinnamon sticks for two days, then serves it in an olive-oil curried stock, with coriander seed and leaves, apple, ginger, and soy sauce, all on a bed of risotto. The ravioli of lobster is a standout. ⊠ *38–40 Howard St.,* ☎ *028/9033–1134. AE, MC, V. Closed Sun.–Mon. and 1 wk in July.*

$$$ ✕ **Shanks.** Golf clubhouses don't usually spell welcome to peripatetic
★ gourmands, but Shanks is decidedly different. Robbie and Shirley Millar's cool temple to the contemporary, designed by London design guru Terence Conran, sits on a vast 3,000-acre estate. The pleasing duplex houses the bar and reception area upstairs with a stylish dining room downstairs. Like many of Ireland's other best young chefs, Robbie Millar studied under Cayenne's Paul Rankin (☞ *above*), and he spares nothing to produce wonderful fish and game dishes. How demanding is he? A scuba diver handpicks large, fresh scallops from the Copeland Islands in the Irish Sea, as they are more tender than scallops dredged by a trawler off the sea bottom. Shanks is about 19 km (12 mi) from Belfast, signposted off the Crawfordsburn Road (turn *right* off the Belfast–Bangor Road, or you can take a train from Belfast to Bangor and then a taxi). ⊠ *Blackwood Golf Centre, Crawfordsburn Rd., Bangor,* ☎ *028/9185–3313. Reservations essential. AE, MC, V. Closed 2 wks in July. No lunch Sat.–Mon.*

$–$$$ ✕ **Chez Delbart.** Better known among locals by an alternative name— Frogities—this is the third and smallest of the trio of eateries founded by French ex-submariner M. Delbart, who promotes his heritage with the Eiffel Tower motif that adorns the exterior. Open in the evenings only, Frogities packs in a student clientele, particularly on weekends, who come back again and again for staples like the crepes and brochettes. ⊠ *10 Bradbury Pl.,* ☎ *028/9023–8020. AE, DC, MC, V. Closed Sun.–Mon. No lunch.*

$–$$$ ✕ **La Belle Époque.** Relaxed and intimate, this well-established restaurant is charmingly French, with art nouveau decor reminiscent of Paris. The very reasonably priced menu features smoked salmon stuffed with fish mousse in a horseradish sauce as an appetizer and a main course of fillet of beef with whole grain mustard cream sauce. For dessert you can't go wrong with the freshly made fruit sorbets. The set-price lunch menu is particularly good value. ⊠ *61 Dublin Rd.,* ☎ *028/9032–3244. Reservations essential. AE, DC, MC, V. Closed Sun. No lunch Sat.*

$$ ✕ **Antica Roma.** Cecil B. DeMille's Rome rubs shoulders with Little Italy in this restaurant's astonishing murals of the interior of a Roman villa, which justify anyone's first visit. The menu has a surprisingly appealing Celtic interpretation of Italian cuisine. Seafood—especially

clams, mussels, and squid—is particularly good. ⊠ *67 Botanic Ave.,* ☎ *028/9031–1121. AE, MC, V. Closed Sun. No lunch Sat.*

$$ ✕ **Café Society.** Though the little tables outside on the sidewalk in the summer may not give Café Society a Parisian air, the second-floor window tables have the best view of bustling Belfast. At this wonderful après-shopping spot, the food is splendid, too. Seared scallops with fennel and olives as well as grilled buffalo mozzarella are typical of the distinctive starters. The mixed fish grill of grouper, red snapper, and salmon served with polenta is a delight that you might find among the entrées. ⊠ *3 Donegall Sq. W,* ☎ *028/9043–9525. MC, V. Closed Sun. No lunch.*

$$ ✕ **Metro Brasserie.** This restaurant has an airy, contemporary feel that complements the trendy cuisine. The combinations of various carefully balanced textures and flavors make for lively, colorful eating. For an entrée you might get peppered monkfish with chorizo-and-lemon orzo, onion rings, and tomato salsa, or pork fillet with colcannon croquettes, braised leeks, and whole grain mustard. If you're in the mood for a drink after dinner, stop in at fashionable Bar Twelve, which shares the ground floor. ⊠ *Crescent Town House, 13 Lower Crescent, off Botanic Ave.,* ☎ *028/9032–3349. AE, DC, MC, V. No lunch Sat.–Sun.*

$–$$ ✕ **Nick's Warehouse.** On a narrow, cobbled street near the increasingly fashionable Laganside area, Nick Price's cool, cozy wine bar and adjacent restaurant are among Belfast's most relaxing watering holes. The busy bar serves warm salads in a range of nut oils, as well as tiny, tasty casseroles. In the slightly more formal restaurant, favorites are duck with red cabbage and apple compote, and halibut with langoustine and sweet peppers. Finish off your meal with a sampling of the cheese selection. The wine and imported beer lists are impressive. ⊠ *35 Hill St.,* ☎ *028/9043–9690. Reservations essential for restaurant. AE, MC, V. Closed Sun. No dinner Mon., no lunch Sat.*

$–$$ ✕ **The Strand.** In the university area, this dark and intimate bistro with candlelit tables attracts students and professors with its adventurous, unusual menu. Recommended dishes include Irish lamb noisettes and baked eggplant. For dessert try the cream-laden gâteaux. Vegetarian entrées are available, such as a flan of broccoli and cashews. ⊠ *12 Stranmillis Rd.,* ☎ *028/9068–2266. AE, DC, MC, V.*

$–$$ ✕ **Sun Kee.** This unpretentious little spot has the mark of all truly good Chinese restaurants—the Chinese people who live in the area eat here, digging into huge portions while watching the large TV in the corner, then rushing upstairs for a quick game of mah-jongg. The decor is simple, but the food is terrific. While you can't go wrong with beef in green pepper sauce and *char sui* (marinated and barbecued) pork, this is also a good place to take a risk with dishes such as duck's web or fish-head soup, eel, and roasted pork belly. The helpful staff will even choose for you if you tell them your tastes. ⊠ *38 Donegall Pass,* ☎ *028/9031–2016. No credit cards. BYOB. Closed mid-July–mid-Aug. No lunch.*

$ ✕ **Kitchen Bar.** A great spot to mingle with city-center office workers, this place is known for its lunches—Irish stew, the Ulster fry, and host Pat Catney's famous Paddy's Pizza, made on a base of traditional Irish soda bread. Wash everything down with the selection of draft beers (real ale aficionados flock here for its annual beer festival during the first week of October). There's traditional music on Friday night. ⊠ *16 Victoria Sq.,* ☎ *028/9032–4901. MC, V.*

$ ✕ **Roscoff Café.** This city-center bakery-café is the perfect spot for enjoying the delights of chefs Paul and Jeanne Rankin of Cayenne fame (☞ *above*) without breaking the bank. It has a Parisian feel to it, especially if the weather is fine, and you can sit outside. Try the walnut bread, sun-dried tomato bread, focaccia, and the delicious soups and desserts. ✉ *21 Fountain St.,* ☎ *028/9031–5090. AE, DC, MC, V. Closed Sun. No dinner Mon.–Wed. or Sat., no lunch Thurs.–Fri.*

Lodging

Airport and Environs

$$$$ 🏨 **Stakis Park Templepatrick.** On 220 acres of wooded parkland with its own 18-hole championship golf course, this modern hotel is 10 minutes from Belfast International Airport and 20 minutes from Belfast city center. Rooms are generously equipped, with satellite TV and full bathroom. The location is particularly good if you're planning a brief visit to the province and don't want to stay in the city. ✉ *Castle Upton Estate, Templepatrick, Co. Antrim BT39 0DD,* ☎ *028/9443–5500,* FAX *028/9443–5511. 129 rooms with bath, 1 suite. Restaurant, bar, indoor pool, sauna, 18-hole golf course, exercise room, meeting rooms. AE, DC, MC, V.* 🐾

$$$ 🏨 **Dunadry Hotel and Country Club.** Ten minutes from Belfast International Airport, this spacious, whitewashed former mill on 10 acres of land is a hotel of considerable charm. Renovations made use of large wooden components from the old mill's massive linen beetling (polishing) engines in the stairwell and a gallery over the bar. Its bedrooms are large; the best open onto the inner courtyard. The restaurant is a popular spot for local weddings, so you may find yourself in the midst of a real Irish celebration. ✉ *2 Islandreagh Dr., Dunadry, Co. Antrim BT41 2HA,* ☎ *028/9438–5050,* FAX *028/9438–5055. 83 rooms with bath. Restaurant, bar, indoor pool, croquet, exercise room, meeting rooms. AE, DC, MC, V.*

Central District

$$$$ 🏨 **Belfast Hilton.** This riverside hotel should be able to cater to your every whim and, with its excellent fitness and leisure facilities, is the perfect place to unwind after the wilds of the countryside. The rooms are well equipped and comfortable, and the restaurant serves contemporary cuisine; along with some of the suites, it has good views of the river and across the city. The hotel is beside Waterfront Hall, in an area undergoing urban renewal. ✉ *4 Lanyon Pl., BT1 3LP,* ☎ *028/9027–7000,* FAX *028/9027–7277. 182 rooms with bath, 13 suites. Restaurant, bar, in-room data ports, indoor pool, beauty salon, sauna, exercise room, business services, meeting rooms. AE, DC, MC, V.* 🐾

Golden Mile

$$ 🏨 **Benedict's of Belfast.** With a facade that stands out from the drab terraces of Bradbury Place, Benedict's of Belfast is a friendly, lively, and convenient base for exploring the Golden Mile and university area. Rooms on the second floor are bright and colorful with wooden floors, while rooms on the third floor are darker with an Asian flavor. If you don't feel like straying too far from home for some nightlife, Bendict's has a buzzing bar and restaurant serving contemporary fare. ✉ *7–21 Bradbury Pl., BT7 IRQ,* ☎ *028/9059–1999,* FAX *028/9059–1990. 32 rooms, 30 with bath. Restaurant, bar. AE, DC, MC, V.*

$$ 🏨 **Jurys Belfast Inn.** The first Jurys north of the border brings the chain's flat-rate pricing formula—one price for up to three adults or two adults and two children—to the Golden Mile. Once you get past the forbidding warehouselike exterior, a spacious, marble-tiled foyer with warm green and salmon hues awaits. Some rooms overlook College Square, the cricket lawn of the elegant dusky-brick Royal Belfast Academical Institution, built in 1814 by Joan Soane. The Arches restaurant offers well-prepared hotel fare. Tartan fabrics and dark wood decorate the Inn Pub, which serves a lunch-only hot buffet. ✉ *Fisher-*

wick Pl., BT2 7AP, ☎ *028/9053–3500,* FAX *028/9053–3511. 190 rooms with bath. Restaurant, bar, meeting rooms. AE, DC, MC, V.* 🕮

Outside the City Center

$$$$ 🏨 **Culloden Hotel.** Eight kilometers (5 miles) from the city center on A2, this 19th-century, former Scottish baronial mansion stands amid 12 acres of parkland. One of only two five-star hotels in Northern Ireland—the other is the Belfast Hilton (☞ *above*)—it's the flagship in a fleet of hotels run by local hotelier Billy Hastings. Public areas have ornate woodwork, Louis XV chandeliers, decorative plasterwork, and stained glass. Guest rooms, both in the original section and in a newer wing, are decorated with silk-and-velvet fabrics and have fine views. The dining areas include the French Mitre restaurant, with mahogany tables and a garden view, and the Grill Bar, which serves both snacks and full meals. The hotel is close to the Ulster Folk and Transport Museum (☞ Side Trips, *below*). No-smoking rooms are available. ⊠ *142 Bangor Rd., Holywood, Co. Down BT18 0EX,* ☎ *028/9042–5223,* FAX *028/9042–6777. 77 rooms with bath, 10 suites. Restaurant, grill, no-smoking rooms, indoor pool, sauna, tennis court, croquet, squash, nightclub, laundry service. AE, DC, MC, V.* 🕮

$$$$ 🏨 **The McCausland Hotel.** Clean and simple lines, a feeling of space and light, and an aura of sumptuous minimalism are the hallmarks of this pair of 1867 grain warehouses, which have become this luxury hotel, with the original cast-iron pillars and beams retained throughout. The well-equipped bedrooms, with entertainment centers, including TVs, VCRs, and stereos, are tastefully color coordinated. Dining, under the capably inspired hands of chef Eamonn O'Cathain, is in the Marco Polo bar-bistro or the more formal Merchants restaurant. On the edge of the blossoming Laganside area, the hotel is a 5-minute walk from the city center and 20 minutes from the start of the Golden Mile (☞ *above*). ⊠ *34–38 Victoria St., BT1 3GH,* ☎ *028/9022–0200,* FAX *028/ 9022–0220. 60 rooms with bath, 4 suites. Restaurant, bar, brasserie, exercise room, meeting rooms. AE, DC, MC, V.* 🕮

$$$ 🏨 **Rayanne House.** This family-owned country house in leafy Holywood, 10 km (6 mi) from Belfast city center, has won numerous national prizes for its food and hospitality, thanks to the devoted owner Anne McClelland. Rooms are airy, each with individual, traditional decor and nice views of the gardens. Lunch and dinner are no longer served, but the breakfast still garners national—and international—praise: a traditional Irish grill along with such specialties as prune soufflé on a puree of green figs and hot Rayanne baked cereal (laced with spices, fresh fruit, whiskey, honey, and cream) are served in the intimate dining room among family antiques, paintings, and candelabra. ⊠ *60 Demesne Rd., Holywood, Co. Down BT18 9EX,* ☎ *028/9042– 5859,* FAX *028/9042–3364. 9 rooms with bath. Dining room. MC, V.*

University Area

$$$ 🏨 **Dukes Hotel.** Although this distinguished redbrick Victorian building has only 21 rooms, it has such big-hotel amenities as a spacious lobby, extensive exercise facilities, and a restaurant that leans toward healthful, local cuisine. The color scheme is smart gray, enlivened with plenty of greenery, and a waterfall splashes down parallel to the stairs. Many of the comfortable rooms have views of the hills beyond the city. ⊠ *65–67 University St., BT7 1HL,* ☎ *028/9023–6666,* FAX *028/9023– 7177. 21 rooms with bath. Restaurant, bar, sauna, exercise room, meeting rooms. AE, DC, MC, V.*

$$$ 🏨 **Wellington Park Hotel.** Formerly a private residence and currently run by the Mooney family, this recently expanded and modernized establishment is among the best in this area of town. The quiet, refurbished bedrooms are well designed, with built-in wooden furniture; some

feature sleeping lofts. Live music and good food are featured at the bar
and restaurant. ⊠ *21 Malone Rd., BT9 6RU,* ☎ *028/9038–1111,* ꜰᴀx
*028/9066–5410. 75 rooms with bath. Restaurant, bar, laundry service,
meeting rooms. AE, DC, MC, V.*

$$–$$$ ⊞ **Ash-Rowan Guest House.** Former restaurateurs Sam and Evelyn Ha-
  ★ zlett own and run this outstanding B&B in a spacious Victorian home
on a tranquil residential avenue. Thomas Andrews, the designer of the
ill-fated *Titanic,* once lived here. Every bedroom has been decorated
in a tasteful, individual style, and each has a private bath and TV. Guests
have access to a library. Breakfasts and dinners, prepared by the owners, are first-rate; the house is no-smoking. ⊠ *12 Windsor Ave., BT9
6EE,* ☎ *028/9066–1758,* ꜰᴀx *028/9066–3227. 8 rooms with bath.
Dining room, library. MC, V. Closed Dec.*

$$–$$$ ⊞ **Madison's.** This is one of Belfast's liveliest spots, with a terrific lo-
cation on tree-, café-, and shop-lined Botanic Avenue, a few minutes'
walk from the university. The hotel is run with gracious aplomb by
the Mooney family (proprietors of the Dunadry Hotel and Country
Club and Wellington Park Hotel [☞ *above* for both]). Its facade and
public areas are decorated in a modish Barcelona-inspired take on art
nouveau. The bedrooms, in cool yellows and rich blues, are sparely
furnished but comfortable. The downstairs bar houses a restaurant that
offers tasty, modern cuisine at reasonable prices and is good for Sunday lunch when many other premises are closed. Guests have access
to the extensive fitness facilities of Queen's University, including a terrific pool. ⊠ *59 Botanic Ave., BT7 1JL,* ☎ *028/9033–0040,* ꜰᴀx *028/
9032–8007. 35 rooms with bath. Restaurant, bar, business services.
AE, MC, V.*

$$ ⊞ **Old Rectory.** Mary and Jerry Callan's well-appointed house, built
in 1896 as a rectory, is decorated in pastels and has good views of the
countryside. Complimentary whiskey is served by the fire each evening.
Rare in Ulster B&Bs, a healthy alternative to the hearty Ulster fry is
served at breakfast. ⊠ *148 Malone Rd., BT9 5LH,* ☎ *028/9066–7882,*
ꜰᴀx *028/9068–3759. 4 rooms with bath. No credit cards.*

Nightlife and the Arts

Nightlife
Belfast has dozens of pubs packed with relics of the Victorian and Ed-
wardian periods. Although pubs typically close around 11:30 ᴘᴍ,
many city-center/Golden Mile nightclubs often stay open until 1 ᴀᴍ.

CITY CENTER/DOCKS
Bittles Bar (⊠ 70 Upper Church La., ☎ 028/9031–1088), on Victoria
Square, has informal music sessions on weekends. **Kelly's Cellars** (⊠
30–32 Bank St., ☎ 028/9032–4835), open since 1720, offers blues on
Saturday nights. The **Kitchen Bar** (⊠ 16 Victoria Sq., ☎ 028/9032–
4901) is a real ale bar with traditional music on Friday nights. **Mad-
den's Bar** (⊠ 74 Smithfield St., ☎ 028/9024–4114) is a popular pub
with traditional tunes. **McHugh's** (⊠ 29–30 Queen's Sq., ☎ 028/9024–
7830), in Belfast's oldest building, dating from 1711, is three floors of
bars, restaurants, and live music on weekends. **Pat's Bar** (⊠ 19–22
Prince's Dock St., ☎ 028/9074–4524) has regular first-rate sessions
of traditional music. The **Rotterdam** (⊠ 54 Pilot St., ☎ 028/9074–6021)
features folk, jazz, and blues performers.

GOLDEN MILE AREA
The glorious **Crown Liquor Saloon** (☞ Sights to See *in* Golden Mile,
above) is far from being the only impressive old pub in the Golden Mile
area—most of Belfast's evening life takes place in bars and restaurants

here. There are a number of replicated Victorian bars with more locals and fewer visitors.

The **Beaten Docket** (✉ 48 Great Victoria St., ☎ 028/9024–2986),
named after a losing betting slip, is a noisy, modern pub that attracts
a young crowd; it features up-to-the-minute music. **Benedict's** (✉ 7–
21 Bradbury Pl., ☎ 028/9059–1999) is a bar, music venue, disco, 150-
seat restaurant, and hotel. Straying from the Victorian-style public house,
the **Limelight** (✉ 17 Ormeau Ave., ☎ 028/9032–5968) is a disco-
nightclub with cabaret on Tuesday, Friday, and Saturday and music on
other nights. The **Manhattan** (✉ 23 Bradbury Pl., ☎ 028/9023–3131),
a.k.a. the M-Club, is Belfast's hottest place for dedicated clubbers, with
TV soap-opera celebrities flown in weekly to mix with the local
nighthawks. **Morrisons** (✉ 21 Bedford St., ☎ 028/9024–8458) is a haunt
of media types. It has a music lounge upstairs, where there's a mix of
jazz, rock, and discussions for film buffs arranged by local directors
in conjunction with the Northern Ireland Film Council; Saturday, it's
rock; Sunday, Irish music. **Robinson's** (✉ 38 Great Victoria St., ☎ 028/
9024–7447), two doors from the Crown, is a popular pub that appeals
to a young crowd with folk music in its Fibber Magee's bar on Saturday and rock in its Rock Bottom basement on Wednesday.

UNIVERSITY AREA

The stylish and modern **Bar Twelve** (✉ Crescent Town House, 13
Lower Crescent, ☎ 028/9032–3349) is an excellent venue for some
fashionable wine sipping. The **Botanic Inn** (✉ 23–27 Malone Rd., ☎
028/9066–0460), known as "the Bot" to its student clientele, is a big,
popular disco-pub. **Cutter's Wharf** (✉ 4 Lockview St., ☎ 028/9066–
2501), down by the river south of the university, is at its best on summer evenings and at the Sunday jazz brunch. The **Eglantine Inn** (✉ 32–
40 Malone Rd., ☎ 028/9038–1994), known as "the Egg," faces the
Bot across Malone Road. The **Empire Music Hall** (✉ 42 Botanic Ave.,
☎ 028/9032–8110), a deconsecrated church, is the city's leading music
venue. Stand-up comedy nights are usually on Tuesday. **Lavery's Gin
Palace** (✉ 12 Bradbury Pl., ☎ 028/9032–7159) mixes old-fashioned
beer drinking downstairs with dancing upstairs. The **Fly Bar** (✉ 56 Lower
Crescent, ☎ 028/9023–5666), with its over-the-top but impressive interior, playing on the fly theme, is a lively spot for a cocktail in the
evenings.

The Arts

The **Northern Ireland Arts Council** (☎ 028/9038–5200) produces the
monthly *Artslink* poster-brochure, which lists what's happening throughout Belfast and the North; it's widely available throughout the city. The
Belfast Festival at Queen's University, which lasts three weeks each
November, is the city's major arts festival. For information, contact
the Festival Office (✉ 25 College Gardens, BT9, ☎ 028/9066–6321).
The **Belfast Folk Festival** has broad-ranging traditional and contemporary music and dance events on weekends during the summer
months. For updates, contact the Northern Ireland Arts Council (☞
above). Information about the **Promenade Concerts,** themed classical
music concerts taking place in June, can be obtained from the Ulster
Orchestra ticket office (☎ 028/9066–8798).

ART GALLERIES

Bell Gallery. Nelson Bell's Victorian home in the leafy university suburbs is a mecca for many of Ireland's more traditional painters. ✉ *13
Adelaide Park, Malone Rd.,* ☎ 028/9066–2998. ☾ *Weekdays 9–5 and
by appointment.*
Fenderesky Gallery. Under the same roof as the Crescent Arts Centre
(☞ *below*), Iranian philosopher Jamshid Mirfenderesky's gallery is one

of the few in Ireland with a stable of modern Irish artists known throughout Europe. ⊠ *Crescent Arts Centre, 2 University Rd.,* ☎ *028/9023–5245.* ⊙ *Tues.–Sat. 11:30–5:30.*

Ormeau Baths Gallery. The white, airy spaces of this former municipal bathhouse now display the work of major contemporary international and Irish artists. ⊠ *18A Ormeau Ave.,* ☎ *028/9032–1402.* ⊙ *Tues.–Sat. 9:30–5:30.*

FILM

Belfast has several city-center movie theaters that show the major new British and American box-office favorites. **Curzon Cinema** (⊠ Ormeau Rd., ☎ 028/9064–1373) has three screens. **Queen's Film Theatre** (⊠ University Sq. Mews, off Botanic Ave., ☎ 028/9024–4857), Belfast's main art cinema, shows domestic and foreign movies on its two screens. **Virgin Cinemas** (⊠ Dublin Rd., ☎ 028/9024–3200 for information, 028/9055–5176 for credit-card booking [both 24 hrs]) has 10 screens.

MAJOR MULTIPURPOSE VENUES

Grand Opera House. This beautifully restored Victorian playhouse has no company of its own but books shows from all over the British Isles and sometimes farther afield. It puts on a constant stream of West End musicals and plays of widely differing kinds, plus occasional operas and ballets. It's worth going to a show if only to enjoy the atmosphere of the opera house itself. ⊠ *Great Victoria St.,* ☎ *028/9024–1919.* 🖾 *U.K.£6–U.K.£30.*

Waterfront Hall. Everyone in Belfast is still singing the praises of this civic structure, which opened in January 1997. From the looks of it, the hall is an odd marriage of *Close Encounters* modern and Castel Sant'Angelo antique. It houses both a major 2,235-seat concert hall (used for ballet, symphony, rock, and Irish music) and a 500-seat studio space (for modern dance, jazz, and experimental theater). If you don't mind the airport-lounge feel, the river-view Terrace Café restaurant and two bars make the hall a convenient place to eat or have a pint before or after your culture fix. ⊠ *Lanyon Pl.,* ☎ *028/9033–4400.*

MUSIC

King's Hall. This is the major venue for pop and rock concerts. ⊠ *484 Lisburn Rd.,* ☎ *028/9066–5225.* **Ulster Hall.** Home to the Ulster Orchestra, the hall has excellent acoustics and a splendid Victorian organ (☞ Sights to See *in* Golden Mile, *above*). ⊠ *Bedford St.,* ☎ *028/ 9032–3900.*

OPERA AND THEATER

Belfast Civic Arts Theatre. Near the university area, this venue specializes in comedies and other lightweight productions. ⊠ *41 Botanic Ave.,* ☎ *028/9031–6900.*

Crescent Arts Centre. "The Crescent" to its habitués, this huge, rambling black stone building off the campus end of Bradbury Place is a focus for experimental theater and dance, provocative art in its Fenderesky Gallery (☞ *above*), and experimental jazz. ⊠ *2–4 University Rd.,* ☎ *028/9024–2338.*

Lyric Theatre. In the south of Belfast, at King's Bridge on the banks of the Lagan, the Lyric stages thoughtful drama inspired by traditional and contemporary Irish culture. ⊠ *Ridgeway St.,* ☎ *028/9038–1081.* 🖾 *U.K.£5.50–U.K.£11; call to confirm prices.*

Old Museum Arts Centre (OMAC). A powerhouse of challenging, avant-garde theater and modern dance, OMAC also has a risk-taking art gallery. ⊠ *7 College Sq. N,* ☎ *028/9023–3332.*

Opera Northern Ireland. Humperdinck's *Hansel and Gretel,* Britten's *A Midsummer Night's Dream,* Leoncavallo's *Pagliacci,* and Puccini's *Gianni Schicchi* were scheduled in past years; performances are at the Grand Opera House (☞ *above*). ☎ *028/9032–2338.*

Shopping

Belfast's main shopping streets include **Donegall Place, High Street, Royal Avenue,** and several of the smaller streets connecting them. The whole area is mostly traffic-free (except for buses and delivery vehicles), so you'll find it pleasant to wander and window-shop. **Castle Court** (⊠ 10 Royal Ave., ☎ 028/9023–4591) is the city's largest, most varied upscale shopping mall. **Craftworks** (⊠ Bedford House, 16–22 Bedford St., ☎ 028/9024–4465) stocks inexpensive crafts by local designers. The long thoroughfare of **Donegall Pass,** running from Shaftesbury Square at the point of the Golden Mile east to Ormeau Road, is a unique mix of biker shops and antiques arcades, and a good place to stroll. **Hoggs** (⊠ 10 Donegall Sq. W, ☎ 028/9024–2232) stocks a good selection of linen, Tyrone crystal, Belleek china, and miniatures. Opposite Castle Court, **Smyth's Irish Linens** (⊠ 65 Royal Ave., ☎ 028/9024–2232) carries a large selection of handkerchiefs, tablecloths, napkins, and other linen goods, which make excellent souvenirs or presents. **Smyth and Gibson** (⊠ Bedford House, Bedford St., ☎ 028/9023–0388) makes and sells beautiful, luxurious linen and cotton shirts and accessories. If you've an interest in bric-a-brac, visit the enormous, renovated **St. George's Market,** an indoor flea market on May Street, every Tuesday and Friday morning. The **Steensons** (⊠ Bedford House, Bedford St., ☎ 028/9024–8268) sells superb, locally designed jewelry.

Side Trips

The three sights below are closer to Belfast than others covered in this chapter. However, none of the sites along the Ards Peninsula and the north coast are more than a few hours' drive from Belfast—perfect for day trips.

⑱ Belfast Castle

Situated in Cave Hill Country Park, Belfast Castle was originally built for the Marquis of Donegall in 1865. In 1934 the castle was passed into the hands of Belfast Corporation. While the castle functions primarily as a restaurant, it also houses the **Cave Hill Heritage Centre** with information about the castle's history and natural surroundings. The best reason to visit the castle for a day trip, however, is to take a stroll in the lovely ornamental gardens and then make the ascent to **McArt's Fort.** This promontory, at the top of sheer cliffs 1,200 ft above the city, affords an excellent view across Belfast. To get there, you will need to take the path uphill from the parking lot, take a right at the next intersection of pathways, and then keep left as you journey up the sometimes steep hill to the fort. It's a good idea to drop into the Northern Ireland Tourist Board (☞ Sights to See *in* Central District, *above*) for detailed directions on walks in this scenic area. You could also take in **Belfast Zoo** (⊠ Antrim Rd., ☎ 028/9077–6277) which is nearby, with its underwater views of the resident penguins and sea lions and a children's farm. City buses 45 and 51 will bring you to both the castle and zoo. ⊠ *About 4 km (2½ mi) north of Belfast on Antrim Rd.,* ☎ *028/ 9077–6925.* 🎫 *Free.* ☉ *Heritage center daily 9–6; tours of castle by appointment.*

⑲ Irish Linen Centre and Lisburn Museum

In the 18th, 19th, and early 20th centuries, linen, a natural fabric woven from the fibers of the flax plant, was the basis of Ulster's most important industry—and thus of much of its folk history and song. A century ago, 240,000 acres were given over to flax, whose pretty blue flowers sparkle for just a week in early July, and 400 acres were designated as "bleach greens," where the woven fabric whitened in the summer sun. Eventually, American cotton and Egyptian flax killed off the mass-production

linen trade, which had been centered on Lisburn, in mills powered by the River Lagan. What now survives of the linen industry does so by producing high-quality designer fabrics, plus traditional expensive damask.

Today at the Irish Linen Centre and Lisburn Museum, a series of rooms trace this history. Weaving is demonstrated on a turn-of-the-20th-century hand loom (although the attached shop has a disappointing choice of linen goods). If you're looking for a more intensive investigation of the linen industry, tours of the **Linen Homelands** are offered. The six-hour bus tour (with a break for lunch) visits three different sites: the Irish Linen Centre; a modern, operational linen spinning and weaving factory; and the last working water-powered scutching mill (where flax fibers are broken down) in Ireland. In July you may catch the splendid sight of just a few fields of lilac-blue flax flowers bending in the light summer breeze. Tours are given May–September, Wednesday 10–4 (the cost is U.K.£9, lunch extra; no tours during factory holidays in July), and begin at the **Banbridge Gateway Tourist Information Centre** (⊠ 200 Newry Rd., Banbridge, ☎ 028/4062–3322). Reservations are essential. ⊠ *12 km (8 mi) southwest of Belfast, Market Sq., Lisburn,* ☎ *028/9266–3377.* ☞ *Free.* ☉ *Mon.–Sat. 9:30–5.*

㉒ Ulster Folk and Transport Museum
Devoted to the province's social history, the excellent Ulster Folk and Transport Museum is 16 km (10 mi) northeast of Belfast, set in some 70 acres around Cultra Manor, encircled by a larger park and recreation area. It vividly brings the North's past to life with a score of reconstructed buildings transported here from around the region; these structures represent different facets of northern life—a traditional weaver's dwelling, terraces of Victorian town houses, an 18th-century country church, a village flax mill, a farmhouse, and a rural school. Inside you'll usually find a cheery fire and an appropriately dressed attendant who will explain what it was like actually to live in them. You start your visit with the **Folk Gallery,** which explains the background of each building. Across the main road (by footbridge) is the beautifully designed **Transport Museum,** where exhibits include locally built airplanes and motorcycles; the iconoclastic car produced by former General Motors whiz kid John De Lorean in his Belfast factory in 1982; and a moving section on the *Titanic,* the Belfast-built luxury liner that sank on her first voyage, in 1912, killing 1,500 of the passengers and crew. A miniature railway runs on Saturday in summer. ⊠ *Cultra, near Holywood,* ☎ *028/9042–8428.* ☞ *U.K.£4.* ☉ *Apr.–June and Sept., weekdays 9:30–5, Sat. 10:30–6, Sun. noon–6; July–Aug., Mon.–Sat. 10:30–6, Sun. noon–6; Oct.–Mar., weekdays 9:30–4, weekends 12:30–4:30.*

AROUND COUNTIES ANTRIM AND DERRY

Starting and finishing in Belfast, you can take a circular route through a portion of the North that allows you to pass through some fair-size towns, as well as drive in open country through splendid natural scenery. From medieval towns such as Carrickfergus, you'll travel past the natural wonder of the Giant's Causeway and the man-made brilliance of the castle at Dunluce before arriving in the old walled city of Derry.

Carrickfergus

㉑ *16 km (10 mi) northeast of Belfast, 24 km (15 mi) south of Larne.*

Carrickfergus, on the shore of Belfast Lough, grew up around its ancient castle. When the town was enclosed by ramparts at the start of the 17th century, it was the only English-speaking town in Northern Ireland. Not surprisingly, this was the loyal port where William of Orange chose to land on his way to fight the Catholic forces at the Battle of the Boyne in 1690. However, the English did have one or two small setbacks, including the improbable victory in 1778 of John Paul Jones, the American naval hero, over the British warship HMS *Drake*. (This, by the way, was America's first naval victory during the Revolutionary War.) After the sea battle, the inhabitants of Carrickfergus stood on the waterfront and cheered Jones because they supported the American Revolution.

Carrickfergus Castle, one of the first and one of the largest of Irish castles, is still in good shape. An impressive sight, perched on a rock ledge, it was built in 1180 by John de Courcy, provincial Ulster's first Anglo-Norman invader. Apart from being captured briefly by the French in 1760, the castle stood as a bastion of British rule right up until 1928, at which time it still functioned as an English garrison.

Walk through the castle's 13th-century gatehouse into the Outer Ward. Continue into the Inner Ward, the heart of the fortress, where the five-story keep stands, a massive, sturdy building with walls almost 8 ft thick. Inside the keep, you'll find the **Cavalry Regimental Museum** with historic weapons and an impressive, vaulted Great Hall. These days Carrickfergus Castle hosts entertaining medieval banquets (inquire at Carrickfergus tourist information office, ☎ 028/9336–6455, or the Northern Ireland Tourist Board, ☎ 028/9023-1221) if you're here at the beginning of August, you can enjoy the annual Lughnasa festival, a lively medieval costume entertainment. ☎ *028/9335–1273.* 🖾 *U.K.£3.* ⊘ *Apr.–Sept., Mon.–Sat. 10–6; Oct.–Mar., Mon.–Sat. 10–4.*

Structures that remain from Carrickfergus's past are **St. Nicholas's Church,** built by John de Courcy in 1205 and remodeled in 1614, and the handsomely restored North Gate in the town's medieval walls. Dobbins Inn on High Street has been a popular hotel for more than three centuries.

The **Andrew Jackson Centre,** in a thatched cottage just outside of town, tells the tale of U.S. president Andrew Jackson, whose parents emigrated from here in 1765. This cottage was not their actual home but a reconstruction of an 18th-century thatched cottage thought to resemble it. 🖾 *2 km (1 mi) northeast of Carrickfergus, Boneybefore, Larne Rd.,* ☎ *028/9336–6455.* 🖾 *U.K.£1.20.* ⊘ *Apr.–May, weekdays 10–4, weekends 2–4; June–Sept., weekdays 10–6, weekends 2–6.*

Dining and Lodging

$$$ ✕🖫 **Galgorm Manor.** The Gillies bar is decidedly Irish, the dining room cosmopolitan, the manor house itself photogenic, and the estate grounds—where guests may go riding and practice archery—cinematic. Full privileges to Galgorm Castle, an 18-hole, par-72 golf course five minutes from the hotel, are an added treat. The River Maine, a good brown-trout river, flows within sight of many of the large rooms. Plans are under way to add a significant number of new bedrooms and facilities, including exercise rooms and a swimming pool. Galgorm is off A42 3 km (2 mi) west of Ballymena, 32 km (20 mi) inland of Larne, 40 km (25 mi) north of Belfast. 🖾 *136 Fenaghy Rd., Ballymena, Co. Antrim BT42 1EA,* ☎ *028/2588–1001,* 🖷 *028/2588–0080. 23 rooms with bath. Restaurant, bar, horseback riding, fishing, meeting rooms. AE, MC, V.* 🕭

En Route As you head away from Carrickfergus on A2, you'll pass through the village of Eden, where **Castle Dobbs** was the home of Arthur Dobbs, the 18th-century British governor of North Carolina. Signposted on the left, 2½ km (1½ mi) off the road, **Dalway's Bawn,** built in 1609, is the best surviving example of an early *bawn,* or fortified farmhouse, occupied by a Protestant Planter.

Glens of Antrim

★ ㉒ *Nine glens in the 86 km (54 mi) between Larne and Ballycastle.*

Soon after Larne, the coast of County Antrim becomes spectacular—wave upon wave of high, green hills curve down to the hazy sea, dotted with lush and gently curved glens, or valleys, first carved out by glaciers at the end of the last Ice Age. A narrow, winding, two-lane road (A2, known locally as the Antrim Coast Road) hugs the slim strip of land between the hills and the sea, bringing you to the magnificent Glens of Antrim, nine wooded river valleys running down from the escarpment of the Antrim Plateau to the eastern shore. Until the building of this road in 1834, the glens were home to isolated farming communities—people who adhered to the romantic, mystical Celtic legends and the everyday use of the Irish language. The Glens are worth several days of serious exploration. Even narrower B-roads curl west off A2, up each of the beautiful glens where trails await hikers.

Carnlough

㉓ *24 km (15 mi) north of Larne, 22½ km (14 mi) east of Ballymena, 43 km (27 mi) from Ballycastle.*

A little resort made of white limestone, Carnlough overlooks an endearing harbor within stone walls. The sandy beaches can be reached by crossing over the limestone bridge on Main Street, built especially for the Marquis of Londonderry. The small harbor, once a port of call for fishermen, now shelters pleasure yachts. Carnlough is surrounded by a group of hills that rise 1,000 ft from the sea. There is a small tourist office inside the post office.

Dining and Lodging

$$$ ✕🏨 **Londonderry Arms Hotel.** This ivy-covered, traditional inn right on Carnlough Harbour was built as a coaching inn in 1848. What awaits are lovely seaside gardens, gorgeous antique furnishings, regional paintings and maps, lots of fresh flowers, and Georgian-period decor. In 1921 Sir Winston Churchill inherited it; since 1947 it has been owned and run by the hospitable O'Neill family. Both the original and the newer rooms have lovely Georgian antiques and luxurious fabrics, and they are immaculately kept. The restaurant serves substantial, traditional Irish meals that rely on fresh, local seafood, simply prepared. ✉ *20 Harbour Rd., Co. Antrim BT44 0EU,* ☎ *028/2888–5255,* 📠 *028/2888–5263. 35 rooms with bath. Restaurant, bar. AE, DC, MC, V.* 🐾

$$$ 🏨 **Ballygally Castle.** At the Larne end of the North Antrim coast drive, 40 km (25 mi) from Belfast, stands an impressive, turreted castle that faces Ballygally Bay. Built by a Scottish lord in 1625, the castle cheerfully invites visitors to enjoy a good night's sleep, a hearty breakfast, and its Dungeon Bar, whose substantial stone walls justify the name. Modern facilities integrate with old Scots baronial design, though an extension jars with the original style. Bedrooms, some in the castle turrets—one complete with milady's ghost—are individually decorated with comfortable furnishings. In the dining room a decent table d'hôte evening meal is served to music, on Saturday, and a Sunday high tea is also available. ✉ *274 Coast Rd., Ballygally, Co. Antrim BT40 2QZ,* ☎ *028/2858–3212,* 📠 *028/2858–3681. 31 rooms with bath. Bar, dining room, fishing, baby-sitting. AE, DC, MC, V.*

En Route   Between Carnlough and Ballycastle the scenery becomes even more stunning. Glenariff, opening onto Red Bay at the village of Glenariff (also known as Waterfoot), is considered the loveliest of the glens. A good day trip is **Glenariff Forest Park,** the largest and most accessible of Antrim's valleys. Inside are picnic facilities and dozens of good hikes, notably the 5½-km (3½-mi) **Waterfall Trail** (follow the blue arrows), which offers outstanding views of Glenariff River and its waterfalls and passes by small but swimmable loughs. Detailed maps are available at the visitor center, which has a small self-serve cafeteria. ⊠ *98 Glenariff Rd.,* ☏ *028/2175–8232.* ⊡ *U.K.£1.* ☉ *Nov.–May, daily 8* AM–8 PM; *June–Oct., daily 8* AM–10 PM.

At Cushendall, you'll see Turnley's Tower—a curious, fortified square tower of red stone, built in 1820 as a curfew tower and jail for "idlers and rioters"—standing at a crossroads in the middle of the village. If you would like a break from the Antrim coast, stay on A2 direct to Ballycastle. But if you would prefer to stay by the sea, turn right at the tower in the direction of **Cushendun,** a tiny jewel of a village designed by Clough Williams-Ellis, who also designed the famous Italianate village of Portmeirion in Wales. From this part of the coast you can see the Mull of Kintyre on the Scottish mainland. If you have firm nerves, take the narrow and precipitous coastal road north past dramatically beautiful **Murlough Bay** to **Fair Head**; others will prefer to rejoin A2 via B92, left, after a few miles and descend—passing on the left the ruins of the Franciscans' 16th-century **Bonamargy Friary**—into Ballycastle.

Ballycastle

㉔ *19⅓ km (12 mi) east of Giant's Causeway, 37½ km (23 mi) north of Carnlough.*

Ballycastle is the main resort town in the glens, at the northern end of the Glens of Antrim drive. People from the province flock here in the summer. The town is shaped like an hourglass—with its strand and dock on one end, its pubs and chippers on the other, and the 1-km (½-mi) Quay Road in between. Beautifully aged shops and pubs line its Castle, Diamond, and Main streets.

From Ballycastle town you have a view of L-shape **Rathlin Island,** where in 1306 the Scottish king Robert the Bruce took shelter in a cave (under the east lighthouse) and, according to the popular legend, was inspired to continue his armed struggle against the English by watching a spider patiently spinning its web. It was on Rathlin in 1898 that Guglielmo Marconi set up the world's first cross-water radio link, from the island's lighthouse to Ballycastle. Bird-watching and hiking are the island's main activities. Unless the sea is extremely rough, a ferryboat makes regular journeys (twice daily in winter, more frequently in summer). Although the island is only 9½ km (6 mi) away from shore, the trip can take 45 minutes; make sure that the weather will permit you to return the same day.

Every year since 1606, on the last Monday and Tuesday in August, Ballycastle has hosted the **Oul' Lammas Fair,** a modern version of the ancient Celtic harvest festival of Lughnasa (Irish for "August"). Ireland's oldest fair, this is a very popular two-day event at which sheep and wool are still sold alongside the wares of more modern shopping stalls. Treat yourself to the fair's traditional snacks, "dulse" (sun-dried seaweed) and "yellow man" (rock-hard yellow toffee).

Off the coast, 8 km (5 mi) west of Ballycastle, you can see the **Carrick-a-Rede** rope bridge, which spans a 60-ft gap between the mainland and Carrick-a-Rede Island. The island's name means "rock in the road" and refers to how it stands in the path of the salmon who follow the coast as they migrate to their home rivers to spawn. For the past 150 years salmon fishermen have set up the rope bridge in late April, taking it down again after the salmon season ends. The bridge is open to the public and offers some heart-stopping views of the crashing waves below. If you summon up the nerve to cross it once, of course you then have to do it again to get back to the mainland. ⊠ *Signposted on B15.* ☑ *Free.* ☉ *Apr.–Sept., daily.*

Giant's Causeway

★ **㉕** *19⅓ km (12 mi) west of Ballycastle, 86 km (54 mi) north of Belfast.*

The Giant's Causeway is Northern Ireland's premier tourist attraction—a singularly strange natural phenomenon consisting of a mass of 37,000 mostly hexagonal pillars of volcanic basalt, clustered like a giant honeycomb and extending hundreds of yards into the sea. Legend has it that the causeway was created 60 million years ago when boiling lava, erupting from an underground fissure that stretched from Northern Ireland to the Scottish coast, crystallized as it burst into the sea, and formed according to the same natural principle that structures a honeycomb. As all Ulster folk know, though, the scientific truth is that the columns were created as stepping-stones by the giant Finn McCool in a bid to reach a giantess he'd fallen in love with on the Scottish island of Staffa (where the causeway resurfaces). Unfortunately, the giantess's boyfriend found out, and in the ensuing battle Finn pulled out a huge chunk of earth and flung it toward Scotland. The resulting hole became Lough Neagh, and the sod landed to create the Isle of Man. Boiling lava, indeed.

To reach the causeway, you can either walk 1½ km (1 mi) down a long, scenic hill or take a minibus from the visitor center. West of the causeway, **Port-na-Spania** is the spot where the 16th-century Spanish Armada galleon *Girona* went down on the rocks. The ship was carrying an astonishing cargo of gold and jewelry, some of which was recovered in 1967 and is now on display in the Ulster Museum in Belfast (☞ Belfast, *above*). Beyond this, **Chimney Point** is the name given to one of the causeway structures on which the Spanish fired, thinking that it was Dunluce Castle, which is 8 km (5 mi) west.

Arriving by car at the Giant's Causeway, you'll first reach a cliff-top parking lot beside the **visitor center,** which houses displays about the area and an audiovisual exhibition explaining the formation of the causeway coast. ⊠ *44 Causeway Rd., near Bushmills,* ☎ *028/2073–1855.* ☑ *Visitor center: exhibition U.K.£1.50, parking U.K.£3.* ☉ *Causeway freely accessible; visitor center May–June, Mon.–Sun. 10–6; July–Aug., Mon.–Sun. 10–7; Sept.–Oct., weekdays 10–5:30, weekends 10–6; Nov.–Feb., daily 10–4:30.*

Bushmills

㉖ *10 km (6 mi) northeast of Coleraine, 14 km (8½ mi) east of Portstewart, 19½ km (12 mi) west of Ballycastle.*

The oldest licensed distillery in the world, Bushmills was first granted a charter by King James I in 1608, though historical records refer to a distillery here as early as 1276. Bushmills produces the most famous of Irish whiskeys—its namesake, Bushmills—and what is widely regarded as the best, the rarer black-label version known to aficionados as Black Bush. One-hour tours begin in the mashing and fermentation room, proceed to the maturing and bottling warehouse, and end with a complimentary shot of *uisce beatha,* the "water of life," in the visitor center–gift shop. ✉ ☎ *028/2073–1521.* 🖃 *U.K.£3.* ⊙ *Apr.–Oct., Mon.–Sat. 10–4; Nov.–Mar., weekdays 10–4.*

Lodging

$$–$$$ 🛏 **Bushmills Inn.** Roy Bolton and Richard Wilson have overseen the transformation of this cozy old coaching inn, found just off the diamond—or main square, as they're referred to in Ulster. Stripped pine, peat fires, and gas lights warm the public rooms. The livery stables now house the informal restaurant, serving fresh and hearty food, and the bar, always full of good spirits; out front are three tables so that you can dine and drink alfresco. Some of the bedrooms are quite small, so ask to see before you decide. The distillery is a stroll away, as is the salmon-filled River Bush. ✉ *25 Main St., Co. Antrim BT57 8QA,* ☎ *028/2073–2339,* 🄵🄰🄷 *028/2073–2048. 32 rooms with bath. Restaurant, bar, meeting rooms. MC, V.* ⊛

Dunluce Castle

★ ㉗ *8 km (5 mi) southwest of Giant's Causeway, 3 km (2 mi) west of Bushmills.*

Halfway between Portrush and the Giant's Causeway, dramatically perched on a cliff at land's end, Dunluce Castle is one of the North's most evocative ruins. Originally a 13th-century Norman fortress, it was captured in the 16th century by the local MacDonnell clan chiefs—the so-called "Lords of the Isles." They enlarged the castle, paying for some of the work with their profits from salvaging the Spanish galleon *Girona* (☞ Ulster Museum *in* Belfast, *above*), and made it an important base for ruling northeastern Ulster. Perhaps they expanded the castle a little too much, for in 1639 faulty construction caused the kitchens (with its cooks) to plummet into the sea during a storm. Nearby is the **Dunluce Centre,** an entertainment complex with rides, a live show about myths and legends, a viewing tower, shops, and a restaurant. ✉ *Port Ballintree,* ☎ *028/7082–4444.* 🖃 *U.K.£4.* ⊙ *Mar.–June and Sept., weekdays noon–5, weekends 10–9; July–Aug., daily 10–9; Oct.–Feb., prebooked group visits only.*

Dining

$$$ ✕ **Ramore Restaurant and Wine Bar.** On Portrush's picturesque har-
★ bor, where a haven of boats are tucked away from the resort's brasher amusements, this spot does double duty. The daily offerings at the wine bar ($) are posted on a blackboard. Upstairs, the draws are panoramic views and chef George McAlpin's Pacific Rim–inflected way with local Atlantic fish and shellfish, which together make up one of Northern Ireland's top dining experiences. Menus change every three months, but Grand Marnier soufflé, a regular dessert, is always an indulgent way to finish. ✉ *The Harbor,* ☎ *028/7082–4313 restaurant, 028/7082–3444 wine bar;* 🄵🄰🄷 *028/7082–3194. MC, V in restaurant only. Restaurant closed Sun.–Mon. Wine bar closed Sun. No lunch in restaurant.*

Outdoor Activities and Sports

Nearby Portrush is home to the **Royal Portrush Golf Club** (☞ Chapter 9), one of Ireland's premier, championship courses. **Portstewart Strand,** to the west of town, has some of Ireland's best surfing.

Coleraine

㉘ *13 km (8 mi) southwest of Dunluce Castle, 48 km (30 mi) east of Derry.*

Dating from the 5th century BC, Coleraine became the seat of the University of Ulster in 1968. The River Bann, flowing through the town, divides the county of Antrim from that of Derry. As well as being a fishing town, Coleraine boasts an important linen industry.

Some of Ireland's oldest remaining relics, dating from the very first inhabitants of this island (about 7000 BC), were found on Mountsandel just to the south of Coleraine. One of the many dolmens in this region is called Slaghtaverty after an evil dwarf who mesmerized women, using his magical harp. He was buried alive and upside down by the great Finn McCool (maker of the Giant's Causeway), so that the sounds of his harp would not escape from the ground.

Lodging

$$ ⊞ **Greenhill House.** This charming Georgian country house, about 13 km (8 mi) south of Coleraine, is a peaceful retreat run by Elizabeth and James Hegarty. Guests enjoy the pleasantly decorated bedrooms, substantial breakfasts, and excellent dinners of locally caught fish, Ulster beef, and homemade bread and cakes. Dinner should be booked by noon. ⊠ *24 Greenhill Rd., Aghadowey, Co. Derry BT51 4EU,* ☎ *028/7086–8241,* FAX *028/7086–8365. 6 rooms with bath. Dining room. MC, V. Closed Nov.–Feb.*

Upperlands

㉙ *32 km (20 mi) south of Coleraine, 56 km (35 mi) northwest of Belfast.*

Upstream from Coleraine, the River Bann—rich in eels for roasting and smoking and in salmon for poaching—flows out of Lough Neagh. On its left bank are the towns and fortifications of the 17th-century Planters, built by London's Livery Companies, whose descendants developed the linen industry. In the tiny town of Upperlands, visitors can tour **William Clark and Sons,** a working linen mill where age-old wooden machinery beetles (polishes) threads for the linen linings of suits for England's Royals. There is also a small linen museum. ⊠ *Maghera,* ☎ *028/7964–2214.* ⊡ *U.K.£1.* ⊙ *Mon.–Thurs. 9–5, Fri. 9–noon.*

Dining and Lodging

$$$ ✕⊞ **Ardtara House.** A 19th-century Victorian home built by a de-
★ scendant of the founder of the town's first linen mill, Ardtara is the North's finest country-house hotel. The gorgeously furnished terra-cotta and pink drawing room, with original plaster moldings and a marble fireplace, looks out on the wide front lawn and tennis court. The eight large bedrooms are furnished with antiques; each has a fireplace, as do some of the elegantly appointed marble bathrooms. The hotel's restaurant is in the former snooker room, with dark paneled walls, a wall-papered hunting scene, and a huge skylight. Either peat-smoked rack of lamb with champ and rosemary gravy, or salmon with champagne sauce, is a stellar entrée. You'll feel the calm and relaxed atmosphere Fenton and the rest of the staff strive for the moment you walk in, and you won't want to leave it behind. ⊠ *8 Gorteade Rd., Co. Derry BT46 5SA,* ☎ *028/7964–4490,* FAX *028/7964–5080. 8 rooms with bath. Restaurant, tennis court, meeting room. AE, MC, V.*

Limavady

㉚ *21 km (13 mi) west of Coleraine, 34 km (21 mi) northwest of Upperlands, 27 km (17 mi) east of Derry.*

In 1851, at No. 51 on Limavady's Georgian main street, Jane Ross wrote down the tune played by a traveling fiddler and called it "Londonderry Air," better known now as "Danny Boy." While staying at an inn on Ballyclose Street, William Thackeray (1811–63) wrote his rather lustful poem "Peg of Limavaddy" about a barmaid. Among the many Americans descended from Ulster emigrants was President James Monroe, whose relatives came from the Limavady area.

Dining and Lodging

$$$$ ✕🏨 **Radisson Roe Park Hotel & Golf Resort.** One of the North's most deluxe resorts, the Radisson rests amid 155 acres of countryside on the banks of the River Roe. Bedrooms are decorated in cream and blue and have satellite TV and other amenities. Guests have a variety of dining options: the Courtyard restaurant is formal and international; the Coach House, an American brasserie, is a relaxed place where golfers congregate; and O'Cahan's bar takes its name from a local chieftain besieged on a riverside promontory, whose Irish wolfhound leapt an impossible chasm to bring relief—doubtless an inspiration to golfers flagging at the ninth. ⊠ *Roe Park, Co. Derry BT49 9LB,* ☎ *028/7772–2222,* 𝖥𝖠𝖷 *028/7772–2313. 64 rooms with bath. 2 restaurants, 2 bars, indoor pool, beauty salon, sauna, steam room, 18-hole golf course, exercise room, horseback riding, fishing, baby-sitting, meeting rooms. AE, DC, MC, V.* 🐾

Derry

③①   *109 km (68 mi) north of Belfast, 53 km (33 mi) north of Omagh, 27 km (17 mi) southwest of Limavady.*

Derry's name is a shadow of its history. Those in favor of British rule call the city Londonderry, its old Plantation-period name; the "London" part was tacked on in 1613 after the Flight of the Earls (☞ Rathmullan *in* Chapter 7), and the city and county were handed over to the Corporation of London, which represented London's merchants. They brought in a large population of English and Scottish Protestant settlers, built new towns for them, and reconstructed Derry within the city walls, which survive almost unchanged to this day. Both before then and after, Derry's sturdy ramparts have withstood many fierce attacks and have never been breached, which explains the city's coy sobriquet, "The Maiden City." The most famous attack was the historic siege of 1688–89, after 13 apprentice boys slammed the city gates in the face of the Catholic king James II. The inhabitants, who held out for 105 days and were reduced to eating dogs, cats, and laundry starch, nevertheless helped to secure the British throne for the Protestant king William III.

Whatever you choose to call it, Derry is one of Northern Ireland's most underrated towns. If Belfast was the Beethoven of Northern Ireland, Derry would be the Mozart—fey, witty, and a touch surreal. Despite the derelict factories along the banks of the River Foyle and a reputation marred by Troubles-related violence, the city has worked hard to move forward. Such efforts show in the quaint, bustling town center, encircled by 20-ft-tall, 17th-century walls. The city's winding streets slope down to the Foyle, radiating from the Diamond—Derry's historic center where St. Columba founded his first monastery in 546. Fine Georgian and Victorian buildings sit side by side with gaily painted Victorian-fronted shops, cafés, and pubs.

Derry, incidentally, has links to Boston that date as far back as the 17th and 18th centuries, when many Derry residents escaped their hardships at home by emigrating to that U.S. city and beyond. Aviation fans, take note: Derry was where Amelia Earhart touched down, on May 21, 1932, after her historic solo flight across the Atlantic. Local lore has it that the first man to reach her airplane greeted her in typically unfazed Derry fashion: "Aye, and what do you want, then?"

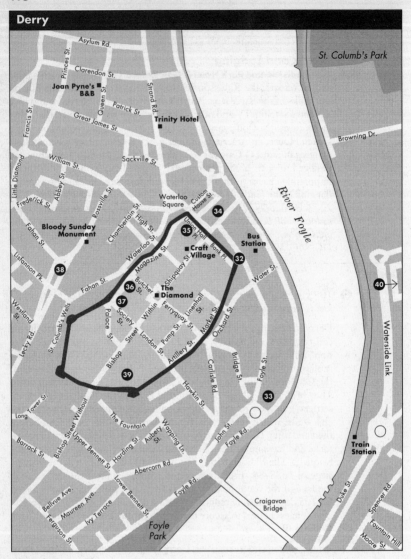

ONE LAST TRAVEL TIP:

Pack an easy way to reach the world.

MCI WORLDCOM   WORLDPHONE

123 456 7891 2345
J.D. SMITH

Wherever you travel, the MCI WorldCom Card℠ is the easiest way to stay in touch. You can use it to call to and from more than 125 countries worldwide. And you can earn bonus miles every time you use your card. So go ahead, travel the world. MCI WorldCom℠ makes it even more rewarding. For additional access codes, visit **www.wcom.com/worldphone**.

MCI WORLDCOM.

EASY TO CALL WORLDWIDE

1. Just dial the WorldPhone® access number of the country you're calling from.
2. Dial or give the operator your MCI WorldCom Card number.
3. Dial or give the number you're calling.

Country	Access Number
Austria ◆	0800-200-235
Belgium ◆	0800-10012
Czech Republic ◆	00-42-000112
Denmark ◆	8001-0022
Estonia ★	800-800-1122
Finland ◆	08001-102-80
France ◆	0-800-99-0019
Germany	0800-888-8000
Greece ◆	00-800-1211
Hungary ◆	06▼-800-01411
Ireland	1-800-55-1001
Italy ◆	172-1022
Luxembourg	8002-0112
Netherlands ◆	0800-022-91-22
Norway ◆	800-19912
Poland ❖	800-111-21-22
Portugal ❖	800-800-123
Romania ❖	01-800-1800
Russia ◆ ❖	747-3322
Spain	900-99-0014
Sweden ◆	020-795-922
Switzerland ◆	0800-89-0222
Ukraine ❖	8▼10-013
United Kingdom	0800-89-0222
Vatican City	172-1022

◆ Public phones may require deposit of coin or phone card for dial tone.   ★ Not available from public pay phones.
▼ Wait for second dial tone.   ❖ Limited availability.

EARN FREQUENT FLIER MILES

Bureau de change

Cambio

外国為替

In this city, you can find money on almost any street.

NO-FEE FOREIGN EXCHANGE

The Chase Manhattan Bank has over 80 convenient
locations near New York City destinations such as:

      Times Square
      Rockefeller Center
      Empire State Building
      2 World Trade Center
      United Nations Plaza

Exchange any of 75 foreign currencies

 CHASE

THE RIGHT RELATIONSHIP IS EVERYTHING.®

To really experience Derry's history, stroll along the parapet walkway atop the ramparts of the **city walls,** built between 1614 and 1618 and one of the few intact sets of city walls in Europe. Pierced by eight gates (originally four) and as much as 30 ft thick, the gray stone ramparts are only 1½ km (1 mi) all around; today most of the life of the town actually takes place outside of them. You can walk the walls on your own, following the sites below in a counterclockwise direction; or, from June through September, you can join one of the guided walks from the city's new Tourist Information Centre (☞ *below*).

The **Tourist Information Centre** is the most strategic place to start your tour of the city, whether by yourself or on one of the guided walks. Tours are currently run by the erudite Tommy Carlin and last just under two hours. ⊠ *44 Foyle St.,* ☎ *028/7126–7284 or 028/7137–7577,* FAX *028/7137–7992.* ☛ *Free, tours U.K.£3.25.* ⊙ *May–Sept., weekdays 9–7, Sat. 10–6; Oct.–Apr., weekdays 9–5, Sat. 10–5.*

Guildhall, at the entrance to the old city, is an ornate Victorian stone and sandstone building dating from 1890. It has impressive stained-glass windows that were actually shattered by two IRA bombs in June 1977 and rebuilt by the Campbell's firm in Belfast, who had installed the original windows in 1890 and still had the plans—now that's a filing system! The Guildhall, where Derry city council meets monthly, is the site of musical recitals and heated political rallies. ⊠ *Guildhall Sq.,* ☎ *028/7137–7335.* ☛ *Free.* ⊙ *Weekdays 9–5; guided tours July–Aug. and by appointment.*

The **Tower Museum,** which chronicles the history of Derry, is inside the reconstructed O'Doherty's Tower, which was originally built in 1615 by the O'Dohertys for their overlords, the O'Donnells, in lieu of tax payments. Highlights include a small section on the eccentric Bishop Frederick Augustus Hervey (1763–1803), who livened up Sunday by making his curates sprint naked along nearby Magilligan Strand while he whipped them. The vivid "Story of Derry" exhibition covers the city's history, from its origins as a monastic settlement in an oak grove and including the beginnings of the Troubles in 1969, after years of institutionalized discrimination in jobs and public housing (a well-known Derry innuendo is that the skeleton in the city's coat of arms was actually a Catholic waiting for a house). It is, in fact, Walter de Burgo, a forebear of singer Chris de Burgh, who was starved to death in the dungeons of Greencastle after a dispute with his cousin William. A small but poignant exhibition details the history of the Troubles in the city, while a large new exhibition on the Spanish Armada was opened in autumn 2000. There's also an excellent virtual museum on-site celebrating the life and legacy of St. Columb. Call ahead if you would like to visit the museum on a Sunday, as Sunday opening was under consideration for 2001 at press time. ⊠ *Union Hall Pl.,* ☎ *028/7137–2411.* ☛ *U.K.£3.75.* ⊙ *Sept.–June, Tues.–Sat. 10–5; July–Aug., Mon.–Sat. 10–5.*

The **Calgach Centre** is the home of the **Fifth Province,** an inspired high-tech celebration of the city's history from its earliest days, as well as its importance in creating the Irish diaspora of 17 million people. You begin by sitting on a Neolithic mound while the voice of veteran actor Richard Harris intones in a ghostly voice the history of Derry, from the sylvan oak grove beloved by the chieftain Calgach right up to the city's finest hour, when local boy Bernardo O'Higgins was made president of Chile. From there it's into a comfortable armchair for a virtual-reality time trip through the coming of the Vikings and the Normans, the flight of the Irish nobility from English persecution in 1601, and the famine of 1845–49, when 1½ million emigrated to the United States and a million more died of starvation. It's moving stuff, grippingly presented. The center is also the home for touring exhibitions. Call for details. ⊠ *4–22 Butcher St.,* ☎ *028/7137–3177.* 🎫 *U.K.£3.* ⊙ *Mon.–Thurs. 9–5:30, Fri. 9–5; shows weekdays at 11:30 and 2:30.*

❸❼ The Scottish baronial edifice, **Apprentice Boys' Memorial Hall,** built in 1867 and extended in 1933 to house the exclusively Protestant organization (which was set up in 1715 to honor the memory of the 13 apprentices who slammed the gate in the face of the Catholic king James in December 1688 and began the famous siege), was only recently opened to the public. Inside you will find the initiation room, in which 20,000 men have sworn allegiance to the code of the organization formed to uphold the defiant spirit of those original 13. An upstairs bar and dance hall has walls lined with 12 banners representing the lost tribes of Israel. In the ladies' room, one of the more curious sights is a photograph of a splendid Italian matriarch wearing the sash of fellow Protestant organization, the Orange Order. She is, in fact, *Signora* E. B. Cabenna, the descendant of one of the Italian workmen brought over by the magnificently eccentric Bishop Frederick Augustus Hervey (☞ *above*) to work on his churches. Naturally, the bishop couldn't have Catholics rebuilding Protestant churches, so the workmen were forced to convert before taking up their tools. A magnificently chaotic museum has shelves and glass cases filled to the brim with furniture and firearms, books and bombs, and swords and sculpture. It's a wonderful glimpse into a hitherto closed world. Roaring Meg, one of the original cannons from the 1688–89 siege, has been moved from the city walls to the hall. ⊠ *Society St.,* ☎ *No phone.* 🎫 *Donations accepted.* ⊙ *Tours by arrangement only. Call Derry TIC 028/7126–7284 or 028/7137–7577.*

Walker Memorial, a statue of the governor of Derry during the siege, is a symbol of Derry's divided nature. It was blown up by the IRA in 1973, and the story goes that the statue's head rolled down the hill into the Catholic Bogside, where it was captured by a local youth. He ransomed it back to the Protestants for a small fortune, and today it sits on the shoulders of a replica of the original statue beside the Apprentice Boys' Memorial Hall.

❸❽ At **Free Derry Corner** (⊠ Fahan and Rossville Sts.) is the white gable wall where Catholics defiantly painted the slogan "You are now entering Free Derry" as a declaration of a zone from which police and the British Army were banned until 1972, when the army broke down the barricades. That same year, 13 civil rights marchers were shot by British soldiers in an event that rankles Catholics to this day. "Bloody Sunday," as it became known, is commemorated by the mural of a civil rights march.

❸❾ **St. Columb's Cathedral,** built in 1633 in simple Planter's Gothic style, was the first Protestant cathedral built in the United Kingdom after the reformation. In the vestibule is the 270-pound mortar ball, which during the siege was fired over the wall with an invitation to surrender sent by King James. Legend has it that when they read it, every man, woman, and child in the city rushed to the walls and shouted, "No surrender!"—a Protestant battle cry to this day. In addition to its intricate, corbeled roof and austere spire, the church contains the oldest and largest bells in Ireland (dating from the 1620s), and it is a treasure house of Derry Protestant emblems, memorials, and relics from the 1688–89 siege. The **Chapter House Museum** has the oldest surviving map of Derry (from 1600) and the Bible owned by Governor George Walker (☞ *above*) during the siege. Nearby is the spot where in 1870 Cecilia Alexander wrote the hymn "There Is a Green Hill Far Away." ⊠ *London St., off Bishop St.,* ☎ *028/7126–7313.* 🎫 *U.K.£1.* ⊙ *Apr.–Oct., daily 9–5; Nov.–Mar., daily 9–1 and 2–4.*

④ Across the River Foyle from the city walls, the **Workhouse** was built in 1832 to alleviate poverty but became the end of the road for people who had tried in vain to make their lives better. During the famine years (1845–49), the city was the main emigration port for Northern Ireland, and many families came to Derry hoping to get on a boat; instead, unable to afford the trip, they ended up in the Workhouse in utter despair. Inside, families were separated, and this was often the last time children saw their parents alive. From the beginning to end of the famine, 1½ million people left Ireland and 1 million died.

Many of the descendants of those who left, of course, came back during the Second World War, when thousands of U.S. servicemen arrived in the city in 1942 to turn it into a base for the Battle of the Atlantic. The **Workhouse Museum,** on the top two floors of the Workhouse, chronicles the story of that battle, from the Yanks' arrival in the January rain (which prompted one of them to ask if the city's barrage balloons were actually there to stop the place from sinking) through the end of the war when 64 U-boats lined up in the harbor to surrender, like a convention of retired sharks, to 1946, when the city's biggest export was G.I. brides. The museum also details life in the Workhouse and has some thoughtful exhibits about famine in general. There is a space for traveling exhibitions that change regularly; call for details. ✉ *23 Glendermott Rd.,* ☎ *028/7131–8328.* ⌧ *Free.* ☺ *Mon.–Sat. 10–4:30; tours by arrangement.*

NEED A BREAK? Derry is packed with agreeable pubs, but **Badgers** (✉ 16 Orchard St., ☎ 028/7136–0763) has the best range of simple wholesome food. Plus it's the watering hole for local media types, artists, writers, and musicians.The **Boston Tea Party** (✉ 10 and 13–15 Craft Village, ☎ 028/7126–9667), a small tea shop down an alley nearly opposite the Richmond Shopping Centre on Shipquay Street, is a nice spot for a snack or lunch break. If you're feeling homesick for an American accent, head for the **Gravy Bistro** (✉ 32 Carlisle Rd., ☎ 028/7136–0300), where home-cooked lunches and dinners have French and Italian leanings; there's no license, so bring your own bottle. **McGilloway's** (✉ 165 Strand Rd., ☎ 028/7126–2050) is an unpretentious but excellent seafood restaurant.

Dining and Lodging

$–$$ ✗ **Oyster's.** All aboard for this cozy hillside restaurant with a nautical theme. Starters include chorizo and linguine or seafood chowder with smoked bacon. Standout mains are Thai seared salmon with egg noodles, sea bass with smoked salmon, vanilla and leek mash, and peppered lamb with rosemary and cherry tomatoes. Upstairs, there's a more informal bistro, which does great fish-and-chips. ✉ *Spencer Rd.,* ☎ *028/7134–4875. MC, V.*

$$$ ✗▥ **Beech Hill.** Past a fairy-tale gatehouse and set among clumps of beech trees, streams, and a duck pond, Beech Hill is a grand 1729 country home very much attuned to the present. Chef Adrian Catterall draws many Northwest politicos, with Eurocrats in tow, who appreciate his sophisticated menu. The vast honeymoon suite, with a four-poster bed, overlooks the gardens. The house is 3 km (2 mi) south of the city, left off A6. ✉ *32 Ardmore Rd., Co. Derry BT47 3QP,* ☎ *028/7134–9279,* ℻ *028/7134–5366. 27 rooms with bath. Restaurant, bar, hot tub, sauna, exercise room, meeting rooms. AE, MC, V.*

$$$ ✗▥ **The Trinity.** On the banks of the River Foyle, past the Guildhall and not far outside the city walls, the cool, stylish, and friendly Trinity is a very reasonably priced city-center hotel. The spacious bedrooms are decorated with rosewood and several hues of green; amenities in-

clude coffeemakers and satellite TV. The hotel is home to a number of watering holes: Nolan's Snug, the European-style café-bar, and the hotel's bistro restaurant, which offers such specialties as scallop of pork stuffed with wild mushrooms and Parmesan. The roof garden makes a pleasant sanctuary. ✉ 22–24 Strand Rd., Co. Derry BT48 7 AB, ☎ 028/7127–1271, FAX 028/7127–1277. 40 rooms with bath, 3 suites. Restaurant, 3 bars, meeting rooms. AE, DC, MC, V.

$ 🏠 **Joan Pyne's.** Many of the architectural sights in the city are in the area around Joan Pyne's, from art deco to neo-Gothic. No. 16 Queen Street was originally a Victorian merchant's family home built to Georgian proportions, then a rectory and bank before Joan began the process of turning it into the city's grandest guest house. Previous guests include the late Hurd Hatfield, star of the movie *The Picture of Dorian Gray.* Joan also owns a similar but smaller house three minutes' walk away, which serves as an annex. ✉ 16 Queen St., Co. Derry BT48 7EQ, ☎ 028/7126–4223, FAX 028/7126–6913. 12 rooms, 4 with bath. MC, V.

Nightlife and the Arts

ART GALLERIES
The **Context Gallery** (✉ 5–7 Artillery St., ☎ 028/7137–3538) shows works by up-and-coming Irish and international artists. The **McGilloway Gallery** (✉ Shipquay St., ☎ 028/7136–6011) stocks a broad selection of representational modern Irish art. Owner Ken McGilloway offers wine on Friday evenings until 9 PM.The **Orchard Gallery** (✉ Orchard St., ☎ 028/7126–9675) has gained a Europe-wide reputation in the fields of political and conceptual art.

The **Verbal Arts Centre** (✉ Mall Wall, ☎ 028/7126–6946) hosts regular exhibitions and storytelling events, re-creating the great old Irish tradition of fireside tales.

PUBS AND CLUBS
The **Gweedore Bar** (✉ 16 Waterloo St., ☎ 028/7126–3513) is a favorite for hip-hop and house music. Traditional Irish music can be found at **Peadar O'Donnell's** (✉ 63 Waterloo St., ☎ 028/7137–2318). **Squire's Nightclub** (✉ 33 Shipquay St., ☎ 028/7126–6017) is the place for disco.

THEATER AND OPERA
Brian Friel, of *Philadelphia Here I Come* fame, premiered much of his work in the Guildhall (☞ above) through the **Field Day Theatre Company** (✉ Foyle Arts Centre, Lawrence Hill, ☎ 028/7136–0196). Other theater productions take place at the **Foyle Arts Centre** (✉ Lawrence Hill, ☎ 028/7126–6657), the **Playhouse** (✉ 5–7 Artillery St., ☎ 028/ 7126–8027), and the **Rialto Entertainment Center** (✉ 5 Market St., ☎ 028/7126–0516).

Shopping
Shopping in town is generally low-key and unpretentious, but some gems of Irish craftsmanship can be found here. Stroll up Shipquay Street to find small stores and an indoor shopping center. Where Shipquay reaches the Diamond, you'll find **Austin's** (✉ 2 the Diamond, ☎ 028/ 7126–1817), a large store stocking Tyrone crystal, Belleek china, and other quality Northern Irish goods. **Bookworm** (✉ 16 Bishop St., ☎ 028/ 7128–2727) is "the best bookshop in Ireland," according to writer Nuala O Faoláin. Off Shipquay Street, the **Derry Craft Village** has a romantic maze of shops, residential apartments, and workshops in an 18th-century setting, complete with crafts demonstrations, costumes, and, of course, souvenirs galore. Stop at the **Donegal Shop** (✉ 8 Shipquay St., ☎ 028/7126–6928) for Irish linen, tweeds, and woolens. The Donegal designer fashions of **Edel MacBride** (✉ 2 Castle Gate, ☎ 028/7126– 6166) are worn by Jane Seymour, Olivia Newton-John, and Hillary Rod-

ham Clinton. **Thomas the Goldsmith** (✉ 7 Pump St., ☎ 028/7137–4549) stocks exquisite work by international jewelry designers.

En Route From Derry, head across County Tyrone toward Enniskillen. Take A5 south via **Strabane**, birthplace of the surreal novelist Brian O'Nolan, alias Flann O'Brien. It has the well-preserved, 18th-century **Gray's Print Shop** (✉ 49 Main St., ☎ 028/7188–4094). John Dunlap (1746–1812), who apprenticed here as a printer before emigrating to Philadelphia, founded America's first daily newspaper, the *Philadelphia Packet,* in 1771, and was also the man who printed and distributed the American Declaration of Independence. James Wilson, grandfather of President Woodrow Wilson, also emigrated from here. The original **Wilson family home** a simple thatched cottage, still with much of the original 18th-century furniture, survives at Dergalt, southeast of Strabane and signposted on the B536 to Plumbridge. It can be visited by knocking at the farmhouse next door, still owned and worked by the Wilson family. ✉ *Ligford Rd., ☎ 028/8224–3292. ☉ July–Aug., Tues.–Sun. 2–5.*

For a delightfully rustic alternative route, drive along the minor road B48, which skirts the foot of the **Sperrin Mountains** and reaches all the way to Omagh. Or, you may want to head north from Derry to the **Inishowen Peninsula,** the northernmost point of Ireland (☞ Chapter 7).

AROUND COUNTIES TYRONE, FERMANAGH, ARMAGH, AND DOWN

During the worst of the Troubles, parts of these four counties that border the Republic were known as bandit country. But now visitors can enjoy a worry-free trip through the calm countryside and stop in at some very "Ulster" towns, distinct from the rest of Ireland. The area includes the great houses of Castle Coole and Florence Court; the ancient, ecclesiastical city of Armagh; and the wild Sperrin Mountains.

Ulster-American Folk Park and Ulster History Park

Folk Park: 51 km (31½ mi) south of Derry; History Park: 6 km (4 mi) northeast of the Folk Park.

41 The **Ulster-American Folk Park** has been designed to re-create a Tyrone village of two centuries ago, a log-built American settlement of the same period, and the docks and ships that the emigrants to America would have used. The centerpiece of the park is an old whitewashed cottage, now a museum, which is the ancestral home of Andrew Mellon (1855–1937), the U.S. millionaire banker and philanthropist. Another thatched cottage is a reconstruction of the boyhood home of Archbishop John Hughes, founder of New York's St. Patrick's Cathedral. Exhibitions trace the contribution of the Northern Irish people to American history. The park also features a crafts shop and café. ✉ *Camphill,* ☎ *028/8224–3292.* ▦ *U.K.£4. ☉ Apr.–Sept., Mon.–Sat. 10:30–6, Sun. 11–6:30; Oct.–Mar., weekdays 10:30–5; last admission 1½ hrs before closing.*

42 The **Ulster History Park** documents Irish history from the first known settlers to the 12th-century arrival of the Normans. The open-air displays include lath and rawhide huts, primitive farms and stockades, a round tower, and an oratory. Hours are identical to those at the Ulster-American Folk Park (☞ *above*). ✉ *Cullion, Lislap, Gortin, off B48,* ☎ *028/8264–8188.* ▦ *U.K.£3.*

Omagh

43 km (27 mi) northeast of Enniskillen, 7½ km (4½ mi) south of the Ulster-American Folk Park.

Omagh, the county town of Tyrone, lies close to the Sperrin Mountains, with the River Strule to the north. Playwright Brian Friel was born here. Sadly, it is more recently known as the scene of the worst atrocity of the Troubles, when an IRA bomb killed 29 people in August 1998. The town has two places of worship—a Church of Ireland church and a Catholic double-spire church.

En Route North of Omagh the country is pretty and rustic, with small farm villages within sight of the bare Sperrin Mountains. Heading east from the town on A505, you'll discover a pensive landscape of moist heath and bog. Left of the road, **Beaghmore** is a strange Bronze Age ceremonial site preserved for millennia beneath a blanket of peat. It has seven stone circles and 12 cairns. Farther along, A505 reaches **Wellbrook Beetling Mill,** where locally made linen was first "beetled," that is, pounded with noisy, water-driven hammers to give it a smooth finish. The mill is kept in working order by the National Trust. ✉ *Corkhill,* ☎ *028/8675–1735.* 🎟 *U.K.£1.60.* ☉ *Apr.–May and Sept., weekends 2–6; Easter and June–Aug., Wed.–Mon. 2–6.*

About 6½ km (4 mi) beyond Wellbrook is **Cookstown,** an odd Plantation village with a single, broad main street more than 1½ km (1 mi) long. From here, head down on the back lanes to **Lough Neagh,** at 396 square km (153 square mi) the largest lake in the British Isles, noted for an abundance of eels. On its shore at **Ardboe** stands a remarkable 10th-century high cross more than 18 ft tall and richly carved with biblical scenes.

Belleek

 41½ km (26 mi) southwest of Omagh.

The old town of Belleek sits on the northwestern edge of Lower Lough Erne and is home to the world-famous Belleek Pottery. On the riverbank stands the visitor center of **Belleek Pottery Ltd.,** producers of Belleek chinaware and porcelain. Here a factory, a showroom, a permanent exhibition, a Belleek pottery museum, and a café are all under one roof. On weekdays, a tour of the factory starts every half hour. You'll find hardly any noise coming from machinery in the workshops, however—everything at Belleek is handmade, using the exact process that was invented in 1857. The showroom is filled with beautiful gifts, but prices are high: a cup and saucer set costs about U.K.£25–U.K.£30, and a bowl in a basket-weave style (very typical of Belleek) could cost you several hundred pounds. ☎ *028/6865–8501.* 🎟 *U.K.£2.* ☉ *Shop and showroom Apr.– June and Sept., weekdays 9–6, Sat. 10–6, Sun. 2–6; July–Aug., weekdays 9–6, Sat. 10–6, Sun. 11–6; Oct.–Mar., weekdays 9–5:30. Tours Mon.– Thurs. 9:15–12:15 and 2:15–4:15, Fri. 9:15–3:15.*

Lough Erne

131 km (82 mi) west of Belfast, 100 km (62 mi) south of Derry.

On the journey beside Lough Erne, pause to catch your breath while eating up the lovely view of green hills extending down to the still lake water.

Castle Archdale Country Park has a lakeside marina, an open-air country museum, and a World War II exhibition featuring the Battle of the

Atlantic. ⊠ *Signposted down a narrow road about 6½ km (4 mi) from Kesh,* ☎ *028/6862–1588.* 🎟 *Free.* ☉ *Call for hrs.*

Lake and River Cruising

Inland cruising on the Erne waterway—777 square km (300 square mi) of lakes and rivers—is one of the North's major treats. Upper and Lower Lough Erne are enclosed by some of Ireland's finest scenery and are studded with more than 100 little islands. Out on the lakes and the River Erne, which links them, you'll have all the solitude you want, but you'll find company at lough-side hostelries. To hire a boat, contact **Erne Charter Boat Association** (⊠ Belleek Charter Cruising, Erne Gateway Centre, Corry, Belleek, ☎ 028/6865–8027). Expect to pay at least U.K.£300 to hire a four-berth cruiser for two or three nights.

White Island and Devenish Island

4 km (2½ mi) and 16 km (10 mi) north of Enniskillen.

From Castle Archdale, a ferry (☎ 028/6862–1333) runs from June through September, Tuesday through Sunday (U.K.£3), taking passengers
44 to see the carved Celtic figures on **White Island.** After you drive 13 km (8 mi) farther from Castle Archdale Park, where B82 joins A32, a small sign shows the way to catch the little boat (☎ 028/6632–3110) that runs from April through September, Tuesday through Sunday (U.K.£2.25)
45 over to **Devenish Island.** The extensive but ruined 12th-century monastery on Devenish features Ireland's best example of a round tower—it is 82 ft tall—and a richly carved high cross.

Enniskillen

46 *43 km (27 mi) southwest of Omagh, 77 km (48 mi) west of Armagh.*

Enniskillen is the pleasant, smart-looking capital of County Fermanagh and the only place of any size in the county. Its town center is strikingly situated on an island in the River Erne between Upper and Lower Lough Erne. The principal thoroughfares, Townhall and High streets, are crowded with old-style pubs and rows of redbrick Georgian flats. The spires of the daunting 19th-century St. Michael's and St. MacArtin's cathedrals, both on Church Street, preside over the town.

The waterfront **Enniskillen Castle** is one of the best-preserved monuments in the North. Built by the Maguire clan in 1670, this stronghold houses the local history collection of the **Fermanagh County Museum** and the polished paraphernalia of the **Royal Inniskilling Fusiliers Regimental Museum.** A **Heritage Centre** also stands within the curtilage of the castle. ⊠ *Castlebarracks,* ☎ *028/6632–5000.* 🎟 *U.K.£2.* ☉ *Mon. 2–5, Tues.–Fri. 10–5. Closed last wk in Dec.*

At the riverside, the 16th-century **Water Gate** is handsomely turreted, a protection against enemies of the town.

Beyond the West Bridge lies **Portora Royal School,** established in 1608 by King James I. Its grounds contain the ruins of Portora Castle. Among the writers educated here were Samuel Beckett and Oscar Wilde, the pride of the school until his trial for homosexuality.

Among the several relaxed and welcoming old pubs in Enniskillen's town center, the one with the most appeal is **Blake's of the Hollow** (⊠ 6 Church St., ☎ 028/6632–2143) on the main street, a place hardly altered since it opened in 1887. Its name derives from the fact that the heart of the town lies in a slight hollow and the pub's landlord is named William Blake. Don't ask if he's related to the great poet of the same name—everybody does, and he isn't!

OFF THE
BEATEN PATH

FLORENCE COURT – Set within an enchanted park—it is reputed that you can hear the "song of the little people" here—this is one of the most impressive of the North's grand Anglo-Irish mansions. Built around 1730 for John Cole, father of the first earl of Enniskillen, the three-story Palladian Florence Court was struck by fire in the 1950s; however, a loving restoration has replicated much of the abundant rococo plasterwork in the dining room, Venetian room, and, particularly, the famous staircase, all ascribed to Robert West, one of Dublin's most famous stuccadores (plaster workers). ⊠ *11 km (7 mi) south of Enniskillen on A4 and A32,* ☎ *028/6634–8249.* ✉ *U.K.£2.80.* ☉ *Mansion Easter, Apr., and Sept., weekends 1–6; May–Aug., Wed.–Mon. 1–6; grounds year-round, 10 AM–1 hr before dusk.*

Castle Coole

★ ㊼ *3 km (2 mi) southeast of Enniskillen.*

In the 18th century and through most of the 19th, the Loughs of Erne and their environs were remote places—far from Ireland's bustling cities. But it was just this isolated green and watery countryside that attracted the Anglo-Irish gentry. They built grand houses—among them, Castle Coole is widely considered to be the finest. This "uncommonly perfect" mansion (to quote the eminent architectural historian Desmond Guinness) stands in its own landscaped oak woods and parkland at the end of a long, tree-lined driveway. Although the Irish architect Richard Johnston made the original drawings in the 1790s and was responsible for the foundation, the castle was, for all intents and purposes, the work of James Wyatt, commissioned by the first Earl of Belmore. One of the best-known architects of his time, Wyatt, who was based in London, did much work in Ireland, but he only visited the country once, and he never came here. Alexander Stewart was the resident builder-architect who oversaw much of the building's construction. The architect wasn't the only imported element; in fact, much of Castle Coole was transported over from England, including the main facade, which is clad in Portland stone shipped from Dorset to Ballyshannon and then hauled over land by horse and cart. And what a facade it is—in perfect symmetry, white colonnaded wings extend from either side of the mansion's three-story, nine-bay center block, with a pedimented central portico. It is perhaps the apotheosis in Ireland of the 18th century's reverence for the Greeks, and it bears a touch of Palladian sensibility.

Inside, the house is remarkably well preserved; most of the lavish plasterwork and original furnishings are still in place. On its completion in September 1798, the construction had cost U.K.£70,000 and the furnishings another U.K.£22,000, compared to the U.K.£6 million cost of a restoration in 1995–96, during which anything not in keeping with the original design was removed. The saloon is one of the finest rooms in the house, with a vast expanse of oak flooring, gilded Regency furniture, and gray scagliola pilasters with Corinthian capitals. The present earl of Belmore still lives on the estate and uses one wing of the house. ⊠ *Dublin Rd. (A4),* ☎ *028/6632–2690.* ✉ *U.K.£3.* ☉ *Apr.–May and Sept., weekends 1–6; June–Aug., Fri.–Wed. 1–6; last tour 5:15 PM; Oct.–Mar., prearranged group bookings only.*

Lodging

$$$ ▣ **Blessingbourne.** This faux Elizabethan, Victorian-era house, with mullioned windows, stables, and carriage museum, sits on a pretty circular lake. Meals can be eaten with the Lowry family, the proprietors.

One of the bedrooms has a four-poster bed. A visit makes the diversion to Fivemiletown—so named as it is five Irish miles from anywhere—worthwhile. ⊠ *Fivemiletown, Co. Tyrone BT75 0QS,* ☎ *028/8952–1221. 4 rooms without bath. Dining room. No credit cards.*

Outdoor Activities & Sports

If you're over in the Enniskillen/Lough Erne area, the **Ulster Lakeland Equestrian Park** (⊠ Necarne Castle, Irvinestown, ☎ 028/6862–1919) can teach you to ride or take you on a pony trek through the 200 rolling acres of this Gothic-looking castle's rolling parkland. Rates begin at U.K.£8 for 30 minutes. There are rooms to stay in, a bar, and a restaurant.

Armagh

48 *64 km (40 mi) west of Belfast, 77 km (48 mi) east of Enniskillen.*

The small but ancient ecclesiastical city of Armagh, despite the pleasing Georgian terraces around the elegant Mall east of the town center, can seem drab. Having suffered as a trouble spot in the sectarian conflict, though, it is now the scene of some spirited and sympathetic renovation. Here St. Patrick founded a church, and the town has remained a religious center to the present day; in fact, *two* Armagh cathedrals are dedicated to Ireland's patron saint. Despite the 1921 partition of Ireland into two parts, the seat of the Catholic Archbishop of All Ireland remains here, as does the seat of the Archbishop of the Anglican Church of Ireland.

Armagh's main attraction is the **Astronomy Centre and Planetarium.** It contains models of spacecraft, video shows of the sky, and hands-on computer displays. The **Earthorium exhibition** explores the world from three levels—its interior, surface, and atmosphere. The outdoor, 30-acre **AstroPark** has a model solar system. A **16-inch telescope** is open two nights per month, September through April (call for specific dates). **Robinson Dome,** also known as "the 10-inch dome" for the 1875 Grub telescope it houses, is open in spring and summer months. ⊠ *College Hill,* ☎ *028/3752–3689.* ⊠ *AstroPark and Robinson Dome free; Earthorium U.K.£1; special shows and other exhibitions U.K.£3.70.* ⊙ *Earthorium and AstroPark weekdays 10–4:45, weekends 1:15–4:45; Robinson Dome Apr.–Sept., weekdays 9:30–4:30.*

Dedicated to St. Patrick, the pale limestone, Victorian-Gothic **Catholic Cathedral,** whose two spires rise above a hill at the north end of Armagh, is best seen from a short distance, allowing the viewer to take in the full majesty of it.

Near the town center, a squat, battlemented tower identifies the **Protestant cathedral,** in simple, early 19th-century Perpendicular-Gothic style. It stands on the site of much older churches and contains several relics of Armagh's long history, including sculpted, pre-Christian idols. This cathedral claims to be the burial place of Brian Boru, the great High King—that is, king of all Ireland—who visited Armagh in 1004 and was received with great ceremony. Ten years later, at the Battle of Clontarf, he drove the Vikings out of Ireland but was killed after the battle was won. ⊠ *Abbey St..* ⊠ *Free.* ⊙ *Call for hrs.*

Past the 13th-century Franciscan friary ruins, in the stables of the former archbishop's demesne, the **Palace Stables Heritage Centre** presents a diorama of everyday life—upstairs and downstairs—in the 18th-century days of the extremely wealthy Baron Rokeby, Church of Ireland Archbishop Richard Robinson. He commissioned local architect Francis Johnston, who had designed much of Georgian Dublin, to create a new Armagh out of the slums into which it had degenerated. The archbishop gave the city a clean water supply and a sewer system, then turned the city's racecourse into an elegant mall. He paved and lit the streets; financed improvements to the Bishop's Palace and the Protestant cathedral; and endowed the public library, the observatory, the Royal School, and the county infirmary. ⊠ *Palace Demesne, Friary Rd., ☎ 028/3752–9629. ⊡ U.K.£3.50. ☉ Apr.–Aug., Mon.–Sat. 10–5, Sun. 1–6; Sept.–Mar., Mon.–Sat. 10–5, Sun. 2–5.*

Just outside Armagh, **Navan Fort** is Ulster's Camelot—the region's ancient capital. Excavations date evidence of activity going back to 700 BC. The fort has strong associations with figures of Irish history and legend. Thousands of years ago it is said to have been the site of the palace of Queen Macha; subsequent legends call it the barracks of the legendary Ulster warrior Cuchulainn and his Red Branch Knights. Remains dating from 94 BC are particularly intriguing: a great conical structure, 120 ft in diameter, was formed from five concentric circles made of 275 wooden posts, with a 276th, about 12 yards high, situated in the center. In a ritual whose meaning is not known, it was filled with brushwood and set on fire. The **Navan Centre** rehearses the Red Branch Knights' tales—Ireland's *Iliad* and Ulster's *Camelot* combined. ⊠ *3 km (2 mi) west of Armagh on A28, ☎ 028/3752–5550. ⊡ Centre U.K.£3.95, fort free. ☉ Fort freely accessible. Centre Apr.–June and Sept., weekdays 10–6, Sat. 11–6, Sun. noon–6; July–Aug., Mon.–Sat. 10–6, Sun. 11–6; Oct.–Mar., weekdays 10–5, Sat. 11–5, Sun. noon–5.*

Lodging

$$$ 🏨 **Drumsill Hotel.** On 15 acres of mature wooded grounds, this modern hotel is 1½ km (1 mi) northwest of Armagh on A29 road, signposted the Moy. The bedrooms are bright and airy, decorated in shades of cream and yellow. Brown's Bistro serves Continental cuisine. There is live music at the bar during summer. ⊠ *35 Moy Rd., Co. Armagh BT61 8DL, ☎ 028/3752–2009, FAX 028/3752–5624. 10 rooms with bath. Restaurant, bar, meeting rooms. MC, V.*

$$ 🏨 **Dean's Hill.** Jill Armstrong's elegant guest house was built, as the name suggests, for the cathedral's dean in 1760, and it has been in the Armstrong family for more than 100 years. Each of the three bedrooms, their period architectural features largely intact, has its own bath. One has a four-poster bed, another a fireplace. A self-catering apartment in the courtyard sleeps four. Despite the rural setting, Armagh's historic center is only a 10-minute walk away. ⊠ *College Hill, Co. Armagh BT61 9DF, ☎ FAX 028/3752–4923. 3 rooms with bath, 1 apartment. Tennis court, croquet. No credit cards.*

En Route   Leave Armagh to the southeast on A28, driving toward Newry. Instead of going the entire way on the main road, after about 9½ km (6 mi), you'll have a more enjoyable drive if you take B133, on the right. This will lead you through a rustic, drumlin landscape of vivid green pastures. The appearance of villages changes as you return toward the River Bann; houses and farms begin to resemble those of Britain rather than those in the Republic.

The Mountains of Mourne

🔵 *51 km (32 mi) south of Belfast, 52½ km (32½ mi) southeast of Armagh.*

In the words of the popular song by Percy French, the Mountains of Mourne "sweep down to the sea"—from 2,000-ft summits. East of the unprepossessing border town of Newry, this area was long considered ungovernable, its hardy inhabitants living from smuggling contraband into the numerous rocky coves on the seashore. Much of the Mourne range is still inaccessible except on foot. The countryside is gorgeous:

high, windswept pasture and moorland threaded with bright streams, bound by a tracery of drystone walls, and dotted with sheep and whitewashed farmhouses snuggled in stands of sycamore. It's the perfect landscape for away-from-it-all walkers, cyclists, and serious climbers. Climbers should inform their hotel or the **Northern Ireland Centre for Outdoor Activities** (✉ Bryansford, Newcastle, ☎ 028/4372–2158) when and where they're heading before setting off.

Newcastle, a bracing Victorian cold-water bathing station, is the main center for visitors to the hills. Looming above Newcastle is **Slieve Donard,** its panoramic, 2,805-ft summit grandly claiming views into England, Wales, and Scotland "when it's clear enough"—in other words, rarely, say the pessimists. **Castlewellan Forest Park** comprises 1,150 acres of forested hills running between the Mourne Mountains and Slieve Croob. With its lake, secluded arbors, and **arboretum,** the park makes an excellent introduction to the area. ✉ *Castlewellan,* ☎ *028/4377–8664.* ☜ *Car U.K.£3.80, pedestrians U.K.£2.* ☉ *Daily dawn–dusk.*

Covering 1,200 acres and entered through picturesque Gothic gateways, **Tollymore Forest Park** extends up the valley of the River Shimna. There are many pretty stone bridges over the sparkling waters. ✉ *Tully-brannigan Rd., Newcastle,* ☎ *028/4372–2428.* ☜ *Car U.K.£3, pedestrians U.K.£1.50.* ☉ *Daily dawn–dusk.*

Farther into the mountains, the road to the **Silent Valley** reservoir parklands leads to more mountain views and excellent photo ops. Take B27 from Kilkeel; after 6 km (4 mi), turn right. ☎ *028/9074–6581.* ☜ *Car U.K.£3, pedestrians U.K.£1.50.* ☉ *Apr.–Sept., daily 10–6:30; Oct.–Mar., daily 10–4.*

Lodging

$$$ ⊞ **Burrendale Hotel & Country Club.** Owner Sean Small's personality has made this low-slung, modern building, shaded by clumps of beech, into one of the most relaxing establishments on the North's east coast. Staff members are cheery; bedrooms are decorated in quiet tones. The Cottage Kitchen and Vine restaurants are competent (the former casual, the latter more formal) and particularly aim to please the local customers, who like their plates overflowing. ✉ *51 Castlewellan Rd., Newcastle, Co. Down BT33 0JY,* ☎ *028/4372–2599,* FAX *028/4372–2328. 68 rooms with bath. 2 restaurants, 2 bars, indoor pool, hot tub, sauna, steam rooms, exercise rooms, meeting rooms. AE, DC, MC, V.* ✍

$$$ ⊞ **Glassdrumman Lodge.** For those who wish to be pampered as well as immersed in the ancient Kingdom of Mourne, Graeme and Joan Hall's eclectically simple and stylish lodge is the place. The outside of the house is less than spectacular, but those at the impressively busy estate grow their own crops, raise their own farm animals, churn their own butter, and bake their own bread. Rooms are decorated in bright colors and have large windows, which take advantage of the glorious views. The Halls think of everything, including overnight laundry service and complimentary car washing. Horseback riding and trekking can also be arranged. ✉ *Mill Rd., Annalong, Co. Down BT34 4RH,* ☎ *028/4376–8451,* FAX *028/4376–7041. 10 rooms with bath, 2 suites. Restaurant, horseback riding, laundry service, business services, meeting rooms. AE, MC, V.*

$$$ ⊞ **Slieve Donard Hotel.** A lavish, redbrick monument to Victoriana, this turreted Victorian hotel stands like a palace on spacious green lawns at one end of Newcastle's 6½-km (4-mi) sandy beach. Guests will feel as if they are stepping back to the town's turn-of-the-20th-century heyday as an elegant seaside resort, even though the rooms now have every modern comfort. Ask for a room overlooking the water. At the entrance to the grounds, the relaxed Percy French gatehouse pub serves adequate seafood dishes; music is presented every Saturday night. The Royal County Down Golf Club is next door. ⊠ *Downs Rd., Newcastle, Co. Down BT33 0AH,* ☎ *028/4372–3681,* FAX *028/4377–4830. 126 rooms with bath. Bar, dining room, indoor pool, beauty salon, hot tub, steam room, 2 tennis courts, 2 exercise rooms. AE, DC, MC, V.*

Outdoor Activities and Sports

The **Royal County Down** (⊠ Newcastle, ☎ 028/4372–3314) is considered by many golfers to be one of the finest courses in the world (☞ Chapter 9).

Downpatrick

⑤⓪ *35 km (22 mi) south of Belfast, 50 km (31 mi) east of Newry.*

Downpatrick used to be called "Plain and Simple Down" but had its name changed by the Norman knight John de Courcy, who moved to the town in 1176 and set about promoting St. Patrick, the 5th-century Briton who, captured by the Irish, became a slave in the Down area and later escaped to France, where he learned about Christianity and bravely returned to try to convert the local chiefs. Although it is not true that Patrick brought a new faith to Ireland—there was already a bishop of Ireland before Patrick got here—he must have been a better missionary than most because he did indeed win influential converts. The clan chief of the Down area gave him land at the village of Saul, near Downpatrick, to build a monastery.

Downpatrick's hilltop **cathedral,** which lay ruined from 1538 to 1790 and was reopened in 1818, preserves parts of some of the earlier churches and monasteries that have stood on the site since the 6th century. Even before that time, the cathedral site had long been an important fortified settlement, and Down takes its name from the Celtic word "dun," or fort. In the churchyard, a somber slab inscribed "Patric" is supposedly the saint's tomb, which is a bit of a fraud, since no one knows where Patrick is buried. It might be here, at Saul, or, some scholars argue, more likely at Armagh. ☑ *Free.* ☉ *Freely accessible.*

For some hard facts concerning the patron saint of Ireland, visit the **St. Patrick Heritage Centre** next to the cathedral; it's housed, together with the **Down Museum,** inside a former 18th-century jail. ⊠ *The Mall,* ☎ *028/4461–5218.* ☑ *Free.* ☉ *June–Sept., weekdays 10–5, weekends 2–5; Oct.–May, Tues.–Fri. 10–5, Sat. 2–5.*

Portaferry

⑤① *30 km (18½ mi) south of Newtownards, 13 km (8 mi) east of Downpatrick.*

You'll have to cross Strangford Lough on the 24-vehicle car ferry from Strangford to reach Portaferry (U.K.£4 per car and driver, 80p per additional passenger), another quiet fishing village with old fortifications to guard this once-strategic channel, which joins the lough to the sea. The ferry crossing takes 10 minutes or less, and boats leave every half hour throughout the day. Departures from Strangford are on the half hour and hour, and from Portaferry on the three-quarter hour and the quarter hour: weekdays 7:30 AM–10:30 PM, Saturday 8 AM–11 PM, and Sunday 9:30 AM–10:30 PM.

۞ **Exploris,** Portaferry's unusual aquarium, has models of the underwater environment in Strangford Lough and examples of 70 species that call the lough their home. Some of these creatures may not be what you expect: seals, found regularly by the aquarium staff and rescued from death on nearby shores (and, in one mysterious episode, the middle of an inland field), as well as several large, long-lived species of fish that still inhabit the lake. ⊠ *The Rope Walk,* ☎ *028/4272–8062.* 📠 *U.K.£3.50.* ☉ *Apr.–Aug., Mon.–Sat. 10–6, Sun. 1–6; Sept.–Mar., Mon.–Sat. 10–5, Sun. 1–5.*

Dining and Lodging

$$$ ✕🏠 **Portaferry Hotel.** Standing on the quayside (or "strand") over-
★ looking the narrow channel that connects Strangford Lough to the sea, this centuries-old, comfortable whitewashed inn has well-kept, simply furnished double rooms. The main action takes place in the popular bar and restaurant, home to huge breakfasts, country lunches, and old-fashioned—and reasonably priced—evening meals. Live Strangford oysters, stuffed mussels, Dublin Bay prawns, scallops with bacon and garlic, and grilled turbot are briskly served to the Belfast and Dublin regulars who appreciate the fresh, frill-and-fad-free seafood. Watch the sun set across the water from the bar window, or better still, book one of the sought-after rooms at the front. ⊠ *10 The Strand Co. Down BT22 1EP,* ☎ *028/ 4272–8231,* 📠 *028/4272–8999. 12 double rooms with bath, 2 single rooms with bath. Restaurant, bar. AE, DC, MC, V.* 🐾

$$ ✕🏠 **Dufferin Arms Coaching Inn.** Next door to Killyleagh Castle, this lively 1803 inn is presided over by Stewart and Morris Crawford. The atmosphere of the beautiful Georgian building is that of a rustic pub; the comfortable decor includes luxurious bedrooms with four-poster beds. Downstairs, the original stables have been converted into the Kitchen Restaurant, a banquet hall with a long bar where medieval feasts and formal dinner parties often take place. Rustic Irish cooking—entrées such as poached salmon and roast duck in cherry sauce—is a specialty. One of the bars has snugs, another an open fire; diversions such as pub quizzes, traditional Irish storytelling, and Cajun and jazz music keep things lively. ⊠ *35 High St., Killyleagh, Co. Down BT30 9QF,* ☎ *028/4482–8229,* 📠 *028/4482–8755. 7 rooms with bath. Restaurant, 3 bars, meeting room. AE, MC, V.*

$$ 🏠 **Killyleagh Castle Towers.** Killyleagh, a pretty heritage area on the
★ east shore of Strangford Lough, is home to this splendidly Baroque edifice. Hans Sloane (1660–1753), physician to George II and the man who founded the British Museum, was a village boy encouraged to educate himself in the castle's library. Travelers can rent three self-catering apartments with room for four; two are in the 17th-century turrets and a larger one is in a Victorian-style turret over the gateway. Royalty-watchers, take note: Fergie, the ex-wife of Prince Andrew, has ancestral links here, and Prince Andrew himself holds the title of Baron of Killyleagh. ⊠ *Killyleagh Castle, Killyleagh, Co. Down BT30 9QA,* ☎ 📠 *028/4482–8261. 3 apartments. Pool, tennis court. No credit cards.*

Mount Stewart

⑤② *21 km (13 mi) north from Portaferry.*

Mount Stewart is the grand 19th-century family home of the Marquesses of Londonderry, who also built one of London's most sumptuous residences on Park Lane. It was constructed in two stages, where an earlier house stood: George Dance designed the west facade (1804–05), and William Vitruvius Morrison designed the neoclassic main part of the building (1845–49). The landscaped gardens are populated with surprising stone carvings of rare and extinct creatures. The house contains one of George Stubbs's most famous portraits, that of the celebrated racehorse Hambletonian, after he had won one of the most prominent contests of the 18th century. The octagonal Temple of the Winds is a copy of a similar structure in Athens, and there's a remarkable bathhouse and pool at the end of the wooded peninsula just before the entrance to the grounds. ✉ *Newtownards,* ☎ *028/4278–8387.* ☕ *U.K.£3.50.* ☉ *May–Sept., Wed.–Mon. 1–6; Apr. and Oct., weekends 1–6.*

Lodging

$$$ 🏠 **The Old Inn.** On the outside, this 1614 coaching inn, which is reputedly Ireland's oldest, looks the part. It's pure 17th-century old-world England, with a sculpted thatched roof, half doors, and leaded windows. Inside there are roaring open fires in winter. Some of the bedrooms have four-poster beds and sitting rooms. The Churn Bistro's menu is solidly Irish, the staff jovial, and the locals inquisitive. Crawfordsburn is 16 km (10 mi) from Belfast. ✉ *15 Main St., Crawfordsburn, Co. Down BT19 1JH,* ☎ *028/9185–3255,* 🖷 *028/9185–2775. 32 rooms with bath. Restaurant, 2 bars. AE, DC, MC, V.*

NORTHERN IRELAND A TO Z

Arriving and Departing

By Bus

Northern Ireland's main bus company, **Ulsterbus,** runs direct service between Dublin and Belfast. Queries about Ulsterbus service, or any other bus service in Northern Ireland, can be dealt with by the central call-center of **Translink** (☎ 028/9033–3000). The Republic's **Bus Éireann** (☎ 01/836–6111 in Dublin) also runs direct services to and from Dublin. Buses arrive at and depart from Belfast's Europa Buscentre (☞ By Bus *in* Getting Around, *below*); the ride takes three hours. Buses to Belfast also run from London and from Birmingham, making the **Stranraer ferry** (☎ 01776/702262) crossing.

By Car

Many roads from the Irish Republic into Northern Ireland were once closed for security reasons, but all are now reinstated, leaving drivers with a choice of legitimate crossing points. Army checkpoints at all approved frontier posts are rare, and few customs formalities are observed. The fast N1/A1 road connects Belfast to Dublin in 160 km (100 mi) with an average driving time of just over two hours.

By Ferry

Norse Irish Ferries (✉ Victoria Terminal 2, West Bank Rd., ☎ 028/9077–9090) has 11-hour daytime or overnight car ferries that connect Belfast with the English west-coast port of Liverpool every other night. **P&O European Ferries** (☎ 0870/598–0980) has a one-hour sailing to Larne from Cairnryan, Scotland; infrequent trains take passengers on to Belfast. You can also cross on the **SeaCat** (☎ 028/9031–2301) or the **StenaLine's HSS** (☎ 0870/598–0980), both fast catamarans that carry cars and passengers from Stranraer directly into Belfast in just 1½ hours. **SeaCat** also sails from Belfast to Heysham on the west coast of England, taking four hours. The **Argyll and Antrim Steam Packet Company** (☎ 0870/552–3523) is a three-hour car-ferry service on the MV *Claymore* linking Campbeltown in Scotland with Ballycastle in County Antrim; it runs July–October. The **Isle of Man Steam Packet Company** (☎ 0870/552–3523) runs summer services to and from the Isle of Man and Belfast.

By Plane

Belfast International Airport at Aldergrove (☎ 028/9442–2888) is the North's principal air arrival point, 30½ km (19 mi) from Belfast. **Belfast City Airport** (☎ 028/9045–7745) is the second airport, 6½ km (4 mi) from the city. It receives flights from U.K. provincial airports, from London Gatwick and Heathrow, and from Stanstead and Luton (both near London). **Aer Lingus** flies once daily on Monday, Thursday, and Saturday from New York's JFK directly to Belfast; inquiries and reservations can be made through the Dublin office (☎ 01/886–8888). Other scheduled services from the United States and Canada are routed through Dublin, Glasgow, London, or Manchester.

Frequent services to Belfast's two airports are scheduled throughout the day from London Heathrow, London Gatwick, Luton, and Stanstead (all of which have fast coordinated subway or rail connections to central London), from 17 other U.K. airports, and from Cork in the Republic of Ireland. Flights take about 1¼ hours from London. **British Airways and BA Express** (both ☎ 0345/222111), **British Midland Airways** (☎ 0345/554554), and **Jersey European Airways** (☎ 0345/676676) operate the majority of flights into Belfast. Direct flights from Amsterdam on **Air UK** (☎ 0345/666777) also arrive in Belfast.

City of Derry Airport (☎ 028/7181–0784) is 8 km (5 mi) from Derry and receives flights from Glasgow and Manchester.

BETWEEN THE AIRPORTS AND THE CITIES
Belfast. Ulsterbus (☎ 028/9033–3000) operates a shuttle bus every half hour (one-way U.K.£5, round-trip U.K.£8) between the International Airport and Belfast city center. From Belfast City Airport, you can travel into Belfast by train from Sydenham Halt to **Central Station** (✉ E. Bridge St.) or catch a taxi from the airport to your hotel.

Derry. If you arrive at the City of Derry Airport, you may need to call a **taxi** (☎ 028/7181–1231 or 028/7126–3905) to get to your destination.

By Train
The Dublin–Belfast Express train, operated by both **Northern Ireland Railways** (☎ 028/9089–9411) and **Iarnród Éireann** (☎ 01/855–4477), travels between the two cities in about two hours. Six trains (check timetables, as some trains are much slower) run daily in both directions (three on Sunday) to and from Belfast's misnamed **Central Station** (✉ E. Bridge St., ☎ 028/9089–9411). However, a free shuttle bus service will drop you off at City Hall or Ulsterbus's city-center **Europa Buscentre** (☎ 028/9033–3000), or you can change trains for the de facto city-center **Great Victoria Street Station** (✉ Great Victoria St., ☎ 028/9043–4424), which is adjacent both to the Europa Buscentre and the Europa Hotel.

Getting Around
By Bus
You can take advantage of frequent and inexpensive Ulsterbus links between all Northern Ireland towns. The main bus stations in Belfast are the **Europa Buscentre** (✉ Glengall St., ☎ 028/9033–3000), which is easiest to find using its Great Victoria Street entrance to the left of the Europa Hotel, and the **Laganside Buscentre** (✉ Donegall Quay, ☎ 028/9033–3000), around the corner from the Albert Clock and about 1 km (½ mi) from Central Station.

If you want to tour the North by bus, a **Freedom of Northern Ireland Ticket** allows unlimited travel on bus or train (U.K.£10 per day, U.K.£25 for three days, and U.K.£37 per week). An **Irish Rover** ticket from Ulsterbus covers Ireland, north and south, and costs U.K.£53 for three days, U.K.£115 for eight. For specific fares and schedules, call **Translink** (☎ 028/9033–3000). Within Belfast, visitors have access to good city-bus service. All routes start from Donegall Square; you'll find a kiosk there where you can pick up a timetable. Another contact is **Citybus** (☎ 028/9024–6485).

By Car

In general, drivers will find roads here are in much better shape and signposted more clearly than in the Irish Republic. Bad rush-hour delays can occur on the West Link joining M1 (heading south or west) and M2 (heading east or north). But on the whole, driving is quicker and easier in the North than in areas south of the border.

PARKING

Belfast has many parking garages, as well as street meter-ticket parking. Before parking on the street, check the posted regulations: during rush hours many spots become no-parking.

By Train

Northern Ireland Railways runs only four rail routes from Belfast's **Central Station** (⊠ E. Bridge St., ☎ 028/9089–9411)—which is not, in fact, that centrally located: northwest to **Derry** via Coleraine and the Causeway Coast; east to **Bangor** along the shore of Belfast Lough; northeast to **Larne** (for the P&O European ferry to Scotland [☞ *above*]); and south to **Dublin**. There are frequent connections to Central Station from the much more central Great Victoria Street Station (☞ Arriving and Departing, *above*) and from **Botanic Station** (⊠ Botanic Ave., ☎ 028/9089–9411) in the university area. **Freedom of Northern Ireland** tickets also apply to trains (☞ *above*). For more information contact **Northern Ireland Railways** (⊠ 28 Wellington Pl., Belfast, ☎ 028/9089–9411).

Contacts and Resources

Banks and Money Exchange

The North uses British currency. Irish *punts,* or pounds, are not accepted. Rates change rapidly, but the British pound is generally worth slightly more than the Irish (☞ Money *in* Smart Travel Tips A to Z). You'll sometimes be given bank notes, drawn on Ulster banks, that are valid only in Northern Ireland; be sure not to get stuck with a lot of these when you leave, because they will be difficult to change at banks back home. Main banks are open weekdays 9:30–4:30, smaller branches weekdays 10:30–3:30. Changing money outside banking hours is possible at **Thomas Cook** branches. ⊠ *Belfast Airport,* ☎ *028/9442–2536.* ☾ *Daily 6:45 AM–8 PM.* ⊠ *11 Donegall Pl.,* ☎ *028/9055–4455.* ☾ *Mon.–Wed. and Fri–Sat. 9–5:30, Thurs. 10–5:30.*

Car Rentals

Visitors can choose among several local rental companies, but car rental isn't cheap. A compact car costs U.K.£150–U.K.£210 per week (including taxes, insurance, and unlimited mileage). If you're planning to take a rental car across the border into the Republic, inform the company and check its insurance procedures. Following are some of the main rental offices.

BELFAST

Avis (⊠ Belfast International Airport, ☎ 028/9442–2333; Belfast City Airport, ☎ 028/9045–2017; Great Victoria St., ☎ 028/9024–0404). **Dan Dooley** (⊠ Belfast International Airport, ☎ 028/9445–2522). **Europcar** (⊠ Belfast International Airport, ☎ 028/9442–3444; Belfast City Airport, ☎ 028/9045–0904). **Hertz** (⊠ Belfast International Airport, ☎ 028/9442–2533; Belfast City Airport, ☎ 020/9073–2451).

DERRY
Ford (✉ Desmond Motors, City of Derry Airport, ☎ 028/7136–0420); a U.K.£180 security deposit is required here.

Consulates
Canada (✉ 378 Stranmillis Rd., Belfast BT9 5EU, ☎ 028/9066–0212). **New Zealand** (✉ New Balance House, 118A Lisburn Rd., Glenavy, Co. Antrim BT29 4NY, ☎ 028/9264–8098). **United States** (✉ Queen's House, 14 Queen St., Belfast BT1 6EQ, ☎ 028/9032–8239).

Emergencies
Police, fire, ambulance, or **coast guard** (☎ 999). **Belfast's main police station** (✉ 6–10 N. Queen St., ☎ 028/9065–0222).

HOSPITALS
Belfast: Belfast City Hospital (✉ Lisburn Rd., ☎ 028/9032–9241) is one of two main hospitals in the city with an emergency room. The **Royal Victoria Hospital** (✉ Grosvenor Rd., ☎ 028/9024–0503) is the other.

Derry: Altnagelvin Hospital (✉ Belfast Rd., ☎ 028/7134–5171) has an emergency room.

Guided Tours
Citybus (✉ Milewater Rd., ☎ 028/9024–6485) offers a Belfast City Tour that takes in the shipyards and heads out from the city center as far as Stormont, 9½ km (6 mi) east, and Belfast Castle on Cave Hill to the north. The cost is U.K.£8.50, including afternoon tea. The City Tour leaves Castle Place June–September, daily at 1 PM. Other Citybus tours include "Lagan Experience" and "A Look at Linen."

Ulsterbus (✉ Milewater Rd., ☎ 028/9033–3000) operates half-day or full-day trips June through September from Belfast to the Glens of Antrim, the Giant's Causeway, the Fermanagh lakes, Lough Neagh, the Mourne Mountains, and the Ards Peninsula.

LOWER LOUGH ERNE
Erne Tours (☎ 028/6632–2882) operates *Kestrel,* a 63-seat water bus, which leaves Round O pier at Enniskillen during the summer at 10:30, 2:15, 4:15, and 7:15 on Tuesday, Thursday, and Sunday for a two-hour trip on beautiful Lough Erne. On weekdays the boat makes a half-hour stop at Devenish Island (☞ *above*). From May to June there are Sunday trips at 2:30, and occasionally tours run at other times of the year.

GIANT'S CAUSEWAY/BUSHMILLS
Ulsterbus has also teamed up with the Old Bushmills Distillery to run the **Bushmills Bus,** an open-top tour bus running from Coleraine to the Giant's Causeway via the coast resorts; you also visit Bushmills to observe whiskey making. Call Ulsterbus in Coleraine for details (☎ 028/7034–3334).

Outdoor Activities and Sports
BICYCLING
Rentals cost around U.K.£7 a day, U.K.£30 a week; local TIOs can offer suggestions for good cycling routes (☞ Visitor Information, *below*). In Belfast rent from **McConvrey Cycles** (✉ 467 Ormeau Rd., ☎ 028/9049–1163). **ReCycle** (✉ 1 Albert Sq., ☎ 028/9031–3113) is another good place to rent in Belfast.

BIRD-WATCHING
Murphy's Wildlife Tours (✉ 12 Belvoir [pronounced beaver] Close, Belvoir Park, Belfast, ☎ 028/9069–3232) leads tours in all seasons, though if you're an advanced birder, you may want to concentrate on wintering wildfowl and waders that have migrated all the way from North

America to the shores of Loughs Foyle, Neagh, and Strangford. For information, ideas, and details of field-study groups, contact Northern Ireland TIOs (☞ Visitor Information, *below*) and the **Royal Society for the Protection of Birds** (⊠ Belvoir Park Forest, ☎ 028/9049–1547).

FISHING
Northern Ireland's system of pricing and administrating fishing licenses and permits can seem anachronistic, unnecessarily complex, and bewildering. No license is needed for sea fishing, but to catch freshwater fish, whether coarse or game, you need a rod license from the **Fisheries Conservancy Board** (⊠ 1 Mahon Rd., Portadown, ☎ 028/3833–4666); another license from the **Foyle Fisheries Commission** (⊠ 8 Victoria Rd., Derry, ☎ 028/7134–2100), depending on the area in which you're fishing; and probably a local permit. The good news is that all licenses and Department of Agriculture and Fisheries permits are available from the **Northern Ireland Tourist Board Information Centre** (☞ Visitor Information, *below*) as well as from a number of TIOs and tackle shops around the province.

In the main angling areas, the following are useful contacts: **Albert Atkins** (⊠ 67 Coleraine Rd., Garvagh, ☎ 028/2955–8555); **Carlton Park Fishing Centre** (⊠ Belleek, ☎ 028/6865–8181); **Hook, Line & Sinker** (⊠ 43 South St., Newtownards, ☎ 028/9181–1671); **Joe Mullan** (⊠ 74 Main St., Portrush, ☎ 028/7082–2209); **Joseph Braddell** (⊠ 11 North St., Belfast, ☎ 028/9032–0525); **Lakeland Tackle & Guns** (⊠ Sligo Rd., Enniskillen, ☎ 028/6632–3774); **Moyle Outdoor Angling** (⊠ 17 Castle St., Ballycastle, ☎ 028/2076–9521); **Tommy McCutcheon** (⊠ 114 Sandy Row, Belfast, ☎ 028/9024–9509).

GOLF
All golf courses and clubs are listed in the Northern Ireland Tourist Board information guide No. 17, "Golf—Where to Play," available from main tourist offices (☞ Northern Ireland *in* Chapter 9).

HIKING AND WALKING
More than 100 places to stay along the Ulster Way are listed in the Northern Ireland Tourist Board information guide *Accommodation for Walkers on the Ulster Way.* The **Sports Council for Northern Ireland** (⊠ House of Sport, Upper Malone Rd., Belfast BT9 5LA, ☎ 028/9038–1222) can also give advice about the Ulster Way; it sells books covering each section of the route. Tougher walks in the hills are outlined in the informative handbook in the Irish Walks series, No. 4, *The North East,* by Richard Rogers, published by **Gill & Macmillan** (⊠ Goldenbridge, Inchicore, Dublin 8, ☎ 01/453–1005), which is available in local book and sporting goods stores in Northern Ireland; it gives precise details of 45 hill walks, complete with descriptions of the wildflowers you'll see along the way. For hikes in the Mountains of Mourne, you can obtain maps and details of suggested routes from the **Mourne Countryside Centre** (⊠ 91 Central Promenade, Newcastle, ☎ 028/4372–4059). **Celtic Journeys** (⊠ 111 Whitepark Rd., Ballycastle, ☎ 028/2076–9651) arranges wildlife and cultural walks.

HORSEBACK RIDING/PONY TREKKING
About 3¼ km (2 mi) south of center-city Belfast, the **Lagan Valley Equestrian Centre** runs pony treks and offers lessons—both group and private. ⊠ *170 Upper Malone Rd., Belfast,* ☎ *028/9061–4853.* ◫ *Group lessons and trekking U.K.£9 hourly, private lessons U.K.£16.* ☯ *Weekdays 10–9, Sat. 10–3:30.*

Student Travel
For details on youth hostels in Belfast and elsewhere, contact **Hosteling International, Northern Ireland** at the Belfast International Youth

Hostel (✉ 22 Donegall Rd., Belfast BT12 5JN, ☎ 028/9032–4733, FAX 028/9043–9699). This modern and comfortable hostel has 128 beds.

Visitor Information

The **Northern Ireland Tourist Board Information Centre** in Belfast is the main TIO for the whole of the North (☞ Exploring, *above*). ✉ *St. Anne's Court, 59 North St., BT1 1NB,* ☎ *028/9023–1221 or 028/9024– 6609,* FAX *028/9023–9936 or 028/9031–2424.* ☉ *Sept.–June, Mon. 9:30–5:15, Tues.–Sat. 9–5:15; July–Aug., Mon. 9:30–7, Tues.–Sat. 9– 7, Sun. noon–4.*

Year-round local offices are also at these locations: **Armagh** (✉ 40 English St., Co. Armagh BT6 17BA, ☎ 028/3752–1800). **Ballycastle** (✉ 7 Mary St., Co. Antrim BT54 6QH, ☎ 028/2076–2024). **Bangor** (✉ Quay St., Co. Down BT20 5ED, ☎ 028/7037–0069). **Carrickfergus** (✉ Heritage Plaza, Co. Antrim BT38 7DG, ☎ 028/9336–6455). **Coleraine** (✉ Railway Rd., Co. Derry BT52 IPE, ☎ 028/7034–4723). **Derry** (✉ Foyle St., Co. Derry BT48 6AT, ☎ 028/7126–7284 or 028/7137– 7577). **Downpatrick** (✉ 74 Market St., Co. Down BT30 6L2, ☎ 028/ 4461–2233). **Enniskillen** (✉ Lakeland Visitor Centre, Shore Rd., Co. Fermanagh BT74 7EF, ☎ 028/6632–3110). **Giant's Causeway** (✉ Visitor Centre, Co. Antrim BT57 8SU, ☎ 028/2073–1855). **Killymaddy** (✉ Ballygally Rd., Co. Derry BT70 ITF, ☎ 028/8776–7259). **Larne** (✉ Narrow Gauge Rd., Co. Antrim BT40 1XB, ☎ 028/2826– 0088). **Limavady** (✉ Connell St., Co. Derry BT49 OHA, ☎ 028/ 7772–2226). **Lisburn** (✉ Market Sq., Co. Antrim BT28 IAG, ☎ 028/ 9266–0038). **Newcastle** (✉ Central Promenade, Co. Down BT33 OAA, ☎ 028/4372–2222). **Newtownards** (✉ Regent St., Co. Down BT23 4AD, ☎ 028/9182–6846). **Newry** (✉ Town Hall, Bank Parade, Co. Armagh BT35 6HR, ☎ 028/3026–8877). During June through August, many more towns and villages open TIOs.

Weather

Call **Weathercall** (☎ 0891/500427) or **Marine Call** (☎ 0891/505365) for a Northern Ireland weather forecast.

9 IRISH GREENS
Golfing in Ireland

If you come to Ireland to golf, you may hear the story about Mick O'Loughlin, a County Clare butcher who spent more time playing at the Lahinch Golf Club than standing behind his meat counter. "He can't be making much money," a visitor remarked, upon hearing where Mick could usually be found. Came the reply: "Maybe not. But he's sure making plenty of friends." In the last decade, Ireland has invested nearly $400 million in a gambit to become Europe's premier golf destination. While its you-know-who neighbor to the northeast still has more courses, Ireland's 390—and counting—are gorgeously scenic and designed by golf's greatest.

ASK MOST GOLFERS WHERE TO FIND the golf vacation of a lifetime—a variety of breathtaking courses, beautiful settings, history seeping into every shot—and they'll probably point you in the direction of Scotland. Unless, of course, they've been to Ireland.

By Jonathan Abrahams

Updated by Dermot Gilleece

Indeed, Ireland's neighbor to the northeast gets more world attention when it comes to tournament golf. It plays host to most of the British Open championships and in many circles is considered the birthplace of the game. But Ireland doesn't lag far behind when it comes to golf history. Its oldest course dates back to 1881, and with more than 390 quality layouts, the Emerald Isle is second only to Scotland in the amount of golf it can offer per square mile. If you ask a local how Ireland's courses stack up against Scotland's, he'll fix you with a steely stare before defending his homeland on his life. Then he very well may buy you a pint of the local stout. But you don't have to be a native to have such passion for the golf courses of Ireland (not to mention the stout). Golfers the world over who are "in the know" have long sung the praises of Irish golf. Tom Watson, winner of five British Opens, lists as his favorite not any Scottish course but Ballybunion, as does the legendary writer Herbert Warren Wind, who, from an American standpoint, is credited with putting Irish golf on the map when he penned, "To put it simply, Ballybunion revealed itself to be nothing less than the finest seaside course I have ever seen." And although Ballybunion is generally considered the prize jewel of the Emerald Isle, it is reflective of the quality of courses found throughout the country.

So what makes Irish golf great? Architecture, perhaps the essence of a golfing experience, is one appropriate place to begin. Connoisseurs of golf in America hold such courses as Cypress Point and Pebble Beach in the highest regard because their designers used the spectacular lay of the land to create a beautiful, challenging, but fair layout. In Ireland, however, there are many such courses. Of the estimated 150 top-quality links courses in the world, 39 of them are in Ireland. Most of the leading courses in Ireland were designed by celebrated British architects, such as Tom Morris, James Braid, Harry Colt, and Alister MacKenzie, who happened to have as their raw material a spectacular landscape: Ireland is one of those remarkable places where mountains and sea meet, so there is no need to manipulate the land. Nature—the scraggly coast of a links-land or rolling hills of heather—dominates the courses here, not the other way around.

There is also something to be said for the sense of history that comes with playing golf on a land that is, most assuredly, "old world." Only 40 minutes from the airport in Shannon is the charming 18-hole course at Adare, complete with a green nestled in the ruins of a 14th-century abbey. Every step you take on an Irish golf course is a step back in history. Where in America can you find something comparable to the "Mass Hole" at Waterville, a par-3 built over a large hollow where Catholic priests used to hold services in secret, because praying was a capital offense at the time?

- **The Weather Factor.** You see all different kinds of weather in Ireland, from high winds to rain and sleet to sunshine, and you may see it all in one round. There are no rain checks here. You play unless there's lightning, so pack your sweaters and rain gear, especially if you're planning your trip for the off-season months of the spring and fall.

- **The Sunday Bag Factor.** If you don't have a golf bag that's light enough for you to carry for 18 holes, invest in one before your trip. Electric carts are generally available only at the leading venues, so you usually have the option of using a caddy or caddy car (pull cart) or carrying your own bag. Many courses have caddies but will not guarantee their availability since they're not employed by the course directly, so it's conceivable that you may have only one option: toting your bag yourself. To be safe, make sure you have a carryall, or Sunday bag.

- **The Private Club Factor.** Unlike those in America, most private golf clubs in Ireland are happy to let visitors play their course and use their facilities. It's important to remember, however, that the course is indeed there for the members first, and the majority of the club's concerns lie with them. Preferred days for visitors are listed below, but it's always a good idea to call in advance and make sure that the club will make time for you.

- **The Northern Ireland Factor.** Some of the best and most beautiful courses are in Northern Ireland, where the leading venues are far less remote than in the Republic. The signing of a peace agreement in April 1998 only enhanced the region's attraction. But keep in mind that this part of the island is under British rule, so all currency is in U.K. pounds.

And finally, a reality check. Ireland's best courses rank with the best of the world, but after that there's a bit of a drop-off. Of the 390-odd courses, only 31 or so are worth crossing an ocean to play. Others are good, but nothing you can't find at home. Of that 31, all are happy to have visitors play, except Royal Belfast, in Northern Ireland. It's the oldest club in Ireland, and it's exclusive. If you belong to a club in America, it must write a letter of introduction to Royal Belfast to secure your playing privilege. The remaining courses are listed below.

North of Dublin

County Louth Golf Club. Like many other Irish courses, County Louth is better known as its hometown, Baltray, a village sandwiched by the Boyne Estuary to the west and the Irish Sea to the east. Long hitters will love the atypical layout, a par-73 that features five par-5s, but beware the well-protected, undulating greens. ⊠ *Baltray, Drogheda, Co. Louth,* ☎ *041/22329. 18 holes. Yardage: 6,783. Par 73.* 🖾 *Fees: weekdays, £50; weekends, £60.* ☉ *Visitors: Mon. and Wed.–Fri. Practice area, caddies (reserve in advance), caddy carts, catering.*

Island Golf Club. Talk about exclusive—until 1960, the only way to reach this club was by boat. It was about as remote as you could get and still be only 24 km (15 mi) from Dublin, but things have changed. The Island has opened its doors and revealed a fine links course that rolls in and around sandhills, with small, challenging greens. ⊠ *Corballis, Donabate, Co. Dublin,* ☎ *01/843–6205. 18 holes. Yardage: 6,625. Par 71.* 🖾 *Fees: weekdays, £60; weekends, £70.* ☉ *Visitors: Mon., Tues., and Fri. Practice area, catering.*

★ **Portmarnock Golf Club.** Across an estuary from the easternmost point of Ireland, Portmarnock is perhaps the most famous of Ireland's "Big Four" (Ballybunion, Royal County Down, and Royal Portrush are the others). Largely because of its proximity to Dublin, this links course has hosted numerous major championships, most recently the 1997 European Men's Amateur Championship. Known for its flat fairways and greens, it provides a fair test for any golfer who can keep it out of the heavy rough. ⊠ *Portmarnock, Co. Dublin,* ☎ *01/846–2968. 27 holes. Yardage: 7,051, 3,449. Par 72, 36.* 🖾 *Fees: weekdays, £75; weekends, £95.* ☉ *Visitors: Mon., Tues., and Fri. Practice area, caddies (reserve in advance), caddy carts, catering.*

Royal Dublin Golf Club. Generally, links courses are in remote, even desolate areas, but this equally captivating one is only 6 km (4 mi) from the center of Dublin, on Bull Island, a bird sanctuary. It's the third-oldest club in Ireland and is routed in the old tradition of seaside links—the front 9 goes out in a line (wind helping), and the back 9 comes back in a line (wind against). Don't expect to make a comeback on the way home if you've struggled going out. ✉ *Dollymount, Clontarf, Dublin 3,* ☎ *01/833–6346. 18 holes. Yardage: 6,763. Par 72.* 🎴 *Fees: weekdays, £65; weekends, £80.* ☉ *Visitors: Mon., Tues., Thurs., and Fri. Practice area, caddies, caddy carts, catering.*

St. Margaret's Golf and Country Club. Not all of the worthwhile golf in Ireland is played on links courses that are a century old. St. Margaret's is a parkland (inland) course that opened in 1992 and immediately received high praise from Ireland's golfing inner circle. If, after getting blown around on the seaside links, you long for a taste of Western golf, this is your haven. ✉ *St. Margaret's, Co. Dublin,* ☎ *01/864–0400. 18 holes. Yardage: 6,965. Par 72.* 🎴 *Fees: weekdays, £45; weekends, £50.* ☉ *Visitors: daily. Practice area, caddies, caddy carts, club rental, catering.*

South of Dublin and the Southeast

Druids Glen Golf Club. Owner Hugo Flinn presented designers Pat Ruddy and Tom Craddock with the brief "Build me the finest parkland course in Ireland, whatever the cost." After an outlay of more than $16 million their handiwork was opened to the public in September 1995. Only a few months later, it had been chosen as the venue for the 1996 Murphy's Irish Open and hosted it again in 1998 for a fourth time. Ruddy unashamedly admits to having copied some key elements of Augusta National—particularly the extensive use of water—in the layout. In any event, the course, situated about 40 km (25 mi) south of Dublin in County Wicklow, is remarkably beautiful, particularly around the glen from which its name derives. It is essentially an American-style target course incorporating some delightful changes in elevation, and its forbidding, par-3 17th has an island green, like the corresponding hole at TPC Sawgrass. ✉ *Newtownmountkennedy, Co. Wicklow,* ☎ *01/287–3600. 18 holes. Yardage: 7,058. Par 72.* 🎴 *Fees: weekdays and weekends, £85.* ☉ *Visitors: daily. Practice area, caddies, caddy carts, catering.*

★ **The K Club.** At just 27 km (17 mi) west of Dublin, this 18-hole, Arnold Palmer–designed parkland course offers a round of golf in lush, wooded surroundings bordered by the River Liffey and is the venue for the 2005 Ryder Cup. The generous fairways and immaculate greens are offset by formidable length, which makes it one of the most demanding courses in the Dublin vicinity. Additional stress is presented by negotiating the numerous doglegs, water obstacles, and sand bunkers. Facilities on the premises are of the highest standard, allowing a wide choice of sporting and nonsporting activities. ✉ *Kildare Country Club, Straffan, Co. Kildare,* ☎ *01/627–3333. 18 holes. Yardage: 7,171. Par 72.* 🎴 *Fees: £140 (residents £80).* ☉ *Visitors: daily except weekdays 1:30–2:30, Sat. 9–1. Practice area, caddies, caddy carts, club rental, shoe rental, catering.*

★ **Mount Juliet Golf Course.** The championship parkland course, 19 km (11 mi) from Kilkenny Town, was designed by Jack Nicklaus and includes practice greens, a driving range, and, for those who feel a little rusty, a David Leadbetter golf academy. The heavily forested course has 8 holes that play over water, including the three signature par-3s. The back 9 presents a series of difficult bunker shots. A sporting day out comes to a welcome end in the Hunter's Yard or Rose Garden lodge, which cater to both the thirsty and the hungry. Greens fees are above average, and although visitors are always welcome, a weekday round is better than a weekend one, as tees can be crowded with members flocking to the course at week's end. ⊠ *Mount Juliet Estate, Thomastown, Co. Kilkenny,* ☎ *056/24455. 18 holes. Yardage 7,172. Par 72.* 🖾 *Fees: weekdays, £75, weekends, £85.* ⊘ *Visitors: daily. Practice area, driving range, caddies, caddy carts, club rental, lessons, catering.*

Tulfarris Golf Club. Less than a year after being officially opened, the $20 million development at Tulfarris was chosen as the venue for the 2000 Irish Senior Professional Open. It was designed by Patrick Merrigan on a 200-acre site beside Poulaphuca Lake, 50 km (31 mi) from Dublin, in an area of outstanding natural beauty. Classic parkland, it has the potential to be among the country's leading venues. ⊠ *Blessington, Co. Wicklow,* ☎ *045/867555. 18 holes. Yardage: 7,116. Par 72.* 🖾 *Fees: weekdays and weekends, £50. Practice area, caddies, caddy carts, catering.*

Southwest

Adare Manor Golf Course. Situated in the ancestral estate of the Earl of Dunraven, this charming parkland stretch was officially opened for play in 1996. Its immediate success was virtually guaranteed by the international profile of its designer, Robert Trent Jones. The "grand old man" of golf-course architects seemed far more comfortable with the wooded terrain than he was when designing the second links at Ballybunion (☞ *below*). As a result, he delivered a course with the potential to play host to events of the highest caliber. The front 9 is dominated by an artificial 14-acre lake with a $500,000 polyethylene base. It is in play at the 3rd, 5th, 6th, and 7th holes. In contrast, the dominant hazards on the homeward journey are the River Mague and the majestic trees. Both combine to make the par-5 18th one of the most testing finishing holes imaginable. ⊠ *Adare, Co. Limerick,* ☎ *061/395044. 18 holes. Yardage: 7,138. Par 72.* 🖾 *Fees: weekdays and weekends, £60.* ⊘ *Visitors: daily. Practice area, caddies, caddy carts, catering.*

★ **Ballybunion Golf Club.** This is one of the finest courses in the world. The Old Course was a virtual unknown until Herbert Warren Wind sang its praises in 1968, and today Ballybunion is universally regarded as one of golf's holiest grounds. On the shore of the Atlantic next to the southern entrance of the Shannon, it has the huge dunes of Lahinch without the blind shots. No pushover, but every hole is a pleasurable experience. Watch out for "Mrs. Simpson," a double fairway bunker on the 1st hole, named after the wife of Tom Simpson, the architect who remodeled the course in 1937. The New Course, which opened in 1985, was designed by Robert Trent Jones. ⊠ *Sandhill Rd., Ballybunion, Co. Kerry,* ☎ *068/27611. 36 holes. Yardage: 6,593 (Old), 6,216 (New). Par 71, 72.* 🖾 *Fees: £60 (Old), £35 (New), £80 (both on same day).* ⊘ *Visitors: weekdays. Practice area, caddies, caddy carts, catering.*

Cork Golf Club. If you know golf-course architecture, you're familiar with the name Alister MacKenzie, who designed Cypress Point in California and Augusta National in Georgia. One of his few designs in Ireland is Cork, better known as Little Island. There's water on this parkland course, but it's not the temperamental ocean; instead, Little Island is in Cork Harbour, a gentle bay of the Irish Sea. The course is little known but one of the Emerald Isle's best. ⊠ *Little Island, Co. Cork,* ☎ *021/435–3451. 18 holes. Yardage: 6,687. Par 72.* 🖾 *Fees: weekdays, £45; weekends, £50.* ⊘ *Visitors: Mon.–Wed. and Fri. Practice area, caddies, caddy carts, club rental, catering.*

Dooks Golf Club. On the second tier of courses in Ireland's Southwest, Dooks doesn't quite measure up to the world-class tracks. It is, nonetheless, a completely worthwhile day of golf if you're touring the area. Built in the old tradition of seaside links, it's shorter and a bit gentler, although the greens are small and tricky. It's an excellent way to take a breath. ✉ *Dooks, Glenbeigh, Co. Kerry,* ☎ *066/976–8205. 18 holes. Yardage: 6,010. Par 70.* 🖼 *Fees: £25.* ⊘ *Visitors: weekdays. Caddy carts, catering.*

Killarney Golf and Fishing Club. Freshwater fishing is the sport here, for Killarney is set among a stunning mixture of mountains, lakes, and forests. There are three golf courses: the Killeen Course, host of the 1992 Irish Open; Mahony's Point, set along the shores of Lough Leane; and the Lackabane, on the far side of the road from the main entrance. Killeen and Lackabane are longer, while Mahony's places a premium on accuracy. Despite the abundance of seaside links, many well-traveled golfers name Killarney their favorite place to play in Ireland. ✉ *Mahony's Point Demesne, Killarney, Co. Kerry,* ☎ *064/31034. 54 holes. Yardage: 7,056 (Killeen), 6,705 (Mahony's), 7,051 (Lackabane). All 3 courses: par 72.* 🖼 *Fees: £43 on all 3 courses.* ⊘ *Visitors: Mon.– Sat. Practice area, caddies, caddy carts, catering.*

Old Head Golf Links. On a celebrated, 215-acre County Cork peninsula, which juts out into the wild Atlantic nearly 300 ft below, it is an awe-inspiring spectacle that defies comparison. The only golfing stretches that could be likened to it are the 16th and 17th holes at Cypress Point and small, Pacific sections of Pebble Beach, from the 7th to the 10th and the long 18th. Even if your golf is moderate, your pulse is certain to race at the stunning views and wonderful wildlife. ✉ *Kinsale, Co. Cork,* ☎ *021/477–8444. 18 holes. Yardage 7,100. Par 72.* 🖼 *Fees: weekdays and weekends, £120.* ⊘ *Visitors: daily. Practice area, caddies (reserve in advance), caddy carts, catering.*

Tralee Golf Club. Tralee is what all modern-golf-course architects *wish* they could do in the States: find unspoiled, seaside links and route a course on it that's designed for the modern game. This is an Arnold Palmer–Ed Seay design that opened in 1984, and the setting is classic, with plenty of cliffs, craters, dunes, and the gale-blowing ocean. Don't let the flat front 9 lull you to sleep—the back 9 can be a ferocious wake-up call. ✉ *West Barrow, Ardfert, Co. Kerry,* ☎ *066/713–6379. 18 holes. Yardage: 6,738. Par 71.* 🖼 *Fees: weekdays, £45; weekends, £60.* ⊘ *Visitors: weekdays. Practice area, caddies, catering.*

Waterville Golf Links. Here's what you should know about Waterville before you play: the 1st hole of this course is aptly named "Last Easy." At 7,184 yards from the tips, Waterville is the longest course in Ireland or Britain, and it is generally regarded as their toughest test. Now the good news—the scenery is so majestic you may not care that your score is approaching the yardage. Six holes run along the cliffs by the sea, surrounding the other 12, which have a tranquil, if not soft, feel to them. ✉ *Waterville, Co. Kerry,* ☎ *066/947–4102. 18 holes. Yardage: 7,184. Par 72.* 🖼 *Fees: £75.* ⊘ *Visitors: weekdays. Practice area, caddies, caddy carts, buggies, catering.*

West

Carne Golf Links. This is a newer, Eddie Hackett–designed links course that takes advantage of its location, far to the west on the shores of Blacksod Bay. From the elevated tees and greens you can see a string of Atlantic islands: Inishkea, Inishglora, and Achill. ✉ *Carn, Belmullet, Co.*

Mayo, ☎ *097/82292. 18 holes. Yardage: 6,608. Par 72.* 🍴 *Fees: £25.* ⊙ *Visitors: daily. Practice area, caddies, caddy carts, catering.*

Connemara Golf Club. The local club for the town of Clifden, Connemara is a links course where you can get carried away not only by the golf but by the surrounding scenery. The Atlantic Ocean and Ballyconneely Bay are immediately to the west, and the Twelve Bens Mountains are to the east. The course starts flat, then rises into the hills for the final, challenging 6 holes. ✉ *Ballyconneely, Clifden, Co. Galway,* ☎ *095/23502. 18 holes. Yardage: 7,174. Par 72.* 🍴 *Fees: £35.* ⊙ *Visitors: Mon.–Sat. Practice area, caddies, caddy carts, catering.*

Lahinch Golf Club. The original course at Lahinch was designed by Old Tom Morris, who, upon the unveiling in 1892, called it "as fine a natural course as it has ever been my good fortune to play over." That was when blind shots (those taken when you can't see your target) were in vogue, and there are many here, where towering sandhills dominate every hole. Only a course with as much charm as this one could get away with that in today's modern game. ✉ *Lahinch, Co. Clare,* ☎ *065/708–1003. 36 holes. Yardage: 6,613 (Old Course), 6,200 (Castle Course). Both par 72.* 🍴 *Fees: £60 (Old Course), £30 (Castle).* ⊙ *Visitors: daily. Practice area, caddies, caddy carts, catering.*

Westport Golf Club. Twice the host of the Irish Amateur Championship, this inland course lies in the shadows of religious history. Rising 2,500 ft above Clew Bay, with its hundreds of islands, is Croagh Patrick, a mountain that legend connects with St. Patrick. The mountain is considered sacred, and it attracts multitudes of worshipers to its summit every year. All the prayers might pay off at the 15th, where your drive has to carry the ball over 200 yards of ocean. ✉ *Carrowholly, Co. Mayo,* ☎ *098/25113. 18 holes. Yardage: 6,667. Par 73.* 🍴 *Fees: weekdays, £20; weekends, £25.* ⊙ *Visitors: weekdays. Practice area, caddies, caddy carts, catering.*

Northwest

County Sligo Golf Club. A century old in 1994, the course at Sligo is one of the grand old venues of Ireland, having hosted most of the country's major championships. At 6,565 yards, this links course isn't particularly long; however, it still manages to have seven par-4s of 400 yards or more. Typical of Ireland's hidden jewels, Rosses Point clings to cliffs above the Atlantic. The third tee offers views of the ocean, the hills, and the unusual mountain Benbulben, which looks like a giant Irish arroyo. ✉ *Rosses Point, Co. Sligo,* ☎ *071/77186. 27 holes. Yardage: 6,565 (Old Course). Par 71.* 🍴 *Fees: weekdays, £35; weekends, £40.* ⊙ *Visitors: Mon., Tues., Thurs., and Fri. Practice area, caddies (summer only), caddy carts, club rental, catering.*

Donegal Golf Club. On the shores of Donegal Bay and approached through a forest, the windswept links are shadowed by the Blue Stack Mountains, with the Atlantic Ocean as a backdrop. The greens are large, but the rough is deep and penal, and there's a constant battle against erosion by the sea. Legendary golf writer Peter Dobereiner called it "hauntingly beautiful," perhaps recalling his experience on the par-3 5th, fittingly called "The Valley of Tears." ✉ *Murvagh, Laghey, Co. Donegal,* ☎ *073/34054. 18 holes. Yardage: 7,153. Par 73.* 🍴 *Fees: weekdays, £25; weekends, £30.* ⊙ *Visitors: daily. Practice area, caddies, caddy carts, catering.*

Enniscrone Golf Club. Eddie Hackett designed this course on the shores of another bay, this time Killala. Hackett may be the Pete Dye of Ireland, due in part to the fact that he's blessed with wonderful land: Enniscrone's setting is a natural for good golf—a combination of flatlands, foothills, and, of course, the Atlantic. It's not overly long on the score-card, but the persistent winds can add yards to almost every hole. It's among the small number of clubs in Ireland with electric carts, or, as they call them here, buggies. ⊠ *Enniscrone, Co. Sligo,* ☎ *96/36297. 18 holes. Yardage: 6,682. Par 72.* ⊠ *Fees: weekdays, £26; weekends, £34.* ☉ *Visitors: weekdays, weekends by appointment. Practice area, caddies (weekends and holidays), caddy carts, buggies, club rental.*

Northern Ireland

Ballycastle Golf Club. Pleasure comes first here, with challenge as an afterthought. It's beautiful (5 holes wind around the remains of a 13th-century friary), short (less than 6,000 yards), and conveniently located right next to Bushmills, the world's oldest distillery, at nearly 400 years. ⊠ *2 Cushendall Rd., Ballycastle BT54 6QP, Co. Antrim,* ☎ *028/2076–2536. 18 holes. Yardage: 5,882. Par 71.* ⊠ *Fees: week-days, U.K. £20; weekends, U.K. £28.* ☉ *Visitors: daily. Practice area, caddy cars, catering.*

Castlerock Golf Club. Where else in the world can you play a hole called "Leg o' Mutton"? Not in America, that's for sure. It's a 200-yard par-3 with railway tracks to the right and a burn to the left—just one of several unusual holes at this course, which claims, year-round, to have the best greens in Ireland. Whether that's true or not, the finish is spec-tacular: from the elevated 17th tee, where you can see the shores of Scot-land, to the majestic 18th, which plays uphill to a plateau green. ⊠ *65 Circular Rd., Castlerock BT51 4TJ, Co. Derry,* ☎ *028/7084–8314. 27 holes. Yardage: 6,499, 2,678. Par 73, 35.* ⊠ *Fees: weekdays, U.K. £35, U.K.£7; weekends, U.K. £40, U.K.£10.* ☉ *Visitors: Mon.–Thurs. Prac-tice area, caddies (reserve in advance), caddy cars, catering.*

Malone Golf Club. Fishermen may find the 22-acre lake at the center of this parkland layout distracting because it's filled with trout. The golf, however, is just as well stocked; large trees and well-manicured, undulating greens combine to provide one of the most challenging in-land tests in Ireland. Bring your power game—there are only three par-5s, but they're all more than 520 yards. ⊠ *240 Upper Malone Rd., Dunmurry, Belfast BT17 9LB,* ☎ *028/9061–2758. 27 holes. Yardage: 6,642, 3,138. Par 71, 36.* ⊠ *Fees: Mon., Tues., Thurs., Fri. U.K. £35 (men), £22 (women); Wed. and weekends, U.K. £40 (men), £30 (women).* ☉ *Visitors: Mon., Thurs., and Fri. Practice area, catering.*

Portstewart Golf Club. A century old in 1994, Portstewart may scare you with its opening hole, generally regarded as the toughest starter in Ireland. Picture a 425-yard par-4 that descends from an elevated tee to a small green tucked between the dunes. The greens are known for uniformity and speed, and seven of the holes have recently been re-designed to toughen the course. Also, if you want a break from the grand scale of championship links, there's the Old Course 18 and the Riverside 9, 27 holes of downsize, executive-style golf. ⊠ *117 Strand Rd., Portstewart BT55 7PT, Co. Derry,* ☎ *028/7083–2015. 45 holes. Yardage: 6,784 (Championship), 4,733 (Old Course), 2,662 (River-side). Par 72, 64, 32.* ⊠ *Fees: weekdays, U.K. £50 (Championship), U.K. £10 (Old Course), U.K. £12 (Riverside); weekends, U.K. £70 (Cham-pionship), U.K. £14 (Old Course), U.K. £17 (Riverside).* ☉ *Visitors: Mon., Tues., and Fri. Practice area, caddies, caddy cars, catering.*

★ **Royal County Down.** This is perhaps the most beautiful course in Ire-land. Catch it on the right day at the right time and you may think you're on the moon; Royal County Down is a links course with a sea of craterlike bunkers and small dunes. Actually, for better players, every day is the right one. Harry Vardon labeled it the toughest course on the Emerald Isle, and if you can't hit your driver long and straight, you might find it the toughest course in the world. It's a true masterpiece. ⊠ *Golf Links Rd., Newcastle BT33 0AN, Co. Down,* ☎ *028/4372– 2419. 36 holes. Yardage: 6,969 (Championship), 4,087 (Annesley). Par 71, 65.* ▨ *Fees: weekdays, U.K. £70 (Championship), £16 (Annesley); weekends, U.K. £80 (Championship), £23 (Annesley).* ☉ *Visitors: Tues., Thurs., and Fri. Practice area, caddies, caddy cars, catering.*

★ **Royal Portrush.** The only club outside Scotland and England to have hosted a British Open, Portrush is perhaps the most understated of Ireland's "Big Four." The championship Dunluce course is named for the ruins of a nearby castle and is a sea of sandhills and curving fairways. The Valley course is a less-exposed, tamer track. Both are conspicuous for their lack of bunkers. The Dunluce, in a poll of Irish golf legends, was voted the best in Ireland. ⊠ *Dunluce Rd., Portrush BT56 8JQ, Co. Antrim,* ☎ *028/7082–2311. 36 holes. Yardage: 6,530 (Dunluce), 6,054 (Valley). Par 72, 70.* ▨ *Fees: weekdays, U.K. £70 (Dunluce), U.K. £25 (Valley); weekends, U.K. £80 (Dunluce), U.K. £32 (Valley).* ☉ *Visitors: weekdays. Practice area, catering.*

10 BACKGROUND & ESSENTIALS

EIRE APPARENT

IF YOU FLY INTO IRELAND, your descent will probably be shrouded by gray clouds. As your plane breaks through the mists, you'll see the land for which the famed Emerald Isle was named: a lovely patchwork of rolling green fields speckled with farmhouses, cows, and sheep. Shimmering lakes, meandering rivers, narrow roads, and stone walls add to the impression that rolled out before you is a luxurious welcome carpet, one knit of the legendary "forty shades of green." (If you're lucky you may even see a rainbow—something you'll see again and again if you travel the countryside.) This age-old view of misty Ireland may be exactly what you imagined. Travelers still arrive expecting Eire to be the land of leprechauns, shillelaghs, shamrocks, and mist. Though we dislike the role of debunker, we feel it but fair to warn that the only known specimens of leprechauns or shillelaghs are those in souvenir shop windows; shamrocks bloom mainly on St. Patrick's Day or around the borders of Irish linen handkerchiefs and tablecloths; and the mists are in reality a soft apologetic rain that can envelope the whole country, cities and towns included, in a matter of minutes. Much can certainly still be sung and said about the "romance" of Ireland and the tear and smile in her eye. Soon enough, however, you'll discover that today's Ireland is this and more—much, much more.

The Celtic Tiger

In fact, Ireland is two-faced, like the Janus-stones and sheela-na-gigs of its pre-Christian past; it's a complex place where the mystic lyricism of Yeats, the hard Rabelaisian passions of Joyce, and the spare, aloof dissections of Beckett grew not only from a rich and ancient culture but also from 20th-century upheavals, few of which have been as dramatic as the transformation that has been changing Ireland for the past decade. Today, the country is racing toward the future. Consider the evidence: more than 150 years since the apocalyptic Great Famine, Ireland's economy—christened the "Celtic Tiger"—is now the fastest-growing in the industrialized world, up 25% in the last three years. Ireland is the second-largest exporter of computer software in the world, after the United States, while unemployment is lower than in France or Spain. Divorce became legal in 1997, and 41% of Ireland's populace are under the age of 24, with 69% younger than 44, making it the youngest nation in Europe. Most telling of all, however, is the fact that Ireland's net emigration has reversed, a profound demographic shift that was unthinkable just 10 years ago. There has been major immigration in each of the last three years—including a record 22,800 in 1999—and that trend shows every sign of continuing. The young who once left for London and New York are now staying, and more college graduates are returning than are leaving.

The foreign capital that has flowed into the country since it joined the Common Market (now the European Union) in 1973 has been crucial to this regeneration. But money alone doesn't guarantee culture, and Irish culture is thriving. Take just a few examples from literature: in 1995, Seamus Heaney claimed Ireland's fourth Nobel Prize in Literature in less than 75 years, and in January 2000 he won the prominent Whitbread Book Award for his translation of *Beowolf*. *Angela's Ashes*, Frank McCourt's memoir of his early life in Limerick, found millions of readers and won every major American literary prize. You name it— food, music, movies, literature, poetry, theater, art, fashion—and something innovative is afoot among the Irish at home and abroad. If you've been moved by seeing *Riverdance,* or *Lord of the Dance,* or reading *How the Irish Saved Civilization,* or hearing the Coors, Enya, Van Morrison, U2, Altan, or any of the hundreds of other prominent Irish musicians, you're likely to feel the spirit that touched you more palpably in Ireland itself, as you meet its people, and witness them imagining—and creating—the Irish spirit anew.

A Friendly People

Liam Neeson, Kenneth Branagh, Daniel Day-Lewis, Neil Jordan, and the Cranberries are just a few of the envoys extraordinaire for Irish culture around the world today. To find the real Ireland, however, you have to actually visit its green land. Venture down its back roads and you'll quickly discover that hospitality is counted among the greatest of Irish virtues, a legacy from Celtic times when anyone not offering the traveler food and drink was shamed. "You are welcome," people say in greeting the moment you cross the threshold of the smallest cottage, while total strangers will take you home for tea or supper and strike up conversations with ease and curiosity, entertaining you perhaps with an account of their second cousin's memorable fortnight in America (a fortnight's worth of stories if you have the time!).

Time, in fact, is one of the greatest luxuries in Ireland—outside fast-forward Dublin, that is. On a fine day, along a lushly green country lane, you may pass a bicycle abandoned against a tree; looking for its owner, you'll find him reclining in the feathery hedgerows or on the long grass, contemplating fast-moving clouds like some philosopher-king. "Oh the dreaming, the dreaming, the heart-scalding bitter, maddening dreaming," cried the playwright George Bernard Shaw, but to knowing travelers in the stressed and industrialized world, this haven of dreamers is a pearl of great price, sought after and kept secret. Forget America's car culture—Ireland has its cow culture. Explore the hills and dales and you'll find the moo-cows seem to own the country lanes, staring haughtily and curiously at interloping motorists, lazily drooping timothy from their soft maws. In the end, with persuasion from harried livery, equipped with frisky dogs and long-knobbed sticks, they'll share the road—but all in their time.

Somehow this may explain why Ireland is what some anthropologists call a "lived" culture, one that doesn't put all its stock in the outward monuments of achievement; where the most potent history is oral, where storytelling is an art, and where people will travel for miles for the "craic," the Irish synonym for a rousing good time. Ireland teaches you patience, reminds you of the rhythms of the natural world, and convinces you, reassuringly, of the essential well-being of humanity.

This is nowhere more the case than in the local pub, the center of social life in Ireland. Even a small town such as Dingle in County Kerry (population 1,000) boasts 52 watering holes, open day and night. Protocol dictates that you enter and greet everyone, taking a seat alone until invited (as you inevitably are) to join a table. Then the ancient custom of rounds begins, with the newcomer offering to buy the first set of drinks, and when the pints are barely half full (or is that half empty?), another imbiber stands the round, and so on, in turn. Dark village pubs, with their scratched wooden counters, dusty tiled floors, and the yeasty smell of Guinness, have a feeling of sanctity and remove from worldly cares not unlike a church. Sit awhile and enjoy your stout, but wit also flows untapped. Nuance and irony are the rules of conversation, and anything less would be considered flat-footed. Irish expertise in double-think and the witty tongue makes for a universally acknowledged aptitude for legal affairs, a gift for words of imagination and persuasiveness that you can find in the crossroads *shebeen* (pub) much as in Dublin's Leinster House, where the Irish *Dáil* (legislature) sits.

Digging up the Past

Despite Ireland's accessibility, you may feel a sense of otherness, attributable not only to the evergreen climate and leisurely pace of life but also to the layering of history and legend dug deep under the country's rich, grassy surface. Standing stones and court graves, mottes and dolmens, raths and cairns, holy wells and mass stones, round towers and Celtic crosses, churches and country houses—the artifacts of Ireland's long, turbulent history are everywhere, from the barren limestone Burren in County Clare to the Neolithic tombs and defenses of Newgrange in County Meath. Even an island off the main island—Inishmore, one of the Aran Islands far out in Galway Bay—claims its antiquity: Dún Aengus, which is 5,000 years older than the pyramids of Giza. Given how tempestuous the fortunes of this small island have been, you may be surprised by just how many of these sights remain.

Iron Age Celts from Central Europe settled in Ireland in the 4th century BC and left a legacy of an agrarian society based on a democratic kingship, a justice system known as the Brehon laws, and an artisan caste proficient in working gold and precious metals. (The National Museum in Dublin displays heaps of this Bronze Age gold jewelry.) Christianity arrived in Ireland in 432 with St. Patrick (or, perhaps, as some scholars suggest, two and possibly more missionaries whose work became conflated into the Patrician story). By the 8th century, Ireland was in its golden age. In general, the country's proliferating religious orders received protection from God-fearing Irish kings. Monks labored for decades to produce the *Book of Kells* (now on display at Trinity College in Dublin). Having set up monasteries throughout Ireland, Irish monks set out for Europe, where they continued their expansion of monastic communities from England to northern Italy. According to the bestseller, Thomas Cahill's *How the Irish Saved Civilization,* the medieval Irish monks who copied and standardized the masterpieces of Virgil and Horace helped to prevent the loss of classical Latin, the written language of Rome, to the vernacular Romance tongues of Italy, Spain, and France.

About 800, Viking longboats scourged the island's coasts. The Norsemen established settlements in Wexford, Cork, and Dublin (and leaving the mark of bright-red hair behind on their Irish descendants). Brian Boru, last of the High Kings to sit at Tara, won the Battle of Clontarf, defeating a troop of Viking raiders off the coast near Dublin in 1014. But Boru's subsequent murder marked the end of an era. Without his leadership, the power of the Irish kings dissipated, and in 1155, English-born Pope Adrian IV boldly granted dominion over Ireland to his fellow Englishman King Henry II. Fourteen years later Norman Strongbow arrived in Ireland, opening the door to more than 800 years of strife between the English and the Irish.

By 1609, the last of the Irish chieftains had lost their land to the British and sailed for exile, making way for the Plantation period. During this era 200,000 Scottish Lowlanders were "planted" on native Irish lands. Oliver Cromwell, "the Avenger," arrived with his troops in 1649, intent on making Ireland a Protestant country. He conducted a ruthless campaign of persecution against the already bitter Irish Catholics—a campaign that included beheading thousands of men, women, and children.

The Great Famine and Its Aftermath

Throughout the early 19th century, poverty was endemic and disease was a simple fact of life. Irish peasants worked for absentee British landlords and either paid exorbitant rents for land that had probably belonged to their parents or grandparents, or simply starved. The system was unjust, but somehow the bulk of Ireland survived the lean years prior to 1845. Within a year, however, potato blight ruined crops throughout the country. In a decade, the population was decimated, reduced from 8 to 6 million inhabitants. Starvation was largely to blame for the decline, but this period also marks the beginning of the large-scale emigration—to America, Canada, and Australia—that continued, albeit at a slower pace, until very recently. At last count, more than 70 million of Ireland's descendants are scattered abroad in the Irish diaspora—including 44 million in the United States.

The mid-19th-century also saw the rise of an Irish Nationalist movement. Various groups, including the Fenians and the Irish Republican Brotherhood, agitated for equal rights for Catholics, land reform, the revival of Ireland's Gaelic heritage, and the expulsion of the British from Ireland. The movement exploded—literally—on Easter Sunday 1916, when Nationalists proclaimed a republic. England's merciless vengeance on the patriots—it shot 15 of the uprising's leaders—galvanized the country to the bitter War of Independence, which ended in 1920 with the partitioning of Ireland into 26 counties in the South, constituting the Irish Free State, and six in the North, making up the British-ruled province of Northern Ireland. The defining event of modern Irish history, the severing of North from South eventually spawned nearly 30 years of Troubles in the North (though the roots of the Troubles date back 800 years) and cast a dark shadow over the country.

The Irish Ascendant

There is a place in an ancient Irish myth called Tír na nóg ("the land of the ever-young"). Ancient though it may be, it's a surprisingly relevant image for Ireland today. The fact that the country is, for the first time in more than 150 years, holding on to many of its young, speaks volumes—it is the era of the ascendant Irish. While past history is still treasured, there's a growing feeling among the young to look ahead, not back. "Get over it!" was the headline cover about Boston's young Irish population and their increasing focus on the years ahead, not on time-stained stories about the Famine. There's a growing

body of evidence for this newfound Irish assuredness—both within Ireland's shores and among the Irish abroad.

Together both the North and South of Ireland welcome more visitors annually (5.2 million) than they have residents (5 million). Not surprisingly, Dublin, the booming capital of the Republic, is the best place to take the pulse of Ireland. Home to half of the Republic's citizens, it is the Celtic Tiger's beating heart, a far cry from Joyce's "our dear, dirty Dublin." Dozens of cranes hover over new office buildings and hotels, and Georgian terrace houses are being brought back to glorious life. Visitors—especially weekenders from the Continent—fill Dublin's buzzing cafés, pubs, restaurants and hotels, and pour out onto busy Grafton Street and the narrow cobblestone alleys of Temple Bar. Outside Dublin, the country's quickening pulse is also palpable. New golf courses, housing developments, and blue-signed divided highways are signs of the changes afoot.

Less conspicuously, in villages throughout the country, heritage and genealogical centers have sprung up to accommodate the surge of interest among the Irish diaspora for information about their roots. This relationship between the past and the present, between those who left and those who stayed, is an elemental part of Ireland's identity. Today, throughout the Irish diaspora, there is a boundless yearning for all that Ireland embodies: indomitable strength against all odds, the romance of an ancient place, the longing for a lost world, the solace and transcendent possibility of art. It's likely that a trip to Ireland in the new millennium will put you in touch with the sources—historical and concrete, ineffable and mysterious—of this longing.

WHAT TO READ AND WATCH BEFORE YOU GO

Autobiography

Since it was published in September 1996, *Angela's Ashes,* Frank McCourt's enormously affecting memoir of growing up desperately poor in Limerick, has garnered every major American literary accolade, from the Pulitzer Prize to the National Book Critics Circle Award. The memoir remains a fixture at the top of American best-seller lists, and is now accompanied by its 1999 sequel,*'Tis.* In *An Only Child* and *My Father's Son* (1969), Frank O'Connor, known primarily for his fiction and short stories, recounts his years as an Irish revolutionary and later as an intellectual in Dublin during the 1920s. Christy Brown's *My Left Foot* is the autobiographical account of a Dublin artist stricken with cerebral palsy (☞ Movies and Videos, *below*).

Guidebooks and Travel Literature

Exploring Ireland (3rd ed.), published by Fodor's, is a full-color guide packed with photographs; it is an excellent companion guide to this edition.

Peter Somerville-Large's *Dublin* is filled with anecdotes relating to the famed Irish city. *Georgian Dublin,* by Desmond Guinness, the founder of the Irish Georgian Society, explores the city's architecture, with photographs and plans of Dublin's most admirable buildings. An excellent work on the Aran Islands is Tim Robinson's award-winning *The Stones of Aran: Pilgrimage.* Robinson has also written a long introduction to the Penguin edition of J. M. Synge's 1907 classic, *The Aran Islands.* Tomas Ó Crohán's *The Islandman* provides a good background on Dingle and the Blasket Islands.

In *Round Ireland in Low Gear* (1988), famed British travel writer Eric Newby breezily pens the story of his bicycle journey with his wife around the wet Emerald Isle. Fifty years older but no less fresh is H. V. Morton's *In Search of Ireland* (1938). Rebecca Solnit uses Ireland as a sounding board for her meditations on travel in *A Book of Migrations: Some Passages in Ireland* (1997).

History and Current Affairs

For two intriguing studies of Irish culture and history, consult Constantine FitzGibbon's *The Irish in Ireland* and Sean O'Faolain's *The Irish: A Character Study,* which traces the history of Ireland from Celtic times. J. C. Beckett's *The Making of Modern Ireland,* a concise introduction to Irish history, covers the years between 1603 and 1923. *Modern Ireland,* by R. F. Foster, spans the years between 1600 and 1972. Thomas Cahill's *How the Irish Saved Civilization* is a lively look at how Irish scholars kept the written word and culture alive in the so-called Dark Ages. Cecil Woodham-Smith's *The Great Hunger* (1962) details the history of the Irish potato famine of the 1840s. For an acclaimed history of Irish nationalism, try Robert Kee's *The Green Flag.* Peter De Rosa's *Rebels: The Irish Rising of 1916* is a popular, novelistic take on the defining event of modern Irish history. John Ardagh's *Ireland and the Irish: Portrait of a Changing Society* (1997) is one of the best sociological and economic analyses of modern Ireland. *"We Wrecked the Place": Contemplating an End to the Northern Irish Troubles* (1996) by Belfast-based journalist Jonathan Stevenson gives an insightful take on the subject. John Conroy's *Belfast Diary: War as a Way of Life* (1995) was reissued with a new afterword on the cease-fire. *The Lost Lives* (1999) is a recent, heart-wrenching collection of biographies about many who have died during the Troubles.

Literature

Ulysses (1922) is the linguistically innovative masterpiece by James Joyce, one of the titans of 20th-century literature. Emulating the structure of *The Odyssey,* and using an unprecedented stream-of-consciousness technique, Joyce follows Leopold and Molly Bloom and Stephen Daedalus through the course of a single day—June 16, 1904—around Dublin. More accessible introductions to Joyce's writing include *A Portrait of the Artist as a Young Man* (1916) and *Dubliners* (1914), a collection of short stories (its most accomplished story, "The Dead," was made into a movie starring Angelica Houston in 1988). Joyce aficionados may want to tackle his final, gigantic work, *Finnegan's Wake* (1939), which takes the linguistic experimentation of *Ulysses* to an almost incomprehensible level. Arguably the greatest literary challenge of the 20th century, its pages include word plays and phonetic metaphors in more than 100 languages. To prepare you for reading Joyce, you might seek out audio recordings in which he reads in his inimitable lilting tenor voice.

Samuel Beckett fills his story collection *More Pricks than Kicks* with Dublin characters; if you enjoy literary gamesmanship, you may also want to try Beckett's trilogy—*Molloy* (1951), *Malone Dies* (1951), and *The Unnameable* (1953).

If you're drawn to tales of unrequited love, turn to Elizabeth Bowen's stories and her novel *The Last September* (1929), set in Ireland during the Irish Civil War. If you prefer reading more magical novels, take a look at James Stephens's *A Crock of Gold* (1912), a charming and wise fairy tale written for adults, and Flann O'Brien's *At Swim-Two-Birds* (1939), a surrealistic tale full of Irish folklore.

One of Ireland's foremost fiction writers working today, Edna O'Brien began her career with the comic novel *The Country Girls* (1960) and has published 17 books since, most recently *House of Splendid Isolation* (1994) and *Down by the River* (1997). Like many of her compatriots, she is a superb short-story writer.

Her collection *A Fanatic Heart* (1985) is one of her best.

Thomas Flanagan's *The Year of the French* is a historical novel about the people of County Mayo, who revolted in 1798 with the help of French revolutionaries. *A Nest of Simple Folk,* by Sean O'Faolain, follows three generations of an Irish family between 1854 and 1916. Leon Uris's *Trinity* covers the years 1840–1916, as seen through the eyes of British, Irish Catholic, and Ulster Protestant families. In *No Country for Young Men,* Julia O'Faolain writes of two Irish families struggling to overcome the effects of the Irish Civil War. In John McGahern's prizewinning novel *Amongst Women,* modern-day Ireland attempts to reconcile itself to the upheavals of the early years of this century. For a more contemporary look at life in urban Ireland, try the phenomenally successful Roddy Doyle. All three works from his "Barrytown Trilogy"—*The Snapper, The Commitments,* and *The Van*—have been made into films; *Paddy Clarke Ha Ha Ha* has followed suit as another success.

Movies and Videos

A plethora of movies have been made in or about Ireland, and the number of Irish characters on screen is legion (the most numerous being priests, drunks, New York cops, and Old Mother Riley). *Juno and the Paycock* (known in the United States as *The Shame of Mary Boyle*) and *The Plough and the Stars* (1936), about the months leading up to the Easter Uprising, are early screen adaptations of Sean O'Casey's theatrical masterpieces. John Ford's superb *The Informer* (1935) is a full-blooded and highly stylized tale of an IRA leader's betrayal during the struggle for independence by a simpleminded hanger-on who wants to emigrate to the United States. Ford's boisterous comedy *The Quiet Man* (1952) is an Irish-village version of *The Taming of the Shrew,* with John Wayne playing a boxer who returns to his ancestor's village in the west of Ireland to claim local beauty Maureen O'Hara, and Barry Fitzgerald. David Lean's epic *Ryan's Daughter* (1970) is a four-hour pastoral melodrama of a village schoolmaster's wife falling for a British officer in the troubled Ireland of 1916; the film was a critical and commercial disaster for Lean, who didn't make another film for 14 years.

Daniel Day-Lewis and Brenda Fricker give Oscar-winning performances in Jim Sheridan's *My Left Foot* (1989), a biography of Christy Brown, the Irish writer and painter crippled from birth by cerebral palsy. Alan Parker's *The Commitments* (1991), from Roddy Doyle's best-seller, humorously recounts the efforts of a group of young, working-class northside Dubliners trying to make it as a soul band. In *A Man of No Importance* (1994), Albert Finney plays a sexually repressed bus conductor whose passion for poetry leads him to stage Wilde's *Salomé*. John Sayles hooked up with acclaimed cinematographer Haskell Wexler to make *The Secret of Roan Inish* (1996), a magical realist fable about a Selkie—a creature from Celtic folklore who is a seal in the water and a woman on land—and the fisherman's family whose lives she changes. *Waking Ned Devine* (1998) is a sidesplitting comedy about a small Irish village thrown into turmoil by a dead man's lottery winnings. *Angela's Ashes* (1999) has left an impact on some as strong as Frank McCourt's memoir.

Some of the best movies made in Ireland deal with the Troubles that have afflicted Northern Ireland. *Four Days in July* (1984), directed by Mike Leigh in classic cinema verité style, is a poignant and compelling portrayal of the sectarian divide in working-class Belfast. Helen Mirren stars as the widow of an executed Protestant policeman in *Cal* (1984), based on Bernard MacLaverty's masterful novel about the troubles. Daniel Day-Lewis was nominated for an Academy Award for his portrayal of Gerry Conlon, the wrongfully imprisoned Irish youth, in Jim Sheridan's *In the Name of the Father* (1993). Neil Jordan's *Michael Collins* (1996), with Liam Neeson and Julia Roberts, depicts the turbulent life of the heroic commander in chief of the Irish Republican Army from the Easter Uprising in 1916, when Collins was 25, until his assassination in West Cork six years later. Day-Lewis appears once again in *The Boxer* (1997), the story of an ex-boxer and former IRA man who tries to put his life back together in contemporary, sectarian Belfast.

Poetry

The poems of William Butler Yeats, Ireland's most celebrated poet, often describe the Irish landscape, including the Sligo and Coole countryside. A favorite poet among the Irish is Patrick Kavanagh, whose distinguished career was devoted to writing exceptionally about ordinary lives. Winner of the *Irish Times*–Aer Lingus Literary prize in 1993, Derek Mahon is the author of *Selected Poems* (1992) and many other books. Northern Ireland serves as the setting for many of Seamus Heaney's poems. *Selected Poems 1996–1987* (1990) and *The Spirit Level* (1996), his first collection published since he won the Nobel Prize in Literature in 1995, are both highly recommended introductions to his work. Though not as well known outside Ireland as Heaney, Paul Muldoon is another major Irish poet. His *Selected Poems: 1968–1986* (1987) and his most recent volume, *The Annals of Chile* (1994), are both good places to start. Eavan Boland is widely regarded as among the top tier of Irish poets and the finest woman writing poetry in Ireland today. *Object Lessons: The Life of the Woman and the Poet in Our Time* (1995) and *An Origin Like Water: Collected Poems 1957–1987* (1996) are two of her acclaimed books.

Theater

Ireland's playwrights are as distinguished as its novelists and short-story writers. Samuel Beckett, who moved from Ireland to Paris and began writing in French, is the author of the comic modernist masterpiece *Waiting for Godot* (1952), among many other plays. Oscar Wilde's finest plays, *The Importance of Being Earnest* and *An Ideal Husband* (both 1895), were playing to packed audiences in London when he was charged by his lover's father as a sodomite, setting in motion the trials that led to his downfall. Among the many plays of George Bernard Shaw, who grew up in Dublin, are *Arms and the Man* (1894), *Major Barbara* (1905), *Pygmalion* (1913), and *Saint Joan* (1923).

The history of Irish theater includes a number of controversial plays, such as J. M. Synge's *The Playboy of the Western World,* which was considered morally outrageous at the time of its opening in 1907 ("Playboy riots" took place in Dublin when the play was produced at the Abbey Theatre) but is appreciated today for its poetic language. Sean O'Casey wrote passionately about social injustice and working-class characters around the time of the Irish Civil War in such plays as *The Plough and the Stars* (1926) and *Juno and the Paycock*

(1924). *The Quare Fellow* (1956), by Brendan Behan, challenged accepted mores in the 1950s and at the time could only be produced in London. Behan is also well known for his play *The Hostage* and for *Borstal Boy* (1958), his memoirs. Two more recently recognized playwrights are Hugh Leonard (*Da* and *A Life*) and Brian Friel (*Philadelphia, Here I Come!, The Faith Healer,* and *Dancing at Lughnasa*), whose work often illuminates Irish small-town life. A new wave of young, brash Irish playwrights has taken London and Broadway by storm. Martin MacDonagh's *The Beauty Queen of Linane* and Conor McPherson's *The Weir* have won awards on both sides of the Atlantic.

IRELAND AT A GLANCE

ca. 3500 BC Neolithic (new Stone Age) settlers (origins uncertain) bring agriculture, pottery, and weaving. They also build massive megaliths—stone monuments with counterparts in England (Stonehenge), Brittany (Carnac), and elsewhere in Europe.

ca. 700 BC Celtic tribes begin to arrive via Britain and France; they divide Ireland into "fifths," or provinces, including Ulster, Leinster, Connaught, Meath, and Munster.

ca. AD 100 Ireland becomes the center of Celtic culture and trade without being settled by the Romans.

432 Traditional date for the arrival of St. Patrick and Christianity; in fact, Irish conversion to Christianity began at least a century earlier.

ca. 500–800 Golden age of Irish monasticism; as many as 3,000 study at Clonard (Meath). Irish missionaries carry the faith to barbarian Europe; art (exemplified by the *Book of Kells,* ca. 8th or 9th century) and Gaelic poetry flourish.

795 First Scandinavian Viking invasion; raids continue for the next 200 years. Viking towns founded include Dublin, Waterford, Wexford, Cork, and Limerick.

1014 Vikings decisively defeated at Clontarf by Irish troops under King Brian Boru of Munster. His murder cuts short hopes of a unified Ireland.

1172 Pope Alexander III confirms Henry II, king of England, as feudal lord of Ireland. Over the next two centuries, Anglo-Norman nobles establish estates, intermarry with the native population, and act in a manner similar to that of the neighboring Celtic chieftains. Actual control by the English crown is confined to a small area known as "the land of peace," or "the Pale," around Dublin.

1366 Statutes of Kilkenny attempt belatedly to enforce ethnic divisions by prohibiting the expression of Irish language and culture and intermarriage between the Irish and English, but Gaelic culture prevails and the Pale continues to contract. Constant warfare among the great landowners keeps Ireland poor, divided, and isolated from the rest of Europe.

1534–40 Henry VIII's break with the Catholic Church leads to insurrection in Ireland, led by Garret Mor's grandson Lord Offaly ("Silken Thomas"). He is executed with five of his brothers.

1558–1603 Reign of Queen Elizabeth I; her fear of Irish intrigue with Catholic enemies of England leads to expansion of English power.

1580–88 Edmund Spenser, an administrator for the Crown in Ireland, writes *The Faerie Queene.*

1591 Trinity College, Dublin, is founded.

1607 The Flight of the Earls and the beginning of the end of Gaelic Ireland. The earl of Tyrone and his ally Tyrconnell flee to Rome; their lands in Ulster are confiscated and opened to Protestant settlers, mostly Scots.

1641 Charles I's policies provoke insurrection in Ulster and, soon after, civil war in England.

1649 August: British leader Oliver Cromwell, having defeated Charles and witnessed his execution, invades Ireland, determined to crush Catholic opposition. Massacres at Drogheda and Wexford.

1652 Act of Settlement—lands of Cromwell's opponents are confiscated, and owners are forced across the Shannon to Connaught. Never fully carried out, this policy nonetheless establishes Protestant ascendancy.

1690 Battle of the Boyne—William of Orange lands in England and Catholic James II flees to Ireland to rally opposition. William pursues him with a large army and defeats him on the banks of the River Boyne in County Meath.

1775 American War of Independence begins, precipitating Irish unrest. Henry Grattan (1746–1820), a Protestant barrister, enters the Irish Parliament.

1782 Grattan's Parliament—Grattan asserts independence of Irish Parliament from Britain. Britain agrees, but independence is easier to declare than to sustain.

1823 Daniel O'Connell (1775–1847), "the Liberator," founds the Catholic Association to campaign for Catholic Emancipation.

1828 O'Connell's election to Parliament (illegal, because he was a Catholic) leads to passage of Catholic Emancipation Act in 1829; later, he works unsuccessfully for repeal of the Union.

1845–49 Failure of potato crop leads to famine; more than a million die, others migrate.

1856 Birth of George Bernard Shaw, playwright (d. 1950).

1858 Fenian Brotherhood founded in New York by Irish immigrants with the aim of overthrowing British rule. A revolt in 1867 fails, but it compels Gladstone, the British prime minister, to disestablish the Anglican Church (1869) and reform landholding (1870) in Ireland.

1865 Birth of William Butler Yeats, the great Irish poet (d. 1939).

1871 Isaac Butts founds parliamentary Home Rule Party, soon dominated by Charles Stewart Parnell (1846–91), descendant of English Protestants, who tries to force the issue by obstructing parliamentary business.

1890 Parnell is named corespondent in the divorce case of Kitty O'Shea; his career is ruined.

1893 Second Home Rule Bill passes Commons but is defeated by Lords. Subsequent policy is to "kill Home Rule with kindness" with land reform, but cultural nationalism revives with founding of Gaelic League to promote Irish language. Yeats, John Synge (1871–1909), and other writers find inspiration in Gaelic past.

1898 On the anniversary of Wolfe Tone's rebellion, Arthur Griffith (1872–1922) founds the Dublin newspaper the *United Irish-*

man, preaching *sinn féin* ("we ourselves")—secession from Britain; Sinn Féin party founded 1905. Socialist James Connolly (executed 1916) founds the *Workers' Republic.*

1904   William Butler Yeats and Lady Gregory found the Abbey Theatre in Dublin.

1914   Despite fierce opposition the Third Home Rule Bill passes the Commons and the Lords but is suspended due to the outbreak of World War I.

1916   Easter Uprising—Irish Republican Brotherhood (IRB) stages insurrection in Dublin and declares independence; the uprising fails, but the execution of 15 leaders by the British turns public opinion in favor of the insurgents. Yeats writes "a terrible beauty is born."

1919   January: Irish Parliamentarians meet as the Dail Éireann (Irish Assembly) and declare independence. September: Dail suppressed; Sinn Féin made illegal.

1920–21   War breaks out between Britain and Ireland: the "Black and Tans" versus the Irish Republican Army (IRA). Government of Ireland Act declares separate parliaments for North and South and continued ties to Britain. Elections follow, but the Sinn Féin majority in the South again declare themselves the Dail Éireann under Eamon de Valera (1882–1975), rejecting British authority. December 1921: Anglo-Irish Treaty grants the South dominion status as the Irish Free State, allowing the North to remain under Britain.

1922   De Valera and his Republican followers reject the treaty; civil war results. The Irish Free State adopts a constitution; William T. Cosgrave becomes president. Michael Collins, chairman of the Irish Free State and commander in chief of the army, is shot dead in County Cork, not far from where he was born. In Paris, James Joyce's *Ulysses* is published.

1923   De Valera is arrested and the civil war ends, but Republican agitation and terrorism continue. William Butler Yeats is the first Irish writer to be awarded the Nobel Prize in Literature; he also takes a seat in the first Irish Parliament.

1938   New constitution creates Republic of Ireland with no ties to Britain.

1939–1945   Despite strong pressure from Britain and the U.S., Ireland remains neutral throughout World War II.

1959   Eamon de Valera resigns as Taoiseach (prime minister) and is later elected president.

1963   John F. Kennedy, the first Irish-American President of the United States, visits Ireland.

1972   Republic of Ireland admitted to European Economic Community. Troubles continue in the North. In Derry on January 30, British troops shoot 13 unarmed demonstrators on "Bloody Sunday." Stormont (the Northern Parliament) is suspended and direct rule from London is imposed. Acts of terrorism on both sides lead to draconian law enforcement by the British. "The Troubles," as the conflict is dubbed, will last 26 years and claim more than 3,000 lives.

1991   Mary Robinson becomes the first female President of the Republic of Ireland. Peace talks begin between the British and Irish governments and the main political parties of the North, excepting Sinn Féin.

1992   Ireland approves European Union. Sixty-two percent of the Irish vote in a referendum in favor of allowing pregnant women to seek an abortion abroad.

1994   The IRA, in response to advances made by the Irish, British, and U.S. governments, announces a complete cessation of activities. Protestant paramilitary groups follow suit one month later. Gerry Adams, the leader of Sinn Féin, speaks on British TV and radio.

1996   Frustrated by the slow progress of the peace talks, the IRA explodes bombs on the British mainland, throwing the whole peace process into doubt. But violence has not returned to the province, and all parties say they are committed to peace.

1997   The Republic of Ireland legalizes divorce. Newly elected British prime minister Tony Blair apologizes for the British government's policies during Ireland's Great Famine, acknowledging that his predecessors' policies prolonged "a massive human tragedy." The IRA reestablishes its cease-fire.

1998   On Good Friday 1998, all sides in the conflict agree on an agreement for sharing power that guarantees the rights of the Catholic minority. Referenda in the North and the Republic show overwhelming support. A splinter IRA group opposed to the agreement explodes a bomb in Omagh, killing more than 20 people. Catholic leader John Hume and Protestant David Trimble share the Nobel Peace Prize.

1999   Despite sporadic violence by splinter loyalist groups, a new executive branch of government, the Northern Ireland Assembly, is formed at Stormont in Belfast on November 27th. Northern Ireland is no longer governed directly from Westminster.

2000   Proposals are made to reform the RUC (Royal Ulster Constabulary) by making it half Catholic and half Protestant and renaming it the "Northern Irish Police Force." Tensions remain high over the decommissioning of weapons.

Irish Family Names

Antrim
Lynch
McDonnell
McNeill
O'Hara
O'Neill
Quinn

Armagh
Hanlon
McCann

Carlow
Kinsella
Nolan
O'Neill

Cavan
Boylan
Lynch
McCabe
McGovern
McGowan
McNally
O'Reilly
Sheridan

Clare
Aherne
Boland
Clancy
Daly
Lynch
McGrath
McInerney
McMahon
McNamara
Molon(e)y
O'Brien
O'Dea
O'Grady
O'Halloran
O'Loughlin

Cork
Barry
Callaghan
Cullinane
Donovan
Driscoll
Flynn
Hennessey
Hogan
Lynch
McCarthy
McSweeney
Murphy
Nugent
O'Casey
O'Cullane
(Collins)

O'Keefe
O'Leary
O'Mahony
O'Riordan
Roche
Scanlon
Sheridan

Derry
Cahan
Hegarty
Kelly
McLaughlin

Donegal
Boyle
Clery
Doherty
Friel
Gallagher
Gormley
McGrath
McLoughlin
McSweeney
Mooney
O'Donnell

Down
Lynch
McGuinness
O'Neil
White

Dublin
Hennessey
O'Casey
Plunkett

Fermanagh
Cassidy
Connolly
Corrigan
Flanagan
Maguire
McManus

Galway
Blake
Burke
Clery
Fah(e)y
French
Jennings
Joyce
Kelly
Kenny
Kirwan
Lynch
Madden
Moran
O'Flaherty
O'Halloran

Kerry
Connor
Fitzgerald
Galvin
McCarthy
Moriarty
O'Connell
O'Donoghue
O'Shea
O'Sullivan

Kildare
Cullen
Fitzgerald
O'Byrne
White

Kilkenny
Butler
Fitzpatrick
O'Carroll
Tobin

Laois
Dempsey
Doran
Dunn(e)
Kelly
Moore

Leitrim
Clancy
O'Rourke

Limerick
Fitzgerald
Fitzgibbon
McKeough
O'Brien
O'Cullane
(Collins)
O'Grady
Woulfe

Longford
O'Farrell
Quinn

Louth
O'Carroll
Plunkett

Mayo
Burke
Costello
Dugan
Gormley
Horan
Jennings
Jordan
Kelly
Madden
O'Malley

Meath
Coffey
Connolly
Cusack
Dillon
Hayes
Hennessey
Plunkett
Quinlan

Monaghan
Boylan
Connolly
Hanratty
McKenna
McMahon
McNally

Offaly
Coghlan
Dempsey
Fallon
(Maher)
Malone
Meagher
Molloy
O'Carroll
Sheridan

Roscommon
Fallon
Flanagan
Flynn
Hanley
McDermot
McKeough
McManus
Molloy
Murphy

Sligo
Boland
Higgins
McDonagh
O'Dowd
O'Hara
Rafferty

Tipperary
Butler
Fogarty
Kennedy
Lynch
Meagher
(Maher)
O'Carroll
O'Dwyer
O'Meara
Purcell
Ryan

Tyrone
Cahan
Donnelly
Gormley
Hagan
Murphy
O'Neill
Quinn

Waterford
Keane
McGrath
O'Brien
Phelan
Power

Westmeath
Coffey
Dalton
Daly
Dillon
Sheridan

Wexford
Doran
Doyle
Hartley
Kavanagh
Keating
Kinsella
McKeogh
Redmond
Walsh

Wicklow
Cullen
Kelly
McKeogh
O'Byrne
O'Toole

ESSENTIAL INFORMATION

Basic Information on Traveling in Ireland, Savvy Tips to Make Your Trip a Breeze, and Companies and Organizations to Contact

ADDRESSES

We have tried to provide full addresses for hotels, restaurants, and sights, though many of Ireland's villages and towns are so tiny they barely have street names, much less house numbers. If in doubt, ask for directions.

AIR TRAVEL

From North America and the United Kingdom, Aer Lingus is the main carrier to Ireland. Indirect flights from the United States and Canada fly via London and then switch to Aer Lingus or Ryanair for the final leg to Dublin. There are no direct flights from Australia or New Zealand. Regular service is available from most major airports in Ireland to most major cities in England and Scotland, including Leeds, Manchester, and Glasgow. In general, flying into Ireland tends to be a relatively hassle-free experience, although an increase in traffic in the last decade has caused a slight increase in flight delays and waiting for baggage to clear customs.

BOOKING

When you book **look for nonstop flights** and **remember that "direct" flights stop at least once.** Try to avoid connecting flights, which require a change of plane.

CARRIERS

When flying internationally, you must usually choose between a domestic carrier, the national flag carrier of the country you are visiting, and a foreign carrier from a third country. National flag carriers have the greatest number of nonstops. Domestic carriers may have better connections to your home town and serve a greater number of gateway cities. Third-party carriers may have a price advantage.

Aer Lingus is the national flag carrier of Ireland, with regularly scheduled flights to Shannon and Dublin from JFK, Newark, Boston's Logan, Chicago's O'Hare, and LAX. Delta has a daily departure from Atlanta that flies first to Dublin and on to Shannon. Continental flies daily direct to Dublin and Shannon, departing from Newark Airport in New Jersey. Aeroflot flies twice weekly from Miami, three times weekly from Washington, DC (Dulles), and once a week from Chicago. With the exception of special offers, the prices of the four airlines tend to be similar.

London to Dublin is now one of the busiest international air routes in the world and four main carriers, as well as numerous smaller airlines, provide daily service on this route. With such healthy competition, there are plenty of bargains to be found. Ryanair, a relatively new Irish airline, is famous for its cheap, no-frills service.

Both Aer Lingus and Ryanair provide service around Ireland.

➤ MAJOR AIRLINES: **Aer Lingus** (☎ 800/223–6537). **Aeroflot** (☎ 888/340–6400). **Continental** (☎ 800/231–0856). **Delta** (☎ 800/241–4141).

➤ FROM THE U.K.: **Aer Lingus** (☎ 0845/973–7747 or 020/8899–4747). **British Airways** (☎ 0345/222–1111). **British Midlands** (☎ 020/8745–7321). **Ryanair** (☎ 0870/156–9569).

CHECK-IN & BOARDING

Checking in and boarding an outbound plane in Ireland tends to be fairly hassle-free. Security is professional but not overbearing, and airport staff are usually helpful and patient. During the busy summer season lines can get longer, and you should play it safe and arrive the suggested two hours before your flight. You'll need to show your passport before checking in.

Assuming that not everyone with a ticket will show up, airlines routinely overbook planes. When everyone does, airlines ask for volunteers to give up their seats. In return, these volunteers usually get a certificate for a free flight and are rebooked on the next flight out. If there are not enough volunteers, the airline must choose who will be denied boarding. The first to get bumped are passengers who checked in late and those flying on discounted tickets, so **get to the gate and check in as early as possible,** especially during peak periods.

Always **bring a government-issued photo I.D. to the airport.** You may be asked to show it before you are allowed to check in.

CUTTING COSTS

The least expensive airfares to Ireland must usually be purchased in advance and are nonrefundable. It's smart to **call a number of airlines, and when you are quoted a good price, book it on the spot**—the same fare may not be available the next day. Always **check different routings** and look into using different airports. Travel agents, especially low-fare specialists (☞ Discounts & Deals, *below*), are helpful.

Consolidators are another good source. They buy tickets for scheduled international flights at reduced rates from the airlines, then sell them at prices that beat the best fare available directly from the airlines, usually without restrictions. Sometimes you can even get your money back if you need to return the ticket. Carefully read the fine print detailing penalties for changes and cancellations, and **confirm your consolidator reservation with the airline.**

When you **fly as a courier,** you trade your checked-luggage space for a ticket deeply subsidized by a courier service. There are restrictions on when you can book and how long you can stay.

Charter carriers such as **Scepter Charters** offer flights to Dublin and Shannon from various U.S. cities. **Air Canada Vacations** and **Regent Holidays** fly from Canada. Note that in certain seasons, usually fall and winter, their charter deals include mandatory hotel and car-rental packages.

To save money on flights from the United Kingdom and back, **look into an APEX or Super-PEX ticket.** APEX tickets must be booked in advance and have certain restrictions. Super-PEX tickets can be purchased at the airport on the day of departure—subject to availability.

➤ CONSOLIDATORS: **Cheap Tickets** (☎ 800/377–1000). **Discount Airline Ticket Service** (☎ 800/576–1600). **Unitravel** (☎ 800/325–2222). **Up & Away Travel** (☎ 212/889–2345). **World Travel Network** (☎ 800/409–6753).

➤ COURIERS: **New Voyager** ☎ 212/431–1616.

➤ CHARTERS: **Air Canada Vacations** (☎ 800/263–0882). **Regent Holidays** (☎ 800/387–4860). **Scepter Charters** (☎ 516/255–9800).

ENJOYING THE FLIGHT

For more legroom, **request an emergency-aisle seat.** Don't sit in the row in front of the emergency aisle or in front of a bulkhead, where seats may not recline. If you have dietary concerns, **ask for special meals when booking.** These can be vegetarian, low-cholesterol, or kosher, for example. On long flights, try to maintain a normal routine, to help fight jet lag. At night, **get some sleep.** By day, **eat light meals, drink water** (not alcohol), and **move around the cabin** to stretch your legs.

FLYING TIMES

Flying time to Ireland is 6½ hours from New York, 7½ hours from Chicago, and 10 hours from Los Angeles.

HOW TO COMPLAIN

If your baggage goes astray or your flight goes awry, complain right away. Most carriers require that you **file a claim immediately.**

➤ AIRLINE COMPLAINTS: U.S. Department of Transportation **Aviation Consumer Protection Division** (✉ C-75, Room 4107, Washington, DC

20590, ☎ 202/366–2220, aircon-sumer@ost.dot.gov, www.dot.gov/air-consumer). **Federal Aviation Administration Consumer Hotline** (☎ 800/322–7873).

RECONFIRMING

Even if an airline says there's no need to reconfirm, it's best to do so anyway 12–14 hours before your flight to ensure that your seat is held; you can also check to see if the flight schedule has changed.

AIRPORTS

The major gateways to Ireland are Dublin Airport, 10 km (6 mi) north of the city center, and Shannon Airport on the west coast, 25½ km (16 mi) west of Limerick. Two airports serve Belfast: Belfast International Airport at Aldergrove, 24 km (15 mi) from the city, handles local and U.K. flights, as well as all other international traffic; Belfast City Airport, 6½ km (4 mi) from the city, handles local and United Kingdom flights only. In addition, the City of Derry Airport receives flights from Manchester, Birmingham, and Glasgow in the United Kingdom and Scotland.

➤ AIRPORT INFORMATION: **Belfast City Airport** (☎ 028/9045–7745). **Belfast International Airport at Aldergrove** (☎ 028/9442–2888). **City of Derry Airport** (☎ 028/7181–0784). **Dublin Airport** (☎ 01/844–4900). **Shannon Airport** (☎ 061/471444).

DUTY-FREE SHOPPING

Duty-free shopping for people traveling between European Union (EU) countries ended July 1, 1999. You can, however, purchase duty-free goods when traveling between any EU country and a non-EU country. For duty-free allowances when entering Ireland from a non-EU country, *see* Customs & Duties, *below*.

BIKE TRAVEL

Ireland is a cyclist's paradise. The scenery is phenomenal, the roads are flat and uncrowded, and the distance from one village to the next is rarely more than 16 km (10 mi). The massive influx of EU money into the roads over the last decade has banished many of the dreaded pothole-covered byways to the distant past.

On the downside, though, foul weather and rough roads in remote areas are all too common, so rain gear and spare parts are a must.

There are plenty of bike rental shops in the country. Most offer 12- to 18-gear mountain bikes with index gears and rear carriers for about £10 per day or £50 per week. A refundable deposit of £50 is often required. For a fee of £12 or so, you can rent a bike at one location and drop it off at another. Raleigh Ireland have dealers all over the country who do repairs and rentals.

➤ BIKE RENTALS: **Raleigh Ireland** (✉ Raleigh House, Kylemore Rd., Dublin 10, ☎ 01/626–1333).

BIKES IN TRANSIT

Most airlines accommodate bikes as luggage, provided they are dismantled and boxed. For bike boxes, often free at bike shops, you'll pay about $5 from airlines (at least $100 for bike bags). International travelers can sometimes substitute a bike for a piece of checked luggage at no charge; otherwise, the cost is about $100. Domestic and Canadian airlines charge $25–$50. Most ferries will transport your bicycle for free. If there's room, Irish buses and Irish Rail will transport bikes for a small fee.

BOAT & FERRY TRAVEL

There are two principal ferry routes to the Irish Republic: to Dublin from Holyhead on the Isle of Anglesea, and to Rosslare from Fishguard or Pembroke in Wales. Two main companies sail the Dublin route: Irish Ferries from Dublin port and Stena Sealink, whose ferries go both to Dublin port and Dun Laoghaire, 4 km (2½ mi) south of the city center. SeaCat Ferries have also started service to Dublin from Liverpool. The trip takes about four hours. Prices and departure times vary according to season, so call to confirm. In summer, reservations are strongly recommended. Dozens of taxis wait to take you into town from both Dublin port and Dun Laoghaire, or you can take DART or a bus to the city center.

Irish Ferries operates the Pembroke–Rosslare route; Stena Sealink operates the Fishguard–Rosslare route. To connect with the Fishguard sailings, take one of the many direct trains from London (Paddington). A connecting train at Rosslare will get you to Waterford by about 8:30 PM, to Cork by about midnight. For the Pembroke sailings, you have to change at Swansea. Sailing time for both routes is 4½ hours.

Swansea Cork Ferries operate a service between Swansea and Cork from mid March to early January. The crossing takes 12 hours, but easy access by road to both ports make this longer sea route a good choice for motorists heading for the Southwest. They also sail from Stranraer, Scotland to Belfast and Larne.

The cost of your trip can vary substantially, so **spend time with a travel agent and compare prices carefully**; flying is sometimes cheaper, and fares to Dublin are cheapest. **Book well in advance at peak periods.** Students and others under 26 should take advantage of the cheap fares offered by Eurotrain.

Car ferries run to Northern Ireland from the Scottish port of Stranraer. Trains leave London (Euston) for Stranraer Harbour several times a day. Sealink Ferries crosses the water to the port of Larne, where you pick up a train to Belfast. The whole trip is around 13 hours. Much faster and more convenient is the SeaCat, a huge, car-ferry catamaran that crosses from Stranraer right into Belfast in just 1½ hours. Trains leave London (Euston) for Liverpool throughout the day.

If you're traveling from County Kerry to County Clare and the West of Ireland, you can take the ferry from Tarbert (in County Kerry), leaving every hour on the half hour. Going the other way, ferries leave from Killimer (in County Clare) every hour on the hour. The 30-minute journey across the Shannon Estuary costs £7 per car, £2 for foot passengers.

A 10-minute car ferry crosses the River Suir between Ballyhack in County Wexford and Passage East in County Waterford. It saves you a boring drive through New Ross on the N25 and also introduces you to two pretty fishing villages, Ballyhack

and Arthurstown. The ferry operates continuously during daylight hours and costs £3.50 per car, 80p for foot passengers.

The Cork Harbour crossing is a scenic route that allows those traveling from west Cork or Kinsale to Cobh and the east coast to bypass the city center. The five-minute car ferry runs from Glenbrook (near Ringaskiddy) in the west to Carrigaloe (near Cobh) in the east and operates continuously from 7:15 AM to 12:45 AM daily. It costs £3 per car, 60p for foot passengers.

You can reach many, but not all, of Ireland's offshore islands by ferry. There are regular services to the Aran Islands from Galway City, Rossaveal in County Galway, and Doolin in County Clare. Ferries also sail to Inishbofin off the Galway coast and Arranmore off the Donegal coast, and to Bere, Sherkin, and Cape Clear islands off the coast of County Cork. The islands are all small enough to explore on foot, so the ferries are for foot passengers and bicycles only. Other islands—the Blaskets and the Skelligs in Kerry, Rathlin, and Tory off the Donegal coast—can be reached by private arrangements with local boatmen (☞ relevant regional chapters). Full details on ferries to the islands are available in a publication from the ITB (☞ Visitor Information, *below*).

FARES & SCHEDULES

You can get schedules and purchase tickets, with a credit card if you like, from the offices listed below. You can also pick them up at Dublin Tourism offices and from any major travel agent in Ireland or the United Kingdom.

➤ BOAT & FERRY INFORMATION: **Cork Swansea Ferries** (✉ 52 S. Mall St., Cork, ☎ 021/271166). **Irish Ferries** (✉ Merrion Row, Dublin, ☎ 01/661–0511). **SeaCat** (✉ Donegal Quay, Belfast, ☎ 028/9031–2301). **Stena Sealink** (✉ Ferryport, Dun Laoghaire, ☎ 01/204–7777 or 01/204–7700).

BUS TRAVEL

IN THE REPUBLIC OF IRELAND

Buses are a cheap, flexible way to explore the countryside. Expressway

bus services, with the most modern buses, cover the country's major routes. Outside the peak season, services are limited, and some routes (e.g., Killarney–Dingle) disappear altogether. There is often only one service a day on the express routes—and one a week to some of the more remote villages!

Long-distance bus services are operated by Bus Éireann, which also provides local services in Cork, Galway, Limerick, and Waterford. To ensure that your proposed bus journey is feasible, **buy a copy of Bus Éireann's timetable**—80p from any bus terminal.

Many of the destination indicators on bus routes are in Irish, so **make sure you get on the right bus.** Asking someone to translate is often the best way to avoid a mishap.

IN NORTHERN IRELAND

In Northern Ireland, all buses are operated by the state-owned Ulsterbus. Service is generally good, with particularly useful links to those towns not served by train. Ulsterbus also offers tours. (For details ☞ Northern Ireland A to Z *in* Chapter 8.)

FROM THE U.K.

Numerous bus services run between Britain and the Irish Republic, but **be ready for long hours on the road and possible delays.** All buses to the Republic use either the Holyhead–Dublin or Fishguard/Pembroke–Rosslare ferry routes. National Express, a consortium of bus companies, has Supabus (as its buses are known) services from all major British cities to more than 90 Irish destinations. Slattery's, an Irish company, has services from London, Manchester, Liverpool, Oxford, Birmingham, Leeds, and North Wales to over 100 Irish destinations.

Buses to Belfast run from London and from Birmingham, making the Stranraer–Larne crossing. Contact National Express (☞ *below*). The numbers listed are in London, so be sure to add the 44 country code and drop the 0 from the area code when dialing from abroad.

CLASSES

Buses have only one class, and prices are similar for all seats.

CUTTING COSTS

A Freedom of Northern Ireland ticket costs U.K.£32 for seven days' unlimited travel. A one-day ticket costs U.K.£9. Several passes offer discounts on both the bus and rail system in the Irish Republic, including the **Irish Explorer Rail & Bus Pass,** the **Go as You Please Rambler Card,** and the **Emerald Isle Card** (☞ Cutting Costs *in* Train Travel, *below*).

FARES & SCHEDULES

Pick up a timetable at any bus station or call the numbers below for a schedule. It's best to avoid Friday-evening and Sunday-morning travel, as this is when throngs of workers from the country return to and depart from Dublin on the weekends.

➤ BUS INFORMATION: **Bus Éireann**(☎ 01/836–6111). **National Express** (☎ 020/7724–0741). **Slattery's** (☎ 020/7482–1604). **Ulsterbus** (☎ 028/9033–3000).

PAYING

You can buy tickets at the main tourist offices, at the bus station, or on the bus (cash only for the latter option).

RESERVATIONS

Check the bus office to see if reservations are accepted for your route; if not, show up early to get a seat. Note: prepaid tickets don't apply to a particular bus time, just a route, so if one vehicle is full you can try another.

BUSINESS HOURS

Business hours are generally 9–5, sometimes later in the larger towns. In smaller towns, stores often close from 1 to 2 for lunch. If a holiday falls on a weekend, most businesses are closed on Monday as well.

BANKS & OFFICES

Banks are open 10–4, Monday–Friday. In small towns they may close from 12:30 to 1:30. They remain open until 5 one afternoon per week; the day of week varies, although it's usually Thursday. Post offices are open weekdays 9–5 and Saturdays 9–1; some of the smaller country offices close for lunch.

In Northern Ireland bank hours are weekdays 9:30–4:30. Post offices are open weekdays 9–5:30, Saturday 9–1. Some close for an hour at lunch.

GAS STATIONS

There are some 24-hour gas stations along the highways; otherwise, hours vary from morning rush hour to late evenings.

MUSEUMS & SIGHTS

Museum and sights are generally open Tuesday–Saturday 10–5 and Sunday 2–5.

PHARMACIES

Most pharmacies are open 9–5:30 or 6, Monday–Saturday. Larger towns and cities often have a 24-hour pharmacy.

SHOPS

Most shops are open 9–5:30 or 6, Monday–Saturday. Once a week—normally Wednesday, Thursday, or Saturday—they close at 1 PM. These times do *not* apply to Dublin, where stores generally stay open later, and they can vary from region to region, so it's best to check locally. Larger shopping malls usually stay open late once a week—generally until 9 on Thursday or Friday.

Shops in Belfast are open 9–5:30, Monday–Friday, with a late closing on Thursday, usually at 9. Elsewhere in Northern Ireland, shops close for the afternoon once a week, usually Wednesday or Thursday; check locally. In addition, most smaller shops close for an hour or so at lunch.

CAMERAS & PHOTOGRAPHY

➤ PHOTO HELP: **Kodak Information Center** (☎ 800/242–2424). *Kodak Guide to Shooting Great Travel Pictures,* available in bookstores or from Fodor's Travel Publications (☎ 800/533–6478; $16.50 plus $5.50 shipping).

EQUIPMENT PRECAUTIONS

Always **keep your film and tape out of the sun.** Carry an extra supply of

batteries, and **be prepared to turn on your camera or camcorder** to prove to security personnel that the device is real. Always **ask for hand inspection of film,** which becomes clouded after repeated exposure to airport X-ray machines, and **keep videotapes away from metal detectors.**

FILM & DEVELOPING

Major brands of film are available throughout Ireland, although 24-hour developing is found only in larger cities. Videotape is also widely available.

CAR RENTAL

If you are renting a car in the Irish Republic and intend to visit Northern Ireland (or vice versa), make this clear when you get your car, and check that the rental insurance applies when you cross the border.

Renting a car in Ireland is far more expensive than organizing a rental before you leave the United States. Rates in Dublin for an economy car with a manual transmission and unlimited mileage begin at $40 a day/$200 a week (January–April and November–December 15); $45 a day/$250 a week (May–June and September–October); and $60 a day/$320 a week (July–August and December 16–31). This includes the Republic's 12½% tax on car rentals.

Rates in Belfast begin at $42 a day/$210 a week (January–June and September–December 15) and $45 a day/$300 a week (July–August and December 16–31). This does not include the 17½% tax on car rentals in the North.

➤ MAJOR AGENCIES: **Alamo** (☎ 800/522–9696; 020/8759–6200 in the U.K.). **Avis** (☎ 800/331–1084; 800/331–1084 in Canada; 02/9353–9000 in Australia; 09/525–1982 in New Zealand). **Budget** (☎ 800/527–0700; 0870/607–5000 in the U.K., through affiliate Europcar). **Dollar** (☎ 800/800–6000; 0124/622–0111 in the U.K., through affiliate Sixt Kenning; 02/9223–1444 in Australia). **Hertz** (☎ 800/654–3001; 800/263–0600 in Canada 020/8897–2072 in the U.K.; 02/9669–2444 in Australia; 09/256–8690 in New Zealand). **National Car Rental** (☎ 800/227–7368; 020/8680–

4800 in the U.K., where it is known as National Europe).

CUTTING COSTS

To get the best deal, **book through a travel agent who will shop around.** Do **look into wholesalers,** companies that do not own fleets but rent in bulk from those that do and often offer better rates than traditional car-rental operations. Payment must be made before you leave home.

➤ LOCAL AGENCIES: Argus (☎ 01/ 490–4444 in Dublin). **Dan Dooley** (☎ 800/331–9301 in the U.S., 0800/ 282–189 in the U.K., 01/677–2723 in Dublin). **ECL Chauffeur Drive** (☎ 01/704–4062) offers chauffeur-driven Mercedes sedans, minivans, and coaches for a journey or daily rate.

➤ WHOLESALERS: **Auto Europe** (☎ 207/842–2000 or 800/223–5555, FAX 800/235–6321, www.autoeurope.com). **Europe by Car** (☎ 212/581–3040 or 800/223–1516, FAX 212/246–1458, www.europebycar.com). **DER Travel Services** (✉ 9501 W. Devon Ave., Rosemont, IL 60018, ☎ 800/782– 2424, FAX 800/282–7474 for information, 800/860–9944 for brochures, www.dertravel.com). **Kemwel Holiday Autos** (☎ 800/678–0678, FAX 914/825–3160, www.kemwel.com).

INSURANCE

When driving a rented car you are generally responsible for any damage to or loss of the vehicle. Before you rent see what coverage your personal auto-insurance policy and credit cards already provide.

Collision policies that car-rental companies sell for European rentals usually do not include stolen-vehicle coverage. Before you buy it, check your existing policies—you may already be covered.

REQUIREMENTS & RESTRICTIONS

In Ireland your own driver's license is acceptable. An International Driver's Permit is a good idea; it's available from the American or Canadian automobile association, and, in the United Kingdom, from the Automobile Association or Royal Automobile Club. These international permits are universally recognized, and having one in your wallet may save you a problem with the local authorities.

Most rental companies require you to be over 23 to rent a car in Ireland (a few will rent to those over 21) and to have had a licence for over a year. Some companies also refuse to rent to visitors over 70.

SURCHARGES

Before you pick up a car in one city and leave it in another, **ask about drop-off charges or one-way service fees,** which can be substantial. Note, too, that some rental agencies charge extra if you return the car before the time specified in your contract. To avoid a hefty refueling fee, **fill the tank just before you turn in the car,** but be aware that gas stations near the rental outlet may overcharge.

CAR TRAVEL

A car journey on Ireland's many back roads and byways is the ideal way to explore the country's predominantly rural attractions. Roads are generally good, although four-lane, two-way roads are the exception rather than the rule. Most National Primary Routes (designated by the letter N) have two lanes with generous shoulders on which to pass. Brand-new divided highways, or motorways— designated by blue signs and the letter M—take the place of some N roads. They are the fastest way to get from one point to another, but use caution: they sometimes end as abruptly as they begin. In general, traffic is light, especially off the national routes, although Dublin is always very congested in rush hour and on weekend evenings. It's also wise to **slow down on the smaller, often twisty roads** and **watch out for cattle and sheep;** they may be just around the next bend. Reckless driving, such as speeding, is not uncommon in the countryside, so stay alert and use caution. Speed limits are 96 kph (60 mph) on the open road, 112 kph (70 mph) on the motorways, and 48 kph (30 mph) in urban areas.

Road signs are generally in both Irish (Gaelic) and English; in the northwest and Connemara, most are in Irish only, so **make sure you have a good road map.** On the new green signposts distances are in kilometers; on the old white signposts they're given in miles. Because of the coexistence of both old and new signs, the route number is not always referred to on the signpost, particularly on National Secondary Roads (also called *N*-numbered routes) and Regional roads (*R*-numbered routes). On such roads, knowing the name of the next town on your itinerary is more important than knowing the route number: neither the small local signposts nor the local people refer to roads by official numbers. At unmarked intersections, a good rule of thumb is to **keep going straight if there's no sign directing you to do otherwise.**

Traffic signs are the same as in the rest of Europe, and roadway markings are standard. Note that a continuous white line down the center of the road prohibits passing. Barred markings on the road and flashing yellow beacons indicate a crossing, where pedestrians have right of way. At a junction of two roads of equal importance, the driver to the right has right of way.

The road network in Northern Ireland is excellent and, outside Belfast, uncrowded. Road signs and traffic regulations conform to the British system. Speed limits are 48 kph (30 mph) in towns, 96 kph (60 mph) on country roads, and 112 kph (70 mph) on two-lane roads and motorways.

All ferries on *both* principal routes to the Irish Republic—Holyhead–Dublin and Fishguard/Pembroke–Rosslare—take cars. Fishguard and Pembroke are relatively easy to reach by road. The car trip to Holyhead, on the other hand, is sometimes difficult: delays on the A55 North Wales coastal road are not unusual.

Car ferries to Belfast leave from the Scottish port of Stranraer and the English city of Liverpool; those to Larne leave from Stranraer and Cairnryan.

For reservations and information, *see* Boat & Ferry Travel, *above.*

AUTO CLUBS

➤ IN AUSTRALIA: **Australian Automobile Association** (☎ 02/6247–7311).

➤ IN CANADA: **Canadian Automobile Association** (CAA, ☎ 613/247–0117).

➤ IN NEW ZEALAND: **New Zealand Automobile Association** (☎ 09/377–4660).

➤ IN THE U.K.: **Automobile Association** (AA, ☎ 0870/550–0600). **Royal Automobile Club** (RAC, ☎ 0870/572–2722 for membership, 0345/121–345 for insurance).

➤ IN THE U.S.: **American Automobile Association** (☎ 800/564–6222).

EMERGENCY SERVICES

Membership in a breakdown service is definitely advisable if you're using your own car in Ireland. The Automobile Association of Ireland is a sister organization of its English counterpart and is highly recommended.

➤ CONTACT: **Automobile Association of Ireland** (☎ 01/677–9481).

GASOLINE

You'll find gas stations along most roads. Self-service is the norm in larger establishments. Major credit cards and traveler's checks are usually accepted.

PARKING

Despite the relatively light traffic, parking in towns can be a problem. Signs with the letter *P* indicate that parking is permitted; a stroke through the *P* warns you to stay away or you'll be liable for a fine of £15 to £50; however, if you get towed, the fine is £150. In Dublin and Cork, parking lots are your best bet, but check the rate first in Dublin; they can vary wildly.

In Northern Ireland there are plenty of parking lots in the towns (usually free except in Belfast), and you should use them. In Belfast, you cannot park your car in some parts of the city center, more because of congestion than security problems.

ROAD CONDITIONS

Most roads are paved and make for easy travel. Watch for traffic at rush hours in Dublin, Cork, Limerick, Belfast, and Galway.

ROAD MAPS

Road maps can be found at most gas stations and bookstores.

RULES OF THE ROAD

The Irish, like the British, **drive on the left-hand side of the road.** Safety belts must be worn by the driver and front passenger, and children under 12 must travel in the back. It is compulsory for motorcyclists and their passengers to wear helmets.

Drunk-driving laws are strict. Ireland has a Breathalyzer test, which the police can administer anytime. If you refuse to take it, the odds are you'll be prosecuted anyway. As always, the best advice is **don't drink if you plan to drive.**

Army checkpoints are a thing of the past between the North and the South, though there are some border checkpoints for cattle (in an effort to contain BSE-contaminated livestock).

CHILDREN IN IRELAND

The Irish go to great lengths to make children welcome. Many hotels offer baby-sitting services, and most will supply a cot if given advance notice. Hotel and pub restaurants often have a children's menu and can supply a high chair if necessary. Unlike Great Britain, Irish licensing laws allow children under 14 into pubs—although they may not consume alcohol on the premises until they are 18, and they are expected to leave by about 5:30 PM (although they may be allowed to stay until 7 PM, depending on how busy the pub gets). This is a boon if you are touring by car because pubs are perfect for lunch or tea stops.

While most attractions and bus and rail journeys offer a rate of half price or less for children, **look for "family tickets,"** which may be cheaper and usually cover two adults and up to four children. The Irish Tourist Board (ITB) publishes "A Tour of Favorite Kids' Places," that covers a week's worth of sights around the country.

Be sure to plan ahead and **involve your youngsters** as you outline your trip. When packing, include things to keep them busy en route. On sightseeing days try to schedule activities of special interest to your children.

If you are renting a car, don't forget to **arrange for a car seat** when you reserve.

FLYING

If your children are two or older, **ask about children's airfares.** As a general rule, infants under two not occupying a seat fly at greatly reduced fares or even for free. When booking, **confirm carry-on allowances** if you're traveling with infants. In general, for babies charged 10% of the adult fare you are allowed one carry-on bag and a collapsible stroller; if the flight is full, the stroller may have to be checked or you may be limited to less.

Experts agree that it's a good idea to use safety seats aloft for children weighing less than 40 pounds. Airlines set their own policies: U.S. carriers usually require that the child be ticketed, even if he or she is young enough to ride free, since the seats must be strapped into regular seats. Do **check your airline's policy about using safety seats during takeoff and landing.** And since safety seats are not allowed just everywhere in the plane, get your seat assignments early.

When reserving, **request children's meals or a freestanding bassinet** if you need them. But note that bulkhead seats, where you must sit to use the bassinet, may lack an overhead bin or storage space on the floor.

LODGING

Most hotels in Ireland allow children under a certain age to stay in their parents' room at no extra charge, but others charge for them as extra adults; be sure to **find out the cutoff age for children's discounts.**

SIGHTS & ATTRACTIONS

Places that are especially appealing to children are indicated by a rubber duckie icon in the margin.

SUPPLIES & EQUIPMENT

Items for babies and children are available in every town and village; check the supermarket or family grocery store.

CONSUMER PROTECTION

Whenever shopping or buying travel services in Ireland, **pay with a major credit card** so you can cancel payment or get reimbursed if there's a problem. If you're doing business with a particular company for the first time, **contact your local Better Business Bureau and the attorney general's offices** in your own state and the company's home state, as well. Have any complaints been filed? Finally, if you're buying a package or tour, always **consider travel insurance** that includes default coverage (☞ Insurance, *below*).

➤ BBBs: **Council of Better Business Bureaus** (✉ 4200 Wilson Blvd., Suite 800, Arlington, VA 22203, ☎ 703/276–0100, FAX 703/525–8277 www.bbb.org).

CUSTOMS & DUTIES

When shopping, **keep receipts** for all purchases. Upon reentering the country, **be ready to show customs officials what you've bought.** If you feel a duty is incorrect or object to the way your clearance was handled, note the inspector's badge number and ask to see a supervisor. If the problem isn't resolved, write to the appropriate authorities, beginning with the port director at your point of entry.

IN AUSTRALIA

Australian residents who are 18 or older may bring home $A400 worth of souvenirs and gifts (including jewelry), 250 cigarettes or 250 grams of tobacco, and 1,125 ml of alcohol (including wine, beer, and spirits). Residents under 18 may bring back $A200 worth of goods. Prohibited items include meat products. Seeds, plants, and fruits need to be declared upon arrival.

➤ INFORMATION: **Australian Customs Service** (Regional Director, ✉ Box 8, Sydney, NSW 2001, ☎ 02/9213–2000, FAX 02/9213–4000).

IN CANADA

Canadian residents who have been out of Canada for at least 7 days may bring home C$500 worth of goods duty-free. If you've been away less than 7 days but more than 48 hours, the duty-free allowance drops to C$200; if your trip lasts 24–48 hours, the allowance is C$50. You may not pool allowances with family members. Goods claimed under the C$500 exemption may follow you by mail; those claimed under the lesser exemptions must accompany you. Alcohol and tobacco products may be included in the 7-day and 48-hour exemptions but not in the 24-hour exemption. If you meet the age requirements of the province or territory through which you reenter Canada, you may bring in, duty-free, 1.14 liters (40 imperial ounces) of wine or liquor *or* 24 12-ounce cans or bottles of beer or ale. If you are 16 or older you may bring in, duty-free, 200 cigarettes and 50 cigars. Check ahead of time with Revenue Canada or the Department of Agriculture for policies regarding meat products, seeds, plants, and fruits.

You may send an unlimited number of gifts worth up to C$60 each duty-free to Canada. Label the package UNSOLICITED GIFT—VALUE UNDER $60. Alcohol and tobacco are excluded.

➤ INFORMATION: **Revenue Canada** (✉ 2265 St. Laurent Blvd. S, Ottawa, Ontario K1G 4K3, ☎ 613/993–0534, 800/461–9999 in Canada, FAX 613/957–8911, www.ccra-adrc.gc.ca).

IN IRELAND

Duty-free allowances have been abolished for those traveling between countries in the European Union (Austria, Belgium, Denmark, Finland, France, Germany, Greece, Ireland, Italy, Luxembourg, the Netherlands, Portugal, Spain, Sweden, the United Kingdom, but not the Channel Islands).

For goods purchased outside the EU, you may import duty-free: (1) 200 cigarettes or 100 cigarillos or 50 cigars or 250 grams of smoking tobacco; (2) 2 liters of wine, and either 1 liter of alcoholic drink over 22% volume or 2 liters of alcoholic drink under 22% volume (sparkling or fortified wine included); (3) 50 grams of perfume and ¼ liter of toilet water; and (4) other goods to a value of £142 per person (£73 per person for travelers under 15 years of age).

Goods that cannot be freely imported to the Irish Republic include firearms, ammunition, explosives, illegal drugs, indecent or obscene books and pictures, oral smokeless tobacco products, meat and meat products, poultry and poultry products, plants and plant products (including shrubs, vegetables, fruit, bulbs, and seeds), domestic cats and dogs from outside the United Kingdom, and live animals from outside Northern Ireland.

No animals or pets of any kind may be brought into Northern Ireland without a six-month quarantine. Other items that may not be imported include fresh meats, plants and vegetables, controlled drugs, and firearms and ammunition.

➤ INFORMATION: **Customs and Excise** (✉ Irish Life Building, 2nd floor, Middle Abbey St., Dublin 1, ☎ 01/878–8811).

IN NEW ZEALAND

Homeward-bound residents 17 or older may bring back $700 worth of souvenirs and gifts. Your duty-free allowance also includes 4.5 liters of wine or beer; one 1,125-ml bottle of spirits; and either 200 cigarettes, 250 grams of tobacco, 50 cigars, or a combination of the three up to 250 grams. Prohibited items include meat products, seeds, plants, and fruits.

➤ INFORMATION: **New Zealand Customs** (Custom House, ✉ 50 Anzac Ave., Box 29, Auckland, New Zealand, ☎ 09/359–6655, FAX 09/359–6732).

IN THE U.K.

If you are a U.K. resident and your journey was wholly within the European Union (EU), you won't have to pass through customs when you return to the United Kingdom. If you plan to bring back large quantities of alcohol or tobacco, check EU limits beforehand.

➤ INFORMATION: **HM Customs and Excise** (✉ Dorset House, Stamford St., Bromley, Kent BR1 1XX, ☎ 020/7202–4227).

IN THE U.S.

U.S. residents who have been out of the country for at least 48 hours (and who have not used the $400 allowance or any part of it in the past

30 days) may bring home $400 worth of foreign goods duty-free. U.S. residents 21 and older may bring back 1 liter of alcohol duty-free. In addition, regardless of your age, you are allowed 200 cigarettes and 100 non-Cuban cigars. Antiques, which the U.S. Customs Service defines as objects more than 100 years old, enter duty-free, as do original works of art done entirely by hand, including paintings, drawings, and sculptures.

You may also send packages home duty-free: up to $200 worth of goods for personal use, with a limit of one parcel per addressee per day (except alcohol or tobacco products or perfume worth more than $5); label the package PERSONAL USE and attach a list of its contents and their retail value. Do not label the package UNSOLICITED GIFT or your duty-free exemption will drop to $100. Mailed items do not affect your duty-free allowance on your return.

➤ INFORMATION: **U.S. Customs Service** (✉ 1300 Pennsylvania Ave. NW, Washington, DC 20229, www.customs.gov; inquiries ☎ 202/354–1000; complaints c/o ✉ Office of Regulations and Rulings; registration of equipment c/o Resource Management, ☎ 202/927–0540).

DINING

In the quite recent past people seldom came to Ireland to eat. In fact, tourists often shared jokes about the stodgy, overcooked, slightly gray food they were often served up. But the last decade has seen rapid change in all aspects of Irish life, and that includes food and drink. The country is going through a culinary renaissance, and Dublin chefs are leading the charge. They are putting nouvelle spins on traditional Irish favorites. And, spurred on by a wave of new immigration, ethnic eateries of all types have sprung up in most major towns and cities.

The restaurants we list are the cream of the crop in each price category. They are indicated in the text by ✗. Establishments denoted by ✗▥ stand out equally for their restaurants and their rooms. For information about restaurants beyond those reviewed in our guide, look for dining guides available from the Irish Tourist Board (ITB) or the Northern Ireland Tourist Board (NITB) (☞ Visitor Information, *below*).

CATEGORY	THE REPUBLIC*	NORTHERN IRELAND*
$$$$	over £25	over UK£25
$$$	£20–£25	UK£15–UK£20
$$	£15–£20	UK£10–UK£15
$	under £15	under UK£10

All prices are per person for a first course, a main course, and dessert, including sales tax, excluding wine or tip.

MEALS & SPECIALTIES

A postmodern renaissance in Irish cuisine has lead to a pursuit for authenticity in traditional Irish food. Many of the finer restaurants in Dublin, Cork, and Galway now offer a couple of dishes which are variations on a traditional theme. *Coddle* is an old Dublin favorite, a boiled stew of bacon, sausage, and smoked meats.

A typical Irish breakfast includes fried eggs, bacon, black and white puddings, sausage, and a pot of tea. A typical lunch might feature a hearty sandwich; dinner meals usually include meat and two vegetables. Some of the best food is found at family bed-and-breakfasts and in inexpensive cafés.

Fresh fish and seafood are at the heart of many specialities. Irish smoked salmon—usually served on brown soda bread with plenty of butter—is among the finest in the world, and many a wondrous dish has been created around the humble cockle and mussel, abundant in the clear Atlantic waters. Galway and the West are rapidly becoming famous for their top-class oyster beds.

Of course there's the omnipresent potato, too. Like snow to the Eskimo, the Irish have many words for the humble spud, and they have invented plenty of ways to serve it up. The best of these is *boxty,* a traditional pancake of once- and twice-cooked potatoes: it makes the perfect bed for a beef-and-Guinness stew, or the equally hearty lamb casserole.

MEALTIMES

Breakfast is served from 7 to 10, lunch runs from 1 to 2:30, and dinners are usually mid-evening occasions.

Pubs are generally open Monday–Saturday 10:30 AM–11:30 PM May–September, closing at 11 the rest of the year. The famous Holy Hour, which required city pubs to close from 2:30 to 3:30, was abolished in 1988, and afternoon opening is now at the discretion of the owner or manager; few bother to close. On Sunday, pubs are open 12:30–2 and 4–11. All pubs close on Christmas Day and Good Friday, but hotel bars are open for guests.

Pubs in Northern Ireland are open 11:30 AM–11 PM Monday–Saturday and 12:30 PM–2:30 PM and 7 PM–10 PM on Sunday. Sunday opening is at the owner's or manager's discretion.

Unless otherwise noted, the restaurants listed in this guide are open daily for lunch and dinner.

PAYING

Traveler's checks and credit cards are widely accepted, although it's cash-only at smaller pubs and take-out restaurants.

RESERVATIONS & DRESS

Reservations are always a good idea: we mention them only when they're essential or not accepted. Book as far ahead as you can, and reconfirm as soon as you arrive. We mention dress only when men are required to wear a jacket or a jacket and tie.

WINE, BEER & SPIRITS

All types of alcoholic beverages are available in Ireland. Beer and wine are sold in shops and supermarkets, and you can get drinks "to go" at some bars, although at inflated prices. Stout (Guinness, Murphy's, Beamish) is the Irish beer; whiskey comes in many brands and is smoother and more blended than Scotch. Most pubs serve until 11:30 PM in the summer and until 11 the rest of the year. In the cities, many bars now stay open until 1 AM, and many small-town pubs ignore closing times and stay open as late as their clientele wish.

DISABILITIES & ACCESSIBILITY

Ireland has only recently begun to provide facilities such as ramps and accessible toilets for people with disabilities. Public transportation also lags behind. However, visitors with disabilities will often find that the helpfulness of the Irish makes up for the lack of amenities.

➤ LOCAL RESOURCES: **National Rehabilitation Board** (⊠ 44 N. Great George's St., Dublin, ☎ 01/874–7503). **Disability Action** (⊠ 2 Annadale Ave., Belfast, ☎ 028/9249–1011.

RESERVATIONS

When discussing accessibility with an operator or reservations agent, **ask hard questions.** Are there any stairs, inside *or* out? Are there grab bars next to the toilet *and* in the shower/tub? How wide is the doorway to the room? To the bathroom? For the most extensive facilities meeting the latest legal specifications, **opt for newer accommodations.**

➤ COMPLAINTS: **Disability Rights Section** (⊠ U.S. Department of Justice, Civil Rights Division, Box 66738, Washington, DC 20035-6738, ☎ 202/514–0301 or 800/514–0301; TTY 202/514–0301 or 800/514–0301, FAX 202/307–1198) for general complaints. **Aviation Consumer Protection Division** (☞ Air Travel, *above*) for airline-related problems. **Civil Rights Office** (⊠ U.S. Department of Transportation, Departmental Office of Civil Rights, S-30, 400 7th St. SW, Room 10215, Washington, DC 20590, ☎ 202/366–4648, FAX 202/366–9371) for problems with surface transportation.

TRAVEL AGENCIES

In the United States, the Americans with Disabilities Act requires that travel firms serve the needs of all travelers. Some agencies specialize in working with people with disabilities.

➤ TRAVELERS WITH MOBILITY PROBLEMS: **Access Adventures** (⊠ 206

Chestnut Ridge Rd., Rochester, NY 14624, ☎ 716/889–9096, dltravel@prodigy.net), run by a former physical-rehabilitation counselor. **CareVacations** (⊠ 5-5110 50th Ave., Leduc, Alberta T9E 6V4, ☎ 780/986–6404 or 877/478–7827, FAX 780/986–8332, www.carevacations.com), for group tours and cruise vacations. **Flying Wheels Travel** (⊠ 143 W. Bridge St., Box 382, Owatonna, MN 55060, ☎ 507/451–5005 or 800/535–6790, FAX 507/451–1685, thq@ll.net, www.flyingwheels.com).

➤ TRAVELERS WITH DEVELOPMENTAL DISABILITIES: **New Directions** (⊠ 5276 Hollister Ave., Suite 207, Santa Barbara, CA 93111, ☎ 805/967–2841 or 888/967–2841, FAX 805/964–7344, newdirec@silcom.com, www.silcom.com/ànewdirec/).

DISCOUNTS & DEALS

Be a smart shopper and **compare all your options** before making decisions. A plane ticket bought with a promotional coupon from travel clubs, coupon books, and direct-mail offers may not be cheaper than the least expensive fare from a discount ticket agency. And always keep in mind that what you get is just as important as what you save.

DISCOUNT RESERVATIONS

To save money, **look into discount reservations services** with toll-free numbers, which use their buying power to get a better price on hotels, airline tickets, even car rentals. When booking a room, always **call the hotel's local toll-free number** (if one is available) rather than the central reservations number—you'll often get a better price. Always ask about special packages or corporate rates.

When shopping for the best deal on hotels and car rentals, **look for guaranteed exchange rates,** which protect you against a falling dollar. With your rate locked in, you won't pay more, even if the price goes up in the local currency.

➤ AIRLINE TICKETS: ☎ 800/FLY-4–LESS. ☎ 800/FLY-ASAP.

➤ HOTEL ROOMS: **Steigenberger Reservation Service** (☎ 800/223–5652, www.srs-worldhotels.com). **Travel Interlink** (☎ 800/888–5898, www.travelinterlink.com).

PACKAGE DEALS

Don't confuse packages and guided tours. When you buy a package, you travel on your own, just as though you had planned the trip yourself. Fly/drive packages, which combine airfare and car rental, are often a good deal. If you **buy a rail/drive pass,** you may save on train tickets and car rentals. All Eurail- and Europass holders get a discount on Eurostar fares through the Channel Tunnel.

ELECTRICITY

To use your U.S.-purchased electric-powered equipment, **bring a converter and adapter.** The electrical current in Ireland is 220 volts, 50 cycles alternating current (AC); wall outlets take plugs with three prongs or two round oversize prongs.

If your appliances are dual-voltage, you'll need only an adapter. Don't use 110-volt outlets marked FOR SHAVERS ONLY for high-wattage appliances such as blow dryers. Most laptops operate equally well on 110 and 220 volts and so require only an adapter.

EMBASSIES

➤ AUSTRALIA: (✉ Fitzwilton House, Fitzwilton Terr., Dublin 2, ☎ 01/676–1517).

➤ CANADA: (✉ 65 St. Stephen's Green, Dublin 2, ☎ 01/478–1988).

➤ UNITED KINGDOM: (✉ 29 Merrion Rd., Dublin 2, ☎ 01/205–3700).

➤ UNITED STATES: (✉ 42 Elgin Rd., Ballsbridge, Dublin 4, ☎ 01/668–8777).

EMERGENCIES

999 is the only emergency number you have to know in Ireland. Wherever you are, this number will connect you with local police, ambulance, and fire services. All three services are very professional and you can expect a prompt response to your call.

ETIQUETTE & BEHAVIOR

The Irish are a casual, comfortable lot who aren't too particular about points of etiquette. Handshakes are more common than hugs although public displays of affection—in moderation—are often seen. Two things to note, though, are the great respect of the younger Irish for their elders and the great respect of all churchgoers for the sermon (hence, no talking during the service).

GAY & LESBIAN TRAVEL

In 1993 the Republic of Ireland began to replace virulently homophobic laws (inherited from British rule and enforced up to the 1970s) with some of the most gay-progressive statutes in the EU. Homosexual acts have been decriminalized and hate crimes and discrimination in the workplace and public accommodation are now illegal. Leading these efforts was Ireland's progressive president, Mary Robinson, the first woman to hold this office. (She was named United Nations High Commissioner for Human Rights in June 1997.)

This enlightened legal environment, however, doesn't readily translate into the same public lesbian and gay presence you find in U.S. and European cities. Outside the Republic's major cities—Dublin, Cork, and Galway—signs of gay life can be difficult to find, and even in these cities you're likely to find them only in small pockets: a pub here, a café there. If you do encounter any difficulties as a gay traveler, it's likely to be with lodging establishments. Proprietors at even some of most upscale places may resist letting a room with one bed to same-sex couples; at other establishments, no one may so much as raise an eyebrow. Test the waters in advance: be explicit about what you want when you make your reservation.

CORK

Ireland's second-largest city has the country's only lesbian and gay community center and a decade-old gay bar. The Cork Film Festival (☞ Festivals and Seasonal Events, *below*), held in October, incorporates the Irish Lesbian and Gay Film Festival.

➤ CORK CONTACTS: **Lesbian and Gay Line** (☎ 021/271087) operates Wednesday 7 PM–9 PM and Saturday 3 PM–5 PM; it functions as a lesbian hot line Thursday 8 PM–10 PM. **Loafers** (✉ 26 Douglas St., ☎ 021/311612) is Cork's main gay bar. **The Other Place** (✉ 8 S. Main St., ☎ 021/278745), the lesbian and gay community center, houses a bookstore and café and hosts Friday- and Saturday-night dances.

DUBLIN

By far, Dublin has more accessible lesbian and gay life than any other city in Ireland. Consult the *Gay Community News*, Ireland's free monthly lesbian and gay newspaper, and *In Dublin* for current information about what's going on in the community. The Gay Switchboard Dublin operates Sunday–Friday 8 PM–10 PM and Saturday 3:30 PM–6 PM. The George is the city's main gay bar, with a mainly male crowd, while Out on the Liffey draws both men and women.

➤ DUBLIN CONTACTS: *Gay Community News* (GCN; ☎ 01/671–9076 or 01/671–0939). **Gay Switchboard Dublin** (☎ 01/872–1055). **The George** (✉ 89 S. Great George's St., ☎ 01/478–2983). *In Dublin* (✉ 3–7 Camden Pl., ☎ 01/478–4322). **Out on the Liffey** (✉ 27 Ormond Quay, ☎ 01/872–2480).

GALWAY

A young populace, a progressive university, and a few outstanding theater companies help make Ireland's bohemian left-coast city one of the country's most gay-friendly places. Neither Le Graal nor Neáchtain's are specifically gay, but they are among the gay-friendlier places in town.

➤ GALWAY CONTACTS: **Galway Gay Helpline** (☎ 091/566134) operates Tuesday 8 PM–10 PM. **Galway Lesbian Helpline** (☎ 091/564611) operates Wednesday 8 PM–10 PM and Saturday noon–2 PM. **Le Graal** (✉ 38 Lower Dominick St., ☎ 091/567614). **Neáchtain's** (✉ 17 Cross St., ☎ 091/561720).

➤ GAY- & LESBIAN-FRIENDLY TRAVEL AGENCIES: **Different Roads Travel** (✉ 8383 Wilshire Blvd., Suite 902, Beverly Hills, CA 90211, ☎ 323/651–5557 or 800/429–8747, FAX 323/651–3678, leigh@west.tzell.com). **Kennedy Travel** (✉ 314 Jericho Tpk., Floral Park, NY 11001, ☎ 516/352–4888 or 800/237–7433, FAX 516/354–8849, main@kennedytravel.com, www.kennedytravel.com). **Now Voyager** (✉ 4406 18th St., San Francisco, CA 94114, ☎ 415/626–1169 or 800/255–6951, FAX 415/626–8626, www.nowvoyager.com). **Skylink Travel and Tour** (✉ 1006 Mendocino Ave., Santa Rosa, CA 95401, ☎ 707/546–9888 or 800/225–5759, FAX 707/546–9891, skylinktvl@aol.com, www.skylinktravel.com), serving lesbian travelers.

HEALTH

Ireland is a very safe country for travel, with virtually no risk of health problems from food, drink, or insects. The weather, however, is another story; be sure to dress for the cold and rain or you may find yourself plagued by a constant cough and sniffles.

HOLIDAYS

Irish national holidays are as follows: January 1 (New Year's); March 17 (St. Patrick's Day); April 13, 2001 (Good Friday); April 16, 2001 (Easter Monday); May 1 (May Day); June 4 and August 6, 2001 (summer bank holidays); October 29, 2001 (autumn bank holiday); and December 25–26 (Christmas and St. Stephen's Day). If you plan to visit at Easter, remember that theaters and cinemas are closed for the last three days of the preceding week.

INSURANCE

The most useful travel insurance plan is a comprehensive policy that includes coverage for trip cancellation and interruption, default, trip delay, and medical expenses (with a waiver for preexisting conditions).

Without insurance you will lose all or most of your money if you cancel your trip, regardless of the reason. Default insurance covers you if your tour operator, airline, or cruise line goes out of business. Trip-delay covers expenses that arise because of bad weather or mechanical delays.

Study the fine print when comparing policies.

If you're traveling internationally, a key component of travel insurance is coverage for medical bills incurred if you get sick on the road. Such expenses are not generally covered by Medicare or private policies. U.K. residents can buy a travel insurance policy valid for most vacations taken during the year in which it's purchased (but check preexisting-condition coverage). British and Australian citizens need extra medical coverage when traveling overseas.

Always **buy travel policies directly from the insurance company**; if you buy them from a cruise line, airline, or tour operator that goes out of business you probably will not be covered for the agency or operator's default, a major risk. Before making any purchase, **review your existing health and home-owner's policies** to find what they cover away from home.

➤ TRAVEL INSURERS: In the United States: **Access America** (✉ 6600 W. Broad St., Richmond, VA 23230, ☎ 804/285–3300 or 800/284–8300, FAX 804/673–1583, www.previewtravel.com), **Travel Guard International** (✉ 1145 Clark St., Stevens Point, WI 54481, ☎ 715/345–0505 or 800/826–1300, FAX 800/955–8785, www.noelgroup.com). In Canada: **Voyager Insurance** (✉ 44 Peel Center Dr., Brampton, Ontario L6T 4M8, ☎ 905/791–8700, 800/668–4342 in Canada).

➤ INSURANCE INFORMATION: In the United Kingdom: **Association of British Insurers** (✉ 51–55 Gresham St., London EC2V 7HQ, ☎ 020/7600–3333, FAX 020/7696–8999, info@abi.org.uk, www.abi.org.uk). In Australia: **Insurance Council of Australia** (☎ 03/9614–1077, FAX 03/9614–7924).

LANGUAGE

Irish (also known as Gaelic)—a Celtic language related to Scots Gaelic, Breton, and Welsh—is the official national language. Though English is technically the second language of the country, it is, in fact, the everyday tongue of 95% of the population.

Nowadays all Irish speakers are fluent in English.

Irish-speaking communities are found mainly in sparsely populated rural areas along the western seaboard, on some but not all offshore islands, and in pockets in West Cork and County Waterford. Irish-speaking areas are known as Gaeltacht (pronounced *gale*-taukt). While most road signs in Ireland are given in both English and Irish, within Gaeltacht areas the signs are often in Irish only. A good touring map will give both Irish and English names to places within the Gaeltacht. You really need only know two Irish words: *Fir* (men) and *mná* (women)— useful vocabulary for a trip to a public toilet.

LODGING

Accommodations in Ireland range from deluxe renovated castles and stately homes to thatched cottages and farmhouses. Room standards are rising all the time, especially in the middle and lower price ranges. Pressure on hotel space reaches a peak from June to September, but it's always a good idea to **reserve in advance.** Many Irish hotels can be booked directly from the United States. Ask your travel agent.

The Irish Tourist Board (ITB) has an official grading system and publishes a list of "approved accommodations," which includes hotels, guest houses, bed-and-breakfasts, farmhouses, hostels, and camping parks. For each accommodation, the list gives a maximum charge that no hotel may exceed without special authorization. Prices must be displayed in every room, so if the hotel oversteps its limit, do not hesitate to complain to the hotel manager and/or the ITB. The ITB and the NITB (Northern Ireland Tourist Board) also distribute five accommodation guides, covering various kinds of lodgings, which are free if obtained in the United States (☞ Visitor Information, *below*).

Ideally, visitors should **sample a range of accommodations.** The very expensive country-house hotels and renovated castles offer a unique combination of luxury and history. Less impressive, but equally charming, are the provincial inns and country hotels with simple but adequate facilities. Many visitors, seeking to meet a wide cross section of Irish people, prefer a different B&B every night. Others enjoy the simplicity of self-catering for a week or two in a thatched cottage. ITB-approved guest houses and B&Bs display a green shamrock outside and are usually considered more reputable than those without. Hotels and other accommodations in Northern Ireland are similar to those in the Republic of Ireland.

The lodgings we list are the cream of the crop in each price category. We always list the facilities that are available—but we don't specify whether they cost extra: when pricing accommodations, always ask what's included and what costs extra. Lodgings are denoted in the text by an 🏠 . Properties indicated by an ✕🏠 are lodging establishments whose restaurant warrants a special trip. Especially in inexpensive places, some baths may contain a tub and shower, while others may have a shower only. Breakfast will likely be included in the price of your accommodation, except at large hotels. Inquire when booking about bathing facilities and meals if you have specific concerns or needs.

CATEGORY	DUBLIN*	ELSEWHERE IN THE REPUBLIC*
$$$$	over £180	over £140
$$$	£140–£180	£100–£140
$$	£100–£140	£80–£100
$	under £100	under £80

CATEGORY	NORTHERN IRELAND*
$$$$	over UK£135
$$$	UK£70–UK£135
$$	UK£40–UK£70
$	under UK£40

*All prices are for two people in a double room, including 12.5% local sales tax (VAT) and a service charge (often applied in larger hotels).

RESERVATIONS

The Irish Tourist Board, known as Bord Fáilte, and Dublin Tourism operate a credit-card central reservations service for hotels and other accommodations, including guest houses, B&Bs throughout Ireland, and self-catering facilities. There's a booking fee of £3 plus a charge of 10% of the cost of the accommodations.

➤ CONTACT INFORMATION: **Bord Fáilte** (☎ 011800/668–66866 in the U.S. or 00800/668–66866). **Dublin Tourism** (☎ 01/605–7700 or 01/602–4129, ℻ 01/605–7787, 01/475–8046 for non–credit card accommodation inquiries).

APARTMENT & VILLA RENTALS

If you want a home base that's roomy enough for a family and comes with cooking facilities, **consider a furnished rental.** These can save you money, especially if you're traveling with a group. Home-exchange directories sometimes list rentals as well as exchanges.

➤ INTERNATIONAL AGENTS: **At Home Abroad** (✉ 405 E. 56th St., Suite 6H, New York, NY 10022, ☎ 212/421–9165, ℻ 212/752–1591, athomabrod@aol.com, www.member.aol.com/athomabrod/index.html). **Hideaways International** (✉ 767 Islington St., Portsmouth, NH 03801, ☎ 603/430–4433 or 800/843–4433, ℻ 603/430–4444, info@hideaways. com, www.hideaways.com; membership $99). **Hometours International** (✉ Box 11503, Knoxville, TN 37939, ☎ 865/690–8484 or 800/367–4668, hometours@aol.com, www.thor.he.net/áhometour/). **Interhome** (✉ 1990 N.E. 163rd St., Suite 110, N. Miami Beach, FL 33162, ☎ 305/940–2299 or 800/882–6864, ℻ 305/940–2911, interhomeu@aol.com, www.interhome.com). **Villas and Apartments Abroad** (✉ 1270 Ave. of the Americas, 15th floor, New York, NY 10020, ☎ 212/897–5045 or 800/433–3020, ℻ 212/897–5039, vaa@altour.com, www.vaanyc.com). **Villas International** (✉ 950 Northgate Dr., Suite 206, San Rafael, CA 94903, ☎ 415/499–9490 or 800/221–2260, ℻ 415/499–9491, villas@best.com, www.villasintl.com).

B&BS

B&Bs are classified by the ITB as either town homes, country homes, or farmhouses. Town and country B&Bs

are listed in the ITB's "Quality Approved Irish Homes Accommodation Guide." Many now have at least one bedroom with a bathroom, but don't expect this as a matter of course. B&Bs often charge an extra 50p–£1 for a bath or shower. If this is taken in the family bathroom, you should ask first whether you can use the facility. Many travelers do not bother booking a B&B in advance. They are so plentiful in rural areas that it's often more fun to leave the decision open, allowing yourself a choice of final destinations for the night. For B&B reservations services, *see* Reservations, *above*.

CAMPING

This is the cheapest way of seeing the country, and facilities for campers and caravaners are improving steadily. An abundance of coastal campsites compensates for the shortage of inland ones. All are listed in *Caravan and Camping Ireland* available from the ITB. Rates start at about £4 per tent, £6 per caravan overnight.

COTTAGES

In more than 100 locations there are clusters of holiday cottages for rent. Although often built in the traditional style, they have central heating and all the other modern conveniences. A three-bedroom cottage equipped for six adults is around £250 per week in mid-season. It is essential to reserve in advance. The ITB's publication *Self-Catering* lists individual properties and clusters of traditional cottages available by the week. For more information, contact the ITB (☞ Visitor Information, *below*).

FARM VACATIONS

Many Irish farms offer holidays with part board or full board on a weekly basis. These are listed in the ITB's illustrated publication *Farmhouse Accommodation*. You will notice at once from the booklet that very few are picturesque: they are more likely to be modern bungalows or undistinguished, two-story houses than creeper-clad, Georgian mansions—though exceptions do exist. Room and part board—breakfast and an evening meal—costs from £170 per week.

GUEST HOUSES

To qualify as a guest house, establishments must have at least five bedrooms, but in major cities they often have many more. Some guest houses are above a bar or restaurant; others are part of a family home. As a rule, they're cheaper (some include an optional evening meal) and offer fewer amenities than hotels. But often that's where the differences end. Most have high standards of cleanliness and hospitality. Some even have a bathroom, a TV, and a direct-dial phone in each room.

HOME EXCHANGES

If you would like to exchange your home for someone else's, **join a home-exchange organization,** which will send you its updated listings of available exchanges for a year and will include your own listing in at least one of them. It's up to you to make specific arrangements.

➤ EXCHANGE CLUBS: **HomeLink International** (✉ Box 650, Key West, FL 33041, ☎ 305/294–7766 or 800/638–3841, ℻ 305/294–1448, usa@homelink.org, www.homelink.org; $98 per year). **Intervac U.S.** (✉ Box 590504, San Francisco, CA 94159, ☎ 800/756–4663, ℻ 415/435–7440, www.intervac.com; $89 per year includes two catalogs).

HOSTELS

No matter what your age, you can **save on lodging costs by staying at hostels.** In some 5,000 locations in more than 70 countries around the world, Hostelling International (HI), the umbrella group for a number of national youth-hostel associations, offers single-sex, dorm-style beds and, at many hostels, rooms for couples and family accommodations. Membership in any HI national hostel association, open to travelers of all ages, allows you to stay in HI-affiliated hostels at member rates; one-year membership is about $25 for adults (C$26.75 in Canada, £9.30 in the United Kingdom, $30 in Australia, and $30 in New Zealand); hostels run about $10–$25 per night. Members have priority if the hostel is full; they're also eligible for discounts around the world, even on rail and bus travel in some countries.

➤ ORGANIZATIONS: **Hostelling International—American Youth Hostels** (✉ 733 15th St. NW, Suite 840, Washington, DC 20005, ☎ 202/783–6161, FAX 202/783–6171, www.hiayh.org). **Hostelling International—Canada** (✉ 400–205 Catherine St., Ottawa, Ontario K2P 1C3, ☎ 613/237–7884, FAX 613/237–7868, www.hostellingintl.ca). **Youth Hostel Association of England and Wales** (✉ Trevelyan House, 8 St. Stephen's Hill, St. Albans, Hertfordshire AL1 2DY, ☎ 01727/855215 or 01727/845047, FAX 01727/844126, www.yha.uk). **Australian Youth Hostel Association** (✉ 10 Mallett St., Camperdown, NSW 2050, ☎ 02/9565–1699, FAX 02/9565–1325, www.yha.com.au). **Youth Hostels Association of New Zealand** (✉ Box 436, Christchurch, New Zealand, ☎ 03/379–9970, FAX 03/365–4476, www.yha.org.nz).

HOTELS

Standard features in most hotels include private bath, air-conditioning, two twin beds (you can usually ask for a king-size instead), TV (often with VCR), free parking, and no smoking rooms. There is usually no extra charge for these services.

➤ TOLL-FREE NUMBERS: **Best Western** (☎ 800/528–1234, www.bestwestern.com). **Choice** (☎ 800/221–2222, www.hotelchoice.com). **Clarion** (☎ 800/252–7466, www.choicehotels.com). **Comfort** (☎ 800/228–5150, www.comfortinn.com). **Forte** (☎ 800/225–5843, www.lemeridien-hotels.com). **Hilton** (☎ 800/445–8667, www.hiltons.com). **Holiday Inn** (☎ 800/465–4329, www.holiday-inn.com). **Le Meridien** (☎ 800/543–4300, www.forte-hotels.com). **Quality Inn** (☎ 800/228–5151, www.qualityinn.com).

MAIL & SHIPPING

Letters take a week to 10 days to reach the United States and Canada, 3 to 5 days to reach the United Kingdom.

POSTAL RATES

Airmail rates to the United States and Canada from the Irish Republic are 45p for letters and postcards. Mail to all European countries goes by air automatically, so airmail stickers or envelopes are not required. Rates are 32p for letters and postcards.

Rates from Northern Ireland are 43p for letters and 37p for postcards (not over 10 grams). To the rest of the United Kingdom and the Irish Republic, rates are 26p for first-class letters and 20p for second class.

RECEIVING MAIL

Mail can be held for collection at any post office free of charge for up to three months. It should be addressed to the recipient "c/o Poste Restante." In Dublin, use the **General Post Office** (✉ O'Connell St., Dublin 1, ☎ 01/705–7000).

MEDIA

NEWSPAPERS & MAGAZINES

In Ireland, there are three national daily broadsheet newspapers, the *Irish Times* and the *Irish Independent*—both Dublin based—and the *Examiner* (formerly the *Cork Examiner*), which is published in Cork. The *Irish Times* is the most authoritative and esteemed of the three, the *Irish Independent* is the most popular, and the *Examiner* is widely read in the southern counties. The British *Daily Star* and the *Sun* also have Irish editions.

The *Evening Herald* is the only nationwide evening newspaper. The *Evening Echo* is published by the Examiner group and sold in the Cork region. There are five Irish Sunday newspapers: the very popular and opinion-focused *Sunday Independent,* the more intellectual *Sunday Tribune,* the business-oriented *Sunday Business Post,* the popular tabloid, *Sunday World,* and the new *Ireland on Sunday.* Regional weekly newspapers are published in almost every county. In Northern Ireland, the main dailies are the *Belfast Telegraph* and the *Belfast Newsletter.* The British broadsheet and tabloid dailies and Sunday newspapers are widely available throughout Ireland.

RADIO & TELEVISION

Radio Telefis Éireann (RTÉ) is Ireland's national television and radio network. There are two television channels—RTÉ 1, which concentrates on news and documentaries, and Network 2, which carries more feature films and light entertainment shows. TV3 is a private channel with a lot of American and British soaps and situation comedies. TG4 is an Irish-language channel (with English subtitles). The British television channels (BBC 1, BBC 2, UTV, Channel 4) and many satellite channels—including SkyNews, SkyMovies, SkySports, CNN, MTV, and TV5 Europe—are also widely available.

There are two 24-hour national radio stations in Ireland—Radio 1 (mainly talk shows) and the popular music-dominated station, 2FM. FM3 is a classical music station which is broadcast in the early mornings and evenings on the same wavelength as the daytime Irish-language radio station, Raidio Na Gaeltachta. There are more than 25 local commercial radio stations whose broadcasting standards vary from county to county. All the BBC radio channels are also available.

MONEY MATTERS

A modest hotel in Dublin costs about £100 a night for two; this figure can be reduced to under £70 by staying in a registered guest house or inn, and reduced to less than £35 by staying in a suburban B&B. Lunch, consisting of a good one-dish plate of bar food at a pub, costs around £6; a sandwich at the same pub, about £2. In Dublin's better restaurants, dinner will run around £20–£30 per person, excluding drinks and tip. Theater and entertainment in most places are inexpensive—about £14 for a good seat, and double that for a big-name, pop-music concert. For the price of a few drinks and (in Dublin and Killarney) a small entrance fee of about £1.50, you can spend a memorable evening at a *seisun* (pronounced *say-shoon*) in a music pub. Entrance to most public galleries is free, but stately homes and similar attractions normally charge about £3 per person. Just about everything is more expensive in Dublin, so add at least 10% to these sample prices: cup of coffee, 80p; pint of beer, £2.20; soda, £1; and 2-km (1-mi) taxi ride, £4.

Hotels and meals in Northern Ireland are less expensive than in the United Kingdom and the Republic of Ireland. Also, the lower level of taxation makes dutiable goods such as gasoline, alcoholic drinks, and tobacco cheaper.

Prices throughout this guide are given for adults. Substantially reduced fees are almost always available for children, students, and senior citizens. For information on taxes, *see* Taxes, *below.*

ATMS

ATMs are found in all major towns. Most major banks are connected to CIRRUS or PLUS systems; there is a four-digit maximum for PIN numbers.

CREDIT CARDS

Throughout this guide, the following abbreviations are used: **AE**, American Express; **DC**, Diner's Club; **MC**, MasterCard; and **V**, Visa. The Discover Card is not honored in Ireland.

➤ REPORTING LOST CARDS: **American Express** (☎ 0353/1205–5111). **Diners Club** (☎ 0353/661–1800). **MasterCard** (☎ 0353/679–8436). **Visa** (☎ 0353/668–5500).

CURRENCY

The unit of currency in the Irish Republic is the pound or punt, pronounced *poont*. It is divided into 100 pence (abbreviated 100p). In this guide, the £ sign refers to the Irish pound; the British pound is referred to as the pound sterling and is written U.K.£.

Irish notes come in denominations of £100, £50, £20, £10, and £5. Coins are available as £1, 50p, 20p, 10p, 5p, 2p, and 1p, and they are not exchangeable outside the Republic of Ireland.

Ireland is a member of the European Monetary Fund (EMU) and since January 1, 1999 all prices have been quoted in pounds and euros. Noncash transactions, including credit-card payments, can be quoted in euros. January 2002 will see the introduction of the euro coins and notes, as well as the gradual withdrawal of the local currency.

CURRENCY EXCHANGE

For the most favorable rates, **change money through banks.** Although ATM transaction fees may be higher abroad than at home, ATM rates are excellent because they are based on wholesale rates offered only by major banks. You won't do as well at exchange booths in airports or rail and bus stations, in hotels, in restaurants, or in stores. To avoid lines at airport exchange booths, **get a bit of local currency before you leave home.**

Dollars and British pounds are accepted only in large hotels and shops geared to tourists. Elsewhere you will be expected to use Irish currency.

At press time, the punt stood at around US$1.15, Canadian $1.70, U.K.£.77, Australian $2.00, and New Zealand $2.64; however, these rates will inevitably change both before and during 2001. Keep a sharp eye on the exchange rate.

➤ EXCHANGE SERVICES: **International Currency Express** (☎ 888/278–6628 for orders, www.foreignmoney.com). **Thomas Cook Currency Services** (☎ 800/287–7362 for telephone orders and retail locations, www.us.thomas-cook.com).

TRAVELER'S CHECKS

Traveler's checks are widely accepted in restaurants, hotels, shops, and stores throughout Ireland. However, if you're going to rural areas and small towns, go with cash; traveler's checks are best used in cities. Lost or stolen checks can usually be replaced within 24 hours. To ensure a speedy refund, buy your own traveler's checks—don't let someone else pay for them: irregularities like this can cause delays. The person who bought the checks should make the call to request a refund.

OUTDOORS & SPORTS

BICYCLING

Ireland is made for the cyclist. In general it's flat with some gently rising hills, it's never too far from one town to the next, repair and support services are good, and the scenery is nonpareil. In summer cycle traffic is at its peak, as winter and early spring tend to be too wet for even the most avid bicycle fan. For information on bike rentals, *see* Bike Travel, *above.*

FISHING

The salmon season is normally from the beginning of January through the end of September, but dates vary from one district to another. The best period for sea trout is from June to late September. Permits are necessary for salmon and sea-trout fishing on privately owned waters or club waters. Besides the permit for the use of a certain stretch of water, those who wish to fish for salmon and sea trout by rod and line must also have a state license. In the Irish Republic, these licenses (£25 annually, or £10 for 21 days) are available in some tackle shops or from the Central Fisheries Board. No license is required for brown trout, rainbow trout, or coarse fish, including pike. Sea angling is available on rocks and piers around the coast.

To game-fish in Northern Ireland, you need a rod license; Foyle Fisheries Commission (FCC) distributes licenses for game fishing in the Foyle area and the Fisheries Conservancy Board (FCB) handles all other regions. A license costs approximately U.K.£10 for eight days. You must also obtain a permit from the owner of the waters in which you plan to fish. Most of the waters in Northern Ireland are owned by the Department of Agriculture, which charges about U.K.£15 for an eight-day permit, U.K.£3.50 for a daily one. If you plan to fish outside the jurisdiction of the Department of Agriculture, you must obtain a permit from one of the local clubs. For more information, and for Department of Agriculture permits and FFC and FCB rod licenses, contact the NITB (☞ Visitor Information, *below*).

➤ INFORMATION: **Central Fisheries Board** (✉ Balngowan House, Mobhi Boreen, Glasnevin, Dublin 9, ☎ 01/837–9206). **Department of Agriculture** (✉ Fisheries Division, Stormont, Belfast BT4 3PW, ☎ 028/9052–3431). **Fisheries Conservancy Board** (✉ FCB, 1 Mahon Rd., Portadown, Craigavon, Co. Armagh BT62 3EE, ☎ 028/3833–4666). **Foyle Fisheries**

Commission (✉ 8 Victoria Rd., Derry BT47 2AB, ☎ 028/7134–2100).

GOLF

What makes Irish Golf so great—and increasingly popular—is quite simply the natural architecture. The wild, wonderful coastline seems to be made for links golf, and 39 of the world's top 150 quality links courses are in Ireland. Most famous of these, of course, is the celebrated Ballybunion. Fortunately, links courses can be played year-round—an asset in a rainy country like Ireland. Pack plenty of sweaters and rain gear, and make sure you're in good shape: electric cars are only available at the most expensive courses. Golf clubs and bags can be rented almost anywhere. With the exception of the ancient Royal Belfast, all golf clubs in Ireland are happy to have visitors (and charge well for the privilege). For details on specific courses, *see* Chapter 9.

➤ INFORMATION: **Golfing Union of Ireland** (✉ 81 Eglington Rd., Dublin 4, ☎ 01/269–4111).

HIKING

Hikers from all over the world spend weeks on the almost 30 major and countless minor trails covering the country. As with biking, the relatively flat landscape, stunning scenery, and nearness of towns to each other make hiking a relatively carefree activity. A tent is always a good idea, but you can certainly plan any walk so that you reach civilization every night. Pack for wind and rain, as there will always be some. A good ordinance survey map is also useful.

The most famous of Ireland's walks is the classic Wicklow Way, a 137-km (85-mi) trail that begins in the Dublin surburbs before winding its way through the Wicklow mountains. Much of the route lies above 1,600 ft and follows rough sheep tracks, forest firebreaks, and old bog roads. Whether you're a novice or veteran hiker, Wicklow's gentle hills are a terrific place to begin an Irish walking vacation. Consider participating in one of the Wicklow walking festivals held at Easter, in May, and in autumn. Other popular hiking options include

the Kerry Way, which starts and ends in Killarney, and the Donegal Walk across the center of wild, rugged County Donegal. For more information, contact Bord Fáilte or the NITB (☞ Visitor Information, *below*).

HORSEBACK RIDING

There are plenty of opportunities for horseback riding throughout the country. You're never more than a few miles from a riding center and the variety of riding possibilities is one of Ireland's major attractions. Short gallops or weeklong guided trips are available. Terrains include beaches, mountain tracks, forests, and flat farmland ideal for cantering. Dublin's environs have excellent horseback riding. Stables on the city's outskirts give immediate access to suitable riding areas. In the city itself, Phoenix Park has superb, quiet riding conditions away from the busy main road that bisects the park. About 20 riding stables in the greater Dublin area have horses for hire by the hour or the day, for novices and experienced riders. A few also operate as equestrian centers and have lessons. Prices vary a great deal, but expect to pay around £15 an hour. For more information, contact Bord Fáilte or the NITB (☞ Visitor Information, *below*).

SPECTATOR SPORTS

The Irish are sports mad, and for an island of only 5 million people they have achieved notable success on the global stage with Olympic champions, World Cup qualifiers, and some of the finest thoroughbreds on the planet. The natives love watching sports almost as much as taking part in them. Horse racing has long been a favorite pastime, with courses ringing Dublin and spread throughout the rest of the country. At Curragh Racecourse, in Dublin's environs, the Irish Derby and other international horse races are run. The capital city is home to two dog racing tracks: Harolds Cross and Shelbourne Park. Soccer has increased in popularity over the last two decades with the dramatic successes of the Republic of Ireland team; most of the major towns and cities have a semiprofessional club in the National League which runs from August to May every year. For a truly

Irish sports experience you should try to attend one of two Gaelic games, either football or hurling; the first is played with a soccer-type ball that is kicked out of the hands, and the second with a wooden stick and a hard ball very much like a baseball. The speed and skill on display in both games can be breathtaking. An inter-county championship takes place from May through September.

➤ INFORMATION: **Curragh Racecourse** (✉ Kildare, ☎ 045/441205). **Football Association of Ireland** (✉ 80 Merrion Sq., Dublin 2, ☎ 01/676–6864). **Gaelic Athletic Association** (✉ Croke Park, Dublin 4, ☎ 01/836–3222). **Harolds Cross** (✉ Harolds Cross, Dublin 6, ☎ 01/497–1081). **Shelbourne Park** (✉ Shelbourne Park, Dublin 4, ☎ 01/668–3502).

PACKING

In Ireland you can experience all four seasons in one day, so pack accordingly. Even in July and August, the hottest months of the year, a heavy sweater and a good waterproof coat or umbrella are essential. You should **bring at least two pairs of walking shoes**: it can and does rain at any time of the year, and shoes can get soaked in minutes.

The Irish are generally informal about clothes. In the more expensive hotels and restaurants most people dress formally for dinner, and a jacket and tie may be required in bars after 7 PM, but very few places operate a strict dress policy. Younger travelers should note that old or tattered blue jeans are forbidden in certain bars and dance clubs.

In your carry-on luggage, **pack an extra pair of eyeglasses or contact lenses** and **enough of any medication you take** to last the entire trip. You may also ask your doctor to write a spare prescription using the drug's generic name, since brand names may vary from country to country. In luggage to be checked, **never pack prescription drugs or valuables.** To avoid customs delays, carry medications in their original packaging. And don't forget to carry with you the addresses of offices that handle refunds of lost traveler's checks.

CHECKING LUGGAGE

How many carry-on bags you can bring with you is up to the airline. Most allow two, but not always, so make sure that everything you carry aboard will fit under your seat or in the overhead bin, and get to the gate early. Note that if you have a seat at the back of the plane, you'll probably board first, while the overhead bins are still empty.

If you are flying internationally, note that baggage allowances may be determined not by piece but by weight—generally 88 pounds (40 kilograms) in first class, 66 pounds (30 kilograms) in business class, and 44 pounds (20 kilograms) in economy.

Airline liability for baggage is limited to $1,250 per person on flights within the United States. On international flights it amounts to $9.07 per pound or $20 per kilogram for checked baggage (roughly $640 per 70-pound bag) and $400 per passenger for unchecked baggage. You can buy additional coverage at check-in for about $10 per $1,000 of coverage, but it excludes a rather extensive list of items, shown on your airline ticket.

Before departure, **itemize your bags' contents** and their worth, and label the bags with your name, address, and phone number. (If you use your home address, cover it so potential thieves can't see it readily.) Inside each bag, **pack a copy of your itinerary.** At check-in, **make sure that each bag is correctly tagged** with the destination airport's three-letter code. If your bags arrive damaged or fail to arrive at all, file a written report with the airline before leaving the airport.

PASSPORTS & VISAS

When traveling internationally, **carry your passport even if you don't need one** (it's always the best form of I.D.) and **make two photocopies of the data page** (one for someone at home and another for you, carried separately from your passport). If you lose your passport, promptly call the nearest embassy or consulate and the local police.

ENTERING IRELAND

All U.S., Canadian, Australian, and New Zealand citizens, even infants, need a valid passport to enter Ireland for stays of up to 90 days. Citizens of the United Kingdom, when traveling on flights departing from Great Britain, do not need a passport to enter Ireland. Passport requirements for Northern Ireland are the same as for the Republic.

PASSPORT OFFICES

The best time to apply for a passport or to renew is in fall and winter. Before any trip, check your passport's expiration date, and, if necessary, renew it as soon as possible.

➤ AUSTRALIAN CITIZENS: **Australian Passport Office** (☎ 131232, www.dfat.gov.au/passports).

➤ CANADIAN CITIZENS: **Passport Office** (☎ 819/994–3500 or 800/567–6868, www.dfait-maeci.gc.ca/passport).

➤ NEW ZEALAND CITIZENS: **New Zealand Passport Office** (☎ 04/494–0700, www.passports.govt.nz).

➤ U.K. CITIZENS: **London Passport Office** (☎ 0870/521–0410) for fees and documentation requirements and to request an emergency passport.

➤ U.S. CITIZENS: **National Passport Information Center** (☎ 900/225–5674; calls are 35¢ per minute for automated service, $1.05 per minute for operator service).

SAFETY

The theft of car radios, mobile phones, cameras, video recorders, and other items of value from cars is common in Dublin and other major cities and towns. Never leave any valuable items on car seats or in the foot space between the back and front seats or in the glove compartments. In fact, never leave anything whatsoever in sight in your car—even if you're leaving it for only a short time. You should also think twice about leaving valuables in your car while visiting tourist attractions anywhere in the country.

SENIOR-CITIZEN TRAVEL

To qualify for age-related discounts, **mention your senior-citizen status up front** when booking hotel reservations (not when checking out) and before you're seated in restaurants (not when paying the bill). When renting a car, ask about promotional car-rental discounts, which can be cheaper than senior-citizen rates.

➤ EDUCATIONAL PROGRAMS: **Elderhostel** (✉ 75 Federal St., 3rd floor, Boston, MA 02110, ☎ 877/426–8056, FAX 877/426–2166, www.elderhostel.org). **Interhostel** (✉ University of New Hampshire, 6 Garrison Ave., Durham, NH 03824, ☎ 603/862–1147 or 800/733–9753, FAX 603/862–1113, www.learn.unh.edu).

SHOPPING

In days gone by, travelers would arrive in Ireland, land of leprechauns, shillelaghs, and shamrocks, and quickly realize that the only known specimens of leprechauns or shillelaghs were those in souvenir-shop windows, while shamrocks bloomed mainly around the borders of Irish linen handkerchiefs and tablecloths. All of this is still true, of course, but today you'll find so much more.

KEY DESTINATIONS

Dublin is the epicenter of shopping in Ireland and items from all over the country can be found in the capital city, though often at a small premium. The variety and sophistication of stores in Dublin are quite remarkable. Department stores stocking internationally known fashion-designer goods and housewares stand beside small boutiques that make shopping in the major city a personalized and pleasurable experience.

Other major cities, such as Belfast, Cork, and Galway, will also have a wide variety of stores, including a few large department stores. The West is the place for those chunky Aran sweaters and hand-knitted knitwear of all types. Donegal is famous for its tweed, of course, and for crystal you can choose between world-famous Waterford and slightly less expensive Cavan. Northern Ireland, especially

Belfast, has a long tradition of producing fine Irish linens.

STUDENTS IN IRELAND

To save money, **look into deals available through student-oriented travel agencies.** To qualify you'll need a bona fide student ID card. Members of international student groups are also eligible.

➤ I.D.s & SERVICES: **Council Travel** (CIEE; ✉ 205 E. 42nd St., 14th floor, New York, NY 10017, ☎ 212/822–2700 or 888/268–6245, FAX 212/822–2699, info@councilexchanges.org, www.councilexchanges.org) for mail orders only, in the United States. **Travel Cuts** (✉ 187 College St., Toronto, Ontario M5T 1P7, ☎ 416/979–2406 or 800/667–2887, www.travelcuts.com) in Canada.

TAXES

VALUE-ADDED TAX

When leaving the Irish Republic, U.S. and Canadian visitors **get a refund** of the value-added tax (VAT), which currently accounts for a hefty 21% of the purchase price of many goods and 12.5% of those that fall outside the luxury category. Apart from clothing, most items of interest to visitors, right down to ordinary toilet soap, are rated at 21%. Most crafts outlets and department stores operate a system called Cashback, which enables U.S. and Canadian visitors to collect VAT rebates in the currency of their choice at Dublin or Shannon Airport on departure. Otherwise, refunds can be claimed from individual stores after returning home. Forms for the refunds must be picked up at the time of purchase, and the form must be stamped by customs before leaving Ireland (including Northern Ireland). Most major stores deduct VAT at the time of sale if goods are to be shipped overseas; however, there is a shipping charge. VAT is not refundable on accommodation, car rental, meals, or any other form of personal services received on vacation.

When leaving Northern Ireland, U.S. and Canadian visitors can also get a refund of the 17.5% VAT by the over-the-counter and the direct-export methods. Most larger stores provide these services upon request and will handle the paperwork. For the over-the-counter method, you must spend more than £75 in one store. Ask the store for Form VAT 407 (you must have identification—passports are best), to be given to customs when you leave the country. The refund will be forwarded to you in about eight weeks (minus a small service charge) either in the form of a sterling check or as a credit to your charge card. The direct-export method, where the goods are shipped directly to your home, is more cumbersome. VAT Form 704/1/93 must be certified by customs, police, or a notary public when you get home and then sent back to the store, which will refund your money.

Global Refund is a V.A.T. refund service that makes getting your money back hassle-free. The service is available Europe-wide at 130,000 affiliated stores. In participating stores, **ask for the Global Refund form** (called a Shopping Cheque). Have it stamped like any customs form by customs officials when you leave the European Union. Then take the form to one of the more than 700 Global Refund counters—conveniently located at every major airport and border crossing—and your money will be refunded on the spot in the form of cash, check, or a refund to your credit-card account (minus a small percentage for processing).

➤ V.A.T. REFUNDS: **Global Refund** (✉ 707 Summer St., Stamford, CT 06901, ☎ 800/566–9828, FAX 203/674–8709, taxfree@us.globalrefund.com, www.globalrefund.com).

TELEPHONES

Ireland's telephone system is up to the standards of the United Kingdom and the United States. Direct-dialing is common; local phone numbers have five to eight digits. You can make international calls from most phones, and some cell phones also work here, depending on the carrier.

Do not make calls from your hotel room unless it's absolutely necessary. Practically all hotels add 200% to 300% to the cost of a call.

AREA & COUNTRY CODES

The country code for Ireland is 353; for Northern Ireland, which is part of the United Kingdom telephone system, 44. When dialing an Irish number from abroad, drop the initial 0 from the local area code. The country code is 1 for the United States and Canada, 61 for Australia, 64 for New Zealand, and 44 for the United Kingdom.

In 2000, local area codes in Northern Ireland changed. The new local area code, 028, replaces the old five- and six-digit codes. A prefix, varying according to region, has also been added before the first digit of the old numbers. The new phone numbers have eight digits. In Belfast, for example, the number 01232/XXXXXX (with the old, five-digit area code of 01232) has changed to 028/90XX–XXXX. For specific details on the change in Northern Ireland, as well as other parts of the United Kingdom, check out the Web site: www.number-change.org. You can also call 020/7634–8700 (from the United States) and 0808/224–2000 (within the United Kingdom).

DIRECTORY & OPERATOR ASSISTANCE

If the operator has to connect your call, it will cost at least one-third more than direct dial.

➤ REPUBLIC OF IRELAND: Call 1190 for directory inquiries within the Republic and Northern Ireland; call 1197 for U.K. numbers; and call 1198 for international numbers. Dial 114 for operator assistance with international calls; dial 10 for operator assistance for calls within Ireland and the United Kingdom.

➤ NORTHERN IRELAND AND THE U.K.: Call 192 for directory inquiries within Northern Ireland and the United Kingdom; 153 for international directory inquiries, which includes the Republic; 155 for the international operator; 100 for operator assistance for calls within the United Kingdom and Northern Ireland.

INTERNATIONAL CALLS

International dialing codes can be found in all telephone directories. The international prefix from Ireland is 00. For calls to Great Britain, dial 0044 before the exchange code, and drop the initial zero of the local code. For the United States and Canada dial 001, for Australia 0061, and for New Zealand 0064.

LOCAL CALLS

To make a local call just dial the number direct. Public phones take either coins (20p for a call) or cards, but not both. At coin phones just pick up the receiver and deposit the money before you dial the number. At card phones pick up the receiver, wait until the display tells you to insert the card, then dial. In the Republic, 20p will buy you a three-minute local call; around 80p are needed for a three-minute long-distance call within the Republic. In Northern Ireland, a local call costs 10p.

LONG-DISTANCE CALLS

To make a long-distance call, just dial the area code, then the number.

If you are dialing Northern Ireland from the Republic, dial 048 or 4428, followed by the new eight-digit number (e.g., For Belfast, dial either 048/90XX–XXXX or 4428/90XX–XXXX).

LONG-DISTANCE SERVICES

AT&T, MCI, and Sprint access codes make calling long distance relatively convenient, but you may find the local access number blocked in many hotel rooms. First ask the hotel operator to connect you. If the hotel operator balks, ask for an international operator, or dial the international operator yourself. One way to improve your odds of getting connected to your long-distance carrier is to travel with more than one company's calling card (a hotel may block Sprint, for example, but not MCI). If all else fails, call from a pay phone.

➤ ACCESS CODES: **AT&T Direct** (☎ 1800/550000 from the Republic of Ireland, 0800/013–0011 from Northern Ireland). **MCI WorldPhone** (☎ 1800/555–1001 from the Republic of Ireland, 0800/890222 from Northern Ireland using BT, 0500/890222 using Mercury). **Sprint International Access** (☎ 1800/552001 from the Republic of Ireland, 0800/890877 from Northern Ireland using BT, 0500/890877 using Mercury).

PHONE CARDS

"Callcards" are sold in all post offices and at most newsagents. These come in denominations of 10, 20, and 50 units, and range in price from £2 for 10 calls to £16 for 100 calls. Card phones are now more popular than coin phones.

PUBLIC PHONES

Public pay phones are in all towns and villages. They can be found in street booths and in restaurants, hotels, bars, and shops, some of which display a sign saying YOU CAN PHONE FROM HERE. There are currently at least three different models of pay phones in operation; read the instructions or ask for assistance.

TIME

Dublin is 5 hours ahead of New York, 8 hours ahead of Los Angeles and Vancouver, 9 hours ahead of Auckland, and 10 hours ahead of Sydney and Melbourne.

TIPPING

In some hotels and restaurants a service charge of around 10%—rising to 15% in a few plush spots—is added to the bill. If in doubt, ask whether service is included. In places where it is included, tipping is not necessary unless you have received particularly good service. But if there is no service charge, add a minimum of 10% to the total.

Tip taxi drivers about 10% of the fare displayed by the meter. Hackney cabs, who make the trip for a prearranged sum, do not expect tips. There are few porters and plenty of baggage trolleys at airports, so tipping is usually not an issue; if you use a porter, 50p is the minimum. Tip hotel porters about 50p per large suitcase. Hairdressers normally expect about £1. You don't tip in pubs, but for waiter service in a bar, a hotel lounge, or a Dublin lounge bar, leave about 50p.

TOURS & PACKAGES

Because everything is prearranged on a prepackaged tour or independent vacation, you'll spend less time planning—and often get it all at a good price.

BOOKING WITH AN AGENT

Travel agents are excellent resources. But it's a good idea to collect brochures from several agencies as some agents' suggestions may be influenced by relationships with tour and package firms that reward them for volume sales. If you have a special interest, **find an agent with expertise in that area**; ASTA (☞ Travel Agencies, *below*) has a database of specialists worldwide.

Make sure your travel agent knows the accommodations and other services of the place they're recommending. Ask about the hotel's location, room size, beds, and whether it has a pool, room service, or programs for children, if you care about these. Has your agent been there in person or sent others whom you can contact?

Do some homework on your own, too: local tourism boards can provide information about lesser-known and small-niche operators, some of which may sell only direct.

BUYER BEWARE

Each year consumers are stranded or lose their money when tour operators—even large ones with excellent reputations—go out of business. So **check out the operator.** Ask several travel agents about its reputation, and try to **book with a company that has a consumer-protection program.** (Look for information in the company's brochure.) In the United States, members of the National Tour Association and the United States Tour Operators Association are required to set aside funds to cover your payments and travel arrangements in the event that the company defaults. It's also a good idea to choose a company that participates in the American Society of Travel Agents' Tour Operator Program (TOP); ASTA will act as mediator in any disputes between you and your tour operator.

Remember that the more your package or tour includes the better you can predict the ultimate cost of your vacation. Make sure you know exactly what is covered, and **beware of hidden costs.** Are taxes, tips, and transfers included? Entertainment and excursions? These can add up.

➤ TOUR-OPERATOR RECOMMENDA-TIONS: **American Society of Travel Agents** (☞ Travel Agencies, *below*). **National Tour Association** (NTA; ⊠ 546 E. Main St., Lexington, KY 40508, ☎ 606/226–4444 or 800/ 682–8886, www.ntaonline.com). **United States Tour Operators Associ-ation** (USTOA; ⊠ 342 Madison Ave., Suite 1522, New York, NY 10173, ☎ 212/599–6599 or 800/468–7862, ℻ 212/599–6744, ustoa@aol.com, www.ustoa.com).

TRAIN TRAVEL

The Irish Republic's train services are generally reliable, reasonably priced, and comfortable. All the principal towns are easily reached from Dublin, though services between provincial cities are roundabout. To reach Cork City from Wexford, for example, you have to go via Limerick Junction. It is often quicker, though perhaps less comfortable, to take a bus. Most mainline trains have two classes: standard and superstandard. Round-trip tickets are usually cheapest.

In Northern Ireland, Northern Ireland Railways has three main rail routes, all operating out of Belfast's **Central Station** (☎ 028/9089–9400). These are north to Derry, via Ballymena and Coleraine; east to Bangor along the shores of Belfast Lough; and south to Dublin and the Irish Republic. Note that **Eurailpasses are not valid in Northern Ireland.**

CUTTING COSTS

To save money, **look into rail passes.** But be aware that if you don't plan to cover many miles you may come out ahead by buying individual tickets.

Ireland (excluding Northern Ireland) is one of 17 countries in which you can **use Eurailpasses,** which provide unlimited first-class rail travel, in all of the participating countries, for the duration of the pass. If you plan to rack up the miles, get a standard pass. These are available for 15 days ($554), 21 days ($718), one month ($890), two months ($1,260), and three months ($1,558). If your plans call for only limited train travel, **look into a Europass,** which costs less

money than a Eurailpass. Unlike with Eurailpasses, however, you get a limited number of travel days, in a limited number of countries, during a specified time period. For example, a two-month pass ($348) allows 5 days of rail travel but costs $200 less than the least expensive Eurailpass; 15 days of travel in two months costs $728. Keep in mind, however, that the Europass is good only in France, Germany, Italy, Spain, and Switzer-land, and the number of countries you can visit is further limited by the type of pass you buy. For example, the basic two-month pass allows you to visit only three of the five partici-pating countries.

In addition to standard Eurailpasses, **ask about special rail-pass plans.** Among these are the Eurail Youthpass (for those under age 26), the Eurail Saverpass (which gives a discount for two or more people traveling together), a Eurail Flexipass (which allows a certain number of travel days within a set period), the Euraildrive Pass and the Europass Drive (which combines travel by train and rental car). Whichever pass you choose, remember that you must **purchase your pass before you leave** for Europe.

The **Irish Explorer Rail & Bus Pass,** for use on Ireland's railroads, bus system, or both, covers all the state-run and federal railways and bus lines throughout the Republic of Ireland. It does not apply to the North or to transportation within the cities. An 8-day ticket for use on buses *and* trains during a 15-day period is $100. Contact Irish Rail International for details.

The **Emerald Isle Card** offers unlim-ited bus and train travel anywhere in Ireland and Northern Ireland, valid within cities as well. An 8-day pass gives you eight days of travel over a 15-day period; it costs $115, $56 for children. A pass for 15 days of travel over a 30-day period costs $200, $100 for children. Irish Rail International provides details on this card as well.

In Northern Ireland, **Rail Runabout** tickets, entitling you to seven days' unlimited travel on scheduled rail services April–October, are available from main Northern Ireland Railway stations. They cost U.K.£35 for adults, U.K.£18 for children under 16 and senior citizens. Interrail tickets are also valid in Northern Ireland.

➤ INFORMATION AND PASSES: **DER Travel Services** (⊠ 9501 W. Devon Ave., Rosemont, IL 60018, ☎ 800/782–2424, FAX 800/282–7474 for information, 800/860–9944 for brochures, www.dertravel.com). **Irish Rail International** (⊠ 108 Ridgedale Ave., Morristown, NJ 07960, ☎ 800/243–7687, www.irishrail.ie). **Rail Europe** (⊠ 500 Mamaroneck Ave., Harrison, NY 10528, ☎ 800/438–7245, FAX 800/432–1329, www.raileurope.com; ⊠ 2087 Dundas E, Suite 106, Mississauga, Ontario L4X 1M2, ☎ 800/361–7245, FAX 905/602–4198).

FARES & SCHEDULES

➤ TRAIN INFORMATION: In the Irish Republic: **Irish Rail** (Iarnrod Éireann; ☎ 01/836–6222), the rail division of CIE. In Northern Ireland: **Northern Ireland Railways** (☎ 028/9089–9411).

RESERVATIONS

Many travelers assume that rail passes guarantee them seats on the trains they wish to ride. Not so. You need to **book seats ahead even if you are using a rail pass**; seat reservations are required on some European trains, particularly high-speed trains, and are a good idea on trains that may be crowded—particularly in summer on popular routes. You will also need a reservation if you purchase sleeping accommodations.

TRANSPORTATION AROUND IRELAND

Ireland is small and relatively flat, so negotiating your way around the island should not be a great difficulty. In the past many of the more remote areas were only accessible by tiny, winding roads usually in pretty dire condition. But in the last decade all this has changed, and a prolonged program of road building and improvement, financed by European grants, has drastically improved driving in every part of Ireland. With long-distance public transport somewhat unreliable and sketchy, a car is the best way to see the country. But

the new prosperity and improved roads mean more traffic, which has had a duel effect of increasing noise and pollution in the countryside and giving rise to traffic jams in the cities.

If public transport is your only option, the trains are comfortable, but they only connect major cities and towns and tend to be overpriced. Buses go to more destinations and are better value, but as they don't always go frequently, and you might find yourself stuck in a small town overnight.

TRAVEL AGENCIES

A good travel agent puts your needs first. Look for an agency that has been in business at least five years, emphasizes customer service, and has someone on staff who specializes in your destination. In addition, **make sure the agency belongs to a professional trade organization.** The American Society of Travel Agents (ASTA), with 27,000 agents in some 170 countries, is the largest and most influential in the field. Operating under the motto "Integrity in Travel," it maintains and enforces a strict code of ethics and will step in to help mediate any agent-client disputes if necessary. ASTA also maintains a Web site that includes a directory of agents. (If a travel agency is also acting as your tour operator, *see* Buyer Beware *in* Tours & Packages, *above.*)

➤ LOCAL AGENT REFERRALS: **American Society of Travel Agents** (ASTA; ☎ 800/965–2782 24-hr hot line, FAX 703/684–8319, www.astanet.com). **Association of British Travel Agents** (⊠ 68–71 Newman St., London W1P 4AH, ☎ 020/7637–2444, FAX 020/7637–0713, abta.co.uk, www.abtanet.com). **Association of Canadian Travel Agents** (⊠ 1729 Bank St., Suite 201, Ottawa, Ontario K1V 7Z5, ☎ 613/521–0474, FAX 613/521–0805, acta.ntl@sympatico.ca). **Australian Federation of Travel Agents** (⊠ Level 3, 309 Pitt St., Sydney 2000, ☎ 02/9264–3299, FAX 02/9264–1085, www.afta.com.au). **Travel Agents' Association of New Zealand** (⊠ Box 1888, Wellington 10033, ☎ 04/499–0104, FAX 04/499–0827, taanz@tiasnet.co.nz).

VISITOR INFORMATION

For information on travel in the Irish Republic, contact the **Irish Tourist Board** (ITB), known as Bord Fáilte (pronounced Board Falcha); its Web site is: www.ireland.travel.ie. Information on travel in the North is available from the **Northern Ireland Tourist Board** (NITB) office; its Web site is: www.ni-tourism.com.

➤ **ITB: Ireland** (✉ Baggot St. Bridge, Dublin 2, ☎ 01/602–4000, 669/792083, or 1850/230330 [within Ireland], FAX 01/602–4100). **U.S.** (✉ 345 Park Ave., New York, NY 10154, ☎ 212/418–0800 or 800/223–6470, FAX 212/371–9052). **U.K.** (✉ Ireland House, 150 New Bond St., London W1Y 0AQ, ☎ 020/7493–3201, FAX 020/7493–9065).

➤ **NITB: Northern Ireland** (✉ 59 North St., Belfast BT1 1NB, ☎ 028/9023–1221, FAX 028/9023–9936). **U.S.** (✉ 551 5th Ave., Suite 701, New York, NY 10176, ☎ 212/922–0101 or 800/326–0036, FAX 212/922–0099). **Canada** (✉ 111 Avenue Rd., Suite 450, Toronto, Ontario M5R 3J8, ☎ 416/925–6368, FAX 416/961–2175). **U.K.** (✉ 4–12 Lower Regent St., London BW1Y 4PQ, ☎ 020/7839–8417).

➤ **U.S. GOVERNMENT ADVISORIES: U.S. Department of State** (✉ Overseas Citizens Services Office, Room 4811 N.S., 2201 C St. NW, Washington, DC 20520, ☎ 202/647–5225 for interactive hot line, 301/946–4400 for computer bulletin board, FAX 202/647–3000 for interactive hot line); enclose a self-addressed, stamped, business-size envelope.

WEB SITES

Do check out the World Wide Web when you're planning. You'll find everything from up-to-date weather forecasts to virtual tours of famous cities. Fodor's Web site, www.fodors.com, is a great place to start your online travels. When you see a ☜ in this book, go to www.fodors.com/urls for an up-to-date link to that destination's site.

For a comprehensive directory of sites on Ireland, visit **www. paddynet.com**. Some of the most popular sites (note that their log-on addresses are subject to change) are: Best of Ireland (www.iol.ie/ádiscover/welcome.htm); Every Celtic Thing on the Web (www.mi.net/users/ang/angris.html); and Heritage Ireland (www.heritageireland.ie). In addition, many of the leading newspapers of Ireland (☞ Media, *above*) have their own Web sites, which can be gold mines of timely information about special events, the latest restaurants, and newest cultural happenings. Track down these newspaper Web sites using a search engine.

WHEN TO GO

Summer remains the most popular time to visit Ireland, and for good reason. The weather is pleasant, the days are long (daylight lasts until after 10 in late June and July), and the countryside is green and beautiful. But there will be crowds in popular holiday spots, and prices for accommodations are at their peak. As British and Irish school vacations overlap from late-June to mid-September, families, backpacking students, and other vacationers descend on popular coastal resorts in the South, West, and East. Unless you are determined to enjoy the short (July and August) swimming season, you would be well advised to **take your vacation in Ireland outside peak travel months.**

Fall and spring are good times to travel (late September can often be dry and warm, although the weather can be unpredictable). Seasonal hotels, restaurants, and accommodations usually close from early- or mid-November until mid-March or Easter. During this off-season, prices are considerably lower than in summer, but your selection of hotels and restaurants is limited, and many minor attractions also close. St. Patrick's Week in March gives a focal point to a spring visit, but some American visitors may find the saint's-day celebrations a little less enthusiastic than the ones back home. Dublin, however, welcomes American visitors on March 17 with a weekend-long series of activities, including a parade and the Lord Mayor's Ball. If you're planning an Easter visit, don't forget that most theaters close from

Thursday to Sunday of Holy Week (the week preceding Easter), and all bars and restaurants, except those serving hotel residents, close on Good Friday.

If you want to feel like the only tourist in town, **try a winter visit.** Many hotels arrange special Christmas packages with entertainment and outdoor activities; horse races and hunting trips abound. Mid-November to mid-February is either too cold or too wet for all but the keenest golfers, but some of the coastal links courses are playable in almost any weather. There are cheerful open fires in almost all hotels and bars, and, with extra time on their hands, people tend to take an added interest in visitors.

CLIMATE

What follows are average daily maximum and minimum temperatures for some major cities in Ireland.

DUBLIN

Jan.	47F	8C	May	59F	15C	Sept.	63F	17C
	34	1		43	6		49	9
Feb.	47F	8C	June	65F	18C	Oct.	58F	14C
	36	2		49	9		43	6
Mar.	50F	10C	July	68F	20C	Nov.	50F	10C
	38	3		52	11		40	4
Apr.	56F	13C	Aug.	67F	20C	Dec.	47F	8C
	40	4		52	11		38	3

CORK

Jan.	49F	9C	May	61F	16C	Sept.	65F	18C
	36	2		45	7		50	10
Feb.	49F	9C	June	67F	19C	Oct.	58F	14C
	38	3		50	10		45	7
Mar.	52F	11C	July	68F	20C	Nov.	52F	11C
	40	4		54	12		40	4
Apr.	56F	13C	Aug.	68F	20C	Dec.	49F	9C
	41	5		54	12		38	3

BELFAST

Jan.	43F	6C	May	59F	15C	Sept.	61F	16C
	36	2		43	6		49	9
Feb.	45F	7C	June	65F	18C	Oct.	56F	13C
	36	2		49	9		45	7
Mar.	49F	9C	July	65F	18C	Nov.	49F	9C
	38	3		52	11		40	4
Apr.	54F	12C	Aug.	65F	18C	Dec.	45F	7C
	50	4		52	11		38	3

➤ FORECASTS: **Weather Channel Connection** (☎ 900/932–8437), 95¢ per minute from a Touch-Tone phone.

FESTIVALS AND SEASONAL EVENTS

In both the Republic and Northern Ireland, festivals devoted to the arts, literature, sports, harvests, and animals fill up the calendar year-round. The Republic's Bord Fáilte and the Northern Ireland Tourist Board jointly produce an annual 80-page Calendar of Events (£1; ☞ Visitor Information, *above*). A horse race is run practically every day of the year in Ireland; the **Irish Horse Racing Authority**'s marketing and promotions department (☎ 01/289–2888) is a good source for information.

➤ EARLY MAR.: **Opera Northern Ireland** (☎ 028/9024–1919) performs at Belfast's Grand Opera House. The annual **Arklow Music Festival** (☎

0402/32732) includes orchestra, choir, solo singing, drama, and verse speaking competitions.

➤ MAR.: For three weeks on either side of St. Patrick's Day, the **Celtic Spring Festival** (☎ 028/7126–7234) brings theatrical and rock music performances, an Irish-language festival, and a parade to **Derry City,** County Derry.

➤ MID-MAR.: At the **Roaring 20's Festival** (☎ 064/32833) in Killarney, County Kerry, which leads up to St. Patrick's Day, revelers turn out in Great Gatsby outfits to enjoy afternoon teas, cocktail parties, and live music. Bands of every stripe and size march in step and blow their horns in the 29th annual **Limerick International Band Festival** (☎ 061/410777), which immediately follows the city's St. Patrick's Day celebrations. The **Adare Jazz Festival** (☎ 061/396118) in County Limerick fills the town's pubs with great jazz. **St. Patrick's Day** celebrations throughout the country get under way three days before the climactic day itself, March 17. Ireland's major St. Patrick's event is the **Dublin Festival and Parade** (☎ 01/ 671–3788), more elaborate every year, which includes a huge fireworks show and guest bands from the United States; there's also a festival of traditional Irish music, the Dublin **Feis Ceoil.**

➤ EARLY APR.: For 10 days, the **Dublin Film Festival** (☎ 01/679–2937) presents an eclectic mix of the best independent and feature films from Ireland and around the world, plus lectures, seminars, and other events for cineastes.

➤ APR.: Easter brings one of the biggest events of the racing calendar, the two-day **Irish Grand National** at Fairyhouse, County Meath (☎ 01/ 825–6167), about 19 km (12 mi) north of Dublin. **Easter walking festivals** also get visitors and locals tootling around on foot at various venues throughout the country, including Rathdrum, County Wicklow (☎ 0404/46262), Glencar, County Kerry (☎ 066/60101), and Kenmare, County Kerry (☎ 064/41034). Contact **Walking World Ireland** (☎ 01/

492–3030) for details on other walking festivals throughout the year.

➤ LATE APR.: The Punchestown Racecourse, just outside **Naas,** hosts the **Punchestown National Hunt Festival** (☎ 045/897704). The **Antiques and Collectables Fair** (☎ 01/670– 8295) brings dealers from all parts of Ireland to the capital.

➤ EARLY MAY: Heritage properties and private gardens open to the public during the **County Wicklow Garden Festival** (☎ 0404/20100). Sixty-plus traditional music sessions take place over the first weekend in May at Kinvara's **Cuckoo Fleadh** (☎ 091/637145).

➤ MAY: Twenty-one days of concerts, competitions, and exhibitions take place during the **Belfast Civic Festival** (☎ 028/9027–0466); festivities kick off with the **Lord Mayor's Show,** a parade. Also during the festival, the **Belfast Marathon** (☎ 028/9027– 0466) fills the streets in early May with 3,500 runners.

➤ MID-MAY: The **Murphy's International Mussel Fair** (☎ 027/50360) in Bantry, County Cork celebrates the peak of the harvest season for this delicacy *na mara* ("of the sea" in Irish).

➤ LATE MAY: The **Galway Early Music Festival** (☎ 091/528166) in Galway City fills the city with the sounds of pre-baroque Irish and European music. The **Fleadh Nua** ☎ 01/280– 0295), the annual festival of traditional Irish music, song, and dance, takes place in **Ennis,** County Clare. Fifteen guided hikewalks around west Cork and parts of Kerry make up the **Kenmare Whit Walking Festival** (☎ 064/42168). Theater, literary readings, and plenty of music fill the calendar of the **Sligo Arts Festival** (☎ 071/69802), which continues into early June.

➤ MAY–JUNE: It's the height of flower season in The Burren in County Clare, and the best time to take a **Burren Flora Tour.** (Contact Mary Angela Keane [☎ 065/74003] or Shane Connolly [☎ 065/77168] for a guided botanical walk.)

➤ EARLY JUNE: **Listowel Writers' Week** (☎ 068/21074), one of Ireland's leading literary festivals, brings writers, poets, and lovers of literature together in this County Kerry town. Cartoonists congregate in the Wicklow village of **Rathdrum** for the annual **Guinness International Cartoon Festival** (☎ 0404/46811). **Carlow** celebrates the arts in its annual **Éigse Carlow Arts Festival** (☎ 0503/40491). The **Weavers' Fair and Vintage Weekend** (☎ 075/41262) comes to **Ardara** in County Donegal in early June, although today the fair has as much to do with music, dance, and having fun as it does with selling homespun.

➤ JUNE: Pick up some decorating tips while you're swooning over Schubert at the **AIB Music Festival in Great Irish Homes** (☎ 01/278–1528), which puts on classical-music concerts in some of Ireland's finest country houses.

➤ MID-JUNE: **Ballycastle** puts on its own lively, three-day music and dance folk festival, the **Fleadh Amhrán agus Rince** (☎ 012657/63703). Devoted Joyceans celebrate the fictional wanderings of *Ulysses*'s Leopold and Molly Bloom and Stephen Daedalus on June 16 (the day the novel was set, in 1904) in **Dublin** with **Bloomsday** (☎ 01/878–8547); readings, dramatizations, and pilgrimages take place around the city (☞ Close-Up: Re-Joyce! *in* Chapter 1).

➤ LATE JUNE: The **Budweiser Irish Derby** (☎ 045/441205) at the **Curragh Racecourse**, County Kildare, is the biggest race event of the year. The Borodin Quartet and other chamber groups perform at the third annual **West Cork Chamber Music Festival** (☎ 027/61105), held at Bantry House in **Bantry**, County Cork.

➤ EARLY JULY: The **Coalisland International Music Festival** (☎ 028/8774–8052) attracts traditional and folk bands from all over Europe to County Tyrone. The **Eagle Wing Festival** (☎ 028/9127–8051) at **Groomsport** in County Down celebrates 300 years of links with America; it has music, line dancing, history lectures, and American food. **Castlebar**, County Mayo, is the venue for the **International Four-Day Walking Festival** (☎ 094/24102). **Murphy's Irish Open Golf Champi**-

onship (☎ 01/662–2433) will be held on one of Ireland's premier links courses (☞ Chapter 9).

➤ MID-JULY: On July 12 **Belfast** and other towns throughout the North commemorate the historic 1690 **Battle of the Boyne** (☎ 028/9032–2801). Bachelors from throughout the country strut their stuff in **Mullingar** for the **Guinness International Bachelor Festival** (☎ 044/45117). Galway is jam-packed for the two-week **Galway Arts Festival** (☎ 091/509705), the West's premier arts event, which includes theater, film, music of all kinds, art exhibits, and a not-to-be-missed kickoff parade. The **James Joyce Summer School** (☎ 01/706–8480) draws academics and aficionados from all over the world to University College Dublin. Also in **Dublin**, the streets and pubs of Temple Bar resound day and night to jazz and blues music for the eighth annual **Temple Bar Blues Festival** (☎ 01/677–2255). **Kilmore Quay** hosts a two-week-long **Seafood Festival** (☎ 053/29922) that runs through to the end of the month.

➤ JULY 25: On the last Sunday in July, thousands of pilgrims, some in bare feet, climb the rocky slopes of **Croagh Patrick** (2,500 ft) in County Mayo to honor St. Patrick.

➤ LATE JULY–EARLY AUG.: The **Galway Races** (☎ 091/753870) start the day after Galway's Arts Festival ends for a week of revelry. **Boyle**, County Roscommon, hosts the **Boyle Arts Festival** (☎ 079/62066), one of the best performing and visual-arts festivals in the region. Would-be beauty queens come to **Dungloe**, County Donegal, from as far away as Australia and New Zealand to compete in the **Mary of Dungloe International Festival** (☎ 075/21254). Across the whole of **County Derry** the best of the country's musicians take part in the **Festival of Popular Irish Music** (☎ 028/7126–7284).

➤ EARLY AUG.: You have even more festivals than usual to choose from at this time of year. The **Ballyshannon Folk and Traditional Music Festival** (☎ 072/51088) in County Donegal is one of the best of the season. Everyone's got the beat at the **Waterford Spraoi**

(☎ 051/353088), an international rhythm festival. The two-week **Yeats International Summer School** (☎ 071/42693) in **Sligo Town** celebrates its 43rd anniversary in 2001.

➤ MID-AUG.: **Kinvara,** County Galway, hosts its long-standing sailing event, **Cruinniú na mBád** ("Festival of the Gathering of the Boats"; ☎ 091/595635), in which traditional brown-sailed Galway hookers laden with turf race across Galway Bay. The **Kerrygold Dublin Horse Show** (☎ 01/668–0866) attracts a fashionable set to watch the best in Irish bloodstock. Aeronautical enthusiasts should check out the **Abbeyshrule Fly-in Festival and Air Show** (☎ 044/57424) in County Longford. The three-day **Puck Fair** (☎ 066/976–2366) in **Killorglin,** County Kerry, one of the country's oldest and more mythical festivals, retains vestiges of old pre-Christian fertility rites, like the garlanding with flowers of a large billy goat to signify his being crowned king.

➤ LATE AUG.: **Kilkenny** hosts **Kilkenny Arts Week** (☎ 056/63663), a marvelous assemblage of classical music, art exhibits, and theater. The highlight of the traditional music calendar is the **Fleadh Ceoil na hEireann** (pronounced *flah kee'yo na erin,* ☎ 01/280–0295). The world-famous **Rose of Tralee International Festival** (☎ 066/712–1322) selects a "Rose of Tralee" from an international lineup of young women of Irish descent, and packs this County Kerry town in the process. The competition coincides with the **Tralee Races.** On the third Thursday of the month, the **Connemara Pony Show** (☎ 095/21863) brings Ireland's finest yearlings and stallions to **Clifden,** County Galway.

If you're in the neighborhood of **Ballycastle,** County Antrim, don't miss Ireland's oldest fair, **Oul' Lammas Fair** (☎ 012657/62024), held every year since 1606 on the last Monday and Tuesday in August. It's a modern version of the ancient Celtic harvest festival of Lughnasa (Irish for "August").

➤ SEPT.: Single people of all ages from throughout Ireland and beyond flock to County Clare for the **Lisdoonvarna Matchmaking Festival** (☎ 065/707–4005) in the hopes of finding a spouse—or at least a date. The **Appalachian and Bluegrass Music Festival** (☎ 028/8224–3292) traces the roots of Appalachian music back to Ireland at the Ulster American Folk Park in **Omagh,** County Tyrone. The hugely popular **Hurling and Gaelic Football Finals** (☎ 01/836–3222) are played in Croke Park Stadium in **Dublin.**

➤ LATE SEPT.: Indulge in the "food of the gods" at the start of the oyster season at the **Galway International Oyster Festival** (☎ 091/522066); the season lasts from September to April. Farmers compete in the **All Ireland Ploughing Championships** (☎ 0507/25125); they are usually held in different locations around the country. **Opera Northern Ireland** (☎ 028/9024–1919) kicks off its autumn season in the Grand Opera House in Belfast. Troupes from all over Europe compete at **Waterford's** Theatre Royal during the annual **International Festival of Light Opera** (☎ 051/375437), which continues into early October.

➤ OCT.: The **Dublin Theatre Festival** (☎ 01/677–8439) puts on 10 visiting international productions, 10 Irish plays (most of them new), a children's festival, and a fringe of 60-plus plays. The beautiful coastal Cork town of **Kinsale** opens its best restaurants for the **International Gourmet Festival** (☎ 021/477–4026).

➤ MID-OCT.: One of Ireland's premier film events, the **Cork Film Festival** (☎ 021/427–1711) shows new feature-length films, documentaries, and short films—a specialty of the festival. Amateur and professional runners fill the streets of **Dublin** in the **Dublin City Marathon** (☎ 01/676–4647).

➤ LATE OCT.: The **Cork Jazz Festival** (☎ 021/427–0463) draws jazz lovers from Ireland and beyond.

➤ LATE OCT.–EARLY NOV.: The **Wexford Opera Festival** (☎ 053/22400) brings in major international stars to stage and perform three rarely heard opera gems in a tiny Georgian theater.

➤ NOV.: The three-day **Millstreet Indoor International Horse Show** (☎

029/70707) brings out-of-season equestrian enthusiasts to this County Cork town. The **Belfast Festival at Queen's University** (☎ 028/9066–7687) is the city's preeminent arts festival, with hundreds of musical, film, theater, and ballet performances.

➤ Nov.: The **Irish Rugby Football season** gets under way in **Dublin** with games between Ireland and nations *not* in the Six Nations group (Scotland, Wales, England, France, Italy, and Ireland). A limited number of tickets are available through the Irish Rugby Football Union (☎ 01/668–4601).

➤ Mid-Dec.: The yearling, foal, and breeding stock sale at **Goff's Bloodstock Sales** (☎ 045/877211), Kill, County Kildare, gives visitors a peek at how the rich and famous buy and sell their prized horses.

➤ Dec. 26: On **St. Stephen's Day,** the traditional Wren Boys in blackface and fancy dress still wander the streets of some rural towns asking for money and singing (these days much of the money goes to charity); by far the most extravagant celebration of this ancient folktale takes place on Sandymount Green in **Dublin** from about 11 AM.

INDEX

Icons and Symbols

★ Our special recommen-
   dations
✕ Restaurant
🏨 Lodging establishment
✕🏨 Lodging establishment
   whose restaurant war-
   rants a special trip
☺ Good for kids (rubber
   duck)
☞ Sends you to another
   section of the guide for
   more information
✉ Address
☎ Telephone number
🕐 Opening and closing
   times
💷 Admission prices
🌐 Sends you to
   www.fodors.com/urls
   for up-to-date links to
   the property's Web site

Numbers in white and black
circles ③❸ that appear on
the maps, in the margins, and
within the tours correspond
to one another.

A

Abbey Presbyterian Church,
   67
Abbey Theatre, 36, 98
Abbeys. ☞ Monasteries and
   abbeys
Achill Island, 337–338, 344
Adare, 281–283
Aghadoe, 267
Ailt an Chorráin (Burtonport),
   376
Ailwee Cave, 310
Albert Memorial Clock Tower,
   395
Allihies, 259
An Clochan Liath, 376
Andrew Jackson Centre, 409
Anglican Parish Church
   (Monkstown), 117
Annaghmakerrig, 175
Annals of the Four Masters,
   365
Annascaul, 273
Anne's Grove Gardens, 249–
   250
Annestown, 215
Antiques, shopping for, 112,
   243
Apartment and villa rentals,
   476
Apprentice Boys' Memorial
   Hall, 418
AquaDome, 278
Aquariums, 428–429

Aran Heritage Centre, 325
Aran Islands, 324–327, 344
   hotels, 325, 326–327
   nightlife, 326
   transportation, 342
   visitor information, 344
Aranmore, 376
Arbour Hill Cemetery, 74
Ardara, 368–369
Ardboe, 422
Ardee, 143
Ardgillan Demesne (park),
   144–145
Ardmore, 218, 225
Ardmore Tower, 217
Ards Forest Park, 374
Ark (children's theater), 56, 57
Arklow, 152–153
Arklow Pottery Factory, 152
Armagh, 425–426, 435
Art galleries and museums
   Belfast, 405–406
   Dublin, 41, 46, 48, 53–54, 64,
      67, 69, 96–97, 115
   Northern Ireland, 418, 419,
      420, 428
   the Northwest, 353, 375, 377–
      378
   the Southwest, 235, 236, 242,
      287
   the West, 323
Arthouse (exhibition space),
   56, 57
Ashtown Castle, 75
Askeaton, 281
Astronomy Centre and
   Planetarium, 425
Athlone, 178–179, 185
Athlone Castle, 178
Athy, 158
ATMs (automatic teller
   machines), 479
Augustine Abbey (Cong),
   328–329
Avoca, 152
Avoca Handweavers, 152
Avondale Forest Park, 152
Avondale House, 152

B

Baily Lighthouse, 122
Ballina, 337, 338–339, 344
Ballinskelligs, 263
Ballsbridge, 115, 117
Ballybunion, 279
Ballycastle, 411–412, 435
Ballycotton, 248
Ballyferriter, 277
Ballyhack, 209
Ballylane Farm, 201
Ballyliffin, 379
Ballymacarbery, 217
Ballymaloe Cookery School
   and Gardens, 247–248
Ballynahinch, 330
Ballyshannon, 363–364

Ballytore, 158–159
Ballyvaughan, 310–311
Balor's Fort, 375
Baltimore, 257
Baltray, 142
Bambrick's (pub), 72, 73
Banagher, 180
Bank of Ireland Arts Center,
   42
Bank of Ireland building, 41,
   42
Banks, hours, 464–465
   Dublin, 129
   Northern Ireland, 432
Bantry, 258–259, 293
Bantry Bay, 259
Bantry House, 258
Bantry 1796 French Armada
   Exhibition Center, 258
Barnacle, Nora, 317
Barry, John, statue of, 204
Beaghmore, 422
Beckett, Samuel, 47, 68, 423
Bed-and-breakfasts, 476–477
Belfast, 392–408
   car rentals, 432
   Central District, 394–396,
      402
   excursions, 407–408
   Golden Mile, 393–394, 402–
      403, 404–405
   guided tours, 433
   High Street, 395–396
   hotels, 402–404
   nightlife and the arts, 404–
      406
   pubs, 395–396, 404–405
   restaurants, 399–402
   shopping, 407
   Stranmillis, 398
   transportation, 430–432
   University area, 396, 398–
      399, 403–404, 405
   visitor information, 395, 396,
      435
   walking tour, 393, 395, 398
Belfast Castle, 407
Bella Cohen's Brothel, 71
Bellamont Forest, 173
Bellamont House, 173
Belleek, 422
Belleek Pottery, 422
Belvedere College, 71
Belvedere House Gardens,
   169
Better Business Bureau, 469
Bewley's Oriental Cafés, 37,
   41, 42
Bicycling, 462, 480
   Dublin, 105–106
   Dublin environs, 133, 147
   Midlands, 164, 179
   Northern Ireland, 388, 433
   the Northwest, 348, 357, 369
   the Southeast, 188, 199, 206,
      216

NOTES

NOTES

NOTES

NOTES

NOTES